Cisco IOS XR Fundamentals

Mobeen Tahir, CCIE No. 12643
Mark Ghattas, CCIE No. 19706
Dawit Birhanu, CCIE No. 5602
Syed Natif Nawaz, CCIE No. 8825

Cisco Press

800 East 96th Street

Indianapolis, IN 46240

Cisco IOS XR Fundamentals

Mobeen Tahir, Mark Ghattas, Dawit Birhanu, Syed Natif Nawaz

Published by:
Cisco Press
800 East 96th Street
Indianapolis, IN 46240 USA

Printed in the United States of America

Fourth Printing, March 2013

Library of Congress Cataloging-in-Publication Data:

Cisco IOS XR fundamentals / Mobeen Tahir ... [et al.].

p. cm.

Includes bibliographical references.

ISBN-13: 978-1-58705-271-2 (pbk.)

ISBN-10: 1-58705-271-7 (pbk.)

1. Cisco IOS. 2. Routing (Computer network management) 3. Routers (Computer networks)
4. Internetworking (Telecommunication) I. Tahir, Mobeen, 1966- II. Cisco Systems, Inc. III. Title.

TK5105.8.C57C548 2009

004.6—dc22

2009019283

ISBN-13: 978-1-58705-271-2

ISBN-10: 1-58705-271-7

Warning and Disclaimer

This book is designed to provide information about the Cisco IOS XR network operating system. Every effort has been made to make this book as complete and as accurate as possible, but no warranty or fitness is implied.

The information is provided on an "as is" basis. The authors, Cisco Press, and Cisco Systems, Inc., shall have neither liability nor responsibility to any person or entity with respect to any loss or damages arising from the information contained in this book or from the use of the discs or programs that may accompany it.

The opinions expressed in this book belong to the authors and are not necessarily those of Cisco Systems, Inc.

Trademark Acknowledgments

All terms mentioned in this book that are known to be trademarks or service marks have been appropriately capitalized. Cisco Press or Cisco Systems, Inc., cannot attest to the accuracy of this information. Use of a term in this book should not be regarded as affecting the validity of any trademark or service mark.

Corporate and Government Sales

The publisher offers excellent discounts on this book when ordered in quantity for bulk purchases or special sales, which may include electronic versions and/or custom covers and content particular to your business, training goals, marketing focus, and branding interests. For more information, please contact: **U.S. Corporate and Government Sales** 1-800-382-3419 corpsales@pearsontechgroup.com

For sales outside the United States please contact: **International Sales** international@pearsoned.com

Feedback Information

At Cisco Press, our goal is to create in-depth technical books of the highest quality and value. Each book is crafted with care and precision, undergoing rigorous development that involves the unique expertise of members from the professional technical community.

Readers' feedback is a natural continuation of this process. If you have any comments regarding how we could improve the quality of this book, or otherwise alter it to better suit your needs, you can contact us through email at feedback@ciscopress.com. Please make sure to include the book title and ISBN in your message.

We greatly appreciate your assistance.

Publisher: Paul Boger

Associate Publisher: Dave Dusthimer

Executive Editor: Brett Bartow

Managing Editor: Patrick Kanouse

Development Editor: Dayna Isley

Project Editor: Tonya Simpson

Editorial Assistant: Vanessa Evans

Book Designer: Louisa Adair

Composition: Mark Shirar

Indexer: Ken Johnson

Business Operation Manager, Cisco Press: Anand Sundaram

Manager Global Certification: Erik Ullanderson

Copy Editor: Mike Henry

Technical Editors: Mukhtiar Shaikh, Syed Kamran Raza

Proofreader: Leslie Joseph

About the Authors

Mobeen Tahir, CCIE No. 12643 (SP, R&S), is a network consulting engineer with the World Wide Service Provider Practice team in Cisco. Mobeen started his career in the communication industry in 1993 with France-based Alcatel. While working for Alcatel between 1993 and 1998, Mobeen engaged in assignments ranging from manufacturing voice switches to planning large-scale telecommunications projects. He joined Cisco in 1999 and has worked on the development testing of the IOS XR operating system for c12000 and CRS-1 platforms. His current role as a network consulting engineer at Cisco consists of designing and deploying NGN networks in the service provider space. Mobeen specializes in IOS XR–based deployments and provides consulting services to Cisco customers. Mobeen has attained master of engineering and B.S.E.E degrees from institutions in Canada and the United States. He lives with his wife and two children in Cary, North Carolina.

Mark Ghattas, CCIE No. 19706 (Service Provider), is a solutions architect focusing on architecture and design. He manages the World Wide Service Provider NGN Core Practice team in Advanced Services. Mark has more than 15 years of experience with data communication technologies. Mark joined Cisco Systems in 1999 and has supported strategic service providers. Mark has supported many of the first CRS-1 customers in Japan and the Asia Pacific theatre, CANSAC, Latin America, and North America. He has presented on various topics at Networkers relating to IOS XR. He holds a bachelor's degree from the University of Maryland and plans to earn his MBA degree.

Dawit Birhanu, CCIE No. 5602, is a technical leader with the World Wide Service Provider Practice team in Cisco Systems, where he is responsible for assisting global service providers with the deployment of new NGN products and technologies. He specializes in IOS XR–based platforms, QoS, MPLS, and BGP. Dawit joined Cisco Systems in 2000 and has worked on the deployment of new technologies for Cisco 12000 and CRS-1 in the service provider space. Dawit has a master of telecommunications degree from the University of Pittsburgh and a master of electronics engineering degree from Eindhoven University of Technology, The Netherlands. Before getting into the networking industry, Dawit was a lecturer of electrical engineering at Addis Ababa University, Ethiopia, between 1992 and 1995. Dawit lives with his wife and two daughters in Raleigh, North Carolina.

Syed Natif Nawaz, CCIE No. 8825 (SP, R&S), has more than ten years of experience in providing networking design, deployments, and escalation assistance to various service provider customers. Syed Natif Nawaz is currently the IOS XE software development manager at Cisco Systems, where he works on customer-focused software qualification/certification/deployment, feature integration, release processes, and other software quality initiatives. He has presented on various MPLS-related topics in the Networkers conference (Florida), MPLS Power Sessions (London), NANOG (Dallas), and APRICOT (Perth) and has contributed to articles such as "L2VPN: Changing and Consolidating Networks" in *Techworld* and "Cell Packing" in *Packet Magazine*. Formerly, Syed Natif Nawaz worked as a development engineer at Assured Access technologies and Alcatel, where he developed software for access concentrators. In addition to higher education in electrical and electronics from the University of Madras, Syed Natif Nawaz also holds an M.S. in computer science and engineering from State University of New York at Buffalo.

About the Technical Reviewers

Mukhtiar Shaikh is a distinguished services engineer at Cisco and a senior member of the central engineering team within the Customer Advocacy Organization. He joined Cisco in October 1996. During his early years at Cisco, he provided technical support to Cisco's large ISP accounts. His areas of focus are IP routing protocols, multicast, and MPLS technologies. Over the past several years, he has led various design projects and has been involved in the deployment of MPLS in the service provider and Enterprise NGN networks. In his current role, he provides technology leadership and architectural and design consulting to the Cisco Advanced Services accounts. Mukhtiar is a regular speaker at various industry forums. He is a CCIE and holds an M.S. degree in electrical engineering from Colorado State University.

Syed Kamran Raza is a technical leader (MPLS software) at Cisco Systems. He joined Cisco in 2000 to work on MPLS architecture and design for Cisco IOS XR and the carrier grade core router platform (CRS-1). For the past eight years, he has been priming the IOS XR MPLS LDP software development and has contributed to various features, including RSVP, LDP, MPLS forwarding, MPLS-based L2/L3 VPNs, SRP, and High Availability. Prior to Cisco, he worked as a software designer at Nortel Networks and as a telecommunications engineer at Alcatel. He completed his B. Eng in computer systems in 1993 from N.E.D. University of Engineering and Technology, Karachi, Pakistan, and completed his M. Eng in 1999 at Carleton University, Ottawa, Canada. He has published several papers and presentations at international conferences and seminars and is also engaged in IETF standardization activities.

Dedications

From Mobeen Tahir:

This book is dedicated to the memory of my father, Tahir Khan. He taught me how to take the first step in life.

To my wife, Sharmeen, and my kids, Mohammad and Iman, for their unconditional love.

To my mother, Sadiqa, and my siblings Noreen, Javaria, and Usman, for their prayers and support.

From Mark Ghattas:

This book is dedicated to my wife and son. I thank my wife, Amy, for her sacrifices, love, patience, and endless support to allow me to pursue my goals.

To my mom, Ehsan, who provided me opportunities, guidance, wisdom, and love, which made me the person, husband, and father I am today.

To my brothers, Matt and Paul, for the great technical discussions that last forever at the dinner table.

To Brian—our friendship keeps me inspired.

From Dawit Birhanu:

This book is dedicated to my wife, Lydia, and daughters, Leah and Blen, for their sacrifice, patience, love, and support. It is also dedicated to my mother, Negesu, and father, Birhanu, for their sacrifice and support to pursue my aspirations.

From Syed Natif Nawaz:

I dedicate this book in loving memory of my grandmother, Ameerunissa Begum, and to my mother, Haseena Begum, for all their sacrifices and support over the years and their love. I also dedicate this to my son, Taha, and my wife, Kouser Fathima, for filling my life with joy. To my sister, Arshiya Afshan, and brother-in-law, Shameeque. May their life be filled with joy and opportunities. Last but not the least, to my late father, Mr. Syed Yakoob Ali.

Acknowledgments

From Mobeen Tahir:

I would like to acknowledge the technical help given to me by several members of the IOS XR development community. I am particularly indebted to Pradosh Mohapatra, Brian Hennies, Muhammad Durrani, Arun Satyanayarana, Deepak Sreekanten, John Plunkett, Rakesh Gandhi, and Syed Kamran Raza, for answering my numerous questions and providing their expert advice. I would also like to point out the help and encouragement given to me by my colleague Muhammad Waris Sagheer.

From Mark Ghattas:

I would like to acknowledge Shahzad Burney and Waris Sagheer, who supported the conception and creativity of this project. A thank you to Anthony Lau, who helped me develop a "world" of experience with the multishelf platform. Thanks to Eddie Chami, Grant Socal, and Nikunj Vaidya for their input on best practices documents. I want to thank my co-authors Mobeen, Dawit, and Syed, who sacrificed personal and family time to meet commitments.

From Dawit Birhanu:

I would like to acknowledge the technical help given to me from several members of IOS XR and CRS development teams, and CRS deployment team. I would also like to acknowledge Lane Wigley, Ken Gray, Joel Obstfeld, and Yeva Byzek for their mentorship, inspiration, and support

Syed Natif Nawaz:

Thanks to all my co-authors for their effort and teamwork. Special thanks to my friends Waris and Shahzad during the inception of this book. I would also like to thank Jeffrey Liang and Lakshmi Sharma for helping me with their expertise and experience. I want to thank Kiran Rane, Srihari Sangli, Sai Ramamoorthy, Ravi Amanaganti, Pankaj Malhotra, and Paresh Shah for their unreserved support. As always I am grateful to my mom, Haseena Begum, my wife, Kouser Fathima, and sister, Arshiya Afshan, for being there for me.

The authors would like to send a special acknowledgement to Brett Bartow at Cisco Press, who has been ultra-supportive and understanding of the hurdles and delays we encountered. In addition, we thank Dayna Isley at Cisco Press, for her input and guidance supporting our content.

Contents at a Glance

Contents

Icons Used in This Book

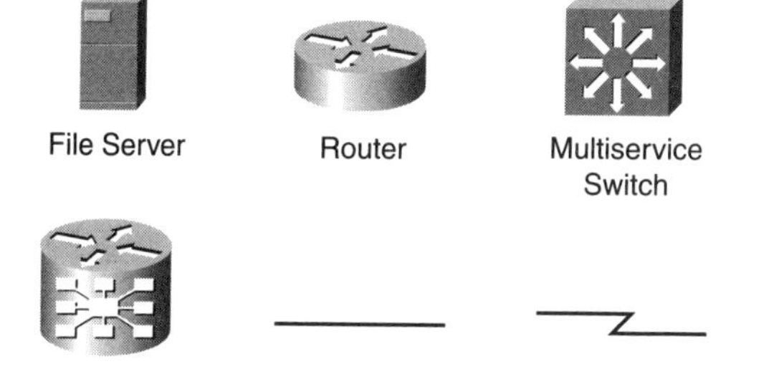

Command Syntax Conventions

The conventions used to present command syntax in this book are the same conventions used in the IOS Command Reference. The Command Reference describes these conventions as follows:

- **Boldface** indicates commands and keywords that are entered literally as shown. In actual configuration examples and output (not general command syntax), boldface indicates commands that are manually input by the user (such as a **show** command).
- *Italic* indicates arguments for which you supply actual values.
- Vertical bars (|) separate alternative, mutually exclusive elements.
- Square brackets ([ ]) indicate an optional element.
- Braces ({ }) indicate a required choice.
- Braces within brackets ([{ }]) indicate a required choice within an optional element.

Foreword

Over the last several years, fiscal discipline has really dominated the industry. Both consumers and businesses expect far more from their communications providers than they did just a few years ago. Offering simple telephone dial tone and an Internet connection are not going to be enough for success. At the same time, however, service providers want to continue to reduce their operational costs. As a result, one of the main challenges telecommunications companies now face is to find ways to cost effectively bring innovative services to their customers. These drivers are why most providers are working on transitioning their disparate legacy networks to one, unified, converged network infrastructure based on IP combined with Multiprotocol Label Switching (MPLS). MPLS is a technology that translates various other telecommunications protocols, such as ATM or frame relay, so they can run over an IP-based network. By eliminating their multiple networks, service providers are greatly reducing their operational costs. And by moving to an IP/MPLS network, they can mix and match all communications types—voice, data, and video—into any service their customers might want.

We believe the CRS-1 will dramatically affect carriers and their capability to successfully transition to this new era in communications. Carriers worldwide are embracing convergence and almost unanimously agree that IP/MPLS is the foundation for their new infrastructures. The CRS-1 provides carriers the means to consolidate their networks in the most efficient and cost-effective way possible. Nothing on the market can match it in terms of scalability, reliability, and flexibility. It is a system that our service provider customers will be able to base their businesses on. And I firmly believe that carriers that deploy the CRS-1 will gain profound competitive advantage over their competition through operational efficiencies and service flexibility. As we like to point out, when service providers work with Cisco, they are not just working with a network equipment maker but, rather, a business partner.

Sameer Padhye
Sr. Vice President, Advanced Services
WW Service Provider Line of Business
Customer Advocacy

Introduction

This book is intended to provide a reference to users who plan or have implemented Cisco IOS XR software in the network. *Cisco IOS XR Fundamentals* provides an overview of IOS XR operation system infrastructure and hardware architecture on the Carrier Routing System. The intention of this book is to provide general networking topics in IOS XR that service providers may implement in the core network. It is not feasible to cover every aspect of IOS XR; however, the key configurations have been explained that are typically deployed in core networks.

Who Should Read This Book?

Readers who have a relatively strong working knowledge of Cisco IOS Software and routing protocols will benefit from the discussions and configuration examples presented.

How This Book Is Organized

Although this book could be read cover to cover, it is designed to provide a configuration overview on Cisco IOS XR to support implementation configuration and features in IOS XR. Chapter 1 provides an overview of the evolution of operating systems and an understanding of the underlying QNX operating system. Chapters 2 through 12 are the core chapters and can be covered in order. If you do intend to read them all, the order in the book is an excellent sequence to use.

Chapters 1 through 12 cover the following topics:

- **Chapter 1, "Introducing Cisco IOS XR":** This chapter discusses the evolution of network operating systems in service provider enviroments. It is important to understand the goals and requirement of service providers that influenced the goals of IOS XR.
- **Chapter 2, "Cisco IOS XR Infrastructure":** This chapter discusses the interworkings of IOS XR. It helps you understand IOS XR microkernel architecture, process scheduling, interprocess communications, system database, and distributed services.
- **Chapter 3, "Installing Cisco IOS XR":** This chapter discusses various procedures for installing IOS XR on the Carrier Routing System.
- **Chapter 4, "Configuration Management":** This chapter provides a deeper insight into how IOS XR is different when configuring interfaces, out of band management, and features such as rollback and commit commands. Understanding these features will help you better manage the system.
- **Chapter 5, "Cisco IOS XR Monitoring and Operations":** This chapter explores how monitoring works in IOS XR. As IOS XR operates as a real-time operating system, there are monitoring tools that provide deeper inspection of activities on the system.
- **Chapter 6, "Cisco IOS XR Security":** This chapter examines inherent policers that provide a layer of security within the operating system. The importance of Local Packet Transport System (LPTS) is discussed.

- **Chapter 7, "Routing IGP":** This chapter covers the basics of routing protocol configurations. It provides configuration examples to show how IGP features are configured in IOS XR.
- **Chapter 8, "Implementing BGP in Cisco IOS XR":** This chapter introduces the IOS XR implementation of BGP. This chapter assumes that you have prior experince and knowledge of the BGP protocol and focuses on unique aspects of IOS XR BGP configuration. This chapter also provides details on Routing Policy Language as a vehicle for implementing BGP routing policies.
- **Chapter 9, "Cisco IOS XR MPLS Architecture":** This chapter discusses Multiprotocol Label Switching (MPLS), an important technology for building converged network infrastructure and services. This chapter assumes that you are familiar with MPLS protocols and operations. This chapter discusses IOS XR MPLS architecture, features, implementation, and configuration. It covers LDP, Layer 3 VPN, VPWS, VPLS, and MPLS Traffic Engineering.
- **Chapter 10, "Cisco IOS XR Multicast":** This chapter discusses when to use queuing and which queuing technique to use. This chapter also examines Weighted Fair Queuing (WFQ), Custom Queuing, and Priority Queuing and addresses the need for compression in today's enterprise network.
- **Chapter 11, "Secure Domain Router":** This chapter covers the concept of SDRs. It discusses the Distributed Route Processor (DRP) hardware needed to implement SDRs and provides configuration examples.
- **Chapter 12, "Understanding CRS-1 Multishelf":** This chapter discusses the Cisco implementation of the CRS-1 multishelf system. The key components are discussed to understand the architecture and troubleshooting of a CRS-1 multishelf system. A fabric troubleshooting section is covered to support implementation and operation.

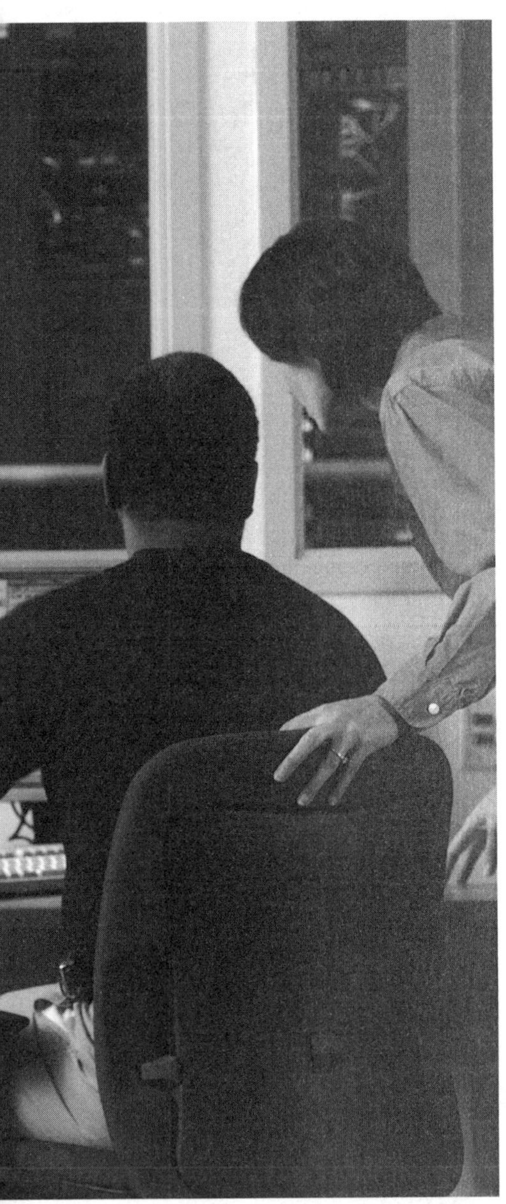

This chapter covers the following topics:

- Evolution of Networking
- Requirements for Carrier-Grade NOS
- Operating System Concepts
- High-Level Overview of Cisco IOS XR
- Cisco IOS XR Platforms
- References

This chapter reviews the evolution of network operating systems (NOS), requirements for current and future networks, and how Cisco IOS XR meets these requirements. The first section of this chapter provides an overview of the evolution of networking. The second section outlines the requirements for a carrier-grade NOS that underpins a converged network with critical applications. The third section reviews basic concepts of operating systems. The final sections provide a high-level overview of Cisco IOS XR.

CHAPTER 1

Introducing Cisco IOS XR

Evolution of Networking

In the 1980s the main network applications were limited to e-mail, web, file, printer, and database. Silicon technology for hardware (HW)-based packet forwarding was not yet fully developed, and transmission speed, CPU power, and memory capacity were very limited. As a result, routers and the underlying NOS were primarily designed to efficiently use CPU and memory resources for packet forwarding. A *NOS* is an operating system that is specifically designed for implementing networking and internetworking capabilities. Network devices such as routers and switches are empowered by a NOS.

Moreover, in the early days of data networking there was a plethora of competing networking protocols in addition to Internet Protocol (IP). Some became industry standards and others remained proprietary. Table 1-1 shows the protocols at different OSI layers that were once prevalent to varying degrees.

Table 1-1 *Protocols That Were in Use in the Early Days of Data Networking*

Protocols	OSI Layer
Token Ring, Fiber Distributed Data Interface (FDDI), Switched Multimegabit Data Service (SMDS)	1–2
ATM, Frame Relay	2–3
Internetwork Packet eXchange (IPX), International Standards Organization ConnectionLess Network Services (ISO CLNS), AppleTalk, DECNet, Xerox Network Services (XNS), IBM System Network Architecture (SNA), Apollo Domain, Banyan Virtual Integrated Network Services (VINES)	3

Routers were designed to support a variety of multiple protocols including IP, Ethernet, SONET/SDH, and some of the protocols shown in Table 1-1.

Network operators had several service-specific networks, each managed and operated by a different team. It was not uncommon for a service provider to maintain a separate PSTN network for telephony, an ATM data network, a Frame Relay data network, a public data network for Internet customers, a separate network for mobile backhaul, and a transport network to support all services. Some network operators still have a legacy of multiple networks; however, they are actively migrating to a converged network.

Although networking services such as e-mail, web browsing, file transfer, instant messaging, VoIP, and so on are taken for granted today, they were either nonexistent or considered privileged services for a few users at large enterprise, academic, and government institutions.

Over the past few decades the network, users, and services have evolved dramatically as follows:

- **Applications:** In the 1980s there were just a few network applications, namely e-mail, file, database, and print services. Today there are countless applications, including video conferencing, instant messaging, IPTV, telepresence, telemedicine, peer-to-peer sharing, video surveillance, online banking, online shopping, and so on.
- **User size:** Until the mid-1990s, data networking usage was limited to large enterprise, government, and academic institutions for limited applications. Based on data from Internet World Stats, Internet usage has grown from 16 million users in 1995 to 1.46 billion users in 2008. Moreover, per-capita bandwidth usage has increased dramatically since the mid 1990s.
- **Transmission capacity:** Transmission capacity of a single fiber pair has increased from 155Mbps in the early 1990s to multi-terabits today (realized with dense wavelength division multiplexing [DWDM] technologies). The Trans-Pacific Express (TPE) submarine cable that connects the United States to mainland China has an initial capacity of 1.28 terabits per second with a designed maximum capacity of 5.12 terabits per second.
- **Processing and memory capacity:** CPU speed and complexity increased from tens of megahertz single core processors in the early 1990s to multigigahertz multicore processors in 2009 following Moore's law. Memory capacity and access speed have seen similar growth—from a few megabytes of memory capacity in the early 1990s to many gigabytes in 2009. Moore's law, which is named after Intel co-founder Gordon E. Moore, states that processor and memory capacity doubles approximately every two years.
- **Protocols:** From several protocols in the early 1990s (as shown in Table 1-1), the network has consolidated toward IPv4/IPv6 and Ethernet protocols.
- **Networks:** Network operators have migrated or are in the process of migrating from multiple networks, each dedicated for specific function to a single converged network capable of supporting multiple services.

Requirements for Carrier-Grade NOS

Service providers are striving to provide solutions that can sufficiently satisfy the needs of their customers. Businesses are demanding integrated data, voice, video, and mobility services with high availability, security, and fast provisioning. Consumers want broadband access with bundled service of voice, video, mobile wireless, and data on a single bill. Governments are pushing for broadband access to every home and a resilient infrastructure that can survive catastrophic failures.

This section describes the requirements that a carrier-grade NOS needs to satisfy to meet the requirements of network operators.

Convergence

A carrier-grade NOS should have the capability to enable infrastructure and service convergence. Network convergence is critical to lowering capital and operational expenditure. Service convergence is vital to meeting customer demands and to offer new revenue-generating services.

Scalability

A converged network infrastructure should be able to scale seamlessly with respect to control plane, data plane, and management plane without interruption to existing services. The growth of customers, access bandwidth, and traffic volume per customer every year is pushing the scalability demand on every aspect of the network infrastructure. To cope with growth, the network operator might have to add additional hardware in the form of network ports, transport links, line cards, route processing cards, power modules or chassis in a multi-chassis system. The NOS should be able to support the addition of different system components without service disruption.

Availability

In a converged network, routers are carrying critical traffic including voice, emergency service traffic, video broadcasting, video conferencing, and business-critical data with availability requirement of 99.999% or better. To achieve carrier-grade availability requirements, a network operating system should be able to support a number of high availability features as described in this section.

Hardware Redundancy

Although it is possible to reduce the probability of hardware failure, it is virtually impossible and cost-prohibitive to reduce it to zero. Therefore, to achieve carrier-grade availability it is important to build the system with redundant hardware modules—particularly for system-critical subsystems. In addition, the NOS should have the necessary software capability to enable the system to operate with no or minimal service disruption when such a module fails, and when it is subsequently removed, upgraded, or replaced.

Failure Recovery and Microkernel-Based NOS

Modern operating systems and applications are complex, and are developed by hundreds of software engineers. It is virtually impossible to have defect-free operating systems. A software component might fail not only due to software defect but also due to memory corruption and malicious attacks. A carrier-grade NOS should be able to contain and recover from most software failures without service disruption.

Modern operating systems have kernel and nonkernel components. In general, a failure in a nonkernel software component will not impact the kernel or other nonkernel components. A kernel failure, however, will cause system reload. This suggests that it is important to keep most software components outside the kernel and to keep only minimal functionality in the kernel. This type of operating system is called a *microkernel-based operating system*. Multitasking, multithreading, and memory protection, which are discussed in the next section, are also critical components of a carrier-grade NOS.

Process Restartability

When a software process fails, the operating system should be able to restart the process. When a process is restarted, it should be able to recover its state so that it can seamlessly continue its functions without disrupting service. This capability is referred to as *process restartability*.

Failure Detection

The network operating system should also support network features that enable quick failure detection and rerouting of traffic around failed links, modules, or routers.

Software Upgrades and Patching

Carrier-grade NOS should support software upgrade and/or patching with no or minimal disruption to service. It is important that it has software patching capability to apply critical software updates and minimize frequent full software upgrades.

Security

A router has two primary security functions:

- To protect customer and service provider infrastructure by supporting network security features such as unicast reverse path forwarding (uRPF), access control list (ACL)–based filtering, and prefix filtering
- To protect the router from malicious or unintended security attacks and intrusions, which is the primary focus here

The operating system must provide effective mechanisms to protect the routing protocols from malicious attacks. It should also provide granular access control to protect the router from unauthorized access. Distributed denial of service (DDoS) attacks are common and becoming sophisticated. The NOS should minimize the impact to data, control, and management plane functions due to such attacks.

Service Flexibility

Carriers are demanding a routing system that has a long life cycle. This requires that the addition of new services should not require a fork-lift upgrade. Carrier-grade NOS needs to support the addition of new software features, line cards, and/or service modules with no or minimal service disruption. This can be achieved with modular software packaging, the support of service modules, and partitioning of systems into multiple routing domains.

Operating System Concepts

Computer systems, including "embedded" systems such as routers, have an operating system that is responsible for providing a number of services to the applications. Coordination of processing activities and access to hardware resources such as memory, network interfaces, and disk are also essential functions provided by an operating system. Figure 1-1 shows the relationships among the operating system, applications, and hardware resources.

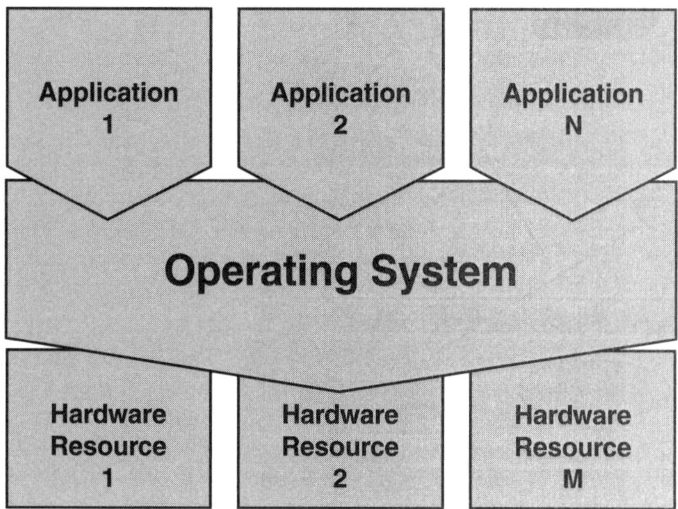

Figure 1-1 *Operating System Interaction with Hardware and Applications*

Basic Functions of an Operating System

Operating systems provide a number of services to applications. The basic functions offered by an operating system include process scheduling, interrupt handling, memory management, interprocess communication, and common routines (or library). These basic functions of OS are discussed in more detail in this section.

Process Scheduling

A *process* is a software program execution instance running on a system that has the capability to execute multiple program instances. Multiple processes can be spawned simultaneously from a single program. In a multitasking operating system multiple processes can time-share CPU resources, giving the user a perception of simultaneous processing. In a multitasking system, a process might have to relinquish control of the CPU before it completes the execution of its current task.

In a *cooperative multitasking* system, a process voluntarily relinquishes control only after completing execution or while waiting for an event. This could result in CPU starvation of other processes while waiting for the current process to relinquish control.

On the other hand, in a *preemptive multitasking* system a currently running process might be forced to relinquish control of the CPU. This is called *preemption*, and it can occur when either a high-priority process becomes ready or after the current process has run for the time allocated to it.

When the operating system preempts a process it is necessary to preserve the state of the process before relinquishing control to another process so that it can resume its execution when it gets to run again. *Context switching* is the mechanism by which a processes state is saved when it is preempted and retrieved when it resumes execution.

Most modern operating systems support running multiple instances of the same process concurrently. These types of operating systems are known as *multithreaded*. A *thread* is the smallest unit of execution within a process.

Interrupt Handling

Interrupt is a signal from hardware or software indicating a need for immediate attention. It causes the operating system to suspend a currently running process and dispatch an interrupt handling routine or process. A running process can also execute an interrupt instruction and trigger context switch to an interrupt handler. When executing a critical routine, the operating system can inhibit certain interrupts until the critical routine is completed. This is known as *interrupt masking*.

Memory Management

The operating system is responsible for managing the entire system memory, including allocation of memory to processes and ensuring that a process does not corrupt memory that belongs to another process. *Memory protection* is a mechanism by which a process is prevented from accessing memory locations other than the memory space allocated to it. With memory protection, each process runs in its own memory space. A defect in one process or a malicious attack to one process will not impact other processes.

In operating systems that support memory protection, some forms of communication between processes are better handled using *shared memory*, which is accessible by multiple processes. The operating system provides different synchronization mechanisms between processes that are writing to or reading from shared memory regions.

In a *monolithic operating system*, all processes share the same address space and the system does not provide fault isolation among processes. A monolithic system can offer better utilization of CPU cycles because it has lower overhead with respect to memory access, interprocess communication, and context switching. It might be useful in scenarios in which CPU resources are expensive and the overall system is simple with small code size.

In operating systems that support memory protection, the OS process that is responsible for managing other processes, memory, and other system resources is known as the *kernel*, and the OS is often referred to as *kernel-based OS*. The kernel can also contain other services, depending on the implementation. It runs in a separate memory space from the rest of the system and is protected from memory corruptions caused by other processes outside the kernel.

A failure in a nonkernel process does not impact the kernel and other processes. However, a failure in the kernel processes impacts all applications. In a *microkernel* system, only essential core OS services reside inside the kernel. All other services, including device drivers and network drivers, reside in their own address space. This has important resilience implications in that a failure in a device or network driver is self-contained and does not propagate to the kernel or other applications. Device and network drivers can also be restarted without restarting the whole system.

Synchronization

When multiple applications are running concurrently and attempt to access a resource such as disk drive, it is important to make sure that data integrity is preserved and resource is allocated fairly. There are different mechanisms that network operating systems provide to synchronize events and resource access.

Interprocess Communication

The operating system provides the interprocess communication (IPC) mechanism for processes running in separate address spaces because they cannot use the memory to exchange data. IPC communication can also occur between processes running on the main route processor and the processes running on different components in the device, including line cards and power supplies.

Dynamic Link Library

It is common for multiple applications to use a set of common routines. When these applications are running in separate protected memory address spaces, the common routines have to be duplicated in each address space, which is a waste of memory space. To avoid this problem, operating systems provide a mechanism to share common routines. This mechanism is called *dynamic linked library (DLL)* or *Libc* (C standard library). This allows the OS to load only active libraries into device memory and enables different processes to share the same libraries. This is a robust fault containment and software modularization mechanism. It also allows the sharing of common code among different applications.

Portable Operating System Interface

Portable Operating System Interface (POSIX) is a set of IEEE specifications that define kernel APIs, thread interfaces, kernel utilities, and more. POSIX also defines a conformance test suite. If an operating system passes the test suite, it is called a POSIX-conforming OS. An OS that adheres to POSIX compliance is considered highly flexible and provides maximum portability for additional features or application development. An application program developed for one POSIX-compliant OS can easily be ported with minimal effort to another POSIX-compliant OS.

High-Level Overview of Cisco IOS XR

As the world is becoming increasingly dependent on IP-based network infrastructure, network operators are demanding a high degree of reliability and availability. Cisco IOS XR Software is designed to meet the stringent requirements of network operators. It is designed to provide the following:

- A high level of scalability
- Distributed forwarding architecture
- Exceptionally high reliability and resiliency
- Service separation and flexibility
- Robust security

- Modularity across all software components
- Hierarchical configuration and robust configuration management
- Better manageability

Cisco IOS XR software is a highly distributed, secure, highly modular, and massively scalable network operating system that allows uninterrupted system operation. It is a microkernel-based operating system with preemptive multitasking, memory protection, and fast context switching. The microkernel provides basic operating system functionalities including memory management, task scheduling, synchronization services, context switching, and interprocess communication (IPC).

The microkernel used in Cisco IOS XR is QNX Neutrino real-time operating system (RTOS) from QNX Software Systems. The kernel is lightweight and does not include system services such as device drivers, file systems, and network stack. Figure 1-2 shows the IOS XR microkernel architecture.

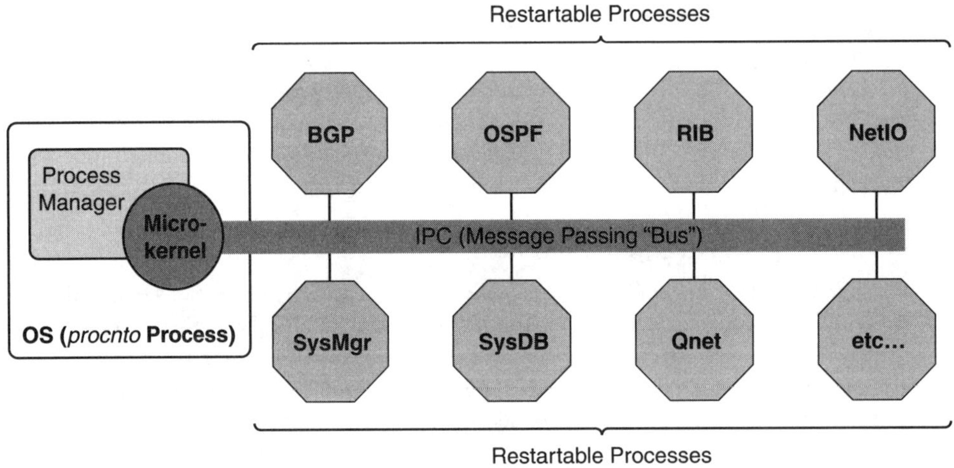

Figure 1-2 *Cisco IOS XR Microkernel Architecture*

All processes outside the microkernel (procnto) are individually restartable. If any of the processes, including SysMgr, SysDB, Qnet, or BGP, is restarted it does not cause the entire system to reload. When a process restarts, it recovers its states from persistent storage or peer processes, also called *collaborators*. For example, if the Routing Information Base (RIB) process restarts it will restore the RIB table from its collaborators, which are routing protocol processes such as OSPF, BGP, IS-IS, and so on. As a result, the RIB table is rebuilt and there is no traffic disruption if the RIB process is restarted.

Cisco IOS XR employs two distribution models to achieve higher performance and scalability. The first distribution model uses localization, which performs processing and storage closer to the resource. With this model, a database specific to a node is located on that node. Also processes are placed on a node where they have greater interaction with the resource. For example, Address Resolution Protocol (ARP), interface manager (IM), Bidirectional Failure Detection (BFD), adjacency manager, and Forwarding Information Base (FIB) manager are located on the line cards and are responsible only for managing resources and tables on that line card. System databases specific to the line card, such as interface-related configurations, interface states, and so on, are stored on the line card. This enables IOS XR to achieve faster processing and greater scalability.

The second distribution model uses load distribution in which additional route processors (RPs or distributed RPs [DRP]) are added to the system and processes are distributed across different RP and/or DRP modules. Routing protocols, management entities, and system processes are examples of processes that can be distributed using this model. For example, we can classify the processes into three groups as follows and allocate each group to run on one RP or active/standby RP pair:

- **Group 1:** All routing protocols or processes, including BGP, ISIS, LDP, RSVP, PIM, MSDP, and RIB
- **Group 2:** All management entities, including SNMP server, SSH, Telnet, XML, and HTTP
- **Group 3:** All other processes

This model enables the operator to add additional RPs or DRPs in the system as needed to offload processing from one RP to another, essentially increasing the overall processing power of the system.

Cisco IOS XR provides a clear separation of management, control, and data plane. Figure 1-3 illustrates the IOS XR architecture and the separation of the management, control, and data planes.

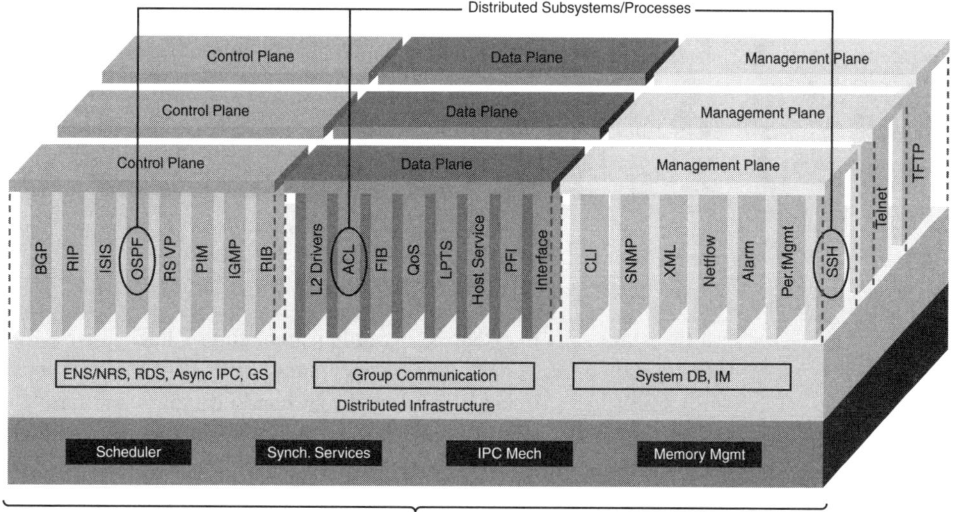

Figure 1-3 *Cisco IOS XR Architecture: Separation of Management, Control, and Data Planes*

Each routing control plane or management plane process runs on one or multiple route processors (RP) and/or distributed RP nodes. Data plane processes are located on each node that participates in packet forwarding, including RP and line card.

Cisco IOS XR supports partitioning of a system into multiple secure domain routers (SDR) at physical boundaries. SDRs share only chassis, power supply, fan tray, and related system components. Each line card or RP belongs to only one SDR. Cisco IOS XR SDRs provide fault and security isolation because they are defined at physical boundaries. A fault, resource starvation, or security breach on one SDR does not impact other SDRs in the same system. An SDR can be defined with just one RP, but it can have multiple RPs and LCs.

Figure 1-4 shows a system partitioned into three SDRs: default SDR, SDR 1, and SDR 2. The SDR that has the designated shelf controller (DSC) is the default SDR. DSC is the main RP (or RP pair for redundancy) on the system.

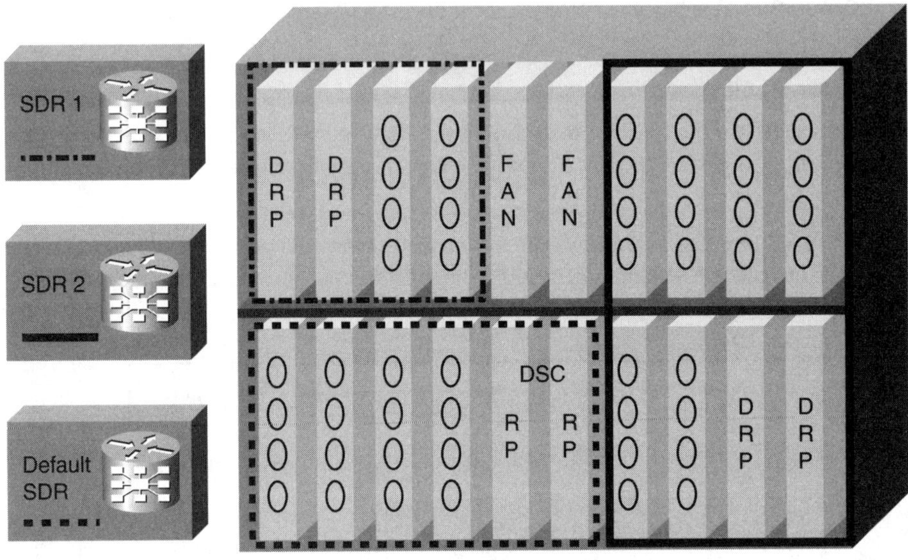

Figure 1-4 *Partitioning System into Secure Domain Routers*

Cisco IOS XR uses a two-stage fully distributed forwarding architecture. Each line card has forwarding information base (FIB) and local adjacency information base (AIB) for local interfaces on that line card. When a packet first enters the system, the ingress line card performs ingress feature processing and FIB lookup. The FIB lookup returns sufficient information for the ingress line card to deliver the packet to the appropriate egress line cards. The ingress line card does not need to know the full adjacency information of the egress interface. The ingress line card sends the packet through the fabric to the egress line card. The egress line card performs egress feature processing and FIB lookup to get full adjacency and layer 2 rewrite information. The packet is then sent to the outbound interface with an appropriate layer 2 header.

The purpose of two-stage forwarding is to get better scalability and performance. This is critical because Cisco IOS XR is designed to achieve a very high degree of scalability in different dimensions, including bandwidth capacity, number of routes, and number of customer connections.

In Cisco IOS XR, all transit traffic is processed in HW and does not involve any LC or RP CPU processing. Only traffic destined to the router or originating from the router is processed by LC or RP CPU. Cisco has developed an innovative processing and delivery mechanism for packets destined to the router. This mechanism is called *local packet transport service (LPTS)*. If a packet enters the system and FIB lookup in HW determines that the packet needs to be delivered to the local system, it will be handed over to LPTS process for additional HW processing. LPTS determines what application it is destined to and sends the packet to the node where the application resides. For example, if a BGP packet is received, the ingress LC will send it directly to the RP where the BGP process is located. The HW forwarding engine on the LC sends the packet through the fabric to the RP. The LC CPU does not touch this packet.

Cisco IOS XR LPTS also acts as a dynamic integral firewall and protects the system from denial of service and other forms of attacks. To protect the system from DoS attacks, it monitors and polices the traffic destined to the router. For example, BGP or any other type of control packets destined to the RP must conform to the policing thresholds set by the LPTS process. In case of BGP, the policer value is set such that regular BGP updates are not impacted. However, if someone maliciously sends a large amount of BGP updates, LPTS protects the RP CPU from being overwhelmed with bogus BGP packets. The policer value also depends on the status of the BGP session for which the packet is sent. If the packet belongs to a configured neighbor and the session is not yet established, the rate will be lower. On the other hand, if the packet matches an established session the rate will be higher. Note that it is very hard to generate bogus BGP packets belonging to an established session because the attacker must know the source and destination port of the BGP session in addition to the source and destination IP addresses.

LPTS does not require user configuration—it is enabled by default and updated dynamically as the system is configured and sessions come up and down. The LPTS policer values, however, are user configurable.

Cisco IOS XR Platforms

This section provides a brief overview of Cisco IOS XR–based platforms. It is not intended to provide a detailed systems architecture for these platforms. Visit the Cisco website (http://www.cisco.com/) to get detailed information on each of the platforms described in this section.

Cisco CRS-1 Carrier Routing System

Cisco CRS-1 is the first platform to run IOS XR. It is designed for high system availability, scale, and uninterrupted system operation. CRS-1 is designed to operate either as a single-chassis or multichassis system. It has two major elements: line card chassis (LCC) and fabric card chassis (FCC). Details about each system follow:

- **CRS-1 16-Slot Single-Chassis System** is a 16-slot LCC with total switching capacity of 1.2 Tbps and featuring a midplane design. It has 16 line card and 2 route processor slots.
- **CRS-1 8-Slot Single-Shelf System** is an eight-slot line card chassis with total switching capacity of 640 Gbps and featuring a midplane design. It has eight line card and two route processor slots.
- **CRS-1 4-Slot Single-Shelf System** is a four-slot line card shelf with total switching capacity of 320 Gbps. It has four line card and two route processor slots.
- **CRS-1 Multi-Shelf System** consists of 2 to 72 16-slot LCC and 1 to 8 FCC with a total switching capacity of up to 92 Tbps. The LCCs are connected only to the FCCs where stage 2 of the three-stage fabric switching is performed. The FCC is a 24-slot system.

Cisco XR 12000 Series

Cisco XR 12000 series is capable of a 2.5 Gbps, 10 Gbps, or 40 Gbps per slot system with four different form factors:

- **Cisco 12016, Cisco 12416, and Cisco 12816** are full-rack, 16-slot, and 2.5-, 10- and 40-Gbps per slot systems, respectively.
- **Cisco 12010, Cisco 12410, and Cisco 12810** are half-rack, 10-slot, and 2.5-, 10- and 40-Gbps per slot systems, respectively.
- **Cisco 12006 and Cisco 12406** are 1/4-rack, 6-slot, and 2.5- and 10-Gbps per slot systems, respectively.
- **Cisco 12404** is a four-slot, 10-Gbps per slot system.

Cisco ASR 9000 Series

ASR 9000 Series Aggregation Service Router is targeted for carrier Ethernet services and delivers a high degree of performance and scalability. It can scale up to 6.4 Tbps per system. It comes with two form factors:

- **Cisco ASR 9010** is a 10-slot, 21-rack unit (RU) system.
- **Cisco ASR 9006** is a 6-slot, 10-rack unit (RU) system.

Summary

Networking has evolved from limited use for specialized applications using several disparate networks to a critical infrastructure that is relied on by businesses, public services, government, and individuals for an increasing number of applications. As a result, network operators are demanding a very high degree of availability, reliability, and security for the routers that constitute their network infrastructure. IOS XR is designed to meet this challenge.

Cisco IOS XR is a microkernel-based operating system with preemptive multitasking, memory protection, a high degree of modularity, and fast context-switching capabilities. Because each process outside the microkernel is restartable without impacting the rest of the system, failure of a process due to memory corruption of software defect does not impact other parts of the system.

To achieve a high degree of scalability and performance, Cisco IOS XR employs two forms of distribution: localization and load distribution. Localization refers to performing processing and storage closer to the resource. *Load distribution* refers to offloading of processing from one RP to another with the objective of increasing overall processing power of the system.

Cisco IOS XR uses a two-stage fully distributed forwarding architecture. When a packet first enters the system the ingress linecard performs ingress feature processing and FIB lookup. The FIB lookup returns sufficient information for the ingress line card to deliver the packet to the appropriate egress line cards. The egress line card performs egress feature processing and FIB lookup to get the full L2 adjacency information.

References

- **Internet World Stats.** http://www.internetworldstats.com/
- **Cisco.** Cisco IOS XR Configuration Guides. http://www.cisco.com/

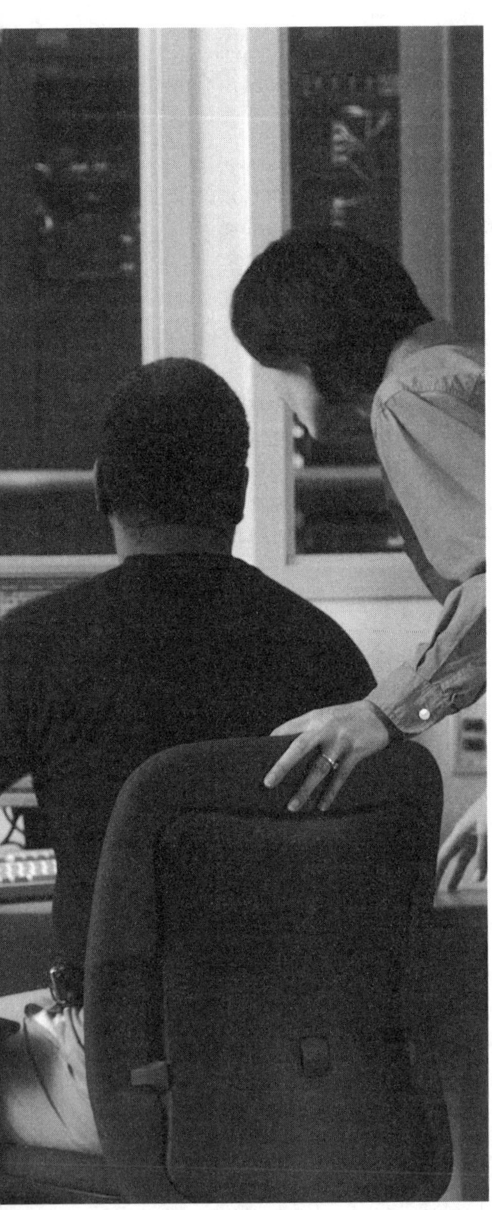

This chapter covers the following topics:

- Cisco IOS XR Kernel
- Cisco IOS XR System Manager
- Interprocess Communication
- Distributed Services
- Process Placement
- Cisco IOS XR System Database
- High Availability Architecture
- Forwarding Path
- References

Cisco IOS XR is designed for massively scalable systems with particular focus on continuous system operation, scalability, security, and performance. This chapter discusses the IOS XR infrastructure and how it achieves the stated goals of IOS XR. The first section discusses the microkernel used by IOS XR. Subsequent sections discuss interprocess communication (IPC), IOS XR System Database, distributed system services, process management, and high availability.

CHAPTER 2

Cisco IOS XR Infrastructure

Cisco IOS XR Kernel

Cisco IOS XR is a highly distributed microkernel-based network operating system. The microkernel used by Cisco IOS XR is QNX Neutrino real-time operating system (RTOS), which is from QNX Systems. The microkernel is lightweight and provides only a few fundamental services. It is responsible for interrupt handling, scheduling, task switching, memory management, synchronization, and interprocess communication. The microkernel does not include other system services such as device drivers, file system, and network stacks; those services are implemented as independent processes outside the kernel, and they can be restarted like any other application.

The microkernel is a POSIX-compliant kernel. POSIX defines OS specifications and test suites for APIs and OS services that a POSIX-compliant OS has to implement. Applications and services developed for a POSIX-compliant kernel can easily be ported to another POSIX-compliant kernel. If the need arises in the future, Cisco IOS XR can easily be ported to another POSIX-compliant OS.

The essential aspect of a microkernel-based OS is modularity. The microkernel provides a very high degree of modularity. The OS is implemented as a team of cooperative processes managed by the microkernel and glued by its message-passing service. Each process is running in its own address space and is protected from memory corruption of other processes. An important aspect of microkernel architecture is its fast context switching capability, which provides the impetus to a high degree of modularity. Because the CPU cost associated with context switching is minimal, it provides greater incentive to implement each application and service as its own process and in its own memory address space. For example, Cisco IOS XR implements BGP, OSPF, OSPFv3, RIBv4, RIBv6, and so on as separate processes. Moreover, if multiple OSPF processes are configured on the router each one will be assigned its own process instance completely separate from other OSPF processes. This greater modularity is made possible due to the fast context-switching capability of the microkernel and efficient interprocess communication provided by QNX and enhanced by Cisco. Interprocess communication is discussed in greater detail in the section "Interprocess Communication," later in this chapter.

Threads

As illustrated in Figure 2-1, the OS is a group of cooperating processes managed by a small microkernel. The microkernel provides thread scheduling, preemption, and synchronization services to the processes. It also serves as a message-passing "bus." The microkernel and the process manager together form the procnto process. Each process runs in its own address space and can be restarted without impacting other processes.

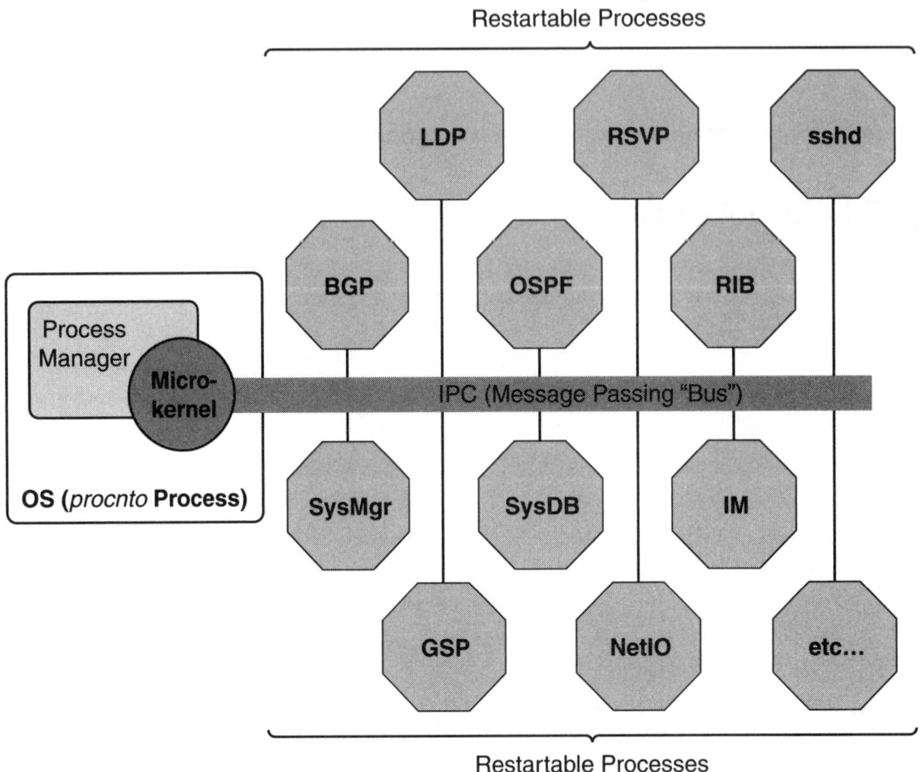

Figure 2-1 *Microkernel-Based Operating System*

When developing an application, it is often desirable to execute several algorithms concurrently. This concurrency is achieved using multiple threads within a process. A *thread* is the minimum unit of execution and scheduling. A *process*, on the other hand, is a container for related threads and defines the memory address space within which the threads can execute. There is at least one thread per process. Threads are discussed in more detail in the section "Cisco IOS XR System Manager."

For example, as you can see from the **show processes threadname** 120 output in Example 2-1, the BGP process in IOS XR has several threads that each perform a specific task, including input, output, import, and so on. In the following sample output, 120 is the jobid of BGP process. Jobid (JID) is a unique number assigned to each process, and it is covered in more detail in the section "Cisco IOS XR System Manager" later in this chapter.

Example 2-1 *Thread Names for the BGP Process*

```
RP/0/RP0/CPU0:CRS-A#show processes threadname 120
! 120 is the jobid of bgp process
JID     TID  ThreadName        pri  state       TimeInState         NAME
120     1    io-control        10   Receive         0:00:04:0166    bgp
120     2    chkpt_evm         10   Receive        96:23:26:0941    bgp
120     3    label-thread      10   Receive         0:00:16:0525    bgp
120     4    rib-update ID 0   10   Receive         0:00:16:0522    bgp
120     5    async             10   Receive        50:49:09:0707    bgp
120     6    io-read           10   Receive         0:01:16:0534    bgp
120     7    io-write          10   Receive         0:00:16:0532    bgp
120     8    router            10   Receive         0:00:16:0533    bgp
120     9    import            10   Receive         0:00:16:0529    bgp
120     10   update-gen        10   Receive         0:00:16:0529    bgp
120     11   crit-event        10   Receive         0:00:16:0525    bgp
120     12   event             10   Receive         0:00:32:0777    bgp
120     13   management        10   Receive         0:00:16:0549    bgp
120     14   rib-update ID 1   10   Receive         0:00:55:0617    bgp
RP/0/RP0/CPU0:CRS-A#
```

Figure 2-2 shows the most common thread states and transitions between the states. The inner circle actually represents two distinct states: ready and running. A thread state can transition from ready to running and vice versa. A thread in running state may also transition to any of the other states shown in Figure 2-2.

Cisco IOS XR microkernel uses a preemptive, priority based, and non-adaptive scheduling algorithm. Each thread is assigned a priority. The scheduler is responsible for selecting the next thread to run based on the priority assigned. The highest priority thread in ready state is selected to run. There is a ready state first in, first out (FIFO) queue for each priority level.

The idle thread is a special thread of the procnto process in that it is the only thread that runs at priority 0 and uses FIFO scheduling. Also, it is either in running or ready state and it never relinquishes CPU voluntarily. However, because it uses the lowest priority, it can be preempted by any other process that is in ready state.

A running thread may be moved to a different state due to system call (such as a kernel call, exception, or hardware interrupt), getting blocked, preempted, or voluntarily yielding. If a running thread is preempted by a higher priority thread, it moves to the head of the ready queue for its priority. On the other hand, if it is preempted after consuming its timeslice or it voluntarily yields the process, it moves to the end of the ready queue for its priority. *Timeslice* is the maximum time that a running thread can consume while one or more threads are in the ready queue for the same priority level as the running thread.

A running thread blocks when it needs to wait for an event to occur such as a reply message. When a thread is blocked it moves to the corresponding blocked state and stays there until it is unblocked. When the process is unblocked, it normally moves to the tail of the ready queue for its priority. There are some exceptions to this rule.

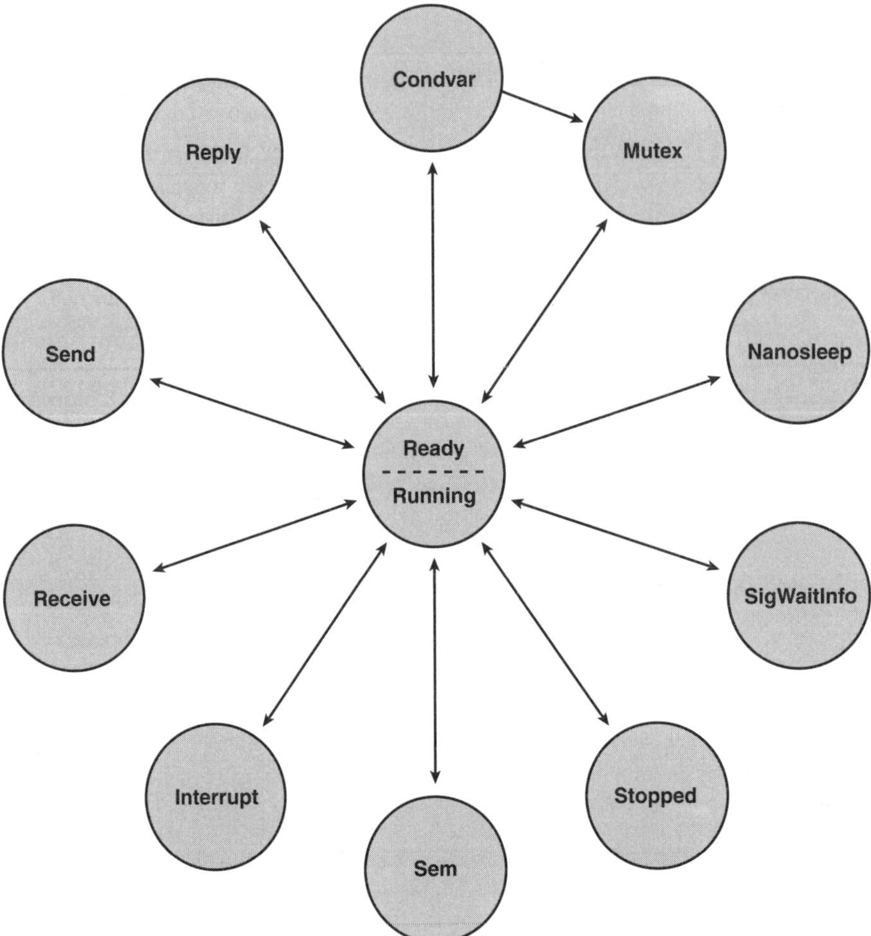

Figure 2-2 *Most Common Thread States and Transitions*

For example, if a server thread is waiting for a client request, it is in a receive blocked state. Suppose the blocked server thread has priority 10 and is unblocked by a client thread at priority 20 sending a request and waiting for a reply. This will unblock the server thread and move the client thread to reply blocked state. If the server thread is moved to the ready queue for priority 10 and there are several threads in ready state at priority 15, it will impact the response time for the client even though the client thread has priority 20. This problem is known as priority inversion. To prevent priority inversion, the microkernel uses priority inheritance, which temporarily boosts the priority of the server thread to match that of the client thread (20) and places the server at the ready queue for the client's priority (20).

Scheduling Algorithms

The microkernel provides the following three scheduling algorithms to meet needs for different scenarios:

- FIFO scheduling
- Round-robin scheduling
- Sporadic scheduling

With FIFO scheduling, a thread continues to run until it voluntarily relinquishes control or is preempted by a higher-priority thread. With Cisco IOS XR, only the idle threads of procnto (kernel) use FIFO scheduling.

Most other processes in IOS XR use round-robin scheduling, which restricts the maximum amount of time (timeslice) a thread can run without relinquishing control. A thread that uses round-robin scheduling runs until it voluntarily relinquishes control, gets preempted by a higher-priority thread, or consumes its timeslice.

Sporadic scheduling algorithm allows a thread to run at its normal priority for a certain amount of time (budget) over a period of replenishment interval before its priority is dropped to a lower priority. Figure 2-3 illustrates how sporadic scheduling works.

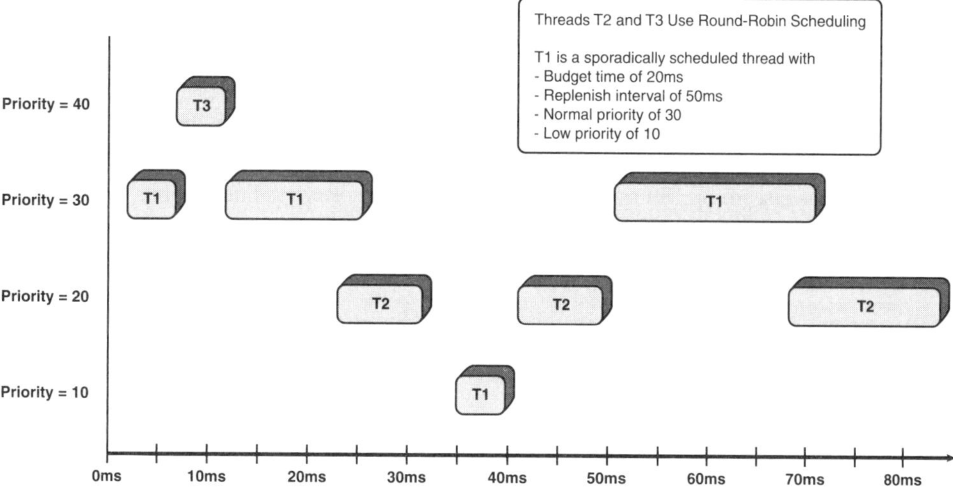

Figure 2-3 *Sporadic Scheduling*

Assume that at time t = 0 ms, threads T1 and T2 are ready to run and all other threads are blocked. Furthermore, assume that T1 is a sporadically scheduled thread with normal priority of 30, low priority of 10, budget time of 20 ms, and replenish interval of 50 ms. T2 is a round-robin scheduled thread with a priority of 20. An example follows:

1. T1 is scheduled to run at t = 0 ms because it has a higher priority than T2.
2. At t = 5 ms, thread T3 with priority of 40 is unblocked and becomes ready.

3. Because T3 has a higher priority than T1, it preempts T1 and starts running. As a result, T1 is moved to the head of the ready queue for priority 30.
4. At t = 10 ms, T3 is blocked and relinquishes CPU. Note that threads T1 with priority 30 and T2 with priority 20 are in the ready state. Therefore, because of its high priority, T1 starts running at t = 10 ms.
5. At t = 25 ms, because T1 has already used its budget time of 20 ms and is a sporadically scheduled thread, its priority is reduced to 10. Because T2 is in ready state and has a priority of 20, it preempts T1 and starts running at t = 25 ms.
6. At t = 50 ms, after the replenish interval lapses, the priority of T1 is restored to its normal priority of 30, which causes T1 to preempt T2 and start running.
7. At t = 70 ms, after T1 has used its budget in the new replenish interval, its priority is reduced to 10 again. This causes T2 to preempt T1 and start running.

Example 2-2 shows a partial output of **show process pidin**, which lists the threads and corresponding process ID (pid), thread ID (tid), process name, priority, scheduling algorithm, and state. The prio column shows the priority and scheduling algorithm of the thread. The scheduling of a thread is denoted as f for FIFO, r for round-robin, or ? for sporadic scheduling. Example 2-2 shows that there are two threads that use FIFO scheduling: procnto threads 1 and 2. These are the idle threads of the kernel. There is one idle thread per CPU. Because this output was taken from the RP of CRS-16/s, which has a two-processor CPU complex, it shows two idle threads, one for each CPU. Example 2-2 also shows that threads 3, 4, and 7 of the eth_server process use sporadic scheduling. All other threads use round-robin scheduling.

Example 2-2 *Output of* show processes pidin

```
RP/0/RP0/CPU0:CRS-A#show processes pidin
     pid tid name                   prio STATE        Blocked
       1   1 procnto                  0f READY
       1   2 procnto                  0f RUNNING
       1   3 procnto                 63r RECEIVE      1
       1   4 procnto                 10r NANOSLEEP
       1   5 procnto                 63r RECEIVE      1
       1   6 procnto                 10r RECEIVE      1
       1   7 procnto                 63r RECEIVE      1
       1   8 procnto                 63r RECEIVE      1
       1   9 procnto                 63r RECEIVE      1
...
   40987   3 pkg/bin/eth_server      50? SEM          29df078
   40987   4 pkg/bin/eth_server      49? SEM          29df080
   40987   5 pkg/bin/eth_server      10r SEM          29defc8
   40987   6 pkg/bin/eth_server      10r RECEIVE      5
   40987   7 pkg/bin/eth_server      55? RECEIVE      9
   40987   8 pkg/bin/eth_server      10r RECEIVE      12
   40987   9 pkg/bin/eth_server      10r RECEIVE      1
```

```
    40987  10 pkg/bin/eth_server   10r RECEIVE      1
    40987  11 pkg/bin/eth_server   55r RECEIVE      1
    45084   1 kg/bin/bcm_process   10r RECEIVE      1
    45084   2 kg/bin/bcm_process   56r RECEIVE      6
    45084   3 kg/bin/bcm_process   56r INTR
    45084   4 kg/bin/bcm_process   56r RECEIVE      10
    45084   5 kg/bin/bcm_process   56r RECEIVE      9
    45084   6 kg/bin/bcm_process   56r RECEIVE      1
    45085   1 pkg/bin/attachd      10r RECEIVE      1
    45085   2 pkg/bin/attachd      55r REPLY        40987
    45085   3 pkg/bin/attachd      55r REPLY        16397
    45086   1 ad_eeprom_protocol   10r RECEIVE      1
    45087   2 pkg/bin/qnet         10r RECEIVE      1
    45087   3 pkg/bin/qnet         10r RECEIVE      4
...
RP/0/RP0/CPU0:CRS-A#

! Count threads that use round-robin scheduling
RP/0/RP0/CPU0:CRS-A#show processes pidin | utility egrep -e "[0-9]+r " count
1025
RP/0/RP0/CPU0:CRS-A#

! List threads that use sporadic scheduling
 RP/0/RP0/CPU0:CRS-A#show processes pidin | include "[0-9]+\\? "
    40987   3 pkg/bin/eth_server   50? SEM          29df078
    40987   4 pkg/bin/eth_server   49? SEM          29df080
    40987   7 pkg/bin/eth_server   55? RECEIVE      9
   180321   5 /bin/parser_server   16? CONDVAR      485f48b4
RP/0/RP0/CPU0:CRS-A#

! List threads that use FIFO scheduling
RP/0/RP0/CPU0:CRS-A#show processes pidin | include "[0-9]+f "
        1   1 procnto                 0f READY
        1   2 procnto                 0f RUNNING
RP/0/RP0/CPU0:CRS-A#RP/0/RP0/CPU0:CRS-A#
```

Synchronization Services

The microkernel provides a message-passing–based synchronous IPC mechanism. This message-passing service copies a message directly from the address space of the sender thread to the receiver thread without intermediate buffering. The content and format of the message are transparent to the kernel. IPC is discussed in greater detail in the section "Interprocess Communication" later in this chapter.

In addition to the message-passing IPC mechanism provided by the microkernel, it is possible to develop other IPC mechanisms that use shared memory space. However, access to the shared memory space must be synchronized to ensure data consistency. For example, if one thread attempts to access a linked list while another thread is in the process of updating it, the result could be catastrophic. The microkernel provides mutex, condvar, and semaphore synchronization tools to address this problem.

Mutual exclusion lock, or mutex, is used to ensure exclusive access to data shared between threads. Before a thread can access the shared data it should first acquire (lock) the mutex. When it completes operation on the shared data, it releases the mutex. Only one thread may acquire a mutex at any given time. If a thread attempts to lock a mutex that is already locked by another thread, it will be blocked until the mutex is unlocked and acquired. When a thread releases a mutex, the highest priority thread waiting to acquire the mutex will unblock and become the new owner of the mutex.

If a higher-priority thread attempts to lock a mutex that is already locked by a lower-priority thread, the priority of the current owner will be increased to that of the higher-priority blocked thread. This is known as *priority inheritance* and solves the priority inversion problem. Priority inheritance and priority inversion are also discussed earlier in this section in the context of client/server thread interaction.

A conditional variable (condvar) is used to wait until some condition (for example, a time-out) is fulfilled. The thread blocks until the condition is satisfied. A condvar is usually used in conjunction with a mutex as follows:

- Lock a mutex
- Wait on a condvar
- Perform an activity (manipulate shared data)
- Unlock the mutex

Semaphore is another form of synchronization in which a thread waits for the semaphore to be positive. If the semaphore is positive, the thread unblocks and decrements the semaphore by 1. A post operation on a semaphore increments it by 1. A semaphore can be used to wake a thread by a signal handler. The thread issues a wait operation on the semaphore to wait for a signal. A signal handler will perform a post operation on the semaphore to wake a thread blocked by the semaphore.

As shown in Example 2-2 earlier in this section, **show process pidin location** *<r/s/m>* shows the state of each thread. Table 2-1 provides a list of states a process may take.

Table 2-1 *Process States*

State	Explanation
dead	The kernel is waiting to release the thread's resources.
running	Actively running on a CPU.
ready	Not running on a CPU but is ready to run.
stopped	Suspended (SIGSTOP signal).
send	Waiting for a client to send a message.

State	Explanation
receive	Waiting for a server to receive a message.
reply	Waiting for a server to reply to a message.
stack	Waiting for more stack to be allocated.
waitpage	Waiting for the process manager to resolve a page fault.
sigsuspend	Waiting for a signal.
sigwaitinfo	Waiting for a signal.
nanosleep	Sleeping for a period of time.
mutex	Waiting to acquire a mutex.
condvar	Waiting for a conditional variable to be signaled.
join	Waiting for the completion of another thread.
intr	Waiting for an interrupt.
sem	Waiting to acquire a semaphore.

As seen in Example 2-2, some of the threads are in a Reply state, which indicates that the client thread is blocked waiting for a reply. If a process is stuck in blocked state, it might be an indication of a problem with the (client/server) process or application. However, the existence of blocked processes on the router does not necessarily indicate a problem because it is expected behavior for selected processes. Other processes stuck in a block state might cause applications not to respond. It is important to understand the typical behavior of a router in your production network.

To display a list of blocked threads, issue the command **show processes blocked location** *<r/s/m>*, as shown in Example 2-3. It is recommended to issue this command several times within a few seconds. Running the command numerous times verifies whether processes are questionably blocked in error versus in a blocked state as it performs its normal IPC exchange. Processes such as ksh and devc-conaux are in a blocked state by design. Ksh is the client process communicating to devc-conaux (the server process). Here the thread is in blocked state until a user provides input on the console server. More specifically, ksh waits for input on the console or the auxiliary port and returns a system message to devc-conaux. When devc-conaux replies to ksh, the process changes the state from blocked to reply.

Example 2-3 *Processes Block*

```
RP/0/RP0/CPU0:CRS1-4#show processes blocked location 0/rp0/cpu0
  Jid       Pid Tid            Name State   TimeInState    Blocked-on
65546     12298   1             ksh Reply 101:26:48:0708   12296  devc-conaux
   52     40988   2         attachd Reply 101:26:50:0679   40985  eth_server
   52     40988   3         attachd Reply 101:26:50:0678   16397  mqueue
   78     40990   6            qnet Reply   0:00:00:0040   40985  eth_server
   78     40990   7            qnet Reply   0:00:00:0038   40985  eth_server
```

```
   78      40990   8              qnet Reply    0:00:00:0032   40985  eth_server
   78      40990   9              qnet Reply    0:00:00:0041   40985  eth_server
   78      40990  10              qnet Reply    0:00:00:0028   40985  eth_server
   78      40990  11              qnet Reply    0:00:00:0033   40985  eth_server
   78      40990  12              qnet Reply    0:00:00:0033   40985  eth_server
   78      40990  13              qnet Reply    0:00:00:0039   40985  eth_server
   51      40996   2     attach_server Reply  101:26:50:0438   16397  mqueue
  394     172114   1       tftp_server Reply  101:25:02:0994   16397  mqueue
  135     499850   4            cethha Reply    0:00:10:0981       1  node
0/RP1/CPU0 kernel
  276     512195   2           lpts_fm Reply    0:00:10:0194  495725  lpts_pa
65742    1470670   1              exec Reply   42:18:14:0620   12296  devc-conaux
65807    1474831   1              exec Reply    2:14:28:0875  512187  devc-vty
65809    4870417   1              exec Reply    0:00:00:0300       1  kernel
65810    4874514   1              more Reply    0:00:00:0094   16395  pipe
65811    4874515   1    show_processes Reply    0:00:00:0000       1  kernel
RP/0/RP0/CPU0:CRS1-4#
```

Cisco IOS XR System Manager

Cisco IOS XR has hundreds of processes running simultaneously on multiple nodes. Some processes are associated with applications and protocols. Examples of such processes include telnetd and isis, which refer to Telnet daemon (server) and the IS-IS routing protocol, respectively. Other processes are dedicated to system functions such as device drivers, interprocess communication, system health monitor, file system, configuration management, software install management, and so on. Such processes are always operational.

IOS XR system manager is the central entity responsible for starting, monitoring, restarting, terminating, and core dumping most IOS XR processes during bootup, RP failover, software activation, and in response to router configuration. System manager can also initiate disaster recovery based on process health. System manger runs on each route processor and line card in the system. Two instances of sysmgr process are running on each node. One of the instances is the primary sysmgr, which is responsible for all system manager responsibilities; the second instance acts as a standby and is ready to assume the primary role if the current primary sysmgr exits for some reason.

The following are the main functions of system manager:

- Start processes during bootup or node reload
- Start processes during route processor (RP) failover
- Start processes in response to user configuration; for example, when a user configures an OSPF process using **router ospf** *<process-name>*, system manager starts a new OSPF process instance

- Act as a central repository for all process-related information
- Initiate disaster recovery based on the process health
- Invoke dumper to collect a core dump when a process terminates abnormally

Process Attributes

System manager uses process attributes stored in a startup file for each process that it manages. Each startup file corresponds to an executable. The startup files are located in the /pkg/startup/ directory and contain tokens that are used by system manager to manage the corresponding process. The startup file for OSPF, FIB manager, and GSP are shown in Example 2-4.

Example 2-4 *Startup Files for OSPF, FIB_mgr, and GSP Processes*

```
# more /pkg/startup/ospf.startup
name:ospf
path:/ios/bin
item:/cfg/gl/ipv4-ospf/proc/
copies:10
tuple_dynamic_tag:ON
placement: ON
check_avail: ON
failover_tier: isis
standby_capable: ON
#
# more /pkg/startup/fib_mgr.startup
name:fib_mgr
path:/ios/bin
check_avail: ON
level:99
standby_capable:ON
#
# more /pkg/startup/gsp-rp.startup
name:gsp
path:/ios/bin
level: 80
check_avail:on
mandatory: on
```

The name token corresponds to the name of the process and the corresponding executable. The path token is the path where the executable is located. If the level token is set it implies that the process is level started during boot. During system boot the system manager uses the level token to determine the sequence in which the processes are started. The startup sequence during boot is shown in Table 2-2. You can use **show process boot location** *<r/s/m>* to see the boot sequence and startup level and at what time each process is ready.

Table 2-2 *IOS XR Startup Levels During Boot*

Band	Levels	Examples
MBI	0–39	dllmgr, nvram, obflmgr, dumpr, syslogd
ARB (arbitration)	40	wdsysmon, redcon
ADMIN	41–90	sysdb, netio, oir_daemon, gsp, envmon, shelfmgr
INFRA	91–100	ifmgr, aib, ipv4_io, fib_mgr
ACTIVE	101–150	ipv4_ma
FINAL	151–999	clns, arp

If the item token is set, it indicates that the corresponding process is started or terminated when a user enters configuration or when the configuration is loaded to the system database (sysdb) during boot. The process is started when the configuration item specified in the startup file is added to sysdb. For example, when the user enters and commits the configuration **router ospf** *<process-name>* system manager starts an OSPF process instance. System database is discussed in more detail in the section "Cisco IOS XR System Database" later in this chapter.

If the mandatory token is set to ON, the process is considered critical for the functioning of the node, which is any subsystem such as line card, route processor, service processor, or switch fabric card module running IOS XR. If a mandatory process exits or dies and fails to be restarted after repeated attempts, system manager will reload the node.

If the placement item is set to ON, the corresponding process is placeable and can run on any active RP or DRP node on the router. Process placement is discussed in the section "Process Placement," later in this chapter.

System manager assigns a unique job id (JID) to each executable. The JID is persistent across restarts. In addition to a JID each process is assigned a unique process ID (PID) when it is started or restarted. If a process is restarted it is assigned a new PID number but it retains its original JID number.

Some processes, such as telnetd, are transient processes that are started in response to a user request (telnetting to the router). These transient processes are not managed by system manager, and their JID is derived from their processed ID (PID). For transient processes a startup file is not needed because they are not started by the system manager.

System Manager and Process Lifecycle

System manager monitors the health of each process. Figure 2-4 shows the system manager and process lifecycle. When system manager starts a process it starts an end of initialization (EOI) timer. After the process starts and completes initialization it notifies system manager by sending an end of initialization signal. If the EOI timer for a process expires before sysmgr receives EOI from the process, sysmgr declares that process initialization failed.

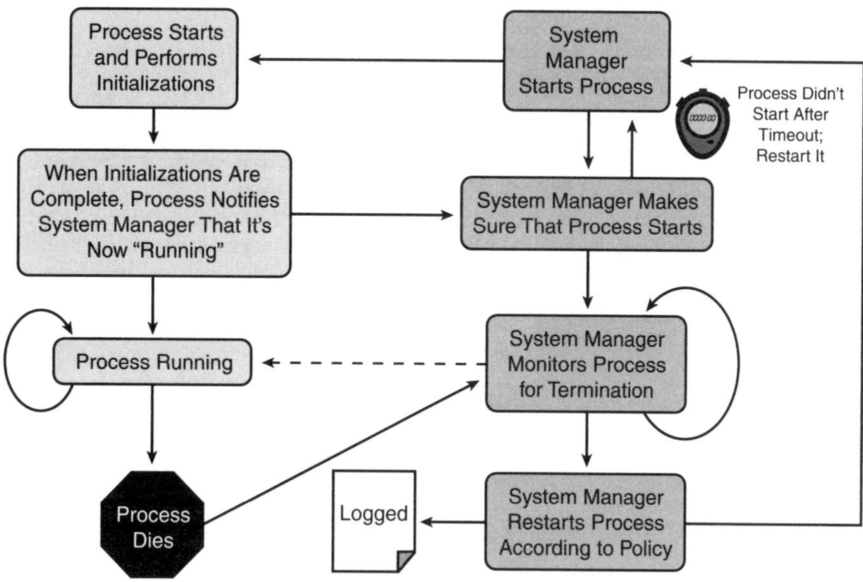

Figure 2-4 *Sysmgr and Process Lifecycle*

CLI for Sysmgr and Processes

System manager provides a rich set of commands to check the status of processes; start, stop, crash, and restart processes; and configure process attributes. Use **show process** [*<process-name>* | *<JID>*] **location** *<r/s/m>* to show the process data and status. Example 2-5 displays an example of such output for an IS-IS process on a primary RP.

Example 2-5 *IS-IS Process and Threads*

```
RP/0/RP0/CPU0:CRS1-4#show processes isis
                  Job Id: 255
                     PID: 12714252
         Executable path: /disk0/hfr-rout-3.6.2/bin/isis
              Instance #: 1
              Version ID: 00.00.0000
                 Respawn: ON
           Respawn count: 5
  Max. spawns per minute: 12
            Last started: Thu Jan 15 05:06:57 2009
           Process state: Run (last exit due to SIGTERM)
           Package state: Normal
       Started on config: cfg/gl/isis/instance/test/ord_A/running
                    core: COPY
```

```
              Max. core: 0
              Placement: ON
           startup_path: /pkg/startup/isis.startup
                  Ready: 2.615s
              Available: 2.664s
      Process cpu time:  0.537 user, 0.130 kernel, 0.667 total
JID     TID  Stack pri state        TimeInState       HR:MM:SS:MSEC NAME
255     1       48K  10 Receive       0:00:14:0377    0:00:00:0284 isis
255     2       48K  10 Receive       0:00:01:0591    0:00:00:0075 isis
255     3       48K  10 Receive     110:34:27:0344    0:00:00:0008 isis
255     4       48K  10 Receive     110:34:18:0331    0:00:00:0002 isis
255     5       48K  10 Receive       0:00:01:0591    0:00:00:0159 isis
255     6       48K  10 Receive       0:00:07:0283    0:00:00:0009 isis
-------------------------------------------------------------------------
RP/0/RP0/CPU0:CRS1-4#
```

The definition of the key attributes of IOS XR processes follow:

- **Job ID (JID):** The JID number remains constant, including process restarts.
- **Process ID (PID):** The PID field changes when a process is restarted.
- **Thread ID (TID):** A single process can have multiple threads executing specific tasks for a process.
- **Executable path:** References a path to the process executable. An additional field called "executable path on reboot" may appear if an in-service software upgrade has been performed.
- **Instance:** There may be more than one instance of a process running at a given time. Each instance is referenced by a number.
- **Respawn count:** The number of times a process has been (re)started. The first time a process is started, the respawn count is set to 1. Respawn mode is on or off. This field indicates whether this process restarts automatically in case of failure.
- **Max spawns per minute:** The number of respawns not to be exceeded in one minute. If this number is exceeded, the process stops restarting as a self-defense mechanism.
- **Last started date and time:** This timestamp shows when the process was last started.
- **Process state:** This shows the current state of the process.
- **Started on config:** Points to the location in system database (SysDB) that contains configuration data that resulted in spawn of the process.
- **core:** Memory segments to include in core file.
- **Max. core:** Shows the number of times to dump a core file. A value of 0 signifies infinity.

- **Mandatory:** Shows whether the process is mandatory. If it is mandatory, and sysmgr fails to start or restart it successfully after repeated attempts, it results in system reload.

As pointed out earlier, each process has several threads, and each thread is identified by a thread ID (TID). In addition, in some cases each thread is assigned a thread name. Use **show process threadname** *<JID>* to find the thread name of each thread of a process. Note that you can obtain the JID of a process using either **show process**, which lists all processes, or **show process** *<process-name>*, which provides detailed information for the process. Example 2-6 shows the thread names for an IS-IS process. Some of the threads shown under a given process might belong to some of the DLL libraries loaded by the process. For example, in the IS-IS case of Example 2-6, chkpt_evm is not an IS-IS thread but a thread owned by a checkpoint DLL library running under IS-IS process space.

Example 2-6 *Display of IS-IS Threads Names*

```
RP/0/RP0/CPU0:CRS-4#show processes threadname 255
Sat Mar 14 10:14:57.262 UTC
JID     TID   ThreadName        pri state     TimeInState        NAME
255     1     Management        10 Receive        0:00:04:0675 isis
255     2     chkpt_evm         10 Receive        0:00:01:0161 isis
255     3     Hello             10 Receive        0:00:01:0024 isis
255     4     Update            10 Receive        0:00:00:0805 isis
255     5     Decision          10 Receive        0:00:01:0003 isis
255     6     TE                10 Receive        0:01:59:0161 isis
255     7     MIB Traps         10 Condvar        0:05:53:0591 isis
RP/0/RP0/CPU0:CRS-4#
```

You can use **process** [**crash** | **restart** | **shutdown** | **start**] [*<process-name>* | *<JID>*] **location** *<r/s/m>* to start, restart, crash, or stop a process on a node.

Interprocess Communication

A robust IPC mechanism is critical for any distributed system. In IOS XR, the importance of efficient and reliable IPC mechanism is even greater in that IOS XR is a highly modular and massively distributed system. Various IPC mechanisms are developed in IOS XR for different purposes and to meet different requirements. This section discusses some of the most common IPC mechanisms used by IOS XR.

Characteristics of IPC Mechanisms

This section discusses major characteristics that define an IPC mechanism and differentiate one IPC mechanism from another.

Synchronous Versus Asynchronous

With synchronous communication, the sender thread blocks until the message is processed by the receiving thread. The basic IPC mechanism provided by the microkernel is an example of a synchronous IPC. With synchronous IPC, the sender can send only one message at a time because it must wait for the receiver to process the message before attempting to send another one. Although this may limit the throughput performance, it has one important advantage in that the sender cannot overrun the receiver. Figure 2-5 shows the execution flow for the sender and receiver thread for synchronous IPC.

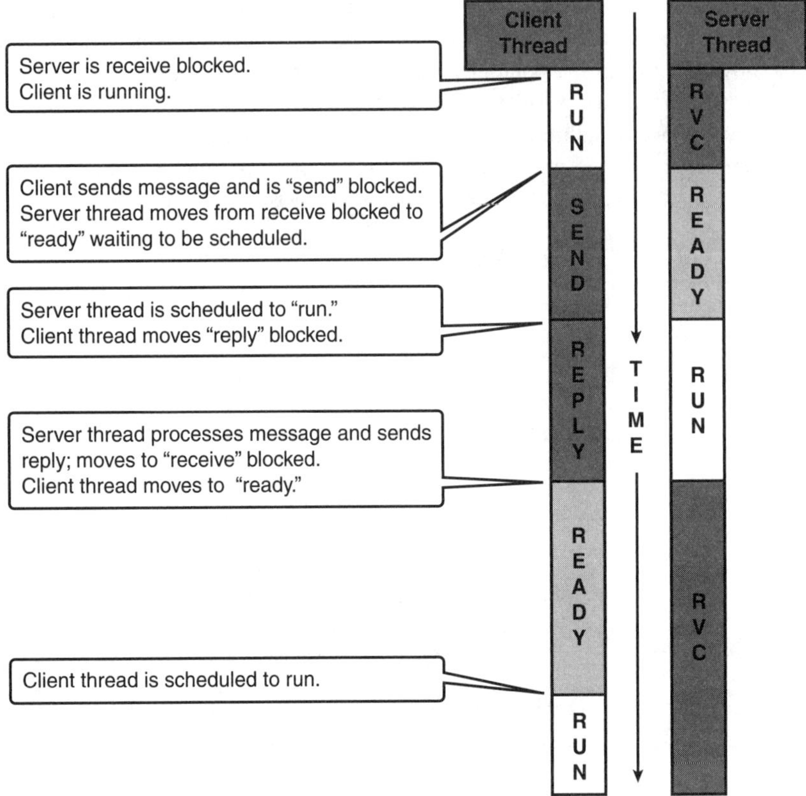

Figure 2-5 *Synchronous IPC*

With asynchronous communication, the sender and receiver are not tightly coupled. The sender is unblocked before the receiver processes the message. In fact, the sender does not know when the receiver processes the message that it sent. The sender can send multiple messages before the receiver processes any of the previously received messages. Although this has the advantage of higher throughput, it also has potential risk of overflowing the receiver buffer. Limiting the maximum number of receive buffers available for a sender prevents the risk of overflowing the receiver. Figure 2-6 shows the execution flow for sender and receiver thread for asynchronous IPC.

Intra-node Versus Inter-node

Cisco IOS XR is designed for massively distributed platforms including multichassis (or multirack) systems. There is significant communication and coordination among different nodes. Some IPC mechanisms can be used only in a single CPU or symmetric multi-processor (SMP) environment, which is referred to here as a *node*. In this context, a node is not necessarily equivalent to a line card or RP/DRP. In fact, some line cards and RP/DRPs have multiple CPUs or SMPs—therefore, they have multiple nodes. For example, a CRS line card (MSC) has two nodes, CPU0 and SP, corresponding to the main CPU and service processor (SP), respectively.

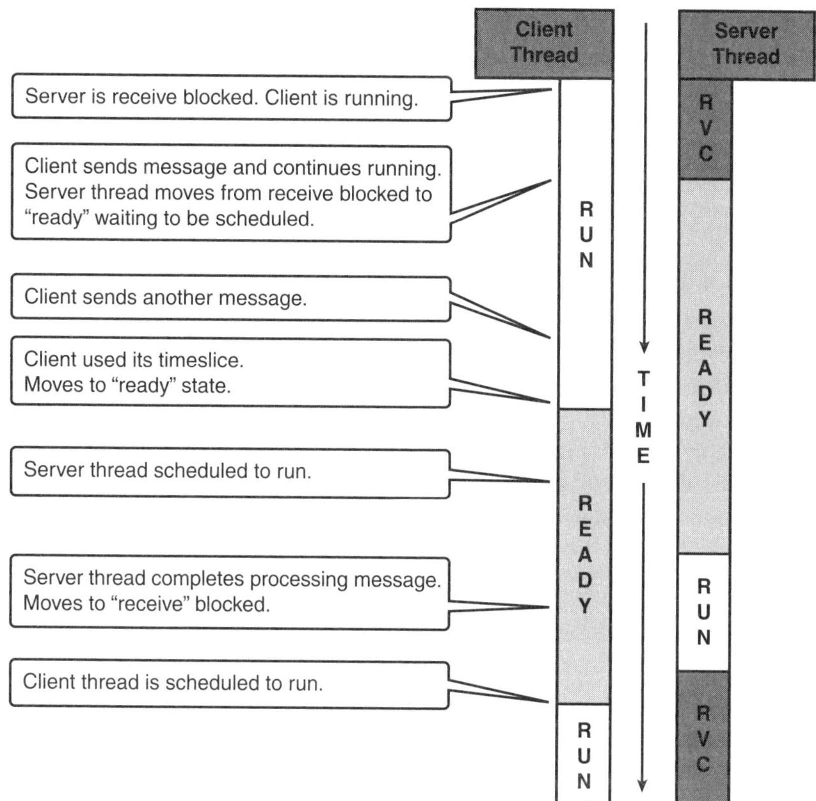

Figure 2-6 *Asynchronous IPC*

An intra-node IPC mechanism can be used only within a single node, whereas an inter-node IPC mechanism can be used between different nodes. Generally the inter-node IPC mechanism supports both inter-node and intra-node communication.

Connection-Oriented Versus Rendezvous

This classification deals with the types of activities preceding the message exchange.

With a connection-oriented scheme the receiver (typically a server) creates and advertises a channel, and the sender (client) connects to the channel before any message is sent by the sender. Both the sender and receiver are aware of the identity of each other. If either the sender or receiver restarts, the connection must be reestablished.

With the rendezvous scheme the data, not the receiver or its channel, is the primary focus of the IPC. The communicating parties find each other through the name of the data structure. The rendezvous scheme is suitable for a producer-consumer model of communication. In a producer-consumer model, a producer process generates data while one or more consumers process the data. The consumers are not interested in the identity of the producer; they are interested in the identity of the data produced.

Point-to-Point Versus Point-to-Multipoint

Point-to-point communication is used between two threads. In some cases it is necessary to send the same message to several threads within a single node or to multiple nodes. This can be achieved using multiple point-to-point communications. However, the use of point-to-point communication for this scenario is inefficient. Moreover, the sender has to know the identity of all the receivers. The use of point-to-multipoint communication solves both problems.

Light Weight Messaging

Light Weight Messaging (LWM) is a point-to-point, synchronous, and connection-oriented communication built on top of QNX synchronous IPC. The microkernel is involved in copying the message from the sender thread memory space to the receiver's memory space. Because the client is blocked after sending each message, there are at least two context switching instances per message. When a client sends a message, it is blocked. If a server is already in receive blocked state, the server thread will run immediately; otherwise, another thread will run until the server thread issues a MsgReceive call. After the server processes the message, the client becomes ready.

LWM can be used both for intra-node and inter-node communication transparently. The sender does not need to know whether the receiver is on a local or remote node.

Group Service Protocol

Group Service Protocol (GSP) is a point-to-multipoint, connectionless, and asynchronous communication mechanism. GSP communication identifies members by a logical group ID (GID) that can be mapped to a multicast address. The multicast address could be an IP multicast address, multicast MAC address, or fabric group ID (FGID).

With GSP the sender does not need to know the identity or location of receivers. GSP provides the sender with a mechanism to send to all members of a GID, a subset of members, or to a single member.

GSP is discussed in more detail in the "Distributed Services" section.

Atomic Descriptor Ring

Atomic descriptor ring (ADR) is a point-to-point, asynchronous, and concurrent IPC mechanism for intra-node communication. The rings are fixed-size FIFO with a configurable data area specified at ring creation time. Data is copied into and out of ADR in user mode and does not require kernel intervention. It is suitable for a producer-consumer type of application.

Qnet

Qnet is a QNX Neutrino protocol for communication between processes residing on different nodes. It enables IPC to work across nodes. For example, LWM uses Qnet transparently to enable inter-node communication.

The use of a symbolic link (symlink) enables location transparency to the Qnet protocol. When a process needs to communicate with another process, it uses the symlink associated with the service and does not need to know where the service is located. A server process registers with Qnet symlink manager (QSM) and publishes its service using symlink.

To verify Qnet connectivity, use **ping control-eth location** *<r/s/m>* from Admin mode, as shown in Example 2-7. Each node has a MAC address associated with it. The Control Ethernet (CE) **ping** command shown in Example 2-7 sends the ping packet to the MAC address of the destination node over the Control Ethernet. When the destination node receives the CE ping packet, it sends a reply back to the originator node much like routers reply to ping packets. Example 2-7 shows the destination node MAC address, number of CE ping packets sent and received, and minimum, maximum, and average round trip time for CE ping packets. CE ping is used to verify Control Ethernet connectivity.

Example 2-7 *Verify Qnet Connectivity*

```
RP/0/RP0/CPU0:CRS-E(admin)#ping control-eth location 0/0/cpu0 count 100

Src node:         513  :  0/RP0/CPU0
Dest node:          1  :  0/0/CPU0
Local node:       513  :  0/RP0/CPU0
Packet cnt:       100  Packet size:    128  Payload ptn type: default (0)
Hold-off (ms):      1  Time-out(s):      2  Max retries: 5
DelayTimeout:       1Destination node has MAC addr 5246.4800.0001

Running CE node ping.
Please wait...
Src: 513, Dest: 1, Sent: 100, Rec'd: 100, Mismatched: 0
Min/Avg/Max RTT (usecs): 0/50/3000
CE node ping succeeded for node: 1
RP/0/RP0/CPU0:CRS-E(admin)#
```

Distributed Services

Cisco IOS XR allows applications to be highly distributed so that the system can achieve very high scalability and service flexibility. IOS XR supports a multichassis or multishelf system with several interconnected racks. It also allows a system to be subdivided into multiple secure domain routers. This chapter discusses some of the key services responsible for enabling IOS XR to achieve a high degree of distributed applications and service flexibility.

GSP

Group service protocol (GSP), which is discussed briefly in the preceding section, is a distributed and reliable group communication protocol. GSP enables a set of distributed processes to function as one application.

GSP communication can be characterized as follows:

- GSP is connectionless and location transparent.
- It is efficient because it supports one-to-many communication, which allows the sender to send once for many targets.
- It uses asynchronous semantics. The sender unblocks before the receivers receive the message. Asynchronous semantics is less prone to deadlock and provides better throughput and performance.
- GSP communication describes members with a logical group ID, not physical (location based) ID.
- Group communication allows members to be reached by a multicast address or, additionally, a logical set on top of a multicast address (selective multicast).
- The sender can send to the entire group, which will deliver to whichever nodes are in the group. The sender need not know anything about the group members.
- The sender can send to a subset of members in the group—a subset of nodes or subset of members.
- GSP supports open group communication and allows nonmembers to send messages to all members in a group.

The GSP process runs on every node in the system. It manages local membership and member nodes. GSP on a local node does not need to know the identity of remote node clients. GSP identifies each group with a unique group ID (GID). The GID maps to a multicast address, which is either fabric group ID (FGID) if it is transported over the fabric or multicast MAC address if it is transported over Control Ethernet. The GID number space is divided into three different ranges as shown in Table 2-3.

Table 2-3 *GID Number Allocation*

GID Range	Description
0–999	Used for admin plane. Scope: All nodes in the system. Transported over Control Ethernet.
1000–1999	Used for SDR control (LR-control). Scope: All SDR node. Transported over Control Ethernet.
> 2000	Used for LR plane. Scope: All SDR nodes. Transported over fabric.

GSP provides a CLI that lists groups and shows group membership and stats for all three planes.

The command **show gsp stats client location** *<r/s/p>* provides the number of messages sent and received for each GSP client process. It also provides an error counter per GSP client process. Example 2-8 shows sample output of the GSP **stats** command.

Example 2-8 *GSP Stats*

```
RP/0/RP0/CPU0:CRS-A#show gsp stats client location 0/0/CPU0
Group stats collected during last 1876575 seconds:

  JID Process          Lookup  Create    Sent  ms/call    Rcv   Error   Eagain   Etime
 --- ---------- ---- ---- ---- ---- --- --- ---
215   qsm                 0       10       96      28    1138       8        8      0
276   sysdb_svr_local     0        2      462       3    6966       0        0      0
275   sysdb_mc            4        4     1269       7    2647       0        0      0
173   lrd                 0        4       11      16     732       0        0      0
135   fabricq_mgr         0        2       21       0      92       0        0      0
160   ingressq            0        1      213       0     256       0        0      0
60    insthelper          0        4       12      60    1317       0        0      0
217   rdsfs_svr           0        8     2650       2   19236     216        0      0
146   ifmgr               1        6      106       5     121       0        0      0
142   hfr_pm              1        5   125214       0    1150       4        0      0
194   pfi_ifh_server      0        1        2      12      70       0        0      0
271   statsd_server       1        3      135       3     138       0        0      0
221   rsi_agent           0        2       12      50    1039       0        0      0
156   ipv6_io             0        2       11      55    1168       0        0      0
149   improxy             0        1        0       0      82       0        0      0
105   bfd_agent           0        4       20      31    1279       0        0      0
152   ipv4_io             0        1        0       0      29       0        0      0
134   fib_mgr             8       13   308232       1  305868       0        0      0
184   netio               1        4    31291       0   63412       0        0      0
169   l2fib_mgr           0        3       11      50    1028       0        0      0
141   fab_svr             0        2        5      17     514       0        0      0
153   ipv4_ma             1        4       11      48    1767       0        0      0
196   pifibm_server       2       12       60      12   94555       0        0      0
.....cut.....
```

You can use the command **show gsp groups [admin | lr-control] location** *<r/s/m>* to list GSP groups in admin, lr-control, or SDR. It lists the groups with GID and group name. Example 2-9 shows sample output for the admin plane group.

Example 2-9 *GSP Admin Plane Group*

```
RP/0/RP0/CPU0:CRS-A#show gsp groups admin location 0/0/cpu0

 List of groups in Admin Plane
Grp_ID Grp_Name
****** ********
     0 gsp_admin
     1 ens_admin_group
     2 _async_admin_group
     3 gang_sched_admin_group
     4 sysdb_medusae_u_admin
     5 sysdb_medusae_u_admin_s
     9 sysdb_medusae_v1_admin
    10 sysdb_medusae_v1_admin_s
    11 FDI0
    16 lrd_admin_grp
    19 QSM_LC_ADMIN_GRP
    24 FDI_SPONGES
RP/0/RP0/CPU0:CRS-A#
```

Example 2-10 shows sample output for the LR-control group.

Example 2-10 *GSP LR-control Group*

```
RP/0/RP0/CPU0:CRS-A#show gsp groups lr-control location 0/rp0/cpU0

 List of groups in Lctrl Plane
Grp_ID Grp_Name
****** ********
  1000 gsp_lctrl
  1001 ens_lctrl_group
  1002 _async_lctrl_group
  1003 gang_sched_lctrl_group
  1004 lrd_lctrl_grp
  1005 sysdb_medusae_u
  1006 QSM_LR_GRP
  1007 sysdb_medusae_v1
  1008 sysdb_medusae_u_s_lr_shared
  1009 sysdb_medusae_v1_s_lr_shared
  1010 PuF group: persisted placement
RP/0/RP0/CPU0:CRS-A#
```

Example 2-11 shows sample output for the SDR group.

Example 2-11 *GSP SDR Scoped Group*

```
RP/0/RP0/CPU0:CRS-A#show gsp groups location  0/14/CPU0

 List of groups in LR Plane
Grp_ID Grp_Name
****** ********
  2000 gsp
  2001 ens_group
  2002 _async_group
  2003 gang_sched_group
  2013 RDS_CGRP_/etc/cfg/lr_1
  2014 RDS_WTR_LWG_GRP_/etc/cfg/lr_1
  2015 RDS_CGRP_/etc/cfg/alt_cfg_1
  2016 RDS_WTR_LWG_GRP_/etc/cfg/alt_cf
  2017 PFI_IFH_GROUP
  2018 IMD_SERVER
  2019 statsd_group
  2020 ifstats_group
  2025 iir_gsp_group
  2026 im_bundle_group
  2027 im_iir_group
  2028 IMD_CLIENT
  2029 ipv4_io_grp
  2030 bcdl_pa_ff
  2031 bcdl_pa_ff_sg0
  2032 im_attr_owners
  2033 IMP_GROUP
  2034 im_attr_clients_async
  2035 im_attr_clients_sync
  2036 L2FIB_MAC_DISTR_GSP_GROUP
  2037 IPSEC_FVRF_GRP
  2042 BFD_GSP_GROUP
  2050 statsd_mgr_lwg
  2052 nd_gsp_group
  2053 bcdl_ipv4_rib
  2054 bcdl_ipv4_rib_sg0
  2055 bcdl_ipv6_rib
  2056 bcdl_ipv6_rib_sg0
  2058 rt_check_ipv4_rib
  2060 rt_check_ipv6_rib
  2062 bcdl_mpls_lsd_v4
  2063 bcdl_mpls_lsd_v4_sg0
  2076 arp_gsp_group
RP/0/RP0/CPU0:CRS-A#
```

Bulk Content Downloader

Bulk Content Downloader (BCDL) is used to download large data tables using GSP. It is primarily used to download routing tables and MPLS label bindings to line cards and FGID tables to fabric cards. It uses the producer/consumer model. Routing information base (RIB) and label switch database (LSD) on the RP are examples of producers. FIB manager processes on the line cards and RP are consumers of the data generated by the producer processes.

BCDL uses GSP to multicast tables over the fabric or control Ethernet to multiple nodes. The following are the services provided by BCDL:

- Downloads data using GSP. BCDL multicasts routing tables and label bindings to line cards over the fabric, and FGID tables to fabric cards over the Control Ethernet. FGID is used on the CRS-1 system because it uses a three-stage switch fabric. FGID is not used on XR12K or ASR9000 systems.
- Handles card insertion or reload. If a line card or fabric card is inserted or reloaded, it needs to receive RIB or FGID tables. Because all other line cards and/or fabric cards have already received the tables, BCDL uses unicast to download tables to the inserted or reloaded line card.
- Handles process restart in a similar way as LC reload.
- Supports multiple tables in RIB to support multiple virtual routing and forwarding tables (VRF). Each table can be sent to a specific set of line cards.

Example 2-12 shows all BCDL consumers on the router. For each BCDL group, the output shows GSP GID, location of producer, number of consumers, location and PID of consumers, and corresponding stats. For example, FGID_BCDL_Srv0 is produced on RP0, uses GSP GID=18, and has four consumers; that is, one consumer (sfe_drvr) on each fabric card (0/SM0/SP, 0/SM1/SP, 0/SM2/SP, 0/SM3/SP).

Example 2-12 *BCDL Consumers*

```
RP/0/RP0/CPU0:CRS1-1#show bcdl consumers
group FGID_BCDL_Svr0, gsp gid 18, 4 consumers, agent jid 111, node 0/RP0/CPU0
(expected 4 consumers to reply, received 4 replies)
      pid        node asg csg  lwg sus  messages        bytes   errs name
    45100    0/SM3/SP   0   0   19   N       460        12472      0 sfe_drvr
    45100    0/SM0/SP   0   0   19   N       460        12472      0 sfe_drvr
    45100    0/SM2/SP   0   0   19   N       460        12472      0 sfe_drvr
    45100    0/SM1/SP   0   0   19   N       460        12040      0 sfe_drvr
```

```
group ipv4_mrib, gsp gid 2080, 4 consumers, agent jid 117, node 0/RP0/CPU0
(expected 4 consumers to reply, received 4 replies)
      pid        node asg csg  lwg sus  messages     bytes  errs name
   434426 0/RP0/CPU0   0   0 2081   N         12      1660     0 ipv4_mfwd_partne
   278761 0/RP1/CPU0   0   0 2081   N         12      1712     0 ipv4_mfwd_partne
   110711   0/0/CPU0   0   0 2081   N         12      1676     0 ipv4_mfwd_partne
   110720   0/7/CPU0   0   0 2081   N         12      1676     0 ipv4_mfwd_partne

group ipv4_rib, gsp gid 2052, 4 consumers, agent jid 110, node 0/2/CPU0
(expected 4 consumers to reply, received 4 replies)
      pid        node asg csg  lwg sus  messages     bytes  errs name
   254081 0/RP1/CPU0   0   0 2053   N         47     47700     0 fib_mgr
    86101   0/0/CPU0   0   0 2053   N         47     47700     0 fib_mgr
    82006   0/7/CPU0   0   0 2053   N         47     47700     0 fib_mgr
   389249 0/RP0/CPU0   0   0 2053   N         47     47700     0 fib_mgr

group ipv6_rib, gsp gid 2055, 4 consumers, agent jid 111, node 0/2/CPU0
(expected 4 consumers to reply, received 4 replies)
      pid        node asg csg  lwg sus  messages     bytes  errs name
   254081 0/RP1/CPU0   0   0 2056   N          1        28     0 fib_mgr
   389249 0/RP0/CPU0   0   0 2056   N          1        28     0 fib_mgr
    82006   0/7/CPU0   0   0 2056   N          1        28     0 fib_mgr
    86101   0/0/CPU0   0   0 2056   N          1        28     0 fib_mgr

group mpls_lsd_v4, gsp gid 2062, 4 consumers, agent jid 115, node 0/RP0/CPU0
(expected 4 consumers to reply, received 4 replies)
      pid        node asg csg  lwg sus  messages     bytes  errs name
   389249 0/RP0/CPU0   0   0 2063   N       3578    806444     0 fib_mgr
   254081 0/RP1/CPU0   0   0 2063   N       3578    806444     0 fib_mgr
    86101   0/0/CPU0   0   0 2063   N       3578    806444     0 fib_mgr
    82006   0/7/CPU0   0   0 2063   N       3578    806444     0 fib_mgr

group mpls_lsd_v6, gsp gid 2064, 0 consumers, agent jid 116, node 0/RP0/CPU0

group pa_ff, gsp gid 2029, 4 consumers, agent jid 112, node 0/RP0/CPU0
(expected 4 consumers to reply, received 4 replies)
      pid        node asg csg  lwg sus  messages     bytes  errs name
   401557 0/RP0/CPU0   0   0 2030   N        428     73876     0 pifibm_server
    86113   0/0/CPU0   0   0 2030   N        428     73876     0 pifibm_server
    82020   0/7/CPU0   0   0 2030   N        428     73876     0 pifibm_server
   266396 0/RP1/CPU0   0   0 2030   N        428     73876     0 pifibm_server
```

Process Placement

In Cisco CRS-1 and Cisco XR12000 series routers, additional route processors can be added to the system in addition to the active and standby RPs. The additional route processors can be used to offload processes from the main RP (or RP pairs), effectively increasing the overall processing capacity of the system. The additional route processors can be paired to form active and standby RPs. The process of moving processes from one RP to another is known as *process placement.*

In the case of CRS-1, the Distributed Route Processor (DRP) card provides additional flexibility and horsepower. The main route processors are placed in dedicated slots.

In the case of XR12000, the PRP used as the main processor can be used as a DRP to provide additional horsepower. The PRP can be placed in any line card slot.

Process placement allows offloading of resource-intensive processes to the DRP from the main RP, resulting in system performance improvement. The DRP does not perform any of the shelf-designated functions normally performed by the RP. Only the main RP can be the designated shelf controller (DSC) in a single or multishelf system.

The process called *placed* (place daemon) manages the process placement feature. There is one placed process per secure domain router. Process placement provides a better distribution of system resources and increases availability.

Configuring process placement requires few commands and an understanding of affinities. *Affinity* can be described as the force of attraction between two heterogeneous objects. Configuring an affinity value essentially sets a degree of preference that determines whether a process would be attracted or repulsed to a particular RP. Process placement can be a triggered event or manually set by an operator. Process placement can also be configured to trigger when a memory threshold is reached and to avoid instability, a resource intensive process's affinity is set to be attractive to another node, or repulse on the existing (D)RP.

Cisco documentation provides details on four affinities that are configurable to influence process placement. The following affinities are referenced from CCO Process Placement on IOS XR software.

The configurable affinities are as follows:

- Affinity location set
- Affinity location type
- Affinity program
- Affinity self

Affinity location set specifies a preference for a process to run on a specific node pair. A *node pair* is either an active and standby pair of nodes (hosted on RPs or DRPs), or a single active node on an RP or DRP that does not have a redundant standby node.

Affinity location type specifies a preference for a process to run on a particular location type. Available location types are as follows:

- **Paired:** RP nodes that have an associated standby node
- **Primary:** Primary RP node for the SDR (also known as the *designated secure domain router system controller* or *DSDRSC*)
- **Current:** Current node. A process's affinity to its current node characterizes its preference to remain on the same node where possible.

You configure the placement policy to allow certain processes to stay where they are (current) or move them by specifying various affinity values. *The higher the value of an affinity, the stronger the requirement that the process run at a particular location.* A low or zero point value indicates a weaker requirement (or no preference) that a process run at a location.

Affinity program specifies a preference for a process to run on the same node as another process or to run on a different node than another process. You would want to use this affinity in a case where certain processes perform better when they are running together on the same node (attract) or on different nodes, apart from each other (repulse).

Affinity self adjusts placement decisions when multiple instances of a process are started. An attract (positive) affinity indicates a preference to have all instances of a process run on the same node, whereas a repulse (negative) affinity indicates a preference to have each instance of a process run on different nodes.

The command **show placement program all** provides a detailed output showing on which node each process or thread resides. Manually moving a process on a router from the default location of an RP to the DRP is done through manipulation of affinities or attractiveness to a node. In Example 2-13, the BGP process has been manually placed on a DRP located in Slot 2 of router 1 (CRS1-1).

Example 2-13 *Output of the* **show placement program all** *Command*

```
RP/0/RP0/CPU0:CRS1-1#show placement program all

If a program is shown as having 'rejected locations' (i.e., locations on which
it cannot be placed), the locations in question can been seen using the "show
placement policy program" command.

If a program has been placed but not yet started, the amount of time elapsed
since the program was placed is shown in the 'waiting to start' field.

Parentheses around the node indicate that the node has not yet fully booted.
  This will be true of standby nodes.
```

```
Program                         Placed at location          # rejected  Waiting
                                                            locations   to start
----------------------------------------------------------------------------------
li_mgr                          0/RP0/CPU0 (0/RP1/CPU0)
statsd_manager                  0/RP0/CPU0 (0/RP1/CPU0)
ipv4_rib                        0/2/CPU0
ipv6_rib                        0/2/CPU0
policy_repository               0/RP0/CPU0 (0/RP1/CPU0)
ipv4_arm                        0/RP0/CPU0 (0/RP1/CPU0)
ipv6_arm                        0/RP0/CPU0 (0/RP1/CPU0)
ipv4_mpa                        0/RP0/CPU0 (0/RP1/CPU0)
ipv6_mpa                        0/RP0/CPU0 (0/RP1/CPU0)
bfd                             0/RP0/CPU0 (0/RP1/CPU0)
domain_services                 0/RP0/CPU0 (0/RP1/CPU0)
ftp_fs                          0/RP0/CPU0 (0/RP1/CPU0)
rcp_fs                          0/RP0/CPU0 (0/RP1/CPU0)
tftp_fs                         0/RP0/CPU0 (0/RP1/CPU0)
ipv4_connected                  0/2/CPU0
ipv4_local                      0/2/CPU0
ipv4_rump                       0/2/CPU0
ipv6_connected                  0/2/CPU0
ipv6_local                      0/2/CPU0
ipv6_rump                       0/2/CPU0
eem_metric_dir                  0/RP0/CPU0 (0/RP1/CPU0)
l2tp_mgr                        0/RP0/CPU0 (0/RP1/CPU0)
l2vpn_mgr                       0/RP0/CPU0 (0/RP1/CPU0)
mpls_vpn_mib                    0/RP0/CPU0 (0/RP1/CPU0)
rt_check_mgr                    0/RP0/CPU0 (0/RP1/CPU0)
cdp_mgr                         0/RP0/CPU0 (0/RP1/CPU0)
ip_expl_paths_daemon            0/RP0/CPU0 (0/RP1/CPU0)
policymgr                       0/RP0/CPU0 (0/RP1/CPU0)
nfmgr                           0/RP0/CPU0 (0/RP1/CPU0)
rsvp                            0/RP0/CPU0 (0/RP1/CPU0)
mpls_ldp                        0/RP0/CPU0 (0/RP1/CPU0)
ipv4_mfwd_ma                    0/RP0/CPU0 (0/RP1/CPU0)
ospf instance 1                 0/RP0/CPU0 (0/RP1/CPU0)
ospf_uv                         0/RP0/CPU0 (0/RP1/CPU0)
ospf instance 10396             0/RP0/CPU0 (0/RP1/CPU0)
bpm                             0/RP0/CPU0 (0/RP1/CPU0)
```

```
ipv4_static                    0/2/CPU0
brib instance 81               0/2/CPU0
brib instance 83               0/2/CPU0
bgp instance 1                 0/2/CPU0
bgp instance 2                 0/2/CPU0
banner_config                  0/RP0/CPU0 (0/RP1/CPU0)
RP/0/RP0/CPU0:CRS1-1#
```

Let us look at a different router (CRS1-4) and view the default placement policy for the BGP process. The command **show placement policy program** *<process-name>* **instance** *[x]* provides the default or configured placement policy for a program (process). It is recommended that you include an instance number in this scenario because more than one instance can be present. The output in Example 2-14 shows placement policy for the BGP process. The affinity location-type attract value of 600 has a default location to the route processor.

Example 2-14 *Output of the* **show placement policy program bgp instance 1** *Command*

```
RP/0/RP0/CPU0:CRS1-4#show placement policy program bgp instance 1
Program: bgp instance 1                                : source
---------------------------------------------------------
  Assumed mem:                      1 MB               : system [default]
  Slow migration interval:        1 second             : system [default]

  affinity location-type current attract 600           : system bgp
  affinity location-type paired attract 50             : system bgp
  affinity location-type primary repulse 50            : system bgp
  affinity self repulse 160                            : system bgp
  affinity program ipv6_rib attract 250                : system bgp
  affinity program ipv4_rib attract 250                : system bgp
```

In Example 2-15, router CRS1-1 is configured to attract BGP process to a DRP located in slot 2. Example 2-15 shows the configuration and output displayed to demonstrate how the BGP process is attracted to the DRP. An affinity location-set is used to specify the node in the chassis. An attract value is configured greater than the default (600) to lure the process.

Example 2-15 *Configuration of BGP Process Placement*

```
RP/0/RP0/CPU0:CRS1-1#show running-config placement program bgp instance 1
placement program bgp instance 1
 affinity location-set 0/2/CPU0 attract 100000

RP/0/RP0/CPU0:CRS1-1##show placement program bgp instance 1
.
.
. <snip>
Program                         Placed at location            # rejected  Waiting
                                                              locations   to start
-----------------------------------------------------------------------------------
bgp instance 1                  0/2/CPU0
RP/0/RP0/CPU0:CRS1-1#
```

In Example 2-15, the BGP process resides on the DRP. Because we have an attract value of 600 on the route process (that is, a value less than what is configured on the DRP), the value of 600 is still significant. If there is a failure or service interruption with the DRP, the BGP process will fail back to the RP. As processes are placed and restarted on new locations, you might see traffic loss with BGP peers, depending on what high-availability features are configured.

The **placement reoptimize** command is important when manipulating affinities in a router. When this command is issued, the system will compare all affinities and execute necessary changes to process placements. One cannot assume the reoptimization will take place every time after this command has been committed in a Cisco IOS XR operating system. If an operator has not made configuration changes, it is not necessary to invoke this command. Instead, allow the IOS XR operating system to optimize based on triggered thresholds.

Cisco IOS XR System Database

Because IOS XR is designed for massively distributed systems, it is important to have a distributed data storage mechanism for both configuration and operational data. In IOS XR, a system contains one or more Secure Domain Routers (SDR). Each LC or RP is associated with one SDR. However, SDRs may share some common hardware components including chassis, power supply, fan tray, fan controller, and fabric cards.

Cisco IOS XR System Database (SysDB) provides a common mechanism for applications to store, modify, and/or access system information. SysDB provides fully distributed in-memory data storage organized as a hierarchical namespace. This is accomplished by partitioning the SysDB namespace into three distinct planes: admin, shared, and local. Each SysDB server process is associated with exactly one of the shared-plane, the local-plane, or the admin-plane and can access items only in its own plane. SysDB is used to store both configuration (cfg) and operational status (oper) items. cfg SysDB items are typically user-configurable entities such as the interface IP address. oper SysDB items are operational status, such as the protocol up/down status of an interface.

Cisco IOS XR SysDB provides the following services:

- Distributed in-memory data storage organized as a hierarchical namespace. SysDB stores both configuration and operation data.
- Access to the data. Application components such as BGP, ARP, and FIB, as well as management entities such as XML, CLI, and SNMP, can create, delete, set, and/or get SysDB items. cfg SysDB items may be created, deleted, or modified only by management entities. oper SysDB items may be created, deleted, or modified only by application components. SysDB also provides list and find operations.
- When an application or management entity attempts to create, update, or delete an item, SysDB sends a verify message to applications that are registered as owner. If the application accepts the change, SysDB sends an apply message to the application so that the change can be applied.
- Provides notification service. Applications registered for notification of an item will receive notification when the item is created, deleted, or changed.
- Application can also register as external data manager (EDM) to manage access to a branch (subtree) of the SysDB name space. An access request to an EDM-registered subtree is redirected by SysDB to the EDM application.

There are four distinct SysDB process types running in a distributed fashion to provide a cohesive SysDB namespace. Table 2-4 lists the SysDB processes. Figure 2-7 shows how SysDB processes interact with one another and with application and management processes.

Table 2-4 *SysDB Processes*

Process	Description
sysdb_mc	SysDB medusa client. One instance per node. It provides transparent access of remote SysDB items for local applications.
sysdb_svr_admin	Admin plane SysDB server. One active instance per system on the designated shelf controller (dSC).
sysdb_svr_shared	Shared plane SysDB server. One active instance per each RP and DRP.
sysdb_svr_local	Local plane SysDB server. One instance per node.

The function and operation of SysDB can be explained using the following example. A user enters into Config mode and makes configuration changes. Note that in Cisco IOS XR the configuration does not get applied to the system until it is committed. The user changes the IP address of interface TenGig0/2/0/0 and adds this interface to OSPF area 0. Then the user attempts to commit the configurations using the **commit** command. The following list demonstrates the SysDB interaction after the user attempts to commit the configuration:

- The config process on an active RP sends a message to the local SysDB client. The SysDB client sends a verification message to the shared plane SysDB server for the

OSPF part of the configuration and to local plane SysDB server in slot 2 (0/2/CPU0) for the interface part of the configuration.

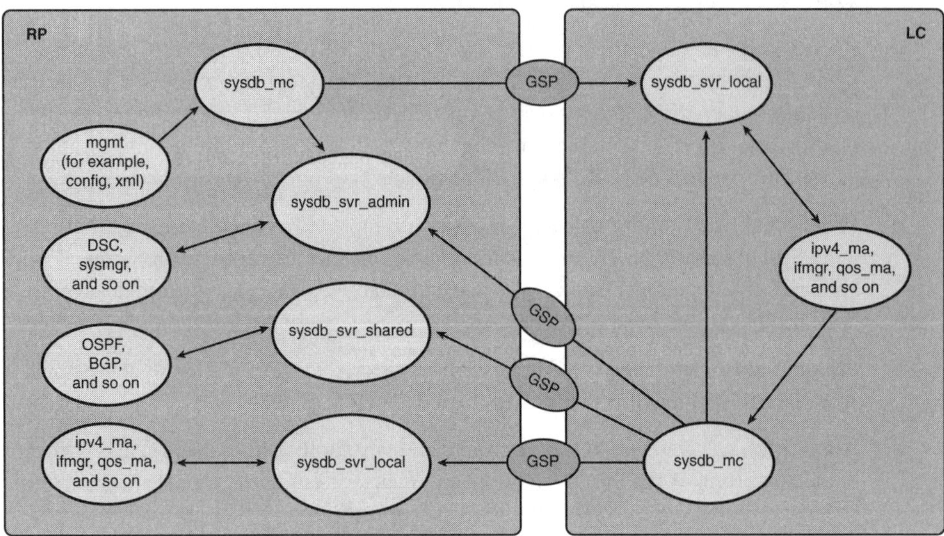

Figure 2-7 *SysDB*

- The shared-plane SysDB server sends a message to the OSPF process because it is already registered for verification of the OSPF configuration items. After the OSPF process accepts the configuration, the SysDB server requests OSPF to apply the configuration. SysDB updates the configuration items.
- At the same time, the local plane SysDB server on 0/2/CPU0 sends a message to the ipv4_ma process because it is already registered for verification of interface IPv4 configuration items. The ipv4_ma process is responsible for the management of IPv4-related configurations for interfaces on the local node. After ipv4_ma accepts the configuration change, SysDB server requests ipv4_ma to apply the configuration. SysDB updates the configuration items.

In summary, an application component or a management entity can register with SysDB to do the following:

- Access or provide configuration data
- Access or provide operation data
- Verify data change
- Be notified of data change
- Manage the SysDB subtree as external data manager.

SysDB provides a CLI to show notification and verification registrations, connections, traces, and more for SysDB client and server.

To determine which SysDB items ipv4_static process has registered for verification, use the command **show sysdb registrations verification** *<ipv4_static JID>* **shared-plane** as shown in Example 2-16.

Example 2-16 *SysDB Verification Registration*

```
RP/0/RP0/CPU0:CRS-A#show processes ipv4_static | inc Job
                  Job Id: 223
RP/0/RP0/CPU0:CRS-A#
RP/0/RP0/CPU0:CRS-A#show sysdb registrations verification job 223 shared-plane
SysDB Verification Registrations:
  jid:      nid:        tid: handle:  reg_path:
  00000223 0/RP1/CPU0 0001 00001145 '/cfg/gl/static/router/max/ipv4'
  00000223 0/RP0/CPU0 0001 00000398 '/cfg/gl/static/router/max/ipv4'
  00000223 0/RP1/CPU0 0001 00001148
    '/cfg/gl/static/router/ord_d/.*/address/ipv4/.*/route/.*/.*/ord_z/'
  00000223 0/RP0/CPU0 0001 00000401
    '/cfg/gl/static/router/ord_d/.*/address/ipv4/.*/route/.*/.*/ord_z/'
  00000223 0/RP1/CPU0 0001 00001147
    '/cfg/gl/static/router/ord_d/.*/address/ipv4/.*/route/.*/.*/.*,.*/'
  00000223 0/RP0/CPU0 0001 00000400
    '/cfg/gl/static/router/ord_d/.*/address/ipv4/.*/route/.*/.*/.*,.*/'
  00000223 0/RP1/CPU0 0001 00001149
    '/cfg/gl/static/router/ord_v/.*/address/ipv4/.*/route/.*/.*/ord_z/'
  00000223 0/RP0/CPU0 0001 00000402
    '/cfg/gl/static/router/ord_v/.*/address/ipv4/.*/route/.*/.*/ord_z/'
  00000223 0/RP1/CPU0 0001 00001146
    '/cfg/gl/static/router/ord_v/.*/address/ipv4/.*/route/.*/.*/.*,.*/'
  00000223 0/RP0/CPU0 0001 00000399
    '/cfg/gl/static/router/ord_v/.*/address/ipv4/.*/route/.*/.*/.*,.*/'
RP/0/RP0/CPU0:CRS-A#
```

To determine which SysDB items the BGP process has registered for notification, use the command **show sysdb registrations notification** *<bgp JID>* **shared-plane** as shown in Example 2-17.

Example 2-17 *Sysdb Notification Registration*

```
RP/0/RP0/CPU0:CRS-A#show processes bgp | i "Job "
                  Job Id: 120
RP/0/RP0/CPU0:CRS-A#
RP/0/RP0/CPU0:CRS-A#show sysdb registrations notification job 120 shared-plane
SysDB Notification Registrations:
  jid:      nid:        tid: handle:  reg_path
  00000120 0/RP1/CPU0 0001 00002942
    '/cfg/gl/vrf/.*/ord_z/afi_safi/.*/.*/ord_b/bgp/'
  00000120 0/RP0/CPU0 0001 00001397
    '/cfg/gl/vrf/.*/ord_z/afi_safi/.*/.*/ord_b/bgp/'
  00000120 0/RP1/CPU0 0001 00002984 '/cfg/gl/snmp/enable/traps/bgpmib'
  00000120 0/RP0/CPU0 0001 00001405 '/cfg/gl/snmp/enable/traps/bgpmib'
```

```
  00000120 0/RP1/CPU0 0001 00002979 '/ipc/gl/ip-bgp/meta/'
  00000120 0/RP0/CPU0 0001 00001404 '/ipc/gl/ip-bgp/meta/'
  00000120 0/RP1/CPU0 0001 00002943 '/ipc/gl/bgp-vrf/rd/'
  00000120 0/RP0/CPU0 0001 00001398 '/ipc/gl/bgp-vrf/rd/'
  00000120 0/RP1/CPU0 0001 00002986 '/ipc/gl/policy_lang/policies/routing/
    Pass-all/pxl'
  00000120 0/RP0/CPU0 0001 00001419 '/ipc/gl/policy_lang/policies/routing/
    Pass-all/pxl'
  00000120 0/RP1/CPU0 0001 00002974 '/oper/ip-bgp/gl/cfg/0x0/0x65/gbl/'
  00000120 0/RP0/CPU0 0001 00001399 '/oper/ip-bgp/gl/cfg/0x0/0x65/gbl/'
  00000120 0/RP1/CPU0 0001 00002975 '/oper/ip-bgp/gl/cfg/0x0/0x65/ord_a/.*/gbl/'
  00000120 0/RP0/CPU0 0001 00001400 '/oper/ip-bgp/gl/cfg/0x0/0x65/ord_a/.*/gbl/'
  00000120 0/RP1/CPU0 0001 00002977 '/oper/ip-bgp/gl/cfg/0x0/0x65/ord_a/.*/nbr/0x0/'
  00000120 0/RP0/CPU0 0001 00001402 '/oper/ip-bgp/gl/cfg/0x0/0x65/ord_a/.*/nbr/0x0/'
  00000120 0/RP1/CPU0 0001 00002976 '/oper/ip-bgp/gl/cfg/0x0/0x65/ord_b/.*/gbl/'
  00000120 0/RP0/CPU0 0001 00001401 '/oper/ip-bgp/gl/cfg/0x0/0x65/ord_b/.*/gbl/'
  00000120 0/RP1/CPU0 0001 00002978 '/oper/ip-bgp/gl/cfg/0x0/0x65/ord_b/.*/nbr/0x0/'
  00000120 0/RP0/CPU0 0001 00001403 '/oper/ip-bgp/gl/cfg/0x0/0x65/ord_b/.*/nbr/0x0/'
RP/0/RP0/CPU0:CRS-A#
```

To determine which SysDB sub-tree is registered with the statsd process as external data manager, use the command **show sysdb registration edm job** *<statsd JID>* **location** *<r/s/m>*, as shown in Example 2-18.

Example 2-18 *Process Registered as EDM with SysDB*

```
RP/0/RP0/CPU0:CRS-A#show processes location 0/2/cpu0 | i "statsd|JID"
JID   TID CPU Stack pri state        TimeInState     HR:MM:SS:MSEC    NAME
271     1    0    24K   10 Receive      0:00:07:0573     0:00:00:0109 statsd_server
271     2    0    24K   10 Receive      228:45:35:0239   0:00:00:0000 statsd_server
RP/0/RP0/CPU0:CRS-A#
RP/0/RP0/CPU0:CRS-A#
RP/0/RP0/CPU0:CRS-A#show sysdb registrations edm job 271 location 0/2/CPU0
SysDB EDM Registrations:
  jid:       nid:        tid: handle:   reg_path:
  00000271 0/2/CPU0    0001 00000053 '/oper/stats/if/'
RP/0/RP0/CPU0:CRS-A#
```

For admin plane SysDB server, use the **show sysdb** command from the Admin mode.

High Availability Architecture

Cisco IOS XR is a modular network operating system designed for fault containment and recovery. The main objective is to contain, manage, and recover from any potential failure scenario. In a complex system, such as IOS XR running platforms, software bugs and hardware failures are inevitable, despite the best design, development, and testing principles followed to develop the systems. IOS XR high availability software and hardware design philosophy is to anticipate various modes of software and hardware failures and to contain the impact of the failure to the smallest unit possible by taking the least aggressive recovery mechanism possible to recover from the fault.

IOS XR uses layered high availability architecture to detect, contain, and recover from various types of failure modes. Figure 2-8 shows the different layers of high availability features in IOS XR.

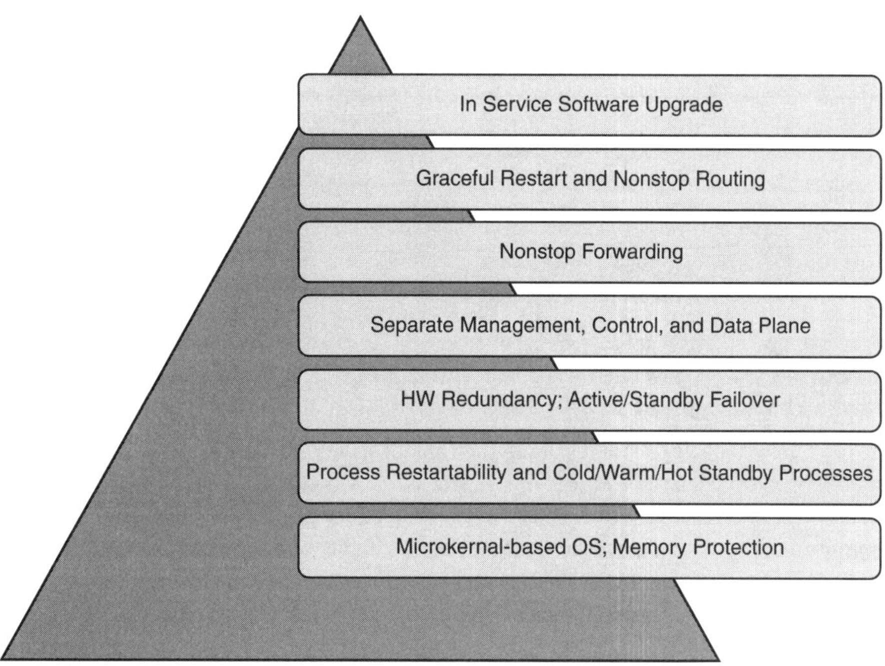

Figure 2-8 *IOS XR Layered High Availability Architecture*

Because IOS XR is a microkernel-based NOS, all processes, with the exception of the small microkernel, are implemented as processes. This includes device drivers and file systems. In addition, because each process runs in its own protected memory, a process crash is self contained and does not impact other processes.

IOS XR processes are designed to be restartable. When a process crashes it can be restarted. A running process saves its vital states to a checkpoint server, which is essentially a shared memory store. When a process crashes and is subsequently restarted by the system manager, the process can recover some of its states from the checkpoint server. This is shown in Figure 2-9. Processes can also recover some of their states from peer processes. For example, the RIB process can recover the RIB table by receiving updates from the routing protocol processes.

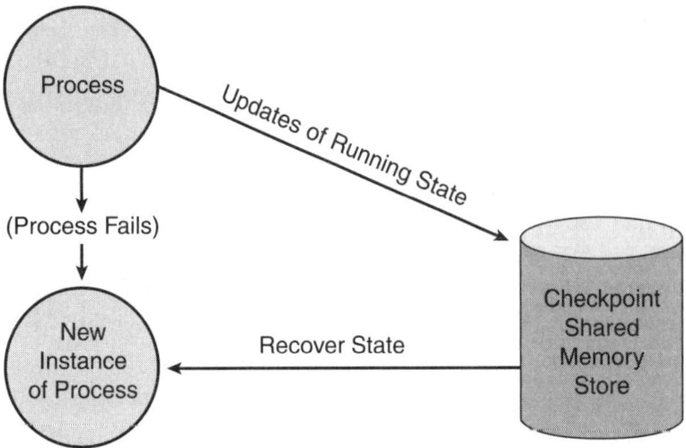

Figure 2-9 *Dynamic State Recovery from Checkpoint Server*

The checkpoint server on the active RP is also mirrored to the checkpoint server on the standby RP. This is useful during failover because processes on the new active RP can recover the states from the local checkpoint server. Figure 2-10 shows how hot, warm, and cold processes recover their state on failover. Active hot processeses sync (checkpoint) their state to the peer process on the standby RP. The standby peer processes the state information immediately. Upon switchover the standby peer takes on the role of active immediately. On the other hand, warm processes on the standby RP do not retrieve state information from the checkpoint server until a failover occurs. When a failover occurs, they immediately retrieve the state of process from the checkpoint server. Cold processes do not mirror their checkpoint state to their standby peer. After failover they must be started by system manager. After they are started they build their state from scratch because there is no checkpointed state. Cold processes can also recover their state from neighboring routers using graceful restart (GR) capability and from peer processes.

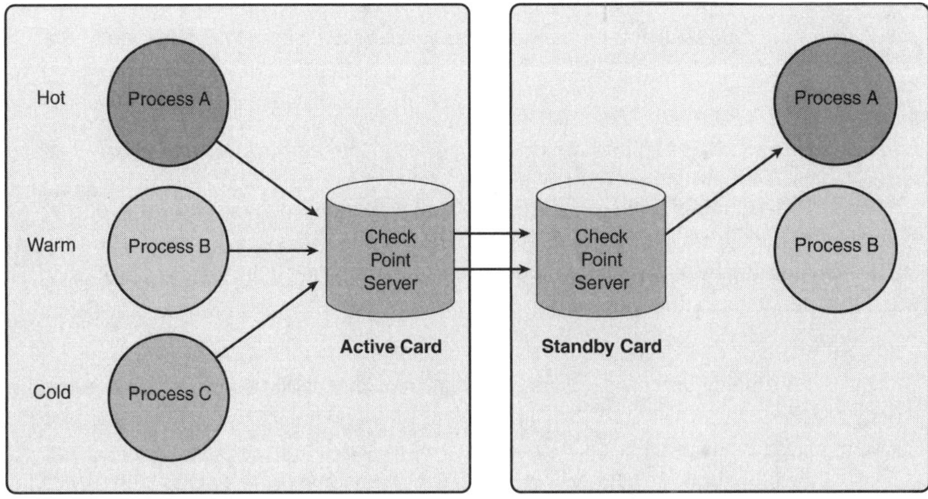

Figure 2-10 *Hot, Warm, and Cold Processes and Mirrored Checkpoint Server*

IOS XR monitors processes to detect CPU hog and memory depletion. It also monitors disk space utilization, deadlocks, kernel thread, file descriptors, and shared memory usage. If a problem is detected the misbehaving processes responsible for the problem are terminated. The process responsible for monitoring CPU hog, memory, and deadlock is wdsysmon (watchdog system monitor). The default behavior for wdsysmon in response to CPU hog, memory hog, or deadlock is to restart the offending process. This behavior can be changed using the configuration **watchdog restart** [**cpu-hog** | **deadlock** | **memory-hog**] **disable**.

Cisco IOS XR platforms use hardware redundancy for critical hardware modules such as route processor, fan tray, and power supply. In the case of RP, a failover from active RP to standby may be triggered for different reasons. Upon failover, processes on standby RP use mirrored checkpointed data to recover their state. The following are reasons for RP failover:

- Hardware errors detected on active RP
- Control plane lockup on active RP
- Mandatory process crashed on active RP and failed to be restarted
- Kernel crash on active RP
- User command **redundancy failover**
- Hardware watchdog timer expired

In IOS XR there is a clear separation of forwarding, control, and management planes. A failure in the management or control plane does not disrupt forwarding. Hardware forwarding on the line cards is not affected by RP failover. In IOS XR platforms, hardware packet forwarding on the line cards can function autonomously during control plane outages. After failover is completed and control plane recovers fully the hardware forwarding table is updated using a mark-and-sweep technique to reconcile the HW forwarding with the latest control plane forwarding.

All IOS XR routing protocols, including BGP, LDP, RSVP, OSPF, and IS-IS, support a graceful restart feature. With a graceful restart (GR) feature, when a process crashes or RP failover occurs the restarting process can recover route updates from neighboring routers if the neighboring routers also have GR capability. The GR capability, coupled with the mark-and-sweep techniques and the separation of control and data plane, enables IOS XR to perform nonstop forwarding (NSF) on RP failover and process crash.

In some cases, network operators might have routers that are not GR capable in their network. Cisco IOS XR has implemented a nonstop routing (NSR) feature so that on RP failover the routing information can be recovered locally. With the NSR feature the routing information and essential routing protocol states are mirrored to the corresponding process on the standby RP. On RP failover the protocol process on the standby RP has all the routing information and essential protocol states to take over the protocol functionality. Neighboring routers do not know that an RP failover has occurred. NSR-capable protocol does not depend on the GR capability of neighboring routers. NSR is supported on a number of protocols, including IS-IS, OSPF, LDP, and BGP.

Cisco IOS XR has the capability to deliver point fixes using the software maintenance unit (SMU) delivery mechanism. SMUs provide fixes for specific components. Most SMU upgrades are hitless because restarting only one or a very few number of processes is required.

Forwarding Path

Forwarding path depicts the life of a packet as it transits through a router or as a router receives it. Understanding the forwarding path helps build the concepts related to the operations a packet goes through inside a router. This section draws its forwarding path using CRS-1 router as an example. The discussion is quite generic and applies equally to IPv4, MPLS, or IPv6 packets; it also applies to CRS-1 routers of all denominations.

Figure 2-11 shows an overview of the CRS-1 forwarding path. It assumes that forwarding and feature information has already been downloaded to a CRS-1 line card based on the control plane computations of the route processor and the features configured on the router.

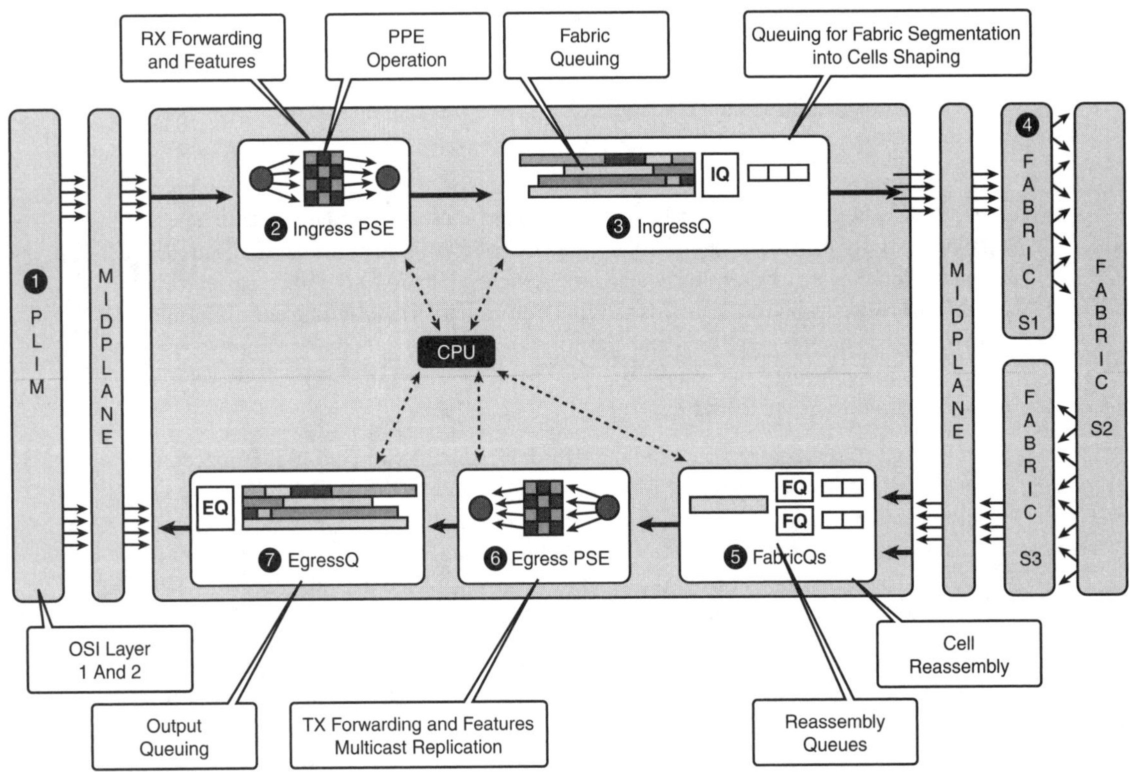

Figure 2-11 *CRS-1 Forwarding Data Path*

A CRS-1 line card consists of a Physical Layer Interface Module (PLIM) and a Modular Services Card (MSC) connected by a midplane. The midplane also provides connectivity between the components on the MSC and the switch fabric. The life of a packet is described as follow:

1. PLIM implements OSI layer 1 and layer 2. It contains the physical interfaces where it receives the frames. It performs CRC checks on the layer 2 frames, and then passes them on as layer 3 packets to the next stage, called the Packet Switching Engine (PSE).

2. Ingress PSE is responsible for forwarding lookups and the application of forwarding-related features such as netflow, ACL, uRPF, policing, and WRED. The PSE consists of 188 parallel processing engines (PPE). Each of the 188 PPEs behaves like a forwarding ASIC and processes an entire packet. The ingress PSE determines the egress line card and the egress FabricQ on that line card.

3. The IngressQ ASIC is the next stage in the forwarding path. Ingress queuing features such as packet-by-packet Modified Deficit Round Robin (P2MDRR), low latency queuing, bandwidth guarantee, and shaping are applied here. These features are applicable to the ingress interface on which they are configured. IngressQ also performs segmentation of packets into fixed-size cells. These cells are then sent into the fabric. IngressQ also takes care of prioritizing cells for fabric access, switch fabric being the next stage in the forwarding path.

4. The switch fabric consists of three distinct stages known as S1, S2, and S3 stages. Switch fabric provides nonblocking switching architecture for the distributed nodes in the CRS. It also provides the architecture for the replication of multicast traffic to the FabricQ ASICs of different MSCs. Its functionality is discussed in more detail in Chapter 12, "Understanding CRS-1 Multishelf."

5. On the egress path of an MSC are two FabricQ ASICs. Each of the FabricQ ASIC services a different set of PLIM ports on the egress path. FabricQ reassembles the cells received from fabric. FabricQ also implements a queuing feature called fabric quality of service, which helps in oversubscription scenarios.

6. The egress PSE de-queues packets from the FabricQ and performs another lookup to determine the egress port. It also performs ACL, policing, WRED, tail-drop lookup, netflow, and other forwarding-related functions. It determines the output queue for the packet based on the QoS policies applied to the EgressQ stage of packet processing. Egress PSE also determines the layer 2 encapsulation string for the packet being processed. In addition, egress PSE performs port-level replication of multicast traffic on the egress path.

7. EgressQ PSE performs output QoS features such as shaping, MDRR, low-latency queuing, and bandwidth guarantee. It passes the packets to the PLIM on the egress path. Note that the same PLIM shares the router's ingress and egress paths.

Summary

Cisco IOS XR uses QNX Neutrino real-time operating system (RTOS), which is a microkernel-based, preemptive, multithreaded, multitasking operating system with memory protection and fast context switching capability. It provides a very high degree of modularity and resilience. The IOS XR microkernel supports FIFO, round-robin, and sporadic scheduling. With FIFO scheduling, a thread runs until it either voluntarily relinquishes control or is preempted by a high priority thread. With round-robin scheduling, a thread can run only until it consumes its allotted timeslice before relinquishing control to another thread. Sporadic scheduling allows a thread to run at normal priority for a period of time (budget) before its priority is dropped to a lower priority.

An efficient and reliable IPC mechanism is critical for any distributed system such as IOS XR. Cisco IOS XR uses various types of IPC mechanisms to meet different requirements. An IPC can be classified as synchronous or asynchronous, intra-node or inter-node, connection-oriented or rendezvous, and point-to-point to point-to-multipoint. Lightweight messaging (LWM) is a synchronous, point-to-point, and connection-oriented IPC. Group service protocol (GSP) is asynchronous, point-to-multipoint, and asynchronous IPC. Bulk Content Downloader (BCDL) is used to download large data tables using GSP.

In IOS XR, the process called system manager performs the role of process management. System manager is the parent of all processes and is responsible for starting, monitoring, stopping, and restarting almost all processes within the system.

Process placement allows offloading of resource-intensive processes and threads to the DRP from the RP, resulting in improvement in system performance. The placed process manages the process placement feature. Process placement can be a triggered event or manually set by an operator.

System Database (SysDB) provides a common mechanism for applications to store, modify, and/or access system information. SysDB provides fully distributed in-memory data storage organized as a hierarchical namespace.

References

- **Cisco.** Cisco IOS XR Software Configuration Guides. http://www.cisco.com/
- **Cisco.** Process Placement on Cisco IOS XR Software. http://www.cisco.com/

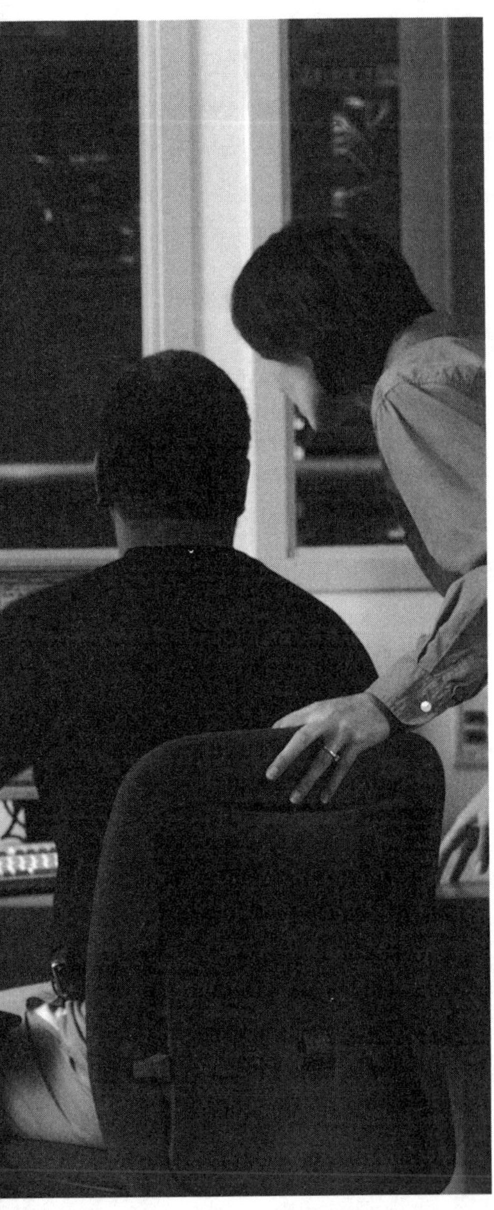

This chapter covers the following topics:

- Introduction to Cisco IOS XR Packages
- Install System Overview
- Preparing to Install Cisco IOS XR
- TURBOBOOT
- Upgrading to a Major Cisco IOS XR Version Using mini.pie
- Disk Backup and Recovery
- Install Health Checks

CHAPTER 3

Installing Cisco IOS XR

This chapter discusses the installation of Cisco IOS XR software. As discussed in Chapter 2, "Cisco IOS XR Infrastructure," IOS XR is not a monolithic image but comprises various packages. It is important to identify the various IOS XR packages and develop an understanding for their naming conventions. This chapter explains the concepts underlying an IOS XR package, details their naming conventions, and outlines the features provided by some of the common packages.

This chapter delves deeper into the features provided by Install Manager in upgrading an IOS XR image and provides examples of the installation or removal of packages and Software Maintenance Upgrade (SMU).

Booting a router is usually considered a simple process by most network engineers, based on their experience in booting a monolithic IOS image. A router that boots an IOS image holds the entire image in its memory. A router running IOS XR does not hold its entire image in memory for continuous operation in live production environments. In fact, IOS XR employs an industrial-grade boot device to install the IOS XR image and the router is booted using the image binaries held on the boot device. This chapter also discusses the various methods a user can employ in protecting and backing up the boot device that was used to install IOS XR.

Introduction to Cisco IOS XR Packages

Cisco IOS XR is made up of independently versioned software components. IOS XR software components exhibit the following properties:

- Functionality that can be individually developed, released, and upgraded on running systems without affecting other software components. IOS XR software components are, therefore, field upgradeable.
- Executable code for running a process or libraries that are shared between the different processes.
- Well-identified functionality. For example, ipv4-bgp, ipv4-acl, and ipv4-mrib components represent some of the BGP, access list, and multicast functionalities.

An IOS XR software package is a modular combination of components that identifies a set of features a user wants to run on the router. An IOS XR package is commonly referred to as a PIE, an abbreviation for *Package Installation Envelope*.

This section discusses the IOS XR naming conventions for PIEs and bootable files and identifies their differences. The most commonly used PIEs are identified and tabulated for ease of reference.

Image Naming Conventions

An IOS XR release version is identified by a numerical suffix value added to the image or PIE file names. For example, a 3.6.0 suffix identifies an IOS XR mainline release 3.6.0. Mainline releases normally end with a zero as the last decimal number in the suffix.

Similarly, a suffix of 3.5.0 identifies a mainline release and a suffix of 3.5.3 identifies a third maintenance release within the 3.5.0 mainline. This chapter draws its examples from 3.6.0 mainline and 3.5.3 maintenance releases of IOS XR. Table 3-1 provides a general naming convention for IOS XR packages. IOS XR naming conventions will become clearer through the course of this chapter.

Table 3-1 *Description of the Filename Components*

Component	Description
comp	Indicates that the file is a composite of multiple packages (for example, **comp**-hfr-mini.vm-3.6.0).
platform	Identifies the platform for which the software package is designed. For packages designed for CRS-1 series of routers, the platform designation is hfr (for example, comp-**hfr**-mini.vm-3.6.0). For packages designed for Cisco XR 12000 Series Routers, the platform designation is c12k (for example, c12k-mini.vm-3.6.0).
composite_name	Identifies a specific composite package. The only composite PIE file at this time is named mini and includes all packages contained in the Cisco IOS XR Unicast Core Routing Bundle (for example, comp-hfr-**mini.vm**-3.6.0).

Component	Description
package_type	Identifies the type of package the file supports. Package types include ■ fwdg for the Forwarding package ■ lc for the Line Card package ■ mcast for the Multicast package ■ mgbl for the Manageability package ■ mpls for the MPLS package ■ k9sec for the Security package ■ rout for the Routing package ■ diags for the Diagnostics package ■ sbc for the Session Border Controller package ■ fpd for field-programmable device package ■ doc for documentation package ■ ipsec-service for IPSec service package hfr-**mcast**-p.pie-3.6.0 is an example of a multicast package required for multicast traffic forwarding.
major	Identifies the major release of this package. A major release occurs when there is a major architectural change to the product (for example, a major new capability is introduced). All packages operating on the router must be at the same major release level. comp-hfr-mini.vm-**3.6.0** is an example.
maintenance	Identifies the maintenance release of this package (for example, comp-hfr-mini.vm-3.5.**3**).
ddts	Used for SMUs. Identifies a Distributed Defect Tracking System (DDTS) number that identifies the software defect this SMU addresses (for example, hfr-base-3.6.0.**CSCsm36321**.pie).

Cisco IOS XR Bootable Files, PIEs, and SMUs

Cisco IOS XR software files can be downloaded from Cisco.com. SMUs for each release are individually downloadable from Cisco.com, whereas the bootable files and optional PIEs come in the form of a tarball. It is important to make a distinction between bootable files, upgrade PIEs, optional packages, and SMUs so that the right files can be used for each specific task.

Table 3-2 lists the various PIEs and bootable .vm files for the mainline 3.6.0 release and provides a description of each file. Only one SMU is listed for release 3.6.0 to help provide an example of the naming conventions used for an IOS XR SMU.

Table 3-2 *Cisco IOS XR Bootable Files, Optional Packages, and MBI Image for Release 3.6.0*

Filename	Purpose	Application
comp-hfr-mini.vm-3.6.0 c12k-mini.vm-3.6.0	Bootable images for CRS-1 and c12000.	Boots IOS XR image from ROMMON
comp-hfr-mini.pie-3.6.0 c12k-mini.pie-3.6.0	Upgrade PIEs for CRS-1 and c12000.	Upgrades a running IOS XR image
hfr-diags-p.pie-3.6.0 c12k-diags.pie-3.6.0	PIEs for running online hardware diagnostics on CRS-1 and c12000.	Optional PIE
hfr-mpls-p.pie-3.6.0 c12k-mpls.pie-3.6.0	PIEs for running MPLS features on CRS-1 and c12000.	Optional PIE
hfr-mcast-p.pie-3.6.0 c12k-mcast.pie-3.6.0	PIEs for running multicast forwarding features on CRS-1 and c12000.	Optional PIE
hfr-doc.pie-3.6.0 c12k-doc.pie-3.6.0	Documentation PIEs for CRS-1 and c12000. The IOS XR manual (man) pages were separated from the base image to make it lighter weight.	Optional PIE
hfr-mgbl-p.pie-3.6.0 c12k-mgbl.pie-3.6.0	Manageability packages for CRS-1 and c12000	Optional PIE
hfr-fpd.pie-3.6.0 c12k-fpd.pie-3.6.0	Field Programmable Device Package for CRS-1 and c12000.	Optional PIE
c12k-sbc.pie-3.6.0	Session Border Controller PIE for c12000.	Optional PIE
c12k-ipsec-service.pie-3.6.0	IPsec services PIE for c12000.	Optional PIE
mbiprp-rp.vm-3.6.0	Minimum boot image for c12000.	Boots standby RP from ROMMON
hfr-base-3.6.0.CSCsm36321.pie	SMU for CRS platform shown as an example of an SMU.	Provides fix for defect ID CSCsm36321

A Cisco IOS XR upgrade that involves an installation upgrade of a major release or a maintenance release causes a reload of the router. This occurs as a result of install operations involved in the upgrade and is a noted behavior at the time of writing this book. Installing an optional PIE such as mpls, multicast, or mgbl is usually a hitless operation and does not cause any downtime of the router. Several SMUs can be hitless. The impact of an SMU can only be determined on a case-by-case basis by studying the documentation readme file that accompanies the SMU.

Composite Bootable Files

Example 3-1 shows an IOS XR 3.6.0 release tarball for the CRS platform. The IOS XR files can be extracted in Microsoft Windows or UNIX using an appropriate untar utility.

Example 3-1 *Extracting CRS-1 Files with* **tar -xvf** *on a Cisco IOS XR 3.6.0 Tarball on a UNIX Workstation*

```
$ tar -xvf CRS-1-iosxr-3.6.0.tar
x comp-hfr-mini.pie-3.6.0, 81851549 bytes, 159867 tape blocks
x comp-hfr-mini.vm-3.6.0, 94079334 bytes, 183749 tape blocks
x hfr-diags-p.pie-3.6.0, 6064539 bytes, 11845 tape blocks
x hfr-doc.pie-3.6.0, 1640953 bytes, 3205 tape blocks
x hfr-fpd.pie-3.6.0, 6024053 bytes, 11766 tape blocks
x hfr-mcast-p.pie-3.6.0, 3911716 bytes, 7641 tape blocks
x hfr-mgbl-p.pie-3.6.0, 9370938 bytes, 18303 tape blocks
x hfr-mpls-p.pie-3.6.0, 2700663 bytes, 5275 tape blocks
```

Refer to the files listed in Example 3-1. Files containing the .vm extension are bootable installation files. These files are installed from ROM Monitor mode. The .vm files are used to install software when the router is booted for the first time or during a last resort disaster recovery. In Example 3-1, comp-hfr-mini.vm-3.6.0 is a bootable image. The .vm file contains the following major functionality areas:

- Operating system kernel
- Base image
- Admin plane features
- Routing and forwarding bundles

Installation of the .vm composite image file results in the installation of a number of individual packages. Their names and functionality are documented in Table 3-3 using the IOS XR maintenance release 3.5.3 as an example. The composite image is therefore itself similar to a tar file containing os-mbi, lc, fwd, admin, and base PIEs.

Table 3-3 *IOS XR Contents of the Composite Image Using 3.5.3 Maintenance Release*

PIE Name	Major Functionality Areas
OS (platform-os-mbi-release; for example, hfr-os-mbi-3.5.3)	System bootup software OS kernel Flash disks, hard disk, and file system support
Base package (platform-base-release; for example, hfr-base-3.5.3)	AAA services, TACACS+ and RADIUS support IPv4, IPv6 forwarding and features Packet forwarding infrastructure Infrastructure components such as Bulk Content Downloader (BCDL), Group Services Protocol (GSP), Q Symbolic Manager (QSM), Netio, Qnet Dependency checker Dynamically Loadable Library (DLL) upgrade Hitless software upgrade or downgrade using PIE files Interface manager Counters MD5 or one-way encryption support SNMP Syslog Version manager (including data translator) Access control lists Quality of Service SONET and SDH Cisco Express Forwarding
Routing package (for example, hfr-rout-3.5.3)	BGP and IGP and Routing Policy Language
Admin (platform-admin-release; for example, hfr-admin-3.5.3)	Admin plane–related features Fabric management SDR
LC (platform-LC-release; for example, hfr-lc-3.5.3)	Line card–related software, SONET, SDH, APS and so on
Forwarding (platform-fwd-release; for example, hfr-fwdg-3.5.3)	Forwarding features, such as CEF and QoS

Example 3-2 shows an extraction of a tarball containing the bootable image and optional packages for the c12000 platform.

Example 3-2 *Extracting c12000 Files with* **tar -xvf** *on an IOS XR 3.6.0 Tarball on a UNIX Workstation*

```
$ tar -xvf XR12000-iosxr-3.6.0.tar
x c12k-diags.pie-3.6.0, 19245474 bytes, 37589 tape blocks
x c12k-doc.pie-3.6.0, 1647132 bytes, 3218 tape blocks
x c12k-fpd.pie-3.6.0, 17009929 bytes, 33223 tape blocks
x c12k-mcast.pie-3.6.0, 5675401 bytes, 11085 tape blocks
x c12k-mgbl.pie-3.6.0, 9318486 bytes, 18201 tape blocks
x c12k-mini.pie-3.6.0, 107423127 bytes, 209811 tape blocks
x c12k-mini.vm-3.6.0, 121593809 bytes, 237488 tape blocks
x c12k-mpls.pie-3.6.0, 2741676 bytes, 5355 tape blocks
x c12k-sbc.pie-3.6.0, 16121856 bytes, 31488 tape blocks
x c12k-ipsec-service.pie-3.6.0, 146688 bytes, 287 tape blocks
x c12k-firewall.pie-3.6.0, 30058058 bytes, 58708 tape blocks
```

Note: All files containing c12k prefix are for the c12000 platform. All files containing hfr as a prefix or in the filename are for the CRS-1 platform.

Composite Upgrade PIE

A composite upgrade PIE is also referred to as *mini.pie* in IOS XR jargon. Examples 3-1 and 3-2 listed the following files for CRS-1 and c12000 platforms:

- comp-hfr-mini.pie-3.6.0
- c12k-mini.pie-3.6.0

The preceding mini.pie files are composite upgrade pies for IOS XR release 3.6.0. These composite upgrade pies are used to install software from the CLI prompt, when the router is in operation and either an older or newer version of the IOS XR operating system is already functional on a routing platform.

Optional PIEs

Optional PIEs provide feature functionality for certain features such as security, manageability, MPLS, and multicast. The optional PIEs are not limited to the four optional feature areas mentioned, although they provide a reference to the more commonly used optional pies. The hfr-mpls-p.pie provides MPLS control plane and forwarding features. The well-known features in hfr-mpls-p.pie include the Label Distribution Protocol (LDP) and MPLS Traffic Engineering, as well as MPLS L2 and L3 VPNs. The hfr-mgbl-p.pie and hfr-diags-p.pie contain software for network management and router diagnostics, respectively.

The hfr-mcast-p.pie, commonly called the *mcast pie*, contains the control and forwarding plane for multicast forwarding. Note that routing protocols use multicast for disseminating routing information. In this case, the mcast pie is not required. The mcast pie is required for the control plane features such as Protocol Independent Multicast (PIM) and Multicast Source Discover Protocol (MSDP) and for the forwarding of multicast traffic for IPv4 and IPv6 protocols.

Table 3-4 *Some of the IOS XR Optional Packages and Their Supported Features*

PIE Name	Functionality
hfr-mpls-p.pie-3.5.3	LDP, MPLS TE, FRR, MPLS L3 and L2 VPN, MPLS OAM
	RSVP
	Optical Unit
hfr-mgbl-p.pie-3.5.3	Configuration editor and manager
	Accounting and statistics management
	Performance management
	Fault or event management
	Extensible markup language (XML) interface and schemas
	Common Object Request Broker Architecture (CORBA) support
	MIB support
hfr-mcast-p.pie-3.5.3	Auto-RP and Bootstrap Router (BSR)
	PIM SM, SSM, Bidirectional
	Dynamic registration using Internet Group Management Protocol (IGMP)
	Explicit tracking of hosts, groups, and channels for IGMPv3
	MBGP
	MSDP
	Multicast NSF
	Multicast Reverse Path Forwarding (RPF)—loose mode
	Multicast Virtual Private Networks (MVPN)
	Multicast out-of-resource handling
hfr-diags-p.pie-3.5.3	Online and scheduled diagnostics

Note: Release 3.5.3 of IOS XR is used to show the optional PIEs and their supported functionality for CRS-1 platform. The feature listing of Table 3-4 for optional PIEs gives a brief overview of feature and therefore is not an exhaustive list.
Note that high availability features are bundled with their feature PIEs. For example, LDP Graceful Restart comes as a part of the MPLS PIE.

Software Maintenance Upgrade

SMU stands for *Software Maintenance Upgrade*. Some of the key facts about SMUs are

- SMU is a software "patch" delivery unit that, after being installed and activated, provides a "point-fix" for a critical issue in a given software release.
- SMUs are release specific. If an issue affects multiple platforms or releases, an SMU will be separately built for each release and each platform depending on the mission-critical need.
- A CRS-1 SMU cannot be applied to a different platform, and vice versa. Furthermore, a release 3.3.4 SMU cannot be applied to release 3.4.2, and vice versa.
- SMUs provide software fixes for critical network-down and qualification-blocking issues. Therefore, every software defect will not have a corresponding SMU. In some cases, it's simply not technically possible to build an SMU for certain issues; for example, ROMMON-related issues where the code base is not IOS XR.
- Some SMUs are hitless, whereas other SMUs might cause a line card or router reload. Cisco documentation must be consulted to understand the impact of an SMU before applying it to a production router.
- Optional PIEs and multiple SMUs can be installed concurrently on the router using just a single install operation via the command line. As mentioned earlier, some SMUs are hitless and others require a reload. Installing multiple hitless SMUs concurrently might cause a reload of a node. Best practices state that all scenarios in which SMU installations involve a concurrent application of a large number of SMUs may be verified in a lab environment prior to attempting installation on a production router.

Install System Overview

The preceding sections provided an insight into the different IOS XR packages and bootable files. This section explains the Install Manager subsystem and its role in booting or upgrading IOS XR. During the course of this discussion, this section refers to a *node* as a generic term for all RPs, DRPs and line cards in an IOS XR router.

As discussed in Chapter 2, Install Manager controls the booting process on each node in the system and determines the proper packages that need to be loaded on each node. Install Manager provides a user with the CLI necessary to carry out install operations. The user initiates an install request from the command line and Install Manager takes care of install-related functions, which might include one of the following tasks:

- Fresh installation of an IOS XR image
- Upgrade or downgrade of an IOS XR release
- Addition and activation of PIEs and SMUs
- Removal of inactive PIEs from boot device
- Provide **show** command outputs related to the state of the installed software or related to the progress of an install operation

Figure 3-1 shows a simplified overview of the process.

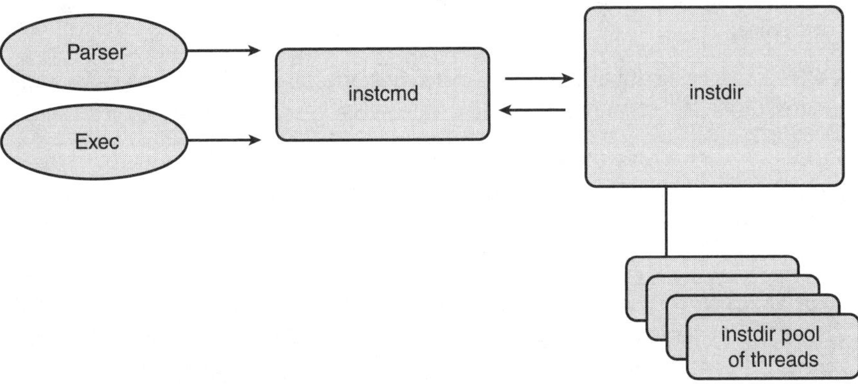

Figure 3-1 *Install Overview*

Figure 3-1 shows two subblocks called exec and parser. The exec subblock represents a user entering a CLI command. The parser subblock verifies that the install-related command is correct in its syntax. The parser and exec blocks together take these CLI inputs and pass them as arguments to a process called instcmd. The process instcmd helps provide output of install-related **show** commands and interacts with a third process shown in Figure 3-1 called instdir (or Install Director). instdir is a continuously running server that provides the bulk of functionality for installing or upgrading the software.

The instcmd process runs only when an install-related operation is started via CLI. The following command shows the querying of the instcmd process using the ksh:

```
RP/0/RP0/CPU0:CRS1-4#run pidin | grep "instcmd"
 6058227    1 pkg/bin/instcmd      10r RECEIVE      1
```

The preceding command output indicates that a CLI operation was passed as an argument to the instcmd process and it is now in receive state. Alternatively, the same can be queried by an exec level command without using the ksh, as shown in Example 3-3.

Example 3-3 *The* show process instcmd *Command Output*

```
RP/0/RP0/CPU0:CRS1-4#show processes instcmd
                  Job Id: 65779
                     PID: 6185203
         Executable name: instcmd
             Instance ID: 1
                 Respawn: OFF
                    core: TEXT SHAREDMEM MAINMEM
JID    TID  Stack pri state         TimeInState      HR:MM:SS:MSEC NAME
65779  1     16K  10 Receive       0:00:01:0349    0:00:00:0062 instcmd
```

Note: The preceding command will produce an output only if an install command is running.

Install Director communicates with the install clients through lightweight messaging and performs install-related operations along with any user error notifications. Install Director is a multithreaded process that relies on a pool of threads to carry out its operations. Its main install thread receives the client request when instcmd is spawned as a result of entering an install CLI. It is also responsible for sending pulses back to instcmd to indicate the status of the install. Example 3-4 shows the command output of querying the instdir process.

Example 3-4 *The* show process instdir *Command Output*

```
RP/0/RP0/CPU0:CRS1-4#show process instdir
                  Job Id: 201
                     PID: 6230121
         Executable path: /disk0/hfr-base-3.5.3/sbin/instdir
              Instance #: 1
                    Args: -b /etc/ena.pie
              Version ID: 00.00.0000
                 Respawn: ON
           Respawn count: 2
  Max. spawns per minute: 12
            Last started: Wed Apr  9 09:04:08 2008
           Process state: Run (last exit due to SIGTERM)
           Package state: Normal
                    core: TEXT SHAREDMEM MAINMEM
               Max. core: 0
                   Level: 90
           MaintModeProc: ON
               Placement: ON
            startup_path: /pkg/startup/instdir.startup
                   Ready: 3.857s
               Available: 4.287s
```

```
         Process cpu time: 0.221 user, 0.117 kernel, 0.338 total
JID    TID  Stack pri state         TimeInState      HR:MM:SS:MSEC NAME
201    1      48K  10 Ready           0:00:00:0000     0:00:00:0210 instdir
201    2      48K  10 Receive         0:00:03:0455     0:00:00:0001 instdir
201    3      48K  10 Receive         0:00:03:0349     0:00:00:0001 instdir
201    5      48K  10 Receive         0:00:03:0304     0:00:00:0000 instdir
201    6      48K  10 Receive         0:00:00:0427     0:00:00:0006 instdir
201    8      48K  10 Receive         0:00:03:0309     0:00:00:0000 instdir
```

The functions of Install Director can be summarized as follows:

- Install Director drives the software installation procedures.
- It keeps a repository of software packages.
- It controls the booting of all nodes in the system and determines which software should run on each node in the system.
- Install Director helps perform general PIE file validation to make sure that a package or an SMU being added is compatible with the running software version.
- Install Director drives software change operations such as software activation, deactivation, removal or rollback.

Figure 3-2 shows the install subsystem in the context of IOS XR software. After presenting a brief overview of Install Manager, this section proceeds to present a view of the various processes that collaborate to enable the installation of IOS XR software as shown in Figure 3-2.

As depicted in Figure 3-2, install operations involve complex interaction of various collaborating processes on the IOS XR operating system. Chapter 2 introduced Sysdb and explained that Sysdb is organized in a tree-like structure. Sysdb collaborates with Install Director and allows instdir to use several trees in its namespace. The command requests passed from the instcmd process and the status of command executions by instdir are all communicated via different trees in the Sysdb.

Configuration Manager is also one of the collaborator processes that places a lock on the configuration when an install operation is in process.

The pkgfs process provides file location information to processes that need to know where files are physically located. The pkgfs process abstracts the locations and version of the files and provides a virtual location known as a *loadpath* to the node so that the software can be run.

Figure 3-2 also shows a collaborating process called install helper or insthlper. Install Helper drives software change operations on a node and its operation is local to the node in question. It not only gets its instructions from instdir but also downloads software through instdir. Install Helper interacts with the Sysmgr process by publishing to it a list of processes that need to be restarted as a result of an install operation.

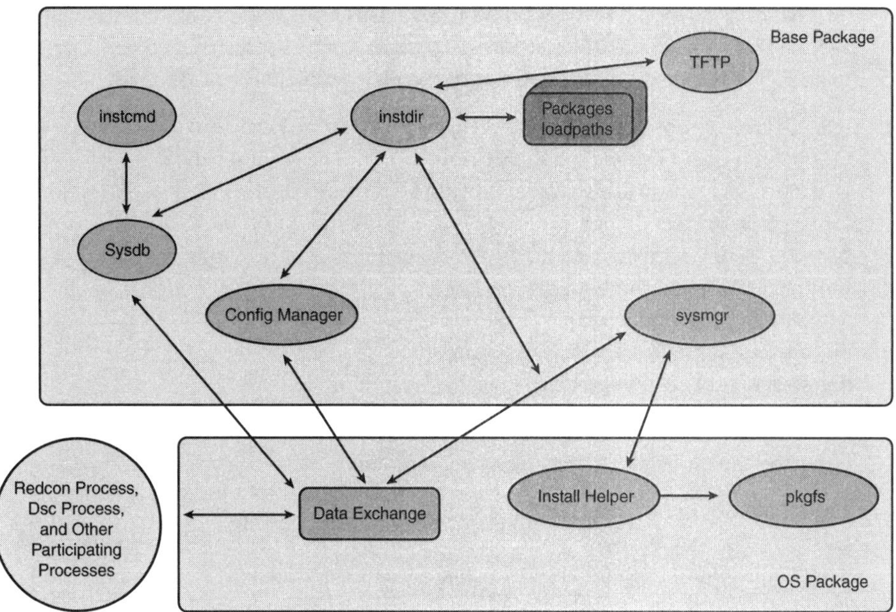

Figure 3-2 *An Overview of Install Subsystems and Collaborating Processes*

Figure 3-2 also indicates other participating processes such as redcon, which is responsible for RP redundancy. The redcon process participation ensures that an RP failover does not occur during an install operation.

Preparing to Install Cisco IOS XR

This section lists the key elements needed to prepare for an IOS XR install. Cisco.com has detailed procedural information on IOS XR install readiness. That information is not repeated here; instead, the key preparation steps follow:

- Identification of an IOS XR release version remains the first and paramount step toward the boot process. The choice of a particular release depends on the supported features and functionality. The desired features further dictate the selection of individual optional packages such as mpls, mcast, and mgbl PIEs.
- An IOS XR installation almost always needs some mandatory SMUs to function properly. Cisco.com documents the SMU information for each IOS XR release. Each SMU must be analyzed in case the software bug addressed by an SMU applies to a particular network scenario.
- The CRS-1 platform natively runs the IOS XR operating system. The c12000 platform, originally being an IOS router, can be upgraded to run IOS XR. However, c12000 hardware, including line cards (LC) as well as route processors (RP), must be checked for XR compliance. In addition, LC and RP memory requirements must be checked for IOS XR support. The c12000 platform additionally requires a boot loader

image that helps with the initial boot process. This boot loader is an IOS-based image. The right boot image for the c12000 platform must be determined corresponding to an IOS XR release. All this information is readily available on Cisco.com.

- IOS XR uses a boot device, usually disk0: or disk1: in the case of CRS-1. In case of c12000, this could include a compact flash as well. The requirement at the time of writing this book specifies 1 Gigabit of Cisco recommended flash disk. An emphasis is placed on the fact that a Cisco-supported flash disk with corresponding part number must be used for this particular operation. Furthermore, Monlib, an executable program, resides on the boot device and loads into RAM for execution by ROMMON during the initial phases of the boot process. Monlib resides only on Cisco-provided boot media; any flash disks procured off the shelf do not contain this important software component.
- Care must be taken in ensuring that the boot device will have sufficient room in bytes to accommodate an ongoing router operation.
- The ROM Monitor (ROMMON) is a bootstrap program that initializes the hardware and helps boot the Cisco IOS XR. It is important to have the correct version of ROMMON. In addition to ROMMON, the line cards' FPGA versions must comply with the requirements of the target IOS XR release.

TURBOBOOT

This section explains the steps needed to boot the IOS XR software on a router. TURBOBOOT refers to a fresh boot of the router from ROMMON. TURBOBOOT is required if an IOS router is being converted to IOS XR or as a last resort disaster recovery in the case of CRS-1. If the router is already running an IOS XR image, there is no need to TURBOBOOT the router for an upgrade or downgrade. Later sections in this chapter address the upgrade scenario. This section deals with a fresh boot of the router from ROMMON.

Setting the TURBOBOOT ROMMON Variable

As a first step in TURBOBOOT, a Cisco-approved nonvolatile storage device is selected. This selection is made possible by setting the TURBOBOOT variable in ROMMON. Example 3-5 depicts querying of ROMMON settings and Example 3-6 sets the ROMMON TURBOBOOT variable to select disk0 as the primary boot device.

Example 3-5 *The ROMMON* set *Command Output*

```
rommon B1 > set
PS1=rommon ! >
IOX_ADMIN_CONFIG_FILE=
IP_ADDRESS=10.1.1.64
IP_SUBNET_MASK=255.255.255.0
DEFAULT_GATEWAY=10.1.1.70
TFTP_SERVER=10.1.1.70
BSI=0
```

```
ReloadReason=0
?=0
TURBOBOOT=
```

Example 3-6 shows the setting of the ROMMON variable to boot from disk0. This example assumes that the .vm composite file has been copied to disk0:/usr directory.

Example 3-6 *Setting TURBOBOOT ROMMON Variable to Boot from Disk0:*

```
rommon B2 > unset BOOT


rommon B4 > TURBOBOOT=on,disk0
rommon B5 > sync
rommon B6 > reset
```

Note: Appendix A provides a handy reference of the different ROMMON variables used for IOS XR booting. Therefore, other ROMMON variables and ROMMON commands are not discussed in detail in this section.

Booting the .vm File from ROMMON

This section shows the booting of .vm image from ROMMON and the accompanying console logs. Refer to Example 3-7.

Example 3-7 *TURBOBOOT from Disk0:*

```
rommon B2 > b disk0:/usr/comp-hfr-mini.vm-3.5.3
......................
##################################################
##################################################
               Restricted Rights Legend
Use, duplication, or disclosure by the Government is
subject to restrictions as set forth in subparagraph
(c) of the Commercial Computer Software - Restricted
Rights clause at FAR sec. 52.227-19 and subparagraph
(c) (1) (ii) of the Rights in Technical Data and Computer
Software clause at DFARS sec. 252.227-7013.
            cisco Systems, Inc.
            170 West Tasman Drive
            San Jose, California 95134-1706

Cisco IOS XR Software for the Cisco XR HFR, Version 3.5.3
Copyright (c) 2008 by Cisco Systems, Inc.
TURBOBOOT: Turboboot process started
TURBOBOOT: Checking size of device disk0:
TURBOBOOT:    OK
```

```
ios con0/RP0/CPU0 is now available
Press RETURN to get started.
TURBOBOOT: Cleaning disk0:
TURBOBOOT: Cleaning disk0: complete
TURBOBOOT: Copying the packages to disk0:
RP/0/RP0/CPU0:Apr 14 16:43:49.033 : instdir[198]: %INSTALL-INSTMGR-6-
   INSTALL_OPERATION_STARTED : Install operation 1 '(admin) install copy-package
   mem: to disk0:' started by user '(Unknown)'
Install operation 1 '(admin) install copy-package mem: to disk0:' started by
user '(Unknown)' via CLI at 16:43:49 UTC Mon Apr 14 2008.
RP/0/RP0/CPU0:Apr 14 16:43:49.122 : alphadisplay[103]: %PLATFORM-ALPHA_DISPLAY-6-
  CHANGE : Alpha display on node 0/RP0/CPU0 changed to XR  PREP in state default
Info:     Checking available free space in disk0:
Info:     Copying installed files from mem: to disk0:
Info:      Copying component 'hfr-boot-mbi-drp' size > 7 MB.
Info:      Copying component 'hfr-boot-mbi-lc' size > 5 MB.
Info:      Copying component 'hfr-boot-mbi-rp' size > 7 MB.
Info:      Copying component 'hfr-boot-mbi-sp' size > 4 MB.
Info:      Copying component 'bundlemgr' size > 1 MB.
Info:      Copying component 'installmgr' size > 4 MB.
Info:      Copying component 'config-cfgmgr' size > 1 MB.
Info:      Copying component 'crypto-pki_base' size > 1 MB.
Info:      Copying component 'ha-lrd' size > 1 MB.
Info:      Copying component 'ifmgr' size > 1 MB.
Info:      Copying component 'infra-distrib' size > 1 MB.
Info:      Copying component 'infra-license' size > 2 MB.
Info:      Copying component 'ip-iarm' size > 1 MB.
Info:      Copying component 'ip-rib' size > 1 MB.
Info:      Copying component 'perl-56' size > 1 MB.
Info:      Copying component 'service-infra-svii' size > 1 MB.
Info:      Copying component 'shellutil' size > 2 MB.
Info:      Copying component 'sysdb' size > 1 MB.
Info:      Copying component 'sysmgr' size > 1 MB.
Info:      Copying component 'drivers-vpa-infra' size > 2 MB.
Info:      Copying component 'hfr-cctl-lib' size > 2 MB.
Info:      Copying component 'hfr-rommon-burner' size > 3 MB.
Info:      Copying component 'hfr-fabricq' size > 1 MB.
Info:      Copying component 'hfr-ingressq' size > 2 MB.
Info:      Copying component 'hfr-drivers-utils' size > 1 MB.
Info:      Copying component 'fabric_driver' size > 3 MB.
Info:      Copying component 'fabric-fsdb' size > 1 MB.
Info:      Copying component 'ipv4-acl' size > 1 MB.
Info:      Copying component 'l2vpn' size > 1 MB.
Info:      Copying component 'fib-common' size > 4 MB.
Info:      Copying component 'platforms-hfr-4695' size > 1 MB.
```

```
Info:      Copying component 'hfr-metro-ucode' size > 1 MB.
Info:      Copying component 'hfr-plim-1p-oc768' size > 2 MB.
Info:      Copying component 'clns-isis' size > 3 MB.
Info:      Copying component 'eigrp' size > 1 MB.
Info:      Copying component 'ipv4-bgp' size > 6 MB.
Info:      Copying component 'ipv4-ospf' size > 2 MB.
Info:      Copying component 'ipv6-ospfv3' size > 2 MB.
Info:     Packages have been copied to disk0:. Removing this device could be
Info:     disruptive to the system.
Info:     New boot image is disk0:hfr-os-mbi-3.5.3/mbihfr-rp.vm
Info:     The newly copied package(s) will be activated upon reload for the
Info:     following card types:
Info:     RP
Info:     UNKNOWN
Info:     UNKNOWN
Info:     UNKNOWN
Info:     DRP
Info:     SP
Info:     LC
Info:     Reload then run this boot image to activate copied packages.
Info:     Package copy operation is complete.
```

The boot command from ROMMON invokes the TURBOBOOT process. The Install Manager subsystem checks the target boot device for free space and copies the operating system from memory to disk0. Once Install Manager has prepared the disk, it sets the BOOT variable to **disk0:hfr-os-mbi-3.5.3/mbihfr-rp.vm,1** in ROMMON. Next, the configuration register is automatically changed to 0x102 and router is reloaded to boot off disk0:, which is already baked with the 3.5.3 image. The router reboots using the 3.5.3 image and completes the TURBOBOOT process. At this point the TURBOBOOT is complete. You can query your boot variables from CLI using the commands shown in the following example.

Example 3-8 shows two commands that display ROMMON variables while IOS XR is running on the router.

Example 3-8 *Using IOS XR* **show** *Commands to See ROMMON Variables*

```
RP/0/RP0/CPU0:CRS1-3#show bootvar
BOOT variable = disk0:hfr-os-mbi-3.5.3/mbihfr-rp.vm,1;
CONFREG variable = 0x102
RP/0/RP0/CPU0:CRS1-3#cd nvram:
RP/0/RP0/CPU0:CRS1-3#more nvram:classic-rommon-var
```

The output of the **show platform** command may be used to ensure that all the nodes are showing IOS XR RUN before any configuration is attempted.

Verifying the Software Installation

This section provides an overview on the install-related commands that help verify the status of IOS XR software installation. Example 3-9 displays the summary of installed packages as a result of booting the .vm composite.

Example 3-9 *Output of* **show install summary** *in Admin Mode*

```
RP/0/RP0/CPU0:CRS1-3(admin)#show install summary
Default Profile:
  Admin Resources
  SDRs:
    Owner
  Active Packages:
    disk0:comp-hfr-mini-3.5.3
```

Example 3-9 shows 3.5.3 composite is the active package on the router.

Refer to Example 3-10 to see a detailed depiction of packages that constitute the .vm composite.

Example 3-10 *Output of* **show install detail** *in Admin Mode*

```
RP/0/RP0/CPU0:CRS1-3(admin)#show install detail
Secure Domain Router: Owner
  Node 0/0/CPU0 [LC] [SDR: Owner]
    Boot Device: mem:
    Boot Image: /disk0/hfr-os-mbi-3.5.3/lc/mbihfr-lc.vm
    Active Packages:
      disk0:comp-hfr-mini-3.5.3
        disk0:hfr-lc-3.5.3
        disk0:hfr-fwdg-3.5.3
        disk0:hfr-admin-3.5.3
        disk0:hfr-base-3.5.3
        disk0:hfr-os-mbi-3.5.3
  Node 0/RP0/CPU0 [RP] [SDR: Owner]
    Boot Device: disk0:
    Boot Image: /disk0/hfr-os-mbi-3.5.3/mbihfr-rp.vm
    Active Packages:
      disk0:comp-hfr-mini-3.5.3
        disk0:hfr-rout-3.5.3
        disk0:hfr-lc-3.5.3
        disk0:hfr-fwdg-3.5.3
        disk0:hfr-admin-3.5.3
```

```
        disk0:hfr-base-3.5.3
        disk0:hfr-os-mbi-3.5.3
Admin Resources:
  Node 0/0/SP [SP] [Admin Resource]
    Boot Device: bootflash:
    Boot Image: /disk0/hfr-os-mbi-3.5.3/sp/mbihfr-sp.vm
    Active Packages:
      disk0:comp-hfr-mini-3.5.3
        disk0:hfr-admin-3.5.3
        disk0:hfr-base-3.5.3
        disk0:hfr-os-mbi-3.5.3
  Node 0/SM0/SP [SP] [Admin Resource]
    Boot Device: bootflash:
    Boot Image: /disk0/hfr-os-mbi-3.5.3/sp/mbihfr-sp.vm
    Active Packages:
      disk0:comp-hfr-mini-3.5.3
        disk0:hfr-admin-3.5.3
        disk0:hfr-base-3.5.3
        disk0:hfr-os-mbi-3.5.3
  Node 0/SM1/SP [SP] [Admin Resource]
    Boot Device: bootflash:
    Boot Image: /disk0/hfr-os-mbi-3.5.3/sp/mbihfr-sp.vm
    Active Packages:
      disk0:comp-hfr-mini-3.5.3
        disk0:hfr-admin-3.5.3
        disk0:hfr-base-3.5.3
        disk0:hfr-os-mbi-3.5.3
  Node 0/SM2/SP [SP] [Admin Resource]
    Boot Device: bootflash:
    Boot Image: /disk0/hfr-os-mbi-3.5.3/sp/mbihfr-sp.vm
    Active Packages:
      disk0:comp-hfr-mini-3.5.3
        disk0:hfr-admin-3.5.3
        disk0:hfr-base-3.5.3
        disk0:hfr-os-mbi-3.5.3
  Node 0/SM3/SP [SP] [Admin Resource]
    Boot Device: bootflash:
    Boot Image: /disk0/hfr-os-mbi-3.5.3/sp/mbihfr-sp.vm
    Active Packages:
      disk0:comp-hfr-mini-3.5.3
        disk0:hfr-admin-3.5.3
        disk0:hfr-base-3.5.3
        disk0:hfr-os-mbi-3.5.3
```

Example 3-10 shows the software installation details on an eight-slot CRS-1. The RP and LC appear under Secure Domain Router resources and carry different packages. Note that routing package is required on the RP only for processing routing protocols.

Admin resources include the Service Processor from MSC and the fabric cards. The admin resources do not have fwd, lc, or routing packages because these functions are relevant only to linecard and RP.

Installing Packages

A TURBOBOOT of the router with the composite .vm image provides only vanilla routing and forwarding capabilities to the router. This section illustrates the installation of optional packages on a router running the IOS XR operating system, thus adding more features that the router can run.

There are two distinct parts of installing a package in IOS XR:

- The addition of a package to disk0
- The activation of this package

Addition and activation of packages can be done separately or the two operations can be specified in the same command line.

The CLI command for adding a package to the boot device takes the following form in admin mode:

```
install add {word | source | tar} {word | activate | synchronous | sdr |
  synchronous | <cr>}
```

The CLI command for activating a package on a boot device takes the following format in admin mode:

```
install activate {package to activate}
```

Example 3-11 shows the addition and activation of multiple packages in the same command line using the TFTP server.

Example 3-11 *Installing Packages*

```
RP/0/RP0/CPU0:CRS1-3(admin)# install add tftp:/10.10.20.100/3.5.3/hfr-mpls-p.pie-
  3.5.3  tftp:/10.10.20.100/3.5.3/hfr-mcast-p.pie-3.5.3
  tftp:/10.10.20.100/3.5.3/hfr-mgbl-p.pie-3.5.3 activate synchronous
RP/0/RP0/CPU0:Apr 15 16:09:12.023 : instdir[198]: %INSTALL-INSTMGR-6-
  INSTALL_OPERATION_STARTED : Install operation 3 '(admin) install add
  /tftp:/10.10.20.100/3.5.3/hfr-mpls-p.pie-3.5.3 /tftp:/10.10.20Install operation
  3 '(admin) install add
.100/3.5.3/hfr-mcast-p.pie-3.5.3 /tftp:/10.10.20.100/3.5.3/hfr-mgbl-p.pie-3.5.3
  activate synchronous' started by user 'cisco' /tftp:/10.10.20.100/3.5.3/
  hfr-mpls-p.pie-3.5.3
/tftp:/10.10.20.100/3.5.3/hfr-mcast-p.pie-3.5.3
/tftp:/10.10.20.100/3.5.3/hfr-mgbl-p.pie-3.5.3 activate synchronous' started by user
```

```
!.
!.
Part 2 of 2 (activate software): Completed successfully
RP/0/RP0/CPU0:CRS1-3(admin)#install commit
RP/0/RP0/CPU0:Apr 15 16:14:34.680 : instdir[198]: %INSTALL-INSTMGR-6-
INSTALL_OPERATION_STARTED : Install operation 4 '(admin) install commit' started
  by user 'cisco'
Install operation 4 '(admin) install commit' started by user 'cisco' via CLI at
16:14:34 EDT Tue Apr 15 2008.
- 100% complete: The operation can no longer be aborted (ctrl-c for
  options)RP/0/RP0/CPU0:Apr 15 16:14:36.092 : instdir[198]: %INSTALL-INSTMGR-4-
  ACTIVE_SOFTWARE_COMMITTED_INFO : The currently active software is now the same
  as the committed software.
RP/0/RP0/CPU0:Apr 15 16:14:36.094 : instdir[198]: %INSTALL-INSTMGR-6-
  INSTALL_OPERATION_COMPLETED_SUCCESSFULLY : Install operation 4 completed
  successfully
Install operation 4 completed successfully at 16:14:36 EDT Tue Apr 15 2008.
```

Example 3-11 shows the installation of various PIEs followed by committing the software at the end of the Install operation. **install commit** signifies an important step at the end of an install operation and ensures that changes to the software are persistent in case the router reloads.

The packages installed in Example 3-11 can be queried as shown in Example 3-12.

Example 3-12 *The* **show install committed detail** *Output in Admin Mode*

```
RP/0/RP0/CPU0:CRS1-3(admin)#show install committed detail
Secure Domain Router: Owner
  Node 0/0/CPU0 [LC] [SDR: Owner]
    Boot Device: mem:
    Boot Image: /disk0/hfr-os-mbi-3.5.3/lc/mbihfr-lc.vm
    Committed Packages:
      disk0:hfr-mcast-3.5.3
      disk0:hfr-mpls-3.5.3
      disk0:comp-hfr-mini-3.5.3
        disk0:hfr-lc-3.5.3
        disk0:hfr-fwdg-3.5.3
        disk0:hfr-admin-3.5.3
        disk0:hfr-base-3.5.3
        disk0:hfr-os-mbi-3.5.3
  Node 0/RP0/CPU0 [RP] [SDR: Owner]
    Boot Device: disk0:
    Boot Image: /disk0/hfr-os-mbi-3.5.3/mbihfr-rp.vm
    Committed Packages:
      disk0:hfr-mgbl-3.5.3
      disk0:hfr-mcast-3.5.3
```

```
    disk0:hfr-mpls-3.5.3
    disk0:comp-hfr-mini-3.5.3
      disk0:hfr-rout-3.5.3
      disk0:hfr-lc-3.5.3
      disk0:hfr-fwdg-3.5.3
      disk0:hfr-admin-3.5.3
      disk0:hfr-base-3.5.3
      disk0:hfr-os-mbi-3.5.3
Admin Resources:
  Node 0/0/SP [SP] [Admin Resource]
    Boot Device: bootflash:
    Boot Image: /disk0/hfr-os-mbi-3.5.3/sp/mbihfr-sp.vm
    Committed Packages:
      disk0:comp-hfr-mini-3.5.3
        disk0:hfr-admin-3.5.3
        disk0:hfr-base-3.5.3
        disk0:hfr-os-mbi-3.5.3
  Node 0/SM0/SP [SP] [Admin Resource]
    Boot Device: bootflash:
    Boot Image: /disk0/hfr-os-mbi-3.5.3/sp/mbihfr-sp.vm
    Committed Packages:
      disk0:comp-hfr-mini-3.5.3
        disk0:hfr-admin-3.5.3
        disk0:hfr-base-3.5.3
        disk0:hfr-os-mbi-3.5.3
  Node 0/SM1/SP [SP] [Admin Resource]
    Boot Device: bootflash:
    Boot Image: /disk0/hfr-os-mbi-3.5.3/sp/mbihfr-sp.vm
    Committed Packages:
      disk0:comp-hfr-mini-3.5.3
        disk0:hfr-admin-3.5.3
        disk0:hfr-base-3.5.3
        disk0:hfr-os-mbi-3.5.3
  Node 0/SM2/SP [SP] [Admin Resource]
    Boot Device: bootflash:
    Boot Image: /disk0/hfr-os-mbi-3.5.3/sp/mbihfr-sp.vm
    Committed Packages:
      disk0:comp-hfr-mini-3.5.3
        disk0:hfr-admin-3.5.3
        disk0:hfr-base-3.5.3
        disk0:hfr-os-mbi-3.5.3
  Node 0/SM3/SP [SP] [Admin Resource]
    Boot Device: bootflash:
    Boot Image: /disk0/hfr-os-mbi-3.5.3/sp/mbihfr-sp.vm
```

```
Committed Packages:
    disk0:comp-hfr-mini-3.5.3
      disk0:hfr-admin-3.5.3
      disk0:hfr-base-3.5.3
     disk0:hfr-os-mbi-3.5.3
```

The preceding command output indicates that the mpls, mgbl, and mcast PIEs have been added to the SDR resources but not to the Admin resources. Both Multicast and MPLS PIEs have line card and RP components and are installed on both. However, the mgbl or manageability PIE has only a RP component, so these PIEs do not appear on the line card hardware.

TURBOBOOT Considerations for the c12000 Platform

The c12000 platform requires a few extra considerations in doing a fresh TURBOBOOT; however, the differences between CRS-1 and c12000 are mostly in fresh reboot. Upgrading an IOS XR image on both platforms follows largely the same concept.

A new c12000 platform can be ordered prebaked as an IOS XR router; however, there will always be cases where an IOS running c12000 needs to install IOS XR. In this case the checklist in the section "Preparing to Install Cisco IOS XR" must be carefully referenced against Cisco.com. This section highlights some key elements in TURBOBOOTing a c12000 router.

The c12000 platform uses a ROMMON variable called BOOTLDR. This BOOTLDR variable needs to point to an IOS boot image that has been copied to bootflash (for example, **BOOTLDR=bootflash:/ c12kprp-boot-mz.120-32.S3.bin**).

Following the setting of BOOTLDR, the following ROMMON variables can be set:

- Rommon>**set BOOTLDR=bootflash:/{filename}**
- Rommon>**unset BOOT**
- Rommon>**unset TFTP_FILE**
- Rommon>**IP_ADDRESS= {IP_address}**
- Rommon>**IP_SUBNET_MASK={subnet_mask}**
- Rommon>**TFTP_SERVER={tftp_server_address}**
- Rommon>**DEFAULT_GATEWAY={default_gateway}**
- Rommon>**TURBOBOOT=on,[disk0] | [disk1] | [compactflash]**
- Rommon>**sync**
- Rommon>**reset**

After setting the preceding ROMMON variables, the router can be booted from ROMMON simply by specifying the path to the .vm file.

Booting the Standby RP

Booting the standby RP is a simple operation and the procedure is platform dependent. When the primary RP has started to boot, the secondary RP can be booted as described in this section.

In the case of CRS-1, on the secondary RP, reset the boot variable as follows:

```
Rommon> unset BOOT
Rommon> confreg 0x2
Rommon> reset
```

The standby RP should reboot on CRS-1 after following the preceding simple steps.

In the case of the c12000 platform, use the following steps:

```
Rommon> unset BOOT
Rommon> sync
Rommon> reset
```

Once the RP returns to ROMMON after reset, the c12000 standby can be booted by booting the mbi image. For example, in the case of the 3.6.0 release the following command can be used to boot the standby RP assuming that the mbi image is on a TFTP server:

```
rommon> b tftp:/mbiprp-rp.vm-3.6.0 {ip_address}
```

Note: The standby RP must always use the same boot device as the active RP. For example, if the active RP uses disk0 for boot process, standby must also use the disk0 as its boot media.
The Standby RP always picks up or synchronizes with the active RP for its image. The IOS XR image contained on the active RP always gets installed on the standby's disk regardless of what image existed on the standby disk.

Upgrading to a Major Cisco IOS XR Version Using mini.pie

Previous sections showed examples of TURBOBOOTing the CRS1-3 router with an IOS XR 3.5.3 image. This section details the steps involved in upgrading an IOS XR image and draws from the previous examples by using the system that was running IOS XR as a result of TURBOBOOT with IOS XR 3.5.3 maintenance release. In this case, the router can be upgraded to the main line IOS XR release 3.6.0 without dropping it into ROMMON mode. In contrast to TURBOBOOT, upgrading an IOS XR using mini.pie is the preferred method for achieving an upgrade and involves the least amount of service interruption.

As previous sections depicted, the CRS1-3 router was running the 3.5.3 base image as well as the mgbl, mcast, and mpls PIEs. When an upgrade is done to 3.6.0, all the PIEs are installed together for consistency or the upgrade is not allowed by Install Manager. The upgrade to 3.6.0 mainline therefore requires the following PIEs:

- **comp-hfr-mini.pie-3.6.0**
- **hfr-mcast-p.pie-3.6.0**
- **hfr-mgbl-p.pie-3.6.0**
- **hfr-mpls-p.pie-3.6.0**

The following command syntax achieves this upgrade, when executed from admin mode:

```
admin) install add {tftp:/location/pie_name ¦ disknum:/location/pie_name}
  activate [synchronous]
```

Note that, in the preceding command, multiple packages are specified together separated by spaces. All the packages specified in the **install** command must match the packages already installed on the router. Although it is not possible to upgrade with a lesser number of packages than those installed, it is possible to install additional packages that currently do not exist within this install operation. That is, to install **hfr-diags-p.pie-3.6.0** to be able to run diagnostics with release 3.6.0, it is possible to do so without affecting the install operation even if this package did not exist with the previous release 3.5.3 that was running before the upgrade.

The command in Example 3-13 starts the upgrade process, upgrading the 3.5.3 maintenance release to 3.6.0.

Example 3-13 *Upgrading from R3.5.3 to R3.6.0 Using mini.pie*

```
RP/0/RP0/CPU0:CRS1-3(admin)# install add tftp:/10.10.20.100/3.6.0/comp-hfr-
  mini.pie-3.6.0 tftp:/10.10.20.100/3.6.0/hfr-mpls-p.pie-3.6.0
  tftp:/10.10.20.100/3.6.0/hfr-mcast-p.pie-3.6.0  tftp:/10.10.20.100/3.6.0/hfr-
  mgbl-p.pie-3.6.0 activate synchronous
RP/0/RP0/CPU0:Apr 15 17:38:53.132 : instdir[198]: %INSTALL-INSTMGR-6-
  INSTALL_OPERATION_STARTED : Install operation 5 '(admin) install add
  /tftp:/10.10.20.100/3.6.0/comp-hfr-mini.pie-3.6.0 /tftp:/10.10.20.100/3.6.0/
  hfr-mpls-p.pie-3.6.0 /tftp:/10.10.20.100/3.6.0/hfr-mcast-p.pie-3.6.0
  /tftp:/10.10.20.100/3.6.0/hfr-mgbl-p.pie-3.6.0 activate synchronous' started by
  user 'cisco'
Install operation 5 '(admin) install add
/tftp:/10.10.20.100/3.6.0/comp-hfr-mini.pie-3.6.0
/tftp:/10.10.20.100/3.6.0/hfr-mpls-p.pie-3.6.0
/tftp:/10.10.20.100/3.6.0/hfr-mcast-p.pie-3.6.0
/tftp:/10.10.20.100/3.6.0/hfr-mgbl-p.pie-3.6.0 activate synchronous' started by
user 'cisco' via CLI at 17:38:53 EDT Tue Apr 15 2008.
Part 1 of 2 (add software): Started
 2,504KB downloaded: The operation can still be aborted (ctrl-c for options)
```

```
:
:
```

The IP address 10.10.20.100 used in Example 3-13 is that of the TFTP address. After upgrading to a major release, the IOS XR router reloads. Following the reload the software must be committed with **install commit**. This ensures consistency and prevents undesirable behavior if a power outage occurs.

The **summary** command in Example 3-14 shows that 3.5.3 packages are now replaced with 3.6.0 packages; the router is now running release 3.6.0 of IOS XR software.

Example 3-14 *Output of* **show install active** *After the Upgrade from 3.5.3 to 3.6.0*

```
RP/0/RP0/CPU0:CRS1-3(admin)#show install active summary
Default Profile:
  Admin Resources
  SDRs:
    Owner
  Active Packages:
    disk0:hfr-mpls-3.6.0
    disk0:hfr-mgbl-3.6.0
    disk0:hfr-mcast-3.6.0
    disk0:comp-hfr-mini-3.6.0
```

Example 3-15 highlights a syslog message that comes from the process instdir. This syslog message identifies the install commit operation as install operation number 6.

Example 3-15 *Committing the Packages*

```
RP/0/RP0/CPU0:CRS1-3(admin)#install commit
RP/0/RP0/CPU0:Apr 16 13:50:53.145 : instdir[204]: %INSTALL-INSTMGR-6-
  INSTALL_OPERATION_STARTED : Install operation 6 '(admin) install commit' started
  by user 'cisco'
Install operation 6 '(admin) install commit' started by user 'cisco' via CLI at
13:50:53 EDT Wed Apr 16 2008.
- 100% complete: The operation can no longer be aborted (ctrl-c for
  options)RP/0/RP0/CPU0:Apr 16 13:50:54.672 : instdir[204]: %INSTALL-INSTMGR-4-
  ACTIVE_SOFTWARE_COMMITTED_INFO : The currently active software is now the same
  as the committed software.
RP/0/RP0/CPU0:Apr 16 13:50:54.674 : instdir[204]: %INSTALL-INSTMGR-6-
  INSTALL_OPERATION_COMPLETED_SUCCESSFULLY : Install operation 6 completed
  successfully
```

Install Manager allows the querying of install operations for troubleshooting or management purposes.

Refer to the Example 3-16 output of the command **show install log from 5**.

Example 3-16 *Output of* show install log

```
RP/0/RP0/CPU0:CRS1-3(admin)#show install log from 5
Install operation 5 started by user 'cisco' via CLI at 17:38:53 EDT Tue Apr 15
2008.
    (admin) install add /tftp:/10.10.20.100/3.6.0/comp-hfr-mini.pie-3.6.0
    /tftp:/10.10.20.100/3.6.0/hfr-mpls-p.pie-3.6.0
    /tftp:/10.10.20.100/3.6.0/hfr-mcast-p.pie-3.6.0
    /tftp:/10.10.20.100/3.6.0/hfr-mgbl-p.pie-3.6.0 activate synchronous
    Install operation 5 completed successfully at 18:05:40 EDT Tue Apr 15 2008.
----------------------------------------
Install operation 6 started by user 'cisco' via CLI at 13:50:53 EDT Wed Apr 16 2008.
```

The preceding command output shows install operations that have transpired since install ID 5. It shows the addition and activation of the composite PIE along with mpls, mgbl, and mcast PIEs. The install ID 6 shows the committing of software, which was the last step in the upgrade performed in previous steps.

Install Rollback

A situation might arise where a router running an IOS XR image might need to be rolled back to the previous release. Or, more simply, a recently installed PIE might need to be removed. Although a single PIE or SMU removal can be achieved with **install deactivate** commands, this section uses the install rollback feature to demonstrate how the packages can be rolled back and to demonstrate some useful **show** commands during the process.

The install rollback scenario in Example 3-17 first adds and activates the SMU **hfr-base-3.6.0.CSCsm36321.pie** and then adds and activates the **hfr-diags-p.pie-3.6.0.** The procedure for addition and activation of an SMU is the same as a PIE, so the steps are not repeated here. However the **show install log from <*install id*>** command is used to show the install operations that transpired.

Example 3-17 *Output of* show install log *After Addition of an SMU and Diagnostics PIE*

```
RP/0/RP0/CPU0:CRS1-3(admin)#show install log from 7
Install operation 7 started by user 'cisco' via CLI at 14:39:10 EDT Wed Apr 16
2008.
    (admin) install add /tftp:/10.10.20.100/3.6.0/hfr-base-3.6.0.CSCsm36321.pie
    activate synchronous
    Install operation 7 completed successfully at 14:40:16 EDT Wed Apr 16 2008.
----------------------------------------
Install operation 8 started by user 'cisco' via CLI at 14:41:07 EDT Wed Apr 16
2008.
    (admin) install commit
    Install operation 8 completed successfully at 14:41:08 EDT Wed Apr 16 2008.
----------------------------------------
Install operation 9 started by user 'cisco' via CLI at 14:44:00 EDT Wed Apr 16
2008.
```

```
    (admin) install add /tftp:/10.10.20.100/3.6.0/hfr-diags-p.pie-3.6.0
    activate synchronous
    Install operation 9 completed successfully at 14:46:00 EDT Wed Apr 16 2008.
----------------------------------------
Install operation 10 started by user 'cisco' via CLI at 14:46:16 EDT Wed Apr 16
2008.
    (admin) install commit
    Install operation 10 completed successfully at 14:46:17 EDT Wed Apr 16
    2008.
----------------------------------------
```

Example 3-17, shown previously, uses the command **show install log 7** to see the details of the install operations. Install operation ID 7 shows the addition and activation of the SMU **hfr-base-3.6.0.CSCsm36321.pie** and the install operation ID 9 shows the addition and activation of the diagnostics PIE for 3.6.0. The install operation IDs 8 and 10 signify install commits.

The concept of install rollback is discussed in this section. Example 3-18 provides insight in the install rollback operations.

Example 3-18 *Rolling Back the Installation of Diagnostics PIE*

```
RP/0/RP0/CPU0:CRS1-3(admin)#install rollback to 7
RP/0/RP0/CPU0:Apr 16 14:59:00.642 : instdir[204]: %INSTALL-INSTMGR-6-
  INSTALL_OPERATION_STARTED : Install operation 12 '(admin) install rollback to 7'
  started by user 'cisco'
Install operation 12 '(admin) install rollback to 7' started by user 'cisco'
via CLI at 14:59:00 EDT Wed Apr 16 2008.
Info:     Install Method: Parallel Process Restart
The install operation will continue asynchronously.
RP/0/RP0/CPU0:CRS1-3(admin)#LC/0/0/CPU0:Apr 16 14:59:26.747 : sysmgr[77]: %OS-
  SYSMGR-7-INSTALL_NOTIFICATION : notification of software installation received
RP/0/RP0/CPU0:Apr 16 14:59:27.257 : sysmgr[84]: %OS-SYSMGR-7-INSTALL_NOTIFICATION
  : notification of software installation received
RP/0/RP0/CPU0:CRS1-3(admin)#show install request
Install operation 12 '(admin) install rollback to 7' started by user 'cisco'
via CLI at 14:59:00 EDT Wed Apr 16 2008.
The operation is 55% complete
The operation can no longer be aborted.
RP/0/RP0/CPU0:CRS1-3(admin)#SP/0/SM1/SP:Apr 16 14:59:36.763 : sysmgr[76]: %OS-
  SYSMGR-7-INSTALL_FINISHED : software installation is finished
Info:     The changes made to software configurations will not be persistent
Info:     across system reloads. Use the command '(admin) install commit' to
Info:     make changes persistent.
Info:     Please verify that the system is consistent following the software
Info:     change using the following commands:
Info:         show system verify
```

```
Info:         install verify packages
RP/0/RP0/CPU0:Apr 16 15:00:11.423 : instdir[204]: %INSTALL-INSTMGR-4-
  ACTIVE_SOFTWARE_COMMITTED_INFO : The currently active software is not committed.
  If the system reboots then the committed software will be used. Use 'install
  commit' to commit the active software.
RP/0/RP0/CPU0:Apr 16 15:00:11.426 : instdir[204]: %INSTALL-INSTMGR-6-
  INSTALL_OPERATION_COMPLETED_SUCCESSFULLY : Install operation 12 completed
  successfully
Install operation 12 completed successfully at 15:00:11 EDT Wed Apr 16 2008.
RP/0/RP0/CPU0:CRS1-3(admin)#show install request
There are no install requests in operation.
RP/0/RP0/CPU0:CRS1-3(admin)#install commit
RRP/0/RP0/CPU0:CRS1-3(admin)#show install active summary
Default Profile:
  Admin Resources
  SDRs:
    Owner
  Active Packages:
    disk0:hfr-mpls-3.6.0
    disk0:hfr-mgbl-3.6.0
    disk0:hfr-mcast-3.6.0
    disk0:hfr-base-3.6.0.CSCsm36321-1.0.0
    disk0:comp-hfr-mini-3.6.0
RP/0/RP0/CPU0:CRS1-3(admin)#show install inactive ¦ incl diag
      disk0:hfr-diags-3.6.0
```

Example 3-18 demonstrates the deactivation of diags PIE by rolling back to install ID 7. A useful command (**show install request**) is also introduced to show the status of an install operation running asynchronously in the background. Finally, the output of **show install active summary** indicates that the diagnostics (diags) PIE has been deactivated. However, a subsequent command **show install inactive** piped to catch a 3.6.0 diags PIE indicates that the diags PIE is still present on the boot media. The important point to note here is that the install rollback performs a deactivation of one or more packages and does not perform a removal.

Example 3-18 was a simple depiction of a PIE deactivation. However, a whole release can be rolled back by providing the right rollback point. The rollback points are noted by the output of **show install log.**

Removing Inactive Packages

Installing an IOS XR image creates a special directory structure on the boot media. Good practices dictate that files should never be copied or removed from disk0:/ or boot_media:/ by the use of **copy**, **delete**, or the UNIX ksh **rm** command; doing so can cause irrecoverable damage to the boot media if an install-related file or directory is accidentally removed. Instead, Install Manager provides an **install remove inactive** command that automates this task for a user.

Example 3-18 shows that the diagnostics PIE remains present on disk0 despite the install rollback operation. Install rollback, therefore, deactivates the packages but does not remove them from the disk. Example 3-19 shows the removal of inactive PIE from the disk.

Example 3-19 *Removal of Inactive PIEs with Install Remove Inactive*

```
RP/0/RP0/CPU0:CRS1-3(admin)#install remove inactive
RP/0/RP0/CPU0:Apr 16 16:42:50.704 : instdir[204]: %INSTALL-INSTMGR-6-
  INSTALL_OPERATION_STARTED : Install operation 17 '(admin) install remove inactive'
  started by user 'cisco'
Install operation 17 '(admin) install remove inactive' started by user 'cisco'
via CLI at 16:42:50 EDT Wed Apr 16 2008.
Info:     This operation will remove the following packages:
Info:         disk0:hfr-admin-3.5.3
Info:         disk0:hfr-base-3.5.3
Info:         disk0:hfr-diags-3.6.0
Info:         disk0:hfr-fwdg-3.5.3
Info:         disk0:hfr-lc-3.5.3
Info:         disk0:hfr-mcast-3.5.3
Info:         disk0:hfr-mgbl-3.5.3
Info:         disk0:hfr-mpls-3.5.3
Info:         disk0:hfr-os-mbi-3.5.3
Info:         disk0:hfr-rout-3.5.3
Info:     After this install remove the following install rollback points will
Info:     no longer be reachable, as the required packages will not be present:
Info:         0, 3, 9
Proceed with removing these packages? [confirm]
The install operation will continue asynchronously.
RP/0/RP0/CPU0:CRS1-3(admin)#show install request
Install operation 17 '(admin) install remove inactive' started by user 'cisco'
via CLI at 16:42:50 EDT Wed Apr 16 2008.
The operation is 1% complete
The operation cannot be aborted.
RP/0/RP0/CPU0:CRS1-3(admin)#
```

In the preceding output, the diags PIE is removed along with other inactive PIEs. After these PIEs are removed, install rollback points are no longer applicable.

Additionally, if bulk operations are not desired and more selective deactivations and removals are necessary, Install Manager provides the **install deactivate** and **install remove** commands in the admin mode.

Performing an Install Audit

The Cisco IOS XR Install subsystem provides a handy tool to perform an audit of all the packages and SMUs installed on a router. The audit performs checks to verify whether the right packages and SMUs are installed on the router by auditing the installed packages against a precreated text file. Although there are **show** commands available to query the same information, the task of verifying the existence of all the desired SMUs and packages can become cumbersome on a large network without the availability of an appropriate tool.

The Package audit tool in IOS XR available from version 3.4.1 helps with the on-demand checking of the active packages on the router against a file stored in a central location. The file contains a listing of the packages that need to be installed and activated on the router. The outcome of an install audit reports as a success if the installed software was found to be compliant or reports on a set of discrepancies.

Example 3-20 illustrates the use of the Install audit tool.

Example 3-20 *Conducting an Install Audit*

```
RP/0/RP0/CPU0:CRS1-3#more disk0:/usr/install_list.txt
hfr-rout-3.6.0.CSCsm76283-1.0.0
hfr-mpls-3.6.0
hfr-mgbl-3.6.0
hfr-mcast-3.6.0
hfr-lc-3.6.0.CSCsl21597-1.0.0
hfr-base-3.6.0.CSCsm36321-1.0.0
comp-hfr-mini-3.6.0
RP/0/RP0/CPU0:CRS1-3(admin)#show install audit file install_list.txt verbose
Info:     Parsing audit file.
Info:     Install Audit file contains 7 packages:
Info:         hfr-rout-3.6.0.CSCsm76283-1.0.0
Info:         hfr-mpls-3.6.0
Info:         hfr-mgbl-3.6.0
Info:         hfr-mcast-3.6.0
Info:         hfr-lc-3.6.0.CSCsl21597-1.0.0
Info:         hfr-base-3.6.0.CSCsm36321-1.0.0
Info:         comp-hfr-mini-3.6.0
Info:     Compare with active packages on the following nodes:
Info:         0/0/SP
Info:         0/0/CPU0
Info:         0/RP0/CPU0
Info:         0/SM0/SP
Info:         0/SM1/SP
Info:         0/SM2/SP
Info:         0/SM3/SP
Install audit operation completed.
Install audit result: SUCCESS
```

Disk Backup and Recovery

A boot device is a critical resource for the router. This section discusses the options available to protect the boot device.

Creating a Backup Disk with Golden Disk

In release 3.4.0, a new feature called Golden Disk was introduced for disk backup and recovery. The Golden Disk feature provides high availability and fault recovery features, which can increase the reliability of the system and help make continued operations of IOS XR more reliable.

Golden Disk allows mitigating a situation where a user faces downtime due to a failed or corrupted disk by creating a backup ahead of time. Creating a backup will help shorten the outage on the router if a primary boot device fails.

By using the disk backup feature it becomes possible to back up the disk before doing an upgrade and downgrade of images. Preparing the Golden Disk helps revert to the known good image in the case of failure. One could argue that you could use the install rollback options available in IOS XR Install Manager. However, the Golden Disk feature is important in case the install- or disk-related issue is more severe in nature, and install rollback is not sufficient to help the router recover from a software fault.

The Golden Disk feature defines two new ROMMON variables: **BOOT_DEV_SEQ_CONF** and **BOOT_DEV_SEQ_OPER.**

This variable **BOOT_DEV_SEQ_CONF** can be set in the Admin mode by the boot sequence command:

```
RP/0/RP1/CPU0:crs4(admin)system boot-sequence disk0: disk1:
```

Disk0: in the preceding command is the primary boot disk and disk1: is the target backup disk.

The **BOOT_DEV_SEQ_OPER** ROMMON variable sets the operational value for the boot sequence and contains devices listed in the **BOOT_DEV_SEQ_CONF** ROMMON variable. This variable will be used by ROMMON to determine the device sequence to be used in booting the RP as well as by TURBOBOOT in determining the target device to install software.

The following commands create backup disk0: on disk1:

```
RP/0/RP1/CPU0:crs4(admin)#system boot-sequence disk0: disk1:
RP/0/RP1/CPU0:crs4(admin)#system backup disk1:
```

The preceding commands specify a boot sequence specifying disk0: as a primary device that needs to be backed up on disk1:

The **system backup disk1:** command creates the backup on disk1:. You then can view its status by using **show system backup verify.**

Since the introduction of Golden Disk feature, a failure of boot media causes an RP failover. Assume a situation in which a router running IOS XR was booted from disk0: and the backup of disk0: was created on disk1:.

The following events might transpire in the case of a boot device failure:

- A backup of disk0: was created on disk1: residing on primary RP to allow mitigating a low probability event of disk failure.
- Disk0: in the primary device fails and that results in a failover of the primary RP to the secondary RP, assuming redundant RPs are present.

- While the new active RP takes over, the failed RP can now be recovered from its backup disk1:.

ROMMON code that shipped alongside Release 3.4.0 did not support the new ROMMON variables **BOOT_DEV_SEQ_CONF** and **BOOT_DEV_SEQ_OPER** created because of introducing the Golden Disk feature. An RP with a failed disk will not automatically boot up from a backup disk, but will need to be booted up from the backup disk manually.

> **Tip:** If a c12000 standby RP is continually resetting, you can bring it into ROMMON by continually entering **send brk** through the console. On a CRS-1, the same is achieved by pressing Ctrl-C.

Disk Mirroring

Although Golden Disk CLI is still available in Release 3.6.0 of IOS XR, a new feature called *disk mirroring* has been introduced in this release. Disk mirroring removes the need for an RP failover if a mirrored disk is present on the primary RP and the primary boot device fails. Therefore, from Release 3.6.0 onward, disk mirroring should always be used for the protection of boot media. At the time of writing this book, disk mirroring is supported only between disk0: and disk1: on both CRS-1 and c12000 platforms.

Disk mirroring works by replicating critical data from the primary boot device onto another storage device on the same RP. This other storage device can be referred to as a *mirrored disk* or simply as a secondary device. If the primary boot device fails, applications continue to be serviced transparently by the secondary device, thereby avoiding a switchover to the standby RP. The failed primary storage device can be replaced or repaired without disruption of service.

Disk mirroring should mirror only critical data from the primary boot device onto a secondary storage device. Any other files, such as crash dumps, text files, and syslog messages, should not be replicated. Furthermore, good practices dictate that noncritical data should be kept away from the primary boot device or at least kept away from disk0:/. To separate critical data from noncritical data, the disk devices need to be partitioned. Disk0: is partitioned into disk0: and disk0a:; disk1: is partitioned into disk1: and disk1a:. Disk0: and disk1: are used for critical data, whereas disk0a: and disk1a: are used for logging data and other noncritical data.

At the time of writing this book, IOS XR is shipping with 1 gigabit boot disks, although 2 and 4 gigabit disks are being actively evaluated. This chapter focuses attention on the currently shipping 1 gigabit disk only. However, a proposed partition of various disk sizes is described in Table 3-5.

Table 3-5 *Possible Partition Ratios Based on Disk Sizes*

Size of Disk	Primary Partition Percentage	Secondary Partition Percentage
Less than 900 MB	Partitioning not supported	Partitioning not supported
900 MB to 1.5 GB	~80%	20%

Size of Disk	Primary Partition Percentage	Secondary Partition Percentage
1.5 GB to 3 GB	60%	40%
More than 3 GB	50%	50%

Note: The partitions shown in Table 3-5 represent partition ratios being discussed at the time of writing this book. They are meant to give you an idea of the ratio of primary and secondary partitions based on disk sizes. Cisco.com must be consulted against the Cisco IOS XR release of interest to see whether these values have changed.

Creating a Disk Partition

The first step toward using disk mirroring is to have a secondary storage device in the primary RP and create a partition on that disk.

Example 3-21 uses a **ksh** command to show what an unpartitioned disk looks like.

Example 3-21 *Output of* **run fdisk** *Command for Disk1:*

```
RP/0/RP0/CPU0:CRS1-3#run fdisk /dev/disk1 show
     _____OS_____        Start       End        ______Number______       Size      Boot
     name      type     Cylinder  Cylinder  Cylinders     Blocks
1. Hü)H dø      11             0        1947        1947     1963521      958 MB
2. ---      -.   ----     ----      ---.   ----    --.
3. ---      -.   ----     ----      ---.   ----    --.
4. ---      -.   ----     ----      ---.   ----    --.
```

The preceding **show** command depicts a single partition on disk1:, the size is 958 MB. Example 3-22 depicts a disk partition after a **format** command has been executed.

Example 3-22 *Creating a Partition on Disk1:*

```
RP/0/RP0/CPU0:CRS1-3#format disk1: partition location 0/rp0/CPU0 force
This operation will destroy all data on "disk1:" and partition device. Continue?
  [confirm]
RP/0/RP0/CPU0:Apr 18 10:36:12.166 : syslog_dev[82]: mkdosfs:
RP/0/RP0/CPU0:Apr 18 10:36:12.166 : syslog_dev[82]: mkdosfs: Format complete:
  FAT16 (4096-byte clusters), 98164 kB available.
RP/0/RP0/CPU0:Apr 18 10:36:12.791 : syslog_dev[82]: mkdosfs:
RP/0/RP0/CPU0:Apr 18 10:36:12.791 : syslog_dev[82]: mkdosfs: Format complete:
  FAT16 (16384-byte clusters), 884192 kB available.
Device partition disk1: is now formated and is available for use.

RP/0/RP0/CPU0:CRS1-3#dir disk1:
Directory of disk1:
2          drwx   16384       Fri Apr 18 10:37:03 2008  LOST.DIR
```

```
905412608 bytes total (905396224 bytes free)
RP/0/RP0/CPU0:CRS1-3#dir disk1a:
Directory of disk1a:
2            drwx  4096        Fri Apr 18 10:37:09 2008  LOST.DIR
100519936 bytes total (100515840 bytes free)
RP/0/RP0/CPU0:CRS1-3#run fdisk /dev/disk1 show
   _____        OS_____Start  End      NumberSizeBoot
   name        type    Cylinder  Cylinder  Cylinders   Blocks
1. Hü)H dø      6          0        1754       1754   1768977    863 MB
2. Hü)H dø      4       1755        1949        194    196560     95 MB
3. ---     -.   ----    ----     ---.  ----   --.
4. ---     -.   ----    ----     ---.  ----   --.
```

Example 3-22 shows a partition created by the execution of the command **disk1: partition location 0/rp0/CPU0 force**. The command creates two partitions. Outputs of the **dir** command and outputs of **run fdisk /dev/disk1 show** depict a disk0: partition of about .9 gigabits and a disk01a: partition of about .1 gigabits.

Turning On Disk Mirroring

The previous section demonstrates the partitioning of a disk. This section explains how to turn on disk mirroring. Example 3-23 demonstrates the enabling of disk mirroring.

Example 3-23 *Enabling Disk Mirroring*

```
RP/0/RP0/CPU0:CRS1-3(config)#mirror location 0/rp0/CPU0 disk0:disk1:
RP/0/RP0/CPU0:CRS1-3(config)#commit
RP/0/RP0/CPU0:Apr 18 14:29:00.265 : config[65788]: %MGBL-CONFIG-6-DB_COMMIT :
  Configuration committed by user 'cisco'. Use 'show configuration commit changes
  1000000008' to view the changes.
RP/0/RP0/CPU0:CRS1-3(config)#RP/0/RP0/CPU0:Apr 18 14:29:00.390 : redfs_svr[80]:
  %OS-REDFS-6-MIRROR_ENABLED : Mirroring has been enabled with configured devices
  of disk0: and disk1:.
RP/0/RP0/CPU0:Apr 18 14:44:28.579 : redfs_svr[80]: %OS-REDFS-6-MIRROR_REDUNDANT :
  Mirroring is now fully redundant for devices disk0: and disk1:.
```

The **mirror location 0/rp0/CPU0 disk0:disk1:** command makes the redfs_svr process start the sync process from the primary device to the primary partition of the secondary device. The command in Example 3-24 queries the redfs_svr while the mirror is synchronizing the files.

Example 3-24 *The redfs Process*

```
P/0/RP0/CPU0:CRS1-3#run pidin | grep "redfs"
   32786    1 pkg/bin/redfs_svr    10r RECEIVE      1
   32786    2 pkg/bin/redfs_svr    10r RECEIVE      5
   32786    3 pkg/bin/redfs_svr    10r NANOSLEEP
   32786    4 pkg/bin/redfs_svr    10r NANOSLEEP
   32786    5 pkg/bin/redfs_svr    10r RECEIVE      5
```

```
   32786     7 pkg/bin/redfs_svr    10r RECEIVE      5
   32786     8 pkg/bin/redfs_svr    10r RECEIVE      5
  364682     1 g/bin/redfs_config   10r RECEIVE      1
RP/0/RP0/CPU0:CRS1-3#
```

Example 3-24 shows the **redfs** process while the synchronization is running between two disks. Knowing the key processes involved in various IOS XR operations helps with troubleshooting the operating system.

Example 3-25 shows the output of the **show mirror** command used for monitoring disk mirroring.

Example 3-25 *Monitoring Disk Mirroring*

```
RP/0/RP0/CPU0:CRS1-3#show mirror
Mirror Information for 0/RP0/CPU0.
=========================================================
 Mirroring Enabled
   Configured Primary:           disk0:
   Configured Secondary:         disk1:
 Current Mirroring State:        Redundant
   Current Physical Primary:     disk0:
   Current Physical Secondary:   disk1:
 Mirroring Logical Device:       disk0:
 Physical Device      State        Flags
---------------------------------------------------------
  disk0:             Available      Enabled
  disk1:             Available      Enabled Formatted
  compactflash:      Not Present
  disk0a:            Not Present
  disk1a:            Available      Formatted
  compactflasha:     Not Present
Mirroring Rommon Variable
 BOOT_DEV_SEQ_CONF = disk0:;disk1:
 BOOT_DEV_SEQ_OPER = disk0:;disk1:
 MIRROR_ENABLE = Y
```

The preceding command output indicates that full redundancy of boot devices has been achieved with disk mirroring.

In the case of disks greater than 1 gigabit, the partitioning of primary boot device is done internally by the redfs_svr process. In the case of 1 gigabit size disk, this will have to be done manually.

Disk mirroring is a useful feature providing high availability for the boot device; it is an improvement over the previous Release 3.4.0 Golden Disk feature in the sense that it does not cause an RP failover in the case of primary boot device failure. For Release 3.6.0 or later, Disk Mirroring should be the preferred way of achieving boot device redundancy.

Install Health Checks

This section deals with install-related operational practices that help avoid install-related issues and aid in troubleshooting. The preemptive measures discussed in this section provide a set of commands that may be run to perform health checks prior to or after an upgrade.

Verifying MD5 Signature of a PIE or an SMU

The Install Manager subsystem performs PIE validation and performs compatibility checks without user intervention. However, it is advisable to check the MD5 signatures of packages offline before the anticipated installation. This practice minimizes chances of failure and saves install time in case a PIE file is corrupted during copying or download. The following command shows the verification of MD5 signature for the 3.6.0 mpls PIE:

```
RP/0/RP0/CPU0:CRS1-3#sam verify tftp:/10.10.20.100/3.6.0/hfr-mpls-p.pie-3.6.0 md5
a8ac40d7d6271edb68c9a930e38e4b40
```

The preceding command shows a Software Authentication Manager (SAM) command that reports the MD5 signature of a PIE or an SMU that resides on a TFTP server. The same command may be used for any storage location where a PIE resides by providing an appropriate path. The command shown belongs to the **crypto-sam** component of IOS XR software.

Anticipating Disk Space Usage

Install operations concerning an IOS XR upgrade involve increased disk space use because two IOS XR images may exist together on the disk during the course of an upgrade. Depletion of disk space has detrimental consequences in IOS XR. Operation of a router whose disk space exceeds 90 percent persistently might be affected due to outage. Example 3-26 depicts using an **install** command in estimating disk space usage for a PIE or a set of PIEs whose installation is anticipated.

Example 3-26 *Estimating the Uncompressed Size of a PIE*

```
RP/0/RP0/CPU0:CRS1-3(admin)#show install pie-info tftp:/10.10.20.100/3.6.0/com-hfr-
  mini.pie-3.6.0
Contents of pie file '/tftp:/10.10.20.100/3.6.0/comp-hfr-mini.pie-3.6.0':
    Expiry date         : Oct 16, 2015 21:51:47 EDT
    Uncompressed size : 212739322
    comp-hfr-mini-3.6.0
        hfr-rout-3.6.0
        hfr-lc-3.6.0
        hfr-fwdg-3.6.0
        hfr-admin-3.6.0
        hfr-base-3.6.0
        hfr-os-mbi-3.6.0
```

Example 3-26 shows a way of estimating the uncompressed byte size of a PIE whose installation is anticipated. The uncompressed sizes of all the PIEs and SMUs can be added, with an extra 10 percent safety factor in estimating the increased disk usage.

Testing a PIE or SMU Installation

Install Manager provides a CLI to conduct a mock SMU or PIE installation. This functionality helps predict the impact of the install on the router. The command for using the test option follows:

```
install activate {pie name and location} test
```

The preceding command shows the impact of installing a particular package and indicates whether the application of a package would trigger a reload of any of the nodes in the system.

Verifying the config-register

Prior to installing any package or SMU, the config-register setting may be checked. The following commands also covered in previous sections show the current config-register setting:

```
show bootvar
more nvram:classic-rommon-var
```

A config-register setting of 0x102 ensures that the router does not go into ROMMON on the application of a reload SMU.

config-register settings can be changed in Admin mode by using the command **config-register 0x102**.

Setting config-register to 0x0 changes the setting for both active and standby RP and drops the router to ROMMON if **reload location all** is executed from Admin mode.

Clearing Configuration Inconsistency

As a matter of good operational practices, router configuration should be backed up prior to attempting an upgrade of IOS XR image. The following command reduces the chances of configuration loss when it is executed from Exec and Admin modes:

```
clear configuration inconsistency
```

Summary

This chapter covered the installation of IOS XR software on the c12000 and CRS-1 platforms. The architectural aspects of Install Manager were explored, along with developing a comprehension for the different PIEs and SMUs that are a part of IOS XR packaging. The chapter also demonstrated the install features of applying PIEs and SMU patches while the router is carrying out its operations and removing inactive PIEs to conserve disk resources. The install rollback feature was explored to back out of a PIE installation. The options of Golden Disk and Disk Mirroring were introduced to provide redundancy to the mission-critical boot device.

The Cisco IOS XR concept of installation is a little more involved than the traditional experience of simply booting a router. This chapter also introduced a checklist that provides preparation guidance for installing IOS XR. When followed closely in conjunction with release-specific information on Cisco.com, the installation checklist can help ease the process of installing IOS XR.

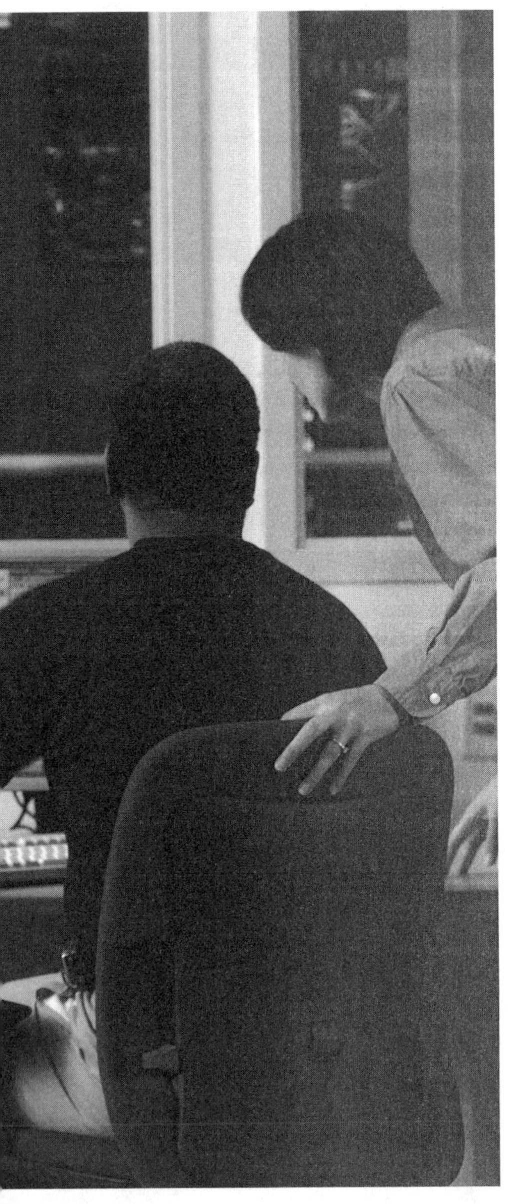

This chapter covers the following topics:

- Understanding Distributed Configuration Management
- Understanding Configuration Planes
- Components of Configuration Management
- Understanding the Two-Stage Commit Model
- Configuration Features in Cisco IOS XR
- Configuration Management During Hardware and Software Change Events
- Configuration Rollback

This chapter discusses the features provided by Cisco IOS XR in facilitating robust configuration management. In accordance with a network engineer's experiences of dealing with an ASCII configuration file, IOS XR introduces the concept of a configuration database where configuration is held like records in a database. This configuration database uses both binary and ASCII structures in providing more management features for network operations.

This chapter also discusses the notion of a two-stage configuration model, where the first stage in applying a configuration acts like a spell checker validating correct syntax, and the second stage explicitly commits the running configuration to the router. The main idea behind IOS XR configuration management is to provide a user-friendly configuration experience and feature-rich options in the implementation of network operations. Additionally, this chapter demonstrates the various configuration management features with examples and provides you with an insight into the basic architecture behind the two stage configuration model.

CHAPTER 4

Configuration Management

Understanding Distributed Configuration Management

Cisco IOS XR has a distributed model for configuration management. IOS XR has different processes, running on every modular service card (MSC) or node, which are responsible for the configuration of that particular node. These processes are responsible for applying configuration and managing operations for their node. The route processor (RP) is responsible only for the summary state information of all interfaces in the system. In IOS XR, the MSC-specific configuration is separated from the control plane–specific configuration.

This section describes control plane and data plane configuration management.

Control Plane Configuration Management

Any routing protocol configuration (IGP or EGP) is considered to be global to the system. The routing protocol configuration is controlled by RPs and distributed route processors (DRP). Border Gateway Protocol (BGP) could be operating in distributed mode; however, it is also part of the global configuration. Control plane services are separated from the physical interfaces from a configuration standpoint; they are unaware of the actual interface's state. When an MSC or Shared Port Adaptor (SPA) is inserted in the system, the control plane configuration becomes active if you have configured any protocol for the interface. When you remove an MSC or SPA, the protocol configuration does not change; however, it becomes inactive for the specific SPA or interface. In IOS XR when you configure a routing protocol, you specify the interface names and not the network address. You can configure the interface (name) under a routing protocol in IOS XR even for an interface that is not yet created or in existence. The protocols will become operational on the interfaces once the interface becomes active. This aspect is also referred to as *interface forward referencing*.

Data Plane Configuration Management

Any data plane features that are specific to the MSC are part of the Data Plane Configuration. Examples of such features include IPv4, IPv6, and Layer 2 protocol. Therefore, these will be provisioned and managed by the MSC. Data plane configurations are unaware of the control plane applications that might be active or enabled over the physical interface. Processes on the node apply the appropriate Layer 2 and Layer 3 protocols to the interface. Control and data plane separation helps to achieve high availability goals. Any change in the control processes (such as BGP) does not impact the MSC operation as they are separated. Configuration scalability is increased as data plane configuration and detailed state information is not held on management node. During reboots, data plane configuration restoration occurs in parallel on multiple nodes, which helps the system to scale.

Understanding Configuration Planes

In Cisco IOS XR the router configuration can be divided into three distinct sections or *planes*. They are

- Admin plane
- Shared plane
- Local plane

This section describes each of these planes in detail.

Admin Plane

The admin plane contains the global configuration that is applicable to the entire physical system. It includes the configuration of SDR carving and Admin user access info. The configuration is accessible from the owner SDR, which has admin privileges. It is applied on the dSC during system bootup.

One example comprises hardware resources shared by all SDRs (for example, the CRS platform's fabric transport) and the configuration that divides a physical system into SDRs.

In Example 4-1 a new SDR, *logical1*, is created in a Cisco CRS-1 router in the admin configuration mode. Using the **location** command, an RP is assigned as the primary node. An additional hardware node in rack 1 slot 0 is then added to the resources available for the *logical1* SDR system.

Example 4-1 *Admin Plane Configuration*

```
RP/0/RP0/CPU0:CRS1-3#admin
RP/0/RP0/CPU0:CRS1-3(admin)#configure
RP/0/RP0/CPU0:CRS1-3(admin-config)#sdr logical1
RP/0/RP0/CPU0:CRS1-3(admin-config-sdr:logical1)#location 1/RP*/* primary
RP/0/RP0/CPU0:CRS1-3(admin-config-sdr:logical1)#location 1/0/*
RP/0/RP0/CPU0:CRS1-3(admin-config-sdr:logical1)#end
RP/0/RP0/CPU0:CRS1-3(admin)#exit
RP/0/RP0/CPU0:CRS1-3#
```

Shared Plane

The shared plane contains global configuration that is applicable to an entire SDR. The shared plane configuration is accessible from throughout the SDR to which it applies, and survives only for as long as the SDR is defined within the physical system. It is applied on the dSDRSC during SDR bootup. Examples are routing protocol configuration, policies for features such as QoS and ACLs, configuration for multicast and MPLS functionality, and configuration for many other global features and services.

Local Plane

The local plane contains configuration that is applicable to an individual node within an SDR. Local plane configuration is applied on each individual node when it boots. It is accessible only from the SDR in which the node resides. It is active only when the node to which it is applied is running. If a node is brought down or removed from the SDR, the local plane configuration relevant to that node is moved to a preconfiguration area from which it will later be restored if the node is added or brought back up again. The preconfiguration concept allows local plane configuration to be added or modified, even when the node to which it applies is not present and running. Examples are interface properties and the attachment of globally defined policies to individual interfaces.

When accessing configuration, the user can access either the admin plane configuration or the configuration for a single SDR (both shared and local planes). It is not possible to simultaneously access the admin plane configuration and the configuration for an SDR; neither is it possible to simultaneously access the configuration for more than one SDR.

Shared plane and local plane configuration are sometimes collectively referred to as *SDR-plane configuration*. Shared and local plane configuration survives for as long as SDR is defined. Similarly, admin plane configuration survives as long as the system is up and running. This implies that the running configuration is persistent over all events that might occur in the lifetime of a system: process restarts, node OIR events, RP/DRP switchovers, and most notably the reboot events. The admin plane configuration is restored after reboot of the physical system, the shared plane configuration is restored after reboot of the SDR, and local plane configuration is restored after reboot of an individual node. When you reboot the entire system the admin, shared, and local plane configurations are brought up sequentially, in that order. Only local plane configurations across different nodes come up in parallel by virtue of parallel booting of the nodes.

Components of Configuration Management

Different components are needed to achieve the separation of control and data plane. This section discusses in detail some of the key components of configuration management, including Configuration Manager (Cfgmgr), Configuration File System (CFS), System Database (SysDB), and Replicated Data Service File System (RDSFS).

Configuration Manager

Cisco IOS XR Configuration Manager is a vital software component that provides the support for management, application, and maintenance of router persistent configuration. Configuration Manager also performs the maintenance of CFS, where CFS is accessed through RDSFS. Furthermore, replication and synchronization of the CFS to all management nodes is done by RDSFS transparently.

Configuration Manager is responsible for the following functionalities:

- It handles large configurations by saving and applying them in a short span of time while the router is up and running.
- In distributed architecture of CRS-1 or GSR XR1200, Configuration Manager is also distributed, where each node is responsible for applying configurations for that particular node.
- Cfgmgr is responsible for storing the configuration on Management nodes for access to all other nodes.
- MSC drivers/clients send config request to Cfgmgr to restore their configuration in the active state.
- Cfgmgr also helps in building and committing bulk configuration at run time.
- Cfgmgr is responsible for management services such as configuration checkpoint and rollback, configuration history, and configuration lock and unlock.

Note: Rollback is simply undoing some of the configuration changes that were done by the user. Configuration rollback is an atomic operation that rolls the active configuration back to a previous known state.

Let's discuss the role of Configuration Manager in the context of a router booting with primary persistent configuration. Configuration Manager on the RP checks the health of the primary persistent configuration. The primary persistent configuration is a new concept in IOS XR and is explained in the following section. Based on the health of the primary persistent configuration, the primary persistent configuration is used to restore the router's running configuration; otherwise, it will fall back to ASCII backup, which is also known as *secondary persistent configuration*. Also under the scenario where the primary persistent configuration is corrupted and/or not backward compatible, version changes of the primary persistent configuration will also resort to the ASCII backup.

Cfgmgr is comprised of a set of processes named Cfgmgr RP and Cfgmgr LCCfgmgr LC. The main purpose of these processes is restoration of the system configuration. Table 4-1 and Table 4-2 summarize the functionality, roles, and responsibilities of Cfgmgr RP and Cfgmgr LC with examples of where it is used.

Table 4-1 *Cfgmgr RP*

Functionality	Description
Distribution model	Runs on all RP and DRP nodes

Functionality	Description
Roles/responsibilities	All instances: Restore their local plane configuration dSC instance only: Restores the admin plane configuration dSDRSC instance only: Restores the shared plane configuration Rebase
Examples	Restoration of global configuration: ACL definitions MQC policy definition Control Plane configuration

Table 4-2 *Cfgmgr LC*

Functionality	Description
Distribution model	Runs on all LC nodes
Roles/responsibilities	Restores the local plane configuration
Examples	Restoration of MSC configuration: IPv4/v6 address Encapsulation Description Shut/no shut

In Figure 4-1 Cfgmgr RP restores the shared plane configuration and its local plane configuration (example management node interface). The Cfgmgr LC process running on each MSC or node applies the configuration for that node independently.

Configuration File System

Configuration File System (CFS) is a set of files and directories used to store the primary persistent configurations in binary format. CFS is managed by Cfgmgr and is replicated to other management nodes (RP and DRP) within the Secured Domain Router (SDR) by RDSFS. It also has the persistent ASCII backup config, configuration history, commits/checkpoints, startup failed configuration files, versioning info, commitdb metadata files, and so on. The configuration files are arranged in a series of directories under a single CFS root directory on a management node. CFS is stored under the directory <media>/config/. By default, Cfgmgr learns about the boot media from the diskutil component.

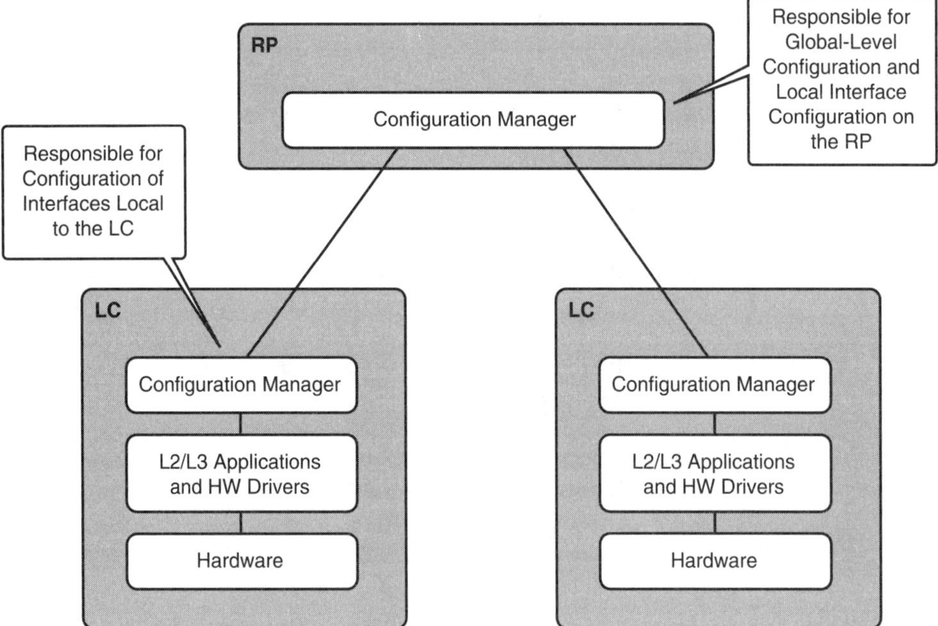

Figure 4-1 *Configuration Manager on RP and LC*

> **Note:** The default behavior of using the media can be changed from disk0 to other media options supported by platforms such as disk1 or compact flash by setting the appropriate ROMMON variable.

The **dir** (directory) command displays an output of flashdisk, also known as disk 0 on the route processor. The config directory displays the configurations parsed in files that are made up of running configurations, history (or committed configurations), and admin configurations as shown in Example 4-2.

Example 4-2 *CFS on disk0*

```
RP/0/RP0/CPU0:CRS1-3#dir disk0:/config



Directory of disk0:/config

22          drwx  16384       Fri Apr 18 15:39:15 2008  admin
24          drwx  16384       Fri Apr 18 15:20:42 2008  running
25          drwx  16384       Fri Apr 18 15:39:15 2008  lr
27          drwx  16384       Fri Apr 18 15:20:43 2008  failed
32          drwx  16384       Fri Apr 18 15:20:43 2008  history
33          drwx  16384       Fri Apr 18 15:20:43 2008  removed_cfg
```

```
905412608 bytes total (319881216 bytes free)
RP/0/RP0/CPU0:CRS1-3#
```

In Example 4-2 the output of disk0:config lists only the main directories that are created:

- The admin directory holds all the admin plane configurations.
- The lr directory has all the SDR-related files.
- The failed directory holds all the configurations that have failed during startup. These failed files can be viewed as well as loaded back, if needed, to restore some of the configurations.
- The history directory holds all the events that have happened in the system related to configuration changes (commit operations). The **show configuration history** output provides the information from the history directory. Consider a system configured with multicast features.
  When you uninstall the multicast PIE from the system, all the configurations related to multicast move into removed_cfg. The removed_cfg directory holds configurations that are removed under scenarios such as PIE uninstallation, unsupported CLIs during upgrade or downgrade, and so on.

CFS is constantly synchronized between Active and Standby RPs to preserve the router's configuration state in the event of an RP failover. You will have a mirror of all the CFS files in the Standby RP, and these are synchronized periodically. CFS is also created and synched in all Management nodes except the MSCs/nodes (because no disk exists there). Figure 4-2 illustrates the pictorial representation of CFS.

As mentioned in the previous section, the primary persistent configuration is a new concept in Cisco IOS XR, and it shouldn't be confused with Startup configuration in IOS. The primary persistent configuration is created based on the absolute refpoints along with the outstanding commit refpoints. The primary persistent configuration is stored in binary format (SysDB native format); hence it can be easily restored directly into memory during bootup. These absolute refpoints and commit refpoints are stored in the CFS, which is updated on every change or commit in the configuration.

Note: For every successful commit operation, a new commit database record gets created. A refpoint is a reference to these records in the database.

Let's take an example to define how these absolute refpoints and commit refpoints are created and used to restore the router configuration. In Figure 4-3 the disk holds all the commit refpoint files from 1000000120 to 1000000219 within CFS. Each of these commit refpoint files refers to a commit operation of the user in the form of a configuration change. The absolute refpoint contains the router configuration as it was after commit 1000000216. Commit change files for the three subsequent commits (1000000217 to 1000000219) can be seen, as well as all prior commits (1000000120 to 1000000219).

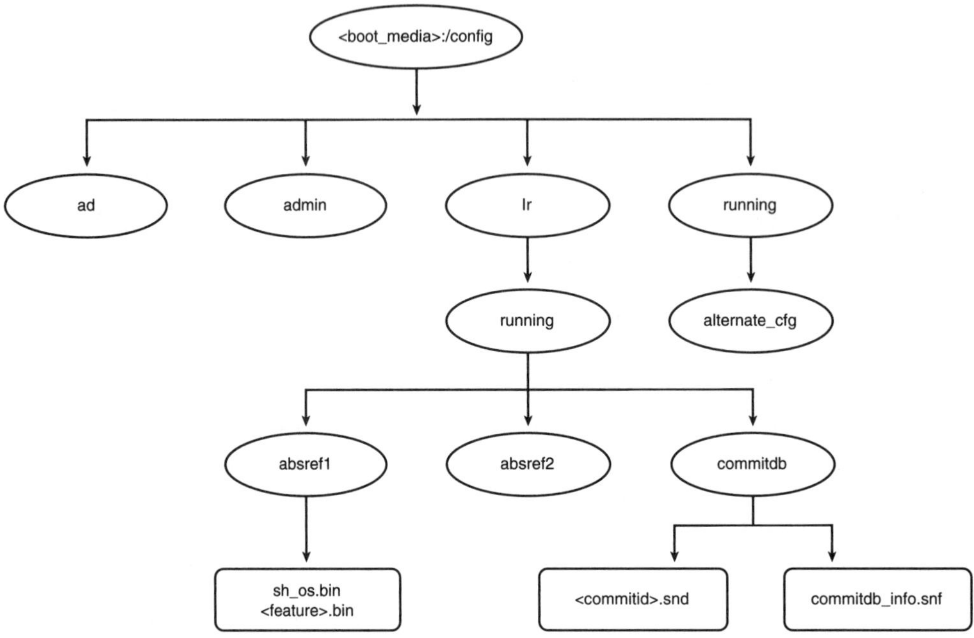

Figure 4-2 *Configuration File System (CFS)*

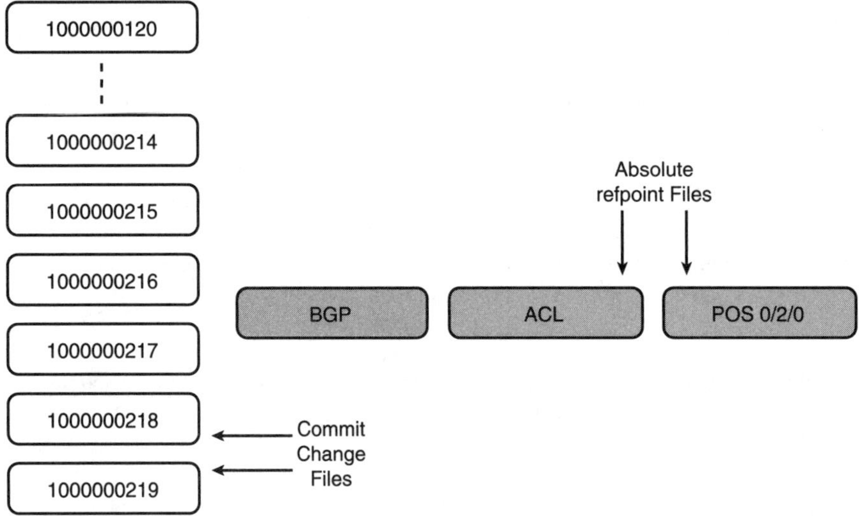

Figure 4-3 *Absolute and Commit Refpoint Files*

When you reload the system the router configuration is restored from the primary persistent configuration, which consists of the absolute refpoint along with the three outstanding commit refpoints.

The secondary persistent configuration, which is also stored in the commit database within CFS, is the IOS equivalent of startup configuration. The secondary persistent configuration is stored in the ASCII format. The ASCII copy comprises a single file containing the entire router configuration in command line interface (CLI) form. The secondary persistent configuration is updated at regular intervals before any reload and during activation of a package or Software Maintenance Update (SMU). The secondary configuration file is parsed to restore configuration on bootup if either of the following occurs:

- Corruption or inconsistency is detected in the binary copy
- The router is booting with upgraded software that is incompatible with the binary configuration copy

The ASCII copy can be used to restore only the most recent contents of the router configuration, and not the history of changes. The capability to display and roll back to previous commit refpoints is lost when configuration is restored from the ASCII copy. All rollback options can be achieved only if the system is restored through primary persistent configuration.

The files and directories in CFS are internal to the router and should not be modified or removed by the user. Modification can result in loss of configuration and can affect service.

Note: An absolute refpoint is the router configuration at some point of time. Commit refpoints are the different commit files that are created for every commit. The last t 100 commit instances are stored as commit refpoint files.

Role of SysDB in Configuration Management

As mentioned in Chapter 2, "Cisco IOS XR Infrastructure," SysDB is a fully distributed database system. Its database structure is similar to a UNIX directory structure where you will see a complete path defined. The primary persistent configuration stored in CFS is in the SysDB native format (binary), which is a proprietary format. All the configuration files stored in CFS are in native SysDB format. By storing in SysDB native format, restoration bypasses the parsing done by the parser, which results in faster recovery.

SysDB, just like any other database, will be locked when changes are made by the user to avoid inconsistencies when different users are trying to modify the same data. It's a database containing tuples for configuration. Data is stored in a binary format, which aids in quicker parsing of the configuration and in turn helps in a quick reboot of the system.

Note: In IOS, the configuration is stored in ASCII format and in IOS XR, the secondary persistent configuration is stored in ASCII format.

Every modification/change to the SysDB must go through the commit process, which also helps in the rollback feature of IOS XR. There is no commit ID during router restoration (namely router bootup) because you are not really committing here. SysDB provides a means for management clients to access operational data from processes providing the data. SysDB is the interface between the user who configures the box through CLI or

SNMP and the features getting provisioned. It allows users to create and modify configuration and stores only accepted configuration.

The configuration distribution to the three different planes—Admin, Shared, and Local Plane—is achieved with the help of SysDB. When configuration is applied to the router, it is parsed (assuming CLI as input). The parser translates the CLI format into internal SysDB format also called as SysDB tuples. When SysDB receives a set of configuration data it must first break up the data into "blocks" to send to different nodes for verification. Local plane data is sent to the appropriate node for its verification. Shared plane data is sent to one RP/DRP card (the dSDRSC) for verification and processing.

SysDB is comprised of a set of server processes for each of the three configuration planes. These server processes are sysdb_svr_admin (Admin SysDB Server), sysdb_svr_shared (Shared/Global SysDB Server), and sysdb_svr_local (Local SysDB Server). In addition, there is a proxy server called medusa, the sysdb_mc process. The server processes store the configuration data for each plane, whereas the medusa (sysdb_mc) process acts as a proxy for manageability agents and configuration-owning applications. It also helps in forwarding information to and from the correct configuration plane servers.

Note: In IOS XR, Management Agent or Client is a process that sits between the Configuration Manager and the external world. Agents are responsible for interacting with the user or external management systems to view or edit the configuration.

Access to SysDB is controlled by the following three different server processes:

- **Shared/Global SysDB Server:** Has the common information for the system, mainly control plane features, such as AAA, routing protocol, and so on. It runs on RP and dRP.
- **Admin SysDB Server:** Responsible for admin information for the system. It runs on RP only.
- **Local SysDB Server:** Runs on every node or LC. It contains the local information of the node (interface information of the node).

The data is separated based on the SysDB namespace subtree. Certain subtrees are defined to be for local plane data, and others are for shared plane data. For example, all data under /cfg/gl is considered shared plane data and is sent to the dSDRSC for verification and updating of the running configuration. The config under /cfg/if/act/<*ifname*> is always local and is sent to the local SysDB server on the node where the interface is hosted.

SysDB data is logically represented as a hierarchical namespace. The namespace provides the following:

- Hierarchical levels for grouping of related information
- Ordered data to enable discovery of, and efficient access to, the items in the datastore

The item data actually held within SysDB is organized in a manner that permits fast lookup. The SysDB datastore provides the hierarchical name space by storing data in a tree format. Each of the three different servers is responsible for covering certain parts of the overall SysDB database.

Briefly, SysDB represents an in-memory copy of the running configuration. It stores the running configuration as provided by the manageability agents and verified by the configuration-owning applications in the different planes. Additionally, it replicates the admin and shared plane configuration between nodes and distributes the storage of local plane configuration between nodes. Figure 4-4 illustrates the local, admin, and global SysDB planes.

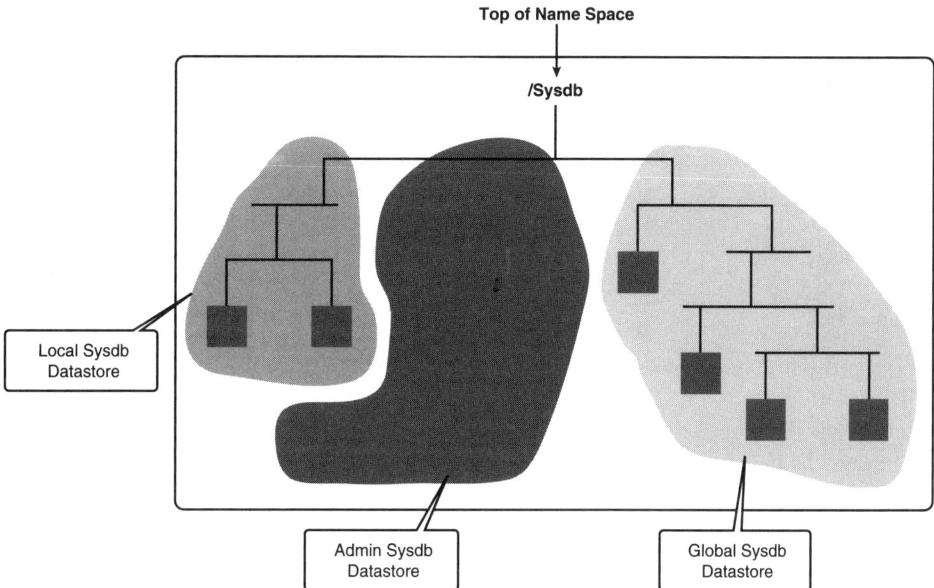

Figure 4-4 *SysDB Name Space*

Replicated Data Service File System

Replicated Data Service File System (RDSFS) is an application that provides the following services:

- A distributed virtual file system.
- High availability via file/data replication. In principle, any object that exports the file system interface can be replicated and accessed using RDSFS.

Nodes can go down and come back online at any time. Applications on these nodes need to access files (CFS) in a location-independent manner. The motivation for RDSFS stems from the scalability, high availability, and reliability requirements of a file system (CFS). RDSFS attempts to address these requirements by replicating file system data (CFS) and providing distributed access to the file system. It maintains coherence across replicas and ensures that no stale data is served out in the presence of disk errors, concurrent writers, and nodes going down or coming back online; all this while ensuring that the performance doesn't take a perceptible hit. MSC, which doesn't have a disk of its own, accesses virtual disk systems with the help of RDSFS to read the CFS files.

Understanding the Two-Stage Commit Model

Cisco IOS XR supports the concept of a two-stage commit model. In a single-stage commit model, each line of the configuration that enters the router takes effect immediately. This approach does not scale because the user configuration is applied serially without the provision to apply the configuration in bulk. In addition, while applying the configuration from a file or script, it is possible for only part of the user-intended configuration to take effect due to syntax or transport errors, which leaves the router configuration in an inconsistent state.

In the two-stage commit model, during the first stage, the user can build a target configuration without affecting the router's running configuration. In this stage, the user can address both syntax and transport errors to ensure that the entire target configuration has entered the router successfully. In the second stage, called the *commit stage*, the entire target is committed and becomes part of the router running configuration. Because the entire target configuration has entered the system, the committed configuration is carried out in bulk.

The two-stage commit process helps in applying the configuration in bulk; this in turn helps in doing subsequent operations such as verification, checkpointing, logging, and so on in bulk. Bulk operation is especially good for performance because it reduces interprocess communication (IPC) overhead.

Figure 4-5 illustrates the two-stage configuration concept.

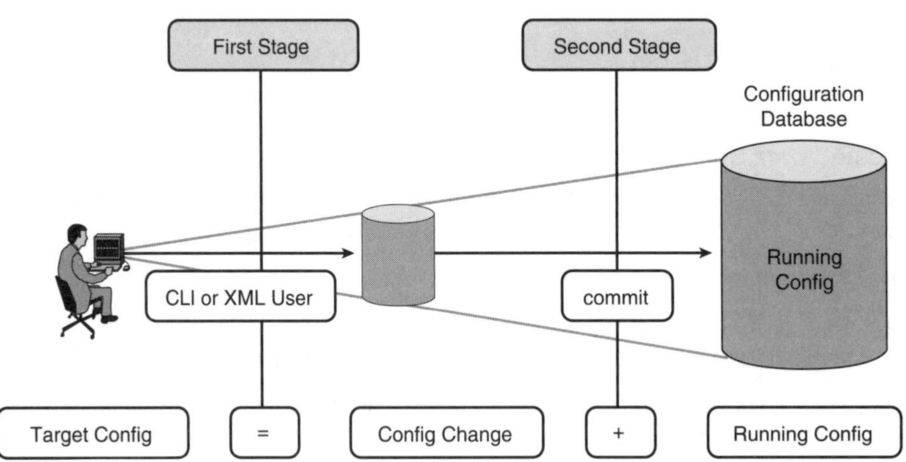

Figure 4-5 *Two-Stage Configuration*

Building the Target Configuration

The target configuration is effectively the cumulative result of the current running configuration with the user-entered configuration. In other words, it is the user-intended configuration if the user were to commit the entered configuration changes. Each user has its own unique target configuration that is not visible to others. However, the latest router running configuration is visible to every user and it forms a base to each user's target configuration instance.

A user can populate the target configuration changes from a previously saved file and browse or modify configuration changes in the target without affecting the current running (that is, active) configuration on the router. The router running configuration can never be set directly. All changes to the running configuration must go through the target configuration where it is explicitly committed by the user to become part of the router's running configuration.

A unique target configuration is created implicitly when the user enters the configuration mode. The target configuration is not a copy of the running configuration; instead, it is an overlay of configuration changes, entered by the user, which have not been committed yet, on top of the router's running configuration. When the user enters the first stage of the configuration and prior to entering configuration changes, the target configuration is identical to the running configuration. This is also the case after each successful commit operation, where the target configuration and running configuration are identical. The user can browse the configuration changes made in the current session but not yet promoted to the active configuration, by using **show configuration**. The user can also browse the resultant configuration produced via the merger of uncommitted configuration and the router's active (also known as running) configuration by using **show config merge**. This is essentially the session's target configuration.

Example 4-3 shows the steps required to build the target configuration.

Example 4-3 *Building Target Configuration*

```
! Let's start with a clean interface with just interface description configured.



RP/0/RP0/CPU0:CRS1-3(config)#show running-config interface tenGigE 0/0/0/1
Building configuration...
interface TenGigE0/0/0/1
 description TO CRS1-1
!
end

! Let's build the target configuration

RP/0/RP0/CPU0:CRS1-3(config)#interface tenGigE 0/0/0/1
RP/0/RP0/CPU0:CRS1-3(config-if)#ipv4 address 10.100.2.31 255.255.255.0
RP/0/RP0/CPU0:CRS1-3(config-if)#exit
```

```
! show config command displays the target configuration

RP/0/RP0/CPU0:CRS1-3#show config
Building configuration...
interface TenGigE0/0/0/1
ipv4 address 10.100.2.31 255.255.255.0
!
end

! show config merge displays the merged running and target configurations

RP/0/RP0/CPU0:CRS1-3(config)#show config merge interface TenGigE 0/0/0/1
interface TenGigE0/0/0/1
 description TO CRS1-1
 cdp
 ipv4 address 10.100.2.31 255.255.255.0
!

RP/0/RP0/CPU0:CRS1-3(config)#
```

Commit Operation

Commit is the operation through which the target configuration is committed to create the new running configuration as shown in Figure 4-6. By default the commit operation is pseudo atomic. In other words, the commit operation could fail for semantics and only valid changes are allowed to get committed.

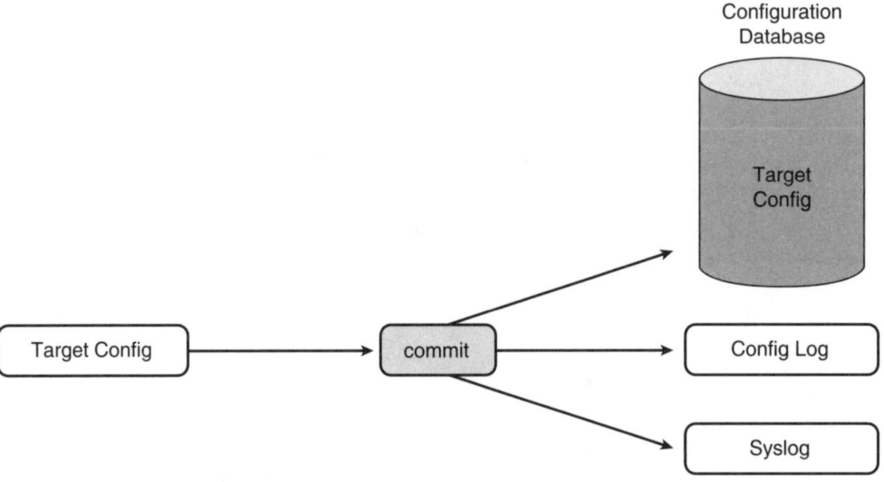

Figure 4-6 *Commit Notification*

The following events take place for every successful commit operation:

1. Before committing, it must first lock the configuration session.
2. Saves the configuration changes in the commit change database, creating a rollback point.
3. Adds a commit change entry to configuration history.
4. Generates a config change notification using syslog.
5. Target configuration is integrated into the running config at the end of successful commit operation.
6. Unlocks the configuration session.

Each time a new configuration is built and committed, Cisco IOS XR adds a commit change entry to the configuration history and generates a configuration change notification using syslog, as shown in Example 4-4.

Example 4-4 *Configuration Log Notification During Commit*

```
RP/0/RP0/CPU0:CRS1-3#
RP/0/RP0/CPU0:CRS1-3#configure
RP/0/RP0/CPU0:CRS1-3(config)#hostname R1
RP/0/RP0/CPU0:CRS1-3(config)#commit
RP/0/RP0/CPU0:Apr 27 16:31:57.534 : config[65790]: %MGBL-CONFIG-6-DB_COMMIT :
  Configuration committed by user 'cisco'. Use 'show configuration commit
  changes 1000000057' to view the changes.
RP/0/RP0/CPU0:R1(config)#end
RP/0/RP0/CPU0:R1#
```

By default the commit operation assigns a commit change ID, allowing you to view the details of the point commit. In Example 4-4, 1000000057 is the commit ID assigned for the configuration changes that went in the last commit. This commit ID is also helpful to quickly verify the changes that went in a specific commit operation.

As shown in Example 4-5, you can use the **show configuration commit changes** *<commit-change-id>* command to view the committed changes.

Example 4-5 *Config Change as Part of the Commit Operation in Example 4-4*

```
RP/0/RP0/CPU0:CRS1-3#show configuration commit changes 1000000057
Building configuration...
hostname R1
end

RP/0/RP0/CPU0:CRS1-3#
```

The target configuration can be committed using either pseudo-atomic or best-effort options. In the case of commit with the pseudo-atomic option, the entire configuration in the target area is committed. In case of any verification errors, the commit operation is rolled back and the errors are returned to the configuration agent.

In the case of the commit with the best-effort option, only that part of the target configuration that has gone through successful verification gets committed, and not necessarily everything in the target buffer. In this case, the errors are returned to the configuration agent. You have a number of **commit** options to try, as shown in Example 4-6.

Example 4-6 *Options Available in a Commit Operation*

```
RP/0/RP0/CPU0:CRS1-3(config)#commit ?
  best-effort       Commit the configuration changes via best-effort operation
  Comment           Assign a comment to this commit
  confirmed         Rollback this commit unless there is a confirming commit
  force             Override the memory checks
  label             Assign a label to this commit
  replace           Replace the contents of running configuration
  <cr>              Commit the configuration changes via atomic operation
```

During a commit operation, Configuration Manager implicitly locks the configuration session to prevent any changes to the configuration by any other configuration agents. The router running configuration is unlocked at the end of the commit operation. Not all the options available in a commit operation are discussed here. Refer to Cisco.com for more details.

Example 4-7 shows the use of the commit operation with the comment option (to add descriptive information to the change) and the label option (to assign a name to the point commit). These options help the user while doing rollback and for easy recovery.

Example 4-7 *Commit Operation with Label and Comments*

```
RP/0/RP0/CPU0:CRS1-3#
RP/0/RP0/CPU0:CRS1-3#configure
RP/0/RP0/CPU0:CRS1-3(config)#hostname R12
RP/0/RP0/CPU0:CRS1-3(config)#commit label hostname comment change of hostname
RP/0/RP0/CPU0:R12(config)#exit
RP/0/RP0/CPU0:R12#
RP/0/RP0/CPU0:R12#show configuration commit list 1 detail

   1) CommitId: 1000000146                 Label: hostname
      UserId:   cisco                      Line:  vty0
      Client:   CLI                        Time:  Tue May 6 05:18:27 2008
      Comment:  change of hostname
```

Commit Confirmed Option

The **commit confirmed** command helps to commit the target configuration on a trial basis and not as a permanent configuration. A user can provide the amount of time to wait before the configuration rollback to the previous configuration. Commit Confirmed is available in global configuration mode. You can configure the amount of time before rollback, and it can range from seconds to minutes. The **commit confirmed** option is not available in administration configuration mode.

In Example 4-8 you are changing the hostname of the system from R1 to CRS1-3 for 30 seconds. After 30 seconds the commit rolls back to the previous state of the router (hostname changes automatically to R1).

Example 4-8 *Commit Operation with Confirmed Option*

```
RP/0/RP0/CPU0:R1#configure
RP/0/RP0/CPU0:R1(config)#hostname CRS1-3
RP/0/RP0/CPU0:R1(config)#commit confirmed ?
  <30-65535>  Seconds until rollback unless there is a confirming commit
  minutes     Specify the rollback timer in the minutes
  <cr>        Commit the configuration changes via atomic operation
RP/0/RP0/CPU0:R1(config)#commit confirmed 30
RP/0/RP0/CPU0:CRS1-3(config)#
! After 30 seconds
RP/0/RP0/CPU0:Mar 16 23:53:23.949 : cfgmgr_trial_confirm[65779]: %MGBL-CONFIG-6-
  DB_COMMIT : Configuration committed by user 'cisco'. Use 'show configuration
  commit changes 1000000652' to view the changes.
RP/0/RP0/CPU0:R1(config)# end
RP/0/RP0/CPU0:R1#
```

Commit Failures

Configuration items that fail to pass semantic verification during commit are known as *failed configuration*. If a failed configuration is generated in an atomic commit, target configuration is left intact and nothing is promoted to active configuration. In IOS XR if a commit attempt fails, the failure of the commit can be viewed through **show configuration failed**, as shown in Example 4-9. The output of the command can be used to view the reason and clues for commit failures and correct the mistakes (if any).

Example 4-9 *Failed Commit Where* **class sample_class** *Is Not Defined*

```
RP/0/RP0/CPU0: CRS1-3#configure
RP/0/RP0/CPU0: CRS1-3 (config)#policy-map sample1
RP/0/RP0/CPU0: CRS1-3 (config-pmap)#class sample_class
RP/0/RP0/CPU0: CRS1-3 (config-pmap-c)#set mpls experimental topmost 3
```

```
RP/0/RP0/CPU0: CRS1-3 (config-pmap-c)#commit

% Failed to commit one or more configuration items during an atomic operation,
  no changes have been made. Please use 'show configuration failed' to view the
  errors

RP/0/RP0/CPU0: CRS1-3 (config-pmap-c)#show config failed
!! SEMANTIC ERRORS: This configuration was rejected by
!! the system due to semantic errors. The individual
!! errors with each failed configuration command can be
!! found below.

policy-map sample1
!!% Entry not found: class map sample_class used in policy map sample1 does not
    exist
end

RP/0/RP0/CPU0: CRS1-3 (config-pmap-c)#
```

Configuration Failures During Startup

When the system boots up, you might experience some configuration failures. This can typically occur when upgrading or downgrading router from one software release to other.

Possible types of configuration failures are

- **Syntax Errors:** Syntax errors are generated by the parser and indicate that a CLI command is not recognized. This is usually due either to a typo or the fact that the command is not present in the current version of the software.
- **Semantic Errors:** Semantic errors are generated by the backend components that verify the startup configuration during bootup. It is up to each backend component owner to analyze the cause of the failure.
- **Apply Errors:** Apply errors occur when configuration passes the verifier's semantic checks and is accepted as part of the running configuration, but the backend component is unable to update its operational state.

You can view configuration failures using the **show configuration failed startup** command as shown in Example 4-10.

Example 4-10 *Configuration Failures During Startup*

```
RP/0/RP0/CPU0: CRS1-3#show configuration failed startup
```

```
!! CONFIGURATION FAILED DUE TO SYNTAX ERRORS
ntp
http server
```

Configuration Features in Cisco IOS XR

The following are some of the similarities between IOS and IOS XR configurations a user can come across:

- Configurations can be viewed in ASCII form
- Configuration entries can be copied and pasted into the console command prompt
- Configurations can be loaded and saved to media devices
- Command syntax is similar to that used in IOS (with some exceptions)

Cisco IOS XR has other unique features, including the following:

- Command return <CR> does not cause the actual configuration change to take place in Cisco IOS XR, as it does in IOS. Users can check and save a configuration without actually committing the configuration to the router (target configuration).
- Cisco IOS XR allows you to lock and unlock a configuration session. It is not used as a security feature but serialization to prevent data/config corruption.
- Configuration tagging (checkpoint) for management and operations.
- Rollback feature for security, recovery, and troubleshooting.
- Configuration verifier to check for user errors.

Let's discuss some of the unique features of IOS XR configurations.

Deleting Physical Interface

In IOS the physical interface cannot be deleted; however, in IOS XR, the physical interface can be deleted. As a result the interface returns to the default configuration state, which means the **show running** command will not display the deleted interface as shown in Example 4-11. The reason being that in SysDB no tuple exists for this configuration, thus nothing is available to nvgen (nonvolatile generation).

Example 4-11 *Deleting Physical Interfaces*

```
RP/0/RP0/CPU0:CRS1-3#show running-config interface tenGigE 0/0/0/7
interface TenGigE0/0/0/7
bundle id 20 mode on
 cdp
 carrier-delay up 300 down 300
 shutdown
 load-interval 30
!
```

```
RP/0/RP0/CPU0:CRS1-3# configure
RP/0/RP0/CPU0:CRS1-3(config)#no interface tenGigE 0/0/0/7
RP/0/RP0/CPU0:CRS1-3(config)#commit
RP/0/RP0/CPU0:CRS1-3(config)#end
RP/0/RP0/CPU0:CRS1-3#show running-config interface tenGigE 0/0/0/7
% No such configuration item(s)

RP/0/RP0/CPU0:CRS1-3#
```

Configuration Navigation

In IOS XR the Configuration Navigation feature is also enhanced. The running configuration can be viewed as a series of functional units. For example, you can view the BGP configuration or OSPF individually or you can parse using **include**, **exclude**, or **begin** options. Example 4-12 illustrates the configuration navigation feature of IOS XR.

Example 4-12 *Configuration Navigation*

```
RP/0/RP0/CPU0:CRS1-3#show running-config router ospf 1
router ospf 1
 area 0
  interface Bundle-Ether10
  !
  interface Bundle-Ether20
  !
  interface TenGigE0/0/0/0
  !
  interface TenGigE0/0/0/2
  !
  interface TenGigE0/0/0/5
  !
 !
!

RP/0/RP0/CPU0:CRS1-3#show running-config router ospf 1 area 0 interface
  TenGigE0/0/0/0
router ospf 1
 area 0
  interface TenGigE0/0/0/0
  !
 !
!
```

Default Running Configuration Behavior

In IOS **show running-config** shows all active configuration and all interfaces present within the system, even if nothing is configured on the interface. However, in IOS XR, as shown in Example 4-13, when you remove all the configurations of an interface, the interface will not appear in the output of **show running-config**.

Example 4-13 *Default* running-config *Behavior for Interfaces Without Any Configs*

```
RP/0/RP0/CPU0:CRS1-3#show running-config interface tenGigE 0/0/0/1
interface TenGigE0/0/0/1
 description TO CRS1-1
 cdp
 ipv4 address 10.100.2.31 255.255.255.0
!

RP/0/RP0/CPU0:CRS1-3#configure
RP/0/RP0/CPU0:CRS1-3(config)#interface TenGigE 0/0/0/1
RP/0/RP0/CPU0:CRS1-3(config-if)#no ipv4 address
RP/0/RP0/CPU0:CRS1-3(config-if)#no description
RP/0/RP0/CPU0:CRS1-3(config-if)#no cdp
RP/0/RP0/CPU0:CRS1-3(config-if)#commit
RP/0/RP0/CPU0:CRS1-3(config-if)#end
RP/0/RP0/CPU0:CRS1-3#show running-config interface tenGigE 0/0/0/1
% No such configuration item(s)

RP/0/RP0/CPU0:CRS1-3#
```

The running configuration of an IOS XR system is the data that defines the setup of the system's hardware resources, the active software features, and the services it provides. It is entirely user-provided; the default configuration for a system is empty. Changes to the running configuration are made only at the request of the user, either directly through one of the access methods or indirectly by changing the system's active software profile.

There are multiple methods by which the user can access the running configuration to view or modify it; these include a command-line interface, a programmatic XML interface, and an SNMP agent.

Troubleshooting Configuration Inconsistencies

Cisco IOS XR software can detect the following error conditions when you restore the primary persistent configuration into running configuration during the bootup or reload process. During restoration of running configuration, semantic checks will be verified. In each case, recovery occurs by using the secondary persistent configuration copy (the ASCII copy) to restore the router configuration.

Some of the common error messages seen during restoration of running configuration are the following:

- Failure to read the primary persistent file due to a reload upgrade or a version change or incompatibility:

```
MGBL_CONFIG-4-VERSION : Version of existing commit database detected to be
incompatible with the installed software. All saved commit points in the
commit database will be removed.
```

- Corruption of the commit database file:

```
MGBL_CONFIG-4-DB_INIT_FAILURE : Commit database initialization Failure. All
configuration rollback points will be lost.
```

- A file that is referenced in the commit database is not present in the CFS:

```
MGBL_CONFIG-3-STARTUP : Configuration Manager detected that the saved running
configuration is corrupt.  All saved commit points in the commit database will
be removed. Configuration will be restored from an alternate backup source.
```

To overcome these configuration inconsistencies between the running configuration and the primary/secondary persistent configurations, you can use the CLI command **clear configuration inconsistency**. The purpose of this command is to overcome the discrepancies by restoring the primary persistent configuration from the running configuration. As you see in Example 4-14, the commit database that holds the persistent configurations is getting synched with the running configuration.

Example 4-14 *Configuration Failures During Startup*

```
RP/0/RP0/CPU0:R1#clear configuration inconsistency
Creating any missing directories in Configuration File system...OK
Initializing Configuration Version Manager...OK
Syncing commit database with running configuration...OK
Regenerating backup files...OK
```

Configuration Session Lock

A configuration session starts when a user enters the configuration mode. From a user configuration protection perspective, Cfgmgr provides a configuration lock to disallow write (for example, commit) and read (for example, OIR config restoration) at the same time. The router running configuration is unlocked at the end of the commit operation.

Configuration sessions can be either normal or exclusive, as shown in Example 4-15. Exclusive target configuration sessions, while in progress, prevent changes being made to the running configuration from any other target configuration session. Users can use the CLI command **show config sessions** to display the connected users who have an exclusive lock on the configuration.

Example 4-15 *Normal Config Session and Exclusive Config Session*

```
RP/0/RP0/CPU0:CRS1-3#configure
RP/0/RP0/CPU0:CRS1-3(config)#hostname R1
RP/0/RP0/CPU0:CRS1-3(config)#do show configuration sessions
Current Configuration Session      Line        User      Date                       Lock
00000201-009d00fe-00000000       vty0        cisco     Sun Apr 27 06:20:51 2008
```

```
RP/0/RP0/CPU0:CRS1-3(config)#exit
Uncommitted changes found, commit them before exiting(yes/no/cancel)? [cancel]:n

RP/0/RP0/CPU0:CRS1-3#configure ?
  exclusive  Configure exclusively from this terminal
  terminal   Configure from the terminal
  <cr>
RP/0/RP0/CPU0:CRS1-3#configure exclusive
RP/0/RP0/CPU0:CRS1-3(config)#hostname R1
RP/0/RP0/CPU0:CRS1-3(config)#do show configuration sessions
Current Configuration Session      Line       User     Date                         Lock
00000201-009d70fe-00000000      vty0       cisco    Sun Apr 27 06:21:32 2008      *
RP/0/RP0/CPU0:CRS1-3(config)#
```

Avoiding a Commit Operation and Clearing the Target Configurations

Every time a user plans to change or create a target configuration, that user goes into the config mode. However, you do have a few options where the user can clear the configuration session or avoid committing the target configurations.

Option 1: Unlock the Configuration Session

You can unlock the configuration session if you know the configuration session identifier of the user. The **show config session** command provides the session ID, and the **clear config session <*id*>** command is used to clear the user session, as shown in Example 4-16.

Example 4-16 *Clearing a Configuration Session Using Clear CLI*

```
RP/0/RP0/CPU0:CRS1-3#
RP/0/RP0/CPU0:CRS1-3#configure
RP/0/RP0/CPU0:CRS1-3(config)#do show configuration sessions
Current Configuration Session  Line       User     Date                         Lock
00000201-00a2e0fe-00000000      vty0       cisco    Sun Apr 27 21:00:10 2008
RP/0/RP0/CPU0:CRS1-3(config)#
RP/0/RP0/CPU0:CRS1-3(config)#do clear configuration
  sessions 00000201-00a2e0fe-00000000
session ID '00000201-00a2e0fe-00000000' terminated
This configuration session was terminated by user 'cisco' from line 'vty0'
RP/0/RP0/CPU0:Apr 27 21:00:34.130 : cfgmgr_cmd_clear_target_session[65792]:
  %MGBL-CONFIG-5-SESSION_CLEAR : Configuration session ID '00000201-00a2e0fe
  -00000000' (started by user 'cisco' from line 'vty0') was terminated by
  user 'cisco' from line 'vty0'.
RP/0/RP0/CPU0:CRS1-3#
```

Option 2: Use the **clear** Command

The **clear** command can be used to wipe the target configuration that is planned for commit. The user can discard the uncommitted changes made in a configuration session using the **clear** command. This effectively starts a new configuration session without requiring the user to exit out of the current configuration session and reenter, as shown in Example 4-17.

Example 4-17 clear *Command to Wipe the Target Configuration*

```
RP/0/RP0/CPU0:CRS1-3#configure
RP/0/RP0/CPU0:CRS1-3(config)#hostname R1
RP/0/RP0/CPU0:CRS1-3(config)#show configuration
Building configuration...
hostname R1
end

RP/0/RP0/CPU0:CRS1-3(config)#clear
RP/0/RP0/CPU0:CRS1-3(config)#show configuration
Building configuration...
end

RP/0/RP0/CPU0:CRS1-3(config)#
```

Option 3: Use the abort Command

The **abort** option is used to abort the current target configuration session as shown in Example 4-18.

Example 4-18 *Abort CLI Option*

```
RP/0/RP0/CPU0:CRS1-3#configure
RP/0/RP0/CPU0:CRS1-3(config)#hostname R1
RP/0/RP0/CPU0:CRS1-3(config)#abort
RP/0/RP0/CPU0:CRS1-3#
```

Option 4: Use the end or exit Commands

You can end the configuration session using the **end** or **exit** command, as shown in Example 4-19. If the target configuration differs from the active configuration, the user is prompted to commit or discard it.

Example 4-19 *Using IOS Options* exit *and* end *Configuration Commands*

```
RP/0/RP0/CPU0:CRS1-3(config)#hostname R1
RP/0/RP0/CPU0:CRS1-3(config)#exit
Uncommitted changes found, commit them before exiting (yes/no/cancel)?
  [Cancel]: no
RP/0/RP0/CPU0:CRS1-3#configure
RP/0/RP0/CPU0:CRS1-3(config)#hostname R1
RP/0/RP0/CPU0:CRS1-3(config)#end
Uncommitted changes found, commit them before exiting (yes/no/cancel)?
  [Cancel]: yes
RP/0/RP0/CPU0:R1#
```

Configuration Management During Hardware and Software Change Events

This section explains the behavior of IOS XR configuration management during different hardware and/or software events, including the following:

- Online insertion and removal (OIR)
- Package activation and deactivation
- Preconfiguration
- Router startup

Configuration Management During Online Insertion and Removal Events

In IOS XR, as discussed in the previous sections, configurations specific to nodes are replicated by RDSFS. However, the CFS system has the master copy of the configuration of all the nodes. As a result, if you remove a node, all the configuration information stored by the node is lost; however, the configuration information of that node moves into the preconfiguration area within the CFS. Upon insertion of an MSC the configuration agent on the node becomes active, downloads the node's configuration from the CFS, and applies it locally. This helps in designing large-scale systems where you have multiple OIR events at any given time.

An OIR event can occur for a node or a SPA. Examples of the OIR scenarios include

- Insert or remove a node
- Replace the node with a different node (different media type)
- Replace a node with a higher density node (same media type)
- Replace a node with a lower density node (same media type)

Case 1: Insert or Remove a Node

When you perform an OIR event of the same SPA, interface configuration will be automatically restored when the SPA or node is up.

Case 2: Replace the Node with a Different Node

When you perform an OIR event of a SPA and replace it with a different SPA (both media and port density are different), all the interface configurations are deleted; however, control plane configuration such as the OSPF or BGP routing protocol configurations will not be changed by this action. The user must change the control plane to remove references to the old interface type.

Case 3: Replace the Node with a Higher Density Node

When you perform an OIR event of a SPA and replace it with a similar SPA (media type) but with higher port density, configurations will be reapplied only to ports that had been configured before. The user has to configure the additional ports and activate the control plane for the same as required. Example 4-20 illustrates the OIR event of a SPA and the effect on final configuration.

Example 4-20 *OIR Event with Higher Density Node*

```
RP/0/RP0/CPU0:CRS1-3#show running-config
interface POS0/1/0/0
 ipv4 address 10.10.10.2 255.255.0.0
!
interface POS0/1/0/1
 ipv4 address 10.11.10.2 255.255.0.0
!
interface POS0/1/0/2
 ipv4 address 10.12.10.2 255.255.0.0
!
interface POS0/1/0/3
 ipv4 address 10.13.10.2 255.255.0.0
!
interface POS0/1/0/4
 shutdown
!
interface POS0/1/0/5
 shutdown
!
<snip>

RP/0/RP0/CPU0:CRS1-3#show running-config router ospf 1
router ospf 1
 area 0
  interface POS0/1/0/0
!
```

```
  interface POS0/1/0/1
!
  interface POS0/1/0/2
!
  interface POS0/1/0/3
!
```

Case 4: Replace the Node with a Lower Density Node

When you perform an OIR event of a SPA and replace it with a similar SPA (media type) but with less port density, interface-level configuration will be reapplied to those ports that are now in existence and had been previously configured. The missing ports will move to preconfigured state. Control plane configuration will remain unaffected and therefore active on the new ports. Example 4-21 illustrates the corresponding changes in the configuration output.

Example 4-21 *OIR Event with Lower Density Node*

```
RP/0/RP0/CPU0:CRS1-3#show running-config
interface POS0/1/0/0
 ipv4 address 10.10.10.2 255.255.0.0

interface POS0/1/0/1
 ipv4 address 10.11.10.2 255.255.0.0

interface POS0/1/0/2
 ipv4 address 10.12.10.2 255.255.0.0

interface POS0/1/0/3
 ipv4 address 10.13.10.2 255.255.0.0

interface preconfigure POS0/1/0/4
 ipv4 address 10.14.10.2 255.255.0.0

interface preconfigure POS0/1/0/5
 ipv4 address 10.15.10.2 255.255.0.0
<snip>

RP/0/RP0/CPU0:CRS1-3#show running-config router ospf 1
router ospf 1
 area 0
  interface POS0/1/0/0

  interface POS0/1/0/1

  interface POS0/1/0/2
```

```
interface POS0/1/0/3

interface POS0/1/0/4
```

In all the preceding scenarios, the control plane configuration, such as OSPF routing, is unaware of the state of the interface. Therefore, the control plane configurations do not move from active to preconfigured and vice versa.

Configuration Management During Package Activation and Deactivation

During package installation there are configuration changes that need to be properly managed by IOS XR. Package deactivation results in a configuration name space version change, and IOS XR removes the affected configuration from the router's running configuration prior to the package being deactivated. Similarly, package activation of a new package version upgrade also results in a configuration name space version change and IOS XR removes the affected configuration from the router's running configuration. The IOS XR saves the removed configuration to a filename with date and timestamp.

You can use the **show configuration removed** command to browse the removed configuration as shown in Example 4-22.

Example 4-22 *Package Deactivation and Restoration of Configs*

```
RP/0/RP0/CPU0:CRS1-3#show configuration removed ?
  20070306121733.cfg   Removed configuration
  20070612120053.cfg   Removed configuration
RP/0/RP0/CPU0:CRS1-3#show configuration removed 20070306121733.cfg
xml agent corba
snmp-server traps sensor
snmp-server traps fru-ctrl
http server
end
RP/0/RP0/CPU0:CRS1-3#

RP/0/RP0/CPU0:CRS1-3#show configuration removed 20070612120053.cfg
xml agent tty
xml agent corba
http server
end
```

After successful package activation, you may browse any removed incompatible configuration and choose to reapply it to the running configuration by using the **load** and **commit** commands as shown in Example 4-23.

Example 4-23 *The* load *and* commit *Commands*

```
RP/0/RP0/CPU0:CRS1-3#configure
RP/0/RP0/CPU0:CRS1-3(config)#load configuration removed 20070612120053.cfg
Loading.
46 bytes parsed in 1 sec (45)bytes/sec
RP/0/RP0/CPU0:CRS1-3(config)#commit
```

Interface Preconfiguration

Cisco IOS XR introduces a new concept called *interface preconfiguration* where you can start configuring the hardware and, to be more specific, the interfaces, even if they are not present in the system.

Preconfiguration helps in the hot swapping of MSCs/SPAs indirectly. It is frequently used to perform the configuration steps of the system in advance of a technician being dispatched to the site for the physical installation of the resource. All the CLI commands specific to the interface can be provisioned much before the node or SPA is installed. All the preconfigured interfaces will show up in the preconfigure area while browsing the router configuration using **show** commands. After you insert the MSC all the preconfiguration gets applied automatically, provided the node matches the location and hardware type as specified in the preconfiguration. It becomes part of the router running configuration.

Preconfiguration helps reduce the time for configuration phase and reduces dependencies (no waiting for onsite hardware installation). It also reduces downtime by allowing the preconfiguration to be done before a replacement node can be found and allowing for quick turnaround after the hardware is installed. Preconfiguration applies to MSC and interface commands only.

Example 4-24 illustrates the concept of preconfiguration.

Example 4-24 *Preconfiguration*

```
RP/0/RP0/CPU0:CRS1-3#configure
RP/0/RP0/CPU0:CRS1-3(config)#interface preconfigure POS 0/4/0/1
RP/0/RP0/CPU0:CRS1-3(config-if-pre)#encapsulation ppp
RP/0/RP0/CPU0:CRS1-3(config-if-pre)#ipv4 address 10.1.1.1 255.255.255.0
RP/0/RP0/CPU0:CRS1-3(config-if-pre)#no shutdown
RP/0/RP0/CPU0:CRS1-3(config-if-pre)#pos crc 32
RP/0/RP0/CPU0:CRS1-3(config-if-pre)#exit
RP/0/RP0/CPU0:CRS1-3(config)#controller preconfigure SONET 0/4/0/1
RP/0/RP0/CPU0:CRS1-3(config-sonet)#clock source internal
RP/0/RP0/CPU0:CRS1-3(config-sonet)#framing sdh
RP/0/RP0/CPU0:CRS1-3(config-sonet)#no shutdown
RP/0/RP0/CPU0:CRS1-3(config-sonet)#path scrambling disable
```

```
RP/0/RP0/CPU0:CRS1-3(config-sonet)#end

RP/0/RP0/CPU0:CRS1-3#show running-config
<snip>
!
interface preconfigure POS0/4/0/1
 ipv4 address 10.1.1.1 255.255.255.0
 encapsulation ppp
 pos
  crc 32
 !
!
controller preconfigure SONET0/4/0/1
 path
  scrambling disable
 !
 framing sdh
 clock source internal
!
```

Configuration Template

The IOS XR CLI provides the Configuration Template feature, which enables the creation and application of configuration templates at the CLI level for later use. This feature will enable end users to group commonly used sets of commands together into a named template with or without parameters. Then by simply applying the templates, a group of configuration tasks can be applied immediately. This feature provides strong modularity and reusability in configuration at the CLI level.

The IOS XR CLI does not support a hierarchical (nested) template definition; that is, a template cannot be defined within another template. Example 4-25 defines a template named config_chapter.

Example 4-25 *Template Configuration*

```
RP/0/RP0/CPU0:CRS1-3#configure
RP/0/RP0/CPU0:CRS1-3(config)#template config_chapter
RP/0/RP0/CPU0:CRS1-3(config-TPL)#policy-map policy1
RP/0/RP0/CPU0:CRS1-3(config-pmap)#class class-default
RP/0/RP0/CPU0:CRS1-3(config-pmap-c)#police rate 1000000
RP/0/RP0/CPU0:CRS1-3(config-pmap-c-police)#exit
RP/0/RP0/CPU0:CRS1-3(config-pmap-c)#exit
RP/0/RP0/CPU0:CRS1-3(config-pmap)#end-policy-map
RP/0/RP0/CPU0:CRS1-3(config-TPL)#end
Uncommitted changes found, commit them before exiting(yes/no/cancel)?
```

For template configuration, *<config-command-list>* is a list of CLI commands that form the body of the template. Any valid configuration command should be allowed in the template body. During the configuration for the template body, other CLI features such as help, command completion, and syntax check are available.

Example 4-26 defines a template named **namechange** with hostname as the parameter. This template is applied with the hostname as the parameter using **apply-template <***template-name***> <***parameters list***>**.

Example 4-26 *Template Configuration with Parameter*

```
RP/0/RP0/CPU0:CRS1-3#configure
RP/0/RP0/CPU0:CRS1-3(config)#template namechange (name)
RP/0/RP0/CPU0:CRS1-3(config-TPL)#hostname $name
RP/0/RP0/CPU0:CRS1-3(config-TPL)#end
Uncommitted changes found, commit them before exiting(yes/no/cancel)? [cancel]:yes

RP/0/RP0/CPU0:CRS1-3#show running-config template namechange
template namechange (name )
 hostname $name
end-template

RP/0/RP0/CPU0:CRS1-3#configure
RP/0/RP0/CPU0:CRS1-3(config)#apply-template namechange (R1)
RP/0/RP0/CPU0:CRS1-3(config)#end
Uncommitted changes found, commit them before exiting(yes/no/cancel)?
  [cancel]:yes
RP/0/RP0/CPU0:R1#
```

Configuration Management During Router Startup

By default, during startup, the router configuration is restored from the primary persistent configuration generated since the previous reload. This is the preferred method, where it is optimized to restore router configuration with the latest configuration since last reload. In addition, it eliminates the need for you to persist the router configuration by issuing **wr mem** after each commit change to the router configuration during run time.

After each **reload** command, Configuration Manager maintains an ASCII equivalent of the running configuration, which is also called the *secondary persistent configuration*. The message "Updating Commit Database. Please wait... [OK]" will appear if Configuration Manager detects that an update of the ASCII-equivalent running configuration is necessary. This ASCII equivalent is used only to restore the router to the previous running configuration if the saved commit points or "commits" cannot be used to restore the previous configuration.

You can override the default behavior by providing the path of the configuration file to use during router reload. This is done using either the **-a** option in boot command or by setting the IOX_CONFIG_FILE variable. The router configuration is restored from the user-specified path instead of the router's latest running configuration. Because the previous router running configuration is overridden by the user option, the entire existing router running configuration is removed. This includes all the checkpointed configuration files prior to restoration of configuration during reload.

While restoring the router configuration from the running configuration, if the running configuration doesn't exist or is corrupted, it will attempt to restore the router configuration from a saved ASCII copy of the running configuration that is maintained by the system and all previous commit points will be removed. In such a case, the previous configuration will still be applied by the user; however, the user will not be able to roll back the configuration to any previous points. If the saved ASCII running configuration file doesn't exist, the default configuration is applied to the router.

Configuration Rollback

In IOS XR the target configuration built by the user is committed to form the new running config. For every successful commit operation, a unique ID or label is generated. This ID or commit point can be used as a rollback point as seen earlier in Figure 4-3.

Rollback is simply undoing some of the configuration changes that were done by the user. Configuration rollback is an atomic operation that rolls the active configuration back to a previous known state. IOS XR has the capacity to roll back up to 100 commits. If an error is encountered in the rollback operation, active configuration is not changed. The **show rollback points** command can be used to list all the rollbacks, as shown in Example 4-27. Each rollback commit is logged with the user information that made the commit along with a timestamp. You can make the rollback point more user friendly by providing a comment using CLI. Because these are different commit files or refpoints, you can view the configuration changes that went in for every commit using **show configuration rollback changes <*commitid*>**. The command **show configuration commit list** can be used to list all the commit IDs that can be used for rollback with the user and timestamp information of every commit as shown in Example 4-27.

Example 4-27 *Displays the List of All Rollback Points*

```
RP/0/RP0/CPU0:R1#show configuration commit list
SNo. Label/ID    User     Line     Client     Time Stamp
~~~~ ~~~~~~~~    ~~~~     ~~~~     ~~~~~~     ~~~~~~~~~~
1    1000000080  cisco    vty0     Rollback   Mon May  5 03:35:14 2008
2    1000000079  cisco    vty0     CLI        Mon May  5 03:34:44 2008
3    1000000078  cisco    vty0     CLI        Mon May  5 02:48:57 2008
4    1000000077  cisco    vty1     CLI        Thu May  1 23:32:35 2008
5    1000000076  cisco    vty1     CLI        Thu May  1 23:31:01 2008
6    1000000075  cisco    vty1     CLI        Thu May  1 19:22:49 2008
7    1000000074  cisco    vty1     CLI        Thu May  1 19:21:29 2008
8    1000000073  cisco    vty1     CLI        Thu May  1 19:19:56 2008
9    1000000072  cisco    vty1     CLI        Thu May  1 18:46:56 2008
10   1000000071  cisco    vty1     CLI        Thu May  1 17:50:15 2008
11   1000000070  cisco    vty1     CLI        Thu May  1 17:47:42 2008
```

```
12    1000000069   cisco      con0_RP0_C   CLI          Thu May  1 14:22:38 2008
```

show configuration commit list <*number*> **detail** provides the last few commit details, as shown in Example 4-28. It displays the list of the last two commits whose corresponding changes can be rolled back to, along with details of the user and the timestamps. If the commit is through a rollback action, the client of the commit operation will reflect the appropriate agent as seen in Example 4-28.

Example 4-28 *Configuration Commit Details*

```
RP/0/RP0/CPU0:CRS1-3#show configuration commit list 2 detail


   1) CommitId: 1000000083                     Label: NONE
      UserId:   cisco                          Line:  vty0
      Client:   Rollback                       Time:  Tue May  6 05:18:37 2008
      Comment:  NONE

   2) CommitId: 1000000146                     Label: hostname
      UserId:   cisco                          Line:  vty0
      Client:   CLI                            Time:  Tue May 6 05:18:27 2008
      Comment:   change of hostname
RP/0/RP0/CPU0:CRS1-3#
```

show configuration rollback changes last <*number*> can also provide the configuration changes of the last few commits as shown in Example 4-29.

Example 4-29 *Configuration of the Last Three Commit Operations*

```
RP/0/RP0/CPU0:R1#show configuration rollback changes last 3
Building configuration...
hostname CRS1-3
end

RP/0/RP0/CPU0:R1#
```

You can use **show configuration rollback changes** <*commit number*> to display the changes that could happen if you roll back to a specific commit ID, as shown in Example 4-30.

Example 4-30 *Configuration of a Specific Commit Operation Using the Commit ID*

```
RP/0/RP0/CPU0:R1#show configuration rollback changes 1000000080
Building configuration...
hostname CRS1-3
end

RP/0/RP0/CPU0:R1#
```

A commit ID is generated for every successful rollback action. In Example 4-31, the configuration is rolled back to the last commit configuration to undo the hostname change from R1 to CRS1-3.

Example 4-31 *Rollback to the Last Configuration*

```
RP/0/RP0/CPU0:R1#rollback configuration last 1
Loading Rollback Changes.
Loaded Rollback Changes in 1 sec
Committing.
1 items committed in 1 sec (0)items/sec
Updating..

Updated Commit database in 1 sec
Configuration successfully rolled back 1 commits.
RP/0/RP0/CPU0:CRS1-3#
```

You can use **show configuration history** to list the history of all configuration events as seen in Example 4-32. A maximum of 1500 events can be displayed.

Example 4-32 *Displays Configuration Events History*

```
RP/0/RP0/CPU0:CRS1-3#show configuration history
Sno.  Event       Info                          Time Stamp
~~~~  ~~~~~~      ~~~~                          ~~~~~~~~~~
1     alarm       inconsistency alarm raised    Mon Apr 14 13:06:59 2008
2     startup     configuration applied         Mon Apr 14 13:08:12 2008
3     OIR config  restore                       Mon Apr 14 13:08:15 2008
4     OIR config  restore                       Mon Apr 14 13:08:55 2008
5     backup      Periodic ASCII backup         Mon Apr 14 14:00:16 2008
158   commit      id 1000000081                 Tue May  6 05:17:56 2008
159   commit      id 1000000082                 Tue May  6 05:18:26 2008
160   commit      id 1000000083                 Tue May  6 05:18:39 2008
```

Summary

This chapter provides detailed concepts of Cisco IOS XR configuration management. Also discussed are some of the key components that are required to achieve the restoration of large-scale configurations—namely Configuration Manager, SysDB, CFS, and RDSFS.

Router configuration in IOS XR is based on a two-stage configuration model. The two-stage commit process, which helps to apply the target configuration in bulk, is also discussed in detail.

Restoration of primary persistent configuration, restoration of configuration during boot and node OIR, package activation and deactivation, configuration handling, and session management are implemented using the IOS XR Configuration Management architecture. Some of the salient points of IOS XR configuration, CLIs, and the output of different **show** commands, are explained with examples.

The rollback feature helps the user to undo a previous configuration commit operation. Preconfiguration helps the user program the configuration in advance before installing the corresponding hardware. Last of all, template configuration improves configuration efficiency by creating reusable configurations.

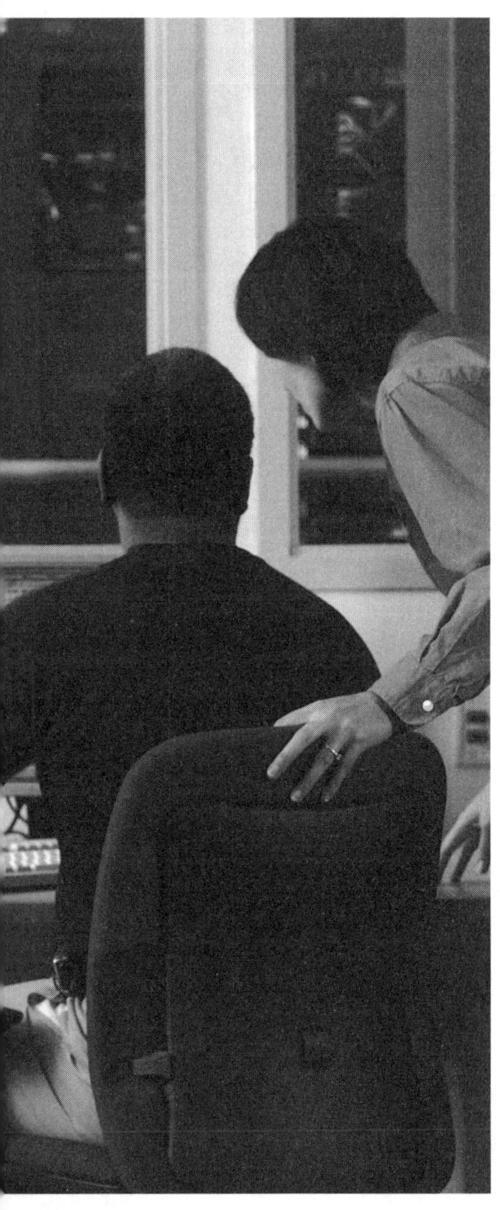

This chapter covers the following topics:

- Using SNMP
- Cisco IOS XR Syslog
- Embedded Event Manager
- Monitoring Processes

Cisco IOS XR finds proven applications in next-generation networks (NGN). Organizations deal with manageability and monitoring aspects as an important part of their day-to-day operations. Monitoring and management functions help reduce the network's operating costs and help improve service response. Therefore, such functions have stringent requirements for accurate measurement of network resources and proactive notification of changes happening on their networks. IOS XR provides features and supports monitoring and troubleshooting commands that integrate well with network management requirements. Monitoring and manageability aspects of the IOS XR operating system have been briefly touched on in the previous chapters. This chapter devotes detailed discussion to these topics.

This chapter outlines the embedded tools and show commands that can be used for monitoring operating system processes and memory. IOS XR also provides real-time monitoring of Layer 2 interfaces and Layer 1 SONET controller counters. This chapter depicts monitoring aspects through examples drawn from a routing platform running IOS XR. Support of syslog and SNMP agent capabilities is an important prerequisite of any OS running on routing and switching devices. IOS XR supports the necessary SNMP management processes that enable it to run as a managed system in compliance with the Internet Network Management Framework. Configuring and monitoring SNMP is also discussed in detail in this chapter.

CHAPTER 5

Cisco IOS XR Monitoring and Operations

This chapter also discusses Embedded Event Management (EEM), where platform or network event stimuli are reported via defined APIs (Application Programming Interfaces). A policy engine then allows a user to trigger responses based on events that might impact a system's health. This chapter devotes a section to demonstrating such policies using a TCL script.

Using SNMP

This section introduces the implementation and configuration of SNMP protocol in IOS XR. As mentioned earlier, SNMP is a protocol used in IP networks for network management. SNMP provides the necessary protocol support to monitor and control network devices, and for network management–related statistics collections. To be managed directly by SNMP, a router must be capable of running an SNMP management process, called an *SNMP agent*. IOS XR has a built-in SNMP agent, whose job is to retrieve and update variables that describe the state of the device or protocols and features enabled in the device. These variables are stored in a data structure called a Management Information Base (MIB).

The Cisco IOS XR software supports the following versions of SNMP:

- Simple Network Management Protocol Version 1 (SNMPv1)
- Simple Network Management Protocol Version 2c (SNMPv2c)
- Simple Network Management Protocol Version 3 (SNMPv3)

There have been several improvements in SNMP as it evolved from v1 to v3; however, the main difference is the improvement in security. The SNMP management stations who have access to the agent MIB are configured by an IP address access control list (ACL) and a community string that serves as a password. In contrast the SNMPv3 ensures security by using Data Encryption Standard (DES) for security. SNMPv3 uses the Hashed Message Authentication Code (HMAC) using the MD5 or SHA-1 algorithm for data integrity. Despite security improvements in SNMP v3, the v2c is still popular and is widespread in SP networks.

Figure 5-1 gives a simplified overview of the exchanges. The figure identifies two devices. One of the devices is a managed device containing the SNMP agent software functionality. The Network Management Station (NMS) contains the applications that helps control or gather the information from the managed device. NMS uses messages called an SNMP

Get or Set. The purpose of Get is to retrieve information from the management device; the purpose of Set is to change certain data on the managed device. The managed device sends to the NMS an unsolicited message known as a *trap*. The purpose of a trap is to indicate an event experienced by the managed device such as a power supply failure, interface flap, and so on. The NMS receiving the trap displays it in an appropriate way so that attention is drawn to the event. SNMP information being exchanged in the form of gets, sets, or traps is defined as managed objects or variables in a Management Information Base (MIB). A MIB, therefore, contains network management information about the managed device.

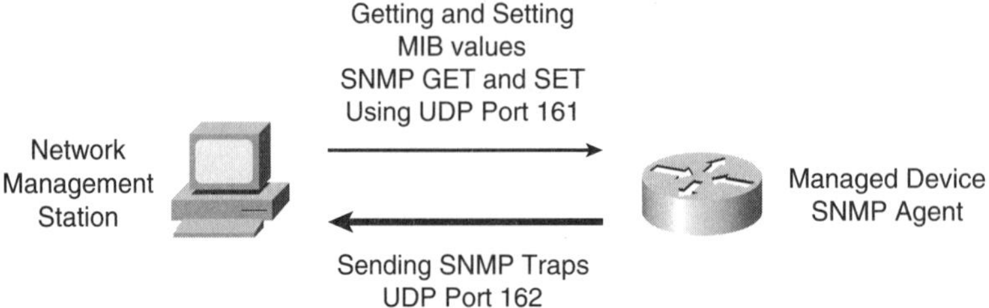

Figure 5-1 *SNMP Traffic*

Some of the IOS XR trap notifications and associated commands are shown in Table 5-1.

Table 5-1 *IOS XR Notification Types and Associated Traps*

Notification Type	Configuration
bgp	**snmp-server traps bgp**
config	**snmp-server traps config**
copy-complete	**snmp-server traps copy-complete**
entity	**snmp-server traps entity**
flash	**snmp-server traps flash** {**insertion** | **removal**}
fru-ctrl	**snmp-server traps fru-ctrl**
hsrp	**snmp-server traps hsrp**
ipsec	**snmp-server traps ipsec tunnel** {**start** | **stop**}
isakmp	**snmp-server traps isakmp tunnel** {**start** | **stop**}
l2vpn	**snmp-server traps l2vpn** {**all** | **vc-down** | **vc-up** }
mpls	**snmp-server traps mpls** {**frr** | **l3vpn** | **ldp** | **traffic-eng**}
msdp	**snmp-server traps msdp peer-state-change**
ntp	**snmp-server traps ntp**

Notification Type	Configuration
ospf	**snmp-server traps ospf** {**errors** | **lsa** | **retransmit** | **state-change** }
pim	**snmp-server traps pim** { **interface-state-change** | **invalid-message-received** | **neighbor-change** | **rp-mapping-change**}
rf	**snmp-server traps rf**
sensor	**snmp-server traps sensor**
snmp	**snmp-server traps snmp**
sonet	**snmp-server traps sonet**
syslog	**snmp-server traps syslog**
vpls	**snmp-server traps vpls** { **all** | **full-clear** | **full-raise** | **status**}

SNMP is considered an application-level protocol and is relatively straightforward to configure. The forthcoming sections depict SNMP configuration.

Configuring SNMP

The following basic steps are needed to configure SNMP on an IOS XR router:

```
snmp-server host address [traps] [version {1¦2c¦3[auth¦noauth¦priv]}] community-
  string [udp-port port] [notification-type]
snmp-server traps [notification-type]
```

The **snmp-server host** command identifies the IP address of the SNMP management station where traps will be sent. This command also provides the options to change the SNMP version and to specify the community string. Moreover, the command allows changing the UDP port to a user-specified port in the range 1 to 65535. This CLI also helps invoke security for SNMP messages and community-string. As a good practice for configuration, **snmp-server community** *value* may be used before configuring the community value through the **snmp-server host** command.

Example 5-1 shows some actual configurations on an IOS XR router. The router is configured to send traps related to the operational states of the CRS fabric planes. A public community has been defined that has only read-only privilege. A timeout of 3 seconds is specified in the configuration. The **SystemOwner** keyword is required to receive traps or poll MIBs related to an admin plane resource, such as the router fabric. The configuration command also specifies a trap-source loopback address that defines the source IP address for the trap messages.

Example 5-1 *SNMP Configuration Example*

```
snmp-server traps fabric plane
snmp-server host 10.10.20.100 traps version 2c public
snmp-server community public RO SystemOwner
snmp-server trap-timeout 3
snmp-server trap-source Loopback0
end
```

SNMP in the Context of a VRF

A network scenario might require SNMP management stations to be present in Layer 3 VPN contexts. This might be necessary due to a number of reasons, a common one being that the IP addresses of the local management network overlap with the router's global routing table. Such a scenario requires that SNMP be configured in the context of a Virtual Routing and Forwarding (VRF) instance. Example 5-2 demonstrates such a configuration.

Example 5-2 *SNMP in the Context of a VRF*

```
 vrf NET_MGMT
 address-family ipv4 unicast
import route-target
   100:111
 export route-target
   100:111
!
snmp-server community public RO
snmp-server community private RW
snmp-server traps snmp
snmp-server trap-source Loopback10
snmp-server vrf NET_MGMT
 host 10.10.20.100 traps version 2c public
!
interface Loopback101
 vrf NET_MGMT
 ipv4 address 10.10.21.1 255.255.255.255
!
interface MgmtEth0/0/CPU0/0
 vrf NET_MGMT
        ipv4 address 10.10.20.21 255.255.255.0
```

Cisco IOS XR Syslog

Syslog is the standard application used for sending system log messages. Log messages are helpful indicators of the health of the device and indicate any encountered problems or simplify notification messages according to their severity level. A flapping physical layer of an interface or state changes of a Layer 3 protocol are some examples for which syslog messages might be generated. The IOS XR router sends its syslog messages to a syslog daemon. The syslog daemon controls the dispatch of syslog messages to the logging buffer, terminal lines, or an external syslog server. The syslog daemon also allows logging to the console. The following shows a syslog message for an interface changing its line protocol state to down:

```
LC/0/7/CPU0:Oct 31 00:15:25.294 : ifmgr[146]: %PKT_INFRA-LINEPROTO-5-UPDOWN : Line
  protocol on Interface GigabitEthernet0/7/0/4, changed state to Down
```

The preceding syslog message indicates the line protocol is going down on an interface in slot 7 of the router. The message is explained by Table 5-2.

Table 5-2 *Dissection of Syslog Message*

Message	Field
LC/0/7/CPU0:Oct 31 00:15:25.294 :	NodeID: Time Stamp:
ifmgr[146]:	process-name [pid]:
%PKT_INFRA-LINEPROTO-5-UPDOWN :	%message-group-severity-message-code :
Line protocol on Interface GigabitEthernet0/7/0/4, changed state to Down	message-text

Logging Destination

Logging messages can be sent to multiple destinations. Logging messages to the console are on by default and this behavior can be changed with the **logging console disable** config mode command. In addition to logging to the console, the logging messages can be sent to terminal lines using the **logging monitor** command.

Example 5-3 shows the logging monitor configuration command followed by a question mark that illustrates all the options available for specifying the severity of the logging message. As depicted by Example 5-3, the lower the severity number, the higher the criticality of the logging message. When a severity level number is specified with a logging configuration command, the messages at or above that severity level are also reported. A user that accesses a router through a vty line can enable logging messages by typing **terminal monitor** or disable it by typing **terminal monitor disable.**

Example 5-3 *Logging Monitor and Severity Levels*

```
RP/0/RP1/CPU0:CRS1-1(config)#logging monitor ?
  alerts         Immediate action needed           (severity=1)
  critical       Critical conditions               (severity=2)
  debugging      Debugging messages                (severity=7)
  disable        Disable logging
  emergencies    System is unusable                (severity=0)
  errors         Error conditions                  (severity=3)
  informational  Informational messages            (severity=6)
  notifications  Normal but significant conditions (severity=5)
  warning        Warning conditions                (severity=4)
```

The syslog output can also be directed to a syslog server using the commands shown in Example 5-4.

Example 5-4 *Directing syslog to an External syslog Server*

```
RP/0/RP1/CPU0:CRS1-1(config)#logging ?
 A.B.C.D or X:X::X  IP v4/v6 address of the logging host
 WORD               Name of the logging host
! output omitted
```

Example 5-4 shows that the **logging** command can be configured with an IPv4/IPv6 or a DNS hostname that specifies an external syslog server where the syslog messages are sent.

In addition to displaying logging messages on terminal lines and directing them to an external syslog server, logging messages may be sent to an internal circular buffer using the configuration command **logging buffered** and specifying a severity level or a size of the circular buffer in bytes.

Example 5-5 shows the configuration of a logging buffer. The configuration command specifies a buffer size of 4194304 bytes and sets the severity level to notification. Example 5-5 also shows a **show logging** command with appropriate pipes to depict the configured values for the logging buffer.

Example 5-5 *Logging Buffered*

```
RP/0/RP1/CPU0:CRS1-1(config)#logging buffered 4194304
RP/0/RP1/CPU0:CRS1-1(config)#logging buffered notifications
RP/0/RP1/CPU0:CRS1-1(config)#commit
Uncommitted changes found, commit them before exiting(yes/no/cancel)? [cancel]:yes
RP/0/RP1/CPU0:CRS1-1#show logging | include Log Buffer | Buffer logging
    Buffer logging: level notice, 7709 messages logged
Log Buffer (4194304 bytes):
```

Cisco IOS XR also allows the logging messages to be sent to an SNMP NMS station using the command **snmp-server enable traps syslog.**

Local Archiving of Logging Messages

Cisco IOS XR provides a feature to allow the creation of a syslog archive on a local disk. The archive can be created on a local storage device and can be particularly useful for having an onboard backup in case communication is lost with an external syslog server. Example 5-6 demonstrates the creation of a logging archive.

Example 5-6 *Logging Buffered*

```
RP/0/RP1/CPU0:CRS1-1(config)#logging archive
RP/0/RP1/CPU0:CRS1-1(config-logging-arch)#frequency weekly
RP/0/RP1/CPU0:CRS1-1(config-logging-arch)#file-size 1
RP/0/RP1/CPU0:CRS1-1(config-logging-arch)#archive-size 10
RP/0/RP1/CPU0:CRS1-1(config-logging-arch)#device harddisk
RP/0/RP1/CPU0:CRS1-1(config-logging-arch)#archive-length 4
RP/0/RP1/CPU0:CRS1-1(config-logging-arch)#show configuration
```

```
Building configuration...
logging archive
 device harddisk
 file-size 1
 frequency weekly
 archive-size 10
 archive-length 4
!
end
```

Example 5-6 shows the creation of a local archive on the hard disk of a CRS-1 router. The archive length of 4 weeks specifies that the log will be kept for a month before getting removed. The frequency specifies whether the log will be collected on a daily or a weekly basis. The archive size specifies the total size that limits the archive and the file size is the maximum size for an individual file. When the file size is exceeded, a new file is created and the files are created on the /var directory of the target device.

Example 5-7 shows the directory and files that are created as the result of configurations in Example 5-6. The logging archive is typically created under /var/log followed by a directory name based on a date. The directory harddisk: /var/log/2008/11/09 indicates an archive that was created on November 9, 2008.

Example 5-7 *Logging Archive Storage*

```
RP/0/RP1/CPU0:CRS1-1#pwd
harddisk:/var/log/2008/11/09
RP/0/RP1/CPU0:CRS1-1#dir
Directory of harddisk:/var/log/2008/11/09
241565792   -rwx 275600      Wed Nov 12 16:11:49 2008 syslog.1
39929724928 bytes total (39905628160 bytes free)
RP/0/RP1/CPU0:CRS1-1#
```

Embedded Event Manager

This section discusses Embedded Event Manager (EEM) and demonstrates EEM policies that can be implemented on the router to help with better fault management and event notification. The EEM is a key software feature that processes events detected by a routing platform running IOS XR. EEM detects events related to fault occurrence and fault recovery as well as maintains process and reliability statistics. An EEM event manifests as a notification that can indicate one of the following occurrences:

- A crucial resource such as memory or CPU oversteps normal operating thresholds
- Online Insertion and Removal (OIR) of hardware such as a fabric card or a CRS Modular Switching Card
- A process crash
- Application defined events

When an event occurs in the system, EEM gets notified by event detectors. In the case of detecting an event, EEM may take a predetermined corrective action specified by a user-defined policy. The policies that specify corrective actions make up a set of routines. These routines must be registered using the EEM configuration CLI. The registration of policy empowers EEM to set the policy in action when an event is detected. EEM can, therefore, be used in the prevention of a fault or it can be used to notify a network administrator by email or syslog based on certain events experienced by the router.

EEM Event Detectors and Events Processing

EEM policies are implemented by a script when an event is detected. The script or the policy handler needs to be registered using the following configuration command:

event manager policy {*name_of-policy_file*}

The EEM script specified by the **event manager policy** command is available for execution until it is negated with the **no event manager policy** command. If an EEM policy is not registered, it does not take any action. Therefore, simply copying an EEM script to a router's disk is not sufficient.

The System Manager Event Detector performs the following roles:

- Keeps track of process reliability metrics
- Performs screening on processes that have outstanding EEM event-monitoring requests
- Publishes the event for a process in case there is an event
- Communicates with sysmgr to take default actions when there are no events
- Communicates with sysmgr to get process startup and termination notifications

Timer Services Event Detector

The Timer Services Event Detector takes care of time-related EEM events. Time-related events are user defined and these events are triggered when the current date or time crosses the date or time specified by the policy.

Syslog Event Detector

The Syslog Event Detector uses syslog messages of interest for generating syslog EEM events. Syslog Event Detector generates an event notification either based on the severity of the message or based on the text in the syslog message. The text in the syslog message can be parsed using POSIX regular expressions.

None Event Detector

When the Event Manager **run** command executes an EEM policy, the None Event Detector publishes an event. This functionality provides users with the ability to run a TCL script using the CLI command.

Watchdog System Monitor Event Detector

The Watchdog System Monitor Event Detector publishes an event when one of the following situations holds true:

- CPU utilization for a process crosses a defined threshold
- Memory utilization for a Cisco IOS XR process crosses a defined threshold
- Utilization of boot media reaches a critical threshold

Distributed Event Detectors

Cisco IOS XR is a distributed architecture, and software processes that have an interest in event detection run not only on route processors but also on the line card modules. The Distributed Event Detector allows publishing of EEM events for processes that are local to a node.

The Distributed Event Detector allows the publishing of events for the following:

- Counter and Statistics Event Detector
- System Manager Fault Detector
- WDSYSMON Fault Detector
- OIR Event Detector

Registering and Using Onboard EEM Policies

Cisco IOS XR software ships with some onboard TCL scripts that can be registered and used. Example 5-8 shows the eight policies that come with the IOS XR software release 3.6.0 from which this example was drawn. These TCL scripts can be browsed by going to the directory /pkg/lib/tcl/fm_scripts/.

Example 5-8 *EEM Onboard Scripts*

```
RP/0/RP1/CPU0:CRS1-1#show event manager policy available system
No.  Type   Time Created              Name
1    system Thu Oct 30 22:52:24 2008 ospf_sysmgr_abort.tcl
2    system Thu Oct 30 22:52:25 2008 ospf_sysmgr_user.tcl
3    system Thu Oct 30 22:40:17 2008 periodic_diag_cmds.tcl
4    system Thu Oct 30 22:40:17 2008 periodic_proc_avail.tcl
5    system Thu Oct 30 22:40:17 2008 periodic_sh_log.tcl
6    system Thu Oct 30 22:46:17 2008 sl_sysdb_timeout.tcl
7    system Thu Oct 30 22:40:18 2008 tm_cli_cmd.tcl
8    system Thu Oct 30 22:40:18 2008 tm_crash_hist.tcl
!
! Register a policy
!
! RP/0/RP1/CPU0:CRS1-1(config)#aaa authorization eventmanager default local
RP/0/RP1/CPU0:CRS1-1(config)#event manager environment __cron_entry_diag 55 8,20 *
  * *
```

```
RP/0/RP1/CPU0:CRS1-1(config)#event manager policy periodic_diag_cmds.tcl username
  cisco
!
! Verify the registered policy
!
RP/0/RP1/CPU0:CRS1-1#show event manager policy registered
No. Type     Event Type           Time Registered           Name
1    system timer cron            Fri Nov 14 16:32:54 2008 periodic_diag_cmds.tcl
 name {diag_cmds} cron entry {55 8,20 * * *}
 nice 0 priority normal maxrun_sec 900 maxrun_nsec 0
persist_time: 3600 seconds, username: cisco
RP/0/RP1/CPU0:CRS1-1#
```

The policy implemented through the TCL script periodic_diag_cmds.tcl is triggered when the _cron_entry_diag entry expires. The output of the set of commands in the script is collected and the output is sent by email. _cron_entry_diag is the cron entry used to dispatch the script. The value configured in Example 5-8 is 55 8,20 * * *, which means that we want to run this script at 8.55 and 20.55 every day.

User-Defined EEM Policy

In addition the onboard TCL scripts that come with the IOS XR operating system, users may write their own TCL-based policies. Example 5-9 shows a TCL script written for the CRS platform. Group Services Protocol (GSP) was introduced in Chapter 2, "Cisco IOS XR Infrastructure." This example shows a script that periodically runs, executes GSP ping, and reports a syslog message in the case of a ping loss.

Example 5-9 *User-Defined EEM Policy*

```
##
###Script written by <Author's name>
# This script runs the command 'gsp_ping -g 2000 -c5 -rv' as a cron entry
# as defined by the variable _gsp_ping_cron_entry. If the #value
# of the late or lost packets are greater than 0, then a #message will be
#logged to syslog as follows.
#RP/0/RP0/CPU0:May 12 15:23:00.495 : syslog_dev[82]: gsp-#test.tcl: The node
  0/0/CPU0 has number late packets and number lost #packets
####
#
::cisco::fm::event_register_timer cron name crontimer1 cron_entry
  $_gsp_ping_cron_entry
# register for cron timer which fires on based on the variable
  _gsp_ping_cron_entry
#
# errorInfo gets set by namespace if any of the auto_path directories do not
# contain a valid tclIndex file. It is not an error just left over stuff.
# So we set the errorInfo value to null so that we don't have left
# over errors in it.
```

```
#
set errorInfo ""
#
namespace import ::cisco::fm::*
namespace import ::cisco::lib::*
#
#
#query the event info and log a message
array set arr_einfo [event_reqinfo]
if {$_cerrno != 0} {
    set result [format "component=%s; subsys err=%s; posix err=%s;\n%s" \
        $_cerr_sub_num $_cerr_sub_err $_cerr_posix_err $_cerr_str]
    error $result
}
#
global timer_type timer_time_sec
set timer_type $arr_einfo(timer_type)
set timer_time_sec $arr_einfo(timer_time_sec)
#log a message
set msg [format "timer event: timer type %s, time expired %s" \
        $timer_type [clock format $timer_time_sec]]
action_syslog priority info msg $msg
# Capture the output of gsp_ping in variable var
#
set var [exec gsp_ping -g 2000 -c5 -rv]
#
# Convert the variable into a searchable list
#
set lst [split $var]
#
# Determine the size of the list so that loop variable can be determined
#
set loop_var [llength $lst]
#
# initialize loop
#
set i 0
#
# Run a while loop to check each list value and find the lost and late packets
#
while {$i < $loop_var} {
 set list_value [lindex $lst $i]
 if {[regexp {CPU0} $list_value] == 1} {
    set node [lindex $lst $i]
    set late [lindex $lst [expr $i + 13]]
```

```
    set lost [lindex $lst [expr $i + 17]]
 #check to see if lost or late packets are > 0
 if {$late || $lost > 0} {
 set logmsg "The node $node has $late late packets and $lost lost packets"
 puts "$logmsg"
# exec logger "$logmsg"
}
 }
 incr i
 }
# End of script
#
```

EEM Reliability Metrics

The EEM proactively monitors the reliability rates achieved by hardware and key processes in the system. The **show** commands depicted in Example 5-10 can be used for monitoring the health of processes and hardware on a router running IOS XR.

Example 5-10 *EEM Reliability Metrics*

```
RP/0/RP1/CPU0:CRS1-1#show event manager metric hardware location 0/0/cpU0
=====================================
node: 0/0/CPU0
Most recent online: Sat Nov 15 16:26:16 2008
Number of times online: 2
Cumulative time online: 15 days, 19:42:06
Most recent offline: Sat Nov 15 16:25:37 2008
Number of times offline: 1
Cumulative time offline: 0 days, 00:00:39
=====================================
RP/0/RP1/CPU0:CRS1-1#
! EEM Metrics for the qnet process
RP/0/RP1/CPU0:CRS1-1#show event manager metric process qnet location 0/0/cPU0
=====================================
job id: 72, node name: 0/0/CPU0
process name: qnet, instance: 1
- - - - - - - - - - - - - - - - -
last event type: process start
recent start time: Fri Oct 31 00:01:04 2008
recent normal end time: n/a
recent abnormal end time: n/a
number of times started: 2
number of times ended normally: 0
number of times ended abnormally: 0
```

```
most recent 10 process start times:
--------------


--------------
most recent 10 process end times and types:
cumulative process available time: 379 hours 58 minutes 12 seconds 770
  milliseconds
cumulative process unavailable time: 0 hours 0 minutes 0 seconds 0 milliseconds
process availability: 1.000000000
number of abnormal ends within the past 60 minutes (since reload): 0
number of abnormal ends within the past 24 hours (since reload): 0
number of abnormal ends within the past 30 days (since reload): 0
RP/0/RP1/CPU0:CRS1-1#
RP/0/RP1/CPU0:CRS1-1#
```

As shown in Example 5-10, EEM maintains reliability information on processes and hardware for a router running IOS XR.

Monitoring Processes

This section discusses process monitoring. As mentioned in previous chapters, the System Manager (sysmgr) process is responsible for monitoring and restarting misbehaving processes. The System Manager handles all the system management duties on a node. This includes tasks such as process creation/startup, respawning, core dumping, node role notification, and so on. Because of a software defect or due to stress conditions, a process deadlock, timeout, or blocked condition can occur. IOS XR provides process-monitoring commands that can be used to collect information that helps debug process-related problems. Table 5-3 lists process-monitoring commands that might be useful to collect in the event a process-level malfunction is observed followed by console messages indicating a problem. Although Table 5-3 provides a list of commands related to process monitoring, detailed troubleshooting might require the intervention of Cisco support services.

Table 5-3 *Process-Monitoring Commands*

Command	Explanation
show process [*process*]	Indicates whether a process is in Run state.
show process blocked	Indicates the blocked processes. A process blocked state may be perfectly normal; therefore, this command is useful when an imminent problem or syslog message is observed that leads one to suspect a process has encountered a deadlock or an unintended blocked state.

Command	Explanation
show process threadname [*job id*]	Helps map a thread ID (TID) to a thread name. Collecting this command's output helps in the debugging process.
follow process [*pid*]	This command performs unobtrusive debugging of a process by following a process and its live threads. This command prints stack trace information similar to a core dump.
monitor processes location {*location*}	Real-time monitoring of process by providing CPU and memory utilization.
monitor threads location {*location*}	Real-time monitoring of threads by providing CPU and memory utilization.
dumpcore {**running** | **suspended**} {**jid** | **process**}	Manually generates a core dump. The **running** option generates a core dump for a running process without affecting services. The **suspended** option suspends a process, generates a core dump for the process, and resumes the process.

A router can be configured with the right commands to direct the core dumps resulting from process crashes to intended storage locations. The following commands configure a TFTP server as the first choice for directing core dumps and the hard disk's directory named crash as the second choice:

```
exception choice 1 filepath tftp://10.10.20.1/coredumps/
exception choice 2 filepath harddisk:/crash/
```

Furthermore, the router can be checked for core dumps by using the **show context location all** command. This command shows whether a process has created a core dump. The output in Example 5-11 shows an excerpt of the information reported by **show context location all.**

Example 5-11 *Output of the* **show context location all** *Command*

```
RP/0/RP1/CPU0:CRS-1#show context location all
Sun Mar 29 10:16:15.434 PST

node:      node0_0_CPU0
----------------------------------------

Core for pid = 94304 (pkg/bin/feature_mgr)
```

```
Core dump time: Sun Mar 29, 2009: 10:15:16
Core for process at
harddisk:/dumper/first.feature_mgr_143.by.sysmgr.node0_0_CPU0.ppc.Z
```

WDSYSMON

WDSYSMON stands for *Watchdog System Monitor*. It is part of the High Availability infrastructure in IOS XR. It runs on RPs, DRPs, and line cards, and its primary function is to detect a problem condition and recover from it. WDSYSMON monitors the processes and memory on each node for memory and CPU usage. It also monitors the use of the boot device because the boot device is considered a critical resource for the continuous operation of an IOS XR system.

Examples 5-12 and 5-13 show the memory states of a given node and gives the default values at which WDSYSMON generates its alarm messages.

Example 5-12 *Output of the* **show watchdog memory-state location 0/rp1/cpu0** *Command*

```
RP/0/RP1/CPU0:CRS1-1#show watchdog memory-state Location 0/rp1/cpu0
Memory information:
    Physical Memory: 4096     MB
    Free Memory:     2969.898 MB
    Memory State:        Normal
```

Example 5-13 *Output of the* **show watchdog threshold memory defaults** *Command*

```
RP/0/RP1/CPU0:CRS1-1#show watchdog threshold memory defaults location 0/rp1/cpu0
 Default memory thresholds:
 Minor:      409       MB
 Severe:     327       MB
 Critical: 204.799 MB
Memory information:
    Physical Memory: 4096     MB
    Free Memory:     2969.898 MB
    Memory State:        Normal
```

If the memory state reaches the default or configured threshold changes from NORMAL to MINOR, a syslog message will generate, as follows:

```
%HA-HA_WD-4-MEMORY_ALARM Memory threshold crossed: [chars] with [x int] [x int]MB
 free
```

The following command manually changes the default minor memory alarm threshold from to 90% or 10% free to 80% (or 20% free). The default Severe and Critical alarms are raised when memory consumption reaches 90% and 95%, respectively. These alarms might be an indication of memory problems, including a memory leak relating to one or more processes. These thresholds can also be reached due to over-subscription of feature scale.

```
P/0/RP1/CPU0:CRS1-1(config)#watchdog threshold memory location 0/rp1/CPU0 minor
  20 severe 10 critical 5
```

If a router node is experiencing out-of-memory conditions, one can look at the list of top memory consumers in order of processes. The **show** command **show process memory**, similar to IOS, can be used to display top memory consumer processes. Another **show** command, **show memory compare**, can be used in identifying possible memory leaks. The memory comparison command tool can help isolate the process or processes that might be culprits of excessive memory consumption. The **show memory compare** command is not recommended for use as an ongoing operational tool under normal operating conditions; instead, its use should be restricted to cases where memory leaks are being investigated. It is more advisable to use the command **show watchdog memory-state location all** as a part of routine operations.

WDSYSMON process has an automatic recovery procedure to prevent memory depletion conditions. After determining the memory state of the node to be SEVERE, WDSYSMON finds top memory consumer process and restarts the process to avoid further memory depletion. This action also triggers a syslog message to alert the network operator of the condition.

The following is a syslog message generated by WDSYSMON:

```
%HA-HA_WD-4-TOP_MEMORY_USER_WARNING [dec]: Process Name: [chars][[dec]], pid:
  [dec][chars], Kbytes used: [dec]
```

Monitoring Memory

The memory comparison tool records a snapshot of details about the heap memory use of all processes on the router at a specific start and end time and then compares the results. The operation of the memory comparison tool can be listed as follows:

- Take an initial snapshot using the following command: **show memory compare start**
- Take another snapshot using the following command: **show memory compare end**
- Print the output using the following command: **show memory compare report**

The memory comparison tool is useful for detecting patterns of memory use during resource-intensive events. Resource-intensive events can be diverse in nature, but a common example would be an event causing a large scale change experienced by the router's control plane. The report generated as a result of **show memory compare** is saved on the active Route Processor disk for extraction and later analysis. When instructed to take a snapshot, the memory comparison tool saves output similar to that of the **show memory heap summary** command for each process running on the router to a file. When instructed to show a report, it reads the files and prints the difference between the values stored there.

Example 5-14 displays the CLI command to implement the memory comparison tool. The result of the processes consuming memory along with the output of **show process memory** can help identify which processes should be restarted. It is highly recommended to contact Cisco technical support to help assess the stability of any commands performed to prevent or minimize service interruption. Example 5-14 displays an example of a running memory comparison tool. In Example 5-14, the Memory Difference column displays reduced memory for the lpts_pa (LPTS port adapter) process and increased memory for the gsp (group services protocol) process. This means that lpts_pa has freed some memory and gsp has allocated more memory during the experiment.

Example 5-14 *Memory Comparison*

```
RP/0/RP1/CPU0:CRS1-1#show memory compare start
Successfully stored memory snapshot /harddisk:/malloc_dump/memcmp_start.out
RP/0/RP1/CPU0:CRS1-1#show memory compare end
Successfully stored memory snapshot /harddisk:/malloc_dump/memcmp_end.out
RP/0/RP1/CPU0:CRS1-1#show memory compare report
JID   name               mem before   mem after    difference mallocs restart
—-    ——                 —————        ————-        ————— ———- ———-
182   gsp                8729272      8743656      14384      4
333   statsd_manager     725560       728000       2440       0
131   cethha             110792       113064       2272       5
145   devc-vty           318692       320772       2080       1
269   netio              890664       891336       672        19
322   shelfmgr           242840       243288       448        6
78    qnet               1151840      1152040      200        5
367   mpls_ldp           740176       740224       48         2
255   lpts_pa            328388       328332       -56        -1
```

After the report is generated, you can now remove the snapshot memcmp_start.out and memcmp_end.out under /harddisk:/malloc_dump.

Using the **show system verify** Command

Cisco IOS XR has a built-in utility that performs a high-level system verification using the **show system verify** command, which has the following syntax:

```
show system verify [start | report | detail]
```

Example 5-15 illustrates output from the **show system verify** command.

Example 5-15 *Output of the* show system verify *Command*

```
RP/0/RP1/CPU0:CRS1-1#show system verify start
Storing initial router status ...
RP/0/RP1/CPU0:CRS1-1#show system verify
Getting current router status ...
System Verification Report
==========================
- Verifying Memory Usage
- Verified Memory Usage                                    : [OK]
- Verifying CPU Usage
- Verified CPU Usage                                       : [OK]
- Verifying Blocked Processes
- Verified Blocked Processes                               : [OK]
- Verifying Aborted Processes
- Verified Aborted Processes                               : [OK]
- Verifying Crashed Processes
- Verified Crashed Processes                               : [OK]
- Verifying LC Status
- Verified LC Status                                       : [OK]
- Verifying QNET Status
- Verified QNET Status                                     : [OK]
- Verifying TCAM Status
- Verified TCAM Status                                     : [OK]
- Verifying PLU ingress Status
- Verifying GSP Fabric Status
- Verified GSP Fabric Status                               : [OK]
- Verifying GSP Ethernet Status
- Verified GSP Ethernet Status                             : [OK]
- Verifying POS interface Status
 interface WARNING messages for router
 POS0/7/5/0: Packets Input has not increased during this period.
 POS0/7/5/0: Bytes Input has not increased during this period.
 POS0/7/5/0: Packets Output has not increased during this period.
 POS0/7/5/0: Bytes Output has not increased during this period.
- Verified POS interface Status                            : [WARNING]
- Verifying TenGigE interface Status
 interface WARNING messages for router
 TenGigE0/0/0/0: Packets Input has not increased during this period.
 TenGigE0/0/0/1: Packets Input has not increased during this period.
 TenGigE0/0/0/2: Packets Input has not increased during this period.
 TenGigE0/0/0/4: Packets Input has not increased during this period.
 TenGigE0/0/0/0: Bytes Input has not increased during this period.
```

```
TenGigE0/0/0/1: Bytes Input has not increased during this period.
TenGigE0/0/0/2: Bytes Input has not increased during this period.
TenGigE0/0/0/0: Packets Output has not increased during this period.
TenGigE0/0/0/1: Packets Output has not increased during this period.
TenGigE0/0/0/2: Packets Output has not increased during this period.
TenGigE0/0/0/0: Bytes Output has not increased during this period.
TenGigE0/0/0/1: Bytes Output has not increased during this period.
TenGigE0/0/0/2: Bytes Output has not increased during this period.
TenGigE0/0/0/4: Bytes Output has not increased during this period.
- Verified TenGigE interface Status                    : [WARNING]
- Verifying TCP statistics
 tcp_udp_raw WARNING messages for router
 TCP Open sockets not the same as recorded initially
- Verified TCP statistics                              : [WARNING]
- Verifying UDP statistics
- Verified UDP statistics                              : [OK]
- Verifying RAW statistics
 tcp_udp_raw WARNING messages for router
 PCB (0x4826bc08, Vrfid: 0x60000000) Packets received has not increased during
  this period.
 PCB (0x4826bc08, Vrfid: 0x60000000) Packets sent has not increased during this
  period.
- Verified RAW statistics                              : [WARNING]
- Verifying RIB Status
- Verified RIB Status                                  : [OK]
- Verifying CEF Status
- Verified CEF Status                                  : [OK]
- Verifying CEF Consistency Status
- Verified CEF Consistency Status                      : [OK]
- Verifying BGP Status
- Verified BGP Status                                  : [OK]
- Verifying ISIS Status
- Verified ISIS Status                                 : [OK]
- Verifying OSPF Status
- Verified OSPF Status                                 : [OK]
- Verifying Syslog Messages
- Verified Syslog Messages                             : [OK]
- Verifying ASIC error status
- Verified ASIC error status                           : [OK]
- Verifying Fabric status
- Verified Fabric status                               : [OK]
- Verifying Fabric statistics
- Verified Fabric statistics                           : [OK]
System may not be stable. Please look into WARNING messages.
```

The **show system verify** command in Example 5-15 performs various checks with regard to memory, blocked or aborted processes, interface counters, and infrastructure health. This command is useful; however, it might produce false positives in certain cases. One of the common false positives is CPU utilization that temporarily spikes as the result of executing the command; therefore, any warning reported by **show system verify** needs to be followed up by further investigation before drawing a conclusion regarding the validity of the warning message. A false positive involving CPU utilization can be further investigated using the **show process cpu** command. Executing the command **show system verify** launches a TCL script that takes a snapshot of the system state at a certain point in time and then takes another snapshot at a later point in time and compares the two reports. Using the **describe show system verify** command, it can be determined that the command spawns /pkg/bin/sys_verify.tcl script.

Operations and Monitoring Best Practices

This section provides a summary of operations and monitoring commands that are useful for day-to-day operations of a CRS-1 router running the IOS XR operating system. As good operational practice, it is important that the router be configured for key features that aid with ongoing operations and debugging of the system. Some of the key operational areas include the following:

- **Correct time zones and NTP configuration:** The router should be configured with the correct time zones, and NTP should be running on the network to allow time synchronization. IOS XR enables timestamps by default, although the timestamp format can be changed using the **service timestamp** command.
- **External syslog, local archives, and SNMP monitoring:** Configuring an external syslog server is advisable for the collection and subsequent analysis of syslog messages. A local logging archive may also be configured to serve as a backup. SNMP is almost a ubiquitous application for managing a device. As good configuration practice, the right SNMP traps should be monitored depending on the configuration of the router.
- **RP redundancy:** The CRS-1 routing platform ships with redundant route processors. It is important to maintain and monitor RP redundancy using the command **show redundancy**, which indicates whether the standby RP is in the STANDBY role. If the router is accessed using its management ports, it is recommended to configure **ipv4 virtual address** {*prefix* | *use-as-src-addr* | *vrf*}. The prefix used for the ipv4 virtual address is in the same subnet as the IP address of the route processors' management ports. The *use-as-src-addr* option of the **ipv4 virtual address** command enables the virtual address to be used as the default sourced address on router-sourced packets.
- **Core dump configuration:** The router must be configured with exception commands in SDR and Admin modes to manage the preferred locations for directing core dumps.

Table 5-4 presents a summary of useful **show** CLI commands from the perspective of operations and monitoring. It is imperative that operations engineers add more IOS XR tools and commands to their arsenal based on the specifics of their environment and as they gain more experience with the operating system. Consult Cisco.com for a comprehensive listing of IOS XR commands.

Table 5-4 *Summary of Operation and Monitoring Commands*

Command	Explanation
show redundancy	Indicates whether the system is redundant with regard to active and standby RP.
(admin) **show environment led**	Indicates any alarms being experienced by system modules such as power supplies and fan trays.
(admin) **show platform**	Indicates the state of each node. **IOS XR RUN** and **OK** states are desirable for line cards/RPs and SPAs, respectively.
show watchdog memory-state location all	Indicates the memory state and the amount of free memory.
show controllers pse tcam summary location {*node*}	Indicates the available memory for line card TCAMs.
monitor interface	Provides real-time monitoring of interface counters. Use of this command should be discretionary for monitoring or troubleshooting purposes. Continuous use of this command is unnecessary.
monitor controller sonet {location}	Provides real-time monitoring of counters related to SONET section, line, and path errors. Again, the use of this command should be discretionary.
monitor controller fabric plane all	Monitors fabric plane counters. Limit the use of this command to special cases requiring monitoring of fabric counters for debugging purposes.
show interfaces | incl error	Indicates whether any interface is seeing errors.
show context	Indicates whether any node has experienced a process crash.
show cef resource detail location {*node*}	Indicates the health of CEF on a node.
show lpts pifib hardware police location	Indicates whether router-destined traffic is being policed by LPTS.

Command	Explanation
(admin)#**hw-module location** {*node*} **reload**	Reloads a node if required due to an operational reason.
(admin-config)#**hw-module shutdown location** {*node*}	Shuts down a module.
(admin-config)#**hw-module reset auto disable location** {*node*}	A critical software failure might reset a node and cause it to reload. This command prevents automatic reset of a node. This command may be configured only on the recommendation of Cisco Technical Support based on a well-thought-out maintenance plan.

Summary

This chapter introduced the monitoring and manageability aspects of IOS XR. IOS XR, being a carrier-class operating system, runs on distributed platforms that have comprehensive monitoring and management requirements. In addition to the standard syslog and SNMP tools that are ubiquitous for most routing platforms, IOS XR offers Embedded Event Management (EEM) to generate notifications or corrective actions based on certain events on the routing system. Onboard TCL scripts and scripts that became foundations for user-defined policies were introduced through examples in this chapter.

This chapter also introduced monitor commands for processes, interfaces, and SONET controllers that allow for real-time monitoring of key router resources. Readers also came across various built-in **show** commands and tools that can effectively be used to discern the health of a router platform running IOS XR.

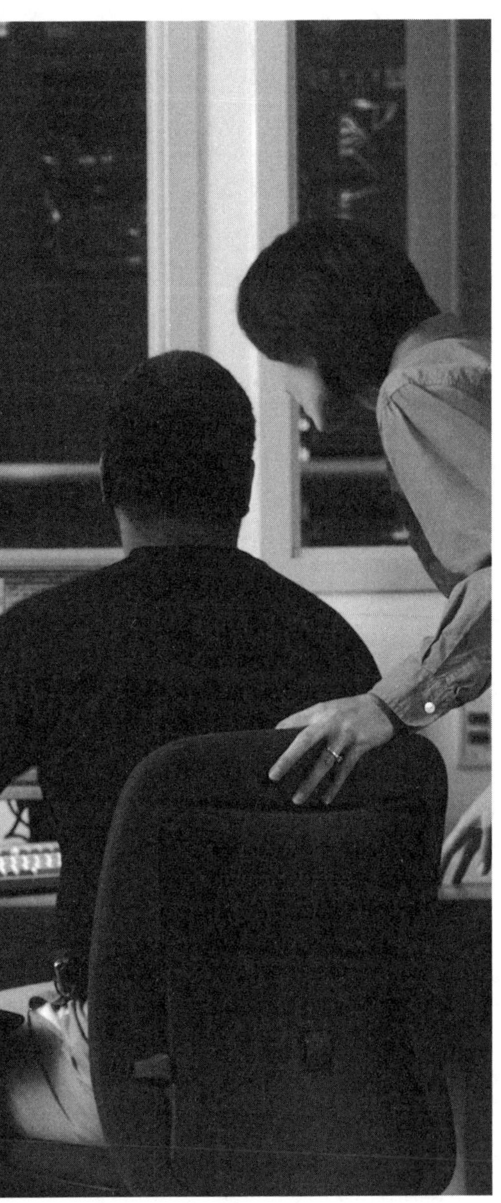

This chapter covers the following topics:

- Secure Operating System
- Securing Access to the Router
- Securing the Forwarding Plane
- References

This chapter discusses the security aspects of the Cisco IOS XR operating system and divides this discussion into two main areas as follows:

- Securing access to the router
- Securing the forwarding plane

CHAPTER 6

Cisco IOS XR Security

It is important to control access to the router to prevent unauthorized or malicious use that might take the router offline or use it to launch an attack on the rest of the network. Cisco IOS XR provides the authentication, authorization, and accounting (AAA) framework that helps provide secure access via the logical vty and the physical tty ports. Furthermore, ensuing sections in this chapter discuss the concepts of task-based authorization and familiarize the user with IOS XR concepts such as admin and SDR planes as well as the uniqueness of user groups and task group configuration.

Forwarding plane refers to the components involved in the various stages during packet forwarding. Forwarding plane refers not only to the flow of a packet through the router but also to the packets destined to the router. Protection of forwarding plane is important and necessitates controlling the type of traffic that traverses the router, and limiting the amount of traffic that's destined to the router itself so that the router does not become a victim of a denial of service (DoS) attack. You might well be familiar with access control lists (ACL) and Unicast Reverse Path Forwarding (uRPF) as popular forwarding plane security features. Additionally, IOS XR has a concept of Local Packet Transport Service (LPTS). LPTS provides protection against traffic destined to the router. This type of traffic is usually related to routing protocols that typically run on the route processor (RP) of the router, though Telnet, SNMP, NTP, ping, traceroute, and various other services create traffic that can be destined to a router's line card or RP CPU. This chapter discusses the details behind LPTS and highlights key elements of forwarding plane security.

Secure Operating System

A router running IOS XR is often used as a backbone router providing core routing capabilities. Cisco IOS XR might also be used on a provider edge router provisioned with edge services such as Layer 2 and Layer 3 VPNs, QoS, and so on. Architectures such as IOS XR often play a critical role in a service provider (SP) network as a core or an edge device, and its security needs are a paramount concern for the network administrator.

Figure 6-1 shows a visual representation of IOS XR secure software design. IOS XR is a microkernel-based operating system. All essential services, such as TCP, UDP, and driver software, run as an independent application on top of its microkernel. Any individual application-level disaster remains contained and has minimal chances of interfering with the core functions of the operating systems. This makes IOS XR internals safe and less vulnerable to exploitation.

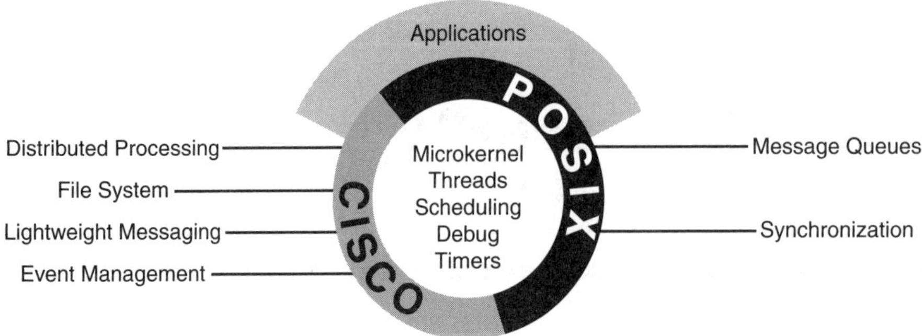

Figure 6-1 *Secure Software Design*

Cisco IOS XR processes run in their own memory space and are "restartable" by design. The software design takes preemptive measures against denial of service–type attacks. IOS XR also mitigates out-of-resource conditions and makes the continuous operation of the system more reliable.

Figure 6-1 illustrates the following main points:

- IOS XR is a microkernel-based operating system offering memory protection and fault tolerance.
- All basic OS and router functionality is implemented as processes. All the distributed services run on top of the microkernel.
- IOS XR follows a UNIX process model with separate, protected memory address spaces for its processes. The microkernel is protected from faults occurring in the protocol or device driver software due to the layered model shown in the figure.

Despite the inherent built-in security and high availability in the operating system, certain configuration measures are inevitable to ensure router and network security. Ensuing sections in this chapter delve deeper into the security considerations of a router or a network of devices running on IOS XR.

Securing Access to the Router

You can access an IOS XR router by using the physical console and auxiliary ports or using the logical vty ports. The console port helps create a terminal session with the router using the standard RS-232 asynchronous serial communications using a commonly found RJ-45 connection. Console ports help configure the router for the first time when it has no configuration and it is advisable to maintain a console connection to the router to aid in debugging or disaster recovery. The auxiliary (aux) port natively runs the Korn Shell (ksh) as its mode of operation. In addition to the physical asynchronous serial ports, IOS XR natively supports router access through 100 vty ports from the range 0 to 99. Furthermore, IOS XR by default enables vty ports in the range 100 to 106 for the embedded event manager (EEM) scripts. This section talks about the access security of the router using local and external AAA.

Note: The IOS XR command **telnet ipv4 server max-servers** is used to limit the number of simultaneous users that can access the router.

AAA authentication commands are defined in Cisco IOS XR to verify a user who attempts to access the system. Cisco IOS XR performs authentication by comparing the incoming user ID and password with what is stored in a security database.

AAA authorization is supported in Cisco IOS XR. It maintains the capability to create audit trails by recording user's actions if specified to do so in Cisco IOS XR.

AAA accounting is the process of tracking user activity and the amount of resources being consumed. Cisco IOS XR provides a method of collecting and sending security server information used for billing, auditing, and reporting, such as user identities, start and stop times, and the executed commands on the router. Cisco IOS XR software supports both the TACACS+ and RADIUS methods of accounting.

Cisco IOS XR operating software maintains two resource management planes from a router access perspective:

- Admin plane
- Secure domain router (SDR) plane

The admin plane consists of resources shared across all secure domain routers. On the other hand, the SDR plane consists of those resources specific to the particular SDR.

IOS XR router security involves concepts of user and task groups. The concepts of user group, task group, and inheritance are important for the understanding of command permissions. These topics will be discussed in more detail later in this chapter. External AAA using TACACS+ and RADIUS are standard access security features. These features will also be illustrated with configuration examples in future sections of this chapter. Configuration examples are provided for Secure Shell (SSH) configurations along with useful show commands.

IOS XR MPP provides the network administrator with the flexibility to restrict interfaces on which network management packets are allowed to enter a device. MPP discussion and examples are a forthcoming topic in this chapter.

Admin Plane

The admin plane maintains responsibility for the owner SDR, and certain administrative responsibilities for all other nonowner SDRs. These functions include user control over power, fan-trays, fabric modules, and environmental aspects of the router required to maintain normal operations. The admin plane is accessible only to a type of user known as the *root-system user*. IOS XR requires configuration of a root-system user using the initial setup dialog. IOS XR router does not allow the system to operate without a user group configuration. If all users and external AAA configurations get deleted, IOS XR prompts the next logged-in user for a new username and password.

SDR Plane

As mentioned in the preceding section, the root-system user has the highest level of privilege for the router operation. This user has the ability to provision SDRs and create root SDR users. After being created, root-lr (the abbreviation *lr* in *root-lr* stands for *logical router*) users take most of the responsibilities from the root-system user for the SDR. The root-lr user is the equivalent of root-system user from an SDR perspective and has jurisdiction only for the particular SDR on which it is defined. A detailed discussion of SDR plane is included in Chapter 11, "Secure Domain Router."

User Groups and Task Groups

Before getting into the details of AAA configuration, this section acquaints you with the concepts of user groups, task groups, and task IDs. The user group concept in IOS XR relates to a group of users with common characteristics. A user that logs in to an IOS XR router may have one or more preconfigured user groups assigned to it. Some user groups are precreated by default and others may be defined via configuration. Table 6-1 lists the predefined user and task groups in IOS XR.

Table 6-1 *Predefined User Groups*

User Groups and Task Groups	Purpose
cisco-support	Used by Cisco Support Team. Provides access to troubleshooting commands.
netadmin	Provides the ability to control and monitor all system- and network-related parameters.
operator	Provides very basic user privileges.
root-lr	Provides the ability to control and monitor the specific SDR.
root-system	Provides the ability to control and monitor the entire system.
sysadmin	Provides the ability to control and monitor all system parameters but cannot configure network protocols.
serviceadmin	Provides the ability to administer session border controllers.

Note: The useful AAA command **show aaa task supported** lists all the available tasks that can be used to select the correct task authorization.

In addition to the predefined task groups, IOS XR provides the ability to custom create task groups consisting of individual tasks. Tasks, in turn, contain a collection of task IDs that define actions such as READ, WRITE, EXECUTE, or DEBUG (R/W/E/D).

The following list elaborates the R/W/E/D task IDs:

- **R:** Permits only a read operation

- **W:** Permits a change (or write) operation and allows an implicit read
- **E:** Permits an access operation (or execution), such as ping or Telnet
- **D:** Permits a debug operation

The concept of tasks, task groups, and task IDs might sound confusing. An example can elucidate this new concept. Suppose a network administrator wants to create a user group called igp-admin that has the capability to execute the following tasks:

- Run **debug** commands for bundle interfaces
- Carry out all configuration and monitoring tasks related to OSPF
- Run only **debug** and **show** commands for MPLS TE

Example 6-1 illustrates the steps needed to meet the preceding requirements.

Example 6-1 *Creating User Groups and Task Groups*

```
! A taskgroup igp-admin is created, the following show command depicts the task-
  group igp-admin
!
RP/0/RP0/CPU0:CRS1-1#show running-config taskgroup igp-admin
taskgroup igp-admin
 task read ospf
 task read mpls-te
 task write ospf
 task execute ospf
 task debug ospf
 task debug bundle
 description OSPF Administrator
! Create a usergroup called igp-admin
RP/0/RP0/CPU0:CRS1-1(config)#usergroup igp-admin
RP/0/RP0/CPU0:CRS1-1(config-ug)#taskgroup igp-admin
RP/0/RP0/CPU0:CRS1-1(config-ug)#commit
RP/0/RP0/CPU0:CRS1-1(config-ug)#exit
!
! Use the following show command to verify the user-group igp-admin
RP/0/RP0/CPU0:CRS1-1#show running-config usergroup igp-admin
usergroup igp-admin
 taskgroup igp-admin
!
! Create a username called igpadmin and configure a secret
RP/0/RP0/CPU0:CRS1-1(config)#username igpadmin
RP/0/RP0/CPU0:CRS1-1(config-un)#group igp-admin
RP/0/RP0/CPU0:CRS1-1(config-un)#secret cisco
RP/0/RP0/CPU0:CRS1-1(config-un)#commit
!
! The following show command verifies the creation of the user-group igpadmin
!
```

```
RP/0/RP0/CPU0:CRS1-1#show running-config username igpadmin
username igpadmin
 secret 5 $1$JodH$mJSA9cRx5IiISitvvOywU.
 group igp-admin
!
```

Example 6-1 creates a task group called igp-admin and assigns the task IDs READ, WRITE, EXECUTE, and DEBUG for OSPF and only READ capability for MPLS-TE and DEBUG capability for bundle tasks, respectively.

A user group called igp-admin is created that references the task group igp-admin. A local AAA username configuration is created that assigns the user group igp-admin to username igpadmin. The username igpadmin is configured with a secret password for authentication purposes. IOS XR supports both a clear text password and a one-way encrypted secret. Using the one-way encrypted secret is ideal for the application shown in Example 6-1.

Example 6-2 demonstrates the **describe** command that can be used to determine the right authorizations if some useful tasks are found to be missing. A user logs in to the router and tries to execute the **show route summary** command only to realize that the command cannot be executed due to missing task authorizations. The **describe** command reveals that the RIB (READ) privilege is required before **show route summary** can be executed.

Example 6-2 *Determining the Right Task ID for an Operation*

```
! Telnet to the router to verify the new configuration. IP address 192.168.254.1
  is that ! of the router on which the new user igpadmin was created.
RP/0/RP0/CPU0:CRS1-1#telnet 192.168.254.1
Trying 192.168.254.1...
Connected to 192.168.254.1.
Escape character is '^^'.
Username: igpadmin
Password:
!
!
RP/0/RP0/CPU0:CRS1-1#show user
igpadmin
! The following command verifies the newly created tasks and their task IDs
RP/0/RP0/CPU0:CRS1-1#show user tasks
Task:                bundle  :                               DEBUG
Task:               mpls-te  : READ
Task:                  ospf  : READ    WRITE    EXECUTE    DEBUG
! Try executing a routing related show command
RP/0/RP0/CPU0:CRS1-1#show route summary
% This command is not authorized
! It appears that an important show command that this user
! needs is not working due to the lack of the right authorization.
```

```
! The "describe" command can be used to find out why this command may not have
! worked, though  to execute the describe command the user logs in again
! with privileges root-system and cisco-support.
!
RP/0/RP0/CPU0:CRS1-1#describe show route
The command is defined in ip_rib_cmds.parser
Node 0/RP0/CPU0 has file ip_rib_cmds.parser for boot package /disk0/hfr-os-mbi-
  3.6.0/mbihfr-rp.vm from hfr-base
Package:
    hfr-base
        hfr-base V3.6.0[00]  Base Package
        Vendor : Cisco Systems
        Desc   : Base Package
        Build  : Built on Mon Dec 17 09:25:24 PST 2007
        Source : By edde-bld1 in /auto/srcarchive2/production/3.6.0/hfr/workspace
          for c2.95.3-p8
        Card(s): RP, DRP, DRPSC, OC3-POS-4, OC12-POS, GE-3, OC12-POS-4, OC48-POS,
  E3-OC48-POS, E3-OC12-POS-4, E3-OC3-POS-16, E3-OC3-POS-8, E3-OC3-POS-4, E3-OC48-
  CH, E3-OC12-CH-4, E3-OC3-CH-16, E3-GE-4, E3-OC3-ATM-4, E3-OC12-ATM-4, E5-CEC,
  E5-CEC-v2, SE-SEC, LC, SP, SC
        Restart information:
          Default:
            parallel impacted processes restart
Component:
    ip-rib V[main/217]  Generic RIB infrastructure
File:
    ip_rib_cmds.parser
        Card(s)              : RP, DRP, SC
        Local view           : /pkg/parser/ip_rib_cmds.parser
        Local install path   : /disk0/hfr-base-3.6.0/parser/ip_rib_cmds
User needs ALL of the following taskids:
        rib (READ)
It will take the following actions:
  Spawn the process:
        show_ipv4_rib -X 0x1 -Y 0x1 -Z ________ -s ipv4 ________
!
! From the highlighted output it is obvious that to
! use "show route" command the task rib must have
! TaskID (READ)
!
! The output of the describe command indicates
! that the tasked "rib (READ)" is required.
!
RP/0/RP0/CPU0:CRS1-1(config)#taskgroup igp-admin
```

```
RP/0/RP0/CPU0:CRS1-1(config-tg)#task read rib
RP/0/RP0/CPU0:CRS1-1(config-tg)#task execute rib
RP/0/RP0/CPU0:CRS1-1(config-tg)#task write rib
RP/0/RP0/CPU0:CRS1-1(config-tg)#task debug rib
RP/0/RP0/CPU0:CRS1-1(config-tg)#commit
RP/0/RP0/CPU0:CRS1-1(config-tg)#exit
!
! A show command showing the newly modified taskgroup
!
RP/0/RP0/CPU0:CRS1-1#show running-config taskgroup igp-admin
taskgroup igp-admin
 task read rib
 task read ospf
 task read mpls-te
 task write rib
 task write ospf
 task execute rib
 task execute ospf
 task debug rib
 task debug ospf
 task debug bundle
 description OSPF Administrator
!
! Login to the router once again to verify the new settings
RP/0/RP0/CPU0:CRS1-1#telnet 192.168.254.1
Trying 192.168.254.1...
Connected to 192.168.254.1.
Escape character is '^^'.
Username: igpadmin
Password:
! show user command shows the new rib task
RP/0/RP0/CPU0:CRS1-1#show user
Igpadmin
RP/0/RP0/CPU0:CRS1-1#show user tasks
Task:                bundle  :                                  DEBUG
Task:               mpls-te  : READ
Task:                  ospf  : READ     WRITE     EXECUTE     DEBUG
Task:                   rib  : READ     WRITE     EXECUTE     DEBUG
!
!show route command can now be executed as the
! authorization issue stands resolved
RP/0/RP0/CPU0:CRS1-1#show route summary
Route Source    Routes     Backup     Deleted     Memory (bytes)
connected       11         5          0           2176
local           16         0          0           2176
```

```
ospf 1          5       0       0       680
isis xr         4       4       0       1216
static          2       0       0       272
bgp 102         0       0       0       0
local SMIAP     1       0       0       136
Total           39      9       0       6656
```

User Group and Task Group Inheritance

User groups and task groups can inherit from other user groups and task groups, respectively. If task group X inherits from task group Y, task group X contains the attributes of X as well as those of Y. In other words, this inheritance produces a "union" of two task groups. The same concept is true for user groups.

Example 6-3 helps illustrate the concept of inheritance. Consider the user group igpadmin created in the previous example. A new user group is created and named deb-eigrp. The user group deb-eigrp has been assigned the debug task for the EIGRP protocol.

Example 6-3 *User Group Inheritance*

```
usergroup igpadmin
 taskgroup igp-admin

! The example shows a user called igpadmin that uses the usergroup igpadmin
username igpadmin
 group igpadmin
 secret 5 $1$laNp$2s/dTtBkqvfkB01B9wqft/

! User igpadmin logs into the router as shown:
RP/0/RP1/CPU0:CRS-1#telnet 192.168.0.1
Trying 192.168.0.1...
Connected to 192.168.0.1.
Username: igpadmin
Password: cisco

! After logging into the router the user checks his tasks with the "show user
! tasks" command.
RP/0/RP1/CPU0:CRS-1#show user tasks
Fri Mar 20 10:26:01.356 PST
Task:                bundle  :                                      DEBUG
Task:               mpls-te  : READ
Task:                  ospf  : READ    WRITE     EXECUTE     DEBUG
Task:                   rib  : READ    WRITE     EXECUTE     DEBUG


! Now a new usergroup called deb-eigrp is created that uses the taskgroup
! debug-eigrp.
```

```
! This configuration is carried out the network administrator and not the
! igpadmin user.
 RP/0/RP1/CPU0:CRS-1#show run taskgroup debug-eigrp
Fri Mar 20 10:31:44.150 PST
taskgroup debug-eigrp
 task debug eigrp
!
 usergroup deb-eigrp
 taskgroup debug-eigrp
!
The administrator assigns the usergroup deb-eigrp to usergroup igpadmin by way of
 inheritance.
usergroup igpadmin
 taskgroup igp-admin
 inherit usergroup deb-eigrp
!
! The user igpadmin logs again into the router and executes the command "show
! user tasks". Note that inheritance has allowed eigrp debug capability to be
! added to the user igpadmin.
RP/0/RP1/CPU0:CRS-1#telnet 192.168.0.1
Trying 192.168.0.1...
Connected to 192.168.0.1.

Username: igpadmin
Password: cisco  Mar 18 07:59:33 2009: 2 days, 2 hours, 34 minutes ago

RP/0/RP1/CPU0:CRS-1#show user tasks
Fri Mar 20 10:33:50.893 PST
Task:                 bundle  :                                   DEBUG
Task:                  eigrp  :                                   DEBUG
Task:                mpls-te  : READ
Task:                   ospf  : READ     WRITE     EXECUTE     DEBUG
Task:                    rib  : READ     WRITE     EXECUTE     DEBUG

RP/0/RP1/CPU0:CRS-1#
```

Let us use another example to demonstrate the concept of inheritance in task groups. A new task group is being created for the user mplsadmin. The requirements for this user are as follows:

- READ, WRITE, EXECUTE, and DEBUG task IDs for MPLS TE
- All the attributes of task group igp-admin

Example 6-4 creates the new task group using inheritance from the already existing task group called igp-admin that was created in Example 6-3.

Example 6-4 *Determining the Right Task ID for an Operation*

```
RP/0/RP1/CPU0:CRS1-1(config)#taskgroup mpls-admin
RP/0/RP1/CPU0:CRS1-1(config-tg)#task debug mpls-te
RP/0/RP1/CPU0:CRS1-1(config-tg)#task execute mpls-te
RP/0/RP1/CPU0:CRS1-1(config-tg)#task read mpls-te
RP/0/RP1/CPU0:CRS1-1(config-tg)#task write mpls-te
RP/0/RP1/CPU0:CRS1-1(config)#inherit taskgroup igp-admin
RP/0/RP1/CPU0:CRS1-1(config-tg)#commit
RP/0/RP1/CPU0:CRS1-1(config-tg)#exit
!
! Use the following show command to verify the configuration from the previous task
RP/0/RP1/CPU0:CRS1-1#show running-config taskgroup mpls-admin
taskgroup mpls-admin
 task read mpls-te
 task write mpls-te
 task execute mpls-te
 task debug mpls-te
 inherit taskgroup igp-admin
!
```

External AAA

Cisco IOS XR supports external AAA using standard IP-based protocols such as TACACS+ and RADIUS. TACACS+ and RADIUS protocols can be used in conjunction with a product such as the Cisco Secure Access Control Server (ACS) to provide an external AAA database. The following describes some key elements of AAA configuration:

- The security server and client are identified by IP addresses and a secret shared key is configured between them.
- The notion of a user group on IOS XR local AAA is unrelated to a user group on an ACS server. The configuration of user groups on the ACS server is a separate ACS-only feature.
- IOS XR task groups are identified as optional attributes on the ACS server. Two methods exist that can help identify task IDs remotely. The first method uses the concept of task maps and the second uses the privilege levels.

Example 6-5 demonstrates the external configuration for tasks. Note that these configurations are on the server side of external AAA and not on the router.

Example 6-5 *Task Configuration Semantics on an External Server*

```
user = igpadmin{
        member = igp-admin-group
        opap = cleartext "cisco"
        service = exec {
        task = "rwxd:ospf,#operator"
        }
}
```

Example 6-5 specifies the task ID as an attribute in the external TACACS+ or RADIUS server. Note that this is shown as an example only. Because the procedure can vary from server to server, consult the TACACS+ or RADIUS server documentation to find out how you can use the optional attributes. A freeware TACACS+ server from Cisco might require an asterisk (*) instead of an equal sign (=) before the attribute value for optional attributes. Example 6-5 shows the task string in the configuration file of the TACACS+ server where tokens are delimited by a comma (,). Each token contains either a task ID name or its permissions in the following format:

```
task = "<permissions>:<taskid name>, #<usergroup name>, ..." .
```

In Example 6-5, the task = "rwxd:ospf,#operator" assigns READ, WRITE, EXECUTE, and DEBUG task IDs to the OSPF task and assigns the user group operator.

Example 6-6 is quoted from Cisco.com and demonstrates the ability to interact with a TACACS+ daemon that does not have the concept of task IDs. In this case a privilege-level mapping is used.

Example 6-6 *Privilege-Level Mappings*

```
!
! TACACS+ example
!
user = admin1{
     member = bar
     service = exec-ext {
          priv_lvl = 5
     }
}
!
!RADIUS Example using Cisco AV-pair
!
user = admin2{
     member = bar
     Cisco-AVPair = "shell:tasks=#root-system,#cisco-support"{
          Cisco-AVPair = "shell:priv-lvl=10"
     }
}
```

Cisco IOS XR AAA supports a mapping between privilege levels that can be defined for a given user in the external TACACS+ server file. The local user group on the router needs to be configured with a user group with a name that matches the privilege level. After TACACS+ authentication, the user gets assigned the task map of the user group mapped to the privilege level received from the external TACACS+ server. Example 6-6 shows a TACACS+ configuration followed by a RADIUS configuration. If the IOS XR router is configured with local user groups priv5 and priv10, they can be mapped to the privilege levels 5 and 10 configured for TACACS+ and RADIUS, respectively. Privilege levels from 1 to 13 may be used in a similar way. Privilege level 15 maps to the root-system and privilege level 14 maps to root-lr.

The following sections discuss the configuration behind external AAA. Various CLI command options for configuring TACACS+ are presented.

Configuring a TACACS+ Server

Figure 6-2 shows an IOS XR router connected to an ACS server. Example 6-7 creates a simple TACACS+ configuration using an external ACS server with an IP address of 172.18.172.16.

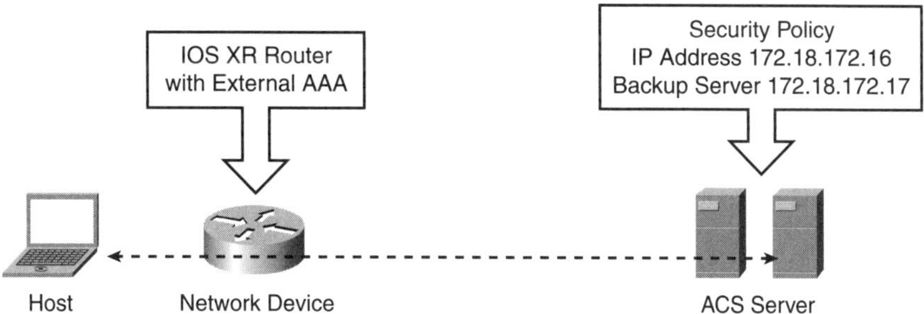

Figure 6-2 *Authentication with an External AAA Server*

Example 6-7 *Configuring AAA with an External TACACS+ Server*

```
RP/0/RP0/CPU0:CRS-A#show run aaa
usergroup priv11
taskgroup netadmin
taskgroup igpadmin
!
tacacs-server host 172.18.172.16 port 49
tacacs-server key 7 06150E2F46411A1C
tacacs source-interface MgmtEth0/0/CPU0/0
!
aaa group server tacacs+ chap6
 server 172.18.172.17
!
aaa authentication login console local
aaa authentication login chap-6 group chap6 local
aaa default-taskgroup root-system
!
line template lab
 login authentication chap-6
 exec-timeout 30 0
!
line console
 login authentication console

vty-pool default 0 99 line-template lab
```

In Example 6-7, a privilege 11 configuration exists on the ACS server. The AAA server is identified with the **tacacs server host** command and a backup server is identified with the **aaa group server** command. The **local** keyword in the **aaa authentication login chap-6 group chap6 local** command ensures that AAA will authenticate locally in the case of failure of both the ACS servers. The AAA method list chap-6 gets assigned to the vty pool.

Authentication Using RADIUS

This section shows some configuration examples for AAA RADIUS client configuration on IOS XR to allow authentication with an external ACS server.

Example 6-8 shows a basic AAA RADIUS configuration. The basic concept is the same as that shown in Example 6-7 except the TACACS+ protocol has been replaced by RADIUS.

Example 6-8 *Configuring AAA with an External RADIUS Server*

```
RP/0/RP0/CPU0:CRS-B_IOX#show run aaa
usergroup priv13
 taskgroup root-system
 taskgroup cisco-support
!
radius-server host 172.18.172.16
 key 7 104D000A0618
!
radius source-interface MgmtEth0/RP0/CPU0/0
aaa authentication login telnet group radius local
aaa authentication login default local
!
line template rads
 login authentication telnet
 exec-timeout 0 0
 session-timeout 0
vty-pool default 0 99 line-template rads
telnet ipv4 server max-servers no-limit
```

Example 6-9 shows AAA RADIUS authentication and introduces a new authorization command: **aaa authorization exec default none**. This command has the same effect as the keyword **if-authenticated** in IOS AAA authorization commands. The configuration states that if a user is authenticated, that user is also authorized.

Example 6-9 *AAA with an External RADIUS Server with Accounting and Authorization*

```
! Configures Radius server dead times and dead-criteria
!
radius-server deadtime 1
radius-server dead-criteria time 15
radius-server dead-criteria tries 2
```

```
!
! Configures the RADIUS server hosts
!
aaa group server radius XR-GROUP
 server 172.18.172.16 auth-port 1645 acct-port 1646
 server 172.18.172.17 auth-port 1645 acct-port 1646
!
! Enables AAA accounting
aaa accounting exec default start-stop group XR-GROUP
aaa accounting commands default start-stop group XR-GROUP
!
! Configure authorization to occur automatically if the user gets authenticated
!
aaa authorization exec default none
!
! sets login authentication to use the default method list and XR-GROUP server
aaa authentication login default group XR-GROUP local
end
```

Configuring Secure Shell

Secure Shell (SSH) is a useful protocol or application for establishing secure sessions with the router. A router configured with SSH server allows a secure connection to the router similar to Telnet. The Telnet application has limited security. SSH provides stronger encryption and deploys public-key cryptography for added confidentiality. SFTP also comes as a component of SSH and enables secure FTP (SFTP) capabilities for downloading software or configuration files. IOS XR supports two versions of SSH:

- SSH version 1 uses Rivest, Shamire, and Adelman (RSA) keys.
- SSH version 2 uses the Digital Signature Algorithm (DSA).

Enabling SSH on IOS XR requires the Hfr-k9sec security PIE to be installed on the router. In addition to installing the k9sec PIE, IOS XR requires RSA or DSA keys to be generated on the router before SSH runs in server mode. Example 6-10 illustrates the SSH configuration on IOS XR.

Example 6-10 *Enabling SSH v2 on IOS XR*

```
!
!The command below verifies the existence of k9sec pie
!
RP/0/RP1/CPU0:CRS1-1(admin)#show install active | include k9sec
      disk0:hfr-k9sec-3.6.0
!
! The following command generates DSA key pairs
!
RP/0/RP1/CPU0:CRS1-1#crypto key generate dsa
```

```
The name for the keys will be: the_default
  Choose the size of your DSA key modulus. Modulus size can be 512, 768, or 1024
    bits. Choosing a key modulus
How many bits in the modulus [1024]: 1024
Generating DSA keys ...
Done w/ crypto generate keypair
[OK]
!
RP/0/RP1/CPU0:CRS1-1(config)#ssh server v2
RP/0/RP1/CPU0:CRS1-1(config)#commit
```

In Example 6-10 the presence of the k9sec PIE is verified first. If this PIE is not present, it needs to be installed. The example shows the generation of DSA keys by executing the **crypto key generate dsa** command, followed by enabling SSH version 2 in Configuration mode.

Example 6-11 demonstrates the debugging of SSH server functionality on a router with the **debug ssh server** command followed by the **show ssh session detail** command.

Example 6-11 *Debugging SSH v2 on IOS XR*

```
! Enable ssh server debugging on the router
!
RP/0/RP1/CPU0:CRS1-1#debug ssh server
RP/0/RP1/CPU0:CRS1-1#show debug
####  debug flags set from tty 'vty0'  ####
ssh server flag is ON
!
! Create an SSH session from a unix server to the IOS XR router
!
$ ssh cisco@10.10.20.31
Password:cisco
Last switch-over Sun Jun  1 08:51:09 2008: 2 weeks, 3 hours, 27 minutes ago
RP/0/RP1/CPU0:CRS1-1#RP/0/RP1/CPU0:Jun 15 12:18:50.284 : SSHD_[364]: Spawned new
  child process 6852847
RP/0/RP1/CPU0:Jun 15 12:18:50.482 : SSHD_[65775]: Client sockfd 3
RP/0/RP1/CPU0:Jun 15 12:18:50.494 : SSHD_[65775]: Connection from 10.10.20.100
  port 61532
RP/0/RP1/CPU0:Jun 15 12:18:50.517 : SSHD_[65775]: Session id 0
RP/0/RP1/CPU0:Jun 15 12:18:50.521 : SSHD_[65775]: Exchanging versions
RP/0/RP1/CPU0:Jun 15 12:18:50.539 : SSHD_[65775]: Remote protocol version 2.0,
  remote software version Sun_SSH_1.1
RP/0/RP1/CPU0:Jun 15 12:18:50.540 : SSHD_[65775]: In Key exchange
RP/0/RP1/CPU0:Jun 15 12:18:51.137 : SSHD_[65775]: Received --------> KEXINIT
RP/0/RP1/CPU0:Jun 15 12:18:51.137 : SSHD_[65775]: Calling Receive kexinit 10
RP/0/RP1/CPU0:Jun 15 12:18:51.137 : SSHD_[65775]: Peer Proposal : diffie-hellman-
  group-exchange-sha1,diffie-hellman-group1-sha1
```

```
RP/0/RP1/CPU0:Jun 15 12:18:51.138 : SSHD_[65775]: Peer Proposal : ssh-rsa,ssh-dss
RP/0/RP1/CPU0:Jun 15 12:18:51.139 : SSHD_[65775]: Peer Proposal : aes128-
  ctr,aes128-cbc,arcfour,3des-cbc,blowfish-cbc
RP/0/RP1/CPU0:Jun 15 12:18:51.139 : SSHD_[65775]: Peer Proposal : aes128-
  ctr,aes128-cbc,arcfour,3des-cbc,blowfish-cbc
RP/0/RP1/CPU0:Jun 15 12:18:51.140 : SSHD_[65775]: Peer Proposal : hmac-md5,hmac-
  sha1,hmac-sha1-96,hmac-md5-96
RP/0/RP1/CPU0:Jun 15 12:18:51.140 : SSHD_[65775]: Peer Proposal : hmac-md5,hmac-
  sha1,hmac-sha1-96,hmac-md5-96
RP/0/RP1/CPU0:Jun 15 12:18:51.141 : SSHD_[65775]: Peer Proposal : none,zlib
RP/0/RP1/CPU0:Jun 15 12:18:51.141 : SSHD_[65775]: Peer Proposal : none,zlib
RP/0/RP1/CPU0:Jun 15 12:18:51.141 : SSHD_[65775]: Peer Proposal : i-default
RP/0/RP1/CPU0:Jun 15 12:18:51.141 : SSHD_[65775]: Peer Proposal : i-default
RP/0/RP1/CPU0:Jun 15 12:18:51.164 : SSHD_[65775]: Negotiated Alg : diffie-hellman-
  group1-sha1
RP/0/RP1/CPU0:Jun 15 12:18:51.168 : SSHD_[65775]: Publikey Alg = ssh-dss
RP/0/RP1/CPU0:Jun 15 12:18:51.173 : SSHD_[65775]: Incoming cipher = 3des-cbc
RP/0/RP1/CPU0:Jun 15 12:18:51.176 : SSHD_[65775]: Outgoing cipher = 3des-cbc
RP/0/RP1/CPU0:Jun 15 12:18:51.179 : SSHD_[65775]: Incoming mac = hmac-md5
RP/0/RP1/CPU0:Jun 15 12:18:51.180 : SSHD_[65775]: Outgoing mac = hmac-md5
RP/0/RP1/CPU0:Jun 15 12:18:51.181 : SSHD_[65775]: Keylen Reqd  = 24
RP/0/RP1/CPU0:Jun 15 12:18:51.204 : SSHD_[65775]: Waiting for KEXDH_INIT
RP/0/RP1/CPU0:Jun 15 12:18:51.215 : SSHD_[65775]: Received KEXDH_INIT
RP/0/RP1/CPU0:Jun 15 12:18:51.269 : SSHD_[65775]: Extracting pubkey from crypto
  engine
RP/0/RP1/CPU0:Jun  15 12:18:51.284 : SSHD_[65775]: Received pubkey from crypto engine
RP/0/RP1/CPU0:Jun 15 12:18:51.285 : SSHD_[65775]: bloblen = 433
RP/0/RP1/CPU0:Jun 15 12:18:51.285 : SSHD_[65775]: prime = 129, subprime = 21, base
  = 128, y =128
RP/0/RP1/CPU0:Jun 15 12:18:51.286 : SSHD_[65775]: Calculating kex hash with
  client_str = SSH-2.0-Sun_SSH_1.1  (len = 19)
RP/0/RP1/CPU0:Jun 15 12:18:51.286 : SSHD_[65775]: server_str = SSH-1.99-Cisco-2.0
  (len = 18)
RP/0/RP1/CPU0:Jun 15 12:18:51.325 : SSHD_[65775]: Sending KEXDH_REPLY
RP/0/RP1/CPU0:Jun 15 12:18:51.328 : SSHD_[65775]: Sending NEWKEYS
RP/0/RP1/CPU0:Jun 15 12:18:51.329 : SSHD_[65775]: Waiting for NEWKEYS
RP/0/RP1/CPU0:Jun 15 12:18:51.362 : SSHD_[65775]: In Authenticate
RP/0/RP1/CPU0:Jun 15 12:18:51.373 : SSHD_[65775]: Request service name - ssh-
  userauth
RP/0/RP1/CPU0:Jun 15 12:18:51.375 : SSHD_[65775]: Sending Servie Accept msg
RP/0/RP1/CPU0:Jun 15 12:18:51.377 : SSHD_[65775]: Waiting for Userauth req
RP/0/RP1/CPU0:Jun 15 12:18:51.391 : SSHD_[65775]: In Interactive shell
RP/0/RP1/CPU0:Jun 15 12:18:51.402 : SSHD_[65775]: Remote channel type - session,
  remote chan id = 0
RP/0/RP1/CPU0:Jun 15 12:18:51.405 : SSHD_[65775]: Winsize = 65536, maxpacksize =
  16384
RP/0/RP1/CPU0:Jun 15 12:18:51.406 : SSHD_[65775]: Sending Channel open success msg
RP/0/RP1/CPU0:Jun 15 12:18:51.437 : SSHD_[65775]: Connecting to VTY Server
```

```
RP/0/RP1/CPU0:Jun 15 12:18:51.494 : SSHD_[65775]: Opening file /dev/vty9999
RP/0/RP1/CPU0:Jun 15 12:18:51.496 : SSHD_[65775]: Allocated pty vty1.
RP/0/RP1/CPU0:Jun 15 12:18:51.497 : SSHD_[65775]: Setting window size row = 24,
  col = 106
RP/0/RP1/CPU0:Jun 15 12:18:51.615 : SSHD_[65775]: Spawned shell
RP/0/RP1/CPU0:Jun 15 12:18:51.677 : SSHD_[65775]: event_contex_init done
!
! Show command to verify the SSH session detail on the router.
!
RP/0/RP1/CPU0:CRS1-1#show ssh session details
SSH version : Cisco-2.0
id  key-exchange  pubkey  incipher  outcipher  inmac   outmac
---------------------------------------------------------------------
Incoming Session
diffie-hellman  ssh-dss  3des-cbc  3des-cbc  hmac-md5  hmac-md5
! A command output showing the incoming SSH TCP session
!
RP/0/RP1/CPU0:CRS1-1#show tcp brief
   PCB       VRF-ID      Recv-Q Send-Q Local Address      Foreign Address      State
0x482e2c30 0x60000000       0      0  :::22              :::0                 LISTEN
0x482e2ea0 0x60000001       0      0  :::22              :::0                 LISTEN
0x482e8248 0x00000000       0      0  :::22              :::0                 LISTEN
0x482e5a38 0x60000000       0      0  10.0.0.11:646      10.0.0.31:35777      ESTAB
0x482cc0a8 0x60000000       0      0  10.0.0.11:646      10.0.0.21:57878      ESTAB
0x482deff4 0x60000000       0      0  10.10.20.31:23     10.10.20.100:61512   ESTAB
0x482e7714 0x60000000       0      0  10.10.20.31:22     10.10.20.100:61532   ESTAB
0x482e8380 0x60000000       0      0  0.0.0.0:22         0.0.0.0:0            LISTEN
0x482e2d68 0x60000001       0      0  0.0.0.0:22         0.0.0.0:0            LISTEN
0x482e8598 0x00000000       0      0  0.0.0.0:22         0.0.0.0:0            LISTEN
0x482d0660 0x60000000       0      0  0.0.0.0:23         0.0.0.0:0            LISTEN
0x482e0dc4 0x00000000       0      0  0.0.0.0:23         0.0.0.0:0            LISTEN
0x482cf2e4 0x60000000       0      0  0.0.0.0:639        0.0.0.0:0            LISTEN
0x482cd9e4 0x60000000       0      0  0.0.0.0:646        0.0.0.0:0            LISTEN
```

Example 6-11 shows an SSH session created from a UNIX host to the router and the corresponding debug output produced on the console. The debug output shows the exchanging of SSH version between the UNIX host and the router as well as the negotiation of the Diffie-Hellman key exchange. The example also presents the **show ssh session detail** command's output showing the details of the SSH session. The output of **show tcp brief** shows the TCP port 22 sessions that identifies the incoming SSH connection.

Management Plane Protection

Management plane refers to a router's architectural components involved in the processing of traffic that is meant for the management of the routing platform. Management Plane Protection (MPP) is a relatively new feature in IOS XR; it was introduced in Release 3.5.0. It helps control the interfaces on which network management traffic can enter the router. The capability helps enhance the router-level security and allows the network administrator better granularity in controlling management access to the router.

Following are the salient features of MPP:

- Enhances the manageability and security aspects of IOS XR.
- Helps alleviate the need to configure more access lists in controlling router access.
- Management ports on RP and DRP are not configurable under MPP because they are out of band by default.
- Controls incoming traffic for protocols, such as TFTP, Telnet, Simple Network Management Protocol (SNMP), SSH, and HTTP.
- Allows control for both in-band and out-of-band interfaces.
- Can specify a peer IPv4 or IPv6 address or subnet from which traffic is allowed, thus providing more control.

In the context of MPP, an *in-band* management interface is an interface that receives and processes management packets as well as forwards Internet traffic. This interface may also be referred to as a *shared management interface*. An out-of-band interface allows only management protocol traffic to be forwarded or processed. This type of interface does not process or receive any customer or Internet traffic and, therefore, has lower potential for becoming a victim of a DoS attack. Out-of-band interfaces are usually also the last hop interfaces in the life of a packet, and these packets are then processed by higher-layer protocols on the router.

Example 6-12 illustrates the configuration steps for MPP.

Example 6-12 *Configuring MPP*

```
RP/0/RP1/CPU0:CRS1-1#configure t
RP/0/RP1/CPU0:CRS1-1(config)#control-plane
RP/0/RP1/CPU0:CRS1-1(config-ctrl)#management-plane
RP/0/RP1/CPU0:CRS1-1(config-mpp)#inband
RP/0/RP1/CPU0:CRS1-1(config-mpp-inband)#interface tenGigE 0/0/0/0
RP/0/RP1/CPU0:CRS1-(config-mpp-inband-TenGigE0_0_0_0)#allow telnet
```

```
RP/0/RP1/CPU0:CRS1-(config-mpp-inband-TenGigE0_0_0_0)#commit
RP/0/RP1/CPU0:CRS1-(config-mpp-inband-TenGigE0_0_0_0)#exit
RP/0/RP1/CPU0:CRS1-1(config-mpp-inband)#exit
RP/0/RP1/CPU0:CRS1-1(config-mpp)#out-of-band
RP/0/RP1/CPU0:CRS1-1(config-mpp-outband)#vrf red
RP/0/RP1/CPU0:CRS1-1(config-mpp-outband)#interface tenGigE 0/0/0/0.1
RP/0/RP1/CPU0:CR(config-mpp-outband-TenGigE0_0_0_0.1)#allow snmp
RP/0/RP1/CPU0:CR(config-mpp-outband-TenGigE0_0_0_0.1)#allow telnet
RP/0/RP1/CPU0:CR(config-mpp-outband-TenGigE0_0_0_0.1)#commit
RP/0/RP1/CPU0:CR(config-mpp-outband-TenGigE0_0_0_0.1)#
! Using an MPP show command
RP/0/RP1/CPU0:CRS1-1#show mgmt-plane
Management Plane Protection
inband interfaces
------------
interface - TenGigE0_0_0_0
        telnet configured -
                All peers allowed
outband interfaces
------------
interface - TenGigE0_0_0_0.1
        telnet configured -
                All peers allowed
        snmp configured -
                All peers allowed
RP/0/RP1/CPU0:CRS1-1#
```

Example 6-12 shows MPP configuration where the Telnet protocol is enabled for only one in-band interface (Tengig0/0/0/0), and the out-of-band management interface Tengig0/0/0/0.1 under vrf red is enabled for telnet and SNMP.

Securing the Forwarding Plane

Forwarding plane refers to a router's forwarding path involved in processing transit traffic or in processing traffic that is destined to the router. The traffic destined to the router is also sometimes termed *for_us* traffic. The forwarding plane constitutes the packet-forwarding, switching, and queuing components involved in the packet flow. This section introduces various forwarding plane features and provides configuration examples of each. The main features covered in forwarding plane security are ACLs, Unicast Reverse Path Forwarding (uRPF), and Local Packet Transport Services (LPTS).

Access Control Lists

ACL filtering allows the network administrator to control packet flow through the network. Such control helps limit undesirable network traffic and helps restrict network use by certain users or devices. ACLs provide the ability to permit or deny packets from passing through specific router interfaces. Access lists also find several uses in providing granularity and control to control plane protocols.

Following are some of the key features of IOS XR access lists:

- **Named access lists:** Cisco IOS XR uses named access lists only. Internally, the access list is treated as a string or name. IOS XR uses only named access lists. Even if a number is used to denote an access list, it is internally treated as a string or a name.
- **Standard or Extended Keywords:** IOS XR does not use standard and extended keywords in specifying an access list. An access list can include mixed Access Control Elements (ACE) that use only source-based filtering or both source- and destination-based filtering that may be combined with protocol port operations.
- **Locally originated traffic:** Cisco IOS XR egress ACLs do not filter traffic originated by the router.
- **ACL numbering and resequence:** Cisco IOS XR ACLs use line numbering to help replace a particular line in an ACL definition. An option is provided to resequence the ACL line numberings if required.
- **Remarks:** Cisco IOS XR ACLs provide the ability to insert remarks in an access list to help explain the purpose of the particular line in an ACL.
- **Log messages:** Cisco IOS XR provides the ability to log an ACL. Logging an ACL produces a syslog message when a packet matches a line with the **log** keyword. This operation is CPU intensive and must not be enabled for high speed traffic rates. Usually an ACL with a **log** keyword can be used for ACLs applied to vty lines. A **log** keyword may also be used for temporary debugging purposes, keeping in mind that its use is CPU intensive.
- **ICMP unreachables:** IOS XR ACL deny packet operation on an interface produces a rate-controlled ICMP unreachable message. This ICMP message can be disabled from the interface by using the CLI **no ipv4 unreachables**.

Example 6-13 shows the creation of an access list that has the following properties:

- ACL with name CRS-Core.
- Permits incoming LDP and BGP sessions from the peer address 67.13.1.1 destined to 67.13.2.1.
- The ACL permits any traffic destined to TCP ports 80 and 8080.
- The ACL permits SSH traffic from host 62.133.1.1.
- The rest of the traffic is denied.

Example 6-13 *Configuring an ACL Named CRS-Core*

```
RP/0/RP1/CPU0:CRS1-1(config)#ipv4 access-list CRS-Core
RP/0/RP1/CPU0:CRS1-1(config-ipv4-acl)#permit tcp host 67.13.1.1 eq ldp host
  67.13.2.1
```

```
RP/0/RP1/CPU0:CRS1-1(config-ipv4-acl)#permit tcp host 67.13.1.1 host 67.13.2.1 eq
  ldp
RP/0/RP1/CPU0:CRS1-1(config-ipv4-acl)#permit tcp host 67.13.1.1 host 67.13.2.1 eq
  bgp
RP/0/RP1/CPU0:CRS1-1(config-ipv4-acl)#permit tcp any eq 80 any
RP/0/RP1/CPU0:CRS1-1(config-ipv4-acl)#permit tcp any any eq 80
RP/0/RP1/CPU0:CRS1-1(config-ipv4-acl)#permit tcp any eq 8080 any
RP/0/RP1/CPU0:CRS1-1(config-ipv4-acl)#permit tcp any any eq 8080
RP/0/RP1/CPU0:CRS1-1(config-ipv4-acl)#permit tcp host 62.133.1.1 any eq 22
RP/0/RP1/CPU0:CRS1-1(config-ipv4-acl)#permit icmp 65.10.20.0 0.0.0.255 any echo
RP/0/RP1/CPU0:CRS1-1(config-ipv4-acl)#permit icmp 65.10.20.0 0.0.0.255 any echo-
  reply
RP/0/RP1/CPU0:CRS1-1(config-ipv4-acl)#commit
RP/0/RP1/CPU0:CRS1-1(config-ipv4-acl)#exit
RP/0/RP1/CPU0:CRS1-1(config)#
```

Example 6-14 shows the application of the access list ingress on the interface tenGigE 0/0/0/0.

Example 6-14 *Applying ACL Named CRS-Core*

```
RP/0/RP1/CPU0:CRS1-1#show access-lists ipv4 CRS-Core
ipv4 access-list CRS-Core
 10 permit tcp host 67.13.1.1 eq ldp host 67.13.2.1
 20 permit tcp host 67.13.1.1 host 67.13.2.1 eq ldp
 30 permit tcp host 67.13.1.1 host 67.13.2.1 eq bgp
 40 permit tcp any eq www any
 50 permit tcp any any eq www
 60 permit tcp any eq 8080 any
 70 permit tcp any any eq 8080
 80 permit tcp host 62.133.1.1 any eq 22
 90 permit icmp 65.10.20.0 0.0.0.255 any echo
 91 permit icmp 65.10.20.0 0.0.0.255 any echo-reply

! Applying the access-list to an interface
RP/0/RP1/CPU0:CRS1-1#configure t
RP/0/RP1/CPU0:CRS1-1(config)#interface tenGigE 0/0/0/1
RP/0/RP1/CPU0:CRS1-1(config-if)#ipv4 access-group CRS-Core ingress
RP/0/RP1/CPU0:CRS1-1(config-if)#commit
```

Example 6-15 shows the access list created in Example 6-14 from the hardware perspective of the node to which it is applied. An access list applied to the forwarding path may be queried using the hardware keyword to ensure that the configuration has been accepted by the linecard hardware.

Example 6-15 *Access List in Hardware*

```
RP/0/RP1/CPU0:CRS1-1#show access-lists ipv4 CRS-Core hardware ingress location
  0/0/cpu0
ipv4 access-list CRS-Core
 10 permit tcp host 67.13.1.1 eq ldp host 67.13.2.1
 20 permit tcp host 67.13.1.1 host 67.13.2.1 eq ldp
 30 permit tcp host 67.13.1.1 host 67.13.2.1 eq bgp
 40 permit tcp any eq www any
 50 permit tcp any any eq www
 60 permit tcp any eq 8080 any
 70 permit tcp any any eq 8080
 80 permit tcp host 62.133.1.1 any eq 22
 90 permit icmp 65.10.20.0 0.0.0.255 any echo
 91 permit icmp 65.10.20.0 0.0.0.255 any echo-reply
```

Table 6-2 lists the key **show** and **debug** commands related to access lists.

Table 6-2 *Key ACL Operations and debug Commands*

Command	Description
show access-lists afi-all	Shows configured access lists for IPv4 and IPv6 address families.
show access-lists maximum [*detail* | *<cr>*]	Shows the maximum configurable and current configured number of ACLs.
show access-lists usage pfilter location *line_card_location*	Indicates which access lists are applied to the node and whether they are applied ingress or egress.
show access-lists hardware {*ingress* | *egress*} **location** *line_card_location*	Shows ACL information as applied to line card hardware.
debug pfilter-ea errors location *line_card_location*	Debugs any errors encountered when applying ACL. Should be used only if there is a problem with applying an ACL.

Unicast RPF

Unicast Reverse Path Forwarding (uRPF) is another useful IOS XR feature that helps prevent malicious traffic from entering a service provider network. uRPF may be used in strict and loose modes. Enabling strict uRPF on an interface helps the forwarding path analyze the incoming traffic's source address. If the reverse path back to the source address of incoming packet is not learned via the interface on which strict uRPF is enabled, the packet is dropped. Loose uRPF is useful when a case of asymmetric routing might be present on the network. In the case of loose uRPF, the route for the source interface must be in the routing table. Configuration options may also allow default routes to satisfy loose uRPF requirements.

The following command configures strict or loose uRPF at the interface level:

```
{ipv4 | ipv6} verify unicast source reachable-via {any | rx} [allow-default]
  [allow-self-ping]
```

The explanation of this command follows:

- Using the **any** option after **verify unicast source reachable-via** enables loose uRPF.
- Using the **rx** option after **verify unicast source reachable-via** enables strict uRPF.
- The **allow-default** option allows uRPF check to be true against a default route. This option is equally applicable to loose and strict uRPF.
- The **allow-self-ping** option allows the router to ping itself and is applicable to both loose and strict uRPF.

Example 6-16 shows the enabling of strict uRPF on a CRS interface and depicts a CEF command to check whether the configuration has been enforced.

Example 6-16 *Strict uRPF on the tenGigE Interface*

```
RP/0/RP1/CPU0:CRS1-1(config)#interface tenGigE 0/0/0/1
RP/0/RP1/CPU0:CRS1-1(config-if)#ipv4 verify unicast source reachable-via rx
RP/0/RP1/CPU0:CRS1-1(config-if)#commit
!
! The following show command shows if the feature has been enabled
RP/0/RP1/CPU0:CRS1-1#show cef ipv4 interface tenGigE 0/0/0/1
TenGigE0/0/0/1 is up (if_handle 0x01080040)
  Interface last modified Jan 12 22:54:42, modify
  Reference count 2
  Forwarding is enabled
  ICMP redirects are never sent
  IP MTU 1500, TableId 0xe0000000
  IP unicast RPF check is enabled
  RPF mode strict
  Protocol Reference count 2
  Primary IPV4 local address 65.10.20.2/32
```

Example 6-17 shows the strict uRPF in action. The router does not have a route to a source of traffic that comes from IP address 171.1.1.1; on receiving the traffic, the strict uRPF feature drops this traffic. Example 6-17 depicts a CEF-related show command for determining uRPF drop statistics.

Example 6-17 *Strict uRPF on the tenGigE Interface*

```
RP/0/RP1/CPU0:CRS1-1#show route 171.1.1.1
% Network not in table
!
```

```
! shows RPF statistics
RP/0/RP1/CPU0:CRS1-1#show cef ipv4 interface tenGigE 0/0/0/1 rpf-statistics
Unicast RPF drops 1000
```

Local Packet Transport Service

The forwarding plane security section has so far discussed features such as ACLs and uRPF, which filter packets based on certain criteria. This section discusses Local Packet Transport Service (LPTS). LPTS provides software architecture to deliver locally destined traffic to the correct node on the router and provides security against overwhelming the router resources with excessive traffic. LPTS achieves security by policing flows of locally destined traffic to a value that can be easily sustained by the CPU capabilities of the platform.

The first question you might ask is what sort of traffic constitutes locally destined traffic. Although routers are in the business of forwarding packets, there are scenarios in which the traffic may be locally destined, including the following:

- All IPv4, IPv6, and MPLS traffic related to routing protocols, or control plane such as MPLS LDP or RSVP. The control plane computations for protocols are done on the Router Processor (RP) of the router. Therefore, whenever routing or MPLS control plane traffic is received on a line card interface, it needs to be delivered to the RP of the router.
- MPLS packets with the Router Alert label
- IPv4, IPv6, or MPLS packets with a TTL less than 2
- IPv4 or IPv6 packets with options
- IP packets requiring fragmentation or reassembly
- Layer 2 keepalives
- Address Resolution Protocol (ARP) packets
- ICMP message generation and response

Table 6-3 lists the various types of locally destined traffic and indicates the router's node on which the traffic may be processed.

Table 6-3 *CRS-1 Release 3.6.0 for_us Packet Processing*

Received Traffic Type	Processed in Packet Switching Engine	Processed by Line Card CPU	Processed by Route Processor
Transit Traffic			
Transit Packets	Undergoes configured features (ACL, QoS, and so on)	-	-

Received Traffic Type	Processed in Packet Switching Engine	Processed by Line Card CPU	Processed by Route Processor
Transit Packets, IP Options	LPTS Policed	X	-
Transit Packets, IP Option "Router Alert"	LPTS Policed	X	X
Packets failed BGP TTL Security Hack (BTSH) and Generalized TTL Security Management (GTSM)	BTSH/GTSM	-	-
Packets that require ARP resolution	LPTS Policed	X	-
Unicast Receive Traffic			
ICMP echo request, packets requiring logging	LPTS Policed	X	-
Any other ICMP (also ICMP with options)	LPTS Policed	X	-
Management traffic (SSH, SNMP, XML, and so on)	LPTS Policed	-	X
Management traffic (Netflow, CDP)	LPTS Policed	X	-
Routing (BGP, OSPF, ISIS, and so on)	LPTS Policed	-	X
Multicast, Broadcast			
Multicast control traffic (OSPF, PIM, HSRP, and so on)	LPTS Policed	-	X
First packet of multicast stream	LPTS Policed	X	-
Broadcasts	LPTS Policed	X	X
Special Cases			
Traffic needing fragmentation	LPTS Policed	X	-
MPLS traffic needing fragmentation	LPTS Policed	X	-
L2 packets (keepalives and so on)	LPTS Policed	X	-

LPTS provides sort of a built-in firewall for an IOS XR router by taking preemptive measures for traffic flows destined to the router. The forthcoming discussions explain how LPTS provides its protection mechanisms.

Mechanics Behind LPTS: A High-Level Overview

Cisco IOS XR runs on platforms with a distributed architecture. Distributed architecture implies that the control plane and the forwarding planes are decoupled for meeting higher routing and forwarding performance objectives. As Table 6-3 in the preceding section shows, an IOS XR router might need to deliver different types of for_us packets to different nodes within the router. Additionally, IOS XR supports process placement on CRS-1 platforms using Distributed Route Processors (DRP). Therefore, a line card receiving a control plane packet needs to make complex decisions regarding the node to which a packet might need to be delivered, keeping in mind that the router may be using a DRP for distributing a control plane process. Furthermore, nonstop routing (NSR) features might require a control packet be replicated both to an active and a standby RP.

Figure 6-3 provides a high-level overview of LPTS.

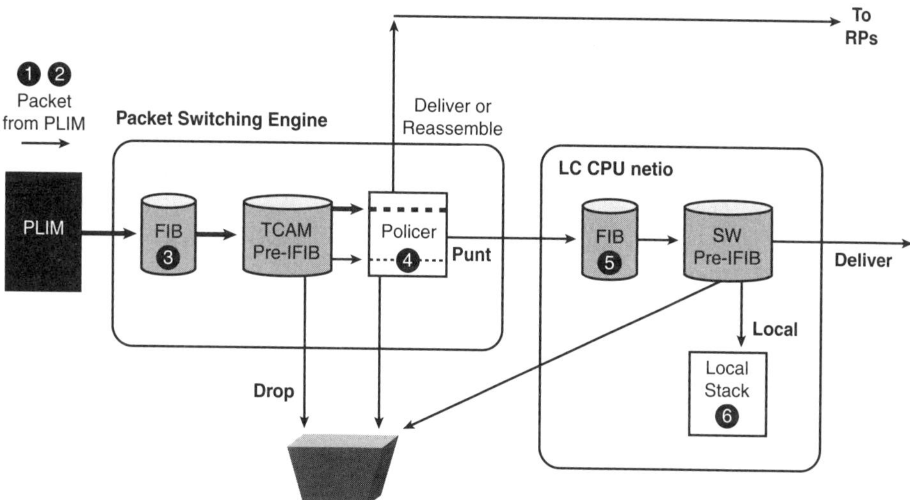

Figure 6-3 *Local Packet Transport Service*

The process follows:

1. On a CRS-1 router, the Physical layer Interface Module (PLIM) receives the frame.
2. On receiving the packet and performing the necessary layer 1 and 2 checks, the PLIM extracts the layer 3 packet and passes it to the forwarding ASIC or the *Packet Switching Engine (PSE)* as it is commonly called.
3. The L3 forwarding engine does a Forwarding Information Base (FIB) lookup and determines whether the packet is a locally destined for_us packet.
4. The LPTS infrastructure maintains tables in the line card's TCAM and also on the RP for handling the for_us packets. The table on the RP is a detailed list of all possible flows of traffic types that can be destined to the router. The detailed table on RP is called the *IFIB*. A smaller table that is a subset of IFIB exists on the line card and this table is referred to as the *pIFIB*. The pIFIB lists flows of critical traffic. These tables are populated by a set of processes known as a LPTS Port Arbitrator (lpts_pa) and LPTS flow manager (lpts_fm). A process called pifibm_server runs on the line card and is responsible for programming hardware for the policing values for different flows. To qualify for a match in the pIFIB, the incoming packet must exactly match the pIFIB table entry in a single lookup.
5. Consider a packet that arrives on a line card and a pIFIB lookup returns a full match. The packet then gets assigned a Fabric Group Identifier (FGID) allocated by the lpts_pa process. FGID serves as an identifier that helps a packet traverse the path through the various ASICs on the switch fabric to be delivered to FabricQ asic on the destination node from where the packet finds its way to the primary/standby RP, DRP, or the line card CPU. The destination node could also be an RP, a DRP, or the line card CPU of the line card on which the packet was received. In case a line card pIFIB entry results in a partial match the incoming packet is referred to the IFIB maintained on the RP.
6. The CPU on the RP, DRP, and line card run the software processes that decapsulate the packet and deliver them to the correct stack.

The discussion related to Figure 6-3 gives a simplified overview of LPTS mostly from the point of view of local packet delivery. However, a key feature of LPTS includes policing the locally destined flows to values deemed safe for CPU resources.

Consider Example 6-18, which shows the LPTS entries accompanying a BGP configuration.

Example 6-18 *BGP Entries in LPTS*

```
! show command indicating the committed BGP configuration
!
RP/0/RP1/CPU0:CRS1-1#show running-config router bgp
router bgp 102
 bgp router-id 192.168.254.1
```

```
  address-family ipv4 unicast
  !
  neighbor 65.10.20.1
   remote-as 101
   address-family ipv4 unicast
   !
  !
 !
 !
! Following show command shows the entries created in IFIB
RP/0/RP1/CPU0:CRS1-1#show lpts ifib brief ¦ include BGP
 BGP4      default  65.10.20.2.179 65.10.20.1.45  TCP   any          0/RP1/CPU0
 BGP4      default  any.179 65.10.20.1            TCP   any          0/RP1/CPU0
! Following show command shows entries in PIFIB.
! The output of the following show command is usually quite large and is
! modified to show only BGP entries in LPTS PIFIB
RP/0/RP1/CPU0:CRS1-1#show lpts pifib brief
RP/0/RP1/CPU0:CRS1-1#show lpts pifib brief
* - Any VRF; I - Local Interest;
X - Drop; R - Reassemble;
 Type        VRF-ID   Local, Remote Address.Port L4    Interface    Deliver
 -----       ----     ---------------          --.   -------      -------.
 ISIS        *         - -                     -     any          0/RP1/CPU0
 IPv4_frag   *        any any                  any   any          R
 IPv4        default  224.0.0.1 any            IGMP  Lo0          0/RP1/CPU0
 IPv4        default  224.0.0.2 any            IGMP  Lo0          0/RP1/CPU0
 IPv4        default  224.0.0.22 any           IGMP  Lo0          0/RP1/CPU0
 IPv4        default  any any                  IGMP  Lo0          0/RP1/CPU0
 IPv4        default  224.0.1.40.496 any       UDP   Lo0          0/RP1/CPU0
 IPv4        default  224.0.0.13 any           103   Lo0          [11295]
 IPv4        default  224.0.0.1 any            IGMP  Lo1          0/RP1/CPU0
 IPv4        default  224.0.0.2 any            IGMP  Lo1          0/RP1/CPU0
 IPv4        default  224.0.0.22 any           IGMP  Lo1          0/RP1/CPU0
 IPv4        default  any any                  IGMP  Lo1          0/RP1/CPU0
 IPv4        default  224.0.0.13 any           103   Lo1          [11295]
 IPv4        default  224.0.0.1 any            IGMP  Lo100        0/RP1/CPU0
 IPv4        default  224.0.0.2 any            IGMP  Lo100        0/RP1/CPU0
 IPv4        default  224.0.0.22 any           IGMP  Lo100        0/RP1/CPU0
 IPv4        default  any any                  IGMP  Lo100        0/RP1/CPU0
 IPv4        default  224.0.0.13 any           103   Lo100        [11295]
 IPv4        default  224.0.0.1 any            IGMP  Lo101        0/RP1/CPU0
 IPv4        default  224.0.0.2 any            IGMP  Lo101        0/RP1/CPU0
 IPv4        default  224.0.0.22 any           IGMP  Lo101        0/RP1/CPU0
 IPv4        default  any any                  IGMP  Lo101        0/RP1/CPU0
 IPv4        default  224.0.0.13 any           103   Lo101        [11295]
```

```
IPv4       default  224.0.0.1 any             IGMP  Lo10             0/RP1/CPU0
IPv4       default  224.0.0.2 any             IGMP  Lo10             0/RP1/CPU0
IPv4       default  224.0.0.22 any            IGMP  Lo10             0/RP1/CPU0
IPv4       default  any any                   IGMP  Lo10             0/RP1/CPU0
IPv4       default  224.0.0.13 any            103   Lo10             [11295]
IPv4       default  any.23 any                TCP   Mg0/RP1/CPU0/0   0/RP1/CPU0
IPv4       default  any.161 any               UDP   Mg0/RP1/CPU0/0   0/RP1/CPU0
IPv4       default  any.639 1.1.1.1           TCP   any              0/RP1/CPU0
IPv4       default  10.0.0.11.646 10.0.0.21.57 TCP  any              0/RP1/CPU0
IPv4       default  10.0.0.11.646 10.0.0.31.35 TCP  any              0/RP1/CPU0
IPv4       default  10.10.20.31.23 10.10.20.10 TCP  any              0/RP1/CPU0
IPv4       default  65.10.20.2.179 65.10.20.1. TCP  any              0/RP1/CPU0
IPv4       default  any.179 65.10.20.1        TCP   any              0/RP1/CPU0
IPv4       default  any.646 any               UDP   any              0/RP1/CPU0
IPv4       default  any.3232 any              UDP   any              [11295]
IPv4       default  any.3503 any              UDP   any              0/RP1/CPU0
IPv4       default  any.50051 any             UDP   any              0/RP1/CPU0
IPv4       default  any.50052 any             UDP   any              0/RP1/CPU0
IPv4       default  any.50053 any             UDP   any              0/RP1/CPU0
IPv4       default  any.50054 any             UDP   any              0/RP1/CPU0
IPv4       default  any any                   103   any              [11295]
IPv4       default  any any                   115   any              0/RP1/CPU0
IPv4       default  any any                   255   any              0/RP1/CPU0
IPv4       *        any.ECHO any              ICMP  any              XI
IPv4       *        any.TSTAMP any            ICMP  any              XI
IPv4       *        any.MASKREQ any           ICMP  any              XI
IPv4       *        any any.179               TCP   any              0/RP1/CPU0
IPv4       *        any.179 any               TCP   any              0/RP1/CPU0
IPv4       *        any any                   TCP   any              0/RP1/CPU0
IPv4       *        any any                   UDP   any              0/RP1/CPU0
IPv4       *        224.0.0.5 any             OSPF  any              0/RP1/CPU0
IPv4       *        224.0.0.6 any             OSPF  any              0/RP1/CPU0
IPv4       *        any any                   OSPF  any              0/RP1/CPU0
IPv4       *        any any                   any   any              0/RP1/CPU0
IPv6_frag  *        any any                   any   any              R
IPv6       *        any any.179               TCP   any              0/RP1/CPU0
IPv6       *        any.179 any               TCP   any              0/RP1/CPU0
IPv6       *        any any                   TCP   any              0/RP1/CPU0
IPv6       *        any any                   UDP   any              0/RP1/CPU0
IPv6       *        any.ECHOREQ any           ICMP6 any              XI
IPv6       *        any.NDRTRSLCT any         ICMP6 any              XI
IPv6       *        any.NDRTRADV any          ICMP6 any              XI
IPv6       *        any.NDNBRSLCT any         ICMP6 any              XI
IPv6       *        any.NDNBRADV any          ICMP6 any              XI
IPv6       *        any.NDREDIRECT any        ICMP6 any              XI
```

```
 IPv6        *         ff02::5 any             OSPF   any           0/RP1/CPU0
 IPv6        *         ff02::6 any             OSPF   any           0/RP1/CPU0
 IPv6        *         any any                 OSPF   any           0/RP1/CPU0
 IPv6        *         any any                 any    any           0/RP1/CPU0
RP/0/RP1/CPU0:CRS1-1#! Hardware Policing values in pifib
!
RP/0/RP1/CPU0:CRS1-1#show lpts pifib hardware police location 0/0/cpu0
-------------------------------------------------------------------------------
                Node 0/0/CPU0:
-------------------------------------------------------------------------------
 Burst = 100ms for all flow types
-------------------------------------------------------------------------------
FlowType                 Policer  Type     Cur. Rate  Def. Rate  Accepted  Dropped
-----------------------  -------  -------  ---------  ---------  --------  -------
unconfigured-default     100      Static   500        500        0         0
Fragment                 106      Static   1000       1000       0         0
OSPF-mc-known            107      Static   20000      20000      248647    0
OSPF-mc-default          111      Static   5000       5000       43431     0
OSPF-uc-known            161      Static   5000       5000       0         0
OSPF-uc-default          162      Static   1000       1000       0         0
ISIS-known               108      Static   20000      20000      536237    0
ISIS-default             112      Static   5000       5000       4         0
BGP-known                113      Static   25000      25000      41        0
BGP-cfg-peer             114      Static   10000      10000      5         0
BGP-default              115      Static   10000      10000      54        0
PIM-mcast                116      Static   23000      23000      0         0
PIM-ucast                117      Static   10000      10000      0         0
IGMP                     118      Static   3500       3500       0         0
ICMP-local               119      Static   2500       2500       20        0
ICMP-app                 120      Static   2500       2500       0         0
na                       164      Static   2500       2500       0         0
ICMP-default             121      Static   2500       2500       0         0
LDP-TCP-known            122      Static   25000      25000      290       0
LDP-TCP-cfg-peer         152      Static   10000      10000      0         0
LDP-TCP-default          154      Static   10000      10000      0         0
LDP-UDP                  158      Static   2500       2500       519490    0
All-routers              160      Static   10000      10000      0         0
LMP-TCP-known            123      Static   25000      25000      0         0
LMP-TCP-cfg-peer         153      Static   10000      10000      0         0
LMP-TCP-default          155      Static   10000      10000      0         0
LMP-UDP                  159      Static   2500       2500       0         0
RSVP-UDP                 124      Static   7000       7000       0         0
RSVP                     125      Static   7000       7000       0         0
IKE                      126      Static   1000       1000       0         0
IPSEC-known              128      Static   3000       3000       0         0
```

```
IPSEC-default           127     Static   1000    1000    0     0
MSDP-known              129     Static   1000    1000    0     0
MSDP-cfg-peer           130     Static   1000    1000    0     0
MSDP-default            131     Static   1000    1000    0     0
SNMP                    132     Static   2000    2000    0     0
NTP                     133     Static   500     500     0     0
SSH-known               134     Static   1000    1000    0     0
SSH-default             135     Static   1000    1000    0     0
HTTP-known              137     Static   1000    1000    0     0
HTTP-default            138     Static   1000    1000    0     0
SHTTP-known             139     Static   1000    1000    0     0
IFIB_FT_SHTTP_DEFAULT   140     Static   1000    1000    0     0
TELNET-known            141     Static   1000    1000    0     0
TELNET-default          142     Static   1000    1000    0     0
CSS-known               143     Static   1000    1000    0     0
CSS-default             144     Static   1000    1000    0     0
RSH-known               145     Static   1000    1000    0     0
RSH-default             146     Static   1000    1000    0     0
UDP-known               147     Static   25000   25000   0     0
UDP-listen              156     Static   4000    4000    0     0
UDP-cfg-peer            157     Static   4000    4000    0     0
UDP-default             101     Static   500     500     69    0
TCP-known               148     Static   25000   25000   0     0
TCP-listen              149     Static   25000   25000   0     0
TCP-cfg-peer            150     Static   25000   25000   0     0
TCP-default             102     Static   500     500     60    0
Mcast-known             151     Static   25000   25000   0     0
Mcast-default           103     Static   500     500     0     0
Raw-listen              104     Static   500     500     0     0
Raw-default             105     Static   500     500     0     0
Ip-Sla                  163     Static   10000   10000   0     0
EIGRP                   109     Static   20000   20000   0     0
RIP                     110     Static   20000   20000   0     0
L2TPv3                  165     Static   3000    3000    0     0
na                      166     Static   100     100     0     0
------------
statistics:
Packets accepted by deleted entries: 1188045
Packets dropped by deleted entries: 0
Run out of statistics counter errors: 0
```

Example 6-18 configures BGP and uses it to demonstrate the LPTS concept. The example creates a BGP process for AS 102 and configures a neighbor 65.10.20.2. On configuring a BGP peer, LPTS creates a flow for the configured peer with TCP port 179. A BGP flow is also created in pIFIB with a destination node of 0/RP1/CPU0 because the BGP routing protocol runs on the RP of the router and the active RP is the destination node for BGP packets.

Example 6-18 shows the policer in line card hardware and shows three different policers for BGP, which exist regardless of BGP configuration. Policer 113 in the example for BGP flow type BGP-known signifies a well established BGP session that actively participates in BGP route advertisement. Policer 114 BGP-cfg-peer represents a new session or recently established session that has not yet elevated to a level of an established session. BGP-default identified by policer 115 represents a default entry for BGP flow. This flow also helps with any latency in hardware programming for new configurations or accounts for a TCP session that might be initiated to port 179 for debugging purposes. The example shows a higher policer rate of 25,000 packets per second (pps) for established sessions compared to 10,000 pps for all other categories of BGP traffic flows.

Configuring LPTS

The LPTS discussion so far has focused on default policers preprogrammed in hardware TCAMs on CRS-1 line cards. Release 3.6 of IOS XR provides the user the ability to configure LPTS policer values. The general syntax for LPTS policer configurations is listed as follows:

lpts pifib hardware police [**location** *node-id*]
flow {*flow_type*} {**rate** *rate*}

The flow rate is in packets per second (pps).

Example 6-19 demonstrates LPTS configuration.

Example 6-19 *Configuring LPTS BGP-default Policer Value to 1000 PPS*

```
RP/0/RP1/CPU0:CRS1-1(config)#lpts pifib hardware police
RP/0/RP1/CPU0:CRS1-1(config-pifib-policer-global)#flow bgp default rate 1000
RP/0/RP1/CPU0:CRS1-1(config-pifib-policer-global)#commit
!
! show command to verify newly configured LPTS policer values
!
RP/0/RP1/CPU0:CRS1-1#show lpts pifib hardware police location 0/0/cpu0 | inc BGP
BGP-known              113     Static   25000      25000      0         0
BGP-cfg-peer           114     Static   10000      10000      0         0
BGP-default            115     Global   1000       10000      237       0
```

Example 6-19 shows a configuration change applied globally to all the line cards in the SDR or logical router to change the policer for BGP-default flow. Alternatively, a configuration may be created for a particular line card location that has the effect of overwriting the global LPTS policing configuration only for the location for which it is created.

Summary

This chapter discussed Cisco IOS XR security aspects. In this chapter we explored the AAA feature and its configuration aspects that are used in managing access to a router running the IOS XR operating system. Although the concepts of AAA are independent of platform and operating system, IOS XR exhibits key characteristics of a large-scale operating system that has unique requirements, such as elaborate access policies. This chapter introduced the IOS XR concepts of predefined users such as root-system, root-lr, netadmin, and cisco-support—each of which has well-defined roles and privileges.

IOS XR's AAA model contains the notion of task permissions for any control, configure, or monitor operation. Tasks are represented as task IDs. A task ID defines the permission to execute an operation for a given user. If the user is associated with a task ID through a user group, that user can execute any of the operations associated with that task ID. All IOS XR CLI are associated with one or more task IDs. Task IDs always imply granted permission and not denied ones. Furthermore, task IDs are always associated with one of the task classes: READ, WRITE, EXECUTE, or DEBUG.

AAA provides transparent use of local, on-the-box authentication as well as remote authentication done with an external TACACS+ or RADIUS server.

This chapter also briefly introduced Secure Shell (SSH), access lists, and uRPF features. This chapter elucidated the concepts behind Local Packet Transport Service (LPTS) in providing an integral firewall for the IOS XR running router.

References

- **Cisco.** Configuring AAA Services on Cisco IOS XR Software. http://www.cisco.com/
- **Cisco.** Implementing Management Plane Protection on Cisco IOS XR Software. http://www.cisco.com/
- **Cisco.** Implementing LPTS on Cisco IOS XR Software. http://www.cisco.com/
- **Cisco.** Implementing Access Lists and Prefix Lists on Cisco IOS XR Software. http://www.cisco.com/

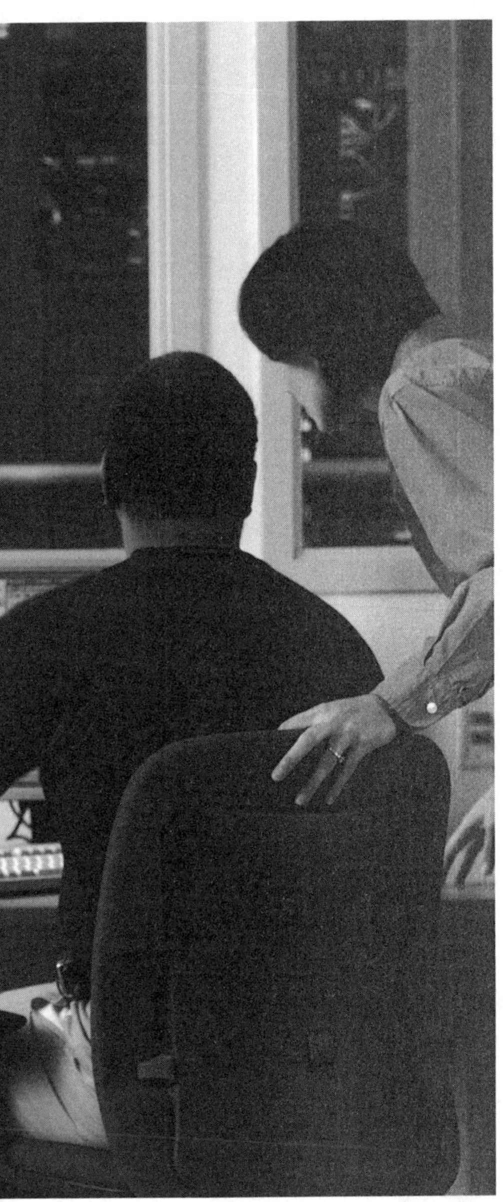

This chapter covers the following topics:

- Routing Information Protocol
- Enhanced Interior Gateway Routing Protocol
- Open Shortest Path First
- Intermediate System to Intermediate System
- References

CHAPTER 7

Routing IGP

An Interior Gateway Protocol (IGP) is used for exchanging routing information between network elements within a single administrative domain (also known as an *autonomous system* or AS). IGP-based routing protocols distribute routing information throughout the AS and consist of either flat or hierarchical network topologies. Four commonly used IGPs are Routing Information Protocol (RIP), Open Shortest Path First (OSPF), Enhanced Interior Gateway Routing Protocol (EIGRP), and Intermediate System to Intermediate System (IS-IS).

Routing protocols are generally categorized as distance vector or link state protocols. Distance vector protocols use routing distance to choose the best path between source and destination. They exchange their entire routing information periodically between all of their neighbors and consume more link bandwidth. Link state protocols, on the other hand, send updates only on link state change and exchange only the routing information that changed between the previous update and the latest update.

This chapter examines the underlying technologies and implementation of different IGPs in IOS XR. It also discusses the steps required for base configuration, authentication, route-policy, and process info, and troubleshooting guidelines with focus on the **show** and **debug** commands.

Routing Information Protocol

RIP is a UDP-based distance vector protocol that broadcasts routes using port number 520. RIP sends out the routing updates at an interval called the *route-update interval* every 60 seconds. It expects the neighbor to send the updates with the same frequency. Routing updates are also sent in the event of any network change. RIP supports different timers—specifically, a timer to control the frequency of the route update and a timer to invalidate a RIP route. This section describes fundamental concepts, and the differences between RIP version 1 (RIPv1) and RIP version 2 (RIPv2), before explaining how to configure RIP for IOS XR.

Understanding RIP Fundamentals

RIP uses a simple hop-count as a metric to compare and compute alternative paths and is limited to networks with diameter of up to 15 hops. A route advertised with distance metric of 16 is marked as invalid and considered unreachable. This value is called infinity because it is larger than the maximum allowable value of 15 for the protocol metric. RIP is generally not the best choice of routing protocol, especially when intelligent route update and calculation method that can incorporate link characteristics for metric are desired.

Unlike other IGP protocols, RIP does not form neighbor relationship (adjacency). Passive configuration command is used in conjunction with RIP to prevent routing updates from being sent out on a given interface. However RIP continues to receive routing updates through that interface from its neighbor.

RIP Versions

Currently, two versions of RIP exist: RIPv1 and RIPv2. Both of these protocols can carry maximum of 25 routes in the protocol packet headers. RIPv1 does not support any subnet masks. In the absence of subnet masks, RIPv1 advertises classful subnets if network addresses fall at major class boundary. If the network addresses do not fall at the major class boundary, the subnet mask of the interface closest to that network address is chosen. RIPv1 does not provide any security against any malicious attacks; there is no check in RIP for the source of the routes received by the router.

RIPv2 eliminates some of the constraints seen with RIPv1 because it supports features such as routing domains, external route tags, route summarization, route distribution, variable length subnet masks (VLSM), next hop addresses, and authentication. Authentication support exists for both clear-text and MD5 and hence is a significant improvement over RIPv1. In comparison with the broadcast updates of RIPv1, RIPv2 packets might be multicast as well. The use of a multicast address (224.0.0.9) reduces the unnecessary processing load on network devices that do not support RIP routing.

RIP is a stable, simple, and easy-to-configure protocol that is compatible with wide varieties of network devices and is still widely deployed in legacy and small or stub networks. IOS XR by default supports RIPv2.

Configuring RIP in Cisco IOS XR

As a first step, IOS XR requires building a target configuration. After the target configuration is built, the user needs to issue an explicit commit to add it to the running configuration of the router. RIP configuration is simplified in IOS XR. Unlike IOS where network addresses are configured under RIP protocol configuration, in IOS XR only the interfaces that are to participate in RIP are configured under the routing process.

The RIP process gets started the moment RIP is configured on the router. After initialization of the process, the configuration is parsed to find interfaces that need to be enabled for RIP.

Figure 7-1 shows a setup that has two routers connected back-to-back over 10 Gigabit Ethernet interfaces. A loopback and a 10 Gigabit Ethernet interface are configured on CRS-1 and a 10 Gigabit Ethernet interface is configured on CRS-2.

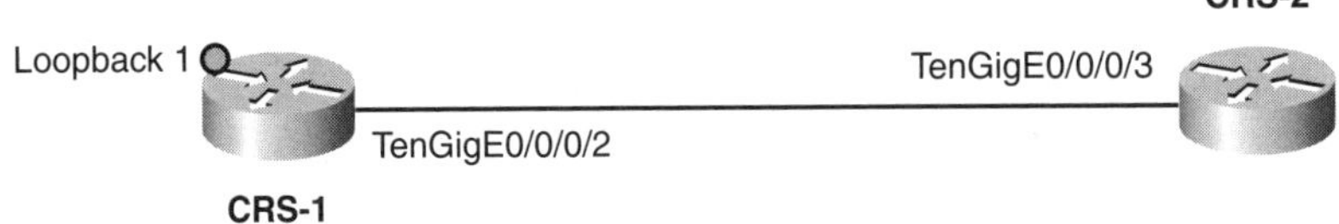

Figure 7-1 *Two Connected Routers*

Note: In Cisco IOS XR, routing protocols can be configured before the interfaces are configured with the IP addresses. However, the routing protocol becomes active only after the network address is configured on at least one of the interfaces.

Example 7-1 shows the configuration for enabling RIP on loopback and 10 Gigabit Ethernet interface on CRS-1. The configuration specific to RIP can be queried by extending the **show running-config** command with the **router rip** option.

Example 7-1 *RIP Configuration on Cisco IOS XR*

```
!Snippet of the base config for CRS-1 and CRS-2

RP/0/RP0/CPU0:CRS-1#show running-config
!
interface Loopback1
 ipv4 address 172.16.1.1 255.255.255.255
!
interface TenGigE0/0/0/2
 ipv4 address 10.0.0.1 255.255.255.0

RP/0/RP0/CPU0:CRS-2# show running-config
!
interface TenGigE0/0/0/3
ipv4 address 10.0.0.2 255.255.255.0

!Now enable RIP on Loopback and TenGigabitEthernet interfaces on CRS-1. Similar
  configuration will be applied on CRS-2

RP/0/RP0/CPU0:CRS-1#conf t
RP/0/RP0/CPU0:CRS-1(config)#router rip
RP/0/RP0/CPU0:CRS-1(config-rip)#interface TenGigE0/0/0/2
RP/0/RP0/CPU0:CRS-1(config-rip-if)#interface Loopback1
RP/0/RP0/CPU0:CRS-1(config-rip-if)#end
Uncommitted changes found, commit them before exiting(yes/no/cancel)? [cancel]:yes
RP/0/RP0/CPU0:CRS-1#

! Displays the rip config which was committed

RP/0/RP0/CPU0:CRS-1#show running-config router rip
router rip
 interface Loopback1
 !
 interface TenGigE0/0/0/2
```

```
 !
RP/0/RP0/CPU0:CRS-1#
```

Configuring Route Policy Language

Route Policy Language (RPL) is used in conjunction with RIP to perform different functionalities. It can be used to set different metrics during redistribution or to filter routing updates from neighboring routers. There are two options in RIP to change the RIP metric: **set rip-metric**, which changes the metric of the route to the newly configured value, and the **add rip-metric** option, which updates the original metric by an offset defined as per the configuration. Example 7-2 shows the usage of routing policy to set the metric for redistributed routes.

Example 7-2 *Redistribution Using* **route-policy**

```
!Configure the route-policy named metric1 which sets a metric for redistributed
  routes

RP/0/RP0/CPU0:CRS-1(config)#route-policy metric1
RP/0/RP0/CPU0:CRS-1(config-rpl)#set rip-metric 5
RP/0/RP0/CPU0:CRS-1(config-rpl)#end-policy
RP/0/RP0/CPU0:CRS-1(config)#commit

!Apply the route-policy metric1 for redistributed routes

RP/0/RP0/CPU0:CRS-1(config)#router rip
RP/0/RP0/CPU0:CRS-1(config-rip)#redistribute static route-policy metric1
RP/0/RP0/CPU0:CRS-1(config-rip)#commit
```

Example 7-3 provides the syntax to configure a route policy used to filter routes. IOS XR supports the **add rip-metric** option of the RPL to change the metric values for RIP.

Example 7-3 *Route Filtering Using route-policy and the* **add rip-metric** *Option*

```
!Lets configure the prefix-set to filter a specific route from the updates

RP/0/RP0/CPU0:CRS-2(config)#prefix-set route1
RP/0/RP0/CPU0:CRS-2(config-pfx)#172.16.1.1/32
RP/0/RP0/CPU0:CRS-2(config-pfx)#end-set
RP/0/RP0/CPU0:CRS-2(config)#commit

!Lets define the route-policy to allow the route defined by prefix-set route1
```

```
RP/0/RP0/CPU0:CRS-2(config)#route-policy filter1
RP/0/RP0/CPU0:CRS-2(config-rpl)#if destination in route1 then
RP/0/RP0/CPU0:CRS-2(config-rpl-if)#pass
RP/0/RP0/CPU0:CRS-2(config-rpl-if)#endif
RP/0/RP0/CPU0:CRS-2(config-rpl)#end-policy

!Apply the route-policy metric1 to rip for incoming routes

RP/0/RP0/CPU0:CRS-2(config)#router rip
RP/0/RP0/CPU0:CRS-2(config-rip)#route-policy filter1 in
RP/0/RP0/CPU0:CRS-2(config-rip)#commit

!Add rip-metric option of RPL is used to change the metric

RP/0/RP0/CPU0:CRS-1(config-rpl)#add rip-metric ?
  <0-16>     decimal number
  parameter  '$' followed by alphanumeric characters
```

Configuring Passive Interface

Passive interfaces in RIP do not advertise routing updates. Example 7-4 provides the syntax to configure a passive interface.

Example 7-4 *Passive Interface Configuration*

```
RP/0/RP0/CPU0:CRS-1(config)#router rip
RP/0/RP0/CPU0:CRS-1(config-rip)#interface TenGigE0/0/0/2
RP/0/RP0/CPU0:CRS-1(config-rip-if)#passive-interface
```

Restarting, Shutting Down, and Blocking RIP

RIP is defined as a cold restart process because the RIP process on the standby RP is not fully initialized. The RIP process can be restarted, shut down, blocked, or started and it can use the checkpoint recovery mechanism of IOS XR to recover. RIP is nonstop forwarding (NSF)–aware, and therefore it can be restarted without impacting data traffic or RIB. It can be monitored using the **show process rip** command.

Examples 7-5 through 7-7 provide the IOS XR commands to restart, shut down, and block the RIP process. The **show process rip** command is used to know the state of the process, and to know the job ID that can be used in conjunction with other commands.

Example 7-5 *RIP Process Status on Active RP*

```
RP/0/RP0/CPU0:CRS-1#show processes rip
                    Job Id: 235
                       PID: 14717173
           Executable path: /disk0/hfr-rout-3.6.1/bin/rip
                Instance #: 1
```

```
                Version ID: 00.00.0000
                   Respawn: ON
             Respawn count: 11
    Max. spawns per minute: 12
              Last started: Wed Nov 12 06:11:08 2008
             Process state: Run (last exit due to SIGTERM)
             Package state: Normal
         Started on config: cfg/gl/rip/ord_A/default/ord_d/config
                      core: TEXT SHAREDMEM MAINMEM
                 Max. core: 0
                 Placement: ON
              startup_path: /pkg/startup/ipv4_rip.startup
                     Ready: 0.678s
         Process cpu time: 0.204 user, 0.116 kernel, 0.320 total
JID    TID  Stack pri state        TimeInState      HR:MM:SS:MSEC NAME
235    1      40K  10 Receive       0:00:03:0731     0:00:00:0190 rip
235    2      40K  10 Receive       0:00:03:0741     0:00:00:0010 rip
235    3      40K  10 Receive       0:00:03:0870     0:00:00:0002 rip
235    4      40K  10 Receive       0:00:03:0732     0:00:00:0002 rip
235    5      40K  10 Receive       0:00:03:0849     0:00:00:0000 rip
-------------------------------------------------------------------------------
RP/0/RP0/CPU0:CRS-1#
```

A RIP process can be restarted, shut down, or blocked using the job ID or the **rip** keyword as shown in Example 7-6.

Example 7-6 *RIP Restart, Shut Down, or Block Process*

```
RP/0/RP0/CPU0:CRS-1#process shutdown rip
RP/0/RP0/CPU0:CRS-1#process blocked 235
RP/0/RP0/CPU0:CRS-1#process restart rip
```

Example 7-7 shows that the standby RIP process is not fully initialized and stays in the queue state.

Example 7-7 *Status of Process Running on Standby RP*

```
RP/0/RP0/CPU0:CRS-1# show processes rip detail location 0/RP1/CPU0---------
                    Job Id: 235
           Executable path: /disk0/hfr-rout-3.6.1/bin/rip
                Instance #: 1
                Version ID: 00.00.0000
                   Respawn: ON
             Respawn count: 0
    Max. spawns per minute: 12
              Last started: Not yet spawned
```

```
            Process state: Queued
            Package state: Normal
        Registered item(s): cfg/gl/rip/
                     core: TEXT SHAREDMEM MAINMEM
                Max. core: 0
                Placement: ON
             startup_path: /pkg/startup/ipv4_rip.startup
             Running path: /disk0/hfr-rout-3.6.1/bin/rip
             Package path: /pkg/bin/rip
   Node redundancy state: standby
              Job-id-link: 235
                group_jid: 1880,0,0,0
               fail_count: 0
                 this pcb: 481fe010
                 next pcb: 60218800
             jobid on RP: 0
```

Verifying and Troubleshooting RIP

Example 7-8 illustrates some of the **show** commands that can be used to verify and troubleshoot RIP on IOS XR.

Example 7-8 *RIP Verification*

```
!Display the information for interfaces enabled for RIP and the version configured


RP/0/RP0/CPU0:CRS-1#show rip interface tenGigE 0/0/0/2

TenGigE0_0_0_2
Rip enabled?:                   Yes
Out-of-memory state:            Normal
Broadcast for V2:               No
Accept Metric 0?:               No
Send versions:                  2
Receive versions:               2
Interface state:                Up
IP address:                     10.0.0.1/24
Metric Cost:                    0
Split horizon:                  Enabled
Poison Reverse:                 Disabled
Socket set options:
    Joined multicast group?:    Yes
    LPTS filter set?:           Yes
RIP peers attached to this interface:
    10.0.0.2
```

```
        uptime: 716    version: 2
        packets discarded: 0    routes discarded: 1


!Display the topology database for RIP on the neighboring router CRS-2

RP/0/RP0/CPU0:CRS-2#show rip database

Routes held in RIP's topology database:
10.0.0.0/24
    [0]    directly connected, TenGigE0/0/0/3
10.0.0.0/8    auto-summary
172.16.1.1/32
    [1] via 10.0.0.1, next hop 10.0.0.1, Uptime: 26s, TenGigE0/0/0/3
172.16.0.0/16    auto-summary
```

Table 7-1 lists some of the key RIP commands in IOS XR.

Table 7-1 *RIP Operation and Debug Commands*

Command	Description
show route rip	Displays the RIP routes that are installed in RIB
show rip statistics **show rip** [**vrf** {**vrf** / **all**}] **statistics** \	Provides the statistics on the sent/received RIP packets
clear rip [**vrf** {**vrf** / **all**}]	Clears the RIP database
debug rip {**auth** | **database** | **events** | **global** | **im** | **oom** | **policy** | **receive** | **rib** | **send** | **show**} [**interface** *type instance*] [**vrf** {**all** | *vrf-name*}]	Used for debugging a RIP database

Note: Cutover, or *switchover*, is a process by which the standby RP assumes control of the system after a failure of the active RP, after removal of the active RP, or as a result of an operator command. Cutover can be planned, as in the case of scheduled maintenance, or unplanned, as in the case of a failure.

Enhanced Interior Gateway Routing Protocol

EIGRP is a distance vector protocol that runs on port number 88. Even though it is considered an IGP, it can also be used for interdomain routing. In addition to variable-length subnet mask (VLSM), route summarization, route tags, and neighbor discovery mechanism, the features that distinguish this protocol from other routing protocols are its fast convergence, low network usage, partial update of the routing table, and support for multiple network layer protocols. This section describes basic EIGRP concepts before outlining the configuration options for EIGRP in IOS XR.

Understanding EIGRP Fundamentals

EIGRP uses 224.0.0.10 as the multicast address for the routing update. EIGRP interface can be active or passive. Active interfaces advertise connected prefixes and form adjacencies with neighbors, whereas passive interfaces only advertise and do not form any neighbor relationship. It uses a distance metric that is a composite metric calculated using available bandwidth, delay, load utilization, and link reliability. Optimal path can be achieved by modifying the link characteristics used in the calculation of the distance metric. By default, the EIGRP metric is a 32-bit quantity.

EIGRP has five types of packets: Hello/Acks, Update, Queries, Replies, and Requests. Goodbye message is another useful message used by EIGRP that helps with faster network convergence. This broadcast message is sent out in the event of EIGRP routing process shutdown and informs adjacent peers about the changed topology. This feature allows supporting EIGRP peers to recompute neighbor relationships more efficiently than would have happened at hold timer expiry.

EIGRP has four basic components: Neighbor Discovery/Recovery, Reliable Transport Protocol (RTP), Diffusing Update Algorithm (DUAL), and Protocol Dependent Modules. This section describes each.

Neighbor Discovery/Recovery

Neighbor discovery/recovery is a process used to discover directly connected neighbors, and is also a method to declare neighbors unreachable or nonfunctional. Discovery/recovery is achieved through small size hello packets sent at periodic intervals.

EIGRP supports secondary IP addresses on the interface, but sources hello packets only from the primary subnet. Neighbors are declared adjacent after exchange of hellos if they have the same AS number, the source IP of the received hello has the same subnet as one of the primary connected interfaces, the K values match, and if they are authenticated successfully. K values are constant values used as multipliers in the calculation of metrics for distance.

Reliable Transport Protocol

The Cisco proprietary TCP-based Reliable Transport Protocol (RTP) is the transport layer that facilitates ordered delivery of EIGRP packets. It allows mixed and reliable delivery of unicast and multicast packets and helps with fast convergence when links with variable speeds are involved in the network. The DUAL algorithm tracks the different routes advertized by the neighbors and uses the EIGRP metrics to calculate the best routes. It is different from other routing protocols in that routing calculations are shared among multiple routers. A router sends routing updates of directly connected routes, instead of every route in the network. In addition it sends an update of a particular route only if a topology change has occurred to that specific route and then is sent to relevant neighbor routers, but not to all routers. This reduces the route computation time by a significant amount.

Diffusing Update Algorithm

DUAL inserts the route into the routing table based on a feasible successor. The *successor* is the neighboring router that would be used for packet forwarding, has the least cost path to a destination, and is not part of a routing loop. DUAL identifies feasible successors after each topology change. A feasible successor is viewed as a neighbor that is downstream with respect to the destination. If a feasible successor exists, it will use any route it finds to avoid any unnecessary recomputation. Lowering recomputation helps reduce processor utilization as well as lower overall convergence time.

Protocol-Dependent Modules

Protocol-dependent modules are used for network layer protocol-specific requirements. This informs DUAL of the protocol-specific messages and route selection related decisions are impacted by this configuration.

The outcome of all EIGRP operations is captured in two tables: a neighbor table and a topology table. A neighbor table stores information about neighbors, hold timer, and sequence numbers used for reliable transmission. A topology table is populated by a protocol-dependent module and is used by DUAL. It records all the advertisements by neighbors along with the metric information.

With such key capabilities to converge fast, low bandwidth utilization, low process utilization, and reliable transmission, EIGRP is one of the most efficient routing protocols available.

Configuring EIGRP in Cisco IOS XR

EIGRP in IOS XR supports both IPv4 and IPv6 address families. Refer to Figure 7-1. In this case CRS-1 and CRS-2 will be configured to form the EIGRP neighbors for IPv4. This can be achieved by enabling the required interfaces under IPv4 address family.

Example 7-9 shows the basic steps required to configure EIGRP in IOS XR.

Example 7-9 *EIGRP Configuration in IOS XR*

```
!Snippet of the base config for CRS-1 and CRS-2

RP/0/RP0/CPU0:CRS-1#show running-config
!
interface Loopback1
 ipv4 address 172.16.1.1 255.255.255.255
!
```

```
interface TenGigE0/0/0/2
 ipv4 address 10.0.0.1 255.255.255.0

RP/0/RP0/CPU0:CRS-2#show running-config
!
interface TenGigE0/0/0/3
ipv4 address 10.0.0.2 255.255.255.0


!Now enable EIGRP for loopback and TenGigabitEthernet interfaces on CRS-1 and
  similar configuration is applied on CRS-2

RP/0/RP0/CPU0:CRS-1#conf t
RP/0/RP0/CPU0:CRS-1(config)#router eigrp 1
RP/0/RP0/CPU0:CRS-1(config-eigrp)#address-family ipv4
RP/0/RP0/CPU0:CRS-1(config-eigrp-af)# interface Loopback1
RP/0/RP0/CPU0:CRS-1(config-eigrp-af-if)# !
RP/0/RP0/CPU0:CRS-1(config-eigrp-af-if)# interface TenGigE0/0/0/2
RP/0/RP0/CPU0:CRS-1(config-eigrp-af-if)#end
Uncommitted changes found, commit them before exiting(yes/no/cancel)? [cancel]:yes
RP/0/RP0/CPU0:CRS-1#

! Use the following command to verify the eigrp config

RP/0/RP0/CPU0:CRS-1#show running-config router eigrp
router eigrp 1
 address-family ipv4
  interface Loopback1
  !
  interface TenGigE0/0/0/2
  !
 !
!
```

Configuring Routing Policy

Example 7-10 gives the steps to use routing policy to set the EIGRP metric for redistributed routes. The addition of **eigrp-metric** with **route-policy** is another way of changing the EIGRP metric values.

Example 7-10 *Set Metric for Redistributed Routes Using route-policy and add eigrp-metric*

```
!Now configure the route-policy metric1 and set the different eigrp metric which
  will be used for redistributed routes
```

```
RP/0/RP0/CPU0:CRS-1(config)#route-policy metric1
RP/0/RP0/CPU0:CRS-1(config-rpl)#set eigrp-metric 5000 50 255 100 1500
RP/0/RP0/CPU0:CRS-1(config-rpl)#end
RP/0/RP0/CPU0:CRS-1(config)#commit

!Apply the route-policy metric1 for redistributed routes

RP/0/RP0/CPU0:CRS-1(config)#router eigrp 1
RP/0/RP0/CPU0:CRS-1(config-eigrp)#address-family ipv4
RP/0/RP0/CPU0:CRS-1(config-eigrp-af)#redistribute static route-policy metric1
RP/0/RP0/CPU0:CRS-1(config-eigrp-af)#commit

!add eigrp-metric support in route-policy metric1 for redistributed routes

RP/0/RP0/CPU0:CRS-1(config)#route-policy metric1
RP/0/RP0/CPU0:CRS-1(config-rpl)#add eigrp-metric ?
  <0-4294967295>  Bandwidth in Kbits per second
```

Configuring Router ID

Cisco IOS XR offers options in EIGRP configuration to set the same or a different router ID for different address families. Example 7-11 shows the steps required to set the same router ID for the IPv4 address family. You can follow the same procedure to set the IPv6 router ID under the IPv6 address family.

Example 7-11 *Configuring Router ID*

```
!Now configure the loopback address as the ipv4 router-id of EIGRP


RP/0/RP0/CPU0:CRS-2#conf t
RP/0/RP0/CPU0:CRS-2(config)#router eigrp 1
RP/0/RP0/CPU0:CRS-2(config-eigrp)#address-family ipv4
RP/0/RP0/CPU0:CRS-2(config-eigrp-af)#router-id 172.16.1.1
RP/0/RP0/CPU0:CRS-2(config)#commit

!show eigrp accounting can be used to verify the router-id of EIGRP with the
  new value

RP/0/RP0/CPU0:CRS-1#show eigrp ipv4 accounting

IPv4-EIGRP accounting for AS(1)/ID(172.16.1.1)

Total Prefix Count: 3  States: A-Adjacency, P-Pending, D-Down
State Address/Source        Interface          Prefix   Restart   Restart/
                                                 Count     Count    Reset(s)
 A    Redistributed         --                  1        0         0
```

Configuring and Verifying NSF

Cisco IOS XR EIGRP supports NSF, which is enabled by default. As long as the neighboring routers are NSF aware, data traffic will not be impacted on an RP cutover scenario. NSF timers can be changed using the **timers** parameters under EIGRP NSF configuration. This feature helps EIGRP to achieve high availability under different fault scenarios such as the EIGRP process failure or RP cutover. Example 7-12 shows how to verify and configure NSF.

Example 7-12 *Verify and Configure NSF*

```
! Show protocols eigrp displays the NSF capability of EIGRP

RP/0/RP0/CPU0:CRS-1#show protocols eigrp

Routing Protocol: EIGRP, instance 1
 Default context AS: 1, Router ID: 192.168.254.3
  Address Family: IPv4
   Default networks not flagged in outgoing updates
   Default networks not accepted from incoming updates
   Distance: internal 90, external 170
   Maximum paths: 4
   EIGRP metric weight K1=1, K2=0, K3=1, K4=0, K5=0
   EIGRP maximum hopcount 100
   EIGRP maximum metric variance 1
   EIGRP NSF: enabled
    NSF-aware route hold timer is 240s
    NSF signal timer is 20s
    NSF converge timer is 120s
    Time since last restart is 00:31:37
   SIA Active timer is 180s
   Interfaces:
    Loopback1
    TenGigE0/0/0/2

! Changing NSF timers for EIGRP

RP/0/RP0/CPU0:CRS-1(config-rip)#router eigrp 1
RP/0/RP0/CPU0:CRS-1(config-eigrp)#address-family ipv4
RP/0/RP0/CPU0:CRS-1(config-eigrp-af)#timers nsf ?
  converge    Route converge time
  route-hold  Route hold time for inactive peer
  signal      Route signal time
```

Verifying EIGRP Process Status

In a dual RP system, EIGRP processes are running only on the Active nodes. It is also a cold restart process because it is not fully initialized on the standby RP. The EIGRP process can be restarted or shut down, and its status can be monitored using **show process eigrp.** The EIGRP process uses checkpoint recovery mechanisms for restarting or shutting down of the process. Example 7-13 provides the commands for verifying the EIGRP process status on active and standby RP. The EIGRP process is in the RUN state in Active RP and in the Queued state in the Standby RP as highlighted in Example 7-13. Just as with RIP, EIGRP is also restartable using **process restart eigrp.**

Example 7-13 *Process Status on Active and Standby RP*

```
! The state of the EIGRP process running on Active (RP0) and Standby (RP1)



RP/0/RP0/CPU0:CRS-1#show processes eigrp detail location all
node:      node0_0_CPU0
--------------------------------------------------------------.
No such process eigrp
--------------------------------------------------------------.
node:      node0_RP0_CPU0
--------------------------------------------------------------.
                   Job Id: 170
                      PID: 15007990
          Executable path: /disk0/hfr-rout-3.6.1/bin/eigrp
               Instance #: 1
               Version ID: 00.00.0000
                  Respawn: ON
            Respawn count: 5
   Max. spawns per minute: 12
             Last started: Wed Nov 12 06:37:03 2008
            Process state: Run
            Package state: Normal
        Started on config: cfg/gl/eigrp/proc/0x1/ord_a/default/ord_a/enabled
                     core: TEXT SHAREDMEM MAINMEM
                Max. core: 0
                Placement: ON
             startup_path: /pkg/startup/eigrp.startup
                    Ready: 0.820s
                Available: 0.833s
             Running path: /disk0/hfr-rout-3.6.1/bin/eigrp
             Package path: /pkg/bin/eigrp
    Node redundancy state: active
              Job-id-link: 170
                group_jid: 1360,0,0,0
               fail_count: 0
```

```
                this pcb: 481fe010
                next pcb: 601ea600
             jobid on RP: 0
              Send Avail: YES
        Process cpu time: 0.278 user, 0.125 kernel, 0.403 total
JID    TID  Stack pri state        TimeInState      HR:MM:SS:MSEC NAME
170    1      52K  10 Receive        0:00:18:0674     0:00:00:0261 eigrp
170    2      52K  10 Receive        0:02:24:0746     0:00:00:0002 eigrp
170    3      52K  10 Receive        0:01:18:0675     0:00:00:0012 eigrp
170    4      52K  10 Receive        0:01:18:0669     0:00:00:0002 eigrp
170    5      52K  10 Receive        0:00:18:0665     0:00:00:0001 eigrp
170    6      52K  10 Receive        0:01:18:0672     0:00:00:0000 eigrp
170    7      52K  10 Receive        0:02:24:0332     0:00:00:0000 eigrp
--------------------------------------------------------------------------.
--------------------------------------------------------------------------.
node:      node0_RP1_CPU0
--------------------------------------------------------------------------.
                  Job Id: 170
         Executable path: /disk0/hfr-rout-3.6.1/bin/eigrp
              Instance #: 1
              Version ID: 00.00.0000
                 Respawn: ON
           Respawn count: 0
  Max. spawns per minute: 12
            Last started: Not yet spawned
           Process state: Queued
           Package state: Normal
       Registered item(s): cfg/gl/eigrp/
                    core: TEXT SHAREDMEM MAINMEM
              Max. core: 0
              Placement: ON
            startup_path: /pkg/startup/eigrp.startup
            Running path: /disk0/hfr-rout-3.6.1/bin/eigrp
            Package path: /pkg/bin/eigrp
   Node redundancy state: standby
             Job-id-link: 170
               group_jid: 1360,0,0,0
              fail_count: 0
                this pcb: 481fe010
                next pcb: 601ea600
             jobid on RP: 0
              Send Avail: YES
```

Verifying and Troubleshooting EIGRP

Example 7-14 illustrates some of the **show** and **debug** commands that can be used for validating and troubleshooting EIGRP.

Example 7-14 *Verify Interface Configuration*

```
!Displays the interface information enabled for EIGRP

RP/0/RP0/CPU0:CRS-1#show eigrp interfaces tenGigE 0/0/0/2  detail

IPv4-EIGRP interfaces for AS(1)

                       Xmit Queue   Mean   Pacing Time   Multicast    Pending
Interface        Peers  Un/Reliable  SRTT   Un/Reliable   Flow Timer   Routes
Te0/0/0/2          1        0/0         6       0/10          50            0
  Hello interval is 5 sec, hold time is 15 sec
  Next xmit serial <none>
  Un/reliable mcasts: 0/3  Un/reliable ucasts: 6/5
  Mcast exceptions: 0  CR packets: 0  ACKs suppressed: 1
  Retransmissions sent: 1  Out-of-sequence rcvd: 0
  Bandwidth percent is 50
  Authentication mode is not set
  Effective Metric:
    Bandwidth: 10000000, Delay: 1, Reliability: 255, Load: 1, MTU: 1500


!The topology database for EIGRP on the neighboring router shows information such
  as successors, feasible distance, metric for the routes.

RP/0/RP0/CPU0:CRS-2#show eigrp topology

IPv4-EIGRP Topology Table for AS(1)/ID(172.16.1.1)

Codes: P - Passive, A - Active, U - Update, Q - Query, R - Reply,
       r - reply Status, s - sia Status

P 10.0.0.0/24, 1 successors, FD is 512
        via Connected, TenGigE0/0/0/3
P 172.16.1.1/32, 1 successors, FD is 128512
        via 10.0.0.1 (128512/128256), TenGigE0/0/0/3


!EIGRP neighbor information can be retrieved on the neighboring router

RP/0/RP0/CPU0:CRS-2#show eigrp neighbors
```

```
IPv4-EIGRP neighbors for AS(1)

H   Address                 Interface        Hold Uptime    SRTT   RTO  Q  Seq
                                              (sec)         (ms)        Cnt Num
0   10.0.0.1                Te0/0/0/3         13 00:00:25    3     200  0   11

RP/0/RP0/CPU0:CRS-2#
```

Table 7-2 lists some of the operational and debug commands related to EIGRP.

Table 7-2 *EIGRP Operational and Debug Commands*

Command	Description
show route eigrp	Displays the EIGRP routes that are installed in RIB
show eigrp traffic	Provides the statistics of the EIGRP packets sent and received
clear eigrp [*as-number*] [**vrf** {*vrf* | **all**}] [**ipv4** | **ipv6**] **neighbors** [*ip-address* | *interface-type interface-instance*] [**soft**]	Clears the EIGRP neighbor database
debug eigrp ipv4 [*as-number* | **vrf** [*vrf-name*]][[*ip-address*] | **neighbor** | **notifications** | **summary**]	Used for debugging EIGRP events

Open Shortest Path First

Open Shortest Path First (OSPF) is an IGP that runs on the IP layer and uses port number 89. It routes packets based on the destination address and the type of service (TOS) byte. It quickly detects the changes in the autonomous system and calculates new routes after a period of convergence. This section describes fundamental OSPF concepts before delving into the configuration details of IOS XR.

Understanding OSPF Fundamentals

OSPF is based on link state technology where each router maintains a database of the link states, which stores information such as IP address, subnet, and cost. This database known as *link state database (LSDB)* is used to build the adjacency and routing table of the router and describes the topology of the autonomous system. These link states are advertised to all the routers in the autonomous system via a flooding process. The router runs Dijktra's algorithm on the LSDB to generate a shortest path first (SPF) tree, which in turn is used to build a routing table with the best route (the one with least cost) to the destination. Unlike RIP, OSPF does not send out periodic updates and after the adjacency is formed between neighbors, only the changed routing information is propagated to the neighbor. These link states are advertised to all the routers within the autonomous system by flooding. This is called *link state advertisement (LSA).*

OSPF allows grouping of networks into areas. The topology of an area is hidden from other areas in an AS. This hierarchy helps reducing routing traffic and protects a network from bad traffic. In case of failure, this hierarchy helps to isolate the impaired network and protects the rest of the network. OSPF routers can have different roles depending on the area they serve. These roles are divided into four categories:

- **Internal routers:** An internal router connects to only one area.
- **Backbone routers:** Backbone routers have one or more links in area 0.
- **Area border router (ABR):** ABR connects more than one area and is generally used to connect a backbone router to a nonbackbone.
- **Autonomous system boundary routers (ASBR):** ASBR connects OSPF AS to another AS.

All routers within the same area have the same LSDBs. Type 1 and Type 2 LSAs are scoped within the area. OSPF supports external route (from EGP) propagation through its AS and such information is stored as separate LSAs called *Type-5 LSAs*. Backbone is always a Type-5-capable area. There are two special types of OSPF areas:

- **Stub area:** A stub area is connected to the backbone area only. It does not receive any external routes and allows no Type-5 LSAs to be propagated.
- **Not-so-stubby area (NSSA):** An NSSA is a type of stub area that allows the injection of external routes into the stub area. Type-7 LSAs allow carrying external route information within NSSA. These are only for one NSSA and are not flooded to backbone or ABR.

OSPF uses 224.0.0.5 for multicasting the LSAs and hello packets. Hello packets are used for establishing neighbors. These packets decide whether the adjacency should be formed with a given neighbor. Some important parameters used in OSPF are hello interval, dead interval, LSA update timer, and minimum time between SPF calculations.

OSPF supports features such as route summarization, VLSM, disjoint subnets, supernetting, loop-free routes, and authentication.

OSPFv3 uses the same mechanism as OSPFv2, with the difference that it supports LSAs for IPv6 address updates. OSPFv3 is not backward compatible with OSPFv2, and networks that have both IPv4 and IPv6 require the presence of both OSPFv2 and OSPFv3 for routing. OSPFv2 recognizes neighbors by using interface addresses on broadcast and nonbroadcast multiple access (NBMA) networks and by using router ID on other types of networks, whereas OSPFv3 only uses router ID to identify neighbors. OSPFv3 does not have OSPF-specific authentication and uses authentication provided by IPv6. This protocol runs on link addresses compared to subnets used in OSPFv3 and uses the link-local address of the interface to exchange the LSAs.

So, with its capability to scale, protect networks through partitioning into various areas, and converge faster for both IPv4 and IPv6 networks, this is one of the protocols of choice when it comes to deploying IGP.

Configuring OSPF in Cisco IOS XR

Refer to Figure 7-1. In this case CRS-1 and CRS-2 will be configured to form the OSPF neighbors for IPv4. Appropriate interfaces will be configured under the OSPF router process. All the interfaces for a given area are enabled by configuring under the defined OSPF area. OSPF and OSPFv2 will be used interchangeably in this section.

Configuring and Verifying OSPFv2

Example 7-15 shows the basic steps required to configure OSPF for a single area in IOS XR.

Example 7-15 *OSPFv2 Configuration*

```
!Snippet of the base config for CRS-1 and CRS-2

RP/0/RP0/CPU0:CRS-1#show running-config
!
interface Loopback1
 ipv4 address 172.16.1.1 255.255.255.255
!
interface TenGigE0/0/0/2
 ipv4 address 10.0.0.1 255.255.255.0

RP/0/RP0/CPU0:CRS-2#show running-config
!
interface TenGigE0/0/0/3
ipv4 address 10.0.0.2 255.255.255.0



!Now enable OSPFv2 for loopback and TenGigabitEthernet interfaces on CRS-1 and
  similar configuration is applied on CRS-2

RP/0/RP0/CPU0:CRS-1#conf t
RP/0/RP0/CPU0:CRS-1(config)#router ospf 1
RP/0/RP0/CPU0:CRS-1(config-ospf)#area 0
RP/0/RP0/CPU0:CRS-1(config-ospf-ar)#interface Loopback1
RP/0/RP0/CPU0:CRS-1(config-ospf-ar-if)# !
RP/0/RP0/CPU0:CRS-1(config-ospf-ar-if)# interface TenGigE0/0/0/2
RP/0/RP0/CPU0:CRS-1(config-ospf-ar-if)#commit
```

```
Uncommitted changes found, commit them before exiting(yes/no/cancel)? [cancel]:yes
RP/0/RP0/CPU0:CRS-1#

! Use the following command to verify the ospf config

RP/0/RP0/CPU0:CRS-1#show running-config router ospf
router ospf 1
 area 0
  interface Loopback1
  !
  interface TenGigE0/0/0/2
  !
 !
!

RP/0/RP0/CPU0:CRS-1#
```

Example 7-16 illustrates the different verification commands for OSPFv2.

Example 7-16 *Verifying the OSPFv2 Configuration*

```
!show ospf neighbor lists out the different IPv4 OSPF neighbors on CRS-2

RP/0/RP0/CPU0:CRS-2# show ospf neighbor

Neighbors for OSPF 1

Neighbor ID     Pri    State           Dead Time    Address         Interface
192.168.254.3   1      FULL/DR         00:00:38     10.0.0.1        TenGigE0/0/0/3
    Neighbor is up for 00:00:04

Total neighbor count: 1

!show ospf interface displays the OSPF attributes for interface enabled for OSPFv2

RP/0/RP0/CPU0:CRS-1#show ospf interface

TenGigE0/0/0/2 is up, line protocol is up
  Internet Address 10.0.0.1/24, Area 0
  Process ID 1, Router ID 192.168.254.3, Network Type BROADCAST, Cost: 1
  Transmit Delay is 1 sec, State DR, Priority 1
  Designated Router (ID) 192.168.254.3, Interface address 10.0.0.1
  Backup Designated router (ID) 10.10.10.222, Interface address 10.0.0.2
  Timer intervals configured, Hello 10, Dead 40, Wait 40, Retransmit 5
```

```
    Hello due in 00:00:05
  Index 2/2, flood queue length 0
  Next 0(0)/0(0)
  Last flood scan length is 2, maximum is 2
  Last flood scan time is 0 msec, maximum is 0 msec
  Neighbor Count is 1, Adjacent neighbor count is 1
    Adjacent with neighbor 10.10.10.222  (Backup Designated Router)
  Suppress hello for 0 neighbor(s)
  Multi-area interface Count is 0
Loopback1 is up, line protocol is up
  Internet Address 172.16.1.1/32, Area 0
  Process ID 1, Router ID 192.168.254.3, Network Type LOOPBACK, Cost: 1
  Loopback interface is treated as a stub Host
RP/0/RP0/CPU0:CRS-1#
```

Hierarchical CLI and Inheritance

Cisco IOS XR OSPF configuration architecture supports hierarchical CLI and inheritance capabilities. Hierarchical CLI allows configuring different OSPF commands at different levels. These commands can be configured at the global (process/instance) level, area level, or interface level. Example 7-17 configures the **cost** parameter at the global level. This global level cost will be used by all the areas and the interfaces configured under OSPFv2 unless overridden by the area or interface level.

Example 7-17 *Hierarchical CLI: Global Level*

```
!parameters defined and verified at global level for OSPF


RP/0/RP0/CPU0:CRS-1(config)#router ospf 1
RP/0/RP0/CPU0:CRS-1(config-ospf)#cost 10
RP/0/RP0/CPU0:CRS-1(config-ospf)#commit
RP/0/RP0/CPU0:CRS-1#show running-config router ospf 1
router ospf 1
 cost 10
 area 0
  interface Loopback1
  !
  interface TenGigE0/0/0/2
  !
 !
!


!Global level value of cost is inherited by all OSPF interfaces as shown in the
  output


RP/0/RP0/CPU0:CRS-1# show ospf interface
```

```
TenGigE0/0/0/2 is up, line protocol is up
  Internet Address 10.0.0.1/24, Area 0
  Process ID 1, Router ID 192.168.254.3, Network Type BROADCAST, Cost: 10
  Transmit Delay is 1 sec, State DR, Priority 1
  Designated Router (ID) 192.168.254.3, Interface address 10.0.0.1
  Backup Designated router (ID) 10.10.10.222, Interface address 10.0.0.2
  Timer intervals configured, Hello 10, Dead 40, Wait 40, Retransmit 5
    Hello due in 00:00:03
  Index 2/2, flood queue length 0
  Next 0(0)/0(0)
  Last flood scan length is 1, maximum is 2
  Last flood scan time is 0 msec, maximum is 0 msec
  Neighbor Count is 1, Adjacent neighbor count is 1
    Adjacent with neighbor 10.10.10.222  (Backup Designated Router)
  Suppress hello for 0 neighbor(s)
  Multi-area interface Count is 0
Loopback1 is up, line protocol is up
  Internet Address 172.16.1.1/32, Area 0
  Process ID 1, Router ID 192.168.254.3, Network Type LOOPBACK, Cost: 10
Loopback interface is treated as a stub Host
```

Example 7-18 defines the cost parameter at the area level. In this case, all the interfaces configured under OSPFv2 will use the value of the cost parameter defined at the area level.

Example 7-18 *Hierarchical CLI: Area Level*

```
!parameters defined and verified at area level for OSPF

RP/0/RP0/CPU0:CRS-1(config)#router ospf 1
RP/0/RP0/CPU0:CRS-1(config-ospf)#area 0
RP/0/RP0/CPU0:CRS-1(config-ospf-ar)#cost 10
RP/0/RP0/CPU0:CRS-1(config-ospf-ar)#commit
RP/0/RP0/CPU0:CRS-1# show running-config router ospf 1
router ospf 1
 area 0
  cost 10
  interface Loopback1
  !
  interface TenGigE0/0/0/2
  !
 !
!

RP/0/RP0/CPU0:CRS-1# show ospf interface
```

```
TenGigE0/0/0/2 is up, line protocol is up
  Internet Address 10.0.0.1/24, Area 0
  Process ID 1, Router ID 192.168.254.3, Network Type BROADCAST, Cost: 10
  Transmit Delay is 1 sec, State DR, Priority 1
  Designated Router (ID) 192.168.254.3, Interface address 10.0.0.1
  Backup Designated router (ID) 10.10.10.222, Interface address 10.0.0.2
  Timer intervals configured, Hello 10, Dead 40, Wait 40, Retransmit 5
    Hello due in 00:00:01
  Index 2/2, flood queue length 0
  Next 0(0)/0(0)
  Last flood scan length is 1, maximum is 2
  Last flood scan time is 0 msec, maximum is 0 msec
  Neighbor Count is 1, Adjacent neighbor count is 1
    Adjacent with neighbor 10.10.10.222  (Backup Designated Router)
  Suppress hello for 0 neighbor(s)
  Multi-area interface Count is 0
Loopback1 is up, line protocol is up
  Internet Address 172.16.1.1/32, Area 0
  Process ID 1, Router ID 192.168.254.3, Network Type LOOPBACK, Cost: 10
  Loopback interface is treated as a stub Host
RP/0/RP0/CPU0:CRS-1#
```

Example 7-19 defines the cost parameter at the interface level. In this scenario the interface, TenGigabitEthernet0/0/2 will use the cost defined at the interface level whereas the default cost will be used for the Loopback interface.

Example 7-19 *Hierarchical CLI: Interface Level*

```
!parameters defined and verified at interface level for OSPF

RP/0/RP0/CPU0:CRS-1(config-ospf-ar)#interface tenGigE 0/0/0/2
RP/0/RP0/CPU0:CRS-1(config-ospf-ar-if)#cost 10
RP/0/RP0/CPU0:CRS-1(config-ospf-ar-if)#commit
RP/0/RP0/CPU0:CRS-1# show running-config router ospf 1
router ospf 1
 area 0
  interface Loopback1
  !
  interface TenGigE0/0/0/2
   cost 10
  !
 !
!

!Use the following command to verify the Cost for the interface
```

```
RP/0/RP0/CPU0:CRS-1(# show ospf interface
TenGigE0/0/0/2 is up, line protocol is up
  Internet Address 10.0.0.1/24, Area 0
  Process ID 1, Router ID 192.168.254.3, Network Type BROADCAST, Cost: 10
  Transmit Delay is 1 sec, State DR, Priority 1
  Designated Router (ID) 192.168.254.3, Interface address 10.0.0.1
  Backup Designated router (ID) 10.10.10.222, Interface address 10.0.0.2
  Timer intervals configured, Hello 10, Dead 40, Wait 40, Retransmit 5
    Hello due in 00:00:07
  Index 2/2, flood queue length 0
  Next 0(0)/0(0)
  Last flood scan length is 1, maximum is 2
  Last flood scan time is 1 msec, maximum is 1 msec
  Neighbor Count is 1, Adjacent neighbor count is 1
    Adjacent with neighbor 10.10.10.222  (Backup Designated Router)
  Suppress hello for 0 neighbor(s)
  Multi-area interface Count is 0
Loopback1 is up, line protocol is up
  Internet Address 172.16.1.1/32, Area 0
  Process ID 1, Router ID 192.168.254.3, Network Type LOOPBACK, Cost: 1
  Loopback interface is treated as a stub Host
```

The inheritance feature of IOS XR OSPFv2 allows various parameters—namely cost, timers, and authentication—to be inherited or used depending on the precedence and the level (global/area/interface) at which these are configured.

Example 7-20 defines cost at both the global level and the interface level. In this case, the cost defined at the ten Gigabit Ethernet interface will supersede the cost defined at the global level and the loopback interface will inherit the global cost based on the precedence.

Example 7-20 *Inheritance*

```
!parameters defined and verified at global and Interface level for OSPF


RP/0/RP0/CPU0:CRS-1#show running-config router ospf 1
router ospf 1
 cost 20
 area 0
  interface Loopback1
  !
  interface TenGigE0/0/0/2
   cost 10
  !
 !
!
```

Hierarchical and inheritance features of OSPFv2 allow better control on assignment of various parameters, provide modularity through grouping of commands, and simplify configuration.

Configuring OSPFv2 Authentication

IOS XR OSPFv2 supports both plain text and MD5 authentication. Example 7-21 demonstrates the steps required for configuring OSPF authentication. This example also uses the inheritance and hierarchical feature support of IOS XR OSPFv2 configuration. CRS-1 is configured with MD5 authentication at the area level as well as at the interface level. Interface TenGigE0/0/0/4 will inherit the area-level authentication, and interface TenGigE0/0/0/2 will use the key 1 MD5 authentication because the interface-level configuration will supersede the area level configuration.

Example 7-21 *Configuring Authentication at Area and Interface Level*

```
!Authentication configured at Area and Interface level

RP/0/RP0/CPU0:CRS-1# configure t
RP/0/RP0/CPU0:CRS-1(config)#router ospf 1
RP/0/RP0/CPU0:CRS-1(config-ospf)# area 0
RP/0/RP0/CPU0:CRS-1(config-ospf-ar)# authentication message-digest
RP/0/RP0/CPU0:CRS-1(config-ospf-ar)# message-digest-key 2 md5 cisco1
RP/0/RP0/CPU0:CRS-1(config-ospf-ar-if)# interface TenGigE0/0/0/2
RP/0/RP0/CPU0:CRS-1(config-ospf-ar-if)#  authentication message-digest
RP/0/RP0/CPU0:CRS-1(config-ospf-ar-if)#  message-digest-key 1 md5 cisco
RP/0/RP0/CPU0:CRS-1(config-ospf-ar-if)# commit
RP/0/RP0/CPU0:CRS-1(config-ospf-ar-if)# end

RP/0/RP0/CPU0:CRS-1(#show running-config router ospf 1
router ospf 1
 area 0
  authentication message-digest
  message-digest-key 2 md5 encrypted 060506324F4158
  !
  interface TenGigE0/0/0/2
   cost 10
   authentication message-digest
   message-digest-key 1 md5 encrypted 030752180500
  !
  interface TenGigE0/0/0/4
  !
  !
 !
!
```

```
!Verification of Authentication using "show ospf interface <>"

RP/0/RP0/CPU0:CRS-1#show ospf interface tenGigE 0/0/0/2

TenGigE0/0/0/2 is up, line protocol is up
  Internet Address 10.0.0.1/24, Area 0
  Process ID 1, Router ID 192.168.254.3, Network Type BROADCAST, Cost: 10
  Transmit Delay is 1 sec, State DR, Priority 1
  Designated Router (ID) 192.168.254.3, Interface address 10.0.0.1
  Backup Designated router (ID) 10.10.10.222, Interface address 10.0.0.2
  Timer intervals configured, Hello 10, Dead 40, Wait 40, Retransmit 5
    Hello due in 00:00:01
  Index 2/2, flood queue length 0
  Next 0(0)/0(0)
  Last flood scan length is 1, maximum is 2
  Last flood scan time is 0 msec, maximum is 1 msec
  Neighbor Count is 1, Adjacent neighbor count is 1
    Adjacent with neighbor 10.10.10.222  (Backup Designated Router)
  Suppress hello for 0 neighbor(s)
  Message digest authentication enabled
    Youngest key id is 1
  Multi-area interface Count is 0


RP/0/RP0/CPU0:CRS-1#show ospf interface tenGigE 0/0/0/4

TenGigE0/0/0/4 is up, line protocol is up
  Internet Address 10.1.34.3/24, Area 0
  Process ID 1, Router ID 192.168.254.3, Network Type BROADCAST, Cost: 20
  Transmit Delay is 1 sec, State WAITING, Priority 1
  No designated router on this network
  No backup designated router on this network
  Timer intervals configured, Hello 10, Dead 40, Wait 40, Retransmit 5
    Hello due in 00:00:08
    Wait time before Designated router selection 00:00:30
  Index 3/3, flood queue length 0
  Next 0(0)/0(0)
  Last flood scan length is 0, maximum is 0
  Last flood scan time is 0 msec, maximum is 0 msec
  Neighbor Count is 0, Adjacent neighbor count is 0
  Suppress hello for 0 neighbor(s)
  Message digest authentication enabled
    Youngest key id is 2
  Multi-area interface Count is 0
```

In Example 7-22, CRS-2 has MD5 authentication configured at global level. All the areas and interfaces in CRS-2 without specific authentication configurations will inherit the authentication defined at the global level.

Example 7-22 *Configuring Authentication at Global Level*

```
!Authentication configured at Global level

RP/0/RP0/CPU0:CRS-2#show running-config router ospf
router ospf 1
 authentication message-digest
 message-digest-key 1 md5 encrypted 030752180500
 area 0
  interface TenGigE0/0/0/3
  !
 !
!
!Verification of Authentication using "show ospf interface <>"

RP/0/RP0/CPU0:CRS-2#show ospf interface tenGigE 0/0/0/3

TenGigE0/0/0/3 is up, line protocol is up
  Internet Address 10.0.0.2/24, Area 0
  Process ID 1, Router ID 10.10.10.222, Network Type BROADCAST, Cost: 1
  Transmit Delay is 1 sec, State DR, Priority 1
  Designated Router (ID) 10.10.10.222, Interface address 10.0.0.2
  Backup Designated router (ID) 192.168.254.3, Interface address 10.0.0.1
  Timer intervals configured, Hello 10, Dead 40, Wait 40, Retransmit 5
    Hello due in 00:00:05
  Index 1/1, flood queue length 0
  Next 0(0)/0(0)
  Last flood scan length is 2, maximum is 2
  Last flood scan time is 0 msec, maximum is 0 msec
  Neighbor Count is 1, Adjacent neighbor count is 1
    Adjacent with neighbor 192.168.254.3  (Backup Designated Router)
  Suppress hello for 0 neighbor(s)
  Message digest authentication enabled
    Youngest key id is 1
Multi-area interface Count is 0
```

Verifying NSF Configuration and Standby RP Status

IOS XR OSPFv2 supports nonstop forwarding (NSF) of traffic to OSPF-learned destinations across RP switchovers with the help of Cisco NSF and IETF Graceful Restart (IETF-GR). OSPF supports *warm standby* where the OSPF process goes through the initialization process completely and reaches the warm standby state. This state helps the RP change the role from standby to active and become operational with much less CPU usage resource. OSPF **show** commands are extended to accommodate the status of the standby process on the standby RP. Commands are also available to enable debug for OSPF on standby RP. LSDB and neighbor information is not synched on the standby RP.

Examples 7-23 through 7-25 show the commands to verify the NSF configs and standby RP OSPF status in IOS XR. The OSPF process state in the Standby RP can be viewed in detail using different command options as shown in Example 7-23. The OSPF process can be restarted, shut down, or blocked using the **process restart ospf** command.

Example 7-23 *Warm Standby*

```
! Displays the different show commands for verifying the state of the OSPF process
  running on Standby(RP1)

RP/0/RP0/CPU0:CRS-1#show ospf standby ?
  bad-checksum             Bad ospf checksum packets queue
  border-routers           Border and Boundary Router Information
  cmd                      Generic command support
  database                 Database summary
  flood-list               Link state flood list
  interface                Interface information
  maxage-list              Maxage List
  message-queue            Hello, TE and router message queue data
  mpls                     MPLS related information
  neighbor                 Neighbor list
  our-address              our address Database
  request-list             Link state request list
  retransmission-list      Link state retransmission list
  routes                   OSPF routes table
  sham-links               Sham link information
  statistics               OSPF statistics information
  summary                  OSPF summary information
  summary-prefix           Summary-prefix redistribution Information
  timers                   OSPF timers information
  trace                    OSPF trace information
  virtual-links            Virtual link information
  vrf                      Show one or more non-default OSPF VRFs in process
  |                        Output Modifiers
```

The NSF information of OSPF can be viewed in detail using the **show ospf <tag> standby** command as shown in Example 7-24.

Example 7-24 *NSF Verification*

```
! Displays the state of the OSPF process running on Standby RP(RP1) and NSF enabled
  for OSPF


RP/0/RP0/CPU0:CRS-1#show ospf 1 standby

Routing Process "ospf 1" with ID 0.0.0.0
Running as standby
NSR (Non-stop routing) is Disabled
Supports only single TOS(TOS0) routes
Supports opaque LSA
Router is not originating router-LSAs with maximum metric
Initial SPF schedule delay 50 msecs
Minimum hold time between two consecutive SPFs 200 msecs
Maximum wait time between two consecutive SPFs 5000 msecs
Initial LSA throttle delay 50 msecs
Minimum hold time for LSA throttle 200 msecs
Maximum wait time for LSA throttle 5000 msecs
Minimum LSA interval 200 msecs. Minimum LSA arrival 100 msecs
Flood pacing interval 33 msecs. Retransmission pacing interval 66 msecs
Maximum number of configured interfaces 255
Number of external LSA 0. Checksum Sum 00000000
Number of opaque AS LSA 0. Checksum Sum 00000000
Number of DCbitless external and opaque AS LSA 0
Number of DoNotAge external and opaque AS LSA 0
Number of areas in this router is 1. 1 normal 0 stub 0 nssa
External flood list length 0
Non-Stop Forwarding enabled
   Area BACKBONE(0) (Inactive)
        Number of interfaces in this area is 3
        SPF algorithm executed 0 times
        Number of LSA 0. Checksum Sum 00000000
        Number of opaque link LSA 0. Checksum Sum 00000000
        Number of DCbitless LSA 0
        Number of indication LSA 0
        Number of DoNotAge LSA 0
       Flood list length 0
```

The standby RP process does not maintain the LSDB, which can be verified using **show ospf standby database** as shown in Example 7-25.

Example 7-25 *Neighbor and Database Information on Standby RP*

```
!

RP/0/RP0/CPU0:CRS-1#show ospf standby database


            OSPF Router with ID (0.0.0.0) (Process ID 1)
RP/0/RP0/CPU0:CRS-1#show ospf standby neighbor
RP/0/RP0/CPU0:CRS-1#
```

Configuring and Verifying Nonstop Routing

OSPFv2 warm standby helps in achieving high availability using Cisco NSF or IETF-GR. However it requires the neighboring routers to be NSF-capable or NSF aware at minimum. This imposes a big limitation where all the routers deployed in a network to be NSF aware. To overcome this limitation, IOS XR introduces *nonstop routing (NSR)*.

NSR is built on the concept of the warm standby process. For NSR, the warm standby concept is extended to a hot standby process. The process running on the standby RP is called *hot standby* because it does not just get initialized but also synchronizes the LSDB, has its own finite state machine (FSM), and maintains the neighbor and adjacency tables. However, SPF calculation and OSPF routes are not done on the standby RP. With NSR, if the switchover happens, OSPFv2 on the standby RP needs minimal CPU to calculate the routes. The neighboring routers remain unaware of the switchover on an NSR enabled router.

NSR can be enabled by configuring NSR under the OSPF process using the **nsr** command. NSR is enabled/disabled for the entire OSPF process instance and cannot be configured at the area or interface level. LSDB, neighbor, and interface information can be verified using the **show ospf standby** command. NSR and NSF can coexist on the same router. Although NSR and NSF can coexist on the same router, the router uses NSR as the default option to recover during failover and NSF serves as a fallback option in such a case.

Examples 7-26 through 7-28 provide the configuration options for NSF and NSR. The **show running-config router ospf** command displays both NSF and NSR coexist in the configuration.

Example 7-26 *NSR Command Options*

```
! Displays the config option for enabling NSR and the running-config after nvgened

RP/0/RP0/CPU0:CRS-1(config-ospf)#?
  nsf                       Enable Cisco Non Stop Forwarding
  nsr                       Enable NSR for all VRFs in this process
! Displays the coexistence of NSF and NSR on the same router

RP/0/RP0/CPU0:CRS-1#show running-config router ospf
router ospf 1
 nsr
 nsf cisco
```

```
 area 0
  interface Loopback1
  !
  interface TenGigE0/0/0/2
  !
  interface TenGigE0/0/0/4
  !
  interface TenGigE0/0/0/6
  !
 !
!
```

Example 7-27 *NSR: Sync of LSDB and Neighbor Information on Standby RP*

```
! Displays the LSDB, neighbor and Interface information on the Standby RP

RP/0/RP0/CPU0:CRS-1#show ospf standby database



            OSPF Router with ID (192.168.254.3) (Process ID 1)

                Router Link States (Area 0)

Link ID         ADV Router      Age         Seq#        Checksum Link count
10.10.10.222    10.10.10.222    534         0x80000006  0x0074a8 1
192.168.254.3   192.168.254.3   135         0x80000097  0x00c8a9 3

                Net Link States (Area 0)

Link ID         ADV Router      Age         Seq#        Checksum
10.0.0.1        192.168.254.3   634         0x80000005  0x00e670

! Neighbor information and Interface information is maintained by the OSPF Process
  running on the Standby RP

RP/0/RP0/CPU0:CRS-1#show ospf standby neighbor

Neighbors for OSPF 1

Neighbor ID     Pri   State           Dead Time   Address         Interface
10.10.10.222    1     FULL/BDR           -        10.0.0.2        TenGigE0/0/0/2
    Neighbor is up for 02:21:57

Total neighbor count: 1
```

```
RP/0/RP0/CPU0:CRS-1#show ospf standby interface brief

Interface      PID    Area             IP Address/Mask      Cost   State Nbrs F/C
Te0/0/0/2      1      0                10.0.0.1/24          10     DR     1/1
Te0/0/0/4      1      0                10.1.34.3/24         20     DR     0/0
Lo1            1      0                172.16.1.1/32        20     LOOP   0/0
```

Example 7-28 *OSPFv2: NSR Process Status on Standby RP*

```
!Standby RP does not perform SPF and OSPF routes calculations

RP/0/RP0/CPU0:CRS-1#show ospf standby routes
RP/0/RP0/CPU0:CRS-1#
RP/0/RP0/CPU0:CRS-1#show ospf standby statistics spf
RP/0/RP0/CPU0:CRS-1#
```

Configuring and Verifying Multiarea Adjacencies

OSPF selects the route based on the route type preference if the same route is learned through an intra-area or inter-area link. To avoid or overcome the route type preference, a Sham-Link can be used. The multiarea interface is yet another mechanism to overcome the route preference behavior of OSPF. Multiarea adjacency allows assigning one physical interface to multiple OSPF areas and hence treating this link as an intra-area link. Only point-to-point networks support multiarea adjacency. A multiarea interface inherits the characteristics of the primary physical link. A multiarea interface will be active in OSPF as long as the primary interface is also active under OSPF, and will be up as long as the primary interface will be up.

Example 7-29 provides the steps required to configure multiarea adjacency. In this example, interface POS 0/7/5/0 is enabled under both Area 0 and Area 1 using the **multi-area-interface** command.

Example 7-29 *Verify Multiarea Interface Configuration*

```
RP/0/RP1/CPU0:CRS1-1(config)#router ospf 1
RP/0/RP1/CPU0:CRS1-1(config-ospf)#area 0
RP/0/RP1/CPU0:CRS1-1(config-ospf-ar)#interface poS 0/7/5/0
RP/0/RP1/CPU0:CRS1-1(config-ospf-ar-if)#area 1
RP/0/RP1/CPU0:CRS1-1(config-ospf-ar)#multi-area-interface poS 0/7/5/0
RP/0/RP1/CPU0:CRS1-1(config-ospf-ar-mif)#commit

RP/0/RP1/CPU0:CRS1-1#show running-config router ospf
ospf 1
 area 0
  interface GigabitEthernet0/7/0/1
  !
```

```
  interface POS0/7/5/0
  !
 !
 area 1
  multi-area-interface POS0/7/5/0
  !
 !
```

You can use **show ospf interface** <*intf-name*> to display the multiarea interface information as shown in Example 7-30.

Example 7-30 *Verify Multiarea Adjacency*

```
RP/0/RP1/CPU0:CRS1-1#show ospf interface poS 0/7/5/0

POS0/7/5/0 is up, line protocol is up
  Internet Address 10.5.5.1/24, Area 1
  Process ID 1, Router ID 192.168.254.1, Network Type POINT_TO_POINT, Cost: 1
  Transmit Delay is 1 sec, State POINT_TO_POINT,
  Timer intervals configured, Hello 10, Dead 40, Wait 40, Retransmit 5
    Hello due in 00:00:02
  Index 2/2, flood queue length 0
  Next 0(0)/0(0)
  Last flood scan length is 0, maximum is 0
  Last flood scan time is 0 msec, maximum is 0 msec
  Neighbor Count is 0, Adjacent neighbor count is 0
  Suppress hello for 0 neighbor(s)
  Multi-area interface Count is 1
    Multi-Area interface exist in area 0 Neighbor Count is 0
```

Configuring and Verifying Bidirectional Forwarding Detection

Normally, OSPF uses the hello protocol for convergence; however, it is slow because it takes seconds before detection occurs. The convergence time can be improved by enabling the Bidirectional Forwarding Detection (BFD) protocol.

The BFD protocol is implemented to detect failures in the range of msecs between two forwarding interfaces and update the routing protocol clients accordingly.

Example 7-31 illustrates the steps required to configure BFD in IOS XR. OSPF is the client of BFD; hence the entire configuration specific to BFD is enabled under the OSPF process.

Example 7-31 *BFD Configuration*

```
RP/0/RP1/CPU0:CRS1-1(config)#router ospf 1
RP/0/RP1/CPU0:CRS1-1(config-ospf)#bfd ?
  fast-detect        Enable Fast detection
```

```
  minimum-interval  Hello interval
  multiplier        Detect multiplier
RP/0/RP1/CPU0:CRS1-1(config-ospf)#bfd fast-detect
RP/0/RP1/CPU0:CRS1-1(config-ospf)#commit
```

BFD can be enabled at the global, area, or interface level. **show bfd session** and **show running-config** commands can be used to verify the BFD state as shown in Example 7-32. BFD is a hot standby process in IOS XR, and **show process bfd detail location all** can be used to verify this.

Example 7-32 *BFD Configuration and Verification*

```
RP/0/RP1/CPU0:CRS1-1#show running-config router ospf
router ospf 1
 bfd fast-detect
 nsf cisco
 area 0
  authentication message-digest
  interface Loopback0
  !
  interface GigabitEthernet0/7/0/1.1
   message-digest-key 1 md5 encrypted 0454181609334D40
  !
  interface TenGigE0/0/0/4
  !
 !
!

!BFD session status

RP/0/RP1/CPU0:CRS1-1#show bfd session
Interface            Dest Addr           Local det time(int*mult)      State
                                             Echo             Async
----------- --------- --------- --------- -----
Te0/0/0/4            10.7.7.4        450ms(150ms*3)   6s(2s*3)         UP
Gi0/7/0/1.1          10.2.2.2        450ms(150ms*3)   6s(2s*3)         UP

!BFD clients

RP/0/RP1/CPU0:CRS1-1#show bfd client detail
Client Process: ospf-1 Node: 0/RP1/CPU0 State: Connected
 Recreate Time: 60 seconds, Num Sessions: 2
```

Configuring OSPF Timers

There are various configuration commands available to fine-tune OSPF throttle timers as well as LSA generations, as shown in Example 7-33. The OSPF **throttle** command has three timer values that can be modified: start-interval, hold-interval, and max-interval. The default values are 500 msec for start-interval, and 5000 msec for hold-interval and max-interval. In this example the default values of throttle timers for OSPF are changed. Use the command **timers lsa min-interval** <*sec*> to limit the frequency of accepting LSAs during flooding. The default value is set to 1 second. Use the **show ospf** command to verify these timer values.

Example 7-33 *OSPF timer Configurations*

```
RP/0/RP0/CPU0:CRS-1#configure
RP/0/RP0/CPU0:CRS-1(config)# router ospf 1
RP/0/RP0/CPU0:CRS-1(config-ospf)# timers throttle lsa all 10 20 20
RP/0/RP0/CPU0:CRS-1(config-ospf)# timers lsa min-interval 2
```

Configuring and Verifying OSPFv3

OSPFv3 is the version of OSPF designed to handle the IPv6 address family. Example 7-34 shows the OSPFv3 configuration commands for IPv6 interfaces in IOS XR.

Example 7-34 *OSPFv3 Configuration*

```
!Snippet of base config for CRS-1 and CRS-2 configured with IPv6 addresses

RP/0/RP0/CPU0:CRS-1#show running-config
!
interface Loopback1
 ipv6 address 2001::1/128
!
interface TenGigE0/0/0/2
 ipv6 address 2002::1/126
!

RP/0/RP0/CPU0:CRS-2#show running-config
!
interface TenGigE0/0/0/3
 ipv6 address 2002::2/126

!Now enable OSPFv3 for loopback and TenGigabitEthernet interfaces on CRS-1 and
  similar configuration is applied on CRS-2

RP/0/RP0/CPU0:CRS-1#configure

RP/0/RP0/CPU0:CRS-1(config)#router ospfv3 1
```

```
RP/0/RP0/CPU0:CRS-1(config-ospfv3)#area 0
RP/0/RP0/CPU0:CRS-1(config-ospfv3-ar)#interface loopback 1
RP/0/RP0/CPU0:CRS-1(config-ospfv3-ar-if)#exit
RP/0/RP0/CPU0:CRS-1(config-ospfv3-ar)#interface tenGigE 0/0/0/2
RP/0/RP0/CPU0:CRS-1(config-ospfv3-ar-if)#commit

! Use the following command to verify the ospfv3 config

RP/0/RP0/CPU0:CRS-1#show running-config router ospfv3
router ospfv3 1
 area 0
  interface Loopback1
  !
  interface TenGigE0/0/0/2
  !
 !
!

RP/0/RP0/CPU0:CRS-1#
```

Example 7-35 shows the OSPFv3 verification commands for IPv6 interfaces in IOS XR.

Example 7-35 *OSPFv3 Verification*

```
! show ospf neighbor lists out the different IPv6 OSPF neighbors on CRS-2

RP/0/RP0/CPU0:CRS-2#show ospfv3 neighbor

Neighbors for OSPFv3 1

Neighbor ID     Pri   State           Dead Time   Interface ID    Interface
192.168.254.3   1     FULL/BDR        00:00:33    2
TenGigE0/0/0/3
    Neighbor is up for 00:00:53

Total neighbor count: 1
RP/0/RP0/CPU0:CRS-2#

! show route ipv6 ospf displays the IPv6 routes installed in RIB learned
  through OSPFv3

RP/0/RP0/CPU0:CRS-2#show route ipv6 ospf

O    2001::1/128
      [110/1] via fe80::217:59ff:fe6e:b50a, 00:09:25, TenGigE0/0/0/3
RP/0/RP0/CPU0:CRS-2#
```

Table 7-3 lists some of the key commands used for verification and debugging on IOS XR OSPFv3.

Table 7-3 *OSPF Operation and Debug Commands*

Command	Description
show ospf [*process-name*] [**vrf** {*vrf-name* | **all**}] **border-routers** [*router-id*]	Provides the ABR routers that are visible to the given process
show ospf bad-checksum	Displays the queue for OSPF updates with bad checksum
show ospf [*process-name*] [**vrf** {*vrf-name* | **all**}] [*area-id*] **database** [**summary**] [*link-state-id*] [**internal**] [**self-originate**] [*link-state-id*]	Displays information about LSDB and LSAs
show ospf [*process-name*] [**vrf** {*vrf-name* | **all**}] **border-routers** [*router-id*]	Displays all the ABRs and ASBRs
clear ospf [*process-name* [**vrf** {*vrf-name* | **all**}]] **redistribution**	Clears the OSPF database specific to the redistributed routes
clear ospf [*process-name* [**vrf** {*vrf-name* | **all**}]] **redistribution**	Clears redistributed routes from other routing protocols
debug ospf adj	Used for debugging adjacencies and neighbor relationship
debug ospf events	Used for debugging OSPF events such as hello packets, SPF calculation, database, and so on
debug ospf *instance-name* **flood** [*access-list-name*]	Used for debugging flooding events namely acknowledgments and updates
debug ospf *instance-name* **rib** [*access-list-name*]	Used for debugging RIB and OSPF interaction

Intermediate System to Intermediate System

Intermediate System to Intermediate System (IS-IS) is a link state routing protocol developed by ISO for routing connectionless network service (CLNS). This is equivalent to OSPF developed for TCP/IP network. This section reviews fundamental IS-IS concepts and then describes configuring IS-IS in IOS XR.

Understanding IS-IS Fundamentals

An ISO network comprises four main components: end systems, intermediate systems, area, and domain. User devices are called *end systems (ES)* and routers are known as *intermediate systems (IS)*. An IS is divided into areas and domains. Domains contain a set of areas. ISO has developed two sets of protocols, known as the ES-IS discovery protocol (routing between ES and IS, also called *Level 0 routing*) and the IS-IS routing protocol.

IS-IS allows intermediate systems within a domain to exchange configuration and routing information. The intradomain IS-IS supports large routing domains. Various kinds of subnetworks supported by this protocol are point-to-point links, multipoint links, X.25 subnetworks, and broadcast subnetworks such as ISO 8802 LANs.

To support large routing domains, IS-IS has support for a topological hierarchy. A large domain may be administratively divided into areas. Each system resides in one area. Intra-area routing is called *Level 1 routing* and inter-area routing is known as *Level 2 routing*. Level 2 routers are called *area routers* and keep track of the paths to destination areas, whereas Level 1 routers (known as *stations*) keep track of the routing within their own area. For a network protocol data unit (NPDU) destined for another area, a Level 1 IS sends the NPDU to the nearest level 2 IS in its own area, regardless of what the destination area is. Then the NPDU travels via Level 2 routing to the destination area, where it again travels via Level 1 routing to the destination end system. Level 2 can be equated to the backbone area in OSPF, Level 1 to the internal nonbackbone area, and Level 1/Level 2 can be compared to ABR. The backbone area is really a set of Level 2 and Level 1/Level 2 routers and has to be contiguous.

The IS-IS protocol supports two address types: Network Service Access Point (NSAP) and Network Entity Title (NET). NSAP is the access point between the network layer and transport layer, and is used to exchange the information from one layer to another. So, there would be one NSAP for each service running on the network. NSAP stores information such as domain identifier, system identifier, area, and selector (equivalent to the port number in the TCP/IP world).

The NET address identifies the network layer component. A NET address can vary in length from 8 bytes to 20 bytes and has information such as area ID, domain, and system ID (field mapped to IP address). IS-IS devices can have more than one of both of these address types.

Intradomain IS-IS routing functions are divided into two groups: subnetwork independent functions (SIF) and subnetwork dependent functions (SDF). One of the important SIFs is determining the path for NPDUs, where the path is defined as a sequence of links and elements between originating and destination end systems. Another important SIF is congestion control that manages the resources at each IS level.

IS-IS has three types of hello messages that are designed to be used with different neighboring devices. An end system uses ES hello (ESH) to discover a router, IS uses IS hello to declare that it is up, and IIH is the hello between two ISs and is responsible for bringing up the adjacency. Unlike OSPF, routers form adjacencies with all routers and send out LSPs (link state packets) to all routers on the LAN. SPF is run based on NETs. IS-IS supports route summarization and NSF, just as OSPFv2 and OSPFv3 do. Integrated IS-IS is an extended version of IS-IS that supports the IP addresses along with NET addresses.

Configuring IS-IS in Cisco IOS XR

Cisco IOS XR IS-IS supports two models: single topology and multitopology. The default model is multitopology. The IS-IS single topology model for IS-IS is used when a router is configured explicitly using the command **single-topology**. This would mean that IS-IS is running single SPF for both IPv4 and IPv6. It uses the link topology information of IPv4 to calculate both IPv4 and IPv6 routes. ISIS uses narrow metric style type length values (TLVs) in the single topology model. IS-IS can have multiple instances of IPv4 and IPv6 in a single topology model.

ISIS multitopology runs separate SPF for IPv4 and IPv6. New multitopology TLVs are introduced to carry IPv6 information and are used to calculate IPv6 route information. This model would be preferred over single topology model if a different topology database is required for IPv6. You can use the command **show isis database detail** to find out the topology model for advertised prefixes.

Refer to Figure 7-1. In this case CRS-1 and CRS-2 will be configured to form the IS-IS adjacencies. Appropriate interfaces will be configured under the IS-IS router process.

Example 7-36 shows the basic steps required to configure IS-IS in IOS XR.

Example 7-36 *IS-IS Configuration and Verification*

```
!Snippet of base config for CRS-1 and CRS-2

RP/0/RP0/CPU0:CRS-1#show running-config
interface TenGigE0/0/0/2
 ipv4 address 10.0.0.1 255.255.255.0
 ipv6 address 2002::1/126
!
interface Loopback1
 ipv4 address 172.16.1.1 255.255.255.255
 ipv6 address 2001::1/128
!

RP/0/RP0/CPU0:CRS-2#show running-config
interface TenGigE0/0/0/3
 ipv4 address 10.0.0.2 255.255.255.0
 ipv6 address 2002::2/126
```

```
!

!Configuring Single Topology ISIS

RP/0/RP0/CPU0:CRS-2#
RP/0/RP0/CPU0:CRS-1#configure
RP/0/RP0/CPU0:CRS-1(config)#router isis 1
RP/0/RP0/CPU0:CRS-1(config-isis)#net 49.0001.0001.0002.00
RP/0/RP0/CPU0:CRS-1(config-isis)#address-family ipv6 unicast
RP/0/RP0/CPU0:CRS-1(config-isis-af)#single-topology
RP/0/RP0/CPU0:CRS-1(config-isis-if)#exit
RP/0/RP0/CPU0:CRS-1(config-isis)#interface tenGigE 0/0/0/2
RP/0/RP0/CPU0:CRS-1(config-isis-if)#address-family ipv4 unicast
RP/0/RP0/CPU0:CRS-1(config-isis-if-af)#address-family ipv6 unicast
RP/0/RP0/CPU0:CRS-1(config-isis-if-af)#exit
RP/0/RP0/CPU0:CRS-1(config-isis-if)#exit
RP/0/RP0/CPU0:CRS-1(config-isis)#interface loopback 1
RP/0/RP0/CPU0:CRS-1(config-isis-if)#address-family ipv4 unicast
RP/0/RP0/CPU0:CRS-1(config-isis-if-af)#address-family ipv6 unicast
RP/0/RP0/CPU0:CRS-1(config-isis-if-af)#commit


!Displays the running-config for Single Topology

RP/0/RP0/CPU0:CRS-1#show running-config router isis
router isis 1
 net 49.0001.0001.0002.00
 address-family ipv6 unicast
  single-topology
 !
 interface Loopback1
  address-family ipv4 unicast
  !
  address-family ipv6 unicast
  !
 !
 interface TenGigE0/0/0/2
  address-family ipv4 unicast
  !
  address-family ipv6 unicast
  !
 !
!
```

```
!Verification of IPv4 and IPv6 routes learned by CRS-2

RP/0/RP0/CPU0:CRS-2#show isis ipv4 route

IS-IS 1 IPv4 Unicast routes

Codes: L1 - level 1, L2 - level 2, ia - interarea (leaked into level 1)
       df - level 1 default (closest attached router), su - summary null
       C - connected, S - static, R - RIP, B - BGP, O - OSPF
       i - IS-IS (redistributed from another instance)

Maximum parallel path count: 8

C  10.0.0.0/24
     is directly connected, TenGigE0/0/0/3
L1 172.16.1.1/32 [20/115]
     via 10.0.0.1, TenGigE0/0/0/3, CRS-1

RP/0/RP0/CPU0:CRS-2#show isis ipv6 route

IS-IS 1 IPv6 Unicast routes

Codes: L1 - level 1, L2 - level 2, ia - interarea (leaked into level 1)
       df - level 1 default (closest attached router), su - summary null
       C - connected, S - static, R - RIP, B - BGP, O - OSPF
       i - IS-IS (redistributed from another instance)

Maximum parallel path count: 8

L1 2001::1/128 [20/115]
     via fe80::217:59ff:fe6e:b50a, TenGigE0/0/0/3, CRS-1
C  2002::/126
     is directly connected, TenGigE0/0/0/3
```

Verifying the Single Topology Model

Example 7-37 illustrates that IPv4 and IPv6 can use the same topology. The command **show isis instance 1** shows that narrow TLV is used for both IPv4 and IPv6, and the command **show isis database detail** confirms that the same TLV is used for both IPv4 and IPv6.

Example 7-37 *Verify the Single Topology Model*

```
RP/0/RP0/CPU0:CRS-1#show isis instance 1


IS-IS Router: 1
  System Id: 0001.0001.0001
```

```
  IS Levels: level-1-2
  Manual area address(es):
    49
  Routing for area address(es):
    49
  Non-stop forwarding: Disabled
  Most recent startup mode: Cold Restart
  Topologies supported by IS-IS:
    IPv4 Unicast
      Level-1
        Metric style (generate/accept): Narrow/Narrow
        ISPF status: Disabled
      Level-2
        Metric style (generate/accept): Narrow/Narrow
        ISPF status: Disabled
      No protocols redistributed
      Distance: 115
    IPv6 Unicast
      Level-1
        Metric style (generate/accept): Narrow/Narrow
        ISPF status: Disabled
      Level-2
        Metric style (generate/accept): Narrow/Narrow
        ISPF status: Disabled
      No protocols redistributed
      Distance: 115
  Interfaces supported by IS-IS:
    TenGigE0/0/0/2 is running actively (active in configuration)
    Loopback1 is running actively (active in configuration)

RP/0/RP0/CPU0:CRS-1#show isis database detail

IS-IS 1 (Level-1) Link State Database
LSPID                 LSP Seq Num  LSP Checksum  LSP Holdtime  ATT/P/OL
CRS-1.00-00         * 0x0000000b   0xe220        627                0/0/0
  Area Address: 49
  NLPID:        0xcc
  NLPID:        0x8e
  Hostname:     CRS-1
  IP Address:   172.16.1.1
  IPv6 Address: 2001::1
  Metric: 10          IS CRS-2.01
  Metric: 10          IP 10.0.0.0/24
  Metric: 10          IP 172.16.1.1/32
  Metric: 10          IPv6 2001::1/128
  Metric: 10          IPv6 2002::/126
```

Configuring and Verifying the Multitopology Model

Example 7-38 shows that unconfiguring the address-family IPv6 unicast converts a single topology model to a multitopology model. The command **show isis instance 1** shows that the multitopology model uses the special TLV called MT-TLV.

Example 7-38 *Configure and Verify the Multitopology Model*

```
RP/0/RP0/CPU0:CRS-1#conf t
RP/0/RP0/CPU0:CRS-1(config)#router isis 1
RP/0/RP0/CPU0:CRS-1(config-isis)#no address-family ipv6 unicast
RP/0/RP0/CPU0:CRS-1(config-isis)#commit


RP/0/RP0/CPU0:CRS-1#show running-config router isis
router isis 1
 net 49.0001.0001.0001.00
 interface Loopback1
  address-family ipv4 unicast
  !
  address-family ipv6 unicast
  !
 !
 interface TenGigE0/0/0/2
  address-family ipv4 unicast
  !
  address-family ipv6 unicast
  !
 !
!

!Verification of Multitopology


RP/0/RP0/CPU0:CRS-1#show isis database detail

IS-IS 1 (Level-1) Link State Database
LSPID                  LSP Seq Num  LSP Checksum  LSP Holdtime  ATT/P/OL
CRS-1.00-00          * 0x0000006d   0x228c        571               0/0/0
  Area Address: 49
  NLPID:         0xcc
  NLPID:         0x8e
  MT:            Standard (IPv4 Unicast)
  MT:            IPv6 Unicast                                        0/0/0
```

```
Hostname:      CRS-1
IP Address:    172.16.1.1
IPv6 Address: 2001::1
Metric: 10          IS CRS-2.03
Metric: 10          IP 10.0.0.0/24
Metric: 10          IP 172.16.1.1/32
Metric: 10          MT (IPv6 Unicast) IS-Extended CRS-2.03
Metric: 10          MT (IPv6 Unicast) IPv6 2001::1/128
Metric: 10          MT (IPv6 Unicast) IPv6 2002::/126
```

Configuring and Verifying Interface States

An IS-IS interface can be configured to be in different states. The default state is active. In this state adjacencies are formed with neighbors and prefixes are advertised. An IS-IS interface can also be configured to be passive. In this state adjacencies are not formed with neighbors, but prefixes are advertised. Use the **passive** command to make an interface configured under IS-IS a passive interface. An interface can be disabled just for IS-IS instead of unconfiguring using the **shutdown** command. Some remote sites might require adjacency establishment, but might not want to advertise the prefixes. Such interfaces can enable the option **suppress**. The command **show isis interface** can be used to verify the state of the interface for all the preceding options. Example 7-39 displays the configuration and verification options for IS-IS interfaces.

Example 7-39 *Configure and Verify Interface States*

```
!Command options available for a ISIS interface


RP/0/RP0/CPU0:CRS-1#configure
RP/0/RP0/CPU0:CRS-1(config)#router isis 1
RP/0/RP0/CPU0:CRS-1(config-isis)#interface tenGigE 0/0/0/2
RP/0/RP0/CPU0:CRS-1(config-isis-if)#?
  no                         Negate a command or set its defaults
  passive                    Do not establish adjacencies over this interface
  shutdown                   Shutdown IS-IS on this interface
  suppressed                 Do not advertise connected prefixes of this interface

!Configuration of ISIS suppressed command

RP/0/RP0/CPU0:CRS-1(config-isis-if)#suppressed
RP/0/RP0/CPU0:CRS-1(config-isis-if)#end

!Verification of ISIS interface in suppressed mode

RP/0/RP0/CPU0:CRS-1#show isis interface
```

```
IS-IS 1 Interfaces
TenGigE0/0/0/2               Enabled
  Adjacency Formation:       Enabled
  Prefix Advertisement:      Disabled (Suppressed in IS-IS cfg)
  BFD:                        Disabled
  BFD Min Interval:          150
BFD Multiplier:            3

RP/0/RP0/CPU0:CRS-1# show running-config router isis
router isis 1
 net 49.0001.0001.0001.00
 interface TenGigE0/0/0/2
  suppressed
  address-family ipv4 unicast

!Configuration of ISIS shutdown command
RP/0/RP0/CPU0:CRS-1(config-isis)#interface tenGigE 0/0/0/2
RP/0/RP0/CPU0:CRS-1(config-isis-if)#shutdown
RP/0/RP0/CPU0:CRS-1(config-isis-if)#commit

!Verification of ISIS interface in shutdown state

RP/0/RP0/CPU0:CRS-1#show isis interface tenGigE 0/0/0/2

TenGigE0/0/0/2               Disabled (Intf shutdown in IS-IS cfg)

RP/0/RP0/CPU0:CRS-1#show running-config router isis
router isis 1
 net 49.0001.0001.0001.00
 interface TenGigE0/0/0/2
  shutdown
  address-family ipv4 unicast
  !
  address-family ipv6 unicast
```

Configuring IS-IS NSF and IS-IS Timers

IS-IS in IOS XR has separate processes for the hello protocol, SPF, and update threads for an IS-IS database. The isis process runs on the standby RP as a warm standby process. It helps the IS-IS to recover faster during cutovers because the standby process is fully initialized. IOS XR isis processes are restartable and use a checkpoint recovery mechanism to have minimal impact on the system. IOS XR IS-IS supports both the IETF and Cisco formats of NSF. The **show processes isis location all** command can be used to verify the IS-IS NSF in IOS XR.

IS-IS uses the incremental shortest path first (iSPF) algorithm rather than running full SPF when there are minimal topology changes. iSPF helps to reduce the load on the processor and it can be enabled by using the command **ispf [level {1 | 2}]**. Whenever there is network instability, label switched paths (LSPs) are generated and flooded in the network. This leads to lot of recalculations for all neighbors, causing load on the CPU as well as increasing the traffic load on the network. To control and throttle the LSP generation under these scenarios, use the command **lsp-gen-interval** {[*initial-wait initial*] [*secondary-wait secondary*] [*maximum-wait maximum*]} **[level {1 | 2}]**. The default value for initial-wait is 50 msec, secondary-wait is 200 msec, and maximum-wait is 5000 msec. You can change these default values based on the network stability as shown in Example 7-40. The amount of time between LSP generations per interface level is also configurable using the command **lsp-interval milliseconds** [**level** {**1** | **2**}]. The default value of lsp-interval is 33 msecs.

Example 7-40 *IS-IS Timers*

```
RP/0/RP0/CPU0:CRS-1#configure
RP/0/RP0/CPU0:CRS-1(config)#router isis 1
RP/0/RP0/CPU0:CRS-1(config-isis)#lsp-gen-interval maximum-wait 40
RP/0/RP0/CPU0:CRS-1(config-isis)#interface tenGigE 0/0/0/2
RP/0/RP0/CPU0:CRS-1(config-isis-if)#lsp-interval 50
```

isis is a restartable process and it can be restarted using the command **process restart isis**, as follows:

```
RP/0/RP0/CPU0:CRS-1#process restart isis
RP/0/RP0/CPU0:CRS-1#
```

IS-IS supports both Cisco and IETF options for NSF as shown in Example 7-41.

Example 7-41 *IS-IS: NSF Configuration and Verification*

```
!ISIS NSF Command options

RP/0/RP0/CPU0:CRS-1(config)#router isis 1
RP/0/RP0/CPU0:CRS-1(config-isis)#nsf ?
  cisco                Cisco Proprietary NSF restart
  ietf                 IETF NSF restart
  interface-expires   # of times T1 can expire waiting for the restart ACK
  interface-timer      Timer used to wait for a restart ACK (seconds)
  lifetime             Maximum route lifetime following restart (seconds)
!ISIS NSF Configuration

RP/0/RP0/CPU0:CRS-1(config)#router isis 1
RP/0/RP0/CPU0:CRS-1(config-isis)#nsf cisco
RP/0/RP0/CPU0:CRS-1(config-isis)#commit
```

```
!ISIS NSF Verification

RP/0/RP0/CPU0:CRS-1# show isis
IS-IS Router: 1
  System Id: 0001.0001.0001
  IS Levels: level-1-2
  Manual area address(es):
    49
  Routing for area address(es):
    49
  Non-stop forwarding: Cisco Proprietary NSF Restart enabled
```

Configuring and Verifying BFD in IS-IS

IS-IS convergence relies on the IS-IS hello protocol, which takes seconds to detect an adjacency failure. You can enable BFD to improve link failure detection and, therefore, the convergence time. It provides timers that can be modified to achieve desirable convergence time. The IS-IS hello protocol registers as a client with BFD. If the BFD session goes down, it notifies its client IS-IS hello process, which in turn brings down the IS-IS adjacency right away, resulting in fast convergence. BFD for IS-IS can be enabled per interface level. The command **show isis interface <*cmd*>** provides the different states of BFD enabled for a given interface as shown in Example 7-42.

Example 7-42 *BFD Configuration and Verification*

```
!BFD Command Options

RP/0/RP0/CPU0:CRS-1(config)#router isis 1
RP/0/RP0/CPU0:CRS-1(config-isis)#interface TenGigE0/0/0/2
RP/0/RP0/CPU0:CRS-1(config-isis-if)#bfd ?
  fast-detect        Enable Fast detection
  minimum-interval  Hello interval
  multiplier         Detect multiplier



!BFD Configuration

RP/0/RP0/CPU0:CRS-1(config-isis-if)#bfd fast-detect ?
  ipv4  Address Family
RP/0/RP0/CPU0:CRS-1(config-isis-if)#bfd fast-detect ipv4
RP/0/RP0/CPU0:CRS-1(config-isis-if)#commit

!BFD Verification
```

```
RP/0/RP0/CPU0:CRS-1#show isis interface tenGigE 0/0/0/2
TenGigE0/0/0/2                Enabled
  Adjacency Formation:        Enabled
  Prefix Advertisement:       Enabled
  BFD:                          Enabled
  BFD Min Interval:            150
  BFD Multiplier:              3
  Circuit Type:                 level-1-2
  Media Type:                   LAN
  Circuit Number:             9
```

Configuring and Verifying IP Fast Reroute

IP Fast Reroute (IPFRR) is another method to improve convergence when there are link or node failures. It is similar to MPLS FRR but is implemented for IP-only network scenarios. In addition to convergence, IPFRR can be used for node or link protection. IPFRR precomputes the repair path for every prefix, and that path is used as soon as the failure (node or link) happens. IS-IS TLVs are extended to advertise the IPFRR capability to other routers and to carry the backup path information. For fast detection of a primary path failure and cutover to the backup path, the trigger for IPFRR includes SONET alarms or BFD-enabled links. IPFRR can be enabled by using the command **ipfrr lfa level 1|2** under IS-IS interface. The backup path information can be verified using the command **show isis neighbor detail.** Example 7-43 provides the steps to configure and verify IPFRR.

Example 7-43 *IPFRR Configuration and Verification*

```
RP/0/RP0/CPU0:CRS-1#configure

RP/0/RP0/CPU0:CRS-1(config)#router isis 1
RP/0/RP0/CPU0:CRS-1(config-isis)#is-type level-2-only
RP/0/RP0/CPU0:CRS-1(config-isis)#address-family ipv4 unicast
RP/0/RP0/CPU0:CRS-1(config-isis-af)#metric-style wide
RP/0/RP0/CPU0:CRS-1(config-isis)#interface Loopback1
RP/0/RP0/CPU0:CRS-1(config-isis-if)#  address-family ipv4 unicast
RP/0/RP0/CPU0:CRS-1(config-isis-if-af)#   ipfrr lfa level 1
RP/0/RP0/CPU0:CRS-1(config-isis-if-af)# interface tenGigE 0/0/0/2
RP/0/RP0/CPU0:CRS-1(config-isis-if-af)#ipfrr lfa level 1


RP/0/RP0/CPU0:CRS-1#show running-config router isis
router isis 1
 is-type level-2-only
 net 49.0001.0001.0001.00
 address-family ipv4 unicast
  metric-style wide
 !
```

```
 interface Loopback1
  address-family ipv4 unicast
   ipfrr lfa level 1
  !
 !
 interface TenGigE0/0/0/2
  address-family ipv4 unicast
   ipfrr lfa level 1
  !
 !
!
```

Configuring and Verifying Authentication in IOS XR IS-IS

IS-IS supports both clear text and MD5 authentication. These can be defined at different levels. Hello packets can be authenticated using the **hello-password** configuration command. This can be defined at the interface level and can be configured for either Level-1 or Level-2 adjacency. Authentication can be enabled at domain level and/or area level by using the **lsp-password** command. This configuration will authenticate LSPs and sequence number protocol (SNP) protocol data units (PDUs) exchanged with the neighbors. The keychain is defined globally and can be used in conjunction with hello packet authentication or LSP authentication. Example 7-44 provides the steps to configure and verify authentication in IOS XR IS-IS.

Example 7-44 *Authentication Configuration and Verification*

```
!Configuration of Hello Password Authentication


RP/0/RP0/CPU0:CRS-1(config)#router isis 1
RP/0/RP0/CPU0:CRS-1(config-isis)#interface tenGigE 0/0/0/2
RP/0/RP0/CPU0:CRS-1(config-isis-if)#hello-password hmac-md5 clear cisco
RP/0/RP0/CPU0:CRS-1(config-isis-if)#commit

!Verification of Committed Configuration

RP/0/RP0/CPU0:CRS-1# show running-config router isis
router isis 1
 net 49.0001.0001.0001.00
 interface TenGigE0/0/0/2
  hello-password hmac-md5 encrypted 13080E020A1F173D24362C
  address-family ipv4 unicast
  !
  address-family ipv6 unicast
  !
 !
```

```
!
!Configuration of LSP Password Authentication
RP/0/RP0/CPU0:CRS-1(config)#router isis 1
RP/0/RP0/CPU0:CRS-1(config-isis)#lsp-password hmac-md5 clear mypassword
RP/0/RP0/CPU0:CRS-1(config-isis)#commit


!Verification of Committed Configuration

RP/0/RP0/CPU0:CRS-1# show running-config router isis

router isis 1
 net 49.0001.0001.0001.00
 nsf cisco
 lsp-password hmac-md5 encrypted 045612160E325F59060B01
 interface Loopback1
  address-family ipv4 unicast
  !
  address-family ipv6 unicast
  !
 !
 interface TenGigE0/0/0/2
  address-family ipv4 unicast
  !
  address-family ipv6 unicast
  !
 !
!


RP/0/RP0/CPU0:CRS-1# show isis database detail

IS-IS 1 (Level-1) Link State Database
LSPID                   LSP Seq Num  LSP Checksum  LSP Holdtime  ATT/P/OL
CRS-1.00-00           * 0x00000090   0x5584        1142              0/0/0
  Auth:         Algorithm HMAC-MD5, Length: 17
```

Table 7-4 lists some of the key commands used for verifying and debugging on IOS XR IS-IS.

Table 7-4 *IS-IS Operation and Debug Commands*

Command	Description
show isis [**instance** *instance-id*] **adjacency** [**level** {**1** | **2**}] [*interface-type interface-instance*] [**detail**] [**systemid** *system-id*]	Provides the IS-IS adjacency information for different instances or levels

Command	Description
show isis [**instance** *instance-id*] **checkpoint lsp**	Provides information on the LSP PDU database
clear isis [**instance** *instance-id*] **process**	Clears the isis process and restarts the adjacency establishment
debug isis [**instance** *instance-id*] **adjacencies** [**interface** *type instance*] [**restarts**] [**level** {**1** | **2**}] [*lsp lsp-id*] [**summary** | **detail**] [**topology** [**ipv4** | **ipv6**] [**unicast** | **multicast**]] [**only**]	Used to debug adjacencies and neighbor relationship
debug isis [**instance** *instance-id*] **configuration** [**interface** *type instance*] [**level** {**1** | **2**}] [**summary** | **detail**] [**topology** [**ipv4** | **ipv6**] [**unicast** | **multicast**]] [**only**]	Used to debug IS-IS configuration and related changes
debug isis [**instance** *instance-id*] **spf** [**full** | **incremental** | **nhc** | **prc** | **trigger** | **ipfrr**] [*prefix/length* [**longer-prefixes**]] [**level** {**1** | **2**}] [**lsp** *lsp-id*] [**prefix-list** *prefix-list-name*] [**summary** | **detail** | **verbose**] [**topology** [**ipv4** | **ipv6**] [**unicast** | **multicast**]] [**only**]	Used to debug SPF calculations

Summary

This chapter discussed and explored the architecture and implementation of the various IGPs supported in IOS XR. It also covered that different IGP processes can be cold restartable, warm restartable, or hot restartable. This chapter also discussed the basic configuration of RIP, EIGRP, OSPF, and IS-IS in IOS XR. This chapter covered some of the salient features and configuration options that can be used for these IGPs, namely process restart, usage of route policy, and MD5 authentication.

This chapter briefly discussed implementation methods of different routing protocols. The configuration and verification commands discussed in this chapter are just a few examples and the focus was to highlight the salient features only. Refer to Cisco.com to get a full list of configuration and verification commands.

References

- **Cisco.** Cisco IOS XR Routing Command Reference, Release 3.6. http://www.cisco.com/
- **Cisco.** Cisco IOS XR Routing Configuration Guide, Release 3.6. http://www.cisco.com/
- **Cisco.** Cisco IOS XR Routing Debug Command Reference, Release 3.6. http://www.cisco.com/

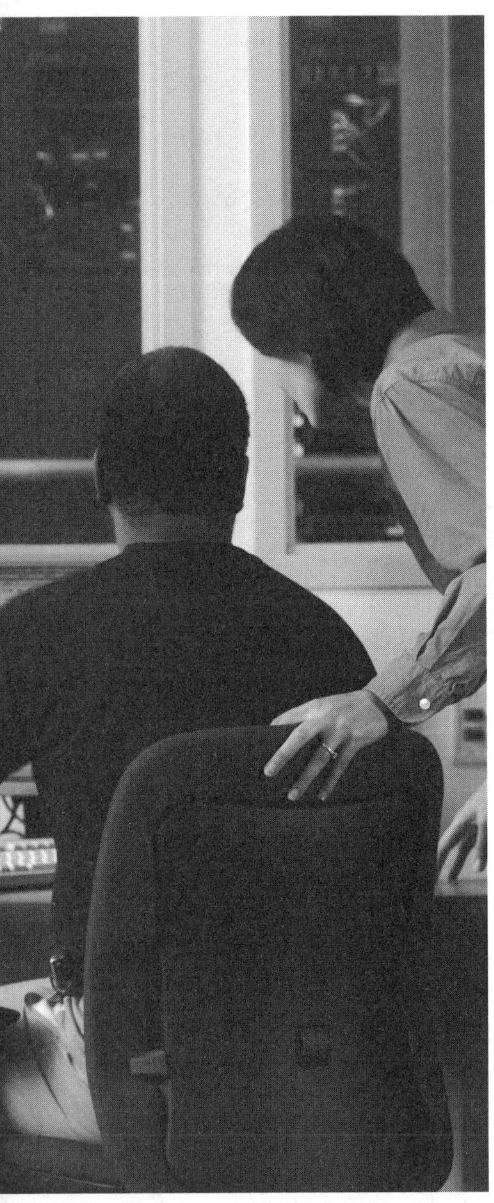

This chapter covers the following topics:

- Cisco IOS XR BGP Architectural Overview
- Cisco IOS XR BGP Hierarchical Configuration
- Implementing BGP Policies
- BGP Policy Accounting
- BGP Remotely Triggered Black Hole
- BGP Graceful Restart
- BGP Distributed Speaker
- Cisco IOS XR BGP Convergence
- References

Border Gateway Protocol (BGP) is the lifeline of the modern Internet. It is a path vector protocol that provides the framework for the exchange of network layer reachability information (NLRI) between different autonomous systems (AS). BGP is very flexible in implementing routing policies because it uses a wide assortment of attributes in making routing decisions.

This chapter introduces BGP architecture and configuration in IOS XR. Many voluminous books have been written about BGP; therefore, this chapter does not aim to address every feature and concept related to the BGP protocol itself. Instead, it highlights key aspects of IOS XR implementation of BGP. This chapter also assumes you are familiar with the details of the BGP protocol, including its attributes and best path calculation algorithm.

CHAPTER 8

Implementing BGP in Cisco IOS XR

Cisco IOS XR BGP provides the ability to exchange IPv4 and IPv6 NLRIs. It also supports the multicast address family for the support of interdomain multicast routing. Additionally, BGP support for propagating VPN prefixes in the single AS or Inter-AS and Carrier Supporting Carrier scenarios is also available. This chapter, however, discusses BGP features and policies as they relate to the IPv4 address family. BGP is periodically discussed throughout this book. This chapter discusses the hierarchical CLI that is a trademark of the IOS XR operating system.

You might be familiar with the concept of peer groups in IOS. This chapter discusses the flexibility provided by IOS XR BGP, especially for large-scale deployments via peer group–like functionality for neighbors, address families, and BGP sessions. These grouping or templates can be implemented using neighbor-group, address-family group, and session-group and are discussed in the upcoming sections of this chapter.

One of the key distinguishing features of IOS XR compared to other predecessor operating systems is its user-friendly implementation of routing policies. Routing polices were briefly introduced in Chapter 7, "Routing IGP," but this chapter provides a more exhaustive overview of Routing Policy Language (RPL) as it relates to BGP. This chapter illustrates examples implementing commonly used BGP policies and provides you with a tutorial where you can implement and customize IOS XR BGP routing policies using RPL.

Cisco IOS XR BGP Architectural Overview

Chapter 2, "Cisco IOS XR Infrastructure," discussed the generic control plane and routing architecture. This section carries forward the architecture discussion with specific focus on the processes involved with BGP routing infrastructure. Figure 8-1 provides a high-level overview of IOS XR BGP architectural blocks.

The previous chapters have discussed the roles of configuration manager, exec, and Sysdb processes in configuring the router and providing the means for executing **clear** and **show** commands. Figure 8-1 shows the communication between exec and CLI operations and a BGP-related process called BGP Process Manager (BPM). This communication occurs via Sysdb. BPM verifies the BGP configuration and determines the conformance of the configuration for correctness. BPM detects configuration errors related to BGP before they can be committed to the commit database. After the BPM process performs the necessary checks, it republishes BGP configuration to the bRIB (BGP RIB) process. BPM also determines the router-id and checks the **clear** commands entered by the user, and then passes them to the BGP process. BPM is responsible for verifying continual configuration changes related to BGP and for calculating and publishing the distribution of neighbors among BGP speaker processes. Figure 8-1 shows the communication of BGP block with RIB and the MPLS label switching database (LSD) processes.

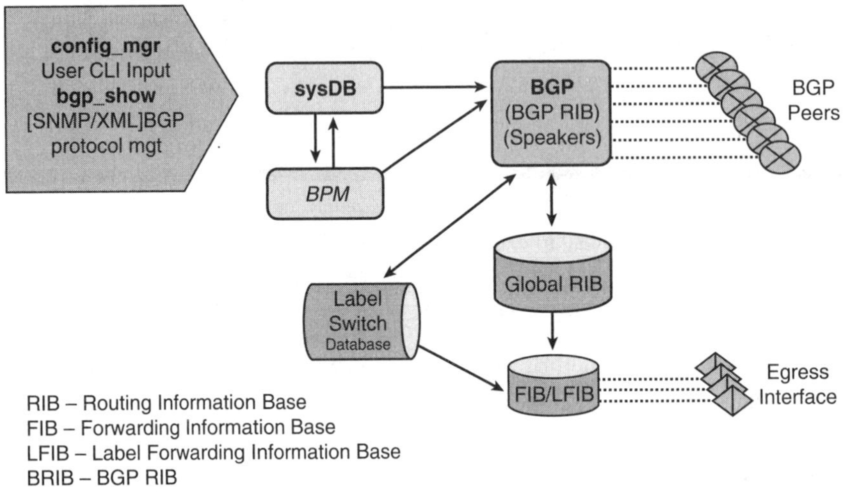

Figure 8-1 *Cisco IOS XR BGP Architectural Overview*

As depicted in Figure 8-1, BPM handles configuration changes related to BGP. BPM is a multithreaded process, and specific details of the process can be examined via the **show process BPM** command in a router running XR. Figure 8-2 adds multiple BGP speakers and the BRIB process to the BGP architectural picture.

Cisco IOS XR has the capability to run BGP in a standalone or distributed mode. BGP speaker is a key concept in IOS XR distributed BGP and is discussed in more detail in the ensuing sections of this chapter. BGP speakers are responsible for handling all BGP peer connections and for imposing neighbor route import and export policies. The speaker stores received paths in the RIB and performs only a partial best path calculation before handing over the result of the partial best paths to the bRIB. Speakers perform a limited best path calculation because a Multi Exit Discriminator (MED) comparison might need to be made with peers that belong to a different speaker. BGP speakers do not have access to the entire BGP local RIB and perform the best path calculation using the following criteria:

- Compare the WEIGHT attribute
- Compare the local preference (LOC_PREF)
- Check LOCAL origination or redistribution
- Check AS_PATH length
- Check ORIGIN
- Compare MED for peers assigned to the speaker

Note: If BGP is configured with the **bgp bestpath med always** command, the speaker process computes the best path taking into account the MED attribute. Otherwise, MED comparisons are undertaken by bRIB in computing the best path.

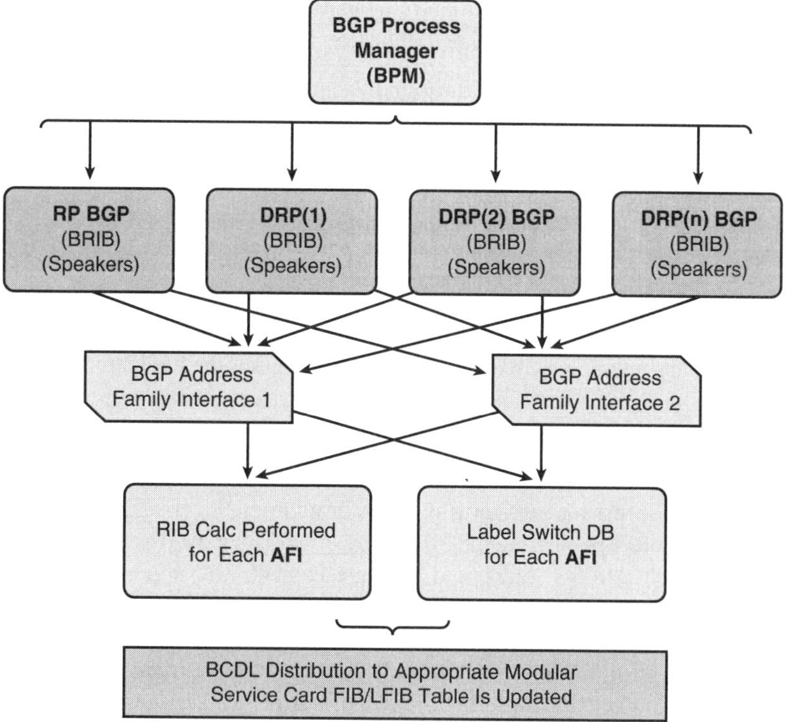

Figure 8-2 *Distributed BGP*

Only the best paths are advertised to the bRIB to reduce speaker IPC overhead and to reduce the number of paths to be processed in the bRIB. BGP speakers can mark a path as active only after learning the result of the full best-path calculation from the bRIB. In distributed mode, up to 15 speaker processes may be used in BGP. Multiple BGP speakers help reduce the collateral damage caused by a fault in one of the address families. For example, a configuration scenario implements IPv6, IPv4, and VPNv4 BGP peers on distributed speakers. In the event of a fault or a reload of a process, say the VPNv4 address family, other IPv6 and IPv4 address families are not impacted.

Cisco IOS XR allows you to control the configuration of the number of distributed speakers and enables you to selectively assign neighbors to specific speakers. On the CRS-1 platform, multiple speaker processes up to 15 may be configured. However, configuring all the different speakers on the primary route processor simply adds to the load on the single RP. Distributed speaker functionality is useful if Distributed Route Processor (DRP) hardware is available to take advantage of process placement. Later sections in this chapter depict distributed BGP and placement of BGP process speakers on DRPs on a CRS-1 router.

In addition to the speaker process, BPM starts the bRIB process once BGP is configured. bRIB process is responsible for performing the best-path calculation based on partial best paths received from the speaker processes. The best route is installed into the bRIB and is advertised back to all speakers. The bRIB process is also responsible for installing routes in the RIB and for handling routes redistributed from the RIB. bRIB runs the rest of the BGP best path algorithm criteria in the final determination of best routes:

- Checks for EBGP versus IBGP
- Compares IGP metric
- Checks the maximum number for Equal Cost Multiple Paths
- If external paths are found to be equal, prefers the oldest
- Compares router ID
- Uses lower cluster ID in case router-ids are equivalent in a route-reflector scenario

bRIB allows route leaking from one RIB to another using configuration. Redistribution between IGP and BGP, and vice versa, are examples of this scenario. bRIB may register for redistribution from multiple RIB routes into a single route in the bRIB process.

bRIB also takes care of BGP aggregate route generation. As Figure 8-2 shows, there is a single instance of bRIB process for each address-family. In addition, Figure 8-2 shows the address-family–specific bRIB populating the RIB and label switching database (LSD). IOS XR supports the different address-family based RIB for each SDR. RIB supports a client/server model and provides distribution of routes between producers of routing information and the consumer entities within the routing platform. RIB downloads the information to forwarding information base (FIB), which is used for forwarding. LSD is the MPLS equivalent of RIB and communicates with bRIB to learn about labels assigned by BGP. The route download happens via BCDL, which was discussed in Chapter 2.

Cisco IOS XR BGP Hierarchical Configuration

BGP uses the hierarchical command-line interface (CLI) configuration, which is a distinctive trait of IOS XR configuration. IOS XR allows grouping of BGP neighbor configuration, making the BGP configuration more intuitive and more easily readable. All BGP parameters can be viewed by simply displaying the BGP configuration using the CLI command **show run router bgp**. This section discusses the various configuration modes and submodes within BGP configuration.

Similar to other routing protocol configuration, IOS XR BGP is configured by typing **router bgp** *<autonomous system number>* in the global configuration mode as illustrated in Example 8-1.

Example 8-1 *BGP Configuration Modes*

```
RP/0/RP1/CPU0:CRS1-1(config)#router bgp 101
RP/0/RP1/CPU0:CRS1-1(config-bgp)#?
  address-family          Enter Address Family command mode
  af-group                Specify a AF group
  bfd                     Configure BFD parameters
  bgp                     BGP commands
  clear                   Clear the uncommitted configuration
  clear                   Clear the configuration
```

```
commit                  Commit the configuration changes to running
default-information     Control distribution of default information
default-metric          default redistributed metric
describe                Describe a command without taking real actions
distributed             Distributed BGP configuration
do                      Run an exec command
exit                    Exit from this submode
mpls                    Enable mpls parameters
neighbor                Specify a neighbor router
neighbor-group          Specify a Neighbor-group
no                      Negate a command or set its defaults
pwd                     Commands used to reach current submode
root                    Exit to the global configuration mode
session-group           Specify a Session group
show                    Show contents of configuration
socket                  set socket parameters
timers                  Adjust routing timers
vrf                     Specify a vrf name
```

The BGP configuration mode allows key global BGP configurations such as IPv4/v6 and VPNv4/v6 address families, BGP timers, and router ID configuration in addition to several other configuration options discussed in the upcoming sections of this chapter.

Cisco IOS XR BGP provides a router ID selection algorithm if one is not configured; however, for production environments, it is strongly advised to configure a router ID using the **bgp router-id** *<IPv4 address>* configuration command. If a router ID is not configured, BGP uses the highest IP address of existing loopbacks or, if no loopbacks exist prior to configuring the BGP process, it assumes the first configured IPv4 address. The upcoming sections discuss some of the key configuration modes under the router BGP stanza.

Note: The BGP router ID should be explicitly configured as a good configuration practice.

Address Family Configuration Mode

BGP provides the address family configuration option under the main BGP routing stanza, as shown in Example 8-2. This output is based on IOS XR release version 3.6.1.

Example 8-2 *Address Family Configuration Submode*

```
! Example output showing the address-families supported under "router bgp"
RP/0/RP1/CPU0:CRS1-1(config-bgp)#address-family ?
  ipv4    IPv4 Address Family
  ipv6    IPv6 Address Family
  vpnv4   VPNv4 Address Family
  vpnv6   VPNv6 Address Family
!
```

```
! Example output showing the options under the ipv4 address-family
!
RP/0/RP1/CPU0:CRS1-1(config-bgp)#address-family ipv4 ?
!
  mdt           Address Family modifier
  multicast     Address Family modifier
  tunnel        Address Family modifier
  unicast       Address Family modifier
!
! Example of configuration options under the ipv4 unicast address-family
RP/0/RP1/CPU0:CRS1-1(config-bgp)#address-family ipv4 unicast ?
  aggregate-address   Configure BGP aggregate entries
  allocate-label      Allocate label for selected prefixes
  bgp                 BGP Commands
  distance            Define an administrative distance
  maximum-paths       Forward packets over multiple paths
  network             Specify a network to announce via BGP
  nexthop             Nexthop
  redistribute        Redistribute information from another routing protocol
  table-policy        Configure policy for installation of routes to RIB
  <cr>
```

Although several address families, including IPv4, IPv6, VPNv4, and VPNv6, are supported, IPv4 address family is the subject of discussion in this chapter. Example 8-2 shows various options under the IPv4 address family, which include *mdt* for multicast VPN (MVPN), *multicast* for interdomain multicast, and *tunnel* for L2TPV3 tunneling applications. The address family *ipv4 unicast* provides the IPv4-specific configuration commands related to BGP routing. Upcoming examples show more detailed usage of the configuration options in the IPv4 unicast address families.

Note: The required address family must be activated in BGP global configuration before a neighbor peer configuration can be assigned that address family.

Configuration Groups

Cisco IOS XR BGP offers various groupings or templates to simplify BGP configuration, as follows:

- **Af-group** allows common parts of address-family specific configuration to be grouped together for reuse of common portions of configuration.
- **Session-group** allows non-AF specific configuration to be grouped together.
- **Neighbor-group** allows grouping and reuse of neighbor-specific configuration.

This section provides configuration examples and explains the IOS XR BGP configuration groupings. Figure 8-3 shows a simple BGP setup in explaining the BGP configuration group templates.

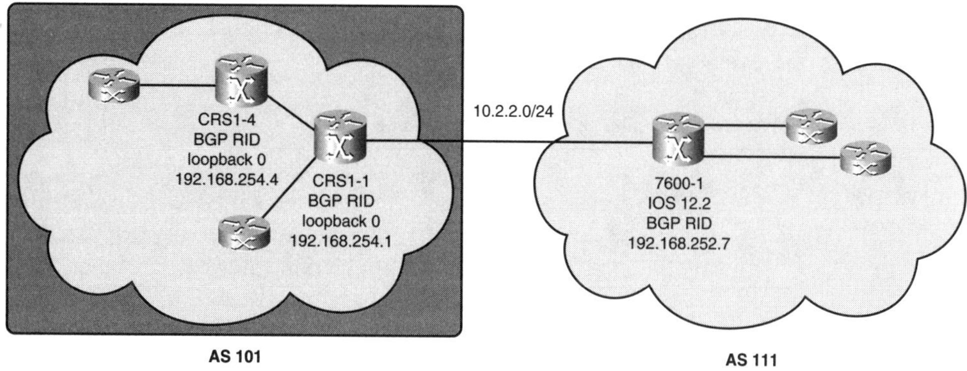

Figure 8-3 *BGP Configuration Topology*

Example 8-3 illustrates IOS XR configurations for a CRS1-1 router as depicted in Figure 8-3. The BGP router-id is explicitly configured to be one of the loopback addresses on the router. The IPv4 unicast address-family is initialized under the router bgp submode, which is then associated with the neighbor using neighbor submode configuration. The iBGP neighbor relationship is defined with the neighbor's loopback address 192.168.254.4, and the parameters necessary to form an iBGP session such as remote-as definition and the BGP update-source loopback address are configured under the hierarchy of the neighbor submode. Example 8-3 shows that default-originate and next-hop self, which are specific to each address family, are configured under the IPv4 address-family submode. If this configuration is found to be repetitive for a large number of peers, neighbor-group and af-group templates can be used to provide configuration constructs that take the tedium out of the configuration. Neighbor-group and af-group lend elegance to BGP configuration and assist with readability and manageability aspects of configuration.

Af-group allows common address-family specific configuration to be grouped. Session-group allows non-AF-specific configurations to be grouped. Neighbor-group allows grouping of neighbor specific configuration.

Example 8-3 *BGP Neighbor Configuration Submode*

```
RP/0/RP1/CPU0:CRS1-1#configure t
RP/0/RP1/CPU0:CRS1-1(config)#router bgp 101
RP/0/RP1/CPU0:CRS1-1(config-bgp)#bgp router-id 192.168.254.1
RP/0/RP1/CPU0:CRS1-1(config-bgp)#address-family ipv4 unicast
RP/0/RP1/CPU0:CRS1-1(config-bgp-af)#exit
RP/0/RP1/CPU0:CRS1-1(config-bgp)#neighbor 192.168.254.4
RP/0/RP1/CPU0:CRS1-1(config-bgp-nbr)#remote-as 101
RP/0/RP1/CPU0:CRS1-1(config-bgp-nbr)#update-source loopback0
RP/0/RP1/CPU0:CRS1-1(config-bgp-nbr)#address-family ipv4 unicast
RP/0/RP1/CPU0:CRS1-1(config-bgp-nbr-af)#next-hop-self
RP/0/RP1/CPU0:CRS1-1(config-bgp-nbr-af)#default-originate
RP/0/RP1/CPU0:CRS1-1(config-bgp-nbr-af)#commit
```

```
!
! Verifying the committed configuration with show command
!
RP/0/RP1/CPU0:CRS1-1#show running-config router bgp 101
router bgp 101
 bgp router-id 192.168.254.1
 address-family ipv4 unicast
 !
 neighbor 192.168.254.4
  remote-as 101
  update-source Loopback0
  address-family ipv4 unicast
   default-originate
   next-hop-self
  !
 !
!
```

An order of precedence dictates the applicability of configuration if a number of templates are used within a BGP configuration:

- If the item is specifically configured directly, the specific settings apply and override the template configuration.
- If the neighbor belongs to a neighbor-group, a session-group, or an af-group, use value from defined group only if no conflict is found with the directly specified configuration.
- If multiple templates are used, the session group and af-group have a higher precedence than the neighbor-group.

Example 8-4 shows the creation of a neighbor-group template called ibgp-peer.

Example 8-4 *session-group, af-group, and neighbor-group Configuration*

```
router bgp 101
 bgp router-id 192.168.254.1
 address-family ipv4 unicast
 !
 neighbor-group ibgp-peer
  remote-as 101
  update-source Loopback0
  address-family ipv4 unicast
   default-originate
   next-hop-self
  !
```

```
!
neighbor 192.168.254.4
 use neighbor-group ibgp-peer
```

The ibgp-peer template defines the remote AS and the update source interface to be used for establishing the BGP session. In addition, the neighbor-group template includes the address family configuration. The ibgp-peer neighbor-group template is applied using the **use neighbor-group ibgp-peer** command under the hierarchy of neighbor configuration submode.

Example 8-5 demonstrates the application of the af-group and session-group template. The configuration is slightly different from Example 8-4 because the example uses distributed speaker configuration.

Example 8-5 *BGP session-group and af-group*

```
router bgp 101
 distributed speaker 1
 distributed speaker 2
 bgp router-id 192.168.254.1
 bgp graceful-restart
 address-family ipv4 unicast
  table-policy bgp-policy-acct
  network 111.1.1.1/32
  redistribute static route-policy RTBH
 !
 address-family vpnv4 unicast
 !
 af-group ibgp-af-group address-family ipv4 unicast
  default-originate route-policy conditional-default
  next-hop-self
 !
 session-group ibgp-session
  remote-as 101
  speaker-id 1
  update-source Loopback0
 !
 neighbor-group ibgp-peer
  use session-group ibgp-session
  address-family ipv4 unicast
   use af-group ibgp-af-group
  !
 !
 neighbor 10.2.2.2
  remote-as 111
  speaker-id 2
```

```
  address-family ipv4 unicast
   route-policy permit-all in
   route-policy permit-all out
  !
 !
 neighbor 192.168.254.4
  use neighbor-group ibgp-peer
  speaker-id 1
  address-family ipv4 unicast
   next-hop-self
  !
 !
!
! This command shows the neighbor inheritance for session and AF
!
RP/0/RP0/CPU0:CRS1-1#show bgp neighbors 192.168.254.4 inheritance
Session:      n:ibgp-peer s:ibgp-session
IPv4 Unicast: n:ibgp-peer a:ibgp-af-group
!
! More show commands related to BGP templates
RP/0/RP0/CPU0:CRS1-1#show bgp neighbor-group ibgp-peer users
Session:      192.168.254.4
IPv4 Unicast: 192.168.254.4
!
RP/0/RP0/CPU0:CRS1-1#show bgp session-group ibgp-session users
Session: 192.168.254.4 n:ibgp-peer
!
RP/0/RP0/CPU0:CRS1-1#show bgp af-group ibgp-af-group users
IPv4 Unicast: 192.168.254.4 n:ibgp-peer
```

Example 8-5 shows an example in which a session-groups and af-groups are created for configuration simplicity. The command **show bgp neighbors** *<ip-address>* **inheritance** shows how to check inheritance of different templates. For neighbor 192.168.254.4, the session parameters come from neighbor-group ibgp-peer and session-group ibgp-session templates. ibgp-peer is shown to be the user of ibgp-af-group.

Implementing BGP Policies

Enforcing policies based on the characteristics of routes and their attributes is a vital part of running BGP in a production network. A routing policy defines the specification of the type of routes that a routing process accepts or advertises.

Following are some of the key aspects of a routing policy. A policy may define one or more of the following actions:

- Accept or advertise BGP routes based on their attributes
- Perform modification on the routes' attributes prior to accepting or advertising them

- Allow redistribution from one routing protocol to another
- Influence a BGP neighbor's routing decisions

Cisco IOS XR uses a CLI construct known as Routing Policy Language (RPL) in defining BGP and IGP routing policies. This section discusses the details behind RPL when used for creating BGP routing policies. Most of the concepts are general and may be applied to IGP protocols as well. RPL provides the following advantages:

- A user-friendly way of specifying routing policies.
- The software architecture behind RPL lends itself well to routing policy definition scale.
- Allows brevity and reuse of common structures through parameterization and hierarchical policy definitions.
- RPL policies are not silently skipped. An RPL policy can be applied only if its actions make sense for its intended use. This reduces chances for misconfiguration.

Routing Policy Language

Cisco IOS XR introduces RPL as a way to support large-scale routing configurations. The RPL grammar employs commonly understood logical constructs defined along the lines of YACC (Yet another Compiler Compiler) and that facilitate a user-friendly way of specifying policies with router CLI. The policy CLI is managed by a process known as policy_repository that compiles these policies into an executable form. Figure 8-4 gives an overview of RPL building blocks involved in configuring and running of routing policies.

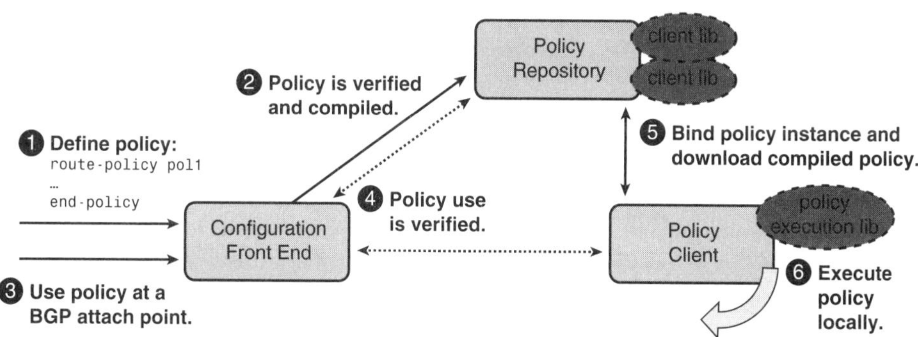

Figure 8-4 *RPL Building Blocks*

In Figure 8-4 the configuration front end refers to the IOS XR CLI used to enter and modify routing policies. RPL configurations are committed to the configuration database in the same way as any IOS XR configuration. There are also standard **show** commands available to support RPL. In addition to IOS XR CLI, the RPL policy may be edited using an appropriate UNIX editor. The choice of an editor is enforced using the configuration command **rpl editor** { **emacs** | **nano** | **vim**}.

Figure 8-4 shows a user defining a route policy in the global configuration. As shown in the figure, a second component of the policy infrastructure, known as *policy repository*, compiles the user-entered configuration into an executable form that the execution engine can understand. The policy repository performs verification of policies and checks to ensure that the policy syntax allows for proper execution. *Policy repository* also keeps track of policy attach-point. An attach-point is a place in the routing protocol where the policy is applied. As an example, if a routing policy is applied for redistribution, its attach-point is known as a redistribution attach-point. Similarly, a policy applied to a neighbor peer has a neighbor attach-point. Some of the common attach-points for BGP are as follows:

- Neighbor inbound
- Neighbor outbound
- Aggregation
- Default originate
- Dampening
- Redistribution
- Table policy
- Network command
- Select cases of BGP **show** commands

Keeping track of the attach-points allows the policy repository to update the right clients when a policy is modified. The policy repository is agnostic of routing protocols and understands the policy syntax and its Boolean logics. It also supports **show** commands used to query an RPL-defined routing policy.

When a policy is used at an attach-point, routing protocols that are policy clients download the compiled form of the policy to their own address space. The RPL execution engine processes routes in client space using this compiled form. Routing protocols or policy clients are responsible for calling the execution engine at the appropriate times to apply the policy to a set of routes. The actions of the policy may include deleting the route if policy indicated that it should be dropped, passing along the route to the protocol's decision tree as a candidate for the best route, or perhaps advertising a policy modified route to a neighbor or peer as appropriate.

Before getting into the nuts and bolts of RPL logical statements, it is important to understand the notion of the various sets that are used to build a routing policy. The concept of set comes from set theory, which is an area of abstract algebra. Set theory defines a set as an unordered grouping of similar objects. In reference to routing policies, this grouping represents route destination prefixes, routing source prefixes, and various attributes such as communities, extended communities, AS paths, and so forth. IOS XR introduces a number of sets that can be used to provide match criteria for an RPL routing policy. The policy language, therefore, provides two kinds of persistent, namable objects. A set is defined as a first namable object that specifies a match criteria, and a policy provides the second namable object. Figure 8-5 shows the two namable objects in a block diagram.

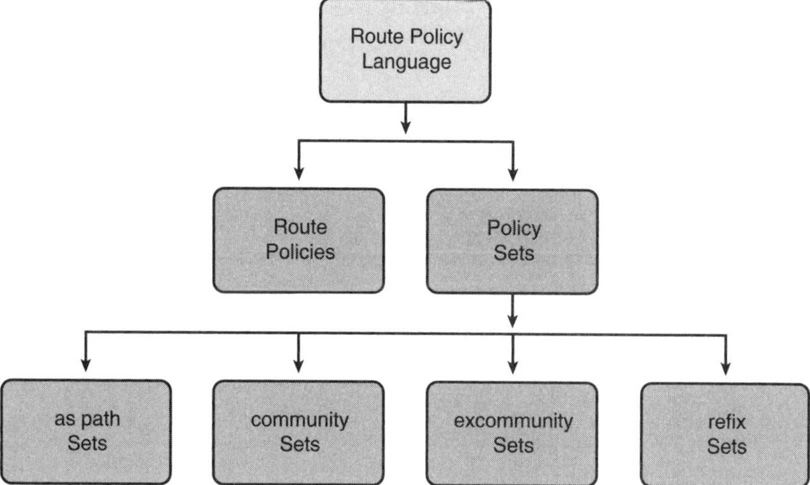

Figure 8-5 *RPL Sets and Policies*

Legal names for policy objects can be any sequence of the uppercase and lowercase alphabetic characters; the numerals 0–9; and the punctuation characters period, minus sign, and underscore. A name cannot begin with a period or underscore. Some of the common sets are discussed in the later sections of this chapter.

Prefix Set

A prefix set holds an unordered collection of IPv4 or IPv6 prefixes used for matching either the source of the route or the incoming and outgoing route prefix advertisement specifications. A prefix listed in a prefix set may have four parts. It defines an address, a mask length, a minimum matching length, and a maximum matching length. The prefix address is required; however, the matching length variables are optional. The address is a standard IPv4 or IPv6 address. Much of the discussion in this chapter revolves around BGP for IPv4; therefore, this section discusses the IPv4 aspects of a prefix set.

The mask length, if specified, presents a nonnegative decimal integer in the range from 0 to 32 following a forward slash (/) that separates the mask from the address. The optional minimum matching length follows the address and optional mask length and is expressed as the keyword **ge** (greater than or equal to), followed by a nonnegative decimal integer in the range from 0 to 32. Finally, the optional maximum matching length follows the rest and is expressed by the keyword **le** (less than or equal to), followed by another nonnegative decimal integer in the range from 0 to 32. The eq (equal) mnemonic denotes an exact match and, therefore, specifies an exact length for prefixes to match.

If a prefix entry in a prefix set has no mask length, the default mask length is 32 and the default minimum matching length is the mask length. If neither minimum nor maximum is specified, the default maximum ends up being the mask length.

The prefix set itself is a comma-separated list of prefix match specifications. Whenever a prefix set is being created, the last prefix is entered without a comma to indicate that an end-set will follow for the completion of the prefix set configuration. Example 8-6 shows the configuration of a prefix set, a namable object called pfx-1.

Example 8-6 *Prefix Set Configuration*

```
RP/0/RP0/CPU0:CRS1-4(config)#prefix-set pfx-1
RP/0/RP0/CPU0:CRS1-4(config-pfx)#192.0.1.1,
RP/0/RP0/CPU0:CRS1-4(config-pfx)#192.0.2.0/24,
RP/0/RP0/CPU0:CRS1-4(config-pfx)#192.0.3.0/24 ge 28,
RP/0/RP0/CPU0:CRS1-4(config-pfx)#192.0.4.0/24 le 28,
RP/0/RP0/CPU0:CRS1-4(config-pfx)#192.0.5.0/24 ge 26 le 30,
RP/0/RP0/CPU0:CRS1-4(config-pfx)#192.0.6.0/24 eq 28
RP/0/RP0/CPU0:CRS1-4(config-pfx)#end-set
RP/0/RP0/CPU0:CRS1-4(config)#commit
```

In Example 8-6, the first element of the prefix set 192.0.1.1 or the host addresses 192.0.1.1/32 must exactly match all four octets. The second element matches prefixes that have the first three octets of 192.0.2, and prefix length of 24. The third element, 192.0.3.0/24 ge 28, matches the first three octets exactly and the prefix length should be greater than or equal to 28. The fourth element matches the first three octets 192.0.4 exactly and the prefix length should be between 24 and 28 inclusive. The fifth element matches the first three octets 192.0.5 and the prefix length is between 26 and 30 inclusive. The sixth element matches any prefix of length 28 while ensuring that the first three octets match 192.0.6. As an example, a prefix 192.0.6.240/28 will provide a match against the sixth line.

Example 8-7 shows an example of choosing an editor for editing sets such as the prefix set. The same editor may also be used for editing routing policies.

Example 8-7 *Using an Editor for Editing Sets or Policies*

```
RP/0/RP0/CPU0:CRS1-4(config)#rpl editor ?
emacs Set default RPL editor to Micro Emacs
nano  Set default RPL editor to nano
 vim  Set default RPL editor to Vim
RP/0/RP0/CPU0:CRS1-4(config)#rpl editor vim
RP/0/RP0/CPU0:CRS1-4(config)#commit
!
RP/0/RP0/CPU0:CRS1-4#edit prefix-set pfx-1
[OK]
prefix-set pfx-1312777" 9 lines, 149 characters
  192.0.1.1,
  192.0.2.0/24,
  192.0.3.0/24 ge 28,
  192.0.4.0/24 le 28,
  192.0.5.0/24 ge 26 le 30,
  192.0.6.0/24 eq 28
end-set
!
```

```
~
~
~
```

Example 8-7 shows a configuration choice of using the VIM editor for editing RPL policies. The users have the choice of using nano and micro emacs editors; it all depends on the user's comfort level and preference with regard to the three supported editors. A user may also reconfigure a set or a route policy using the IOS XR CLI—this causes an overwriting of the previously defined set or policy.

AS-path Set

An AS-path set contains a listing of AS paths for matching an AS path attribute. The AS-path set allows regular expressions. Example 8-8 shows the creation of AS-path sets.

Example 8-8 *AS-Path Set Configuration*

```
RP/0/RP0/CPU0:CRS1-4(config)#as-path-set path-1
RP/0/RP0/CPU0:CRS1-4(config-as)#ios-regex '_101_',
RP/0/RP0/CPU0:CRS1-4(config-as)#ios-regex '_101$'
RP/0/RP0/CPU0:CRS1-4(config-as)#end-set
RP/0/RP0/CPU0:CRS1-4(config)#commit
```

The first line in the AS-path set represents a route that passed through AS 101 and the second line represents a route that originated in AS 101.

Table 8-1 provides a review of commonly used regular expressions that can be used to match AS paths in an AS-path set.

Table 8-1 *Review of ios-regex (Regular Expressions)*

AS Path Regular Expression	Usage
.*	Matches any AS path
^$	Indicates an empty AS path or a locally originated route
^101_	Route learned from AS 101
_101$	Originated from AS 101
_101_	Passed through AS 101
^[0-9]+$	Directly connected Autonomous Systems

Community Set

A community set comprises community values for providing a match against the BGP community attribute. A community is a 2*16 bit quantity. Community values are commonly expressed as two unsigned decimal integers in the range 0 to 65,535, separated by a colon. IOS XR allows the use of wildcards, range operators, and regular expressions in matching community sets. This chapter demonstrates community set matching in the forthcoming sections.

Example 8-9 shows a community set called com-1 that provides matching capabilities against user-defined 2*16 bit quantities; namely 100:300 and 100:200.

Example 8-9 *Community Set Configuration*

```
RP/0/RP0/CPU0:CRS1-4(config)#community-set com-1
RP/0/RP0/CPU0:CRS1-4(config-comm)#  100:300,
RP/0/RP0/CPU0:CRS1-4(config-comm)#  100:200,
RP/0/RP0/CPU0:CRS1-4(config-comm)#  ios-regex '10:[0..50]',
RP/0/RP0/CPU0:CRS1-4(config-comm)#  ios-regex '_10:[0-9]0_',
RP/0/RP0/CPU0:CRS1-4(config-comm)#?
  #-remark       Remark beginning with '#'
  *              Wildcard (any community or part thereof)
  <0-65535>      16-bit half-community number
  [              Left bracket to begin range
  abort          Discard RPL definition and return to top level config
  internet       Internet (BGP well-known community)
  ios-regex      Traditional IOS style regular expression
  local-AS       Do not send outside local AS (BGP well-known community)
  no-advertise   Do not advertise to any peer (BGP well-known community)
  no-export      Do not export to next AS (BGP well-known community)
  private-as     Match within BGP private AS range [64512..65534]
  show           Show partial RPL configuration
  <cr>
```

In Example 8-9, the third and fourth lines of the community set demonstrate the ability to use regular expressions and range operators. The third line shows the range operator expressed as two dots. The range operator in line three shows that the lower 16 bits of the community can have a range from 0 to 50, inclusive. Finally, after demonstrating regular expression usage within a community set, a question mark is entered to show the options available for specifying the well-known communities such as internet, no-advertise, no-export, and private-as. These well-known communities may be specified via predefined keywords in a community set.

Routing Policies

So far we have discussed routing policies without actually showing the anatomy of RPL. This section discusses the composition and structure of RPL in IOS XR. An RPL route policy starts with the route-policy keyword followed by the policy name. A policy that permits everything can be specified as follows:

```
route-policy rpl-1
  pass
end-policy
```

A policy may also be configured to drop all the routes; such a policy follows the following nomenclature:

```
route-policy drop-all
  drop
end-policy
```

RPL uses if statements to provide conditional expression to decide which actions or dispositions should be taken for the given set of routes. The if-then-else statements or elseif statements provide a set of conditions and actions. The conditions are specified via if or elseif, and actions come after the then keyword. Example 8-10 shows a routing policy that drops a route if it passes through AS 103, 104, and 105. In other words, if the BGP AS path attribute contains any of the mentioned autonomous systems, the route is dropped.

Example 8-10 *A Routing Policy Based on if-then-else*

```
RP/0/RP1/CPU0:CRS1-1#show rpl as-path-set poison
as-path-set poison
  ios-regex '_103_',
  ios-regex '_104_',
  ios-regex '_105_'
end-set
!
!
RP/0/RP1/CPU0:CRS1-1#show rpl route-policy drop-based-on-aspath
route-policy drop-based-on-aspath
  if as-path in poison then
    drop
  else
    pass
  endif
end-policy
!
```

The number of AS paths in Example 8-10 that need to be checked is only three. These AS paths may be specified in a single line using an OR-based Boolean operator. The OR operator returns true for an if statement if any one or more of the conditions provides a match. Example 8-11 demonstrates this concept.

Example 8-11 *Specifying AS-paths Inline Using Boolean OR Operator*

```
route-policy drop-based-on-aspath
  if as-path passes-through '103' or as-path passes-through '104' or as-path
    passes-through '105' then
    drop
  else
    pass
```

```
  endif
end-policy
!
```

Example 8-11 specifies an alternative way of specifying the RPL policy in Example 8-10. This example describes a policy using a simple Boolean condition that evaluates true or false states. The routing policy language also provides means to build compound conditions from simple conditions by means of Boolean assignments. There are three Boolean operators:

- **Negation (NOT):** Statement using NOT returns true if converse is matched.
- **Conjunction (AND):** All the conditions being evaluated with the AND operator must match before an if statement returns a true.
- **Disjunction (OR):** If any of the conditions being evaluated provides a match, the result of the if statement returns true.

RPL statements are evaluated from left to right. In RPL, negation (NOT) has the highest precedence, followed by conjunction, and then by disjunction. Use of parentheses helps to group compound conditions and to override precedence. Furthermore, the appropriate use of parentheses helps improve readability. Consider the following Boolean statement used within an RPL policy:

```
if local-preference ge 110 and (not destination in (176.1.1.0/24)) or  community
  matches-every (100:1, 100:2, internet) then
```

The preceding if statement represents a complex Boolean expression. The negation within the parentheses is evaluated first to ensure that the prefix does not match 176.1.1.0/24. The conjunction AND is evaluated next to ensure that the local preference is ge 110. The OR statement is evaluated next. The OR part of the Boolean statement presents an interesting way of specifying a list of values without using a community set. This is known as an *inline set*, and it is specified within the body of a policy when the match criteria present a fewer number of items to match. Inline sets lend simplicity and readability to an RPL policy.

Most of the RPL attributes involved in specifying match criteria are user friendly and self explanatory. Table 8-2 explains some unique attributes that require explanation.

Table 8-2 *RPL Attributes*

RPL Attribute	Explanation
source	source is usually a prefix that represents the source or the router-id of the router that advertised the prefix.
destination	Represents an advertised route or prefix.
route-type	Provides a match on the type of IGP route. Useful for redistribution.

RPL Attribute	Explanation
rib-has-route	Provides a conditional advertisement based on the presence of a route in the routing table. For example, advertisement of a default route based on certain prefixes being present in the RIB.
rib-has-label	Conditional advertisement based on whether rib has label.

Note: Table 8-2 is not an exhaustive list of RPL attributes but rather a partial list of the RPL lexicon that might need an explanation. Most of the RPL lexicon is self explanatory for readers who have prior knowledge of the BGP and IGP protocols.

Figure 8-6 shows the various BGP attach-points and types of actions permissible at each attach-point.

AttachPoint/ Attribute	pass / drop	destination	orf-prefix	next-hop	weight	local-preference	med	origin	as-path	as-path length	community	ext community (cost)	ext community (rt)	ext community (soo)	suppress	unsuppress	dampening	treffic-index	source	route-type	rib-has-route	label	Notes m = match s = set * = supported
neighbor in	*	m		m/s	s	s	m/s	m/s	m/s	m	m/s	s	m/s	m					m				
neighbor out	*	m		m/s			m/s	m/s	m/s	m	m/s	s	m/s	m		s			m				
neighbor orf	*		m																				
network	*	m		s	s	s	s	s	m/s		s	s	s	s									
aggregation	*	m		m/s	s	s	m/s	m/s	m	m	m/s	s			s				m				'Set' attributes applied only to aggregate NLRI
default originate	*						s														m		
redistribute	*			s	s		s	s	s		s	s								m			
dampening	*	m		m			m	m	m	m	m						s		m				
table policy	*	m		m			m	m	m	m	m							s	m				
VRF import	*	m		m/s			m	m	m	m	m		m	m					m				
VRF export	*	m		m	s	s	m	m	m	m	m/s		m/s	m					m				
allocate-label	*	m		m			m	m	m	m	m											s	
Show cmd	*	m		m			m	m	m	m	m		m	m					m				

Figure 8-6 *RPL Attach-Points*

Now that you have some background in RPL policies, we will demonstrate an RPL policy and apply it to a neighbor attach-point in BGP. The main intent of such an example is to see more complex policies in action and demonstrate what **show** commands might be available in RPL to support their use in a production environment. Furthermore, this example allows us to demonstrate show commands as they relate to an inbound or an outbound policy.

Example 8-12 demonstrates an RPL policy that uses three community sets and the inline form of expressing the AS-path attribute to specify certain conditions and actions. (Note that Examples 8-12 through 8-14 refer to the topology shown in Figure 8-3.)

Example 8-12 *RPL Policy*

```
RP/0/RP1/CPU0:CRS1-1#show rpl community-set
Listing for all Community Set objects
community-set CUST-COMM1
  100:300,
  100:301,
  100:302,
  100:303
end-set
!
community-set CUST-COMM2
  200:300,
  200:301,
  200:302,
  200:303
end-set
!
community-set CUST-COMM3
  300:300,
  300:301,
  300:302,
  300:303
end-set
!
RP/0/RP1/CPU0:CRS1-1#show rpl route-policy Nextlink-peer
route-policy Nextlink-peer
  if as-path originates-from '10000' and community matches-any CUST-COMM1 then
    set community (0:0)
  elseif as-path originates-from '10001' and community matches-any CUST-COMM2 then
    set local-preference 60
    set community (6389:20103, 6389:46198) additive
  elseif as-path originates-from '10002' or community matches-any CUST-COMM3 then
    set local-preference 80
    set community (6389:80, 6389:20103, 6389:46198) additive
  elseif as-path originates-from '10003' then
    set community (6389:20103, 6389:46198) additive
  endif
end-policy
```

Example 8-13 applies the RPL policy from Example 8-12 to a neighbor attach-point in BGP in the inbound direction and various **show** command outputs are explored. The CRS1-1 applies the route policy Nextlink-peer ingress for an iBGP neighbor. For illustration purposes, the iBGP neighbor advertises a prefix 173.1.1.1/32 using the network statement and a route-policy to set community to a value that matches the CUST-COMM3 referenced in the policy Nextlink-peer. Example 8-13 shows a sequence of configuration steps and **show** commands for the topology diagram shown in Figure 8-3.

Example 8-13 *Outbound Policy*

```
! Configuration on CRS1-4 sending a routing update with community of 300:301
route-policy set-com
  set community (300:301)
end-policy
!
!
router bgp 101
 bgp router-id 192.168.254.4
 address-family ipv4 unicast
  network 173.1.1.1/32
 !
 address-family vpnv4 unicast
 !
 neighbor 192.168.254.1
  remote-as 101
  update-source Loopback0
  address-family ipv4 unicast
   route-policy set-com out
  !
!
!
! Using a show command to check the attributes of prefix 173.1.1.1/32
! being advertised to the neighbor.
!
RP/0/RP0/CPU0:CRS1-4#show bgp policy sent-advertisements
173.1.1.1/32 is advertised to 192.168.254.1
  Path info:
    neighbor: Local            neighbor router id: 192.168.254.4
    valid  local  best
  Attributes after inbound policy was applied:
    next hop: 0.0.0.0
    MET ORG AS
    origin: IGP  metric: 0
    aspath:
  Attributes after outbound policy was applied:
    next hop: 192.168.254.4
```

```
    MET ORG AS COMM
    origin: IGP  metric: 0
    aspath:
    community: 300:301
! show command on CRS1-4 to verify the policy applied to neighbor 192.168.254.1

!
RP/0/RP0/CPU0:CRS1-4#show bgp ipv4 unicast policy neighbor 192.168.254.1
173.1.1.1/32 is advertised to 192.168.254.1
  Path info:
    neighbor: Local           neighbor router id: 192.168.254.4
    valid  local  best
  Attributes after inbound policy was applied:
    next hop: 0.0.0.0
    MET ORG AS
    origin: IGP  metric: 0
    aspath:
  Attributes after outbound policy was applied:
    next hop: 192.168.254.4
    MET ORG AS
    origin: IGP  metric: 0
    aspath:
!
! show BGP up-date group which identifies a grouping of neighbors using common
  outbound polices.
RP/0/RP0/CPU0:CRS1-4#show bgp update-group neighbor 192.168.254.1

Update group for IPv4 Unicast, index 0.1:
  Attributes:
    Outbound policy: set-com
    Internal
    Common admin
    Send communities
    Send extended communities
    4-byte AS capable
    Minimum advertisement interval: 0
  Update group desynchronized: 0
  Sub-groups merged: 0
  Messages formatted: 1, replicated: 1
  All neighbors are assigned to sub-group(s)
    Neighbors in sub-group: 0.1
      192.168.254.1
RP/0/RP0/CPU0:CRS1-4#
! Shows which neighbors have update-group specified in the show command.
RP/0/RP0/CPU0:CRS1-4#show bgp update-group 0.1
```

```
Update group for IPv4 Unicast, index 0.1:
  Attributes:
    Outbound policy: set-com
    Internal
    Common admin
    Send communities
    Send extended communities
    4-byte AS capable
    Minimum advertisement interval: 0
  Update group desynchronized: 0
  Sub-groups merged: 0
  Messages formatted: 1, replicated: 1
  All neighbors are assigned to sub-group(s)
    Neighbors in sub-group: 0.1
      192.168.254.1
RP/0/RP0/CPU0:CRS1-4#
```

Now that we have seen the prefix advertised by the router CRS1-4, Example 8-14 depicts the configuration that binds the ingress RPL policy to the neighbor attach-point. The main aspect of Example 8-14 is to illustrate various RPL **show** commands that can be used in IOS XR.

Example 8-14 *BGP Attach-Point and RPL* show *Commands*

```
RP/0/RP1/CPU0:CRS1-1#configure t
RP/0/RP1/CPU0:CRS1-1(config)#router bgp 101
RP/0/RP1/CPU0:CRS1-1(config-bgp)#neighbor 192.168.254.4
RP/0/RP1/CPU0:CRS1-1(config-bgp-nbr)#address-family ipv4 unicast
RP/0/RP1/CPU0:CRS1-1(config-bgp-nbr-af)#route-policy Nextlink-peer in
RP/0/RP1/CPU0:CRS1-1(config-bgp-nbr-af)#commit

RP/0/RP1/CPU0:CRS1-1#show rpl active route-policy

ACTIVE — Referenced by at least one policy which is attached
INACTIVE — Only referenced by policies which are not attached
UNUSED — Not attached (directly or indirectly) and not referenced

The following policies are (ACTIVE)
-------------------------
    Nextlink-peer

RP/0/RP1/CPU0:CRS1-1#

RP/0/RP1/CPU0:CRS1-1#show rpl route-policy Nextlink-peer attachpoints
```

```
BGP Attachpoint: Neighbor

Neighbor/Group  type  afi/safi   in/out   vrf name
---------------------------------------------
192.168.254.4    -     IPv4/uni   in         default
!
!
RP/0/RP0/CPU0:CRS1-1#show route 173.1.1.1

Routing entry for 173.1.1.1/32
  Known via "bgp 101", distance 200, metric 0, type internal
  Installed Jan 21 21:13:29.020 for 00:00:01
  Routing Descriptor Blocks
    192.168.254.4, from 192.168.254.4
      Route metric is 0
  No advertising protos.
RP/0/RP0/CPU0:CRS1-1#

RP/0/RP0/CPU0:CRS1-1#show bgp ipv4 unicast 173.1.1.1/32 detail
BGP routing table entry for 173.1.1.1/32
Versions:
  Process           bRIB/RIB  SendTblVer
  Speaker                  2           2
Paths: (1 available, best #1)
  Not advertised to any peer
  Path #1: Received by speaker 0
  Flags:0x1000007
  Local
    192.168.254.4 (metric 4) from 192.168.254.4 (192.168.254.4)
      Origin IGP, metric 0, localpref 80, valid, internal, best
      Community: 300:301 6389:80 6389:20103 6389:46198
RP/0/RP0/CPU0:CRS1-1#
```

Example 8-14 shows how an RPL policy is attached to a neighbor attach-point and the RPL show commands that show whether the policy is active, the attach-point of policy, and the direction (ingress/egress) of application.

Example 8-15 shows how to generate a conditional advertisement by using an RPL match called rib-has-route. This attribute provides conditional checks based on the presence of a route in the local RIB. Example 8-15 shows how the results are different when the rib-has-route check returns a positive match.

Example 8-15 *Generating a Conditional Default Route*

```
! Route policy looks for 173.1.2.1/32 in the local RIB but the RIB has no
! matching entry
route-policy conditional-default
```

```
  if rib-has-route in (173.1.2.1/32) then
    set community (101:101)
  endif
end-policy
!
RP/0/RP0/CPU0:CRS1-1#show route 173.1.2.1

% Network not in table

! BGP Configuration showing the conditional advertisement policy attach-point
RP/0/RP0/CPU0:CRS1-1#
!
router bgp 101
 bgp router-id 192.168.254.1
 address-family ipv4 unicast
 !
 neighbor-group ibgp-peer
  remote-as 101
  update-source Loopback0
  address-family ipv4 unicast
   default-originate route-policy conditional-default
  !
 !
 neighbor 192.168.254.4
  use neighbor-group ibgp-peer
  address-family ipv4 unicast
   route-policy Nextlink-peer in
  !

! BGP show command to check the neighbor configuration
RP/0/RP0/CPU0:CRS1-1#show bgp neighbors 192.168.254.4 configuration
neighbor 192.168.254.4
 remote-as 101                                       [n:ibgp-peer]
 update-source Loopback0                             [n:ibgp-peer]
 address-family ipv4 unicast                         []
  default-originate policy conditional-default       [n:ibgp-peer]
  policy Nextlink-peer in                            []
RP/0/RP0/CPU0:CRS1-1#show bgp neighbors 192.168.254.4 advertised-routes

! This command produces no output

! Now RIB has a matching entry for the condition being checked by the RPL policy
RP/0/RP0/CPU0:CRS1-1#show route 173.1.2.1

Routing entry for 173.1.2.1/32
```

```
  Known via "static", distance 1, metric 0 (connected)
  Installed Jan 21 23:10:03.650 for 00:00:09
  Routing Descriptor Blocks
    directly connected, via GigabitEthernet0/7/0/1
      Route metric is 0
  No advertising protos.
RP/0/RP0/CPU0:CRS1-1#
!
! show command showing the generation of a default route
!
RP/0/RP0/CPU0:CRS1-1#show bgp neighbors 192.168.254.4 advertised-routes
Network            Next Hop        From             AS Path
0.0.0.0/0          0.0.0.0         Local            i
RP/0/RP0/CPU0:CRS1-1#
!
!
RP/0/RP0/CPU0:CRS1-4#show bgp 0.0.0.0/0 detail
BGP routing table entry for 0.0.0.0/0
Versions:
  Process           bRIB/RIB  SendTblVer
  Speaker                 11          11
    Flags:0x361000
Paths: (1 available, best #1)
  Not advertised to any peer
  Path #1: Received by speaker 0
  Flags:0x1000007
  Local
    192.168.254.1 (metric 2) from 192.168.254.1 (192.168.254.1)
      Origin IGP, localpref 100, valid, internal, best
      Community: 101:101
RP/0/RP0/CPU0:CRS1-4#
```

Hierarchical Policies and Parameterization

Cisco IOS XR RPL allows the reuse of common RPL structures in building hierarchical policies. These common policy actions are applied using the **apply** statement. Assume a case where a network administrator applies a common set of dispositions based on certain match criteria. Instead of specifying the common dispositions repeatedly in every policy, a hierarchical policy may be created defining the common policy first. Example 8-16 demonstrates the use of the **apply** command and shows some useful RPL commands that can be employed.

Example 8-16 *Using Hierarchical Policies*

```
RP/0/RP0/CPU0:CRS1-4#show rpl route-policy child
route-policy child
  set local-preference 100
  set community none
end-policy
!
RP/0/RP0/CPU0:CRS1-4#
RP/0/RP0/CPU0:CRS1-4#
RP/0/RP0/CPU0:CRS1-4#show rpl route-policy parent
route-policy parent
  if destination in (171.1.1.0/24) then
    apply child
  endif
end-policy
!
!
!
RP/0/RP0/CPU0:CRS1-4#show rpl route-policy child references

Usage Direct — Reference occurs in this policy
Usage Indirect — Reference occurs via an apply statement

Status UNUSED — Policy is not in use at an attachpoint (unattached)
Status ACTIVE — Policy is actively used at an attachpoint
Status INACTIVE — Policy is applied by an unattached policy

     Usage/Status          count
-------------------------------
     Direct                1
     Indirect              0

     ACTIVE                0
     INACTIVE              0
     UNUSED                1


     Usage      Status      Route-policy
-------------------------------

     Direct     UNUSED      parent

RP/0/RP0/CPU0:CRS1-4#
!
!
```

```
RP/0/RP0/CPU0:CRS1-4#show rpl route-policy parent uses all

Policies directly and indirectly applied by this policy:
----------------------------------
    child


Sets used directly or indirectly in this policy
--------------------
type community-set:
    none
```

We saw in Example 8-15 how common policy structures can be configured as an individual route policy and brought into use with the **apply** statement in a hierarchical relationship. Example 8-16 demonstrates the RPL concept of parameterization, where a parameter can be passed to an RPL policy. Users with programming backgrounds should have experience in parameter passing, either by value or by reference, to functions or subroutines. Passing a parameter by value refers to passing the value held in a variable to the function or the RPL policy. Passing a parameter by reference means passing an address, instead of a value, of a variable. Passing a parameter by reference allows the called function to change the value of the variable itself. Note that RPL supports parameter pass by value only—passing by reference, although popular with programmers, finds no real use in defining RPL policies with IOS XR configuration.

Note: RPL parameterization supports passing of parameters to policy statements by value only. Parameter passing by reference is not supported in IOS XR.

Example 8-17 defines an AS-path based RPL policy that calls an AS-path-set based on the value of a parameter passed to the policy. The part where the RPL policy is expecting a parameter is preceded by a dollar ($) sign.

Example 8-17 *Using Parameterization*

```
! shows the parameterized policy. $AS is the part where a parameter is being
! expected.
route-policy filter-based-on-asregex($AS)
  if (as-path in $AS) then
    pass
  else
    drop
  endif
end-policy

!
as-path-set 10000
  ios-regex '^(_10000)+$'
```

```
end-set
!
!
as-path-set 11000
  ios-regex '^(_11000)+$'
end-set

! shows the application of RPL policy to a neighbor attach-point with a parameter
! value of 10000
  router bgp 101
 bgp router-id 192.168.254.4
 address-family ipv4 unicast
  network 173.1.1.1/32
 !
 address-family vpnv4 unicast
 !
 neighbor 192.168.254.1
  remote-as 101
  update-source Loopback0
  address-family ipv4 unicast
   route-policy filter-based-on-asregex(10000) in
   route-policy set-com out
  !
! show command that depicts the selection of as-path-set 10000 based on the
! parameter passed to the RPL policy filter-based-on-asregex.
!
RP/0/RP0/CPU0:CRS1-4#show rpl as-path-set 10000 attachpoints
BGP Attachpoint: Neighbor

Neighbor/Group  type  afi/safi   in/out   vrf name
--------------------------------------------------
192.168.254.1    —     IPv4/uni   in         default
 RP/0/RP0/CPU0:CRS1-4#show rpl route-policy filter-based-on-asregex references

Usage Direct — Reference occurs in this policy
Usage Indirect — Reference occurs via an apply statement

Status UNUSED — Policy is not in use at an attachpoint (unattached)
Status ACTIVE — Policy is actively used at an attachpoint
Status INACTIVE — Policy is applied by an unattached policy

     Usage/Status          count
------------------------------------------------------------
     Direct                0
     Indirect              1
```

```
    ACTIVE              1
    INACTIVE            0
    UNUSED              0


    Usage       Status      Route-policy
-------------------------------------------------------------

    Indirect   ACTIVE       filter-based-on-asregex(10000)
```

Example 8-17 shows a parameterized policy name filter-based-on-regex that is expecting a parameter for $AS. The dollar sign preceding AS shows that it is a variable whose value may change when the policy is called at an attach-point. The RPL policy is called with a parameter of 10000, which leads to a match being done against as-path-set 10000. If the variable 11000 was used, the match criteria would have changed to a different as-path-set.

BGP Policy Accounting

This section discusses an important BGP feature known as BGP policy accounting (BGP PA). Although BGP PA is not a unique feature to IOS XR, this section shows some important points in how to configure it using an RPL policy. BGP PA works by assigning index values to BGP routes in the RIB and then using Cisco Express Forwarding (CEF) commands to check the counters for these index values. The RPL policy for BGP PA is applied to an attach-point known as *table-policy* under the address-family. The match and set criteria for the BGP RPL policy at the table-policy attach-point were listed in Figure 8-6 shown earlier.

After the policy is specified and attached to BGP, the interface on which accounting needs to be initialized gets configured with the following command:

ipv4 bgp policy accounting {input | output {destination-accounting [source-accounting] | source-accounting [destination-accounting]}}

BGP policy accounting provides

- Input/output source accounting
- Input/output destination accounting
- Input/output source and destination accounting

The BGP PA counters can then be checked by using the command **show cef ipv4 interface** {*interface name*} **bgp-policy-statistics.** Example 8-18 demonstrates BGP PA on a CRS-1 running IOS 3.6.2.

Example 8-18 *BGP Policy Accounting*

```
! Define an RPL route policy
RP/0/RP0/CPU0:CRS1-1#show rpl route-policy bgp-policy-acct
route-policy bgp-policy-acct
  if destination in (75.15.0.0/16) then
```

```
    set traffic-index 1
  elseif destination in (209.66.0.0/16) then
    set traffic-index 2
  else
    set traffic-index 3
  endif
end-policy
!
router bgp 101
 bgp router-id 192.168.254.1
 address-family ipv4 unicast
  table-policy bgp-policy-acct
!
interface GigabitEthernet0/7/0/1
 cdp
 mtu 9194
 ipv4 address 65.1.1.1 255.255.255.0
 ipv4 bgp policy accounting output destination-accounting
 load-interval 30
!
! show command that shows the different traffic indexes.
RP/0/RP0/CPU0:CRS1-1#show route bgp

B    75.15.0.0/16 [20/0] via 10.2.2.2, 10:54:20
      Traffic Index 1
B    180.1.1.0/24 [20/0] via 10.2.2.2, 10:57:26
      Traffic Index 3
B    209.66.0.0/16 [20/0] via 10.2.2.2, 10:53:16
      Traffic Index 2
 !
! BGP PA accounting command.
RP/0/RP0/CPU0:CRS1-1#show cef ipv4 interface gigabitEthernet 0/7/0/1 bgp-policy-
  statistics
GigabitEthernet0/7/0/1 is UP
Output BGP policy accounting on dst IP address enabled
  buckets       packets          bytes
  0             1524243       62044448
  1                   5            500
  2             4446485      444648500
  3               33333        3333300
!
!

!
```

Example 8-18 shows an RPL policy applied to the table-policy attach-point. Although this policy is used to classify prefixes into indexes, the implicit deny in the RPL policy holds. If a certain type of prefix is assigned an index, the RPL policy must remember to pass the remaining prefixes or they will be implicitly dropped.

BGP Remotely Triggered Black Hole

The BGP remotely triggered black hole (RTBH) is a security technique used to divert undesirable traffic away from POP routers to an appropriate point in the network where it can be black holed. This technique is accomplished by using a trigger router. The trigger router generates a BGP advertisement toward all the other routers in an autonomous system and serves as a black hole for undesirable traffic. This concept is commonplace in live networks and may be used to create a black hole for traffic to mitigate a DOS attack or to place a barrier for traffic destined to undesirable websites. Note that the BGP remotely triggered black hole is among a myriad of security techniques available and should be deployed only with careful understanding of the problem at hand.

This section illustrates the IOS XR configuration for implementing a BGP RTBH. The following is a step-by-step process for RTBH configuration:

Step 1. Create a static route destined to the null 0 interface. The IP address used for the static route may come from an RFC 1918 address or simply the 192.0.2.0/24 address allocated by IANA for use in documentation. The 192.0.2.0/24 address commonly known as *test-net* finds its use in internetworking documentation so that its verbatim use does not cause problems on the Internet. It is an address that does not appear on the Internet.

Step 2. Create an RPL policy that sets the next hop of prefix to be black holed to the static route pointing to null 0.

Step 3. Set the community for this route to **no export**.

Step 4. Advertise this route with a local preference so that the router with RTBH configuration attracts traffic destined to the prefix and serves as a "sink" for this traffic.

Example 8-19 shows the static route pointing to Null0 and the steps that implement RTBH via RPL. Again refer to Figure 8-3 for a reference to the BGP topology.

Example 8-19 *Configuring RTBH*

```
router static
 address-family ipv4 unicast
  192.0.2.1/32 Null0 tag 666


Configure an RPL route-policy so that the next hop of the prefix to be black
  holed gets set to null 0
!
route-policy RTBH
  if tag eq 666 then
```

```
    # set the next hop to the Test-net prefix that points to null 0
    set next-hop 192.0.2.1
    # Set community to no-export as a precaution to prevent inadvertant
        advertisements
    set community (no-export)
    # For additional safeguard add a community to allow further policies to be
        enforced
    set community (666:666)
    # set local prefernece to 50
    set local-preference 50
    # set origin to IGP
    set origin igp
  endif
end-policy
!
! Apply the RPL policy
router bgp 101
 bgp router-id 192.168.254.1
 address-family ipv4 unicast
  redistribute static route-policy RTBH
!
! Show command now shows 192.0.2.1 as a next hop
RP/0/RP0/CPU0:CRS1-1#show bgp nexthops

Gateway Address Family: IPv4 Unicast
Table ID: 0xe0000000
Nexthop Count: 4
Critical Trigger Delay: 3000msec
Non-critical Trigger Delay: 10000msec

Nexthop Version: 1, RIB version: 1

Status codes: R/UR Reachable/Unreachable
              C/NC Connected/Not-connected
              L/NL Local/Non-local
              I    Invalid (Policy Match Failed)
Next Hop        Status          Metric        Notf      LastRIBEvent     RefCount
10.2.2.2        [R][C][NL]           0         1/0        2d15h (Cri)    27/33
192.0.2.1       [R][C][NL]           0         0/0     01:32:26 (Reg)    2/4
192.168.254.4   [R][NC][NL]          4         4/2        2d15h (Non)    2/5


Now lets say traffic to a prefix 172.16.1.0/24 needs to be black holed, a static
  route will be created for the prefix 172.16.1.0/24 with a tag 666


router static
```

```
 address-family ipv4 unicast
  172.16.1.0/24 Null0 tag 666
  173.1.2.1/32 GigabitEthernet0/7/0/1
  192.0.2.1/32 Null0 tag 666
 !
! show command depicts the advertised prefix for which black holing is intended.
!
RP/0/RP0/CPU0:CRS1-1#show bgp 172.16.1.1
BGP routing table entry for 172.16.1.0/24
Versions:
  Process           bRIB/RIB  SendTblVer
  Speaker                119         119
Paths: (1 available, best #1, not advertised to EBGP peer)
  Advertised to peers (in unique update groups):
    192.168.254.4
  Path #1: Received by speaker 0
  Local
    192.0.2.1 from 0.0.0.0 (192.168.254.1)
      Origin IGP, metric 0, localpref 50, weight 32768, valid, redistributed, best
      Community: 666:666 no-export

RP/0/RP0/CPU0:CRS1-1#show bgp advertised ¦ begin 172.16
172.16.1.0/24 is advertised to 192.168.254.4
  Path info:
    neighbor: Local          neighbor router id: 192.168.254.1
    Not advertised to any EBGP peer.
    valid  redistributed  best
  Attributes after inbound policy was applied:
    next hop: 192.0.2.1
    MET ORG AS LOCAL COMM
    origin: IGP  metric: 0  local pref: 50
    aspath:
    community: 666:666 no-export
```

Example 8-19 shows how black holing is implemented for the prefix 172.16.1.0/24. Taking additional measures for protection, this prefix is set with a community no-export, an additional user defined community 666:666 to help implement additional policies by matching on this community value. Finally the example shows a local preference of 50; this local preference might have to be adjusted based on the requirements of a network so that the prefix can be advertised from the correct trigger router.

BGP Graceful Restart

BGP graceful restart (GR) is a high availability mechanism supported in IOS XR. GR mechanism helps ensure that the forwarding path continues to function while a BGP crashing or restarting node recovers. Graceful restart for BGP is invoked with the CLI command **bgp graceful-restart** under BGP. Invoking the graceful restart configuration allows BGP to exchange a capability with a type code 64. It indicates to the neighbor that BGP has the capability to preserve the forwarding path while the control plane has been reset due to a BGP process or RP failure on the neighboring node. As a result of advertising BGP GR capability, BGP has to generate an End-of-Rib marker after its initial update. The mechanisms behind BGP GR are briefly described as follows:

The node on which the BGP process restarts after a reload or a manual process restart marks the BGP routes as Stale in its RIB but continues to forward traffic to the destinations. An important point to note is that the BGP session will flap due to BGP process restart, or due to missing keepalives, and ultimately hold time expiration. However, the forwarding plane will continue to function. The neighboring router that sees the BGP neighbor restarting and has successfully exchanged the GR capability marks his RIB stale only for routes learned from the restarting neighbor. Example 8-20 shows BGP GR from the perspective of a BGP speaker that itself is working fine but sees one of its neighbors restarting.

Example 8-20 *BGP Graceful Restart*

```
RP/0/RP0/CPU0:CRS1-1#show bgp neighbors 192.168.254.4 | begin Graceful Restart
Tue Jan 27 12:57:49.176 PST
    Graceful Restart Capability advertised
      Local restart time is 120, RIB purge time is 600 seconds
      Maximum stalepath time is 360 seconds
  Route refresh request: received 2, sent 1
  2 accepted prefixes, 2 are bestpaths
  Prefix advertised 88, suppressed 0, withdrawn 2, maximum limit 524288
  Threshold for warning message 75%
  An EoR was received during read-only mode

  Connections established 2; dropped 1
  Last reset 5d20h, due to BGP Notification sent: hold time expired
  Time since last notification sent to neighbor: 5d20h
  Error Code: hold time expired
  Notification data sent:
    None
!
RP/0/RP0/CPU0:CRS1-1#RP/0/RP0/CPU0:Jan 27 13:06:29.985 : bgp[122]: %ROUTING-BGP-5-
  ADJCHANGE : neighbor 192.168.254.4 Down - Peer closing down the session
!
!
RP/0/RP0/CPU0:CRS1-1#show bgp
Tue Jan 27 13:06:34.986 PST
BGP router identifier 192.168.254.1, local AS number 101
BGP generic scan interval 60 secs
BGP table state: Active
Table ID: 0xe0000000
```

```
BGP main routing table version 123
BGP scan interval 60 secs

Status codes: s suppressed, d damped, h history, * valid, > best
              i - internal, S stale
Origin codes: i - IGP, e - EGP, ? - incomplete
   Network            Next Hop            Metric  LocPrf  Weight  Path
*> 75.15.0.0/16       10.2.2.2                 0               0  111 i
*> 111.1.1.1/32       0.0.0.0                  0           32768  i
*> 172.16.1.0/24      192.0.2.1                0      50   32768  i
S>i173.1.1.1/32       192.168.254.4            0     100       0  i
S>i173.1.1.2/32       192.168.254.4            0     100       0  i
```

The restarting BGP speaker recomputes the routes after an End-of-Rib marker is received from all its GR-capable neighbors who begin re-advertising to the restarting BGP speaker under discussion when the BGP session is established. The maximum time to wait for the End-of-Rib marker is dictated by the stalepath timer value. Following route selection, the stale state in the RIB is removed. At this stage the restarting neighbor can send an outbound update where the initial update is followed by the End-of-Rib marker.

BGP graceful restart involves other timers such as restart-time, purge-time, and stalepath-time. The restart time specifies a time limit for the BGP speaker that sees its neighbor restart. The time limit indicates that the BGP routes received from the restarting neighbor will be marked stale while maintaining the forwarding state unless the BGP session does not reestablish within the restart time. If the TCP session for BGP does not form within the restart time, the stale entries in the BGP rib are removed. The stalepath timer indicates the maximum time to wait for End-of-Rib marker, and purge time dictates the maximum time after which stale routes are purged. The default values of these timers are as follows:

- **Restart-time:** 120 seconds
- **Stalepath-time:** 360 seconds
- **Purge-time:** 600 seconds

BGP Distributed Speaker

The "Cisco IOS XR BGP Architectural Overview" section earlier in this chapter discussed route computations based on distributed speakers. This section shows the configuration of distributed speaker BGP. The process placement aspects were already discussed in Chapter 2 and are not repeated here.

Example 8-21 depicts the distributed speaker configuration in IOS XR and commands to change the mode from BGP standalone to BGP distributed speaker mode. As a first step, various distributed speakers are configured using the command **distributed speaker** *number*. The maximum number supported is 15 on the CRS-1 router. Note that distributed speaker configuration leverages the DRP hardware, so although it's possible to configure distributed speakers without DRPs, it makes no sense to do so. The neighbors are assigned to a distributed speaker using the command **speaker-id** *number*. The command **clear bgp current-mode** changes the standalone mode to distributed mode.

Example 8-21 shows the BGP distributed speaker concept by creating a distributed speaker BGP configuration and assigning speaker IDs. The example demonstrates some popular **show** commands and log messages when BGP changes mode from standalone mode to distributed mode.

Example 8-21 *BGP Distributed Speaker Configuration*

```
RP/0/RP0/CPU0:CRS1-1(config)#router bgp 101
RP/0/RP0/CPU0:CRS1-1(config-bgp)#distributed speaker 1
RP/0/RP0/CPU0:CRS1-1(config-bgp)#distributed speaker 2
RP/0/RP0/CPU0:CRS1-1(config-bgp)#neighbor 192.168.254.4
RP/0/RP0/CPU0:CRS1-1(config-bgp-nbr)#speaker-id 1
RP/0/RP0/CPU0:CRS1-1(config-bgp-nbr)#exit
RP/0/RP0/CPU0:CRS1-1(config-bgp)#neighbor 10.2.2.2
RP/0/RP0/CPU0:CRS1-1(config-bgp-nbr)#speaker-id 2
RP/0/RP0/CPU0:CRS1-1(config-bgp-nbr)#commit
!
! Despite configuration the current-mode of BGP operation is "standalone"
!
RP/0/RP0/CPU0:CRS1-1#show bgp summary
Tue Jan 27 17:02:18.132 PST
BGP router identifier 192.168.254.1, local AS number 101
BGP generic scan interval 60 secs
BGP table state: Active
Table ID: 0xe0000000
BGP main routing table version 33
BGP scan interval 60 secs

BGP is operating in STANDALONE mode.

Process         RecvTblVer    bRIB/RIB   LabelVer  ImportVer   SendTblVer
Speaker                 33          33         33         33           33

Neighbor        Spk    AS MsgRcvd MsgSent    TblVer  InQ OutQ  Up/Down  St/PfxRcd
10.2.2.2          0   111      14       9        33    0    0 00:04:39 27
192.168.254.4     0   101       8      13        33    0    0 00:04:39 2
!
!
! The following command clears bgp current-mode to "distributed"
RP/0/RP0/CPU0:CRS1-1#clear bgp current-mode
Tue Jan 27 17:05:35.476 PST
 !
! Syslog messages followed by command "clear bgp current-mode"
!
```

```
RP/0/RP0/CPU0:Jan 27 17:05:46.485 : bgp[408]: %ROUTING-BGP-5-ADJCHANGE : neighbor
  192.168.254.4 Up
RP/0/RP0/CPU0:Jan 27 17:05:46.524 : bgp[407]: %ROUTING-BGP-5-ADJCHANGE : neighbor
  10.2.2.2 Up
!
! Note that BGP mode changes to distributed.
!
RP/0/RP0/CPU0:CRS1-1#show bgp summary
Tue Jan 27 17:06:55.442 PST
BGP router identifier 192.168.254.1, local AS number 101
BGP generic scan interval 60 secs
BGP table state: Active
Table ID: 0xe0000000
BGP main routing table version 33
BGP scan interval 60 secs

BGP is operating in DISTRIBUTED mode.

Process    Id    RecvTblVer    bRIB/RIB   LabelVer  ImportVer  SendTblVer
Speaker    1             3           3         33         33          33
Speaker    2            28          28         33         33          33
bRIB       1            33          33         33         33          33

Neighbor        Spk    AS  MsgRcvd  MsgSent    TblVer  InQ  OutQ  Up/Down   St/PfxRcd
10.2.2.2          2   111       10        5        33    0     0  00:01:09  27
192.168.254.4     1   101        5       10        33    0     0  00:01:09  2
!
!
! Note: a show command "show bgp paths" shows BGP paths for each speaker.
RP/0/RP0/CPU0:CRS1-1#show bgp paths
Tue Jan 27 17:09:02.682 PST

Proc        IID   Refcount    Metric    Path
Spk  1      0            2         0    i
Spk  1      0            2         0    i
Spk  1      0            2         0    111 701 ?
Spk  1      0            2         0    111 i
Spk  1      0            2         0    i
Spk  1      0            2         0    111 701 10 10 10 10 ?
Spk  2      0            2         0    i
Spk  2      0            2         0    i
Spk  2      0            2         0    111 701 ?
Spk  2      0            2         0    111 i
Spk  2      0            2         0    i
Spk  2      0            2         0    111 701 10 10 10 10 ?
bRIB 1      0            2         0    i
```

```
bRIB 1      0           2        0      i
bRIB 1      0           2        0      111 701 ?
bRIB 1      0           2        0      111 i
bRIB 1      0           2        0      i
bRIB 1      0           2        0      111 701 10 10 10 10 ?
!
! show bgp process command showing the processes and the nodes on which they are
! running.
!
RP/0/RP0/CPU0:CRS1-1#show bgp process
Tue Jan 27 17:11:09.966 PST

BGP Process Information:
BGP is operating in DISTRIBUTED mode
Autonomous System: 101
Router ID: 192.168.254.1 (manually configured)
Cluster ID: 192.168.254.1
Fast external fallover enabled
Neighbor logging is enabled
Enforce first AS enabled
Default local preference: 100
Default keepalive: 60
Graceful restart enabled
Restart time: 120
Stale path timeout time: 360
RIB purge timeout time: 600
Update delay: 120
Generic scan interval: 60

Address family: IPv4 Unicast
Dampening is not enabled
Client reflection is enabled
Scan interval: 60
Main Table Version: 33
IGP notification: IGPs notified
RIB has converged: version 0

Node            Process     Nbrs  Estb  Rst  Upd-Rcvd  Upd-Sent  Nfn-Rcv  Nfn-Snt
node0_RP0_CPU0  Speaker 1      1     1    2         2         3        0        1
node0_RP0_CPU0  Speaker 2      1     1    6         7         2        0        1
node0_RP0_CPU0  bRIB 1         0     0    0         0         0        0        0
node0_RP0_CPU0  bRIB 3         0     0    0         0         0        0        0
```

The next step is that of placing the different speaker processes on RPs/DRPs, which is a concept already discussed in Chapter 2 with regard to other processes.

Cisco IOS XR BGP Convergence

High availability and fast convergence requirements are of paramount importance in next generation (NGN) backbone networks. BGP traditionally converges slower compared to link state IGP protocols due to the nature of the BGP protocol itself. The BGP keepalive and hold-down timers have default values of 90 seconds and 180 seconds, respectively. These timer values are high in comparison to the traditional counterpart timers of IGP protocols. BGP is a TCP-based protocol and to benefit from TCP retransmission mechanisms, the timers cannot be very small values. Reducing the BGP keepalive and hold-down timer might have a negative impact on the performance of the router due to increased control traffic. In addition, the BGP scanner is a periodic BGP function that runs every 60 seconds to check the validity of BGP next hops. Note that BGP scanner is a generic function and is not specific to IOS XR only. Even if a change in BGP next hop is detected and installed in the RIB at a given point in time, the next hop change could take up to 60 seconds to take effect.

The following configuration command was executed on a router running IOS XR release 3.6.2 and shows the scan timer range that can be configured:

```
RP/0/RP0/CPU0:CRS1-4(config-bgp)#bgp scan-time ?
  <5-3600>  Scanner interval (seconds)
```

Example 8-22 shows BGP timers as shown in the output of the **show bgp process** CLI command.

Example 8-22 *Output of the* **show bgp process** *Command*

```
RP/0/RP0/CPU0:CRS1-4#show bgp process



BGP Process Information:
BGP is operating in STANDALONE mode
Autonomous System: 101
Router ID: 192.168.254.4 (manually configured)
Cluster ID: 192.168.254.4
Fast external fallover enabled
Neighbor logging is enabled
Enforce first AS enabled
Default local preference: 100
Default keepalive: 60
Update delay: 120
Generic scan interval: 60

Address family: IPv4 Unicast
Dampening is not enabled
```

```
Client reflection is enabled
Scan interval: 60
Main Table Version: 118
IGP notification: IGPs notified
RIB has converged: version 0

Node             Process    Nbrs  Estb  Rst  Upd-Rcvd  Upd-Sent  Nfn-Rcv  Nfn-Snt
node0_RP0_CPU0   Speaker       2     1    2        41        27        0        1
```

Example 8-22 highlights certain key parts of **show bgp process** output. The BGP scanner discussion of Example 8-22 helps build the right convergence-related concepts, but it is not recommended that the BGP scanner values be configured as a standard practice to improve convergence. The command output shows a generic scan interval as well as a scan interval for address-family ipv4, which is the only configured address family on the router that produced the command output. Reducing the scan time can be CPU-intensive and is generally not recommended. Moreover, the BGP scanner might be tricked by the presence of summary and default routes that provide a certain degree of match to a downed BGP next hop. This matching of a downed next hop with an aggregate or a summary route might have the effect of BGP relying on the expiration of the hold-down timer to detect a downed next hop—a time value of astronomical proportions from a convergence standpoint.

So far we have described a convergence problem that comes into play by relying only on the traditional BGP scanner; this discussion is independent of operating system and is a general BGP characteristic. IOS XR, being an NGN operating system, considers all these factors and implements some key features that improve convergence.

Cisco IOS XR Routing Information Base (RIB) contains the next hops in use by BGP. BGP gets information from RIB to determine the following factors with regard to next hops:

- Determine the reachability of the next hop.
- Perform best path calculations to a next hop considering the next hop may be recursive
- Verify connected neighbor reachability
- Perform validation on received next hops
- Compute outgoing next hops

As a start, any changes occurring in RIB with regard to BGP next hop are immediately treated as critical or noncritical events. RIB events that trigger a notification to BGP are as follows:

- Loss of reachability to next hop (Critical)
- Gaining reachability to the next hop (Critical)
- Change of first hop or interface network address (Critical)
- Next hop becomes connected or unconnected, local or nonlocal (Critical)
- IGP metric change to next hop (Noncritical)

Although critical events are greater in number, noncritical events are more likely to occur in live production environments. These critical and noncritical events are buffered and handled with different urgencies. Furthermore, critical events are handled in subseconds (100msec), whereas the event handling for a noncritical event is on the order of seconds (10 seconds).

Notifications from RIB are handled by BGP Next Hop Tracking (NHT). Being event driven by nature, NHT offers much faster reaction to a change in BGP next hop than the legacy BGP scanner. NHT is enabled by default in IOS XR, and a command can be executed per address family to change the NHT processing delay for critical and noncritical events.

Example 8-23 shows this configuration example along with supporting **show** commands.

Example 8-23 *NHT Trigger Delay for Critical and Noncritical Events*

```
router bgp 101
 bgp router-id 192.168.254.4
 address-family ipv4 unicast
  nexthop trigger-delay critical 50
  nexthop trigger-delay non-critical 5000

 !
 address-family vpnv4 unicast
  nexthop trigger-delay critical 40
  nexthop trigger-delay non-critical 4000
!
! show command to depict the configured changes.
RP/0/RP0/CPU0:CRS1-4#show bgp nexthops statistics
Total Nexthop Processing
  Time Spent: 0.000 secs

Maximum Nexthop Processing
  Received: 00:00:07
  Bestpaths Deleted: 0
  Bestpaths Changed: 29
  Time Spent: 0.000 secs

Last Notification Processing
  Received: 00:00:07
  Time Spent: 0.000 secs

Gateway Address Family: IPv4 Unicast
Table ID: 0xe0000000
Nexthop Count: 3
Critical Trigger Delay: 50msec
Non-critical Trigger Delay: 5000msec
```

```
Nexthop Version: 1, RIB version: 1

Total Critical Notifications Received: 5
Total Non-critical Notifications Received: 0
Bestpaths Deleted After Last Walk: 0
Bestpaths Changed After Last Walk: 29
Nexthop register:
  Sync calls: 3, last sync call: 1d17h
  Async calls: 2, last async call: 1d17h
Nexthop unregister:
  Async calls: 3, last async call: 1d17h
Nexthop batch finish:
  Calls: 11, last finish call: 1d17h
Nexthop flush timer:
  Times started: 17, last time flush timer started: 1d17h
RIB update: 0 rib update runs, last update: 00:00:00
            0 prefixes installed, 0 modified, 0 removed
!
!
RP/0/RP0/CPU0:CRS1-4#show bgp nexthops

Gateway Address Family: IPv4 Unicast
Table ID: 0xe0000000
Nexthop Count: 3
Critical Trigger Delay: 50msec
Non-critical Trigger Delay: 5000msec

Nexthop Version: 1, RIB version: 1

Status codes: R/UR Reachable/Unreachable
              C/NC Connected/Not-connected
              L/NL Local/Non-local
              I    Invalid (Policy Match Failed)
Next Hop        Status       Metric      Notf     LastRIBEvent     RefCount
11.2.2.2        [UR]         4294967295   2/0      1d17h (Cri)          0/4
192.168.254.1   [I]          4294967295   3/0   00:16:16 (Cri)        29/32
```

Note: IOS XR BGP NHT automatically excludes default routes from consideration as candidates for determining a next hop when a specific next hop goes away. In case aggregate or summarized routes are present in the RIB, IOS XR allows implementing a routing policy using the command **nexthop route-policy** *name*, for example:

```
route-policy NHT
  if protocol is ospf 10 and destination in (192.168.254.1/32) then
    pass
  else
    drop
  endif
end-policy
```

The route-policy allows matching of source protocols from where the next hop becomes available to RIB and the next hop's mask length. This helps reduce the pitfalls associated with a next hop learned from an undesirable source and mitigates the presence of aggregate or summary routes in the RIB.

BGP NHT plays a critical role in convergence. It is recommended that unless network behavior is very well understood, the NHT timers are best left at default values.

The output of the **show bgp process** command seen earlier includes a line in the output showing **Fast external fallover enabled.** BGP fast external failover is enabled by default in IOS XR because we know that the failure of a local interface is a critical NHT event that is processed immediately. Besides the processing of event by NHT, BGP fast external failover provides an immediate resetting of the eBGP session and aids in faster convergence. This feature is enabled by default and can be disabled by the CLI command **bgp fast-external-fallover disable** under the BGP neighbor submode.

Summary

This chapter discusses the architectural aspects of BGP. The overall architecture of BGP is discussed along with the distributed speaker BGP, which can be configured in the presence of DRP hardware. This chapter familiarizes the readers with the hierarchical configuration behind BGP and the various templates that can be used in the form of neighbor-group, session-group, and af-groups. The chapter introduces the reader to the concepts behind the routing policy language that is a focal point in implementing BGP-based policies. Finally, some implementation examples and high-availability concepts are discussed, depicting application of BGP concepts along with the various IOS XR–related **show** commands that can be used to discern BGP-related information.

References

- **Cisco.** Implementing Cisco Express Forwarding on Cisco IOS XR Software. http://www.cisco.com/
- **Cisco.** Implementing BGP on Cisco IOS XR Software. http://www.cisco.com/en

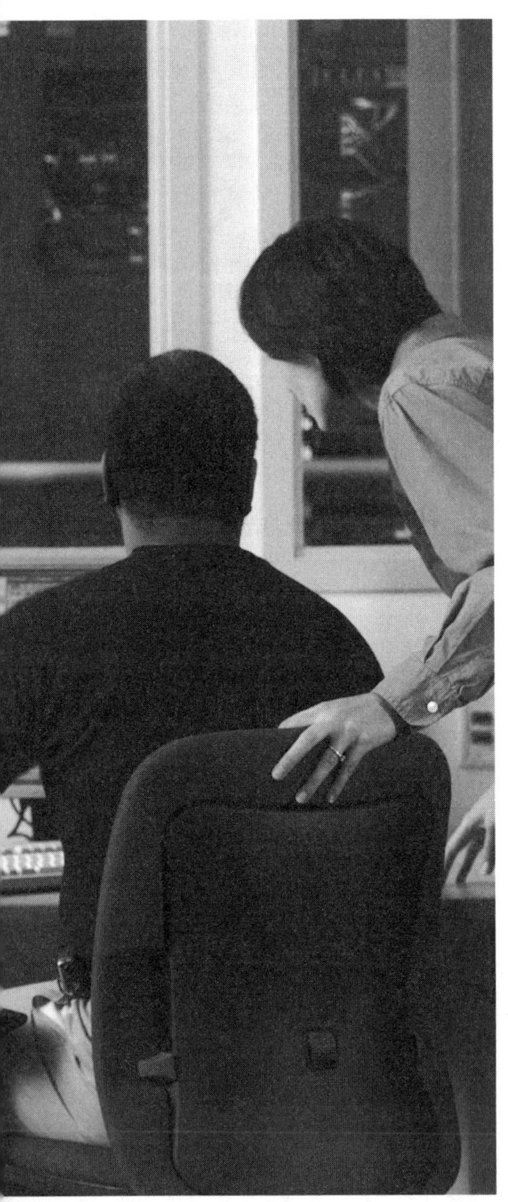

This chapter covers the following topics:

- Understanding Cisco IOS XR MPLS Architecture Fundamentals
- Label Distribution Protocol
- MPLS Traffic Engineering
- Cisco IOS XR Peer-to-Peer L3VPN
- L2VPN

Service providers deploy Multi-Protocol Label Switching (MPLS) as a foundational technology for converged network architecture. MPLS is used to enable L2- or L3-based VPN services, traffic engineering, and fast rerouting.

This chapter discusses IOS XR MPLS architecture, features, implementation, and configuration. A detailed discussion of MPLS protocols and standards is a broad topic that deserves a book or more on its own. The focus of this chapter is to provide you with some knowledge of MPLS implementation in IOS XR. You are expected to be familiar with MPLS protocols and operations before reading this chapter.

Note: Although IOS XR supports a variety of MPLS features this book focuses on the basic features and concepts. The support section of Cisco Systems website (http://www.cisco.com) provides a configuration, troubleshooting, and design guide for specific releases and features of IOS XR software.

CHAPTER 9

Cisco IOS XR MPLS Architecture

Understanding Cisco IOS XR MPLS Architecture Fundamentals

This section provides an overview of basic MPLS concepts, followed by IOS XR MPLS architecture. MPLS is a framework that has control plane and forwarding plane components. The basic function of the control plane component is to assign a locally significant label to a forwarding equivalence class (FEC) and advertise this label binding to its neighbors. The goal of the label exchange is to set up a Label Switched Path (LSP) for forwarding traffic.

Table 9-1 lists the protocols that are used to assign and advertise label bindings for some FEC types. The table also shows the types of FEC advertised by each protocol.

Table 9-1 *MPLS Control Protocols and Corresponding FEC Types*

Label Exchange/Binding Protocol	Forwarding Equivalence Class Type
Label Distribution Protocol (LDP)	IPv4 prefix IPv6 prefix L2VPN Pseudo-Wire (S,G) multicast
RSVP (TE-Control)	Traffic Engineering Tunnel
BGP	IPv4 prefix IPv6 prefix VPNv4 prefix VPNv6 prefix

The MPLS forwarding component is responsible for forwarding received traffic based on the top label contained in the packet, incoming interface, IP address, and/or MAC address. Furthermore, at the entry of the MPLS network, the ingress Label Switch Router (LSR) classifies traffic based on incoming interface, IP address, and/or MAC address and imposes a label that is advertised by the downstream neighbor. Subsequent LSRs classify the traffic based on the label contained in the received packet and swap the label with an outgoing label that is advertised by a downstream neighbor. If the LSR is the exit point for the MPLS network, it will remove (or pop) the label and forward the packet to the downstream router. This behavior, in which the egress LSR removes the top label and forwards the packet, is known as *ultimate-hop popping*. An egress LSR may also advertise a well-known implicit-null label for directly connected prefix FECs to its upstream LSR neighbors. When an MPLS-labeled packet is received by an LSR and if it matches a FEC for which an implicit-null label advertisement is received from the corresponding next-hop router, the penultimate LSR will remove the label and forward the packet to the egress LSR. This is known as *penultimate hop popping*.

Figure 9-1 illustrates IOS XR MPLS architecture.

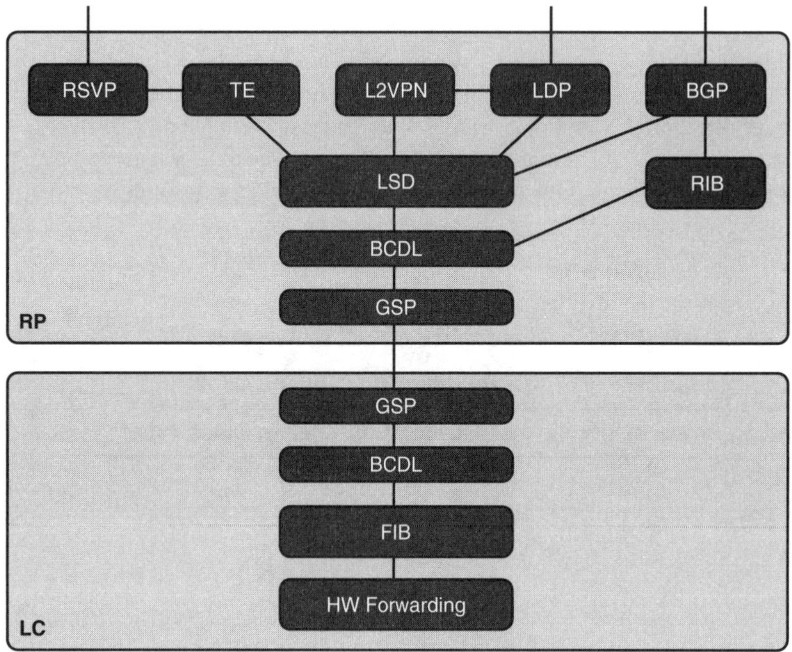

Figure 9-1 *Cisco IOS XR MPLS Architecture*

The Label Switch Database (LSD) is a central repository of label switching information. LDP, TE, L2VPN, and BGP act as LSD clients or applications and are responsible for binding labels to a FEC and downloading label forwarding data to LSD. When it was first standardized by IETF, LDP was used primarily for creating and exchanging label binding for IGP prefixes. Since then, its application has expanded to include label binding exchange for L2VPN's pseudo-wires and multicast's (S,G). MPLS TE is used to create bindings for MPLS Traffic Engineering tunnels and then to download the label-forwarding data of these tunnels to LSD. MPLS TE and L2VPN are not protocols but frameworks. The MPLS TE label exchange protocol is implemented using Resource Reservation Protocol (RSVP), which sets up the tunnel path and advertises the label binding for the tunnel. The label-binding exchange for L2VPN's pseudo-wires is handled by LDP.

The command **show mpls lsd applications** shows a list of applications that are registered with LSD to set up LSPs. Example 9-1 lists L2VPN, LDP, TE-Control, BGP, and LSD processes as applications that are registered with LSD to set up the MPLS forwarding plane (LSPs). Example 9-1 shows that only one instance of each application is registered with LSD. In some cases, some applications may have more than once instance registered with LSD. For example, LDP Non-Stop Routing (NSR) has two instances registered with LSD. Distributed BGP can have multiple instances registered with LSD.

Example 9-1 *Output of* **show mpls lsd applications**

```
RP/0/RP0/CPU0:CRS-A#show mpls lsd applications
Application                  State    RecoveryTime    Location
---------------              ----     --------        ------
LSD                          Active   0/0 (0)         0/RP0/CPU0
L2VPN                        Active   0/0 (600)       0/RP0/CPU0
TE-Control                   Active   0/0 (600)       0/RP0/CPU0
LDP:Active                   Active   0/0 (15)        0/RP0/CPU0
BGP-VPNv4:bgp-0              Active   0/0 (600)       0/RP0/CPU0
```

The LSD is responsible for maintaining the label database, receiving label-forwarding updates (also called *rewrites*) from applications, and downloading the LSD rewrite table to the FIB process on the line cards. LSD downloads label rewrites to line cards using BCDL, which uses GSP to distribute the data via multicast to line cards. BCDL and GSP are discussed in Chapter 2, "Cisco IOS XR Infrastructure."

The MPLS forwarding component is responsible for

- Classifying incoming traffic based on the received label, incoming interface, IP address, and/or MAC address
- Performing label operation on the incoming packet: push, swap, or pop
- Forwarding the packet to the outgoing interface

Table 9-2 shows possible label operations, and under what scenario each label operation is carried out.

Table 9-2 *MPLS Label Operations*

Label Operations	Descriptions
Swap	When an LSR receives an MPLS-labeled packet, it swaps the incoming label with the outgoing label advertised by the downstream LSR.

Label Operations	Descriptions
Push	When an ingress LSR receives an unlabeled packet that matches a FEC that has a binding from the downstream LSR, it pushes or imposes the label advertised by the downstream LSR and forwards the packet.
Pop	When a penultimate LSR receives an MPLS-labeled packet, and if the label corresponds to a FEC for which a downstream LSR has advertised an implicit-null label, it pops the topmost label and forwards the packet to the downstream LSR. This operation is also referred to as *penultimate hop popping*.
Unlabeled	When an egress LSR receives an MPLS-labeled packet that corresponds to a FEC for which no label advertisement is received from the downstream router, it removes the label and forwards the unlabeled packet to the downstream router if the underneath packet is IP. However, if label pop exposes underneath MPLS packet, the packet is dropped if the outgoing path is unlabeled.
De-aggregate	When an LSR receives an MPLS-labeled packet that corresponds to a FEC that requires secondary lookup to be forwarded, it removes the top label and performs a Layer 3 lookup on the packet. A special case of a de-aggregate operation is when an LSR receives an explicit-null labeled packet (label=0). Another example is when a PE router in L3VPN case advertises a label for a connected interface in a VRF.
Swap and push	A swap and push operation is typically done on boundary LSRs such as ASBR PE and CsC PE in L3VPN cases and LDP over MPLS TE at TE head-end LSRs. It involves swapping the incoming label for an outgoing label advertised from a remote boundary LSR, and imposing another label advertised from an adjacent downstream LSR.

Example 9-2 shows the output of the **show mpls forwarding** command.

Example 9-2 *Output of* show mpls forwarding

```
RP/0/RP0/CPU0:CRS-A#show mpls forwarding
Local  Outgoing    Prefix             Outgoing     Next Hop        Bytes
Label  Label       or ID              Interface                    Switched
------ ----------- ------------------ ------------ --------------- ------------
16000  Pop         192.168.0.3/32     Te0/0/0/4    192.168.1.2     0
```

```
        Pop         192.168.0.3/32     Te0/0/0/6     192.168.2.2     0
16001   Pop         192.168.6.0/30     Te0/0/0/4     192.168.1.2     0
        Pop         192.168.6.0/30     Te0/0/0/6     192.168.2.2     0
16002   Unlabelled  192.168.4.0/30     Te0/0/0/0.61  192.168.3.2     0
16003   Unlabelled  192.168.5.0/30     Te0/0/0/0.61  192.168.3.2     0
16004   16002       192.168.0.4/32     Te0/0/0/4     192.168.1.2     22289
        16002       192.168.0.4/32     Te0/0/0/6     192.168.2.2     0
        Unlabelled  192.168.0.4/32     Te0/0/0/0.61  192.168.3.2     0
16005   Unlabelled  192.168.0.2/32     Te0/0/0/0.61  192.168.3.2     0
16007   Aggregate    red: Per-VRF Aggr[V]    \
                                          red                    0
16009   Pop         192.168.100.2/32   tt1           point2point     0
16010   Pop         192.168.100.1/32   tt1           point2point     0
16011   Pop         192.168.100.3/32   tt2           point2point     0
16012   Pop         192.168.100.4/32   tt2           point2point     0
```

Example 9-3 shows the output for the **show mpls forwarding label 0** command, which is for the explicit null label.

Example 9-3 *Output of* **show mpls forwarding label 0** *for Explicit Null Label*

```
RP/0/RP0/CPU0:CRS-A#show mpls forwarding labels 0
Local  Outgoing    Prefix             Outgoing     Next Hop        Bytes
Label  Label       or ID              Interface                    Switched
------ ----------- ------------------ ------------ --------------- ----------
0      Aggregate   Exp-Null-v4
```

Example 9-4 shows output for the **show mpls forwarding label 16004 detail** command, which shows three equal cost multi-paths (ECMP). The first two paths use label swapping, whereas the third uses unlabel.

Example 9-4 *Output of* **show mpls forwarding label 16004 detail**

```
RP/0/RP0/CPU0:CRS-A#show mpls forwarding labels 16004 detail
Local  Outgoing    Prefix             Outgoing     Next Hop        Bytes
Label  Label       or ID              Interface                    Switched
------ ----------- ------------------ ------------ --------------- ----------
16004  16002       192.168.0.4/32     Te0/0/0/4    192.168.1.2     22424
     Updated Feb 22 11:45:01.113
     MAC/Encaps: 14/18, MTU: 9202
     Label Stack (Top -> Bottom): { 16002 }
     Packets Switched: 331

       16002       192.168.0.4/32     Te0/0/0/6    192.168.2.2     0
```

```
     Updated Feb 22 11:45:01.113
     MAC/Encaps: 14/18, MTU: 9202
     Label Stack (Top -> Bottom): { 16002 }
     Packets Switched: 0

       Unlabelled 192.168.0.4/32      Te0/0/0/0.61 192.168.3.2      0
     Updated Feb 22 11:45:01.113
     MAC/Encaps: 18/18, MTU: 9202
     Label Stack (Top -> Bottom): { }
     Packets Switched: 0
```

Example 9-2 and 9-4 show that the LSR has assigned local label **16004** for FEC representing IPv4 destination prefix **192.168.0.4/32**. The LSR has determined that there are three forwarding paths for the FEC and it has received label binding 16002 from a downstream LSR for the first two paths but has not received label binding for the third path (hence unlabeled). If this LSR receives a packet with an MPLS top label of 16004 and the label has end of stack (EOS) set to indicate that it is the only label, it will perform a load-balancing decision (hashing) to pick one of the three paths. If it selects one of the first two paths, it performs label swapping with 16002 and forwards the packet on the selected path. If it selects the third (unlabeled) path, it will remove the label and forward the IP packet over the path. On the other hand, if EOS is not set, which indicates that there are multiple labels, only one of the first two paths is used in the hashing decision. The third (unlabeled) path is not used for a multi-label stack case. MPLS load balancing is discussed in more detail later in this section.

To display the owner process of each MPLS label, use **show mpls label table** as shown in Example 9-5.

Example 9-5 *Output of* **show mpls label table**

```
RP/0/RP0/CPU0:CRS-A#show mpls label table
Sun Feb 22 12:41:41.640 PST
Table Label   Owner                          State Rewrite
----- ------- ------------------------------ ----- -------
0     0       LSD                            InUse Yes
0     1       LSD                            InUse Yes
0     2       LSD                            InUse Yes
0     16000   LDP:Active                     InUse Yes
0     16001   LDP:Active                     InUse Yes
0     16002   LDP:Active                     InUse Yes
0     16003   LDP:Active                     InUse Yes
0     16004   LDP:Active                     InUse Yes
0     16005   LDP:Active                     InUse Yes
0     16006   TE-Control                     InUse Yes
0     16007   BGP-VPNv4:bgp-0                InUse Yes
0     16008   TE-Control                     InUse Yes
```

```
0      16009   LDP:Active                    InUse Yes
0      16010   LDP:Active                    InUse Yes
0      16011   LDP:Active                    InUse Yes
0      16012   LDP:Active                    InUse Yes
```

TTL Processing

When an ingress LSR receives an IP packet that matches a FEC with a label binding from the downstream LSR, it imposes an MPLS label and forwards the labeled packet. Depending on the time to live (TTL) propagation setting, the LSR either copies the TTL value of the incoming IP packet to the TTL field of the MPLS packet header after decrementing it by one or sets the MPLS TTL to 255. The default behavior is to copy the IP TTL value to the MPLS header. This behavior can be changed by configuring **mpls ip-ttl-propagation disable**, in which case the TTL value of the MPLS header is set to 255 irrespective of the TTL value in the received IP packet.

Also, when an egress or penultimate hop LSR performs an unlabeled or pop operation and the resulting payload is an IP packet, the default behavior is to copy the TTL value of the MPLS packet header to the IP header, essentially accounting for all the hops traversed by the packet. If **mpls ip-ttl-propagation disable** is configured, it does not overwrite the IP header TTL value on egress and all the hops the packet traverses through the MPLS network remain unaccounted for. Some service providers use **mpls ip-ttl-propagation disable** to hide their network from traceroute probes. With **mpls ip-ttl-propagation disable** configured, the service provider MPLS network appears as a single hop to a trace-route probe.

Cisco IOS XR MPLS Load Balancing

In IOS XR, when there are multiple equal cost paths, also called Equal Cost Multi Path (ECMP), for a FEC, the path for an incoming packet is selected using hashing function in the data plane. Also, if a path uses Layer2 bundle interface as the outgoing interface, a member of the bundle is selected using a bundle-hashing function. The fields from the packet used in the hashing function depend on the payload type and **cef load-balancing fields** setting. For an MPLS-labeled packet, if the payload is non-IP (for example, L2VPN service), the bottommost label and the router-id of the LSR are used in the hashing function.

For an MPLS-labeled packet with IP payload, no MPLS label is used as input to the hashing function. The default hashing function uses the source IP address, destination IP address, and router-id of the LSR. This is referred to as *3-tuple*, or L3, hashing. The configuration **cef load-balancing fields L4** changes the default to 7-tuple, or L4, hashing. L4 (or 7-tuple) hashing uses the router ID, IP source and destination addresses, IP protocol, source and destination port numbers, and ingress interface handle as input to the hashing function. If the IP protocol is not UDP, TCP, SCTP, or L2TPv3, the source and destination port numbers are set to 0. For the L2TPv3 protocol, the session ID is used for source and destination port number.

IOS XR provides a CLI to check the exact path on which a specific packet is forwarded given the hashing field values. For an MPLS-labeled packet with non-IP payload, use **show mpls forwarding exact-route label** *<top-label>* **bottom-label** *<bottom-label>* as shown in

Example 9-6. In the case of L2VPN, the bottom label represents a pseudo-wire (PW) and can be obtained from the corresponding L2VPN command, which is discussed in the L2VPN section later in this chapter. Bottom labels 55, 56, and 57, in Example 9-6, correspond to one PW each.

Example 9-6 *Output of* **show mpls forwarding exact-route** *for Non-IP Payload*

```
RP/0/RP0/CPU0:CRS-A#show mpls forwarding labels 16004
Local  Outgoing    Prefix             Outgoing     Next Hop       Bytes
Label  Label       or ID              Interface                   Switched
------ ----------- ------------------ ------------ -------------- --------
16004  16002       192.168.0.4/32     Te0/0/0/4    192.168.1.2    49964
       16002       192.168.0.4/32     Te0/0/0/6    192.168.2.2    0
       Unlabelled  192.168.0.4/32     Te0/0/0/0.61 192.168.3.2    0

RP/0/RP0/CPU0:CRS-A#show mpls forwarding exact-route label 16004 bottom-label 55
Local  Outgoing    Prefix             Outgoing     Next Hop       Bytes
Label  Label       or ID              Interface                   Switched
------ ----------- ------------------ ------------ -------------- --------
16004  Unlabelled  192.168.0.4/32     Te0/0/0/0.61 remote         N/A
     Via: Te0/0/0/0.61, Next Hop: remote
     MAC/Encaps: 4/4, MTU: 1500
     Label Stack (Top -> Bottom): { Unlabelled }

RP/0/RP0/CPU0:CRS-A#show mpls forwarding exact-route label 16004 bottom-label 56
Local  Outgoing    Prefix             Outgoing     Next Hop       Bytes
Label  Label       or ID              Interface                   Switched
------ ----------- ------------------ ------------ -------------- --------
16004  16002       192.168.0.4/32     Te0/0/0/4    remote         N/A
     Via: Te0/0/0/4, Next Hop: remote
     MAC/Encaps: 4/8, MTU: 1500
     Label Stack (Top -> Bottom): { 16002 }

RP/0/RP0/CPU0:CRS-A#show mpls forwarding exact-route label 16004 bottom-label 57
Local  Outgoing    Prefix             Outgoing     Next Hop       Bytes
Label  Label       or ID              Interface                   Switched
------ ----------- ------------------ ------------ -------------- --------
16004  16002       192.168.0.4/32     Te0/0/0/6    remote         N/A
     Via: Te0/0/0/6, Next Hop: remote
     MAC/Encaps: 4/8, MTU: 1500
     Label Stack (Top -> Bottom): { 16002 }
```

For an MPLS-labeled packet with IP payload and default L3 hash setting, use **show mpls forwarding exact-route label** *<top-label>* {**ipv4** | **ipv6**} *<source IP address>* *<destination IP* **address**> to get the exact path for a specific incoming packet as shown in Example 9-7.

Example 9-7 *Output of* **show mpls forwarding exact-route** *for IP payload with Default Hashing Function*

```
RP/0/RP0/CPU0:CRS-A#show mpls forwarding exact-route label 16004 ipv4 1.1.1.6
  192.168.0.4
Local  Outgoing    Prefix              Outgoing     Next Hop       Bytes
Label  Label       or ID               Interface                   Switched
------ ----------- ------------------ ------------ --------------- ------------
16004  16002       192.168.0.4/32      Te0/0/0/6    remote         N/A
     Via: Te0/0/0/6, Next Hop: remote
     MAC/Encaps: 4/8, MTU: 1500
     Label Stack (Top -> Bottom): { 16002 }

RP/0/RP0/CPU0:CRS-A#show mpls forwarding exact-route label 16004 ipv4 1.1.1.7
  192.168.0.4
Local  Outgoing    Prefix              Outgoing     Next Hop       Bytes
Label  Label       or ID               Interface                   Switched
------ ----------- ------------------ ------------ --------------- ------------
16004  16002       192.168.0.4/32      Te0/0/0/4    remote         N/A
     Via: Te0/0/0/4, Next Hop: remote
     MAC/Encaps: 4/8, MTU: 1500
     Label Stack (Top -> Bottom): { 16002 }

RP/0/RP0/CPU0:CRS-A#show mpls forwarding exact-route label 16004 ipv4 1.1.1.8
  192.168.0.4
Local  Outgoing    Prefix              Outgoing     Next Hop       Bytes
Label  Label       or ID               Interface                   Switched
------ ----------- ------------------ ------------ --------------- ------------
16004  Unlabelled  192.168.0.4/32      Te0/0/0/0.619 remote        N/A
     Via: Te0/0/0/0.619, Next Hop: remote
     MAC/Encaps: 4/4, MTU: 1500
    Label Stack (Top -> Bottom): { Unlabelled }
```

For an MPLS-labeled packet with IP payload and L4 (7-tuple) hashing configuration, use the following command to get the exact path for a specific incoming packet as shown in Example 9-8.

```
show mpls forwarding exact-route label <top-label> {ipv4 | ipv6} <source IP
  address> <destination IP address> protocol <protocol> source-port <src port>
  destination-port <dst port> ingress-interface <ingress intf>.
```

Example 9-8 *Output of* **show mpls forwarding exact-route** *for IP Payload With 7-Tuple Hashing Configuration*

```
RP/0/RP0/CPU0:CRS-A(config)#cef load-balancing fields L4
RP/0/RP0/CPU0:CRS-A(config)#commit
RP/0/RP0/CPU0:CRS-A(config)#end
```

```
RP/0/RP0/CPU0:CRS-A#show mpls forwarding exact-route label 16004 ipv4 1.1.1.1
   192.168.0.4 protocol TCP source-port 105 destination-port 80 ingress-interface
   Ten 0/0/0/4
Local  Outgoing    Prefix              Outgoing     Next Hop        Bytes
Label  Label       or ID               Interface                    Switched
---    ------.     ----------         ------       ---------.      ------
16004  16002       192.168.0.4/32      Te0/0/0/4    remote          N/A
      Via: Te0/0/0/4, Next Hop: remote
      MAC/Encaps: 4/8, MTU: 1500
      Label Stack (Top -> Bottom): { 16002 }

RP/0/RP0/CPU0:CRS-A#show mpls forwarding exact-route label 16004 ipv4 1.1.1.1
   192.168.0.4 protocol TCP source-port 106 destination-port 80 ingress-interface
   Ten 0/0/0/4
Local  Outgoing    Prefix              Outgoing     Next Hop        Bytes
Label  Label       or ID               Interface                    Switched
---    ------.     ----------         ------       ---------.      ------
16004  Unlabelled 192.168.0.4/32     Te0/0/0/0.619  remote          N/A
      Via: Te0/0/0/0.619, Next Hop: remote
      MAC/Encaps: 4/4, MTU: 1500
      Label Stack (Top -> Bottom): { Unlabelled }

RP/0/RP0/CPU0:CRS-A#show mpls forwarding exact-route label 16004 ipv4 1.1.1.1
   192.168.0.4 protocol TCP source-port 107 destination-port 80 ingress-interface
   Ten 0/0/0/4
Local  Outgoing    Prefix              Outgoing     Next Hop        Bytes
Label  Label       or ID               Interface                    Switched
---    ------.     ----------         ------       ---------.      ------
16004  16002       192.168.0.4/32      Te0/0/0/6    remote          N/A
      Via: Te0/0/0/6, Next Hop: remote
      MAC/Encaps: 4/8, MTU: 1500
      Label Stack (Top -> Bottom): { 16002 }
```

Label Distribution Protocol

MPLS uses various control plane protocols to set up an MPLS forwarding table. The Label Distribution Protocol (LDP) is one of the MPLS control plane protocols standardized by IETF. It is defined in RFC 5036. LDP is a mechanism by which an LSR creates label bindings for FECs and informs other LSRs about the bindings.

Before exchanging label bindings, two LSRs have to establish an LDP session and become LDP peers. TCP is used as a reliable transport for an LDP session. To avoid manual configuration of LDP peering, the protocol specifies a discovery mechanism that enables an LSR to discover potential LDP peers.

RFC 5036 specifies two discovery mechanisms:

- **Basic discovery** is used between directly connected LSRs. LDP link hello packets are sent as UDP with a destination IP address of 224.0.0.2, which is a reserved address for all routers on this subnet and UDP port number 646. LDP discovery message carries LDP identifier, which is typically built using the LDP router-id. When an LSR receives an LDP hello packet on an interface, it first creates a Hello adjacency on this interface and then attempts to establish an LDP session using the LDP identifier of the peer.

- **Extended discovery** is typically used between LSRs that are not directly connected. With extended discovery, an LSR sends LDP targeted hellos to a specific IP unicast address using UDP port 646. LDP extended discovery is used by some applications including L2VPN. This section focuses primarily on basic discovery mechanisms.

Cisco IOS XR supports both basic and extended discovery for LDP neighbor relationships.

After LDP session establishment, two LSRs can exchange label bindings for a given FEC. RFC 5036 defines a single FEC type, called the Address Prefix FEC element. Additional FEC types are defined by other IETF specifications and LDP applications, but our focus in this section is the address prefix FEC element.

Cisco IOS XR LDP operates in the following modes:

- **Downstream unsolicited:** LSR advertises its label bindings to all its peers without any need for explicit binding request.
- **Independent label distribution control:** LSR advertises its label binding to all its peers without waiting for label binding reception from a downstream peer.
- **Liberal label retention mode:** LSR keeps all label bindings received from peers. In contrast, a conservative retention mode LSR retains only label bindings that can be used for forwarding at a given time. The use of liberal retention mode enables IOS XR to react quickly to network changes.

Normally an IOS XR router advertises label binding for all IGP prefixes to all its LDP peers and, by inference, it also receives label bindings for all IGP prefixes from all its LDP peers. To illustrate this behavior consider the routers in Figure 9-2. All four routers are in the same OSPF area 0 and are configured for LDP, with given IP addresses and OSPF costs.

Take, for example, CRS-A from Figure 9-2. It forms two LDP sessions: one with CRS-B and another with CRS-C. Therefore, it sends label bindings for all IGP prefixes to both CRS-B and CRS-C and it receives label binding for the same IGP prefixes from both CRS-B and CRS-C.

Table 9-3 shows the label bindings received by CRS-A from both CRS-B and CRS-C. The bindings are shown side by side for easy comparison. The FECs (prefixes) advertised by both CRS-B and CRS-C are identical; however, the label binding for the FECs, shown as remote-bindings in the table, may be different.

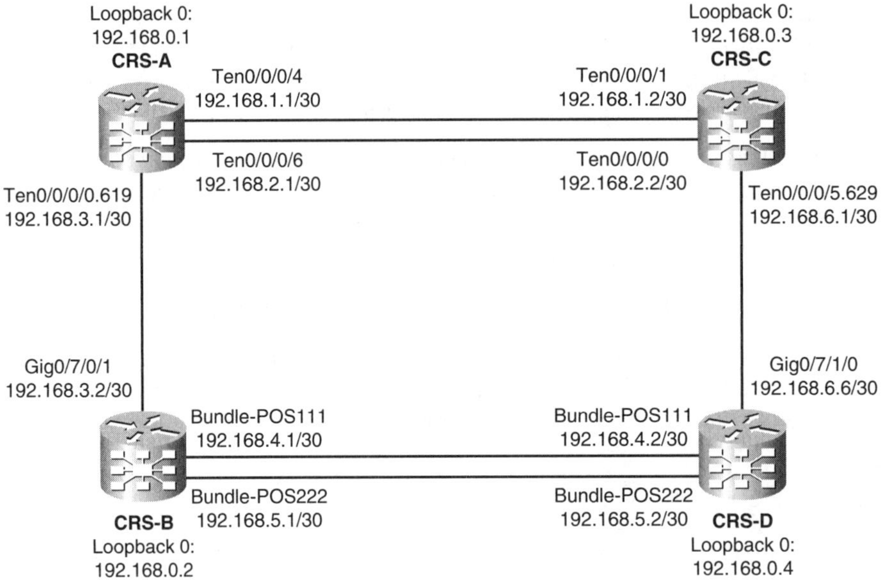

Figure 9-2 *MPLS Network*

Table 9-3 *Label Bindings Received by CRS-A from CRS-B and CRS-C*

Bindings from CRS-B	Bindings from CRS-C
RP/0/RP0/CPU0:CRS-A#**show mpls ldp bindings neighbor 192.168.0.2**	RP/0/RP0/CPU0:CRS-A#**show mpls ldp bindings neighbor 192.168.0.3**
192.168.0.1/32, rev 2	192.168.0.1/32, rev 2
Local binding: label: IMP-NULL	Local binding: label: IMP-NULL
Remote bindings:	Remote bindings:
LSR: 192.168.0.2:0, label: 16000	LSR: 192.168.0.3:0, label: 16000
<...cut...>	<...cut...>
192.168.0.4/32, rev 33	192.168.0.4/32, rev 33
Local binding: label: 16004	Local binding: label: 16004
Remote bindings:	Remote bindings:
LSR: 192.168.0.2:0, label: 16002	LSR: 192.168.0.3:0, label: 17002
<...cut...>	<...cut...>
192.168.6.0/30, rev 34	192.168.6.0/30, rev 34
Local binding: label: 16001	Local binding: label: 16001
Remote bindings:	Remote bindings:
LSR: 192.168.0.2:0, label: 16003	LSR: 192.168.0.3:0, label: IMP-NULL

If an LSR receives label binding for all IGP prefixes from all its peers, how does it determine which binding to use to set up the forwarding? The forwarding path selection decision is made by IGP protocol. For example, consider prefix 192.168.0.4/32 from Figure 9-2. CRS-A receives label binding for this prefix from both CRS-C and CRS-B. CRS-B and CRS-C have advertised a label value of 16002 and 17002, respectively, for 192.168.0.4/32.

Based on the OSPF cost, the best path to 192.168.0.4/32 is via CRS-B. Therefore, CRS-A uses the outgoing label of 16002 and outgoing interface as Ten0/0/0/0.619. MPLS forwarding setup for a given IP prefix can be seen from the output of **show mpls forwarding prefix 192.168.0.4/32** shown in Example 9-9.

Example 9-9 *Output of* **show mpls forwarding prefix 192.168.0.4/32**

```
RP/0/RP0/CPU0:CRS-A#show mpls forwarding prefix 192.168.0.4/32
Local  Outgoing    Prefix            Outgoing      Next Hop         Bytes
Label  Label        or ID            Interface                      Switched
-----  ----------- ----------------  ------------  ---------------  --------
16004  16002       192.168.0.4/32    Te0/0/0/0.619 192.168.3.2      5005
```

Subsequent subsections discuss LDP basic configurations, LDP parameters, label control, and solutions for traffic black-holing problems.

LDP Basic Configuration

In IOS XR, similar to other routing protocols and applications, LDP has its own global configuration mode and all the relevant LDP commands are configured under LDP configuration mode. LDP is enabled on interfaces that connect the router to potential LDP peer routers either by explicitly specifying the interfaces under **mpls ldp** configuration mode or by using LDP auto-configuration under the IGP protocol configuration mode. For CRS-A in Figure 9-2, explicit configuration of interfaces is shown in Example 9-10.

Example 9-10 *MPLS LDP Explicit Configuration of Interfaces*

```
mpls ldp
 router-id 192.168.0.1
 interface TenGigE0/0/0/0.619
 !
 interface TenGigE0/0/0/4
 !
 interface TenGigE0/0/0/6
```

Example 9-11 shows LDP auto-configuration.

Example 9-11 *MPLS LDP Auto-Configuration*

```
mpls ldp
 router-id 192.168.0.1
!
router ospf mpls-test
 router-id 192.168.0.1
 mpls ldp auto-config
 area 0
 interface Loopback0
 !
 interface TenGigE0/0/0/0.619
```

```
 !
 interface TenGigE0/0/0/4
 !
 interface TenGigE0/0/0/6
 !
 !
!
```

With MPLS LDP auto-configuration, LDP is enabled on all interfaces for which the IGP protocol is enabled. Because in most cases LDP and IGP protocols are enabled on the same set of interfaces, LDP auto-configuration eliminates the need to specify the same list of interfaces under LDP and simplifies the configuration task for network operators.

LDP Parameters

On each LDP-enabled interface, LDP sends a discovery hello packet every 5 seconds and it has a hold time of 15 seconds. If it does not receive a discovery hello from peer for more than 15 seconds, it brings down the corresponding adjacency and removes the LDP session, if the session belonged to only this adjacency. For extended discovery of neighbors, LDP uses targeted hellos with an interval of 10 seconds and a hold time of 90 seconds. After the LDP session is established, it sends a session Keepalive message every 60 seconds and has a session hold time of 180 seconds. LDP session Keepalive messages are used to maintain session liveness and are sent only if there is no other LDP protocol message to send. The LDP parameters in use can be displayed using the **show mpls ldp parameters** command. The desired parameters for both session and discovery hellos can also be changed by configuration. Example 9-12 shows nondefault parameters for discovery and session timers.

Example 9-12 *LDP Parameter Configuration*

```
mpls ldp
 router-id 192.168.0.1
 discovery hello holdtime 30
 discovery hello interval 10
 discovery targeted-hello holdtime 135
 discovery targeted-hello interval 15
 holdtime 60
!
```

LDP Label Control

As stated earlier in this section, LDP creates label bindings for all IGP prefixes and receives label bindings for all IGP prefixes from all its peers. If an LSR receives label bindings from several peers for thousands of IGP prefixes, it consumes significant memory and CPU cycles. Most of the LDP label bindings are not useful for any application. In fact, label bindings for looback addresses of boundary routers, such as PE for L3VPN or L2VPN, and eBGP peering router for BGP free core application, are sufficient in most LDP applications.

Cisco IOS XR provides a robust and flexible label control mechanism to limit the allocation of local label bindings, received label bindings, and advertised label bindings. Configuring **mpls ldp label allocate for** **<*ipv4-access-list*>** limits the allocation of the local label to only IPv4 prefixes that match the ACL. For Figure 9-2, the configuration shown in Example 9-13 limits the local label bindings to only the loopback addresses of the routers.

Example 9-13 *LDP Label Allocation Control Configuration*

```
RP/0/RP1/CPU0:CRS-1#show running-config ipv4 access-list MPLS-PE
ipv4 access-list MPLS-PE
 10 permit ipv4 192.168.0.0/24 any
!
RP/0/RP1/CPU0:CRS-1#show running-config mpls ldp label
mpls ldp
 label
 allocate for MPLS-PE
 !
!
```

Example 9-14 shows label bindings of CRS-A after the configuration shown in Example 9-13 is applied to all four routers.

Example 9-14 *Label Binding of CRS-A After Applying Preceding Configuration to All Routers*

```
RP/0/RP0/CPU0:CRS-A#show mpls ldp binding

192.168.0.1/32, rev 2
        Local binding: label: IMP-NULL
        Remote bindings:
            LSR: 192.168.0.3:0, label: 16000
            LSR: 192.168.0.2:0, label: 16000
192.168.0.2/32, rev 7
        Local binding: label: 16005
        Remote bindings:
            LSR: 192.168.0.3:0, label: 16005
            LSR: 192.168.0.2:0, label: IMP-NULL
192.168.0.3/32, rev 6
        Local binding: label: 16000
        Remote bindings:
            LSR: 192.168.0.3:0, label: IMP-NULL
            LSR: 192.168.0.2:0, label: 16001
192.168.0.4/32, rev 8
        Local binding: label: 16004
```

```
      Remote bindings:
         LSR: 192.168.0.3:0, label: 16002
         LSR: 192.168.0.2:0, label: 16002
```

Although **label allocate** is the most effective and simple way to control label binding allocation and advertisement, IOS XR LDP provides two more knobs to control label binding. The configuration **mpls ldp label advertise for** *<FEC-ACL>* [**to** *<peer-ACL>*] is used to control the label bindings advertised to specific peers. The configuration **mpls ldp label accept for** *<FEC-ACL>* [**from** *<peer-IP-address>*] is used to control which label bindings to accept from specific peers.

LDP-IGP Sync and LDP Session Protection

When a link or node goes down, some traffic loss is expected while an alternative route is calculated and traffic is rerouted around the failed link or node. The duration of traffic loss can be reduced using one or more of the fast convergence mechanisms, such as MPLS TE Fast Re-route (FRR), IP-FRR, BFD, IGP tuning, prefix prioritization, and Prefix Independent Convergence (PIC). At the link-up event, however, network operators may expect zero or minimal traffic loss. Although this sounds logical, it is a challenging requirement in an MPLS LDP environment, as explained in the next paragraph.

When a new link or node comes up, it is possible that routing adjacency is established first before the LDP session is established. Therefore, IP routing might converge before label bindings are exchanged and label forwarding is set up. This means that an LSR might start forwarding traffic to the new path/link before it receives bindings for the same prefix from the downstream peer. This can result in traffic loss if the traffic carried over the MPLS network is L2VPN, L3VPN, or BGP-free core traffic.

As an example, consider the network with BGP-free core depicted in Figure 9-3, which has an AS 100 network with two eBGP sessions to two ISPs (AS 200 and 300). AS 100 core routers CRS-1, CRS-2, CRS-3, and CRS-4 do not participate in BGP, and only the edge routers PE-1 and PE-2 participate in BGP protocol. The regular traffic path from PE-1 to PE-2 is via { CRS-A, CRS-B, CRS-D }, but it changes to {CRS-A, CRS-C, CRS-D} if the link between CRS-A and CRS-B is down.

Now assume the following information:

- Router R300 advertises prefix 192.168.64.0/20 to PE-2 using eBGP.
- PE-2 advertises 192.168.64.0/20 with its loopback address as the next hop [nh=10.10.10.6] to PE-1 using iBGP.
- PE-1 advertises the same prefix to R200 using eBGP.
- PE-2 LDP advertises an implicit null label binding for its loopback address (FEC=10.10.10.6/32, label=Implicit-null) to its peer CRS-D.
- CRS-D advertises label 400 as the label binding for the given FEC (FEC=10.10.10.6/32, label=400) to its peers.
- CRS-C advertises (FEC=10.10.10.6/32, label=300) binding to its peers.

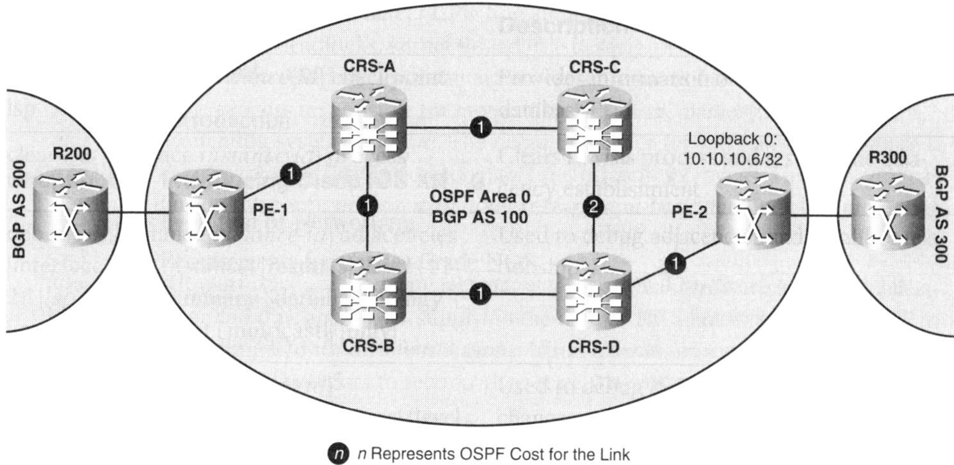

Figure 9-3 *Traffic Black-Holing on Link-Up Event*

- CRS-B advertises (FEC=10.10.10.6/32, label=200) binding to its peers.
- CRS-A advertises (FEC=10.10.10.6/32, label=100) binding to its peer.
- The LSP from PE-1 to PE-2 for the destination prefix 10.10.10.6/32 is as follows:
  - PE-1 imposes label 100 on the incoming packet, nh=CRS-A.
  - CRS-A swaps label 100 for 300, nh=CRS-C.
  - CRS-C swaps label 300 for 400, nh=CRS-D.
  - CRS-D pops label 400 and forwards the packet to PE-2.

Suppose there is traffic stream destined to 192.168.64.1 incoming into PE-1. The forwarding for the traffic stream is carried out as follows:

- At PE-1, the destination address 192.168.64.1 matches BGP prefix 192.168.64.0/20 with next hop of 10.10.10.6.
- The BGP next hop is recursively resolved in forwarding via IGP/LDP path and, therefore, PE-1 forwards the traffic using routing information for 10.10.10.6, which corresponds to an LSP path.
- Subsequent routers CRS-A, CRS-C, and CRS-D forward the traffic based on the MPLS label.
- PE-2 receives an IP packet because the label was popped by CRS-D. This packet is now the same packet that had arrived at the PE-1 ingress.
- At PE-2, destination address 192.168.64.1 matches a BGP prefix received from R300; therefore, PE-2 forwards the packet to R300.
- As demonstrated in the preceding paragraphs, the core routers forward the traffic destined to BGP learned prefix while they do not have BGP prefixes in their routing table. This implementation is known as *BGP-free core*.

Assume that at some point the link between CRS-A and CRS-B is restored. As a result, traffic will be rerouted over the new link because it is the least cost path with an OSPF metric of 2. The following examines what happens from the time the link is restored until traffic is rerouted over the new path:

- At time t=T_0, the link between CRS-A and CRS-B is restored.
- Both CRS-A and CRS-B start sending LDP discovery hello packets and OSPF hello packets over the new link immediately.
- It is possible that OSPF adjacency establishment and LSA exchange are completed before LDP session establishment and binding exchange completion. As a result, forwarding entries in CRS-A and CRS-B are programmed as "unlabeled" for all the routes they learn from each other.
- As a result, when CRS-A receives an MPLS packet with label 100 for the traffic stream destined to 192.168.64.1, it removes the label and forwards the unlabeled IP packet to CRS-B. CRS-B ends up performing an IP lookup and drops the packet because it does not run BGP and, therefore, destination 192.168.64.1 in AS 300 is not in its forwarding table.
- After some time, the LDP session is reestablished, CRS-A receives a label binding for 10.10.10.6/32 from CRS-B, and the forwarding is updated accordingly. Subsequent MPLS packets received by CRS-A with label 100 are forwarded to CRS-B after swapping the label with 200.

As demonstrated, after a link-up event occurs in an MPLS core network, it is possible that LDP and IGP might not be in synchronization, which can lead to traffic loss—albeit for a short time. MPLS networks are designed to support multiple services, of which some are acutely sensitive to latency and/or loss. IOS XR provides two mitigation mechanisms to traffic loss induced by link-up events:

- **LDP Session Protection** mechanism allows LDP sessions between adjacent LSRs to stay up even after the link between them is down. Because the LDP session remains up, the bindings received from the peer are not removed. Therefore, there is no or minimal impact to labeled traffic when the link is restored. As soon as IP forwarding converges, MPLS is ready to converge because it can use the label binding that is already available.
- **LDP-IGP synchronization** keeps the IGP cost of the link between LSRs to be maximum metric until MPLS LDP converge on a link between peers. We are using the term *converge* loosely here to refer to the time when all label bindings have been exchanged between the peers after session establishment. When MPLS control plane convergence completes, the IGP cost is restored to its configured or default value. Because the IGP link cost is kept maximized until the MPLS control plane converges, the link is not used for forwarding before the LSR has label binding for the forwarding.

LDP session protection is configured as follows. It can be enabled for all peers or for selected peers. Also, it is possible to specify the maximum duration for protecting a session once protection becomes active.

```
mpls ldp
 session protection [for <peer-ACL>] [ duration { infinite ¦ <seconds> } ]
 !
!
```

When session protection is enabled for a peer, LDP starts sending targeted hello (directed discovery) in addition to basic discovery link hellos. When the direct link goes down, the targeted hellos can still be forwarded to the peer LSR over an alternative path as long as there is one. As a result, the session stays up after the link goes down.

LDP session protection has a few shortcomings:

- It does not protect from node failures because both the link and targeted LDP sessions terminate on the same neighbor node.
- It does not protect from software failures that impact the LDP protocol; therefore, both the link and targeted session could tear down simultaneously, rendering this feature ineffective.
- Both LSRs need to have, at minimum, configuration to accept and/or send targeted hellos.

LDP-IGP synchronization is supported for both OSPF and ISIS protocols and is configured under the corresponding IGP protocol configuration mode. For OSPF, it can be configured globally, per area, or per interface level. For ISIS, it is configured per interface.

The following shows the global configuration for LDP IGP synchronization for OSPF:

```
router ospf <process-name>
 mpls ldp sync
!
```

The following shows the per-area configuration for LDP IGP synchronization for OSPF:

```
router ospf <process-name>
 area <area ID>
 mpls ldp sync
 !
!
```

The following shows the per-interface configuration for LDP IGP synchronization for OSPF:

```
router ospf <process name>
 area <area ID>
 interface <intf>
   mpls ldp sync
 !
 !
!
```

The following shows the ISIS configuration for LDP IGP synchronization:

```
router isis <process name>
```

```
  interface <intf>
  address-family ipv4 unicast
    mpls ldp sync
  !
  !
!
```

The following shows the LDP IGP synchronization delay parameter configuration:

```
mpls ldp
 igp sync delay <delay-in-seconds>
!
```

The LDP IGP synchronization mechanism does not suffer from the limitations of session protection. It can protect against adjacent node failure and it does not depend on the capability of the peer LSR. It has one limitation, nonetheless. When a link comes up, the IGP cost of the link is advertised with the maximum metric. After the LSR has completed sending its label bindings, it assumes that it has also received all label bindings from its peer. At this point, it then starts advertising regular metric for the link. However, there is no guarantee that it has received all the label bindings from the adjacent peer. If the adjacent peer is very slow to send its label bindings or uses the ordered label distribution control mode, it is possible that the LSR can prematurely advertise regular metric for the link and start to send traffic before it receives label bindings from its peer. This could cause traffic loss for L2VPN, L3VPN, and BGP-free core type of traffic. IOS XR provides a configuration knob to configure a delay to accommodate slow LSR peers.

MPLS Traffic Engineering

MPLS TE is used primarily for one or both of the following purposes:

- **Traffic Engineering:** This enables the network operator to use network bandwidth more efficiently by steering the traffic away from congestion points in the network, taking into account the link bandwidth and traffic size.
- **Fast Re-Routing (FRR):** MPLS TE enables Fast Re-Routing of traffic around a failed link or node.

The rest of this section focuses primarily on basic MPLS TE operations and configurations. The basic operations of MPLS TE can be summarized as follows:

- MPLS TE establishes Label Switched Path (LSP) tunnel from a head-end to a tail-end router via zero or more midpoint routers. The tunnel is set up by the RSVP protocol, which also reserves the requested bandwidth on the links that are part of the LSP tunnel.
- The tunnel interface along with its bandwidth, affinity to interface attributes, and/or destination address are configured on the head-end router.
- The LSP tunnel path is either explicitly configured at the head-end router or dynamically calculated by the head-end router.

- Dynamic tunnel path computation utilizes IGP protocol (OSPF or ISIS) with MPLS TE extensions. The IGP protocol provides the topology of the network along with available bandwidth and attribute parameters on each link of the topology.
- The head-end router performs constrained shortest-path first (CSPF) computation to find the best tunnel path with available bandwidth.
- CSPF is SPF performed on the subset of the topology that is obtained by removing infeasible links from the topology. Infeasible links are links that do not satisfy the bandwidth and other criteria of the TE tunnel.

MPLS TE configuration involves multiple configuration modes including RSVP, MPLS Traffic Engineering, IGP (OSPF or ISIS), explicit path, and TE tunnel interface. The first three are configured on all routers and interfaces in the MPLS traffic engineering network. Explicit path and TE tunnel interfaces are configured only on head-end routers. MPLS TE configuration tasks are summarized as follows:

1. Under **rsvp** configuration mode, add interfaces that are part of the MPLS TE network. For each interface, configure the bandwidth available for TE.
2. Under **mpls traffic-eng** configuration mode, define *affinity-map*. This is necessary only if interface attributes are used.
3. Under **mpls traffic-eng** configuration mode, add interfaces that are part of the MPLS TE network. Optionally, for each interface, configure the bandwidth available for TE.
4. If OSPF is the IGP protocol, under **router ospf** *<id>* **area** *<area-id>* configuration mode, enable MPLS TE for each OSPF area that participates in MPLS traffic engineering (use **mpls traffic-eng**). Also, under **router ospf** configuration mode specify router ID for MPLS TE using **mpls traffic-eng router-id Loopback***<i>*.
5. If ISIS is the IGP protocol, under **router isis** *<id>* **address-family ipv4 unicast** configuration mode, enable MPLS TE for either or both levels using **mpls traffic-eng** {**level-1** | **level-1-2** | **level-2-only**}. Also, in the same configuration mode, specify MPLS TE router ID using **mpls traffic-eng router-id Loopback***<i>*.
6. At the head-end, using **explicit-path name** *<path-name>* or **explicit-path identifier** *<id>*, configure explicit path(s) for each MPLS TE tunnel that uses explicit path option.
7. At the head-end, configure each MPLS TE tunnel using **interface tunnel-te** *<number>*. Under the **tunnel-te** interface mode, configure the following parameters:
   - **ipv4 unnumbered Loopback** *<loopback-address-number-for-MPLS-TE-router-id>*.
   - **destination** *<ip-address-of-tail-end-router>*.
   - **autoroute announce** to use the tunnel in the routing table via announcing it to IGP.
   - **signaled-bandwidth** *<tunnel-BW-in-Kbps>* to signal the BW reservation.
   - **signalled-name** *<tunnel-name>* to signal the name for the TE tunnel. This is useful in troubleshooting at midpoint or tail-end routers.

- **record-route** so that the actual TE tunnel path is recorded. This is also useful for troubleshooting.
- Configure one or more explicit and/or dynamic path options in preference order. If there is a dynamic path option, it should be configured as the last option. Use **path-option** <*preference*> {**dynamic** | **explicit** {**name** <*path-name*> | **id** <*id*>}} to configure each path option.
- Optionally, set affinity by **affinity** {**include** | **exclude** | **exclude-all** | **include-strict**} <*affinity-name*> [<*affinity-name*> [<*affinity-name*] ...]].

Example 9-15 shows MPLS traffic configurations for a head-end router. The configurations include RSVP, MPLS TE, OSPF, explicit-paths, and one TE tunnel interface.

Example 9-15 *MPLS TE Configuration on Head-End Router*

```
interface tunnel-te55
 ipv4 unnumbered Loopback0
 signalled-name Testing
 signalled-bandwidth 550000
 autoroute announce
 destination 192.168.0.3
 record-route
 path-option 1 explicit name P1-to-PE3
 path-option 2 explicit name P2-to-PE3
 path-option 3 dynamic
!
rsvp
 interface TenGigE0/0/0/4
 bandwidth 8000000
 !
 interface TenGigE0/0/0/6
 bandwidth 8000000
 !
!

mpls traffic-eng
 interface TenGigE0/0/0/4
 !
 interface TenGigE0/0/0/6
 !
!
```

```
router ospf mpls-test
 router-id 192.168.0.1
 area 0
 mpls traffic-eng
 interface Loopback0
 !
 interface TenGigE0/0/0/4
 !
 interface TenGigE0/0/0/6
 !
 !
 mpls traffic-eng router-id Loopback0
!

explicit-path name P1-to-PE3
 index 10 next-address strict ipv4 unicast 192.168.1.2
 index 20 next-address strict ipv4 unicast 192.168.0.3
!
explicit-path name P2-to-PE3
 index 10 next-address strict ipv4 unicast 192.168.2.2
 index 20 next-address strict ipv4 unicast 192.168.0.3
!
```

Example 9-16 shows the status of the MPLS TE tunnel configured in Example 9-15. It shows the tunnel status (up/up/valid/connected), the recorded path, outgoing MPLS label (implicit-null), and other details.

Example 9-16 *Output of* show mpls traffic-eng tunnels 55 detail

```
RP/0/RP0/CPU0:CRS-A-PE1#show mpls traffic-eng tunnels 55 detail

Signalling Summary:
              LSP Tunnels Process: running
                     RSVP Process: running
                       Forwarding: enabled
          Periodic reoptimization: every 3600 seconds, next in 1494 seconds
           Periodic FRR Promotion: every 300 seconds, next in 171 seconds
          Auto-bw enabled tunnels: 0 (disabled)

Name: tunnel-te55 Destination: 192.168.0.3
 Status:
    Admin:    up Oper:   up   Path: valid   Signalling: connected
```

```
    path option 1, type explicit P1-to-PE3 (Basis for Setup, path weight 1)
    path option 2, type explicit P2-to-PE3
    path option 3, type dynamic
    G-PID: 0x0800 (derived from egress interface properties)
    Bandwidth Requested: 550000 kbps CT0

  Config Parameters:
    Bandwidth:   550000 kbps (CT0) Priority: 7 7 Affinity: 0x0/0xffff
    Metric Type: TE (default)
    AutoRoute: enabled LockDown: disabled   Policy class: not set
    Loadshare:           0 equal loadshares
    Auto-bw: disabled
    Direction: unidirectional


    Endpoint switching capability: unknown, encoding type: unassigned
    Transit switching capability: unknown, encoding type: unassigned
    Fast Reroute: Disabled, Protection Desired: None

  History:
    Tunnel has been up for: 00:11:33
    Current LSP:
      Uptime: 00:11:33
  Current LSP Info:
    Instance: 70, Signaling Area: OSPF mpls-test area 0
    Uptime: 00:11:33
    Outgoing Interface: TenGigE0/0/0/4, Outgoing Label: implicit-null
    Router-IDs: local      192.168.0.1
                downstream 192.168.0.3
    Path Info:
      Outgoing:
      Explicit Route:
        Strict, 192.168.1.2
        Strict, 192.168.0.3
      Record Route: None
      Tspec: avg rate=550000 kbits, burst=1000 bytes, peak rate=550000 kbits
      Session Attributes: Local Prot: Not Set, Node Prot: Not Set, BW Prot: Not Set
    Resv Info:
      Record Route:
        IPv4 192.168.1.2, flags 0x0
      Fspec: avg rate=550000 kbits, burst=1000 bytes, peak rate=550000 kbits
Displayed 0 (of 3) heads, 0 (of 1) midpoints, 0 (of 0) tails
Displayed 0 up, 0 down, 0 recovering, 0 recovered heads
```

Example 9-17 shows the MPLS TE topology information for the router. For each link, it shows the reservable BW as well as the total bandwidth that is already allocated (reserved).

Example 9-17 *Output of* **show mpls traffic-eng topology** *<router-id>*

```
RP/0/RP0/CPU0:CRS-A-PE1#show mpls traffic-eng topology 192.168.0.1

IGP Id: 192.168.0.1, MPLS TE Id: 192.168.0.1 Router Node (OSPF mpls-test area 0)

 Link[0]:Broadcast, DR:192.168.1.2, Nbr Node Id:41, gen:164016
      Frag Id:70, Intf Address:192.168.1.1, Intf Id:0
      Nbr Intf Address:0.0.0.0, Nbr Intf Id:0
      TE Metric:1, IGP Metric:1, Attribute Flags:0x0
      Switching Capability:, Encoding:
      BC Model ID:RDM
      Physical BW:10000000 (kbps), Max Reservable BW Global:8000000 (kbps)
      Max Reservable BW Sub:0 (kbps)
                                  Global Pool       Sub Pool
                Total Allocated  Reservable        Reservable
                BW (kbps)         BW (kbps)         BW (kbps)
                ---------------  -----------       ----------
        bw[0]:              0       8000000                 0
        bw[1]:              0       8000000                 0
        bw[2]:              0       8000000                 0
        bw[3]:              0       8000000                 0
        bw[4]:              0       8000000                 0
        bw[5]:              0       8000000                 0
        bw[6]:              0       8000000                 0
        bw[7]:         550000       7450000                 0
```

Cisco IOS XR Peer-to-Peer L3VPN

This section and the one that follows assume that you are familiar with basic concepts of Layer 3 and Layer 2 Virtual Private Networks (L3VPN and L2VPN). This section discusses IOS XR peer-to-peer L3VPN fundamentals, operations, and configurations. In a peer-to-peer model, the provider edge (PE) router exchanges routing information with the customer edge (CE) router. Using this peer-to-peer L3VPN model, a service provider (SP) can provide IP connectivity between multiple sites of a customer. The collection of sites with IP connectivity over a common IP backbone (SP network) is referred to as Virtual Private Network (VPN). The VPN routes are exchanged between PE routers using multiprotocol BGP (MP-BGP), and customer VPN traffic is transported over the provider network using MPLS or IP GRE tunnels. The peer-to-peer VPN model is specified by IETF in RFC 4364, "BGP/MPLS IP Virtual Private Networks (VPNs)."

In this section, you first learn about Virtual Routing and Forwarding (VRF) tables and how they are configured in IOS XR. You then explore how routes are exchanged between PE routers using Multi-Protocol internal BGP (MP-iBGP). You also cover the relevant configurations for MP-iBGP session. Finally, you learn about various routing protocols used for the route exchange between PE and CE routers.

Virtual Routing Forwarding Tables

Whereas VPN represents a collection of sites that have IP connectivity over a common backbone, VRF is the forwarding table used for the VPN on a given PE router. A PE router maintains a number of separate forwarding tables. In IOS XR, each forwarding table is a Virtual Routing Forwarding (VRF) table. One of the forwarding tables is *default VRF*. The other VRFs are defined and named by user configuration. In IOS XR, each interface is associated with exactly one VRF. Configuring **vrf** *<vrf-name>* under the interface associates the interface with the VRF. If a VRF name is not explicitly configured under an interface, the interface is automatically associated with the default VRF.

Suppose three customers are connected to a PE router of a service provider as shown in Figure 9-4. Customer A has two connections to the PE, whereas customers B and C have one connection each. Example 9-18 shows the PE configuration that defines the VRFs associated with each customer and associates each customer-facing interface to the corresponding VRF.

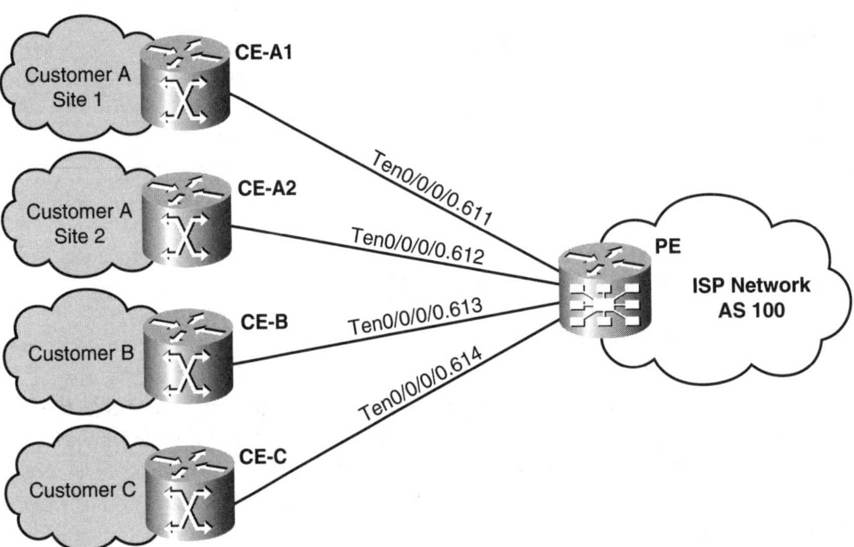

Figure 9-4 *PE with Three VPN Customers*

Example 9-18 *VRF Configuration*

```
RP/0/RP0/CPU0:CRS-A-PE1#show running-config vrf
vrf vrf-red
 description Customer A
 address-family ipv4 unicast
 !
!
vrf vrf-blue
 description Customer B
 address-family ipv4 unicast
 !
!
vrf vrf-mgmt
 address-family ipv4 unicast
 !
!
vrf vrf-green
 description Customer C
 address-family ipv4 unicast
 !
!

RP/0/RP0/CPU0:CRS-A-PE1#show running-config interface Ten0/0/0/0.61*
interface TenGigE0/0/0/0.611
 vrf vrf-red
 ipv4 address 192.168.111.1 255.255.255.0
 dot1q vlan 611
!
interface TenGigE0/0/0/0.612
 vrf vrf-red
 ipv4 address 192.168.112.1 255.255.255.0
 dot1q vlan 612
!
interface TenGigE0/0/0/0.613
 vrf vrf-blue
 ipv4 address 192.168.113.1 255.255.255.0
 dot1q vlan 613
!
interface TenGigE0/0/0/0.614
 vrf vrf-green
 ipv4 address 192.168.114.1 255.255.255.0
 dot1q vlan 614
!
interface TenGigE0/0/0/0.615
 vrf vrf-mgmt
```

```
 ipv4 address 192.168.115.1 255.255.255.0
 dot1q vlan 615
!
interface TenGigE0/0/0/0.619
 ipv4 address 192.168.3.1 255.255.255.252
 dot1q vlan 619
!


RP/0/RP0/CPU0:CRS-A-PE1#show ipv4 vrf all interface brief

Interface                    IP-Address      Status          Protocol

vrf: vrf-blue
TenGigE0/0/0/0.613           192.168.113.1   Up              Up

vrf: vrf-green
TenGigE0/0/0/0.614           192.168.114.1   Up              Up

vrf: vrf-mgmt
TenGigE0/0/0/0.615           192.168.115.1   Up              Up

vrf: vrf-red
TenGigE0/0/0/0.611           192.168.111.1   Up              Up
TenGigE0/0/0/0.612           192.168.112.1   Up              Up

vrf: default
Loopback0                    192.168.0.1     Up              Up
Loopback9                    98.99.99.1      Up              Up
TenGigE0/0/0/0               unassigned      Up              Up
TenGigE0/0/0/0.619           192.168.3.1     Up              Up
```

MP-iBGP Between PE Routers

PE routers exchange customer VPN prefixes using multi-protocol BGP (MP-BGP). The address family of the network layer reachability information (NLRI) for VPN IPv4 prefixes is VPN-IPv4, which is a concatenation of route-distinguisher and VPN prefix. In IOS XR, CLI uses VPNv4 to refer to the VPN-IPv4 address family. The configuration steps for MP-iBGP are as follows:

1. Under the router bgp configuration mode, activate VPNv4 using **address-family vpnv4 unicast.**
2. For each MP-iBGP session, define the neighbor by entering the neighbor IP address and AS number. In addition, you need to set the session source to the IP address of the loopback address using **update-source Loopback0** and activate

VPNv4 address family. Note that the same MP-iBGP session can be used to exchange other address families including IPv4, IPv6, and VPNv6.

Consider the MPLS VPN network shown in Figure 9-5, which has three VPNs and three PE routers. Example 9-19 shows part of the BGP configuration for the MP-iBGP sessions on PE1, which uses full-mesh MP-iBGP configuration.

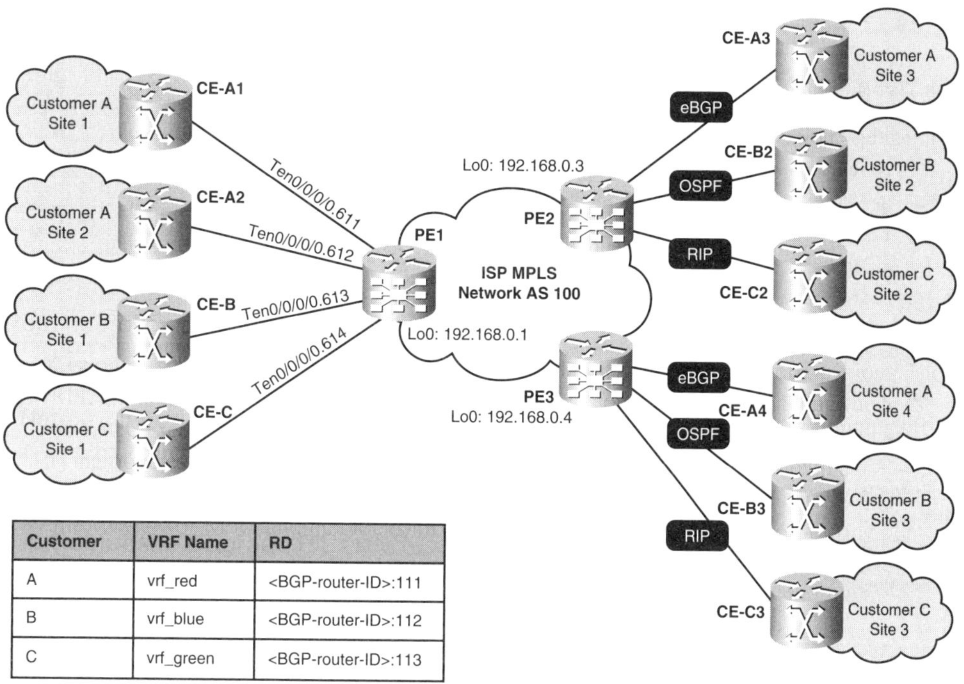

Customer	VRF Name	RD
A	vrf_red	<BGP-router-ID>:111
B	vrf_blue	<BGP-router-ID>:112
C	vrf_green	<BGP-router-ID>:113

Figure 9-5 *MPLS VPN Network with Three PEs and Three VPNs*

Example 9-19 *MP-iBGP Configuration*

```
router bgp 100
 bgp router-id 192.168.0.1
 address-family vpnv4 unicast
 !
 neighbor 192.168.0.3
 remote-as 100
 update-source Loopback0
 address-family vpnv4 unicast
 !
 !
 neighbor 192.168.0.4
 remote-as 100
 update-source Loopback0
```

```
address-family vpnv4 unicast
!
!
```

Use **show bgp vpnv4 unicast summary** to display the status of BGP sessions for which VPNv4 address family is activated. The output for PE1 in Figure 9-5 is shown in Example 9-20.

Example 9-20 *Output of* **show bgp vpnv4 unicast summary** *for PE1*

```
RP/0/RP0/CPU0:CRS-A-PE1#show bgp vpnv4 unicast summary
BGP router identifier 192.168.0.1, local AS number 100
BGP generic scan interval 60 secs
BGP table state: Active
Table ID: 0x0
BGP main routing table version 91
BGP scan interval 60 secs

BGP is operating in STANDALONE mode.


Process       RcvTblVer   bRIB/RIB   LabelVer ImportVer SendTblVer StandbyVer
Speaker              91         91         91        91         91         91

Neighbor          Spk     AS MsgRcvd MsgSent    TblVer  InQ OutQ  Up/Down  St/PfxRcd
192.168.0.3         0    100    1116    1121        91    0    0 18:25:13          0
192.168.0.4         0    100    1112    1118        91    0    0 18:23:24          0
```

When a PE router learns routes from a local CE attached to an interface that is associated with a VRF, the route is automatically installed in the corresponding VRF table. However, when a PE receives routes from a remote PE router via an MP-iBGP session, the routes need to be explicitly installed into VRF(s). This is achieved using route target (RT) attributes that are associated with each VPNv4 route received from remote PE routers.

Route target is a BGP-extended community attribute, which is structured in the same way as route distinguisher (RD) and has three possible formats:

- ***<IP-Address>:<ID>:*** ID is from 0–65535
- ***<AS-Number>:<ID>:*** ID is from 0–4294967295
- ***<4-Byte AS>:<ID>:*** ID is from 0–65535

A VPNv4 route received by a PE should have one or more RT attributes for it to be installed in one or more VRF tables. To associate RT attributes to VPN routes, configure **export route-target** or **export route-policy** *<export-policy>* under the VRF address family mode. The first option, **export route-target**, associates one or more RT attributes to all routes of the VRF received from local CEs. The second option, **export route-policy** *<export-policy>*, is used to assign RT attributes to selected prefixes.

Example 9-21 shows both types of RT export configuration for vrf-red on PE1. The first option is used to assign all local vrf-red routes on PE1 with RT value of 100:111. The second option is used to assign an additional RT value of 100:999 for two subnets of directly connected interfaces. The two prefixes are defined using **prefix-set** configuration, and the RT value is defined using **extcommunity-set rt** configuration.

Example 9-21 *Route Target Export Configuration*

```
RP/0/RP0/CPU0:CRS-A-PE1#show running-config prefix-set VPN-MGMT
prefix-set VPN-MGMT
 192.168.111.0/24,
 192.168.112.0/24
end-set
!

RP/0/RP0/CPU0:CRS-A-PE1#show running-config extcommunity-set rt MGMT-RT
extcommunity-set rt MGMT-RT
 100:999
end-set
!

RP/0/RP0/CPU0:CRS-A-PE1#show running-config route-policy VRF-MGMT-EXPORT
route-policy VRF-MGMT-EXPORT
 if destination in VPN-MGMT then
    set extcommunity rt MGMT-RT additive
 endif
end-policy
!

RP/0/RP0/CPU0:CRS-A-PE1#show running-config vrf vrf-red
vrf vrf-red
 description Customer A
 address-family ipv4 unicast
 export route-policy VRF-MGMT-EXPORT
 export route-target
   100:111
 !
 !
!

RP/0/RP0/CPU0:CRS-A-PE1#
```

When a PE router receives a VPNv4 prefix from remote PE routers, it compares the route target associated with the prefix against the RT import setting of each VRF. If one or more of the RT values of the VPNv4 prefix matches with an RT import configured for a VRF, the prefix is installed in the VRF table. It is possible that a VPNv4 prefix may be installed on multiple VRF tables.

RT import for a VRF is configured in the same way as RT export using the keyword **import** instead of **export**. With RT import and export you can enable various forms of VPN connectivity. Consider the MPLS VPN network shown in Figure 9-6.

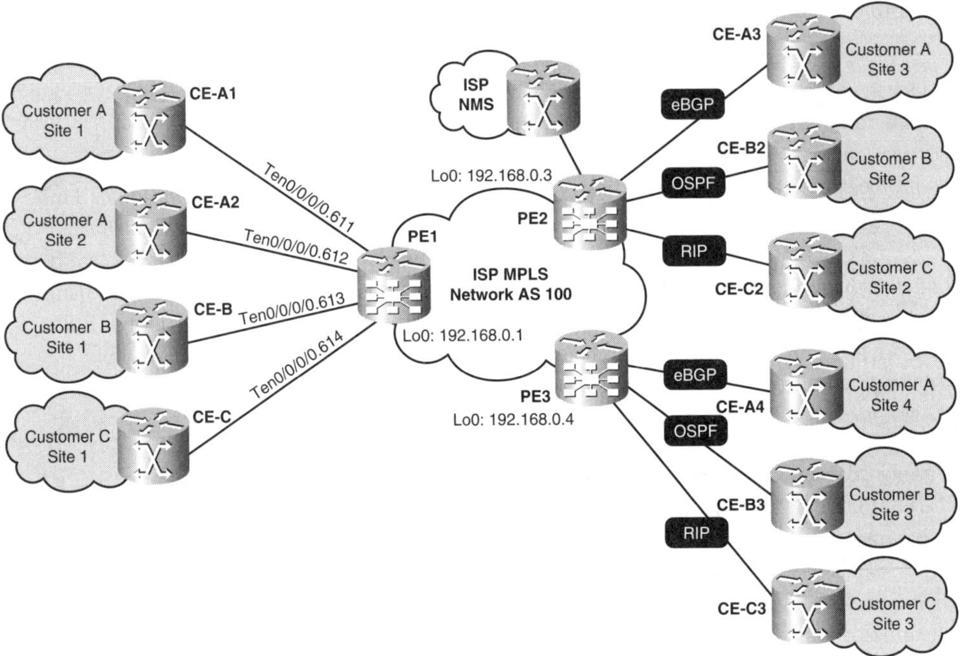

Figure 9-6 *MPLS VPN Connectivity Options*

The VPN connectivity requirements for the ISP and its customers are as follows:

- The ISP network operations team requires that it should be able to monitor and verify CE-PE connectivity from their Network Management System (NMS) network. In particular, they want to be able to ping each CE device from the NMS network. For this, the ISP connected their NMS network to PE2 using vrf-mgmt. ISP uses an RT export value of 100:998 and RT import value of 100:999 for vrf-mgmt.
- Customer A needs full connectivity between its sites. It uses RT 100:111 for both import and export. In addition it uses 100:999 as RT export for directly connected subnet prefixes so that it can be reached by the NMS network. Similarly, it imports 100:998 so that it can reach the NMS network.
- Customer B has headquarters at site 1 and wants all remote sites to connect to the headquarters. However, direct connectivity between remote sites is not allowed. To

fulfill this requirement, hub site 1 exports RT 100:112 and imports RT 100:212, whereas the remote sites (site 2 and site 3) export RT 100:212 and import RT 100:112. In addition, it uses RT 100:999 and 100:998 in the same way as customer A.

- Customer C wants full connectivity between its sites, and it uses RT 100:113 for both import and export. In addition, it uses RT 100:999 and 100:998 in the same way as customers A and B.

The VRF configurations for PE1, PE2, and PE3 that meet the preceding requirements are shown in Example 9-22, 9-23, and 9-24, respectively.

Example 9-22 *VRF Configuration for PE1*

```
RP/0/RP0/CPU0:CRS-A-PE1#show running-config prefix-set VPN-MGMT
prefix-set VPN-MGMT
 192.168.111.0/24,
 192.168.112.0/24,
 192.168.113.0/24,
 192.168.114.0/24
end-set
!

RP/0/RP0/CPU0:CRS-A-PE1#show running-config extcommunity-set rt MGMT-RT
extcommunity-set rt MGMT_RT
 100:999
end-set
!

RP/0/RP0/CPU0:CRS-A-PE1#show running-config route-policy VPN-NMS-EXPORT
route-policy VPN-NMS-EXPORT
 if destination in VPN-MGMT then
    set extcommunity rt MGMT-RT additive
 endif
end-policy
!

RP/0/RP0/CPU0:CRS-A-PE1#show running-config vrf
vrf vrf-red
 description Customer A
 address-family ipv4 unicast
 import route-target
   100:111
   100:998
 !
 export route-policy VPN-NMS-EXPORT
 export route-target
   100:111
 !
```

```
 !
!
vrf vrf-blue
 description Customer B
 address-family ipv4 unicast
 import route-target
   100:212
   100:998
 !
 export route-policy VPN-NMS-EXPORT
  export route-target
   100:112
 !
 !
!
vrf vrf-green
 description Customer C
 address-family ipv4 unicast
 import route-target
   100:113
   100:998
 !
 export route-policy VPN-NMS-EXPORT
 export route-target
   100:113
 !
 !
!

RP/0/RP0/CPU0:CRS-A-PE1#
```

Example 9-23 *VRF Configuration for PE2*

```
RP/0/RP0/CPU0:CRS-C-PE2#show running-config prefix-set VPN-MGMT
prefix-set VPN-MGMT
 192.168.122.0/24,
 192.168.123.0/24,
 192.168.124.0/24
end-set
!

RP/0/RP0/CPU0:CRS-C-PE2#show running-config extcommunity-set rt MGMT-RT
extcommunity-set rt MGMT-RT
 100:999
end-set
```

```
!

RP/0/RP0/CPU0:CRS-C-PE2#show running-config route-policy VPN-NMS-EXPORT
route-policy VPN-NMS-EXPORT
 if destination in VPN-MGMT then
    set extcommunity rt MGMT-RT additive
 endif
end-policy
!

RP/0/RP0/CPU0:CRS-C-PE2#show running-config vrf
vrf pip
 address-family ipv4 unicast
 import route-target
   100:1
 !
 export route-target
   100:1
 !
 !
!
vrf vrf-red
 description Customer A
 address-family ipv4 unicast
 import route-target
   100:111
   100:998
 !
 export route-policy VPN-NMS-EXPORT
 export route-target
   100:111
 !
 !
!
vrf vrf-blue
 description Customer B
 address-family ipv4 unicast
 import route-target
   100:112
   100:998
 !
 export route-policy VPN-NMS-EXPORT
 export route-target
   100:212
 !
```

```
 !
!
vrf vrf-mgmt
 description NMS
 address-family ipv4 unicast
 import route-target
   100:999
 !
 export route-target
   100:998
 !
 !
!
vrf vrf-green
 description Customer C
 address-family ipv4 unicast
 import route-target
   100:113
   100:998
 !
 export route-policy VPN-NMS-EXPORT
 export route-target
   100:113
 !
 !
!

RP/0/RP0/CPU0:CRS-C-PE2#
```

Example 9-24 *VRF Configuration for PE3*

```
DRP/0/5/CPU0:CRS-D-PE3#show running-config prefix-set VPN-MGMT
prefix-set VPN-MGMT
 192.168.132.0/24,
 192.168.133.0/24,
 192.168.134.0/24
end-set
!

DRP/0/5/CPU0:CRS-D-PE3#show running-config extcommunity-set rt MGMT-RT
extcommunity-set rt MGMT-RT
 100:999
end-set
!
```

```
DRP/0/5/CPU0:CRS-D-PE3#show running-config route-policy VPN-NMS-EXPORT
route-policy VPN-NMS-EXPORT
 if destination in VPN-MGMT then
    set extcommunity rt MGMT-RT additive
 endif
end-policy
!

DRP/0/5/CPU0:CRS-D-PE3#show running-config vrf
vrf vrf-red
 description Customer A
 address-family ipv4 unicast
 import route-target
   100:111
   100:998
 !
 export route-policy VPN-NMS-EXPORT
 export route-target
   100:111
 !
 !
!
vrf vrf-blue
 description Customer B
 address-family ipv4 unicast
 import route-target
   100:112
   100:998
 !
 export route-policy VPN-NMS-EXPORT
 export route-target
   100:212
 !
 !
!
vrf vrf-green
 description Customer C
 address-family ipv4 unicast
 import route-target
   100:113
   100:998
 !
 export route-policy VPN-NMS-EXPORT
 export route-target
   100:113
```

```
  !
  !
!
DRP/0/5/CPU0:CRS-D-PE3#
```

Cisco IOS XR provides a set of **show** commands to check VPN routes. Table 9-4 lists some of the **show** commands for VPN.

Table 9-4 *Commonly Used* show *Commands for MPLS VPN*

Commands	Description
show bgp vpnv4 unicast	Lists all VPN routes on PE router that are received by BGP (both local and remote)
show bgp vpnv4 unicast rd *<RD-value>*	Lists all VPN routes with a specific RD value
show bgp vpnv4 unicast vrf *<vrf-name>*	Lists all VPN routes that are imported into a specific VRF
show bgp vpnv4 unicast rd *<rd>* **labels**	Lists all VPN routes with a specific RD value along with incoming and outgoing MPLS label
show bgp vpnv4 unicast vrf *<vrf>* **labels**	Lists all VPN routes that are imported into a specific VRF value along with the incoming and outgoing MPLS label
show bgp vpnv4 unicast rd *<rd>* *<prefix>/<len>*	Shows VPNv4 route detail for a specific VPN prefix using the RD value and prefix
show bgp vpnv4 unicast vrf *<vrf>* *<prefix>/<len>*	Shows VPNv4 route detail for a specific VPN prefix using the VRF name and prefix
show route vrf *<vrf-name>*	Shows the routing table for a specific VRF
show route vrf *<vrf-name>* *<prefix/len>*	Displays the routing info for specific prefix in a given VRF
show cef vrf *<vrf-name>* *<prefix/len>*	Displays the FIB entry detail for a prefix on the RP
show cef vrf *<vrf-name>* *<prefix/len>* **location** *<r/s/m>*	Displays the FIB entry detail for a prefix on a specific line card
show cef vrf *<vrf-name>* *<prefix/len>* **hardware** {**ingress** | **egress**} **location** *<r/s/m>*	Displays ingress or egress hardware FIB entry detail for a prefix on a specific line card

Captures of some of the commands listed in Table 9-4 are shown next. Example 9-25 lists all VPN routes with specific RD value along with the incoming and outgoing MPLS labels.

Example 9-25 show bgp vpnv4 unicast rd *<rd> Labels*

```
RP/0/RP0/CPU0:CRS-C-PE2#show bgp vpnv4 unicast rd 192.168.0.1:111 labels
BGP router identifier 192.168.0.3, local AS number 100
BGP generic scan interval 60 secs
BGP table state: Active
Table ID: 0x0
BGP main routing table version 108
BGP scan interval 60 secs

Status codes: s suppressed, d damped, h history, * valid, > best
              i - internal, S stale
Origin codes: i - IGP, e - EGP, ? - incomplete
   Network            Next Hop       Rcvd Label      Local Label
Route Distinguisher: 192.168.0.1:111
*>i3.3.3.3/32          192.168.0.1     16008           nolabel
*>i4.4.4.4/32          192.168.0.1     16007           nolabel
*>i192.168.111.0/24    192.168.0.1     16000           nolabel
*>i192.168.112.0/24    192.168.0.1     16000           nolabel
*>i192.168.200.0/24    192.168.0.1     16002           nolabel
*>i192.168.201.0/24    192.168.0.1     16005           nolabel
*>i192.168.202.0/24    192.168.0.1     16006           nolabel

Processed 7 prefixes, 7 paths
```

Example 9-26 lists all VPNv4 routes that are imported into a specific VRF.

Example 9-26 *Output of* show bgp vpnv4 unicast vrf

```
RP/0/RP0/CPU0:CRS-C-PE2#show bgp vpnv4 unicast vrf vrf_red 192.168.111.0/24
BGP routing table entry for 192.168.111.0/24, Route Distinguisher: 192.168.0.3:111
Versions:
 Process           bRIB/RIB SendTblVer
 Speaker                 80          80
Last Modified: Feb 26 13:13:54.656 for 00:59:29
Paths: (1 available, best #1)
 Not advertised to any peer
 Path #1: Received by speaker 0
 Local
    192.168.0.1 (metric 2) from 192.168.0.1 (192.168.0.1)
      Received Label 16000
      Origin incomplete, metric 0, localpref 100, valid, internal, best, import-
        candidate, imported
     Extended community: RT:100:111 RT:100:999
```

Example 9-27 displays the routing table for a given VRF.

Example 9-27 *Output of* show route vrf

```
RP/0/RP0/CPU0:CRS-C-PE2#show route vrf vrf-red

Codes: C - connected, S - static, R - RIP, M - mobile, B - BGP
       D - EIGRP, EX - EIGRP external, O - OSPF, IA - OSPF inter area
       N1 - OSPF NSSA external type 1, N2 - OSPF NSSA external type 2
       E1 - OSPF external type 1, E2 - OSPF external type 2, E - EGP
       i - ISIS, L1 - IS-IS level-1, L2 - IS-IS level-2
       ia - IS-IS inter area, su - IS-IS summary null, * - candidate default
       U - per-user static route, o - ODR, L - local, A - access/subsciber

Gateway of last resort is not set

B    3.3.3.3/32 [200/0] via 192.168.0.1 (nexthop in vrf default), 00:58:45
B    4.4.4.4/32 [200/0] via 192.168.0.1 (nexthop in vrf default), 00:58:45
B    192.168.111.0/24 [200/0] via 192.168.0.1 (nexthop in vrf default), 00:58:45
B    192.168.112.0/24 [200/0] via 192.168.0.1 (nexthop in vrf default), 00:58:45
B    192.168.121.0/24 is directly connected, 00:43:34, TenGigE0/0/0/5.621 (nexthop
     in vrf vrf-mgmt)
C    192.168.122.0/24 is directly connected, 01:22:03, TenGigE0/0/0/5.622
L    192.168.122.1/32 is directly connected, 01:22:03, TenGigE0/0/0/5.622
B    192.168.132.0/24 [200/0] via 192.168.0.4 (nexthop in vrf default), 00:58:40
B    192.168.200.0/24 [200/0] via 192.168.0.1 (nexthop in vrf default), 00:58:45
B    192.168.201.0/24 [200/0] via 192.168.0.1 (nexthop in vrf default), 00:58:45
B    192.168.202.0/24 [200/0] via 192.168.0.1 (nexthop in vrf default), 00:58:45
```

Example 9-28 show the forwarding (CEF) information for a specific prefix in a given VRF.

Example 9-28 *Output of* show cef vrf *<vrf-name> <prefix/len>*

```
DRP/0/5/CPU0:CRS-D-PE3#show cef vrf vrf-red 3.3.3.3/32
3.3.3.3/32, version 1, internal 0x40040001 (0x9d054d64) [1], 0x0 (0x0), 0x4100
(0x9d9b4278)
 Updated Feb 26 13:14:04.553
 Prefix Len 32, traffic index 0, precedence routine (0)
   via 192.168.0.1, 3 dependencies, recursive
```

```
    next hop 192.168.0.1 via 16003/0/21
     next hop 192.168.4.1      BP111         labels imposed {16000 16008}
     next hop 192.168.5.1      BP222         labels imposed {16000 16008}
```

Example 9-29 displays the HW forwarding (CEF) information on a line card for a specific prefix in a given VRF.

Example 9-29 *Output of* **show cef vrf** *<vrf-name> <prefix/len>* **hardware ingress location** *<node>*

```
DRP/0/5/CPU0:CRS-D-PE3#show cef vrf vrf-red 3.3.3.3/32 hardware ingress loc
  0/7/CPU0
3.3.3.3/32, version 1, internal 0x40040001 (0x9f922d64) [1], 0x0 (0x0), 0x4100
  (0xa01ec2c0)
 Updated Feb 26 13:14:04.599
 Prefix Len 32, traffic index 0, precedence routine (0)
   via 192.168.0.1, 3 dependencies, recursive
    next hop 192.168.0.1 via 16003/0/21
     next hop 192.168.4.1      BP111         labels imposed {16000 16008}
     next hop 192.168.5.1      BP222         labels imposed {16000 16008}

 INGRESS PLU
   SW: 0x06000000 00fa2010 00200000 004a0000
   HW: 0x06000000 00fa2010 00200000 004a0000
 entry_type:          FWD    rpf ptr:      0x00000000
 prefix len:           32    BGP policy a/c:        0
 QoS group:             0    as number:             0
 num entries:           1    next ptr:     0x00004a00
 label:             16008    Label(1) Ptr(0)

    Recursive load info:
    Flag: 0x00040021
    TLU1 0x00004a00
    TLU1 ENTRY          0
     SW: 0x00000000 00013c12 c0a80001 00000200
     HW: 0x00000000 00013c12 c0a80001 00000200
    label:               0   num of labels:         0
    PBTS:                0   extra lbe:             0
    entry type:        FWD   next ptr:      0x00013c12
    num of entries:      2
   Recursive next-hop:   192.168.0.1
```

Routing Between CE and PE

Different routing protocols are supported between CE and PE including static, eBGP, OSPF, RIP, and EIGRP. For the network shown in Figure 9-5, we use the following:

- Static routing between PE and CE-A1
- eBGP between PE and CE-A2
- OSPF between PE and CE-B
- RIP between PE and CE-C

This section provides examples of CE-PE protocols.

Static Routing for CE-PE

Static routing is used when the number of routes exchanged is few. Static routing must be configured on both CE and PE. On a PE router, a VRF static is configured as shown in Example 9-30, which also shows the routing table for vrf-red after static route is configured. Example 9-30 shows four static routes. The first two routes use CE-A1 as the next hop, the third static route uses next-hop address in another VRF (vrf-blue), and the fourth static route uses next-hop address in the default VRF.

Example 9-30 *Static Routing for CE-PE*

```
RP/0/RP0/CPU0:CRS-A-PE1#show running-config router static vrf vrf-red
router static
 vrf vrf-red
 address-family ipv4 unicast
   192.168.200.0/24 192.168.111.2
   192.168.201.0/24 192.168.111.2
   192.168.202.0/24 vrf vrf-blue 192.168.113.2
   192.168.202.0/24 vrf default 192.168.0.3
  !
  !
!

RP/0/RP0/CPU0:CRS-A-PE1#show route vrf vrf-red

Codes: C - connected, S - static, R - RIP, M - mobile, B - BGP
       D - EIGRP, EX - EIGRP external, O - OSPF, IA - OSPF inter area
       N1 - OSPF NSSA external type 1, N2 - OSPF NSSA external type 2
       E1 - OSPF external type 1, E2 - OSPF external type 2, E - EGP
       i - ISIS, L1 - IS-IS level-1, L2 - IS-IS level-2
       ia - IS-IS inter area, su - IS-IS summary null, * - candidate default
       U - per-user static route, o - ODR, L - local, A - access/subsciber

Gateway of last resort is not set

C    192.168.111.0/24 is directly connected, 05:45:46, TenGigE0/0/0/0.611
```

```
L      192.168.111.1/32 is directly connected, 05:45:46, TenGigE0/0/0/0.611
C      192.168.112.0/24 is directly connected, 05:45:46, TenGigE0/0/0/0.612
L      192.168.112.1/32 is directly connected, 05:45:46, TenGigE0/0/0/0.612
S      192.168.200.0/24 [1/0] via 192.168.111.2, 00:08:48
S      192.168.201.0/24 [1/0] via 192.168.111.2, 00:08:48
S      192.168.202.0/24 [1/0] via 192.168.0.3 (nexthop in vrf default), 00:01:09
                        [1/0] via 192.168.113.2 (nexthop in vrf vrf-blue), 00:01:09
RP/0/RP0/CPU0:CRS-A-PE1#
```

eBGP as CE-PE Protocol

The recommended CE-PE protocol is eBGP if the CE device is capable of running BGP. There are a couple of reasons for this. First, because the routing protocol between PE routers is also BGP, it makes it seamless to use eBGP between CE and PE. If any other CE-PE protocol is used, it might require configuration of mutual redistribution of routes between BGP and the CE-PE protocol. Another reason for this recommendation is that BGP is designed for exchange of routes between different administrative domains, and it has flexibility and route control embedded in the protocol and implementations. On the other hand, IGP is designed to be used within a single administrative domain and lacks the control and flexibility of BGP. Finally, it is better to use BGP because it scales much better than IGP.

For the example, we use eBGP between PE and CE-A2. However, it is important to highlight one key point. PE routers exchange customer VPN prefixes using MP-iBGP. When exchanging VPN prefixes, a PE router has to prepend each prefix with an identifier, known as a route distinguisher (RD), that uniquely identifies the specific VPN.

In this example, BGP on CE-A2 is assigned a private AS number of 65112. The configuration on the PE router for CE-PE eBGP protocol is done under BGP VRF configuration mode. The relevant configuration steps are as follows:

1. Assign the route distinguisher (RD) to the VRF using **rd** {**<***rd-value***>** | **auto**}. RD value can be specified in three different ways:
   - <*AS-number*>:<*nn*>: In this format, the operator can use its AS number followed by a unique number for each VRF.
   - <*IP-address*>:<*nn*>: With this option, the operator can use the BGP router ID IP address followed by a unique number for each VRF.
   - **auto:** With this option, BGP will automatically use the BGP router ID IP address followed by a unique number for each VRF sequentially starting from 0.
2. Configure a neighbor by specifying the neighbor's IP address and AS number.
3. Under the relevant address family of the neighbor configuration, configure inbound and outbound route-policy to allow all updates to be received and advertised. In IOS XR, no updates are accepted or advertised on eBGP peers unless explicitly permitted by **route-policy** configuration. The route policy named **pass-**

all, which allows all updates, is defined and attached as inbound and outbound policy for the neighbor IPv4 unicast address family.

4. Because static routing is used on another interface for the same VRF, it is necessary to redistribute the static routes into BGP. This is configured under **address-family ipv4 unicast** submode of the BGP VRF configuration mode.

Example 9-31 shows the configuration of eBGP.

Example 9-31 *Configuration of eBGP as the CE-PE Protocol*

```
RP/0/RP0/CPU0:CRS-A-PE1#show running-config route-policy pass
route-policy pass-all
 pass
end-policy
!

RP/0/RP0/CPU0:CRS-A#show running-config router bgp
router bgp 100
 bgp router-id 192.168.0.1
 vrf vrf-red
 rd 100:111
 address-family ipv4 unicast
   redistribute static
 !
 neighbor 192.168.112.2
   remote-as 65112
   address-family ipv4 unicast
    route-policy pass-all in
    route-policy passa-ll out
   !
 !
 !
!

RP/0/RP0/CPU0:CRS-A-PE1#show route vrf vrf-red

Codes: C - connected, S - static, R - RIP, M - mobile, B - BGP
       D - EIGRP, EX - EIGRP external, O - OSPF, IA - OSPF inter area
       N1 - OSPF NSSA external type 1, N2 - OSPF NSSA external type 2
       E1 - OSPF external type 1, E2 - OSPF external type 2, E - EGP
       i - ISIS, L1 - IS-IS level-1, L2 - IS-IS level-2
       ia - IS-IS inter area, su - IS-IS summary null, * - candidate default
       U - per-user static route, o - ODR, L - local, A - access/subsciber

Gateway of last resort is not set

B    3.3.3.3/32 [20/0] via 192.168.112.2, 00:00:55
```

```
B    4.4.4.4/32 [20/0] via 192.168.112.2, 00:01:26
C    192.168.111.0/24 is directly connected, 06:24:15, TenGigE0/0/0/0.611
L    192.168.111.1/32 is directly connected, 06:24:15, TenGigE0/0/0/0.611
C    192.168.112.0/24 is directly connected, 06:24:15, TenGigE0/0/0/0.612
L    192.168.112.1/32 is directly connected, 06:24:15, TenGigE0/0/0/0.612
S    192.168.200.0/24 [1/0] via 192.168.111.2, 00:47:18
S    192.168.201.0/24 [1/0] via 192.168.111.2, 00:47:18
S    192.168.202.0/24 [1/0] via 192.168.0.3 (nexthop in vrf default), 00:39:38
                      [1/0] via 192.168.113.2 (nexthop in vrf vrf-blue), 00:39:38
RP/0/RP0/CPU0:CRS-A-PE1#

RP/0/RP0/CPU0:CRS-A-PE1#show bgp vrf vrf-red summary
BGP VRF vrf-red, state: Active
BGP Route Distinguisher: 100:111
VRF ID: 0x60000004
BGP router identifier 192.168.0.1, local AS number 100
BGP table state: Active
Table ID: 0xe0000004
BGP main routing table version 58

BGP is operating in STANDALONE mode.


Process       RcvTblVer   bRIB/RIB   LabelVer ImportVer SendTblVer StandbyVer
Speaker              58         58         58        58         58         58

Neighbor        Spk    AS MsgRcvd MsgSent   TblVer InQ OutQ  Up/Down  St/PfxRcd
192.168.112.2     0 65112      15      20       58   0    0 00:02:25          2

RP/0/RP0/CPU0:CRS-A-PE1#


RP/0/RP0/CPU0:CRS-A-PE1#show bgp vrf vrf-red
BGP VRF vrf-red, state: Active
BGP Route Distinguisher: 100:111
VRF ID: 0x60000004
BGP router identifier 192.168.0.1, local AS number 100
BGP table state: Active
Table ID: 0xe0000004
BGP main routing table version 58

Status codes: s suppressed, d damped, h history, * valid, > best
              i - internal, S stale
```

```
Origin codes: i - IGP, e - EGP, ? - incomplete
   Network            Next Hop            Metric LocPrf Weight Path
Route Distinguisher: 100:111 (default for vrf vrf_red)
*> 3.3.3.3/32         192.168.112.2            0             0 65112 i
*> 4.4.4.4/32         192.168.112.2            0             0 65112 i
*> 192.168.200.0/24   192.168.111.2            0         32768 ?
*> 192.168.201.0/24   192.168.111.2            0         32768 ?
*> 192.168.202.0/24   192.168.0.3              0         32768 ?

Processed 5 prefixes, 5 paths
RP/0/RP0/CPU0:CRS-A-PE1#
```

OSPF as CE-PE Protocol

Although eBGP is the preferred CE-PE protocol, some customers might prefer to be connected using OSPF. The following steps summarize the configuration tasks needed on a PE router to configure OSPF as the CE-PE protocol for a VRF:

1. Create a loopback interface with IP address and associate it with the VRF. The IP address is used as the OSPF router ID for VRF.
2. Configure the VRF OSPF instance under an OSPF process. You can use a single OSPF process for global OSPF (ISP core) and for all VRFs. It is also possible to separate the OSPF instances into a few OSPF processes.
3. Under the VRF OSPF instance, configure the following:
   - The OSPF router ID
   - The VRF OSPF interface(s) under the corresponding area
   - The **redistribute bgp** **<*as-num*>** [**route-policy** <*rpl*>] command to redistribute routes received from remote PE into the VRF OSPF instance
4. Under the BGP VRF address family mode, configure **redistribute ospf** <*id*> [**route-policy** <*rpl*>] to redistribute VRF OSPF routes into BGP.

Example 9-32 shows the relevant configuration of OSPF as the CE-PE protocol on PE1 for vrf-blue.

Example 9-32 *OSPF as the CE-PE Protocol for vrf-blue on PE1*

```
interface Loopback112
 vrf vrf-blue
 ipv4 address 192.168.1.112 255.255.255.255
!
router ospf mpls-test
 vrf vrf-blue
 router-id 192.168.1.112
 redistribute bgp 100
 area 0
```

```
    interface TenGigE0/0/0/0.613
    !
  !
  !
!
router bgp 100
 vrf vrf-blue
 address-family ipv4 unicast
   redistribute ospf mpls-test
  !
  !
!
```

RIP as CE-PE Protocol

The following steps summarize the configuration tasks needed on the PE router to configure RIP as CE-PE protocol for a VRF:

Configure the VRF RIP instance under **router rip** configuration mode.

1. Under the VRF RIP instance, configure the following:
   - VRF interface(s) that participate in RIP
   - The default metrics used for redistributed routes using **default-metric** *<1-15>*
   - The **redistribute bgp** *<as-num>* [**route-policy** *<rpl>*] command to redistribute routes received from the remote PE into the VRF RIP instance
2. Under BGP VRF address family mode, configure **redistribute RIP** [**route-policy** *<rpl>*] to redistribute VRF RIP routes into BGP.

Example 9-33 shows the relevant configuration of RIP as CE-PE protocol on PE1 for vrf-green.

Example 9-33 *RIP as CE-PE Protocol for vrf-green on PE1*

```
router rip
 vrf vrf-green
 interface TenGigE0/0/0/0.614
  !
 redistribute bgp 100
 default-metric 5
  !
!
router bgp 100
 vrf vrf-green
 address-family ipv4 unicast
```

```
    redistribute rip
  !
  !
!
```

L2VPN

The preceding section discussed L3VPN, how it is implemented in IOS XR, and how VPN routes are exchanged between different sites of a VPN. In particular, it showed that the service provider plays an important role in route exchange between different sites of a VPN customer. In contrast, the service provider does not get involved in route exchange between different sites for L2VPN. The customer has full responsibility and full control in the route exchange between its sites. The service provider needs only to provide Layer 2 connectivity service between the VPN sites.

For customers, the primary motivations for L2VPN connectivity service as opposed to L3VPN are the following:

- Customer might want to have full control of the routing between sites so that when the customer needs to make routing changes, it does not depend on the service provider.
- Customer might need to transport non-IP traffic between sites because of legacy applications, which excludes the use of L3VPN service.

Broadly speaking, there are two types of L2VPN services:

- **Virtual Private Wire Service (VPWS):** VPWS is a point-to-point connectivity service that is provided between a pair of sites.
- **Virtual Private LAN Service (VPLS):** VPLS is a Layer 2 service that emulates a VLAN across an IP or MPLS network. It interconnects multiple sites and provides LAN emulation for the sites.

Virtual Private Wire Service

VPWS is a point-to-point (p2p) service that provides L2 connectivity between two sites. Figure 9-7 shows a VPWS service scenario in which a customer has four sites. Site 3 is the hub site and needs VPWS connectivity to each of the other three sites. In addition site 2 and site 4 need direct VPWS connectivity.

CE1 in Figure 9-7 is connected to PE1 using an attachment circuit (AC), which could be an Ethernet port, a VLAN, or a POS port. Similarly, CE3 is connected to PE3 using three attachment circuits (AC), one to each of the three sites. To interconnect sites 1 and 3 (CE1 and CE3), a pseudo-wire (PW) is established between PE1 and PE3. The CE1-PE1 attachment circuit is cross-connected to this PW at PE1. The CE3-PE3 attachment circuit is cross-connected to the same PW at PE3. Consequently, the VPWS connectivity between CE1 and CE3 is a concatenation of AC (CE1-PE1), PW (PE1-PE3), and AC (PE3-CE3).

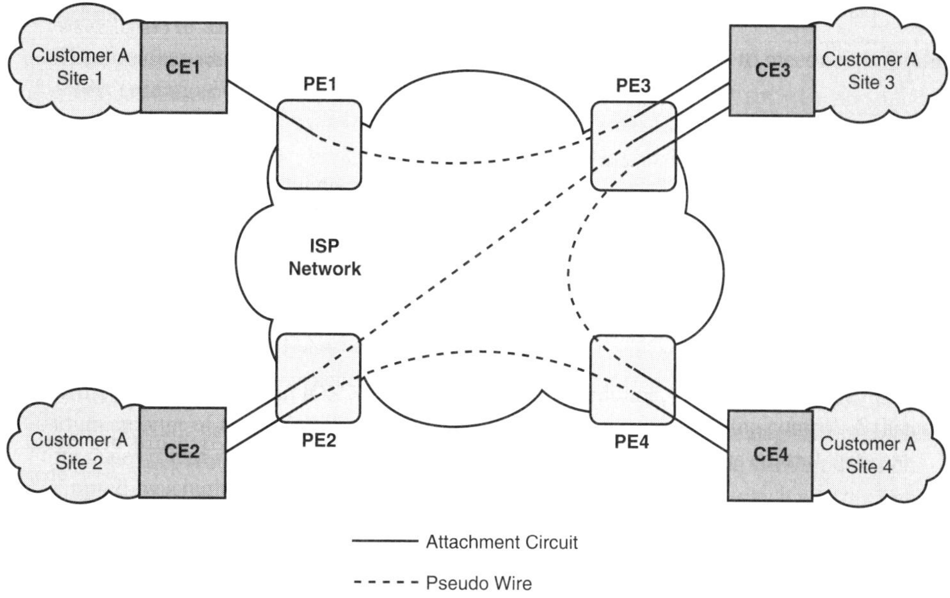

Figure 9-7 *Virtual Private Wire Service*

VPWS architecture is specified by IETF in Pseudo Wire Emulation Edge-to-Edge (PWE3) Architecture (defined in RFC 3985). The encapsulation mechanism used for the pseudo wire (PW) can be either L2TPv3 or MPLS LDP. Any Transport over MPLS (AToM) refers to the VPWS service using MPLS encapsulation and LDP signaling.

VPWS Configuration in IOS XR

The configuration steps for VPWS with MPLS encapsulation for PW are as follows:

1. Configure the interface or subinterface as an attachment circuit (AC) using the **l2transport** qualifier.
2. Enter into L2VPN configuration mode using **l2vpn**. All other L2VPN-specific configurations are made under L2VPN configuration mode.
3. Under **l2vpn** configuration mode, create a pw-class with MPLS encapsulation.
4. Create **xconnect group** under **l2vpn** configuration mode.
5. Under this xconnect group, create a P2P connection using **p2p** configuration.
6. Under the **p2p** configuration mode, specify the AC by configuring **interface** <*intf*>.
7. Under the **p2p** configuration mode, specify the PW and encapsulation type by configuring **neighbor** <*remote-PE-IP*> and **pw-clas** <*pw-class-name*>.

Figure 9-8 shows VPWS connectivity requirement for a customer.

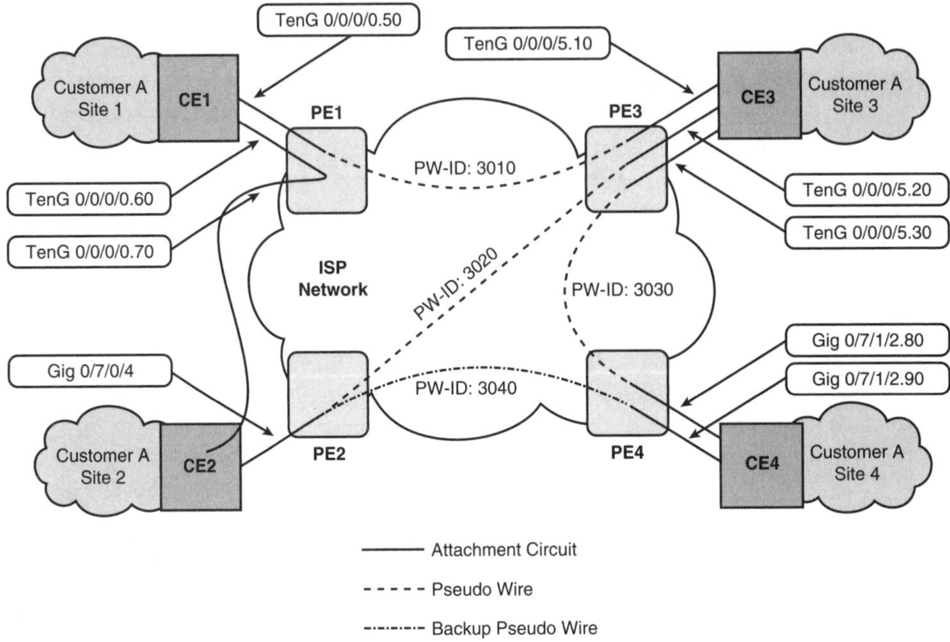

Figure 9-8 *Connectivity Requirement for a VPWS Customer*

Example 9-34 shows relevant VPWS configurations for PE3 to achieve the VPWS service shown in Figure 9-8.

Example 9-34 *VPWS Configuration for PE3*

```
RP/0/RP0/CPU0:CRS-C-PE2#show running-config int Ten 0/0/0/5*
interface TenGigE0/0/0/5
 mtu 9216
!
interface TenGigE0/0/0/5.10 l2transport
 dot1q vlan 10
!
interface TenGigE0/0/0/5.20 l2transport
 dot1q vlan 20
!
interface TenGigE0/0/0/5.30 l2transport
 dot1q vlan 30
!

RP/0/RP0/CPU0:CRS-C-PE2#show running-config l2vpn
l2vpn
 pw-class my-mpls
  encapsulation mpls
```

```
  !
  !
 pw-class mpls-ether
  encapsulation mpls
    transport-mode ethernet
  !
  !
  xconnect group my-group
  p2p to-pe1-ce1
    interface TenGigE0/0/0/5.10
    neighbor 192.168.0.1 pw-id 3010
     pw-class my-mpls
    !
  !
  p2p to-pe2-ce2
    interface TenGigE0/0/0/5.20
    neighbor 192.168.0.2 pw-id 3020
     pw-class mpls-ether
    !
  !
  p2p to-pe4-ce4
    interface TenGigE0/0/0/5.30
    neighbor 192.168.0.4 pw-id 3030
     pw-class my-mpls
    !
  !
  !
 !
```

The command **show l2vpn xconnect** displays the status of VPWS connections. Example 9-35 shows that for all connections the attachment circuits (segment 1) are up, whereas the PWs (segment 2) are down (DN). Consequently all VPWS end-to-end connections are also down (DN). Because MPLS LDP is used for PW signaling between PEs, you can use LDP **show** commands to check the status of LDP discovery and session with remote PE. First, use **show mpls ldp discovery** to check the status of the directed LDP discovery with remote PE.

Example 9-35 *L2VPN Cross-Connect Status for PE3*

```
RP/0/RP0/CPU0:CRS-C-PE2#show l2vpn xconnect
Legend: ST = State, UP = Up, DN = Down, AD = Admin Down, UR = Unresolved,
        LU = Local Up, RU = Remote Up, CO = Connected

XConnect                     Segment 1                      Segment 2
Group        Name        ST  Description              ST   Description             ST
-------------------------    ------------------------     ------------------------
```

```
my-group    to-pe1-ce1 DN    Te0/0/0/5.10          UP    192.168.0.1      3010    DN

----------------------------------------------------------------------------
my-group    to-pe2-ce2 DN    Te0/0/0/5.20          UP    192.168.0.2      3020    DN

----------------------------------------------------------------------------
my-group    to-pe4-ce4 DN    Te0/0/0/5.30          UP    192.168.0.4      3030    DN

----------------------------------------------------------------------------
```

Example 9-36 shows that targeted hellos are sent by PE3 to all remote PEs, but PE3 has not received targeted hellos. The reason for this is that L2VPN is not yet configured on the remote PEs.

Example 9-36 *Output of* show mpls ldp discovery

```
RP/0/RP0/CPU0:CRS-C-PE2#show mpls ldp discovery

Local LDP Identifier: 192.168.0.3:0
Discovery Sources:
 Interfaces:
    TenGigE0/0/0/0 : xmit/recv
      LDP Id: 192.168.0.1:0, Transport address: 192.168.0.1
          Hold time: 15 sec (local:15 sec, peer:15 sec)

    TenGigE0/0/0/1 : xmit/recv
      LDP Id: 192.168.0.1:0, Transport address: 192.168.0.1
          Hold time: 15 sec (local:15 sec, peer:15 sec)

 Targeted Hellos:
    192.168.0.3 -> 192.168.0.1 (active), xmit

    192.168.0.3 -> 192.168.0.2 (active), xmit

    192.168.0.3 -> 192.168.0.4 (active), xmit
```

Example 9-37 shows the relevant L2VPN configurations for PE1. Note that PE1 has two VPWS connections. The first one interconnects local AC from CE1 to remote AC PE3-CE3. The second VPWS connects local AC to CE1 and another local AC to CE2. This type of VPWS connectivity, which does not require PW, is known as *local switching*.

Example 9-37 *L2VPN Configurations for PE1*

```
interface TenGigE0/0/0/0.50 l2transport
 dot1q vlan 50
!
interface TenGigE0/0/0/0.60 l2transport
 dot1q vlan 60
!
interface TenGigE0/0/0/0.70 l2transport
 dot1q vlan 70
!

l2vpn
 pw-class my-mpls
 encapsulation mpls
 !
 !
 xconnect group my-group
 p2p to-pe3-ce3
   interface TenGigE0/0/0/0.50
   neighbor 192.168.0.3 pw-id 3010
    pw-class my-mpls
   !
 !
 p2p local-ce1-to-ce2
   interface TenGigE0/0/0/0.60
   interface TenGigE0/0/0/0.70
 !
 !
```

Example 9-38 shows the status of the two VPWS connections on PE1.

Example 9-38 *Output of* **show l2vpn xconnect** *on PE1*

```
RP/0/RP0/CPU0:CRS-A-PE1#show l2vpn xconnect
Legend: ST = State, UP = Up, DN = Down, AD = Admin Down, UR = Unresolved,
        LU = Local Up, RU = Remote Up, CO = Connected

XConnect                    Segment 1                   Segment 2
Group       Name        ST  Description             ST  Description            ST
--------------------------  ------------------------    ----------------------
my-group    to-pe3-ce3  UP  Te0/0/0/0.50            UP  192.168.0.3     3010   UP

--------------------------------------------------------------------------------
my-group    local-ce1-to-ce2
```

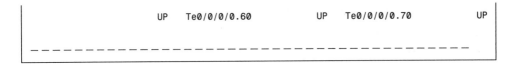

```
                    UP    Te0/0/0/0.60            UP    Te0/0/0/0.70            UP

-----------------------------------------------------------------------
```

Pseudo Wire Redundancy

Consider a scenario in which a critical service is made available at two locations for the purpose of redundancy. If connectivity to one site is disrupted, the remote site can fall back to the second site. This capability is achieved using *pseudo wire redundancy*. In Figure 9-8, PE2 has two PWs for one attachment circuit (AC). One of the PWs (PW-ID 3020) is the primary PW, whereas the second PW (PW ID 3040) is a backup PW. As long as the primary PW is active, the backup is kept down. When the primary PW fails, the backup PW is brought up. Example 9-39 shows L2VPN configuration for PE2, which includes PW redundancy.

Example 9-39 *PW Redundancy Configuration for PE2*

```
interface GigabitEthernet0/7/0/4
 mtu 9216
 l2transport
  !
!

l2vpn
 pw-class my-mpls
 encapsulation mpls
  !
  !
 xconnect group my-group
 p2p to-pe3-ce3
   interface GigabitEthernet0/7/0/4
   neighbor 192.168.0.3 pw-id 3020
    pw-class my-mpls
    backup neighbor 192.168.0.4 pw-id 3040
     pw-class my-mpls
    !
   !
  !
  !
!
```

The **show l2vpn xconnect neighbor** *<remote-PE-IP>* **pw-id** *<pw-id>* **detail** command displays detailed information for a specific VPWS connection. It shows MTU, MPLS labels, PW type, and so on for both local and remote PEs. Example 9-40 shows the detailed output for PW ID=3020.

Example 9-40 *Detailed Output for a Specific VPWS Connection*

```
RP/0/RP0/CPU0:CRS-C-PE2#show l2vpn xconnect neighbor 192.168.0.2 pw-id 3020 detail
Group my-group, XC to-pe2-ce2, state is up; Interworking none
 AC: TenGigE0/0/0/5.20, state is up
    Type VLAN; Num Ranges: 1
    VLAN ranges: [20, 20]
    MTU 9202; XC ID 0x1080002; interworking none; MSTi 0
    Statistics:
      packets: received 417, sent 0
      bytes: received 56433, sent 0
      drops: illegal VLAN 0, illegal length 0
 PW: neighbor 192.168.0.2, PW ID 3020, state is up ( established )
    PW class mpls-ether, XC ID 0x1080002
    Encapsulation MPLS, protocol LDP
    PW type Ethernet, control word disabled, interworking none
    PW backup disable delay 0 sec
    Sequencing not set
      MPLS         Local                           Remote
      ------ ------------------------------ ------------------------------
      Label        16017                           16005
      Group ID     0x10800c0                       0x17800a0
      Interface    TenGigE0/0/0/5.20               GigabitEthernet0/7/0/4
      MTU          9202                            9202
      Control word disabled                        disabled
      PW type      Ethernet                        Ethernet
      VCCV CV type 0x2                             0x2
                   (LSP ping verification)         (LSP ping verification)
      VCCV CC type 0x2                             0x2
                   (router alert label)            (router alert label)
      ------ ------------------------------ ------------------------------
    Create time: 28/02/2009 16:20:28 (00:36:58 ago)
    Last time status changed: 28/02/2009 16:20:42 (00:36:44 ago)
    Statistics:
      packets: received 417, sent 0
      bytes: received 56433, sent 0
```

Virtual Private VLAN Service

Virtual Private VLAN Service (VPLS) is a Layer 2 service that interconnects multiple sites and emulates a LAN or VLAN across an MPLS or IP network. Figure 9-9 shows a VPLS scenario in which a customer has seven sites and the CE routers from each site is connected to an emulated LAN service.

The three attachment circuits of customer A and the Virtual Forwarding Instance (VFI), which has PW to all three remote PE routers, are on the same bridge domain. VFI creates the bridging domain among all ACs and PWs. Packets received on one attachment circuit are switched to other attachment circuits or PWs based on the destination MAC address.

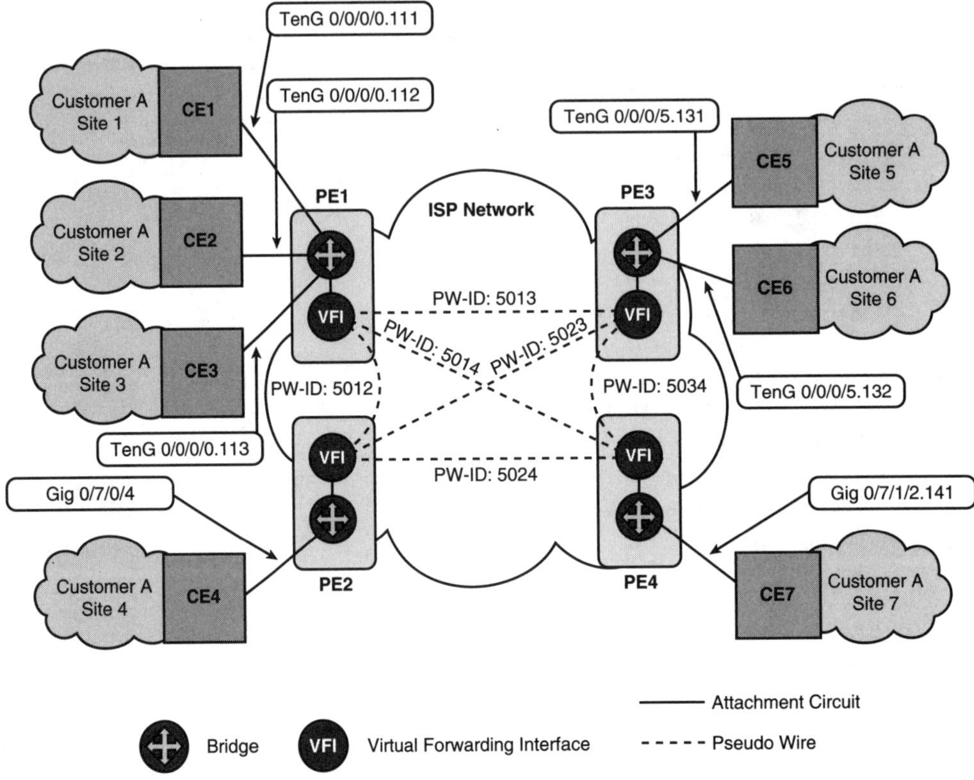

Figure 9-9 *VPLS Service Scenario*

If a MAC address is not present in the table, packets are flooded on all other ACs and on all PWs associated with the bridge domain.

When a packet is received on a PW, it has an MPLS label. The MPLS label is used to select the bridge domain associated with the PW. The packet is forwarded to one of the attachment circuits depending on the destination MAC address. Note that a packet received on a PW is not forwarded back to another PW because split-horizon is enabled by default on the VFI. The reason for this is that there is a full mesh PW between PE routers of an emulated LAN.

When a packet is received on a PW and the destination MAC address is not known, then the packet is forwarded to all attachment circuits. The same is true if either a broadcast or multicast packet is received on a PW.

As in the case of VPWS, VPLS configuration is well structured and hierarchical. It also shares similar characteristics with VPWS configuration. The configuration steps for VPLS with MPLS encapsulation for PW follow:

1. Configure the interface or subinterface as an attachment circuit (AC) using **l2transport**.

2. Enter into L2VPN configuration mode using **l2vpn**. All other L2VPN-specific configurations are made under L2VPN configuration mode.
3. Under **l2vpn** configuration mode create a pw-class with MPLS encapsulation.
4. Create **bridge group** under **l2vpn** configuration mode.
5. Under the **bridge group** just created, create a **bridge-domain.**
6. Under the **bridge-domain** configuration mode, specify the AC by configuring **interface** *<intf>*. Repeat this step for each AC.
7. Optionally, under the **bridge-domain** configuration mode, configure the bridge MTU.
8. Under the **bridge-domain** configuration mode, create a **vfi**.
9. Under the **vfi**, specify the PW and encapsulation type by configuring **neighbor** *<remote-PE-IP>* and **pw-class** *<pw-class-name>*. Repeat this step for each remote PE participating in a VPLS emulated VLAN.

Example 9-41 shows relevant VPLS configurations for PE1 to achieve the VPLS service shown in Figure 9-9.

Example 9-41 *VPLS Configuration for PE1*

```
interface TenGigE0/0/0/0.111 l2transport
 dot1q vlan 111
!
interface TenGigE0/0/0/0.112 l2transport
 dot1q vlan 112
!
interface TenGigE0/0/0/0.113 l2transport
 dot1q vlan 113
!

l2vpn
 pw-class my-mpls
 encapsulation mpls
 !
 !
 bridge group BG1
 bridge-domain Customer_A
   mtu 9202
   interface TenGigE0/0/0/0.111
   !
   interface TenGigE0/0/0/0.112
   !
   interface TenGigE0/0/0/0.113
   !
   vfi VFI_A
```

```
        neighbor 192.168.0.2 pw-id 5012
         pw-class my-mpls
        !
        neighbor 192.168.0.3 pw-id 5013
         pw-class my-mpls
        !
        neighbor 192.168.0.4 pw-id 5014
         pw-class my-mpls
        !
       !
     !
     !
    !
```

The command **show l2vpn forwarding summary location** *<r/s/m>* provides a summary of L2VPN connections for both VPLS and VPWS. Example 9-42 shows L2VPN forwarding summary output for PE1.

Example 9-42 *L2VPN Forwarding Summary for PE1 on 0/0/CPU0*

```
RP/0/RP0/CPU0:CRS-A-PE1#show l2vpn forw summary location 0/0/CPU0
Major version num:1, minor version num:0
Shared memory timestamp:0xa49fb3d780
Number of forwarding xconnect entries:8
 Up:8 Down:0
 AC-PW:1 (1 mpls)  AC-AC:1 AC-BP:3 AC-Unknown:0
 PW-BP:3 PW-Unknown:0
Number of xconnects down due to:
 AIB:0 L2VPN:0 L3FIB:0
Number of p2p xconnects: 2
Number of bridge-port xconnects: 6
Number of nexthops:3
 MPLS:    Bound:3 Unbound:0 Pending Registration:0
Number of bridge-domains: 1
Number of static macs: 0
Number of locally learned macs: 3
Number of remotely learned macs: 0
Number of total macs: 3
```

The **show l2vpn bridge-domain brief** command lists all bridge domains configured on the router. For each bridge domain, the output shows the status of the bridge and number of ACs and PWs. Example 9-43 lists the **bridge-domain** command output for PE1.

Example 9-43 show l2vpn bridge-domain brief *for PE1*

```
RP/0/RP0/CPU0:CRS-A-PE1#show l2vpn bridge-domain brief
Bridge Group/Bridge-Domain Name  ID    State      Num ACs/up     Num PWs/up
-------------------------------- --.  -----    ---------     --------
BG1/Customer_A                   1     up         3/3            3/3
```

The **show l2vpn bridge-domain bd-name** *<BD-name>* command displays the ACs and PWs for the specified bridge domain, as shown in Example 9-44.

Example 9-44 *Showing ACs and PWs for a Bridge Domain*

```
RP/0/RP0/CPU0:CRS-A-PE1#show l2vpn bridge-domain bd-name Customer_A
Bridge group: BG1, bridge-domain: Customer_A, id: 1, state: up, ShgId: 0, MSTi: 0
 Aging: 300 s, MAC limit: 4000, Action: none, Notification: syslog
 Filter MAC addresses: 0
 ACs: 3 (3 up), VFIs: 1, PWs: 3 (3 up)
 List of ACs:
    Te0/0/0/0.111, state: up, Static MAC addresses: 0, MSTi: 0
    Te0/0/0/0.112, state: up, Static MAC addresses: 0, MSTi: 0
    Te0/0/0/0.113, state: up, Static MAC addresses: 0, MSTi: 0
 List of Access PWs:
 List of VFIs:
    VFI VFI_A
      Neighbor 192.168.0.2 pw-id 5012, state: up, Static MAC addresses: 0
      Neighbor 192.168.0.3 pw-id 5013, state: up, Static MAC addresses: 0
      Neighbor 192.168.0.4 pw-id 5014, state: up, Static MAC addresses: 0
```

Use the **detail** option to get more detailed information including statistics for each PW and AC of the bridge domain, as shown in Example 9-45.

Example 9-45 *Display Detailed Information for a Bridge Domain*

```
RP/0/RP0/CPU0:CRS-A-PE1#show l2vpn bridge-domain bd-name Customer_A detail
Bridge group: BG1, bridge-domain: Customer_A, id: 1, state: up, ShgId: 0, MSTi: 0
 MAC learning: enabled
 MAC withdraw: disabled
 Flooding:
    Broadcast & Multicast: enabled
    Unknown unicast: enabled
 MAC aging time: 300 s, Type: inactivity
 MAC limit: 4000, Action: none, Notification: syslog
 MAC limit reached: no
 Security: disabled
 DHCPv4 snooping: disabled
 Bridge MTU: 9202
```

```
 Filter MAC addresses:
 ACs: 3 (3 up), VFIs: 1, PWs: 3 (3 up)
 List of ACs:
    AC: TenGigE0/0/0/0.111, state is up
      Type VLAN; Num Ranges: 1
      VLAN ranges: [111, 111]
      MTU 9202; XC ID 0x1080004; interworking none; MSTi 0
      MAC learning: enabled
      Flooding:
        Broadcast & Multicast: enabled
        Unknown unicast: enabled
      MAC aging time: 300 s, Type: inactivity
      MAC limit: 4000, Action: none, Notification: syslog
      MAC limit reached: no
      Security: disabled
      DHCPv4 snooping: disabled
      Static MAC addresses:
      Statistics:
        packets: received 47483, sent 20042
        bytes: received 3725666, sent 1362856
! Output omitted for brevity
 List of Access PWs:
 List of VFIs:
    VFI VFI_A
      PW: neighbor 192.168.0.2, PW ID 5012, state is up ( established )
        PW class my-mpls, XC ID 0xfff80008
        Encapsulation MPLS, protocol LDP
        PW type Ethernet, control word disabled, interworking none
        PW backup disable delay 0 sec
        Sequencing not set
          MPLS         Local                          Remote
          ------------ ------------------------------ -------------------------
          Label        16017                          16007
          Group ID     0x1                            0x0
          Interface    VFI/A                          VFI/A
          MTU          9202                           9202
          Control word disabled                       disabled
          PW type      Ethernet                       Ethernet
          VCCV CV type 0x2                            0x2
                       (LSP ping verification)        (LSP ping verification)
          VCCV CC type 0x2                            0x2
                       (router alert label)           (router alert label)
          ------------ ------------------------------ -------------------------
        Create time: 28/02/2009 23:44:57 (09:44:08 ago)
        Last time status changed: 28/02/2009 23:45:01 (09:44:03 ago)
```

```
        MAC withdraw message: send 0 receive 0
        Static MAC addresses:
        Statistics:
          packets: received 0, sent 0
          bytes: received 0, sent 0
! Output omitted for brevity
      VFI Statistics:
       drops: illegal VLAN 0, illegal length 0
```

Summary

This chapter discusses the fundamentals of a key service provider technology, MPLS, and its architecture, services, and configurations in IOS XR. MPLS has control and data plane components. The control plane components are responsible for binding labels to forwarding equivalence classes (FECs) and exchanging label bindings with neighboring label switch routers (LSRs). The forwarding component is responsible for forwarding received traffic based on the top label contained in the packet, incoming interface, IP address, and/or MAC address. It is also responsible for label operations: push, swap, pop, unlabeled, or de-aggregate.

An essential component of IOS XR MPS architecture is Label Switch Database (LSD), which is the central repository of label-switching information and is responsible for receiving label-forwarding updates from applications and multicasting the LSD rewrite table to FIB process on the line cards using BCDL. LDP, TE, L2VPN, and BGP act as LSD clients or applications and are responsible for binding labels to a FEC and downloading label forwarding data to LSD.

When ingress LSR receives an IP packet, it copies the IP TTL value to the TTL field of the MPLS header after decrementing it by one. This behavior can be changed using **mpls ip-ttl-propagation disable** configuration, which sets the MPLS TTL to 255. Some service providers use this feature to hide their network from traceroute probes.

Like most other applications in IOS XR, MPLS LDP has its own configuration mode that contains all LDP related configurations including discovery and session parameters, label control, interfaces, session protection, GR, and NSR. IOS XR also supports LDP auto-configuration via IGP protocol, which automatically enables LDP on all interfaces for which IGP is enabled.

Normally, LDP allocates and binds a label for each IGP prefix. IOS XR label allocation feature enables you to limit the set of IGP prefixes for which LDP binds and allocates labels.

Cisco IOS XR supports two features that prevent traffic black-holing on a link-up event. The LDP session protection mechanism allows an LDP session between adjacent LSRs to stay up even after the link between them is down. The LDP-IGP synchronization feature keeps the IGP cost of the link between LSRs to be the maximum metric until LDP converges between the LSRs.

Network operators use MPLS TE primarily for traffic engineering purposes to achieve optimal network link utilization and/or for fast enabling rerouting on link or node failure.

MPLS TE is configured by enabling interfaces for MPLS TE and RSVP under **mpls traffic-eng** and **rsvp** configuration modes, respectively, throughout the MPLS TE domain. In addition, if a dynamic tunnel path computation is desired, MPLS TE has to be configured under the IGP protocol throughout the MPLS TE domain. At the head-end router of a TE tunnel, the tunnel interface and zero or more corresponding explicit path(s) have to be configured using **interface tunnel-te** *<id>* and **explicit-path** {**name** *<path-name>* | **id** *<path-id>*}, respectively.

Cisco IOS XR peer-to-peer L3VPN feature uses a hierarchical configuration and supports a variety of connectivity options. Protocol- and interface-independent VRF-specific configurations are done under VRF configuration mode. Protocol-specific VRF configurations are done under the respective protocol. MP-iBGP is used between PE routers to exchange L3VPN routes. Static routing, BGP, OSPF, RIP, and EIGRP are supported as CE-PE protocols. An interface is associated with a VRF using **vrf** *<vrf-name>* configuration under the interface.

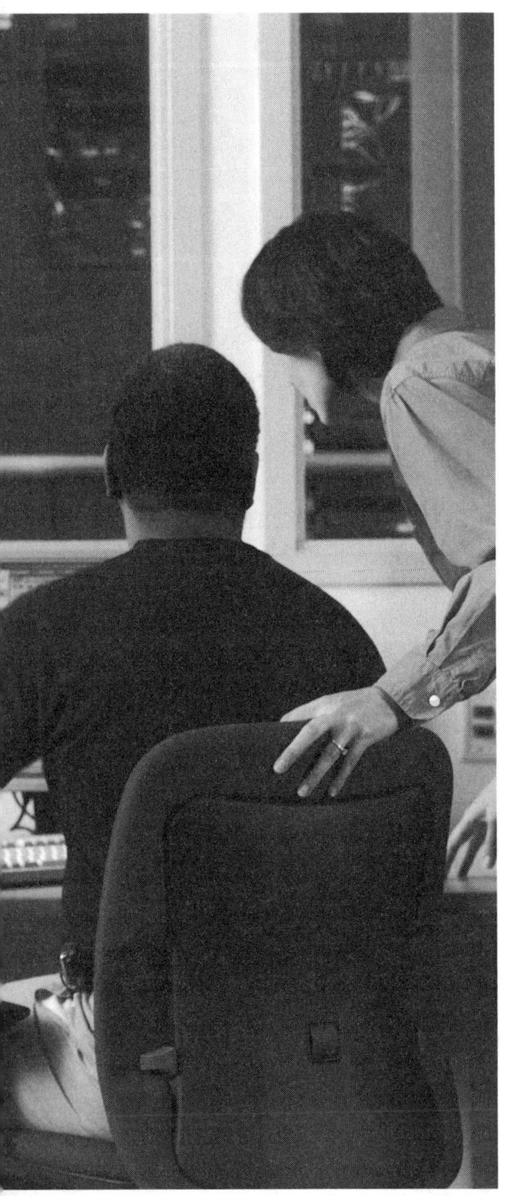

This chapter covers the following topics:

- Understanding Multicast Routing Fundamentals
- Understanding Cisco IOS XR Multicast
- Configuring Cisco IOS XR Multicast
- Monitoring and Troubleshooting Cisco IOS XR Multicast
- References

IPv4 multicast routing has been around since the mid-1980s. Multicast is becoming more prevalent in services provider (SP) networks as the transition to next-generation network (NGN) architectures gains momentum. As the high-definition video market grows, multicast is gaining popularity and finding applications in the SP networks as a bandwidth-conserving video delivery technology. Multicast is also finding a place in the financial sector, such as in the common financial stock ticker applications.

This chapter introduces the concepts of Cisco IOS XR multicast routing and forwarding. A high-level overview of IOS XR architecture is presented, followed by an in-depth discussion of PIM Sparse mode. This chapter also presents the configuration basics related to IOS XR multicast and introduces a section on IOS XR operations and troubleshooting.

CHAPTER 10

Cisco IOS XR Multicast

Understanding Multicast Routing Fundamentals

This section discusses key underlying concepts behind multicast routing and forwarding to set the stage for upcoming IOS XR multicast-specific topics. Fundamentals of Internet Group Management Protocol (IGMP) and Protocol Independent Multicast (PIM) are briefly discussed to provide a refresher and serve as precursors to IOS XR multicast configuration and troubleshooting topics.

IPv4 multicast provides an efficient data delivery mechanism in scenarios where more than one receiver is interested in receiving the same IP datagram transmission. Instead of sending a copy of the traffic stream to each interested party, the sender of multicast traffic sends one stream and allows multicast protocols to take care of the replication of traffic as the traffic stream draws near its destinations. The function of replicating the multicast stream resides in the network that is configured for multicast routing. Following are some of the basic requirements of multicast forwarding:

- **Class D IP address:** A method needs to be provided so that the groups of receivers interested in receiving multicast traffic can be identified. This is accomplished by using a Class D IPv4 address in the destination address field of the IPv4 header. IANA has dedicated the Class D IP address from the range 224.0.0.0–239.255.255.255 for multicast traffic.
- **Internet Group Management Protocol (IGMP):** A method needs to be provided where groups can join or leave the attending of IPv4 multicast transmission, similar to a radio listener tuning in and out of a radio station. This functionality is provided by IGMP.
- **Protocol Independent Multicast (PIM):** Multicast routing follows a reverse paradigm from that adopted by unicast routing. Instead of routing based on destination address, multicast routing works by using reverse path forwarding (RPF) to deliver traffic from source to receivers. The protocol constructs for multicast routing are provided by Protocol Independent Multicast (PIM) that uses unicast routing for performing reverse path lookups. Multicast streams are identified by a source and group pair known as an (S,G), where S is an IP unicast source address and G is a Class D IP address that denotes a group.

The following sections discuss these ideas in a little more detail.

Internet Group Management Protocol

IGMP provides a communication medium between the router and the host attached directly to the router's link layer. A host that wants to become a member of a multicast group runs IGMP with the router to indicate its intent of joining or leaving the membership of a multicast group. IGMP was introduced to the Internet community as IGMPv1 via RFC 1112 and later improved to IGMPv2 documented in RFC 2236. Further enhancements in the form of IGMPv3 were introduced in RFC3376.

The following sections include some key features of IGMPv2 and IGMPv3.

IGMPv2

A router queries its connected subnet to discern a host interested in joining a multicast group. The query is sent to the address 224.0.0.1, which means that it is intended for all systems (routers and hosts) on that subnet. A router's query message contains a field called Max Response Time. This allows the host to set a random timer leading up to the expiration of which the host responds with a membership report. The default value of Max Response Time is 10 seconds. The router forwards the multicast traffic to this subnet based on the outcome of its query.

When a host wants to join a multicast stream and has not received a router's query, the host takes the initiative to send a join request message to the router. This join request is known as a *report*. Reports help reduce join latency by allowing hosts to join a multicast group without having to wait for a router's query. A report may also be sent in response to a router query. All IGMP messages are exchanged with an IP TTL of 1 so that they are never forwarded beyond the directly connected segment. The membership reports are sent to the group address so that other hosts on the subnet can hear the message and avoid duplicate transmissions of reports.

When a host wants to leave a group, it announces its departure by sending a Leave Group message to all routers on the subnet using the IANA reserved address of 224.0.0.2. The connected router responds to the leave message by sending out a group-specific query and checks for more hosts on its subnets that might still be interested in being members of the group. IGMPv1 does not have leave messages and group-specific queries; these are IGMP-specific enhancements. As a result, leave and join latency is improved.

Note: IGMPv2 has improvements over IGMPv1 with regard to group join and leave latency.

IGMPv3

IGMPv3 has added capabilities beyond IGMPv2 in the sense that it introduces group- and source-specific querying. A group may be serviced by multiple sources; IGMPv3 reports have include and exclude filters that allow it to filter a source and group combination (S, G) from which it wants to receive traffic. IGMPv3 is important in supporting Source Specific Multicast (SSM), which is discussed in subsequent sections.

By default, Cisco IOS XR supports IGMPv3; however, the IGMP version can be changed via CLI. IGMPv3 provides backward compatibility with IGMPv2. When an IOS XR router with a default setting of IGMPv3 receives an IGMPv2 report, it turns on the old host compatibility mode and treats the report as (*,G) EXCLUDE {none}. This indicates that IGMPv3 filters do not exclude any source from sending traffic to this multicast group.

Protocol Independent Multicast

Protocol Independent Multicast (PIM) is used to build multicast distribution trees by using the information provided by the unicast routing table. Multicast traffic is forwarded on the distribution tree by moving it from the source toward hosts that have requested to be members of the concerned multicast group. A source originates the multicast traffic; the recipients of this stream may be multiple hosts scattered in different parts of a given network. Multicast traffic flows downstream from the source toward its destination. This form of forwarding is commonly referred to as *Reverse Path Forwarding*.

Multicast forwarding requires the maintenance of multicast forwarding states known as (S,G) entries in the multicast routing and forwarding tables. To avoid forwarding loops, multicast routing ensures that traffic is received only on the shortest path back to the source; otherwise, it discards the traffic. A multicast routing table keeps track of the information needed to successfully forward multicast traffic. The multicast tables keep information such as the IP address of upstream node (also called the *RPF neighbor*), the interface along the shortest path to the source (also called the *incoming interface*), and a list of the downstream interfaces on which explicit join messages are receiving from the interested receivers.

This information about distribution tree and the resulting multicast routing and forwarding are populated via PIM protocol signaling. The multicast trees can be based on the shortest path to the source of multicast traffic, or they can be based on a shared central point through which the traffic from source to receiver can flow in the network. The first type of multicast tree is known as a *source-based tree* or *Shortest Path Tree* (*SPT*), and the second type is commonly referred to as a *shared tree*. The shared trees are rooted at routers in the network known as Rendezvous Points (RP).

Cisco IOS XR router supports a variety of multicast features, including the commonly used PIM Sparse Mode (SM). PIM SM uses a shared tree for multicast distribution but has the capability to switch to a shortest path tree rooted at the source of the traffic (assuming a shorter path to the source is discovered after the traffic is received natively via the shared tree). As in Cisco IOS, the SPT threshold for traffic to switchover from shared to shortest path tree is zero in IOS XR.

Note: Cisco IOS XR does not support PIM Dense Mode as a configurable option at the time of writing this book—that is, up to IOS XR release 3.6.2.

This chapter depicts key Cisco IOS XR PIM concepts using only the Sparse Mode of multicast routing and forwarding.

Understanding Cisco IOS XR Multicast

This section provides an overview of IOS XR multicast routing and some of its components. Figure 10-1 provides a high-level reference to the various building blocks involved in the implementation of multicast routing and forwarding features. This section describes those building blocks.

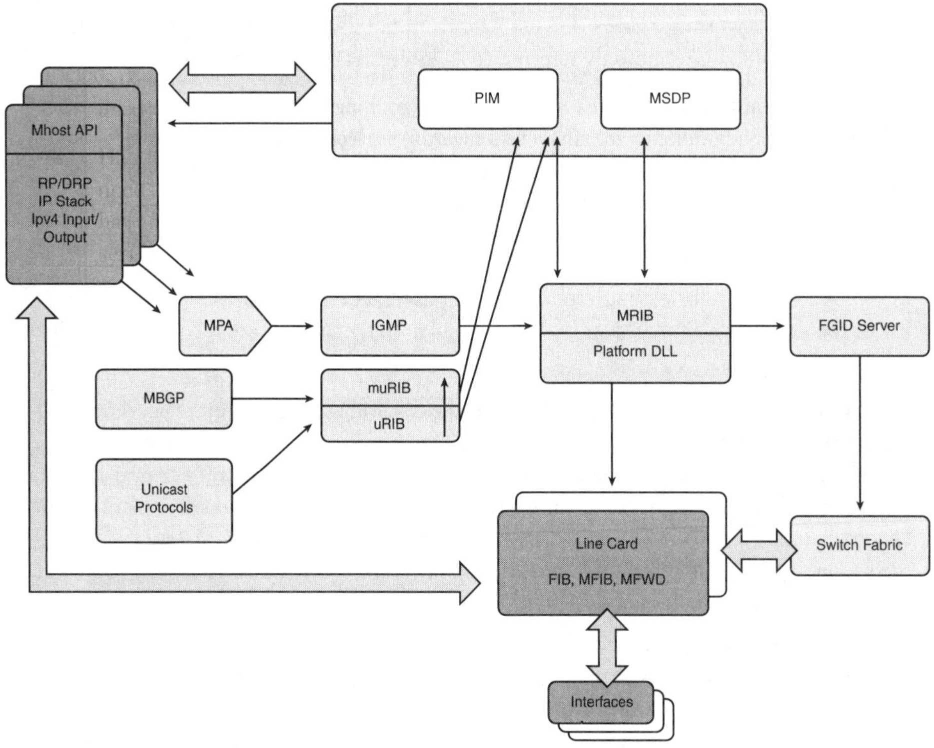

Figure 10-1 *Multicast Software Building Blocks*

As shown in Figure 10-1, IP multicast host stack Mhost provides an interface to multicast applications. In certain cases of processing multicast control plane traffic, data is sent or received from the IP stack via Mhost. Cisco IOS XR provides some rudimentary configurable options with Mhost. In the following configuration CLI dictates the router's address used as a source for multicast ping:

```
mhost {ipv4 | ipv6} default-interface {interface}
```

A process known as MPA is shown in Figure 10-1. One of the purposes of this process is to aggregate the IGMP join information for the SDR and pass it on to the processes that create pIFIB entries. The concept of pIFIB was explained in Chapter 6, "Cisco IOS XR Security."

The multicast routing information base (MRIB) resides in the route processor and has a central position in IOS XR multicast implementation. It helps manage multicast routing (mroute) entries for PIM, IGMP, and forwarding. MRIB is the central database through which information on multicast routing and host group interest is exchanged between various routing and forwarding multicast components. MRIB is a protocol-independent representation of multicast routing information containing the source (S), group (G), incoming interface (IIF), outgoing interfaces, and RPF neighbor information for each multicast route, among other multicast-related information. The MRIB acts as the consolidated routing information base in which all multicast routing protocols reflect the routes they learn. It also acts as a passive server for the selection of routing information among its clients. Subsequent sections in this chapter show how information received from IGMP will be redistributed to PIM using the MRIB.

The multicast unicast RIB (muRIB), similar to MRIB, operates and resides in route processors. This table is similar in many ways to the regular unicast RIB except that it is never used for forwarding unicast data. It is updated by protocols such as Multicast BGP (MBGP) or by multi-topology routing enabled via address-family multicast configuration command in IS-IS. muRIB comes into play where certain routing features need to be invoked to circumvent RPF issues in the network.

Note: Some of the features involved with muRIB are mutually exclusive and, therefore, cannot co-exist. A common example of such features is that the multicast-intact knob for MPLS TE and IS-IS multicast address family cannot be run simultaneously on the same IOS XR router.

MFIB is a protocol-independent multicast forwarding table that contains unique multicast forwarding entries for each (S,G) pair for multicast routes. There is a separate MFIB for every logical network (VPN) in which the router is configured. Each MFIB entry resolves a given source/group pair to an incoming interface (IIF) for RPF checking and an output list, commonly referred to as *O-list*, for multicast forwarding. Multicast forwarding information is downloaded to the line cards for the fast forwarding of multicast packets. The replication of multicast within the IOS XR router is enabled by Fabric Group Identifiers (FGID) memberships within the router.

Figure 10-1 also shows a process known as MFWD. MFWD partner process helps in the programming of multicast forwarding information in the hardware.

The preceding discussion sets the stage for understanding the mechanics behind PIM SM on IOS XR. Forthcoming discussion provides a refresher to PIM Sparse Mode and details the IOS XR–specific details of the PIM SM protocol.

Understanding Cisco IOS XR PIM Sparse Mode

This section explains the mechanics involved with the multicast forwarding of IOS XR using PIM SM. The configuration details are not presented yet; however, the control plane behavior is discussed with the help of **show** commands. Configuration details are discussed in the "Configuring Cisco IOS XR Multicast" section of this chapter.

Figure 10-2 shows a network that is preconfigured for PIM SM multicast routing. All the CRS-1 and GSR routers shown in the topology are running Release 3.6.0 of Cisco IOS XR software. The 7200-Paris router running IOS is configured for bootstrap router (BSR) and functions as a rendezvous point for this network. The GSR1-SJC router receives an IGMP join for a multicast group 231.1.1.1. Example 10-1 shows the IGMP and MRIB debugs and illustrates the process of creating multicast route entry when an IGMP join is received on an IOS XR router configured for PIM SM.

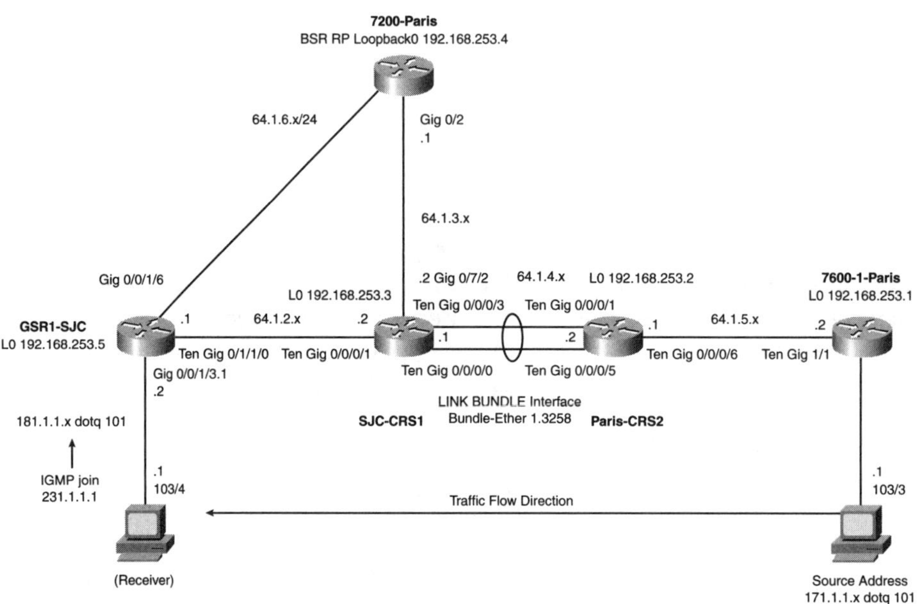

Figure 10-2 *Multicast Topology*

Example 10-1 *IGMP and MRIB Debugs Showing the Joining of Group 231.1.1*

```
! IGMP Debug collected from IGMP trace buffer
Nov  2 09:07:44.630 igmp/group 0/8/CPU0 t1  Added a new group 231.1.1.1 on
GigabitEthernet0/0/1/3.1
!
!
! MRIB Debug collected from the output of the following debug command:
####  debug flags set from tty 'vty0'  ####
```

```
ipv4 mrib route flag is ON with value '#'
!
RP/0/8/CPU0:GSR1-SJC#RP/0/8/CPU0:Nov  2 09:07:44.830 : mrib[291]:   [  0] TID:
  0xe0000000 (*,231.1.1.1) Received   [Gi0/0/1/3.1  LI*]
RP/0/8/CPU0:Nov  2 09:07:44.831 : mrib[291]:   [  0] TID: 0xe0000000
  (*,231.1.1.1) Added   #A=0, #F=0 [Gi0/0/1/3.1  LI*] Route Ver = 0x4325
RP/0/8/CPU0:Nov  2 09:07:44.831 : mrib[291]:   [  0] TID: 0xe0000000
  (*,231.1.1.1) Wakeup Clients  Force = FALSE
RP/0/8/CPU0:Nov  2 09:07:44.832 : mrib[291]:   [  1] TID: 0xe0000000
  (*,231.1.1.1) Redistributed   [Gi0/0/1/3.1  LI*]
RP/0/8/CPU0:Nov  2 09:07:44.833 : mrib[291]:   [  1] TID: 0xe0000000
  (*,231.1.1.1) Received   C* RPF=64.1.6.2
RP/0/8/CPU0:Nov  2 09:07:44.833 : mrib[291]:   [  1] TID: 0xe0000000
  (*,231.1.1.1) Updated   C* #A=0, #F=0 RPF=64.1.6.2 Route Ver = 0x4326
RP/0/8/CPU0:Nov  2 09:07:44.833 : mrib[291]:   [  1] TID: 0xe0000000
  (*,231.1.1.1) Wakeup Clients  Force = FALSE
RP/0/8/CPU0:Nov  2 09:07:44.833 : mrib[291]:   [  1] TID: 0xe0000000
  (*,231.1.1.1) Received   [Gi0/0/1/6  A*]
RP/0/8/CPU0:Nov  2 09:07:44.834 : mrib[291]:   [  1] TID: 0xe0000000 (*,231.1.1.1)
  Updated   C* #A=1, #F=0 RPF=64.1.6.2 [Gi0/0/1/6  A*] Route Ver = 0x4327
RP/0/8/CPU0:Nov  2 09:07:44.834 : mrib[291]:   [  1] TID: 0xe0000000
  (*,231.1.1.1) Wakeup Clients  Force = FALSE
RP/0/8/CPU0:Nov  2 09:07:44.834 : mrib[291]:   [  1] TID: 0xe0000000
  (*,231.1.1.1) Received   [Gi0/0/1/6  NS*]
RP/0/8/CPU0:Nov  2 09:07:44.835 : mrib[291]:   [  1] TID: 0xe0000000
  (*,231.1.1.1) Updated   C* #A=1, #F=0 RPF=64.1.6.2 [Gi0/0/1/6  A* NS*] Route
  Ver = 0x4328
RP/0/8/CPU0:Nov  2 09:07:44.835 : mrib[291]:   [  1] TID: 0xe0000000
  (*,231.1.1.1) Wakeup Clients  Force = FALSE
RP/0/8/CPU0:Nov  2 09:07:44.835 : mrib[291]:   [  1] TID: 0xe0000000
  (*,231.1.1.1) Received   [Gi0/0/1/3.1  F* NS*]
RP/0/8/CPU0:Nov  2 09:07:44.836 : mrib[291]:   [  1] TID: 0xe0000000
  (*,231.1.1.1) Updated   C* #A=1, #F=1 RPF=64.1.6.2 [Gi0/0/1/3.1  F* NS* LI]
  [Gi0/0/1/6  A* NS*] Route Ver = 0x4329
RP/0/8/CPU0:Nov  2 09:07:44.836 : mrib[291]:   [  1] TID: 0xe0000000
  (*,231.1.1.1) Wakeup Clients  Force = FALSE
RP/0/8/CPU0:Nov  2 09:07:44.837 : mrib[291]:   [  2] TID: 0xe0000000 (*,231.1.1.1)
  Redistributed   C* [Gi0/0/1/3.1  F* NS* LI] [Gi0/0/1/6  A* NS*]
```

Example 10-1 shows an IGMP debug trace highlighting the joining of a multicast group 231.1.1.1 on the GigabitEthernet0/0/1/3.1 interface. Messages in Example 10-1 indicate the mrib process with job ID of 291. Following the process name and job ID, the debug lists another square bracket showing a decimal number [0], [1], or [2]. The value 0 in the square bracket indicates that the debug message pertains to IGMP, whereas the values 1 and 2 indicate PIM and BCDL processes, respectively.

The highlighted output indicates the following:

- Because the join message is coming from a directly connected host, the Local Interest (LI) flag indicates IGMP's interest in this update. IGMP tells mrib of the group 231.1.1.1 join event by sending a (*,G) update with the Local Interest flag. The internal router version in mrib is 0x4325. This route version updates throughout the debug output as multicast routing and signaling information is modified.

- PIM is interested in the LI flag, and mrib redistributes this information to PIM, which creates a (*,G) entry in the PIM topology table.
- PIM is a designated forwarder on the subnet where the join for 231.1.1.1 was received. Hence, PIM is responsible for sending the (*,G) toward the rendezvous point. The mrib trace shows the directly connected flag C being modified. The modification of the flag is indicated by the asterisk (*), and RPF 64.1.6.2 is the RPF neighbor to the RP. The setting of the directly connected C flag checks to see whether a new source is directly connected to the router under discussion. The PIM topology outputs will subsequently show the flags set by PIM. The route version in the mrib output changes to 0x4326 to indicate the updating of this information.
- PIM updates the Accept (A) flag as indicated by the presence of an asterisk (that is, A*). mrib now has information about the incoming interface from the RP with the presence of A flag. This incoming interface in our example is Gig 0/0/1/6 with the RPF of 64.1.6.2.
- The very last line in the debug illustrates mrib updating the MFIB using the BCDL transport (indicated by [2]). Here the Forwarding (F) flag for Gig 0/0/1/3.1 indicates the interface that will forward multicast traffic, and Accept (A) flag for interface Gig 0/0/1/6 points to the root of the shared tree—that is, toward the RP located on the 7200-Paris router. Note that once traffic switches from a shared tree to a shortest path tree, the A flag shows the RPF interface or the source of multicast traffic stream.

Example 10-2 lists the output of a PIM **show** command for the interface on which the IGMP join is received, the output of PIM topology, and the routing entry in MRIB.

Example 10-2 *PIM Topology*

```
RP/0/8/CPU0:GSR1-SJC#show pim interface gigabitEthernet 0/0/1/3.1
PIM interfaces in VRF default
Address               Interface                    PIM  Nbr   Hello  DR    DR
                                                            Count Intvl  Prior
181.1.1.2       GigabitEthernet0/0/1/3.1     on   1     30     1      this system
!
RP/0/8/CPU0:GSR1-SJC#show pim topology 231.1.1.1
IP PIM Multicast Topology Table
Entry state: (*/S,G)[RPT/SPT] Protocol Uptime Info
Entry flags: KAT - Keep Alive Timer, AA - Assume Alive, PA - Probe Alive,
    RA - Really Alive, LH - Last Hop, DSS - Don't Signal Sources,
    RR - Register Received, SR - Sending Registers, E - MSDP External,
    DCC - Don't Check Connected,
    ME - MDT Encap, MD - MDT Decap,
    MT - Crossed Data MDT threshold, MA - Data MDT group assigned
Interface state: Name, Uptime, Fwd, Info
Interface flags: LI - Local Interest, LD - Local Dissinterest,
```

```
    II - Internal Interest, ID - Internal Dissinterest,
    LH - Last Hop, AS - Assert, AB - Admin Boundary
(*,231.1.1.1) SM Up: 00:03:07 RP: 192.168.253.4
JP: Join(00:00:41) RPF: GigabitEthernet0/0/1/6,64.1.6.2 Flags: LH
  GigabitEthernet0/0/1/3.1    00:03:07  fwd LI LH
 !
!
```

```
RP/0/8/CPU0:GSR1-SJC#show mrib route 231.1.1.1
IP Multicast Routing Information Base
Entry flags: L - Domain-Local Source, E - External Source to the Domain,
    C - Directly-Connected Check, S - Signal, IA - Inherit Accept,
    IF - Inherit From, D - Drop, MA - MDT Address, ME - MDT Encap,
    MD - MDT Decap, MT - MDT Threshold Crossed, MH - MDT interface handle
    CD - Conditional Decap
Interface flags: F - Forward, A - Accept, IC - Internal Copy,
    NS - Negate Signal, DP - Don't Preserve, SP - Signal Present,
    II - Internal Interest, ID - Internal Disinterest, LI - Local Interest,
    LD - Local Disinterest, DI - Decapsulation Interface
    EI - Encapsulation Interface, MI - MDT Interface
(*,231.1.1.1) RPF nbr: 64.1.6.2 Flags: C
  Incoming Interface List
    GigabitEthernet0/0/1/6 Flags: A NS
  Outgoing Interface List
    GigabitEthernet0/0/1/3.1 Flags: F NS LI
RP/0/8/CPU0:GSR1-SJC#
```

The output of the **show pim interface** command for interface gigabitEthernet 0/0/1/3.1 indicates that this system (GSR1-SJC) is the designated router (DR) elected by PIM on this segment. Upon learning about (*,G) through MRIB, the PIM process generates and sends a (*,G) join toward the rendezvous point located at 192.168.253.4 on the router 7200-Paris. Example 10-2 shows that the (*,G) topology entry is created with an RP address of 192.168.253.4. Because the RPF neighbor for an (*,G) entry always points to the RP, in this example the RPF neighbor toward RP is populated as 64.1.6.2.. PIM sets the last hop (LH) flag in the PIM topology table to indicate that this router is the PIM DR and is the designated last hop router for the group entry 231.1.1.1.

Output of the **show mrib route 231.1.1.1** command shows that PIM updates MRIB with the Accept (A) flag for the GigabitEthernet 0/0/1/6 interface, which is the interface toward the RP. The command output also shows the setting of the Forward (F) flag on GigabitEthernet 0/1/3.1, which is the interface on which the IGMP join was received.

The MRIB is then used to derive the forwarding table MFIB entry, and MFIB data structures are downloaded to the line card to enable fast forwarding of multicast packets. Example 10-3 shows the MFIB entry that is used to derive the line card forwarding table.

Example 10-3 *MFIB Entry for 231.1.1.1*

```
RP/0/8/CPU0:GSR1-SJC#show mfib route 231.1.1.1
IP Multicast Forwarding Information Base
Entry flags: C - Directly-Connected Check, S - Signal, D - Drop,
  IA - Inherit Accept, IF - Inherit From, MA - MDT Address,
  ME - MDT Encap, MD - MDT Decap, MT - MDT Threshold Crossed,
  MH - MDT interface handle, CD - Conditional Decap,
  DT - MDT Decap True
Interface flags: F - Forward, A - Accept, IC - Internal Copy,
  NS - Negate Signal, DP - Don't Preserve, SP - Signal Present,
  EG - Egress, EI - Encapsulation Interface, MI - MDT Interface
Forwarding Counts: Packets in/Packets out/Bytes out
Failure Counts: RPF / TTL / Empty Olist / Encap RL / Other
(*,231.1.1.1),    Flags:  C
  Last Used: never
  SW Forwarding Counts: 0/0/0
  Failure Counts: 0/0/0/0/0
  GigabitEthernet0/0/1/6 Flags:  A NS
  GigabitEthernet0/0/1/3.1 Flags:  NS
RP/0/8/CPU0:GSR1-SJC#
```

Example 10-3 shows the MFIB entry that retains only the flags needed for forwarding, such as the Accept and Forwarding flags. Protocol-related flags, such as the Local Interest (LI) flag, are not retained in this output.

Example 10-4 introduces a command called **show pim topology**.

Example 10-4 *The* show pim topology *Command Output*

```
RP/0/8/CPU0:GSR1-SJC#show pim topology 231.1.1.1

IP PIM Multicast Topology Table
Entry state: (*/S,G)[RPT/SPT] Protocol Uptime Info
Entry flags: KAT - Keep Alive Timer, AA - Assume Alive, PA - Probe Alive,
    RA - Really Alive, LH - Last Hop, DSS - Don't Signal Sources,
    RR - Register Received, SR - Sending Registers, E - MSDP External,
    DCC - Don't Check Connected,
    ME - MDT Encap, MD - MDT Decap,
    MT - Crossed Data MDT threshold, MA - Data MDT group assigned
Interface state: Name, Uptime, Fwd, Info
Interface flags: LI - Local Interest, LD - Local Dissinterest,
    II - Internal Interest, ID - Internal Dissinterest,
    LH - Last Hop, AS - Assert, AB - Admin Boundary
(*,231.1.1.1) SM Up: 00:03:07 RP: 192.168.253.4
JP: Join(00:00:41) RPF: GigabitEthernet0/0/1/6,64.1.6.2 Flags: LH
```

```
  GigabitEthernet0/0/1/3.1    00:03:07  fwd LI LH
!
```

```
!
RP/0/8/CPU0:GSR1-SJC#show pim rpf
* 192.168.253.4/32 [115/20]
    via GigabitEthernet0/0/1/6 with rpf neighbor 64.1.6.2
RP/0/8/CPU0:GSR1-SJC#
```

Example 10-4 shows the PIM topology for the last hop router as it relates to the shared tree. The multicast routing protocol is SM, or sparse mode. The command output indicates the RP address corroborated by the output of **show pim rpf**, and indicates the interface on which the IGMP join for group 231.1.1.1 is received by indicating LI or local interest. Note that this output relates to the shared tree because only a (*,G) entry is shown. After a source starts to send traffic, this command output indicates the source. Example 10-5 shows the output of **show mrib route** at core routers that are not part of the multicast shared tree.

Example 10-5 *State of mrib on the Routers That Are Not on the Shared Tree*

```
RP/0/RP0/CPU0:PARIS-CRS2#show mrib route 231.1.1.1
No matching routes in MRIB route-DB
!
RP/0/RP0/CPU0:SJC-CRS1#show mrib route 231.1.1.1
No matching routes in MRIB route-DB
```

Example 10-5 shows no (*,G) entry for 231.1.1.1 because the core CRS routers are not part of the shared tree and have no knowledge of the PIM join messages sent toward the RP by the last hop router.

Consider a situation where a source on 7600-1-Paris router starts to send traffic for group address 231.1.1.1.

When the first hop router 7600-paris router receives a multicast packet from a source for the first time, it will encapsulate the first multicast packet into a PIM register message and send it toward the 7200-Paris router that is functioning as the RP. Via the standard PIM SM mechanism, packets will first be forwarded natively via shared tree by the RP, but then will be switched to the SPT by the last hop router.

The PIM register message from the first hop router is sent unicast toward the RP. The RP receives this packet and forwards it based on its multicast routing table outgoing interface list, or O-list. The RP then sends a Join/Prune message using multicast toward the source. The purpose of this Join/Prune is to enable building of an (S,G) entry and the shortest path tree between the RP and Source. After traffic starts arriving at the RP by ways of the multicast (S,G) entry, the RP sends a register stop message to inform the source to no longer send encapsulated register messages. If the RP does not have an MRIB entry for the route, it will perform registration stop or suppression as there is no route available in this scenario.

So far the discussion has revolved around the forwarding of packets on the shared tree taking the path through the RP. When the last hop router receives the multicast traffic, it can see the source address of the incoming stream. Furthermore, the router can discern the RPF interface for this multicast traffic source address and observe that it is not the same as the one on which the traffic arrives at that moment via the rendezvous point router. The last hop router can initiate a PIM join message toward the source on the shortest path route (also known as the SPT) for the source. When the traffic is received on the SPT, the last hop router can prune itself from the RP tree.

Example 10-6 shows the mrib route for the group address 231.1.1.1 after the multicast traffic has converged to the SPT for the source.

Example 10-6 *State of mrib on Last Hop After SPT*

```
RP/0/8/CPU0:GSR1-SJC#show mrib route 231.1.1.1
IP Multicast Routing Information Base
Entry flags: L - Domain-Local Source, E - External Source to the Domain,
    C - Directly-Connected Check, S - Signal, IA - Inherit Accept,
    IF - Inherit From, D - Drop, MA - MDT Address, ME - MDT Encap,
    MD - MDT Decap, MT - MDT Threshold Crossed, MH - MDT interface handle
    CD - Conditional Decap
Interface flags: F - Forward, A - Accept, IC - Internal Copy,
    NS - Negate Signal, DP - Don't Preserve, SP - Signal Present,
    II - Internal Interest, ID - Internal Disinterest, LI - Local Interest,
    LD - Local Disinterest, DI - Decapsulation Interface
    EI - Encapsulation Interface, MI - MDT Interface
(*,231.1.1.1) RPF nbr: 64.1.6.2 Flags: C
  Incoming Interface List
    GigabitEthernet0/0/1/6 Flags: A NS
  Outgoing Interface List
    GigabitEthernet0/0/1/3.1 Flags: F NS LI
(171.1.1.1,231.1.1.1) RPF nbr: 64.1.2.2 Flags:
  Incoming Interface List
    TenGigE0/1/1/0 Flags: A
  Outgoing Interface List
    GigabitEthernet0/0/1/3.1 Flags: F NS
!
!
RP/0/8/CPU0:GSR1-SJC#show pim topology 231.1.1.1
IP PIM Multicast Topology Table
Entry state: (*/S,G)[RPT/SPT] Protocol Uptime Info
Entry flags: KAT - Keep Alive Timer, AA - Assume Alive, PA - Probe Alive,
    RA - Really Alive, LH - Last Hop, DSS - Don't Signal Sources,
    RR - Register Received, SR - Sending Registers, E - MSDP External,
    DCC - Don't Check Connected,
    ME - MDT Encap, MD - MDT Decap,
    MT - Crossed Data MDT threshold, MA - Data MDT group assigned
```

```
Interface state: Name, Uptime, Fwd, Info
Interface flags: LI - Local Interest, LD - Local Dissinterest,
    II - Internal Interest, ID - Internal Dissinterest,
    LH - Last Hop, AS - Assert, AB - Admin Boundary
(*,231.1.1.1) SM Up: 01:58:21 RP: 192.168.253.4
JP: Join(00:00:28) RPF: GigabitEthernet0/0/1/6,64.1.6.2 Flags: LH
  GigabitEthernet0/0/1/3.1     01:58:21   fwd LI LH
(171.1.1.1,231.1.1.1)SPT SM Up: 01:21:07
JP: Join(00:00:38) RPF: TenGigE0/1/1/0,64.1.2.2 Flags: KAT(00:03:01) RA
  No interfaces in immediate olist
```

Example 10-6 shows the mrib entry for source-based SPT. Notice the A flag has changed from being on the RPF interface toward RP to the TenGigE0/1/1/0 interface pointing toward the source on the SPT. The output of **show pim topology** indicates a Keep Alive Timer (KAT). The KAT timer duration is 3.5 minutes and is used to periodically check whether traffic is flowing for an (S,G) route. The output also shows a Really Alive (RA) flag for the (S,G) entry; PIM sets this flag when it receives an indication that the (S,G) route has seen traffic.

As mentioned earlier, all communications between PIM and MFIB take place via MRIB. MFIB is the line card–forwarding component in the multicast architecture, and it is aware of multicast traffic arriving on the line card interface. When PIM KAT expires and traffic is no longer running for an (S,G) route, PIM sets an Assume Alive (AA) flag, restarts the KAT for a duration of 1 minute and 5 seconds, and removes the Negate Signal (NS) flag from the MFIB on the incoming interface. In the context of SM forwarding, the purpose of the NS flag is to provide a signal for PIM based on the state of the (S,G) flow and the state of the KAT timer.

On arrival of the next data traffic, PIM gets signaled by MFIB using the MRIB as the communication path. PIM then resets the KAT and replaces the Assume Alive (AA) flag with Really Alive (RA) flag. The NS flag is again set on the MRIB and MFIB entries until the expiration of the KAT, at which point the whole cycle is repeated again. Therefore, IOS XR PIM maintains a way to age out a multicast PIM topology entry by triggering data traffic. PIM topology entries can also be added and deleted by the regular PIM join/prune mechanism.

The flags discussed in the preceding discussion are shown in Table 10-1.

Table 10-1 *Overview of Common Multicast Flags for Sparse Mode Forwarding*

Flag	Process	Description
Keep Alive Timer (KAT)	PIM	KAT is used to check that traffic is flowing for the (S,G) route on which it is set. As long as traffic is running for an (S,G) route, KAT is running and the route will not be timed out. The KAT runs for 3.5 minutes, and then the route goes into KAT-probing mode for as long as 65 seconds. If no traffic is seen during the probing interval, the route is deleted.
Really Alive (RA)	PIM	RA is seen with the KAT. PIM sets this flag when it has been signaled that the route has seen traffic.
Assume Alive (AA)	PIM	AA is set for (S,G) routes after the route has been alive once and the KAT 3.5 minute timer has expired.
Negate Signal (NS)	MRIB/MFIB	NS provides a signal for PIM based on the state of the (S,G) flow and the state of KAT.
Accept A	MRIB/MFIB	For shared tree, the A flag indicates the RPF interface to the rendezvous point. For SPT, it is set against the RPF interface on the shortest path to the source.
Forward	MRIB/MFIB	Shows the interface in the forwarding path.

Example 10-7 shows the PIM topology entries on the CRS routers on the SPT.

Example 10-7 *PIM Topology and MRIB on SPT Router PARIS-CRS1*

```
RP/0/RP0/CPU0:PARIS-CRS2#show pim  topology 231.1.1.1
IP PIM Multicast Topology Table
Entry state: (*/S,G)[RPT/SPT] Protocol Uptime Info
Entry flags: KAT - Keep Alive Timer, AA - Assume Alive, PA - Probe Alive,
    RA - Really Alive, LH - Last Hop, DSS - Don't Signal Sources,
    RR - Register Received, SR - Sending Registers, E - MSDP External,
    DCC - Don't Check Connected,
    ME - MDT Encap, MD - MDT Decap,
    MT - Crossed Data MDT threshold, MA - Data MDT group assigned
Interface state: Name, Uptime, Fwd, Info
Interface flags: LI - Local Interest, LD - Local Dissinterest,
    II - Internal Interest, ID - Internal Dissinterest,
    LH - Last Hop, AS - Assert, AB - Admin Boundary
(171.1.1.1,231.1.1.1)SPT SM Up: 01:29:08
JP: Join(00:00:45) RPF: TenGigE0/0/0/6,64.1.5.2 Flags:
  Bundle-Ether1.3258          01:29:08  fwd Join(00:03:25)
!
!
RP/0/RP0/CPU0:PARIS-CRS2#show mrib route 231.1.1.1
IP Multicast Routing Information Base
```

```
Entry flags: L - Domain-Local Source, E - External Source to the Domain,
    C - Directly-Connected Check, S - Signal, IA - Inherit Accept,
    IF - Inherit From, D - Drop, MA - MDT Address, ME - MDT Encap,
    MD - MDT Decap, MT - MDT Threshold Crossed, MH - MDT interface handle
    CD - Conditional Decap
Interface flags: F - Forward, A - Accept, IC - Internal Copy,
    NS - Negate Signal, DP - Don't Preserve, SP - Signal Present,
    II - Internal Interest, ID - Internal Disinterest, LI - Local Interest,
    LD - Local Disinterest, DI - Decapsulation Interface
    EI - Encapsulation Interface, MI - MDT Interface
(171.1.1.1,231.1.1.1) RPF nbr: 64.1.5.2 Flags:
  Incoming Interface List
    TenGigE0/0/0/6 Flags: A
  Outgoing Interface List
    Bundle-Ether1.3258 (0/0/CPU0) Flags: F NS
!
!
RP/0/RP0/CPU0:PARIS-CRS2#show mfib route 231.1.1.1
IP Multicast Forwarding Information Base
Entry flags: C - Directly-Connected Check, S - Signal, D - Drop,
  IA - Inherit Accept, IF - Inherit From, MA - MDT Address,
  ME - MDT Encap, MD - MDT Decap, MT - MDT Threshold Crossed,
  MH - MDT interface handle, CD - Conditional Decap,
  DT - MDT Decap True
Interface flags: F - Forward, A - Accept, IC - Internal Copy,
  NS - Negate Signal, DP - Don't Preserve, SP - Signal Present,
  EG - Egress, EI - Encapsulation Interface, MI - MDT Interface
Forwarding Counts: Packets in/Packets out/Bytes out
Failure Counts: RPF / TTL / Empty Olist / Encap RL / Other
(171.1.1.1,231.1.1.1),   Flags:
  Last Used: never
  SW Forwarding Counts: 0/0/0
  Failure Counts: 0/0/0/0/0
  Bundle-Ether1.3258 Flags:  NS
  TenGigE0/0/0/6 Flags:  A
!
!
```

Example 10-7 shows the interfaces on which PIM joins are received and shows the interfaces with Accept and Forward Flags, indicating the flow of the multicast (S,G) traffic.

Example 10-8 shows PIM topology and MRIB entries on the router SJC-CRS1.

Example 10-8 *PIM Topology and MRIB on SPT Router SJC-CRS1*

```
RP/0/RP0/CPU0:SJC-CRS1#show pim topology
IP PIM Multicast Topology Table
Entry state: (*/S,G)[RPT/SPT] Protocol Uptime Info
Entry flags: KAT - Keep Alive Timer, AA - Assume Alive, PA - Probe Alive,
    RA - Really Alive, LH - Last Hop, DSS - Don't Signal Sources,
    RR - Register Received, SR - Sending Registers, E - MSDP External,
    DCC - Don't Check Connected,
    ME - MDT Encap, MD - MDT Decap,
    MT - Crossed Data MDT threshold, MA - Data MDT group assigned
Interface state: Name, Uptime, Fwd, Info
Interface flags: LI - Local Interest, LD - Local Dissinterest,
    II - Internal Interest, ID - Internal Dissinterest,
    LH - Last Hop, AS - Assert, AB - Admin Boundary
(*,224.0.1.40) DM Up: 2d07h RP: 0.0.0.0
JP: Null(never) RPF: Null,0.0.0.0 Flags: LH DSS
  TenGigE0/0/0/1               06:53:40  off LI II LH
  GigabitEthernet0/7/0/2       2d07h     off LI LH
(171.1.1.1,231.1.1.1)SPT SM Up: 00:01:13
JP: Join(00:00:40) RPF: Bundle-Ether1.3258,64.1.4.2 Flags:
  TenGigE0/0/0/1               00:01:12  fwd Join(00:03:13)

RP/0/RP0/CPU0:SJC-CRS1#show mrib route 231.1.1.1
IP Multicast Routing Information Base
Entry flags: L - Domain-Local Source, E - External Source to the Domain,
    C - Directly-Connected Check, S - Signal, IA - Inherit Accept,
    IF - Inherit From, D - Drop, MA - MDT Address, ME - MDT Encap,
    MD - MDT Decap, MT - MDT Threshold Crossed, MH - MDT interface handle
    CD - Conditional Decap
Interface flags: F - Forward, A - Accept, IC - Internal Copy,
    NS - Negate Signal, DP - Don't Preserve, SP - Signal Present,
    II - Internal Interest, ID - Internal Disinterest, LI - Local Interest,
    LD - Local Disinterest, DI - Decapsulation Interface
    EI - Encapsulation Interface, MI - MDT Interface
(171.1.1.1,231.1.1.1) RPF nbr: 64.1.4.2 Flags:
  Incoming Interface List
    Bundle-Ether1.3258 Flags: A
  Outgoing Interface List
    TenGigE0/0/0/1 Flags: F NS
```

Example 10-8 shows the interfaces on which PIM joins are received and shows the interfaces with Accept and Forward flags, indicating the flow of the multicast (S,G) traffic. Although there were no mrib entries in the absence of traffic, the SPT joins create (S,G) states on the routers in the shortest path tree.

Even though the topic of discussion is Cisco IOS XR, Example 10-9 illustrates the mroute entries on the IOS-based RP router and the first hop IOS 7600-1-Paris router.

Example 10-9 *mroute Entries on the Rendezvous Point and First Hop Routers*

```
7200-Paris#show ip mroute 231.1.1.1
IP Multicast Routing Table
Flags: D - Dense, S - Sparse, B - Bidir Group, s - SSM Group, C - Connected,
       L - Local, P - Pruned, R - RP-bit set, F - Register flag,
       T - SPT-bit set, J - Join SPT, M - MSDP created entry,
       X - Proxy Join Timer Running, A - Candidate for MSDP Advertisement,
       U - URD, I - Received Source Specific Host Report,
       Z - Multicast Tunnel, z - MDT-data group sender,
       Y - Joined MDT-data group, y - Sending to MDT-data group
Outgoing interface flags: H - Hardware switched, A - Assert winner
 Timers: Uptime/Expires
 Interface state: Interface, Next-Hop or VCD, State/Mode
(*, 231.1.1.1), 01:45:20/00:03:11, RP 192.168.253.4, flags: S
  Incoming interface: Null, RPF nbr 0.0.0.0
  Outgoing interface list:
    GigabitEthernet0/1, Forward/Sparse, 01:45:20/00:03:11
(171.1.1.1, 231.1.1.1), 01:33:07/00:01:52, flags: PT
  Incoming interface: GigabitEthernet0/2, RPF nbr 64.1.3.2
  Outgoing interface list: Null
!
7600-1-PARIS#show ip mroute 231.1.1.1
IP Multicast Routing Table
Flags: D - Dense, S - Sparse, B - Bidir Group, s - SSM Group, C - Connected,
       L - Local, P - Pruned, R - RP-bit set, F - Register flag,
       T - SPT-bit set, J - Join SPT, M - MSDP created entry, E - Extranet,
       X - Proxy Join Timer Running, A - Candidate for MSDP Advertisement,
       U - URD, I - Received Source Specific Host Report,
       Z - Multicast Tunnel, z - MDT-data group sender,
       Y - Joined MDT-data group, y - Sending to MDT-data group,
       V - RD & Vector, v - Vector
Outgoing interface flags: H - Hardware switched, A - Assert winner
 Timers: Uptime/Expires
 Interface state: Interface, Next-Hop or VCD, State/Mode
(*, 231.1.1.1), 01:33:51/stopped, RP 192.168.253.4, flags: SPF
  Incoming interface: TenGigabitEthernet1/1, RPF nbr 64.1.5.1, RPF-MFD
  Outgoing interface list: Null
(171.1.1.1, 231.1.1.1), 01:33:51/00:03:21, flags: FT
  Incoming interface: GigabitEthernet2/11.1, RPF nbr 0.0.0.0, RPF-MFD
  Outgoing interface list:
    TenGigabitEthernet1/1, Forward/Sparse, 01:33:51/00:02:42, H
```

Example 10-9 shows the mroute entry on the Rendezvous Point router after the multicast traffic has switched to the shortest path tree and is no longer running through this router. This entry was created after receiving an (S,G) RPT-bit prune message from the last hop IOS XR router GSR1-SJC.

This example also shows the mroute entry at the first hop 7600 router depicting a hardware-switched (S,G) entry that now follows the SPT.

Understanding PIM Source Specific Multicast on IOS XR

Source Specific Multicast (SSM) introduces a multicast forwarding paradigm based on a source-based tree. The subscription to an SSM-based transmission is commonly provided via IGMPv3. As mentioned earlier, IGMPv3 is the default IGMP version on an IOS XR router. IGMPv3 provides hosts with the capability to express interest in a group membership based on a certain source. This allows a simple and more efficient control for routing multicast traffic where only a specified source can send to a multicast group address. Because SSM forwarding is based entirely on a source-based tree, there is no concept of the rendezvous point that was required in the forwarding of multicast traffic using sparse mode. This section depicts IOS XR implementation via SSM-specific multicast routing and forwarding entries using Figure 10-2 as an example. Examples 10-10 and 10-11 show PIM SSM mrib states for PIM SSM where IOS XR is a first hop and a last hop router, respectively.

Example 10-10 *PIM SSM Using IOS XR as a Last Hop Router*

```
7600-1-PARIS#show ip mroute 232.0.0.0
IP Multicast Routing Table
Flags: D - Dense, S - Sparse, B - Bidir Group, s - SSM Group, C - Connected,
       L - Local, P - Pruned, R - RP-bit set, F - Register flag,
       T - SPT-bit set, J - Join SPT, M - MSDP created entry, E - Extranet,
       X - Proxy Join Timer Running, A - Candidate for MSDP Advertisement,
       U - URD, I - Received Source Specific Host Report,
       Z - Multicast Tunnel, z - MDT-data group sender,
       Y - Joined MDT-data group, y - Sending to MDT-data group,
       V - RD & Vector, v - Vector
Outgoing interface flags: H - Hardware switched, A - Assert winner
 Timers: Uptime/Expires
 Interface state: Interface, Next-Hop or VCD, State/Mode
(171.1.1.1, 232.0.0.0), 00:17:03/00:03:24, flags: sT
  Incoming interface: GigabitEthernet2/11.1, RPF nbr 0.0.0.0, RPF-MFD
  Outgoing interface list:
    TenGigabitEthernet1/1, Forward/Sparse, 00:17:03/00:03:24, H
!
! Last hop router running IOS XR
!
RP/0/8/CPU0:GSR1-SJC#show mrib route 232.0.0.0
IP Multicast Routing Information Base
Entry flags: L - Domain-Local Source, E - External Source to the Domain,
```

```
    C - Directly-Connected Check, S - Signal, IA - Inherit Accept,
    IF - Inherit From, D - Drop, MA - MDT Address, ME - MDT Encap,
    MD - MDT Decap, MT - MDT Threshold Crossed, MH - MDT interface handle
    CD - Conditional Decap
Interface flags: F - Forward, A - Accept, IC - Internal Copy,
    NS - Negate Signal, DP - Don't Preserve, SP - Signal Present,
    II - Internal Interest, ID - Internal Disinterest, LI - Local Interest,
    LD - Local Disinterest, DI - Decapsulation Interface
    EI - Encapsulation Interface, MI - MDT Interface
(171.1.1.1,232.0.0.0) RPF nbr: 64.1.2.2 Flags:
  Incoming Interface List
    TenGigE0/1/1/0 Flags: A
  Outgoing Interface List
    GigabitEthernet0/0/1/3.1 Flags: F NS LI
!
!
RP/0/8/CPU0:GSR1-SJC#show pim topology 232.0.0.0
IP PIM Multicast Topology Table
Entry state: (*/S,G)[RPT/SPT] Protocol Uptime Info
Entry flags: KAT - Keep Alive Timer, AA - Assume Alive, PA - Probe Alive,
    RA - Really Alive, LH - Last Hop, DSS - Don't Signal Sources,
    RR - Register Received, SR - Sending Registers, E - MSDP External,
    DCC - Don't Check Connected,
    ME - MDT Encap, MD - MDT Decap,
    MT - Crossed Data MDT threshold, MA - Data MDT group assigned
Interface state: Name, Uptime, Fwd, Info
Interface flags: LI - Local Interest, LD - Local Dissinterest,
    II - Internal Interest, ID - Internal Dissinterest,
    LH - Last Hop, AS - Assert, AB - Admin Boundary
(171.1.1.1,232.0.0.0)SPT SSM Up: 00:33:36
JP: Join(now) RPF: TenGigE0/1/1/0,64.1.2.2 Flags:
  GigabitEthernet0/0/1/3.1    00:33:36  fwd LI LH
```

Example 10-10 shows the first hop IOS router where (S,G) SSM traffic arrives for group 232.0.0.0 and source 171.1.1.1. The sT flags on the first hop 7600-1-Paris IOS router represent SSM-based forwarding with SPT bit set. The last hop GSR1-SJC router is receiving an IGMPv3 join for source 171.1.1.1 and group 232.0.0.0. This last hop router only creates an (S,G) entry in mrib.

Example 10-11 shows PIM and MRIB entries for a case where IOS XR is a first hop router and the IGMP v3 join is being received on 7600-1-Paris router's GigabitEthernet2/11.1 interface for (S,G) pair 181.1.1.1 as source and 232.0.0.1 group address.

Example 10-11 *PIM SSM Using Cisco IOS XR as a First Hop Router*

```
7600-1-PARIS#show ip mroute 232.0.0.1
IP Multicast Routing Table
Flags: D - Dense, S - Sparse, B - Bidir Group, s - SSM Group, C - Connected,
       L - Local, P - Pruned, R - RP-bit set, F - Register flag,
       T - SPT-bit set, J - Join SPT, M - MSDP created entry, E - Extranet,
       X - Proxy Join Timer Running, A - Candidate for MSDP Advertisement,
       U - URD, I - Received Source Specific Host Report,
       Z - Multicast Tunnel, z - MDT-data group sender,
       Y - Joined MDT-data group, y - Sending to MDT-data group,
       V - RD & Vector, v - Vector
Outgoing interface flags: H - Hardware switched, A - Assert winner
 Timers: Uptime/Expires
 Interface state: Interface, Next-Hop or VCD, State/Mode
(181.1.1.1, 232.0.0.1), 00:03:15/00:02:56, flags: sTI
  Incoming interface: TenGigabitEthernet1/1, RPF nbr 64.1.5.1, RPF-MFD
  Outgoing interface list:
    GigabitEthernet2/11.1, Forward/Sparse, 00:03:15/00:02:44, H
!
!
RP/0/8/CPU0:GSR1-SJC#show mrib route 232.0.0.1 detail
IP Multicast Routing Information Base
Entry flags: L - Domain-Local Source, E - External Source to the Domain,
    C - Directly-Connected Check, S - Signal, IA - Inherit Accept,
    IF - Inherit From, D - Drop, MA - MDT Address, ME - MDT Encap,
    MD - MDT Decap, MT - MDT Threshold Crossed, MH - MDT interface handle
    CD - Conditional Decap
Interface flags: F - Forward, A - Accept, IC - Internal Copy,
    NS - Negate Signal, DP - Don't Preserve, SP - Signal Present,
    II - Internal Interest, ID - Internal Disinterest, LI - Local Interest,
    LD - Local Disinterest, DI - Decapsulation Interface
    EI - Encapsulation Interface, MI - MDT Interface
(181.1.1.1,232.0.0.1) Ver: 0x464f RPF nbr: 181.1.1.1 Flags:, FMA: 0x20000
  Incoming Interface List
    GigabitEthernet0/0/1/3.1 Flags: A
  Outgoing Interface List
    TenGigE0/1/1/0 Flags: F NS
RP/0/8/CPU0:GSR1-SJC#
RP/0/8/CPU0:GSR1-SJC#show pim topology 232.0.0.1
IP PIM Multicast Topology Table
Entry state: (*/S,G)[RPT/SPT] Protocol Uptime Info
Entry flags: KAT - Keep Alive Timer, AA - Assume Alive, PA - Probe Alive,
    RA - Really Alive, LH - Last Hop, DSS - Don't Signal Sources,
    RR - Register Received, SR - Sending Registers, E - MSDP External,
    DCC - Don't Check Connected,
```

```
    ME - MDT Encap, MD - MDT Decap,
    MT - Crossed Data MDT threshold, MA - Data MDT group assigned
Interface state: Name, Uptime, Fwd, Info
Interface flags: LI - Local Interest, LD - Local Dissinterest,
    II - Internal Interest, ID - Internal Dissinterest,
    LH - Last Hop, AS - Assert, AB - Admin Boundary
(181.1.1.1,232.0.0.1)SPT SSM Up: 00:04:45
JP: Join(never) RPF: GigabitEthernet0/0/1/3.1,181.1.1.1* Flags:
  TenGigE0/1/1/0              00:04:45  fwd Join(00:02:48)
RP/0/8/CPU0:GSR1-SJC#
```

Example 10-11 shows the last hop IOS router's mroute entry that indicates an sTI flag. The sTI flag implies that PIM is using SSM mode, as indicated by the presence of the lowercase s flag. In this case the forwarding is being done on the SPT indicated by the T flag. Furthermore, the flag I indicates the reception of a source-specific host report for the group 232.0.0.1. The PIM topology for the first hop IOS XR GSR1-SJC router indicates SSM (S,G) entry and RPF entry toward the source of traffic. The fwd Join is shown for the TenGigE0/1/1/0 interface, which is in the forwarding shortest path toward the last hop 7600-1-Paris router.

Configuring Cisco IOS XR Multicast

This section describes how to configure IOS XR multicast. The first step is to enable multicast routing. Configuring IGMP and PIM follows.

Enabling Multicast Routing

To configure multicast in Cisco IOS XR, the first step is to enable multicast routing an IPv4 or an IPv6 address family. As mentioned earlier, IOS XR IGMPv3 is enabled by default. Multicast routing and forwarding can be enabled on all or selective interfaces under the multicast routing process:

```
configure
multicast-routing
          address-family {ipv4 | ipv6}
                interface {interface | all} enable
exit
```

Configuring IGMP

The IGMP version can be specified with the **version** command. Moreover, the IGMP configuration stanza allows the configuration of **static-group** and **join-group**. It also allows the setting of IGMP query interval. The configuration CLI is shown as follows:

```
router {igmp|mld}
        version {1|2|3}
        interface {interface}
```

```
        static-group {group-address [inc-mask mask count cnt] [source-address]}
        join-group {group-address [source-address]}
       query-interval {seconds}
```

Configuring PIM

To configure PIM-specific parameters, the router pim configuration mode is used. The default configuration prompt is for IPv4 and will be seen as config-pim-default-ipv4. To change the configuration mode for IPv6-related PIM configuration, issue the command **router pim address-family ipv6** from the global configuration mode.

To ensure the election of a router as PIM DR on a LAN segment, use the **dr-priority** command. The router with the highest DR priority will win the election.

By default, at a preconfigured threshold, the last hop router can join the shortest path tree to receive multicast traffic. To change this behavior, use the command **spt-threshold infinity** under the router pim configuration mode. This will result in the last hop router permanently joining the shared tree.

The frequency at which a router sends PIM hello messages to its neighbors can be configured by the **hello-interval** command. By default, PIM hello messages are sent once every 30 seconds. If the **hello-interval** is configured under router pim configuration mode, all the interfaces with PIM enabled will inherit this value. To change the hello interval on the interface, use the **hello-interval** command under interface configuration mode, as follows:

```
router pim [address-family {ipv4 | ipv6}]
        dr-priority {value}
        spt-threshold infinity {[group-list {access-list}]| <cr>}
        hello-interval {seconds}
        interface {interface} enable
        hello-interval {seconds}
```

Configuring Static RP

To configure static RP for SM operation, use the **rp-address** command under the router pim configuration mode. Use the **group-access-list** keyword to configure RP for a specific multicast group or a range of multicast groups. If a router is statically configured as a PIM RP and it receives information about another RP for the same group via Auto-RP or BSR, the latter will take precedence. To ensure static RP is always preferred in this scenario, use the **override** keyword with the **rp-address** command:

```
configure
router pim [address-family {ipv4 | ipv6}]
rp-address {ip-address} [group-access-list] [bidir] [override]
```

Auto-RP

To configure Auto-RP in the network, at least one router must be the candidate RP. The candidate RP is configured using the **auto-rp candidate-rp** command under router pim configuration mode. The **instance** keyword in the auto-rp configuration is the interface from which the candidate RP messages are sourced. The number of hops for the candidate RP messages in IOS XR can be controlled using the **scope** keyword. A router can also advertise itself to be the candidate RP for a specific multicast group or a range of multicast groups. This is configured by using the **group-list** keyword. The frequency of candidate RP messages can be controlled by using the **interval** keyword.

For the dynamic RP assignment using Auto-RP, one router in the network must be selected to function as the mapping agent. The mapping agent is configured using the **auto-rp mapping-agent** command in the router pim configuration mode. The interface from which the mapping agent messages are sourced has to be specified.

The syntax follows:

```
configure
router pim
auto-rp candidate-rp {interface}   scope {ttl-value} [group-list access-list-
  name] [interval seconds] [bidir]
auto-rp mapping-agent {interface} scope {ttl-value} [interval seconds]
exit
```

BSR

To configure dynamic RP assignment in the network via BSR, use the **candidate-bsr** command under the router pim configuration mode to announce the candidacy as a BSR. The *ip-address* keyword is the IP address of the BSR candidate. The **priority** value is used to decide between multiple routers. The higher the priority, the more weight it has in the BSR election. If the priority results in a tie, the router with the higher IP address is preferred. To advertise a router's candidacy as a PIMv2 RP, use the **bsr candidate-rp** command in the router pim configuration mode. The RP candidacy can also be advertised for specific multicast groups using the **group-list** keyword. The frequency of announcement of the candidate RP messages can be controlled via the **interval** keyword. The syntax follows:

```
configure
router pim [address-family {ipv4 | ipv6}]
        bsr candidate-bsr {ip-address} [hash-mask-len length] [priority value]
        bsr candidate-rp {ip-address} [group-list access-list] [interval
          seconds] [priority value]

exit
```

PIM SSM Configuration

By default, PIM SSM is enabled for multicast addresses of the 232.0.0.0/8 range. SSM can be disabled on the router using the **disable** keyword. The range for multicast addresses for SSM can be changed using the **range** keyword with an access list, as follows:

```
configure
multicast-routing [address-family {ipv4 | ipv6}]
ssm [allow-override | disable | range access-list]
```

Monitoring and Troubleshooting Cisco IOS XR Multicast

This section addresses the monitoring and troubleshooting aspects of Cisco IOS XR multicast. This section draws its examples from a CRS-1 router platform running an IOS XR image release 3.6.0 or greater. The platform-dependent commands might vary among IOS XR platforms, although the monitoring and troubleshooting concepts still prevail. Example 10-12 shows an output of **show run multicast-routing** command from a CRS-1.

Example 10-12 *Enabling Multicast PIM Logging, Counters, and OOM*

```
RP/0/RP0/CPU0:CRS1-1#show running-config multicast-routing
multicast-routing
 address-family ipv4
  log-traps
  oom-handling
  rate-per-route
  interface all enable
  accounting per-prefix
 !
!
```

The configurations shown in Example 10-12 help with monitoring and troubleshooting. The configuration command **log-traps** helps in the logging of messages if the PIM neighbor relationship goes down for some reason. The **oom-handling** (out of memory handling) command helps protect depleted memory resources from getting overwhelmed by any further pim joins. Finally, **rate-per-route** and **accounting per-prefix** provide important counter functionality that is useful for monitoring and troubleshooting (S,G) flows.

Table 10-2 represents some general guidelines for developing a multicast health check methodology.

Table 10-2 *Multicast Health Checks*

Health Check Items	Cisco IOS XR Commands
Number of (S,G) flows expected on your router	**show pim summary**
Expected incoming and outgoing interfaces for an (S,G)	**show mrib route** <*group_address*> detail | <cr> **show mfib route** <*group_address*>
Knowing your RPF addresses and interfaces. Also checks whether muRIB has been invoked.	**show pim rpf** [*IP_address* | *summary*]
Be aware of an (S,G) rate	**show mfib route rate**
show route ipv4 multicast	muRIB entries

Health Check Items	Cisco IOS XR Commands
Fabric health Verify that fabric planes are up and that Fabric group identifiers are correctly programmed	(admin) **show controller fabric plane all** (admin) **#show controllers fabric fgid information id** <*fgid*> **brief**

On a CRS-1 router, the methodology described in the following sections proceeds from ingress to egress using **show** commands at different stages to debug multicast forwarding issues.

Debugging Multicast on the CRS Router's Ingress Path

Verify ingress multicast Layer 2 counters with the following command syntax. The same command may be used on the egress:

```
show int tenGigE <interface_> | incl multicast
show int bundle-ether <bundle> | incl multicast
show int tenGigE <interface> accounting
```

The following commands help verify whether packets are dropped on the ingress PLIM ASIC of a CRS line card:

```
show controllers <tenGigE interface_>  stats
show controllers plim asic statistics interface tenGigE <interface_number> |
  include MulticastPkts
```

The following command checks the Layer 3 forwarding engine. It indicates multicast drops due to a wrong incoming interface and whether traffic might be getting punted.

```
show controllers pse statistics ingress location <location>
show controllers ingressq statistics location <location>| be Ingressq Drops
```

Debugging Multicast in Router's Fabric and Egress Path

Verify that all fabric planes are up and the Uncorrectable Cell Error (UCE) statistics are not incrementing. Also the following commands give high and low priority multicast and unicast counters in the S2 and S3 stage of the fabric.

Verify all planes are up and none show multicast down:

```
(admin)#show controllers fabric plane all  -
```

Verify UCE count is not incrementing:

```
(admin)#show controllers fabric plane all statistics -
```

Clear previous fabric plane error statistics with this command:

```
(admin)#clear controller fabric statistics plane all -
```

The following commands can be used to look for drops in the FabricQ:

```
show controllers fabricq statistics location <location>
```

The following command looks at PSE counters in the egress path:

```
show controllers pse statistics egress location <location>
```

The following command looks for drops related to egressQ:

show controllers egressq statistics location *<location>* | **incl drop**

show controller plim asic statistics summary location *<location>*

In most cases the above mentioned commands will be applicable to both unicast and multicast traffic.

Debugging an RPF Failure Using a Line Card MFIB Command

Earlier in this chapter, the command **show pim rpf** was used to see the control plane RPF information. The command shown in Example 10-13 gives forwarding plane information on multicast RPF using the counter HW Drop Counts: Ingress / Egress. The ingress HW drops are due to RPF and egress drops may be due to no output list or O-list.

Example 10-13 *Determining an RPF Failure Using an MFIB Command*

```
RP/0/RP0/CPU0:SJC-CRS1#show mfib ipv4 route statistics detail location 0/0/cpu0
IP Multicast Forwarding Information Base
Entry flags: C - Directly-Connected Check, S - Signal, D - Drop,
  IA - Inherit Accept, IF - Inherit From, MA - MDT Address,
  ME - MDT Encap, MD - MDT Decap, MT - MDT Threshold Crossed,
  MH - MDT interface handle, CD - Conditional Decap,
  DT - MDT Decap True
Interface flags: F - Forward, A - Accept, IC - Internal Copy,
  NS - Negate Signal, DP - Don't Preserve, SP - Signal Present,
  EG - Egress, EI - Encapsulation Interface, MI - MDT Interface
SW/HW Forwarding Counts: Packets in/Packets out/Bytes out
SW Failure Counts: RPF / TTL / Empty Olist / Encap RL / Other
HW Drop Counts: Ingress / Egress
HW Forwarding Rates: bps In/pps In/bps Out/pps Out
(*,231.1.1.1),   Flags:  C
  Last Used: never
  SW Forwarding Counts: 0/0/0
  SW Failure Counts: 0/0/0/0
  HW Forwarding Counts: N/A /N/A /N/A
  HW Drop Counts: N/A /N/A
  HW Forwarding Rates: N/A /N/A /N/A /N/A
  GigabitEthernet0/7/0/2 Flags:  A
  TenGigE0/0/0/1 Flags:  NS EG
(171.1.1.1,231.1.1.1),   Flags:
  Last Used: never
  SW Forwarding Counts: 0/0/0
  SW Failure Counts: 0/0/0/0
  HW Forwarding Counts: 4212583/4212240/5804466720
  HW Drop Counts: 0/0
  HW Forwarding Rates: 24274921/2201/24309536/2204
  TenGigE0/0/0/1 Flags:  NS EG
  Bundle-Ether1.3258 Flags:  A
```

Summary

This chapter explained the basic concepts behind Cisco IOS XR Multicast. IOS XR follows the same multicast routing protocols as other operating systems such as IOS; however, the configuration and **show** commands are quite different between the two operating systems.

This chapter introduced the MRIB components and its strategic position in the IOS XR multicast control and forwarding plane architecture. The various components that interact with MRIB to provide notifications to PIM were illustrated, along with examples on how multicast routing entries are formed. This chapter culminated in a discussion of multicast troubleshooting using the CRS-1 platform as an example. The troubleshooting methodology involves a combination of control plane and forwarding plane commands in systematically troubleshooting multicast forwarding issues.

References

- **Cisco.** Cisco IOS XR Multicast Configuration Guide, Release 3.6. http://www.cisco.com/
- **Cisco.** Cisco IOS XR Multicast Command Reference, Release 3.6. http://www.cisco.com/

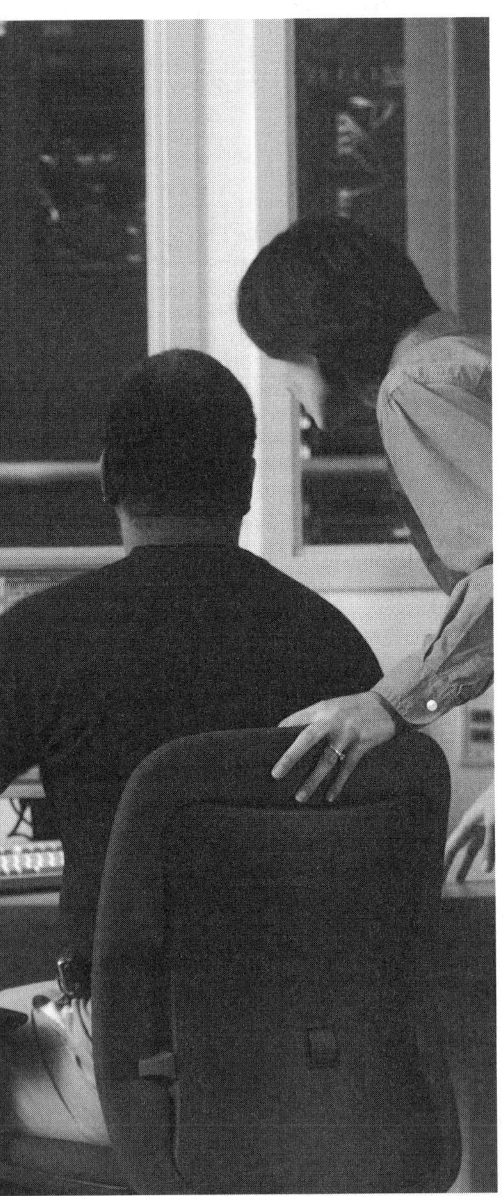

This chapter covers the following topics:

- Owner and Non-Owner SDR
- Understanding SDR Privileges
- Creating a Secure Domain Router
- DRP
- Configuring a Secure Domain Router
- Process Placement
- References

You might consider the Cisco CRS-1 router as a system; however, it is capable of functioning as a collection of one or more routers that share the same hardware infrastructure. This concept of a collection of routers is commonly referred to as *logical routers (LR)*, and Cisco calls this feature *Secure Domain Router (SDR)*. SDR is an IOS XR feature that provides secure partitioning isolation of hardware and software resources within a single system. A feature such as SDR is attractive to network planners because it allows a reduction in operating expense by consolidating multiple network layers while maintaining redundancy and network security. This capability allows network planners to target a higher return of investment. For network planners and engineering, this approach allows more control over the distribution of forwarding and control plane resources for specific services and applications.

CHAPTER 11

Secure Domain Router

The following sections provide more detail on SDRs, including configuration examples and the introduction of hardware, known as *distributed route process (DRP)*. A distributed route processor is necessary for the implementation of the SDR feature on a CRS-1. Distributed router processor can also be used to implement a feature called process placement, which is covered in the following sections. Note that SDR functions can also be implemented in the Cisco 12000 series running IOS XR using a performance route processor (PRP). Cisco XR 12000 series generally follow the same subset of configurations; however, detailed discussions and configurations are not covered in this chapter.

Owner and Non-Owner SDR

As the name suggests, each partitioned router provides a secure entity within the host CRS-1 system, or owner SDR, which is a feature first introduced in IOS XR version 3.3.0. An owner SDR is created by default when the system is first booted and cannot be deleted; therefore, it is always present. Use the command **show sdr summary** in admin mode to view the nodes to which the owner SDR is assigned an ID number of zero by the system. The function of the owner SDR is mandatory to facilitate all necessary and shared functions of the router. It assumes ownership of all unassigned resources (to a defined SDR). Therefore, the owner SDR oversees the function of all nodes in the CRS-1 system that require administrative-level privileges.

The owner SDR has the administrative privileges to create, view, and log non-owner SDR(s). User-defined SDRs are also referred to as *named SDRs*. When a user creates a named SDR, the SDR is considered a non-owner SDR. The task of creating named SDRs is allowed only from the admin mode of the owner SDR in an IOS XR operating system and is performed by a user who is logged in with root system privileges. This minimum set of privilege access is necessary or users will not have authority to create non-owner SDRs or assign any resources to the named SDR. It is imperative for security that the privilege level be sustained because assigning resources to a named SDR will cause service interruption to the node. When a named SDR is created, there is no impact to services or traffic associated with existing resources. However, resources assigned to the newly created named SDR from the owner SDR or another named SDR simulates an online insertion and removal (OIR). In other words, it is equivalent to removing the resource from one slot in the system and inserting into another. You should expect to see the resource reload as service and data traffic will be interrupted.

There are shared attributes and resources common to all SDRs. It is important to note that the shared resources are critical to the system's overall operation. Access is granted to any and all resources only from the owner SDR. It is critically important that security policy be properly applied. A security breach in this manner could lead to a systemwide or networkwide disruption. Some examples of shared resources that are common to SDR are

- Environmental resources
- Power supplies
- Fan trays
- Fan controllers
- Fabric cards

Figure 11-1 displays the separation of planes between the owner SDR and SDR1 (a named SDR). The separate SDRs share common resources essential for the system operation.

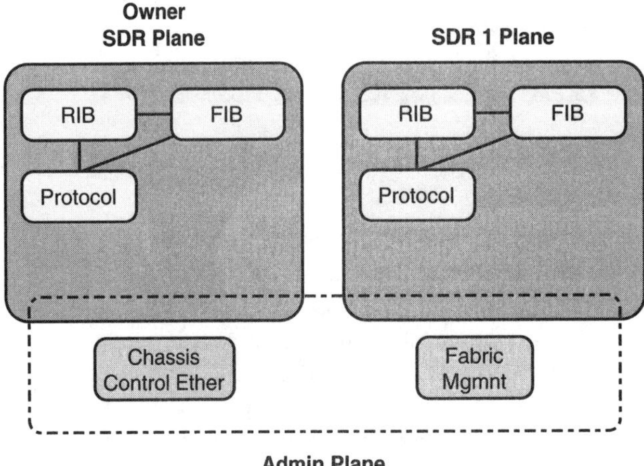

Figure 11-1 *SDR Shared Resources*

Distinguishing the differences between privilege levels can assist in troubleshooting and correcting administrative issues when creating SDRs. The next section explains SDR privileges.

Understanding SDR Privileges

SDRs are treated as separate secure logical entities where each SDR (owner and non-owner) has its own set of privileges and operates independently. The owner SDR contains the administrative privileges to the router and the privilege level to create named SDR within the owner-SDR. The root-system privilege is needed in administrative mode to create non-owner SDRs. Owner SDR users need root-lr (root logical router) privileges to access non-owner SDR administrative functions.

In the case of the owner SDR, the administrative and control function is upheld by the active route processor (RP). This functionality is called *Designated Secure Domain Router System Controller (DSDRSC)*. Each SDR has a DSDRSC preserving administrative and control function. In the case of a non-owner SDR, the DSDRSC function is maintained on the distributed route processor (DRP).

Table 11-1 is a reference of which resources are dedicated to SDRs and which are shared among SDRs.

Table 11-1 *Dedicated and Shared SDR Resources*

Area	Component	Specific per SDR	Shared Among SDRs
Hardware	RP	Yes	No
	DRP	Yes	No
	Line card	Yes	No
	System power	No	Yes
	Fan tray and fan controllers	No	Yes
	Fabric cards	No	Yes
Software	Exec-level config	Yes	Yes. Configurations in admin mode can affect all SDRs.
	Routing tables	Yes	No
	Forwarding tables	Yes	No
	Admin-level config	Yes	Yes. Admin-level command can impact owner SDR and non-owner SDRs.
	Process instances	Yes	A few processes are shared, systemwide processes such as LRd (SDR Deamon).
Management	SNMP traps	Yes	Yes. For example, shared power, fans, and fabric-related traps.
	SNMP polling	Yes	Shared for power, fans, and fabric-related MIBS.
	Syslogs	Yes	Yes. Some non-owner SDRs are logged to the owner SDR.
	Shared environment variables	N/A	Yes
Security	AAA	Yes	No
	LPTS	Yes	No

Creating a Secure Domain Router

Designated System Controller (DSC) can be configured as a pair for redundancy. The DSC should not be confused with the Designated Shelf Controller associated with the Cisco CRS-1 multishelf implementation. In the case of the owner SDR, the active and standby RP are redundant by default. The active RP maintains this role of DSDRSC.

In the CRS-1 family, DRPs can be inserted only into the data forwarding slots (in place of an MSC in the rear of the chassis) of the CRS-1. The DRP behaves in the same fashion as the route processor and contains two CPU processors enabling more processing power.

The DRP consists of two modules:

- The CRS-DRP-B-CPU board that hosts the two dual processor SMP complexes
- The CRS-DRP-PLIM board that hosts the access to management, auxiliary, and console ports and accessories such as the hard drive

Both modules are required for DRP operation. A DRP has two CPU and 4 gigabytes of memory for each SMP, for a total of 8 gigabytes. The DRP supports the suite of protocols equivalent to the dedicated route processors shipped with the system.

When creating an SDR, follow these steps:

Step 1. Plan which forwarding slots will occupy the DRPs. Take into account power zones for each chassis type.

Step 2. Insert the DRPs appropriately into the allotted forwarding slots. Take into consideration power zones for each chassis type when considering redundancy.

Step 3. Verify DRPs are able to boot properly and are functional.

Step 4. Optionally, pair the DRPs for redundancy and choose appropriate DRP slots.

Step 5. Create a named secure domain router through the command-line interface.

Step 6. Assign resources (modular service cards) to the newly created named SDR.

Step 7. Create AAA authentication on the new SDR.

Step 8. Log in and complete the configuration of preferred routing protocols and other related configurations to forward traffic as desired.

It is feasible to configure an SDR with a single DRP because a second DRP can be added without impact to services. However, Cisco recommends DRPs configured as pairs to optimize redundancy. Configuring SDR with single and redundant DRPs is explained in this chapter.

DRP

When DRP hardware is inserted for the first time in the CRS-1, the default configuration on the DRP is empty. It is up to the operator to provide all necessary configurations. The IOS XR operating system synchronizes the same IOS XR version configured on the owner SDR. IOS XR does not support different versions of IOS XR among SDRs within the same system. It's important to verify that the features intended to be implemented on a named SDR are supported in the IOS XR version of the owner SDR.

Example 11-1 displays output of the **show platform** command from the admin mode on a CRS-1 router to verify whether DRP have booted successfully. Notice that the output in slot 5 and slot 7 contains a DRP. The DRP in slot 5 is designated as 0/5/CPU0 and 0/5/CPU1. As mentioned earlier, there are two CPUs per DRP. The hardware containing CPUs is inserted on the rear slots of the chassis and DRP management cards inserted in the front (PLIM) slots.

Example 11-1 *Output of* show platform

```
RP/0/RP0/CPU0:CRS-2(admin)#show platform
Node             Type              PLIM           State             Config State
-----------------------------------------------------------------------------
0/5/SP           DRP(SP)           N/A            IOS XR RUN        PWR,NSHUT,MON
0/5/CPU0         DRP(Active)       DRP-ACC        IOS XR RUN        PWR,NSHUT,MON
0/5/CPU1         DRP(Active)       DRP-ACC        IOS XR RUN        PWR,NSHUT,MON
0/7/SP           DRP(SP)           N/A            IOS XR RUN        PWR,NSHUT,MON
0/7/CPU0         DRP(Active)       DRP-ACC        IOS XR RUN        PWR,NSHUT,MON
0/7/CPU1         DRP(Active)       DRP-ACC        IOS XR RUN        PWR,NSHUT,MON
0/RP0/CPU0       RP(Active)        N/A            IOS XR RUN        PWR,NSHUT,MON
0/RP1/CPU0       RP(Standby)       N/A            IOS XR PREP       PWR,NSHUT,MON
```

Slot allocation requires some consideration to maintain high availability within your CRS-1 system. See Figure 11-2 for the CRS-1 16-slot and Figure 11-3 for the CRS-1 8-slot display power distribution zone under consideration for higher availability. It is advised to configure DRPs in different power zones to increase redundancy and reliability. Cisco.com provides an excellent reference, which provides detailed reference of how power distribution is allocated to the CRS-1 to each node. The CRS-1 is comprised of two power shelves that distribute power across the chassis in six load zones providing redundancy in the event of multiple power module failure. The Power Shelves (PS-0 and PS-1) consist of three power modules within each power shelf (A0, A1, A2 and B0, B1, B2) that pair together to provide redundant power supply across the six load zones (Z1, Z2, Z3, Z4, Z5, Z6). For continuous operation of the SDRs in the event of power module failures, Cisco recommends placing the primary and secondary DRPs in different load zones. An MSC in a particular load zone can function until a power module in each power shelf fails. The power zones have slight differences between the CRS-1 8- and 16-slot chassis.

Figure 11-3 shows the power zone distribution for the CRS-1 8-slot chassis. Equal consideration should be given to all Cisco CRS-1 chassis.

Configuring a Secure Domain Router

This section discusses command-line interface (CLI) examples of SDR. DRPs have been inserted and assumed functional for the discussions and examples that follow. All configurations of SDR presented assume no previous configurations have been applied. This section covers verifying DRP booting, configuring an SDR, pairing DRPs for redundancy, and finally, assigning a resource to a named SDR.

Power Distribution Zones

Line Card Chassis Front View (PLIM-side) Slot Numbers

Line Card Chassis Slot Numbers and Module Location Rear (Line Card Side) View

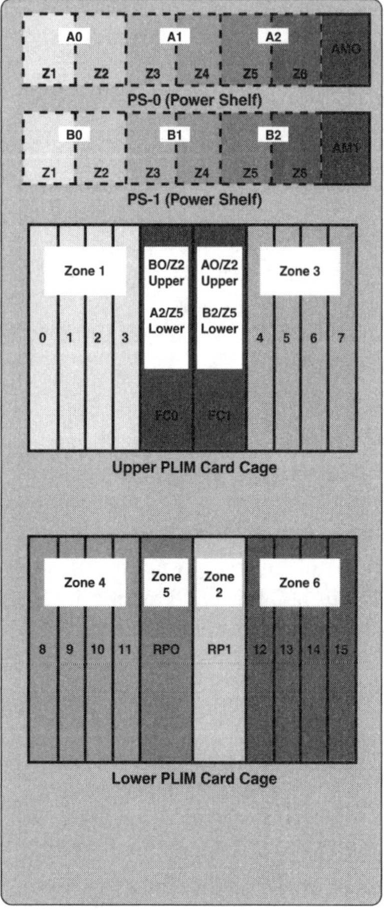

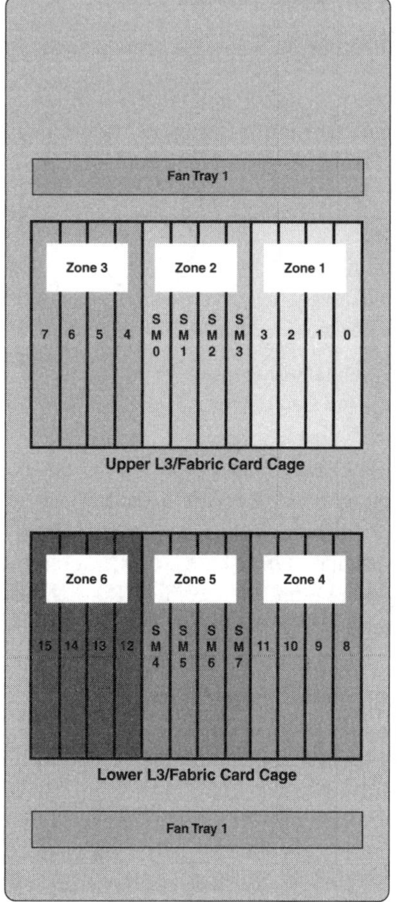

AM = Alarm Module
RP = Route Processor
SM = Switch Module
FC = Fan Controller (Note: One fan tray is powered from load zone 2; the other is powered from load zone 5.)

Figure 11-2 *CRS-1 16-Slot Power Zones*

DRPs have been inserted in slots 5 and 7 as indicated in Example 11-1. Issue the command **show platform** in admin mode from the owner SDR. Example 11-2 displays the full output of **show platform** in admin mode. Notice there is one MSC with an 8-port 10 GB PLIM in slot 0. Slot 5 and slot 7 each have a DRP installed as each DRP has two CPUs. The operating system implements a sophisticated algorithm to load-balance processing cycles between the CPUs. Notice that, in owner-SDR admin mode, a user has visibility to critical environmental and fabric cards.

HQ System Power Distribution Zones

PLIMs and RP Side (Front View)

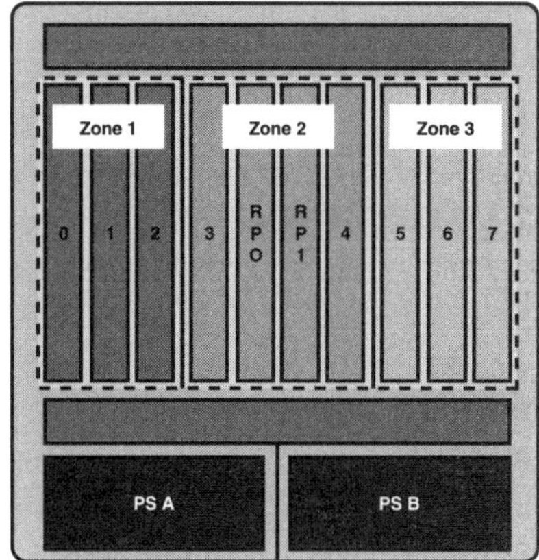

MSC and Switch Fabric (Rear View)

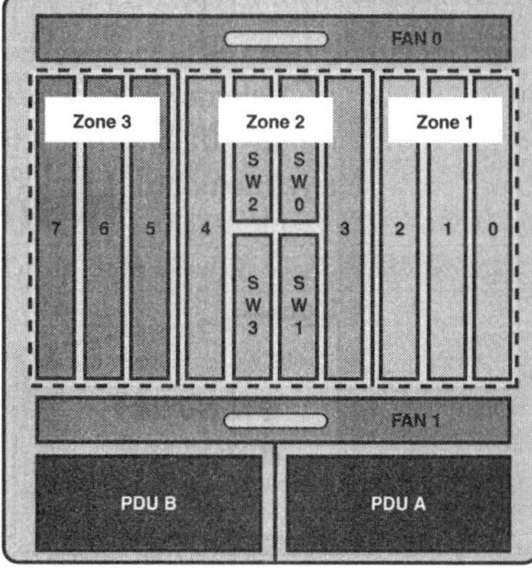

PLIMs = Slots 0 to 3 and 4 to 7
RPs = Two Middle Slots
PS = Power Supply

MSCs = Slots 0 to 3 and 4 to 7
SF = Four Middle Slots
Half-Height Card Per Slot
PDU = Power Distribution Unit

Figure 11-3 *CRS-1 8-Slot Power Zones*

Example 11-2 *The* **show platform** *Command Output from CRS-1 8-Slot Chassis*

```
RP/0/RP0/CPU0:CRS-2(admin)#show platform
Node            Type            PLIM            State           Config State
-----------------------------------------------------------------------------
0/0/SP          MSC(SP)         N/A             IOS XR RUN      PWR,NSHUT,MON
0/0/CPU0        MSC             8-10GbE         IOS XR RUN      PWR,NSHUT,MON
0/5/SP          DRP(SP)         N/A             IOS XR RUN      PWR,NSHUT,MON
0/5/CPU0        DRP(Active)     DRP-ACC         IOS XR RUN      PWR,NSHUT,MON
0/5/CPU1        DRP(Active)     DRP-ACC         IOS XR RUN      PWR,NSHUT,MON
0/7/SP          DRP(SP)         N/A             IOS XR RUN      PWR,NSHUT,MON
0/7/CPU0        DRP(Active)     DRP-ACC         IOS XR RUN      PWR,NSHUT,MON
0/7/CPU1        DRP(Active)     DRP-ACC         IOS XR RUN      PWR,NSHUT,MON
0/RP0/CPU0      RP(Active)      N/A             IOS XR RUN      PWR,NSHUT,MON
0/RP1/CPU0      RP(Standby)     N/A             IOS XR PREP     PWR,NSHUT,MON
0/SM0/SP        FC/S(SP)        N/A             IOS XR RUN      PWR,NSHUT,MON
0/SM1/SP        FC/S(SP)        N/A             IOS XR RUN      PWR,NSHUT,MON
0/SM2/SP        FC/S(SP)        N/A             IOS XR RUN      PWR,NSHUT,MON
0/SM3/SP        FC/S(SP)        N/A             IOS XR RUN      PWR,NSHUT,MON
RP/0/RP0/CPU0:CRS-2(admin)#
```

Now that a DRP has been inserted and is booted in the chassis, we can begin creating an SDR.

Creating a Named Secure Domain Router

To create a named SDR, a user must be logged in the owner SDR, in admin mode, with appropriate privileges. A user cannot configure an SDR from global executive plane, regardless of privilege access; therefore, admin access is a must. A user must also have group root-system privilege assigned. In admin mode, the user can invoke the command **show running-config** to verify the correct privilege has been assigned to the user ID. Example 11-3 shows the sample output.

Example 11-3 show running-config *in Admin Mode*

```
P/0/RP0/CPU0:CRS-2(admin)#show running-config
Building configuration...
username cisco
 secret 5 $1$1j.C$S45xztld/P/K4YzwqnuH21
 group root-system
end

RP/0/RP0/CPU0:CRS-2
```

After the appropriate privilege has been established, you can create a named SDR. Example 11-4 provides the commands to initially create a named SDR from the owner SDR. To designate the DRP pair as the controller for a new SDR, two DRPs can be grouped and identified as a pair by assigning an alias via explicit **pairing** command. As shown in Example 11-4, the DRP are being paired using an alias of drp-Edge. After creating the DRP pair, the CLI will create a subconfiguration mode. Here you can instruct the system where the DRPs are located in order to pair the appropriate hardware slots. Notice in Example 11-4 that asterisks are used for slot 5 and slot 7 after the keyword **location**. Asterisks indicate the entire slot is allocated. At the time of writing of this book, SDRs cannot assign resources on a per port basis; instead, when a resource is assigned, the entire slot is allocated. If a single DRP is used (as opposed to a DRP pair, for redundancy), the **pairing** keyword can still be used to assign one DRP to a slot.

Example 11-4 *Pairing DRPs*

```
RP/0/RP0/CPU0:CRS-2(admin-config)#pairing drp-Edge
RP/0/RP0/CPU0:CRS-2(admin-config-pairing:drp-Edge)#location 0/5/* 0/7/*
RP/0/RP0/CPU0:CRS-2(admin-config)#commit

RP/0/RP0/CPU0:CRS-2(admin)#show running-config
Building configuration...
username cisco
 secret 5 $1$1j
```

```
 group root-system
!
pairing drp-Edge
 location 0/5/* 0/7/*
```

Assigning Resources to a Named SDR

After the DRPs have been configured, nodes such as line cards or MSCs can be assigned as resources to the named SDR. Owner SDRs will assign ownership of resources to the named SDR. The DRPs will maintain routing updates, control plane connectivity to assigned resources, and all related functions. The relationship of DRPs associated to resources in a named SDR behaves in the same sense as route processors managing all unassigned resources.

In Example 11-5, the command-line output displays how to create an SDR and assign a 10-gigabit line card to the newly created SDR. An SDR name is created by the keyword **sdr**. sdr-Edge1 is created as the named SDR. In the example, drp-Edge (a pair of named DRPs configured in Example 11-4) is associated with sdr-edge1. A resource such as a 10-gigabit line card (slot 0) is assigned to the SDR. If the system has several DRP or several named SDRs, the **pair** keyword command associates the DRP to our named SDR. Finally, the resource can be assigned to the SDR that was created and associated.

When resources become assigned to a named SDR, in this case sdr-Edge1, the software emulates a soft reboot of the nodes. Therefore, the MSC in slot 0 is removed from the owner-SDR and (in software) it will be reinserted in sdr-Edge1. It is normal behavior for the MSC to be offline during the time it goes through normal bootup procedures.

Example 11-5 *Creating an SDR and Assigning Resources*

```
RP/0/RP0/CPU0:CRS-2(admin)#configure terminal
RP/0/RP0/CPU0:CRS-2(admin-config)#sdr sdr-Edge1
RP/0/RP0/CPU0:CRS-2(admin-config-sdr:sdr-Edge1)#pair drp-Edge primary
RP/0/RP0/CPU0:CRS-2(admin-config-sdr:sdr-Edge1)#location 0/0/*
RP/0/RP0/CPU0:CRS-2(admin-config-sdr:sdr-Edge1)#commit

RP/0/RP0/CPU0:CRS-2(admin)#show run
Building configuration...
sdr sdr-Edge1
 pair drp-Edge primary
 location 0/0/*
!
username cisco
 secret 5 $1$1j.C$S45xztld/P/K4YzwqnuH21
 group root-system
!
pairing drp-Edge
```

```
 location 0/5/* 0/7/*
!
end
```

As SDR sdr-Edge1 resources boots and becomes operational, CLI verification can be invoked to ensure that the named SDR is configured correctly. The CRS-1 router should see two SDRs based on the current configurations depicted in the example. As shown in Example 11-6, the command **show sdr summary** provides details on the SDR ID, which DRPs are assigned to the SDR, and which resource belongs to each SDR. The owner SDR is assigned a default SDR ID of 0. The first named SDR (sdr-Edge1) is assigned the next number in sequence; that is, SDR ID 1. Because there is only one resource, the 10-gigabit PLIM and associated MSC, the owner sdr will not have any resources assigned and sdr-Edge will have the 10-gigabit PLIM and MSC associated. When the MSC and PLIM have been associated with sdr-Edge1, it will not appear in the inventory output from the owner SDR when **show platform** CLI command is invoked.

Example 11-6 *The* **show sdr summary** *Command Output*

```
RP/0/RP0/CPU0:CRS-2(admin)#show sdr summary


SDRs Configured:
SDR-Names   SDRid   dSDRSC       StbydSDRSC Primary1    Primary2    MacAddr
-------------------------------------------------------------------------
Owner       0       0/RP0/CPU0   NONE       0/RP0/CPU0  0/RP1/CPU0  0017.5a75.3b00
sdr-Edge1   1       0/5/CPU0     0/7/CPU0   0/5/CPU0    0/7/CPU0    0017.5a75.3b01
RP/0/RP0/CPU0:CRS-2(admin)#
```

As previously explained, the MSC that was assigned to the named SDR will appear in admin mode, as shown in Example 11-7, but will not appear in the inventory list in global mode.

Example 11-7 *Admin Mode Platform Inventory*

```
P/0/RP0/CPU0:CRS-2(admin)#show platform
Node            Type            PLIM             State           Config State
-----------------------------------------------------------------------------
0/0/SP          MSC(SP)         N/A              IOS XR RUN      PWR,NSHUT,MON
0/0/CPU0        MSC             8-10GbE          IOS XR RUN      PWR,NSHUT,MON
0/5/SP          DRP(SP)         N/A              IOS XR RUN      PWR,NSHUT,MON
0/5/CPU0        DRP(Active)     DRP-ACC          IOS XR RUN      PWR,NSHUT,MON
0/5/CPU1        DRP(Active)     DRP-ACC          IOS XR RUN      PWR,NSHUT,MON
0/7/SP          DRP(SP)         N/A              IOS XR RUN      PWR,NSHUT,MON
0/7/CPU0        DRP(Standby)    DRP-ACC          IOS XR RUN      PWR,NSHUT,MON
```

```
0/7/CPU1          DRP(Standby)      DRP-ACC            IOS XR RUN        PWR,NSHUT,MON
0/RP0/CPU0        RP(Active)        N/A                IOS XR RUN        PWR,NSHUT,MON
0/RP1/CPU0        RP(Standby)       N/A                IOS XR PREP       PWR,NSHUT,MON
0/SM0/SP          FC/S(SP)          N/A                IOS XR RUN        PWR,NSHUT,MON
0/SM1/SP          FC/S(SP)          N/A                IOS XR RUN        PWR,NSHUT,MON
0/SM2/SP          FC/S(SP)          N/A                IOS XR RUN        PWR,NSHUT,MON
0/SM3/SP          FC/S(SP)          N/A                IOS XR RUN        PWR,NSHUT,MON
```

The MSC in slot 0 does not appear in global mode, as shown in Example 11-8.

Example 11-8 *Global Mode Platform Inventory*

```
RP/0/RP0/CPU0:CRS-2#show platform
Node              Type              PLIM               State             Config State
----------------------------------------------------------------------------------
0/RP0/CPU0        RP(Active)        N/A                IOS XR RUN        PWR,NSHUT,MON
0/RP1/CPU0        RP(Standby)       N/A                IOS XR PREP       PWR,NSHUT,MON
RP/0/RP0/CPU0:CRS-2#
```

Logging In to a Newly Named SDR

DRPs maintain responsibilities similar to route processors. Access to DRPs is provided through the console and management Ethernet ports. However, logging in to the newly created SDR poses a challenge because no username is configured inside the SDR. Each user ID is local to each SDR. IOS XR allows a user to log in a named SDR before the usernames are created within the SDR. The user first authenticates and authorizes the named SDR from the Owner_LR AAA rules via a command in the owner SDR. By using the command **aaa authentication login remote local** in the admin plane, the user authenticated in the owner SDR can initially log in with the credential of username@admin. Example 11-9 shows this configuration.

Example 11-9 *The* **aaa authentication login remote local** *Configuration*

```
RP/0/RP0/CPU0:CRS-2(admin)#configure term
RP/0/RP0/CPU0:CRS-2(admin-config)#aaa authentication login remote local
RP/0/RP0/CPU0:CRS-2(admin-config)#commit
```

Before customizing the configuration, log in to SDR sdr-Edge1. In Example 11-10, we will console through admin mode into the DRP and authenticate as cisco@admin. The same password used to authenticate the owner SDR is used to access the newly created named SDR, sdr-Edge1. Notice that the 8-port 10-gigabit interface card appears in the named SDR as configured in the owner SDR.

Example 11-10 *Console to SDR sdr-Edge1*

```
Console connection to DRP in slot 0/5/cpu0
Escape character is '^]'.

Press RETURN to get started!

User Access Verification

Username: cisco@admin
Password:
DRP/0/5/CPU0:ios#show running-config
Building configuration...
!! No configuration change since last restart
!
interface MgmtEth0/5/CPU0/0
 shutdown
!
interface MgmtEth0/5/CPU1/0
 shutdown
!
interface MgmtEth0/7/CPU0/0
 shutdown
!
interface MgmtEth0/7/CPU1/0
 shutdown
!
interface TenGigE0/0/0/0
 shutdown
!
interface TenGigE0/0/0/1
 shutdown
!
interface TenGigE0/0/0/2
 shutdown
!
interface TenGigE0/0/0/3
 shutdown
!
interface TenGigE0/0/0/4
 shutdown
!
interface TenGigE0/0/0/5
 shutdown
!
interface TenGigE0/0/0/6
 shutdown
```

```
!
interface TenGigE0/0/0/7
 shutdown
!
end

DRP/0/5/CPU0:ios#
```

The SDR is now in a state available for configuration per user specifications. The first step is to create AAA configurations for user access. Each named SDR maintains its own independent AAA model (that is, local AAA, RADIUS, TACACS, and so on) and operates autonomously from other SDRs within the chassis.

SDRs are carved from the original router and share only environment resources with the owner SDR. The Cisco CRS-1 supports a maximum of four SDRs per system. If there are multiple SDRs in a router, the SDRs can be connected to one another only through an existing port associated to the named SDR. Therefore, SDRs are treated as separate physical routers.

Process Placement

Because Cisco IOS XR aims to achieve high availability and stable performance, the Cisco IOS XR software is built on a modular system of processes. Each process provides specific functions for the system and runs in a protected memory space to ensure that problems within one process cannot impact other processes or the entire system. Multiple instances of a process can run on a single node, and multiple threads of execution can run on each process instance.

Under normal operating conditions, processes are managed automatically by the Cisco IOS XR software. Processes are started, stopped, or restarted as required by the running configuration of the router. In addition, processes use checkpointing to optimize performance during process restart and automatic switchover.

Cisco IOS XR offers an important feature called *process placement* that allows strategic placement of processes to specific locations, such as a DRP installed in a CRS-1 router. By default, processes are distributed using a predefined policy across the set of available RPs that is without requiring any user placement configuration. Process placement can be configured manually or triggered based on a threshold setting if memory or disk place is exceeded. User configuration can still be applied to explicitly modify the way applications are distributed. Refer to Chapter 2, "Cisco IOS XR Infrastructure," for more detailed explanation of process placement and configuring with DRPs.

Summary

Secure Domain Routers (SDR) can be used to reduce capital expense of creating new routers within the current CRS-1 system. SDRs require dedicated DRP (Distributed Route Processor) hardware for the Cisco CRS-1 platform. When an SDR is created and configured, the SDR is treated as a separate router. This delivers a layer of security for each layer of the network attached to an SDR. SDRs can neither view nor manipulate resources of the other SDR. Routing protocols and configurations remain completely autonomous. The administration mode remains in control of all critical resources of the host system, known as the owner SDR. Administration configuration mode maintains authority to make future changes to the SDRs.

References

- **Cisco.** Cisco CRS-1 Distributed Route Processor. http://www.cisco.com/en/US/prod/collateral/routers/ps5763/product_data_sheet0900aecd80501c66.html
- **Cisco.** Process Placement on Cisco IOS XR Software. https://www.cisco.com/en/US/docs/ios_xr_sw/iosxr_r3.3/system_management/configuration/guide/yc33pp.html

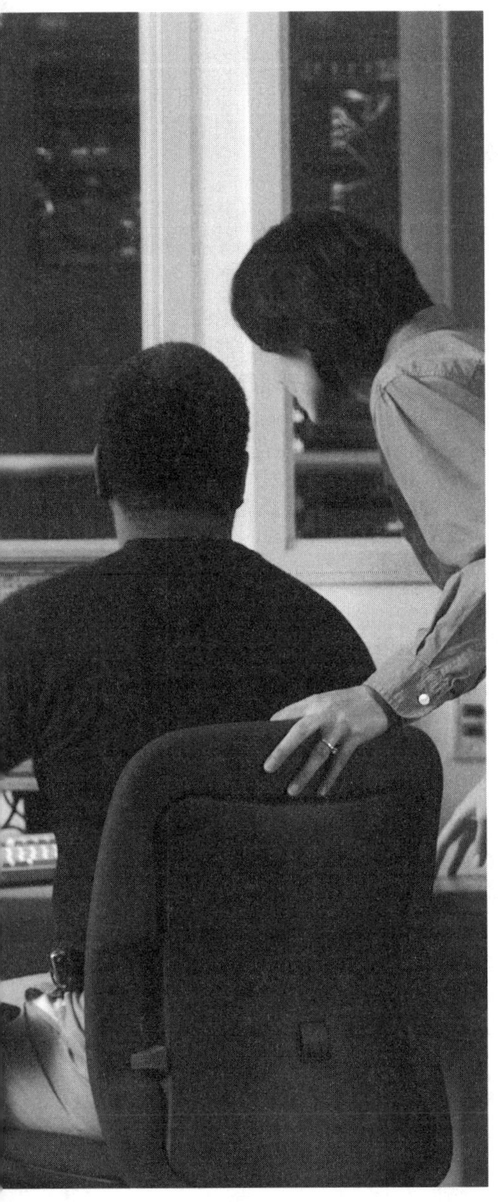

This chapter covers the following topics:

- Multishelf Overview
- Line Card Chassis
- Fabric Card Chassis
- Switch Fabric Cards
- Multishelf Fabric Interconnect
- Multishelf Control Ethernet
- Multishelf Configuration
- Reference

The CRS-1 16-slot single chassis highly scalable platform is leveraged to a larger scalable system to meet demands and growth of service providers. Service providers had developed multiservice networks to provide services over the same infrastructure and require more bandwidth and port density, and are increasingly becoming more complex to manage.

The Cisco CRS-1 multishelf system is a natural evolution of the Cisco CRS-1 16-slot single chassis system. Powered by the IOS XR operating system, a CRS-1 multishelf system offers additional capacity by adding line cards to increase throughput capabilities to the existing system. The multishelf system is intended to address the scalability and requirements in the core of service providers' next-generation networks (NGN). As the name implies, a multishelf system consists of multiple chassis. However, like Cisco CRS-1 single router, the multishelf acts as a single entity that operates as one unit or a router system, and is managed as a single unit regardless of the added hardware in its configuration. Multishelf system complexity does not increase with growth because it remains one management system.

CHAPTER 12

Understanding CRS-1 Multishelf

Multishelf Overview

The CRS-1 multishelf system consists of the same building blocks as the CRS-1 single chassis system. A fabric *plane* is considered the fabric data path of Stages 1, 2, and 3 of the fabric architecture. The path of packet forwarding remains similar to the CRS-1 single line card chassis (LCC). Multishelf's fabric is parsed to support growth and scalability. This is explained further in detail in this chapter; however, for now, keep in mind that within a multishelf system, you can add line card chassis as the network grows in a manner that does not impact services running across the network.

The major component that changes in a multishelf system is the fabric card of the CRS-1 single LCC. The fabric card in the CRS-16 single LCC has a fabric called the S123. The S123 represents that fabric has all three stages of fabric switching embedded in the card. We conclude all fabric switching is performed intrachassis. When the CRS-1 single shelf system participates in a multishelf system, only the fabric card is replaced with an S13. A fabric card chassis (FCC) is introduced to perform the essential stage 2 fabric switch. The LCC and FCC chassis are connected via fabric array cables to support the fabric data links between them. The fabric components to identify a multishelf system are

- CRS-1 line card chassis
- S13 fabric card
- CRS-1 fabric card chassis
- S2 fabric cards and optical interface module (OIM)
- Fabric array cables

Careful planning was considered to avoid multishelf migration as a forklift upgrade. Instead, the migration of a single LCC to multishelf offers a number of options including hitless migration. All discussions in this chapter assume full fabric connectivity of all eight planes for fabric high availability. In this chapter, you will learn the building blocks to interconnect the LCC and FCC and configurations of a multishelf system.

Line Card Chassis

The line card chassis (LCC) carries the following key hardware components:

- Modular services cards (MSC)
- Physical layer interface modules (PLIM)

- S13 fabric cards (SFC)
- Route processor (RP) cards
- Distributed route processor (DRP) cards (optional)

The LCC contains its own power and cooling systems. A minimum of one line card chassis and one fabric card chassis are required to configure a multishelf system. This minimum configuration is called a one plus one (1+1) system.

The LCC can be deployed, and operated independently, as a single CRS-1 router. The system descriptions presented in this section focus on line card chassis and fabric card chassis operating as a multishelf system.

Fabric Card Chassis

The fabric card chassis (FCC) enclosure houses the following key hardware components:

- 8 or 24 switch fabric cards (SFC)
- Two shelf controller gigabit Ethernet 22 port (SCGE-22) cards
- Two fan trays
- 8 or 24 optical interface module (OIM) cards
- Two OIM light emitting diode (OIM-LED) cards
- Two alarm modules
- Two AC or DC power shelves

Except for the SCGE-22 cards, OIM cards, and fan trays, each of these components houses its own service processor with two backplane Fast Ethernet links to the SCGE cards. The two SCGE cards have one internal Fast Ethernet link between them. The SCGE-22 card has integrated controllers to control fan speed and monitors the status of the fan trays.

The SFCs and SCGE-22 cards reside in the front of the chassis, whereas the rear of the chassis houses OIM and OIM-LED cards. Similar to the line card chassis, the fabric card chassis contains its own power and cooling systems.

OIM modules host a set of nine connectors. The external sides of these modules connect to the S13 SFCs located in the 16-slot LCC through the use of optical cables called fabric *array cables*. The internal side of the OIM module mates with the S2 SFCs inside the FCC. Figure 12-1 illustrates the relationship between the S13, OIM, and S2 cards on the LCC and FCC.

The OIM is a passive device that provides fiber connectivity functions. The OIM modules connect S2 fabric to the S13 fabric on the LCC. The external connectors on OIM cards are called *bulkhead array adapters* (BAA). BAAs are used to terminate the fabric array cables on the OIM side of an FCC. The other end of the fabric cables are terminated in the same manner on the BAA of the S13 fabric cards in the LCCs.

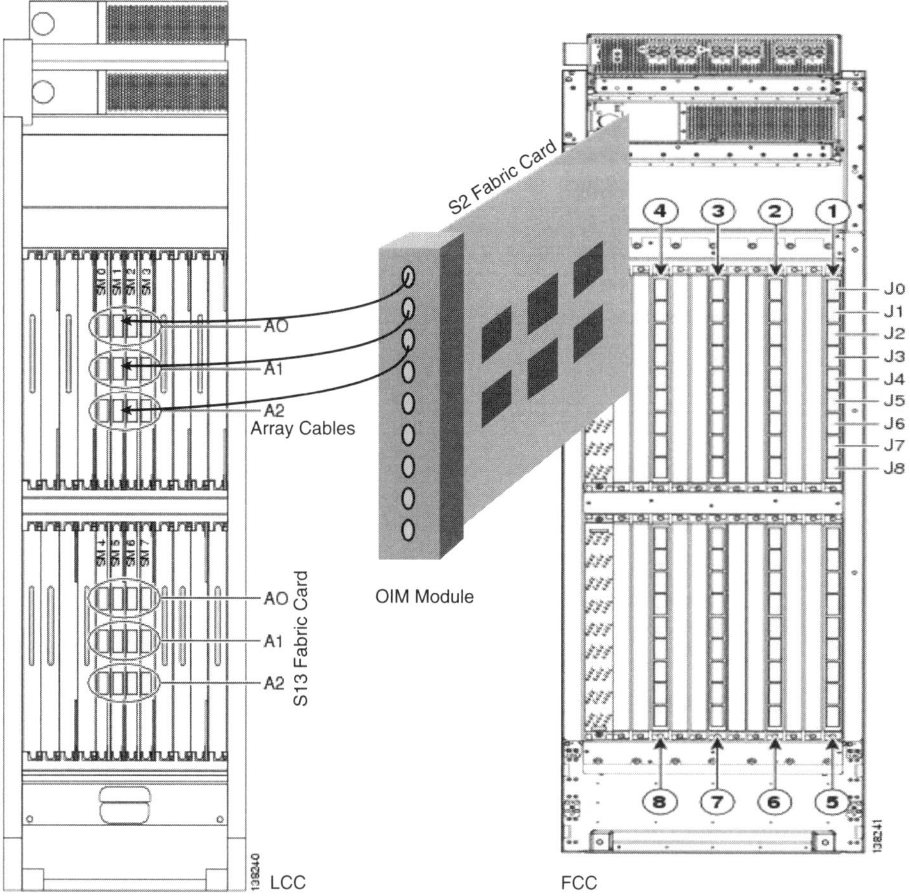

Figure 12-1 *Fabric Overview*

The FCC contains an OIM-LED module that indicates the status of each fabric cable bundle that connects the fabric cards between the FCC to a LCC. The module gives visual indications of fabric cables that are operationally up or down or incorrectly connected. It also specifies the correct place to connect or reconnect a fabric cable. The OIM-LED card is used to aid cable installation and troubleshooting. The status of an array cable is indicated through various colors and states of the LED array.

Table 12-1 lists possible LED states for OIM-LED.

Table 12-1 *LED States for OIM-LED*

LED State	Explanation
Off	A card to which this fabric cable is attached is either powered off or not recognized within the chassis, or the fabric cable is not connected at one end of the connection.

LED State	Explanation
Green	The fabric cable is properly connected at both ends and data transmission is occurring.
Yellow	The fabric cable is properly connected at both ends, although some data errors are occurring.
Red	More than one fabric cable is not connected to the correct location.
Blinking red	A single fabric cable is not connected to the correct location.
Blinking green	The location where the incorrectly connected fabric cable should be connected is shown. This LED corresponds to the blinking red LED described previously for cases in which a single fabric cable is connected incorrectly.

With regard to nomenclature, (1+1) describes *one line card chassis* and *one fabric card chassis*, respectively. Therefore, two line card chassis and one fabric chassis would be represented by two plus one (2+1) multishelf system. The configuration (1+1) is the minimum hardware required for a multishelf system. Additionally, in many references, multishelf and multichassis are used interchangeably. Each LCC has a switching capacity of up to 1.28 Tbps, assuming all fabric cards are in operation.

Switch Fabric Cards

The packet flow from MSC to fabric architecture in a multishelf system is not different from that of a single-shelf chassis. The differences between the two sets of platforms come in the breakout or placement of Stage 2 switch fabric cards. These differences in switch fabric cards (SFC) provide the following benefits for multishelf:

- Scalability of growth for additional line cards chassis added to an existing multishelf system
- Migration and in-service hardware upgrade from single chassis to multishelf CRS-1

Fabric Data Path

Traffic is forwarded from an incoming (ingress) interface to an outgoing (egress) interface using a three-stage switching fabric. Data traffic crosses all eight fabric cards (planes). The eighth card provides redundancy because the loss of one fabric card (seven active fabric cards) will not diminish bandwidth to any slot of the router. In a single CRS-1 16-slot router, the fabric card is called S123 card (Stage 1, 2, 3), known as a *three-stage fabric architecture* because all three switch fabric stages exist within the same fabric card. Refer to Figure 12-2 for a high-level view of data traffic path in a multishelf fabric architecture.

The fabric process consists of the following three stages:

- Stage 1 consists of data that enters the system from a line card ingress port and is sent to the fabric chassis. Stage 1 (located on the line card chassis) distributes incoming traffic (cells) evenly across all Stage 2 components within the same plane to achieve load balancing using a round-robin algorithm.

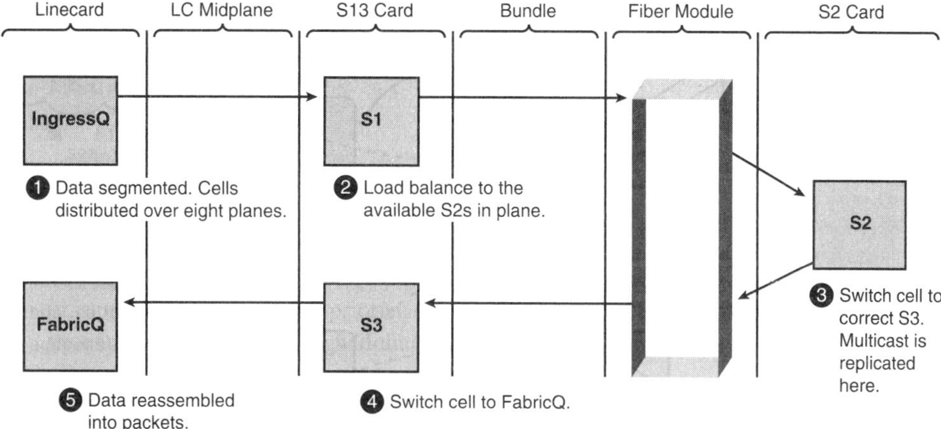

Figure 12-2 *Traffic Path in a Multishelf Fabric Architecture*

- Stage 2 data cells are routed to the appropriate Stage 3 line card chassis. This is based on the destination address of the incoming cells. There are two types of traffic classifications: unicast and multicast. Multicast is first replicated at Stage 2 in the fabric. If multicast replication is required, the cells are replicated to the Stage 3 fabric ASIC (application-specific integrated circuit). Stage 3 is located on the line card chassis fabric card (S13). The S2 card now must know on which line card chassis to replicate the traffic based on the destination egress modular service card.
- Stage 3 data is routed to the appropriate destination modular service card, and then continues forwarding through the appropriate egress port on the PLIM.

In a multishelf system, Stage 1 and Stage 3 are located in the LCC on fabric cards, also known as S13 (Stage 1, 3) cards, and Stage 2 is located in the FCC on switch fabric cards (SFC), also called *S2 cards*. In a multishelf system, the LCC requires the replacement of S123 switch fabric cards with S13 switch fabric cards.

For the fabric cards to provide functionality, they are connected with fiber optic cables that interconnect between the line card chassis and fabric chassis. For the system to route data, the Cisco IOS XR software configuration must match this physical cable configuration. This is discussed later in this chapter in the "Multishelf Configuration" section.

High Availability

From inception of the CRS-1 single shelf platform, redundancy has been accounted in multishelf components to meet 99.999% availability goals. The redundancy is available for fabric or SEA ASICs, links, fabric cards, power, and other environmental components. In software, the feature redundancy supporting Designated Shelf Controller (DSC) migration and Secure Domain Router (SDR) redundancy can occur across LCCs.

Multishelf Fabric Interconnect

This section describes the role of fabric planes, switch fabric elements, backpressure, and optical array cables.

Fabric Planes

As reviewed earlier, in the section "Fabric Data Path," traffic can travel across the eight planes that comprise the switching fabric. Eight is the magic number to provide absolute high availability in the fabric.

In the CRS-1 16-slot line card chassis, each S13 fabric card represents one fabric plane and is connected to one of the S2 fabric cards in the fabric chassis. Traffic is evenly distributed between the fabric planes for redundancy. If any of the fabric planes is removed from operation, the traffic for that plane is rerouted to the remaining planes without impacting router performance.

SEA Links

Switch fabric elements (SEA) are the fabric ASICs that make up the core fabric and provide the ingress and egress interface into the fabric. The following are the key switch fabric elements:

- Ingressq
- Fabricq
- SEA
- Qlink

Ingressq and Fabricq are ingress and egress ASICs, respectively, on the modular service card served to interface with the fabric nonblocking architecture.

The SEA ASIC is the building block of the fabric cards and is used to construct the previously mentioned three-stage switch fabric. SEA ASIC comprises three modes, S1, S2, and S3, which form the three stages of the fabric.

Qlink is a interconnecting ASIC that connects the line card, RP, and DRP to the fabric. It bridges the single-ended bundled interface links on the connected card side to the differential 2.5 Gbps unilink on the fabric side.

The switch fabric is constructed with eight identical, independent, and unsynchronized switch planes. Each switch fabric plane comprises S1, S2, and S3 ASICs.

In a Cisco CRS-1 16-slot chassis, each switch fabric plane has two S1 ASICs, represented by an upper and lower ASIC on the fabric card. The MSCs in slots 0 through 7 connect to the upper S1 ASIC on each switch fabric plane. The two route processors (RP) in slots RP0 and RP1 and MSCs in slots 8 through 15 connect to the lower S1 ASIC of each of the switch fabric planes.

Every MSC has four 2.5-Gbps serial connections to the S1 ASICs on each of the eight switch fabric planes. Therefore, each MSC has 32 connections to the S1 ASICs on the eight switch fabric planes (4 connections for each S1 × 8 switch fabric plane). Each MSC thus provides a raw "to fabric" bandwidth of 80 Gbps (32 connections at 2.5 Gbps = 80 Gbps). The effective "to fabric" bandwidth is less than 80 Gbps due to the following reasons:

- **Packet to Cell Conversion:** Cell header represents about 12 percent in overhead.
- **Segmentation:** Whenever the size of a packet is not a multiple of the cell size, segmentation results in the last cell containing that packet to be partially unused. The cell can strategically insert two packets in one cell aligned on 30-byte boundaries (within the 120-byte payload). This action can reduce overhead greatly and improve throughput. Improvement is based on packet lengths. The worst-case overhead is 28 percent (61-byte packets).
- **Error Correction:** A 4-byte FEC code is transmitted with each cell. The FEC code is not the same as the error control that is done with the encoding (8B10B is electronic Layer 1 correction), and this error correction is at the cell layer (or Layer 2 roughly). The FEC code is checked and regenerated at each stage of the switch fabric (it must be regenerated because the cell header is modified at each stage of the switch fabric).

The final result of all the combined overhead is an approximate ingress bandwidth of approximately 50 Gbps. Each RP has a 2.5-Gbps connection to the lower S1 ASIC in each switch fabric plane.

The number of links within each fabric plane, from Stage 1 fabric to Stage 2, sums to a total of 72 links. The Stage 1 (S1) ASICs have redundant links to each of the Stage 2(S2) ASICs, each made up of 18 links. Stage 2 ASICs have two links to each of the Stage 3 ASICs, creating 144 links between Stage 2 and Stage 3. Stage 3 has a sum of four ASICs on each plane to speed up traffic or reduce any potential latency. The total links per plane in the SEA for data forwarding is 216.

From Figure 12-3, it is important to note that for a plane to be UP there is a threshold of links that must maintain an UP state for the plane to be in operation.

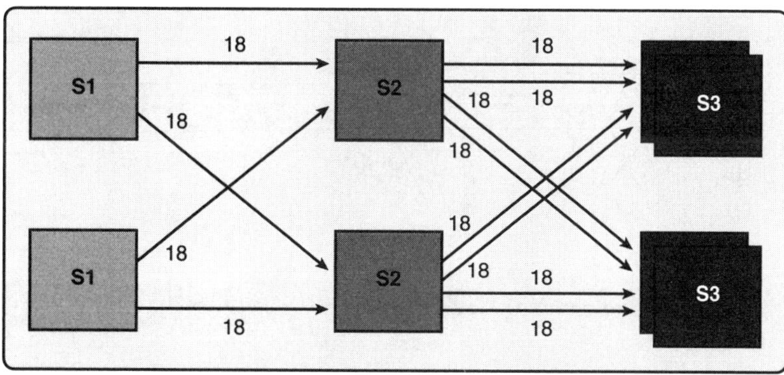

Figure 12-3 *Three-Stage Fabric Architecture*

When the plane exceeds the threshold of down links, the plane will automatically switch to a down state and will remain out of service until the condition has been resolved.

- **S1-S2 links:** Minimum 26 links of 72 links must be UP
- **S2-S3 links:** Minimum 49 links of 144 links must be UP
- **S3-Fabricq:** Minimum 3 links of 8 links must be UP

Fabric Backpressure

Backpressure is a message carried in cell headers from an S3 to all ingress queues indicating that a per priority, per destination queue in an S3 is becoming congested. For example, the path to a fabric destination is congested. The S3 out of resource (OOR) turns on backpressure to all S3 destination queues. S2 queue status is forwarded to the S3 so that above-threshold S2 queues also turn on back pressure for all S3 destinations served by the S2 queue. At the source of the backpressure message, a per priority per destination queue in S3, or per priority per S3 queue in S2, exceeds its backpressure threshold, indicating that it is becoming congested. In this case, the path to a fabric destination is congested. Once the ingress queue receives the backpressure notification it is expected to stop sending packets to the backpressured destination and priority on a cell boundary.

A *discard* is a notification issued as a result of backpressure. More specifically, it is a broadcast message carried in a fabric control cell from a Fabricq to all ingress queues, indicating that a raw queue in a Fabricq has exceeded its tail drop threshold (somewhere in the range of 100mS to 400mS). When a Fabricq raw queue exceeds its tail drop threshold, all reassembled packets destined for that queue are discarded.

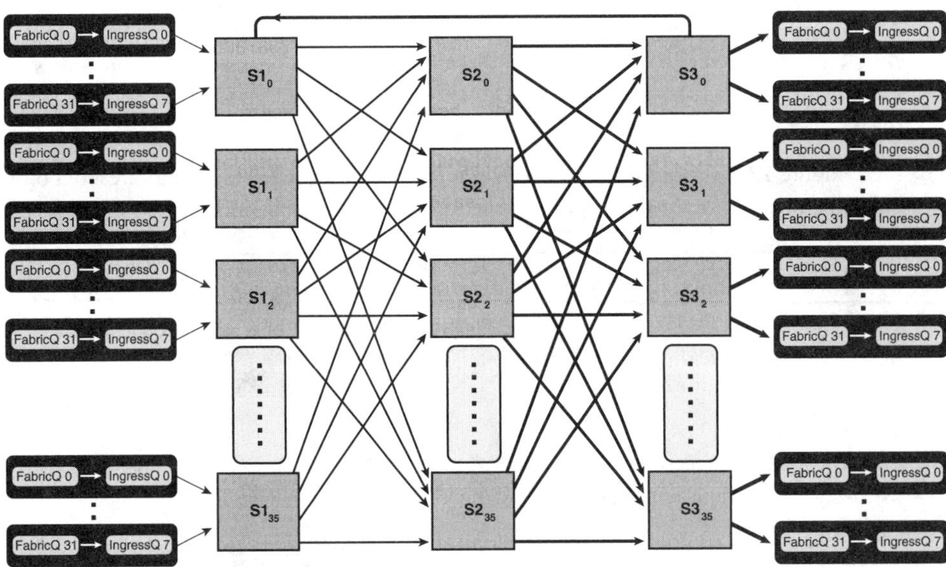

Figure 12-4 *Three-Stage Fabric Links*

Optical Array Cables

Optical array cables are used in a multishelf system. Array cables are a solution to implement an approach of nondisruptive system scalability while managing network growth. Optical array cables connect S2 ASICs of SFCs in the FCC to the S13 fabric cards in the modular service card in the LCC. The optical array cables provide the connectivity of the three stages in the switch fabric described earlier in the section “Fabric Data Path.”

Depending on your multishelf system (MSS) configuration, you need up to 48 array cables for a single multishelf system (24 cables for each LCC); cables must be long enough to span the distance between the LCCs and FCCs. Currently, cable lengths can be ordered as short as 10 meters. The maximum cable distance between the FCC and an LCC with an array cable is 100 meters. In this example of 48 array cables, we are describing a 2+1 multishelf system while assuming all eight fabric planes are connected. As each additional line card chassis is added to the multishelf system, an additional 24 array cables will be added to the fabric card chassis.

There are two cabling schemes to choose when implementing multishelf system:

- **Vertical:** Vertical cabling is also referred to as *single-module cabling*. *Module* refers to the SFC.
- **Horizontal:** Horizontal cabling is referred to as *multimodule cabling*. Horizontal cabling is first supported in Cisco IOS XR release 3.5.

A single card or multiple cards can be grouped as a fabric plane. Single-module cabling requires eight S2 cards in the fabric card chassis. In this mode, each S2 is dedicated to a plane number and cabled to the appropriate line card chassis plane. If your network requires more than three LCC in the multishelf system, this is achieved using the multimodule configuration. Multimodule configuration provides capacity to add up to nine LCCs.

Recommended Practices and Considerations

There are considerations and criteria that define the requirements for positioning S2 OIMs in the multishelf system and connecting them to the S13 cards in the LCCs. Stage 2 (S2) fabric cards can service only one plane. In a single-module configuration, each S2 is dedicated to a plane and vertical mode has three S2 fabric cards dedicated to a plane. Vertical cabling requires eight S2 fabric cards to support up to three line card chassis.

There are advantages and slight drawbacks to each method. If you choose vertical cabling, you will use less hardware with equal fabric redundancy; however, this cabling scheme will limit you to a maximum of three line card chassis to a multishelf system.

If you anticipate network growth and require more than three line card chassis, you must install or convert 24 S2 cards; therefore, horizontal cabling is needed. The drawback to horizontal cabling is the cost associated with the additional hardware. The S2 card is one of the most complex cards in the system. Multimodule configuration will support up to nine line card chassis with one, two, four, or eight fabric card chassis.

You can choose additional redundancy by adding multiple fabric chassis to reduce traffic impact in the event of catastrophic failure to the fabric chassis. Currently, you can select one, two, or four fabric chassis in a single multishelf system. Let's consider the advantages of adding additional fabric card chassis. The fabric card chassis has built-in one-to-one redundancy in hardware. The power shelves, shelf controllers, and fabric provide high availability for any single point of failure. However, in the event of some external events that might cause the fabric card chassis to fail, the multishelf system will be unable to continue to forward data traffic given the elimination of S2 forwarding in the fabric path, managed by the S2 cards.

The flexibility of the CRS-1 multishelf system allows up to four fabric chassis. Therefore, an additional layer of redundancy can be implemented in the fabric to minimize the loss of bandwidth. If the multishelf system is configured to utilize more than one FCC, the S2 fabric cards should be equally distributed among the fabric card chassis. If the two fabric card chassis is chosen, the S2 cards must be distributed equally. In the event of a complete failure of a single fabric chassis within the multishelf system, less than 50 percent of bandwidth will be lost. It's important to note *less than 50 percent*. When you divide the fabric planes between two fabric chassis, you will divide eight planes equally among the two fabric chassis. Let's assume that one of the two fabric chassis is taken out of service. You have four fabric planes in service and four planes out of service. Keep in mind that with the inherent redundancy of the fabric, one of the eight fabric planes is redundant. Therefore, the multishelf is functional with seven planes sans a redundant plane. As a result, three of the four planes pulled out of service will affect bandwidth. Three out of seven planes removed yields approximately 42 percent traffic loss.

The FCC power distribution system divides the 24 S2 fabric card slots into several power zones. In certain multiple-failure scenarios, all the cards in one zone could lose power. For a multishelf system to operate, one odd-numbered plane and one even-numbered plane must be active. For maximum fault tolerance, S2 fabric cards should be distributed among power zones so that the loss of one zone does not disable all odd-numbered or all even-numbered fabric planes. Figure 12-5 shows the power zones of the fabric card chassis.

Single Module Fabric Configuration

You may choose to perform interchassis cabling before or after powering the chassis. If you connect the cabling (array cables) after powering up the chassis, you can take advantage of the OIM LED module to check the LED status and ensure the cabling is connected correctly.

In a multishelf system, each S13 fabric card in a line card chassis is connected to the S2 fabric cards in the fabric chassis with a set of three fiber optic cables. This equipment is installed so that each fabric plane is mapped to a specific set of cards. In other words, Plane 0 cards in each line card chassis are connected to the Plane 0 cards in a fabric chassis. For the system to route data properly, Cisco IOS XR software must be configured to match the physical cabling. Specifically, you must define which slots (S2) in the fabric chassis operate each fabric plane.

The array cables connect the fabric cards of the line card chassis and the OIM on the fabric card chassis. On the LCC, the array cables connect to the designated S13 fabric plane number. The plane numbering is determined by the slot; for example, slot SM0 is plane 0 and not configurable. The remote end of each array cable must connect to a fabric card chassis, specifically to the OIM (mated to the S2 card) designated for the same plane number. Unlike the line card chassis, each slot of the fabric card chassis is configurable and can be assigned a plane numbering. It is important to consider power zones to take full advantage of high availability and minimize traffic impact.

Connecting the array cables from the line card chassis to the OIM/S2 fabric card requires three array cables for each plane. Each array cable has a total of 72 fibers bundled per array cable. The total is 216 fibers bundled between the three cables per plane.

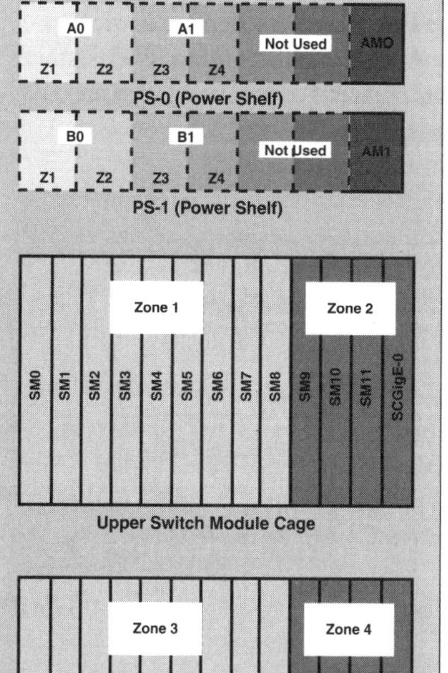

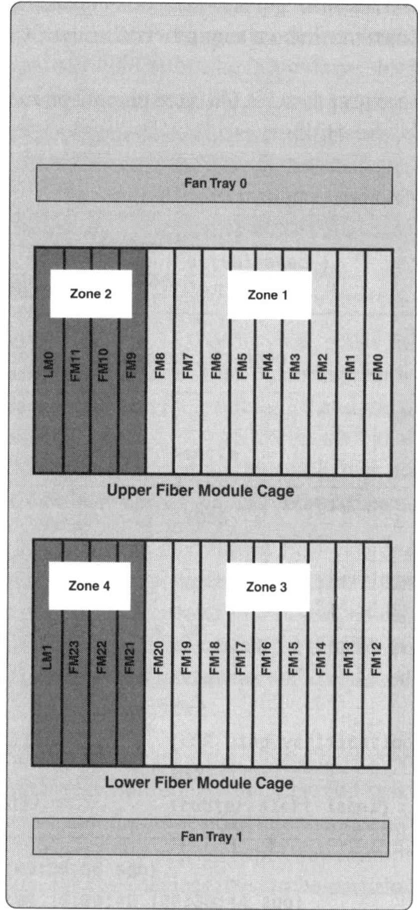

Figure 12-5 *FCC Power Zones*

Refer to Figure 12-3. In a 2+1 multishelf system, you will have line card chassis 0. The other is line card chassis 1, in addition to the fabric chassis, which is by default fabric chassis 0. For example, in vertical (single module) the connectors for Rack 0, plane 2 connect to connectors J0 through J2 on the S2 card, all fabric cables for Rack 0 must connect to connectors J0 through J2 on the respective OIM modules/S2 cards. The connector sequence on the S13 cards must match the connector sequence on the S2 cards. For example, if Rack 1 connectors connect to S2 connectors J3 through J5, S13 card connector A0 must connect to S2 connector J3, S13 card connector A1 must connect to S2 connector J4, and S13 card connector A2 must connect to S2 connector J5. Any cable mismatch will cause the plane to be in a down state because it will exceed the threshold of links down.

Figures 12-6 and 12-7 provide a detailed and high-level view of fabric connectivity. Figure 12-6 illustrates the plane numbers on the LCC. The FCC planes are defined in the CLI. Each plane on the LCC has three BAA connectors: A0, A1, and A2. Figure 12-7 illustrates LCC0 connect to an FCC where plane 0 on the LCC connects to (configured) plane 0 on the FCC (J0, J1, J2).

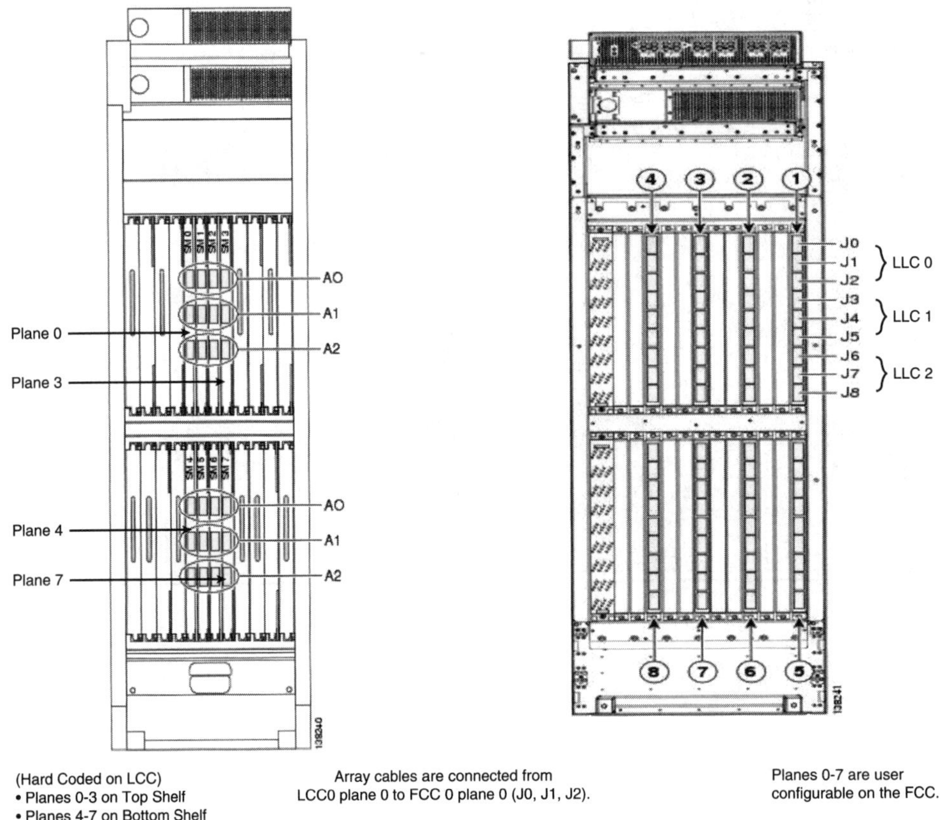

Figure 12-6 *Multishelf Fabric Labeling*

Multimodule Configuration

Software release IOS XR 3.5 introduces the support of configuring three fabric cards (S2 cards) as a single fabric plane. This configuration enables supporting up to nine LCC. Referring to Figure 12-8, we see that three adjacent slots are configured as a single plane on the fabric card chassis. Assume the cards below are configured as plane 0. The topmost jack on each of the OIM (jack 0) is dedicated only for line card chassis 0 or rack 0 and connected only to plane 0. If these cables are connected to another line card chassis or a different plane, it is considered a cabling error and the plane will not be operational. Jack 1 is dedicated to line card chassis 1 and also destined to plane 0. The same logic applies for each additional jack until we reach to jack 8. As we see, from jack 0 to jack 8 we have support for up to nine line card chassis after configuring horizontal cabling. The same method of connecting fabric cables, from the fabric card chassis to the line card chassis, would apply to the other seven fabric planes.

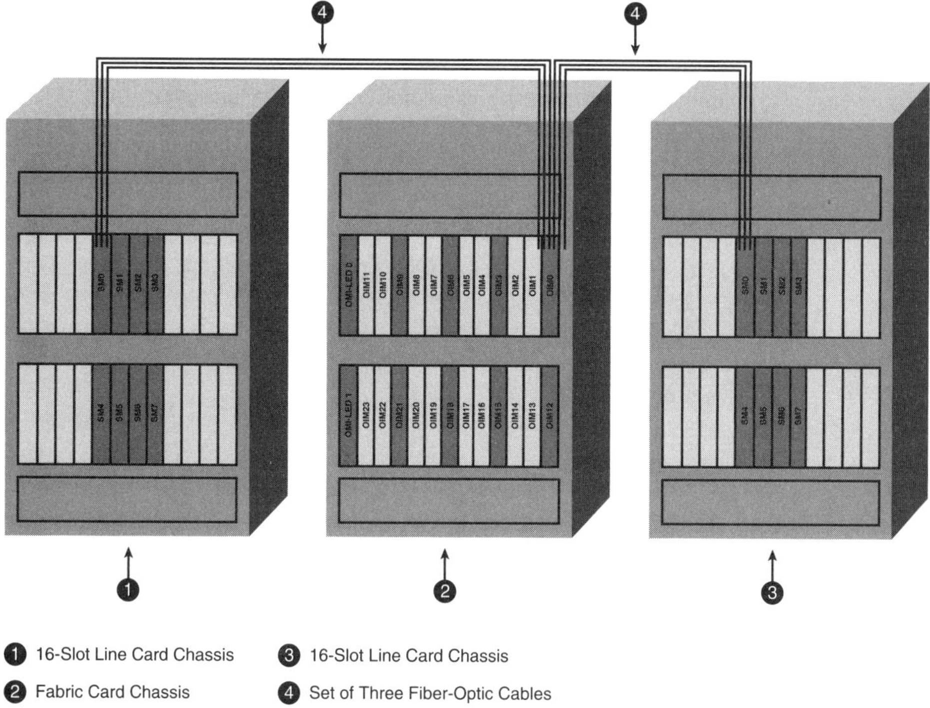

Figure 12-7 *Multishelf Plane 0 Connectivity*

Multishelf Control Ethernet

On the CRS-1 16-slot line card chassis, control Ethernet is responsible for internal synchronizations and communication between all nodes to the route processor. On the single-shelf chassis, this communication is done internally. A multishelf system must maintain the same communications and synchronizations to the designated shelf controller's (DSC) route processor. The active route processor becomes the master for all nodes in the multishelf system. To maintain this communication, external links are connected between the line card chassis in the multishelf system.

The shelf controller (SC) function is carried out by a process on RP for a line card chassis and by a process on SCGE-22 module on the fabric chassis. At least one SC must be operational at all times for a chassis to function as part of a routing system. Redundant SCs are provided for each chassis so that loss or removal of any single SC does not bring down a chassis. The SC instructs individual service processors to power up nodes, provides code images for each card or module to download, and resets any node that it determines is unresponsive. The master SC is a single control-and-arbitration point in the chassis and determines master and standby RP status when necessary.

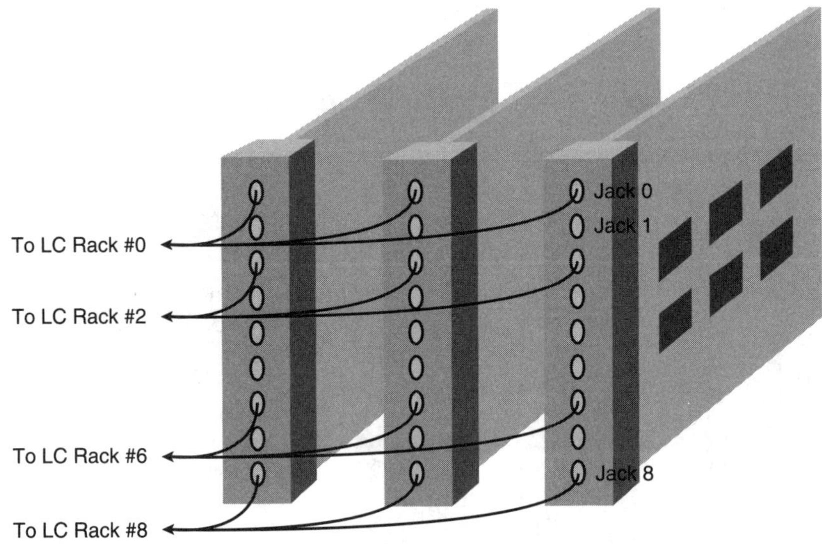

Figure 12-8 *Multimodule Fabric Configuration Cabling*

The SCGE-22 card is the local system management node for an FCC. The shelf controller has an integrated 22-port switch on the FCC. The SCGE-22 card does not need any feature tuning. Spanning-tree, root bridge, timers, election process, UDLD, and so on are preconfigured and tuned. The end user can simply utilize a plug-and-play method of deployment.

In a multishelf 2+1 system, the multishelf is connected with two paths: LCC0 and LCC1. Both have fiber Gigabit Ethernet (GE) connections (on the RP) that are used only for external control of Ethernet during multishelf setup. The Gigabit Ethernet connects to one or more GE connections (on the 22-port SCGE cards) in the FCCs. An important note: Dual paths to all chassis are interconnected through a path via the 22-port SCGE card network controller. The 22-port SCGE card provides the GE path, or control Ethernet network, between all chassis.

In comparison to the CRS-1 16-slot single chassis, the control Ethernet connection is done internally because the architecture maintains an internal fast Ethernet connection from the route processor to the each of the nodes on the chassis. The array cables carry data traffic only via switch fabric; we need control traffic to manage the multishelf system. Control traffic consists of heartbeat and many other IPC processes for bootup and operation. Each route processor contains two fiber Gigabit Ethernet connections for redundancy. The redundancy provides one-to-one redundancy on the node. After the 22-port SCGE cards are installed, the control network topology becomes a more involved topology utilizing hub-and-spoke set of connections.

A control network topology provides the following functions. Each RP in a line card chassis is connected to alternate SCGE-22 cards in a fabric chassis for redundancy. The 22-port SCGE cards are interconnected in a full mesh to provide an available control network with multiple redundant Ethernet connections. The SCGE-22 cards behave as a backbone in which different RPs are connected from the outside. Both the SCGE-22 cards and RPs run Multiple Spanning Tree (MST) protocol to provide a loop-free topology. The spanning-tree algorithm decides the flow of control traffic based on MAC address and cost for its algorithm.

In a 2+1 multishelf system, you need nine single-mode fiber cables to create a full mesh control Ethernet topology. In Figure 12-9, note there is a fiber link between shelf controller 0 (SC0) and shelf controller 1 (SC1). By default, the architecture maintains a fast Ethernet connection between the active and standby shelf controllers (SC0 and SC1). The control Ethernet traffic might take a suboptimal route without the external fiber 1 GB link.

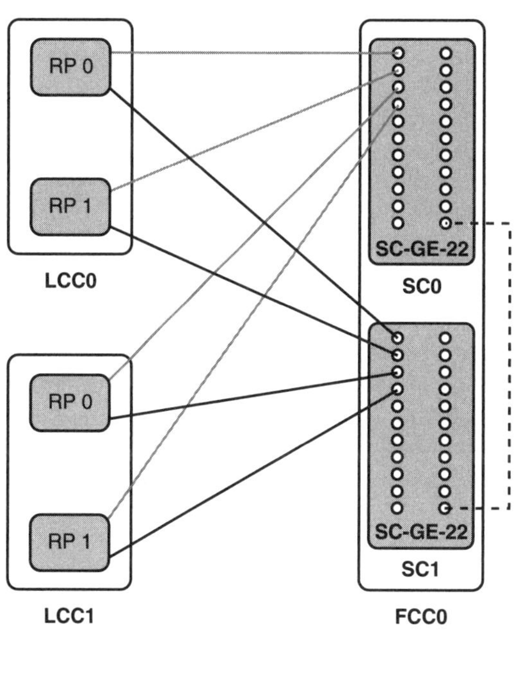

Figure 12-9 *2+1 Control Ethernet Connectivity*

In the case where there are two fabric chassis, a full mesh control Ethernet topology must be implemented. In Figure 12-10, there are two fabric card chassis, FCC0 and FCC1, with

15 external fiber links to create a full mesh between the line card chassis and both fabric chassis.

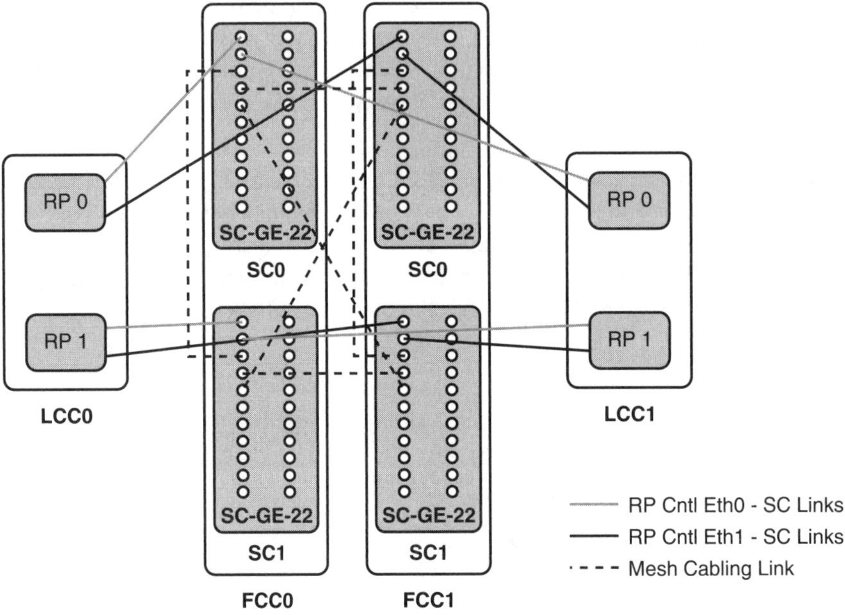

Figure 12-10 *Multishelf 2+2 Control Ethernet Connectivity*

Multishelf Configuration

In a multishelf system, each chassis must be assigned a unique rack number. These rack numbers are used to identify the chassis and related equipment in the system and to maintain the software and configurations for each chassis.

Caution: Failure to assign a unique rack number to each chassis in the system can result in system error and potential downtime. Unique rack numbers must be assigned and committed on rack 0 before the additional chassis are powered on and brought online.

Rack 0 is known as the designated shelf controller (DSC). In a multichassis system, the DSC assumes matership for the entire multishelf session.

The configuration of the rack numbers should match the physical wiring of the fiber cables. This means the three array cables must be connected in an order to represent LCC0, LCC1, and so on, in sequential order along the OIM module. Only the top OIM connectors are considered rack 0 by the hardware. This is not configurable. The configuration of rack number assignment should match the physical cabling and assigned rack 0. As an example, let's walk through connecting plane 0 of the line card chassis 0 to fabric chassis in SUM. Plane 0 on the line card chassis will connect to switch fabric chassis SM 11 on jack 0, jack 1, and jack 2. The OIM has a total of nine jacks. Therefore, line card chassis 0, also known as the DSC, will always connect to the top three jacks in single module configuration. Figure 12-11 details how the plane 0 from each line card chassis is cabled to the fabric chassis.

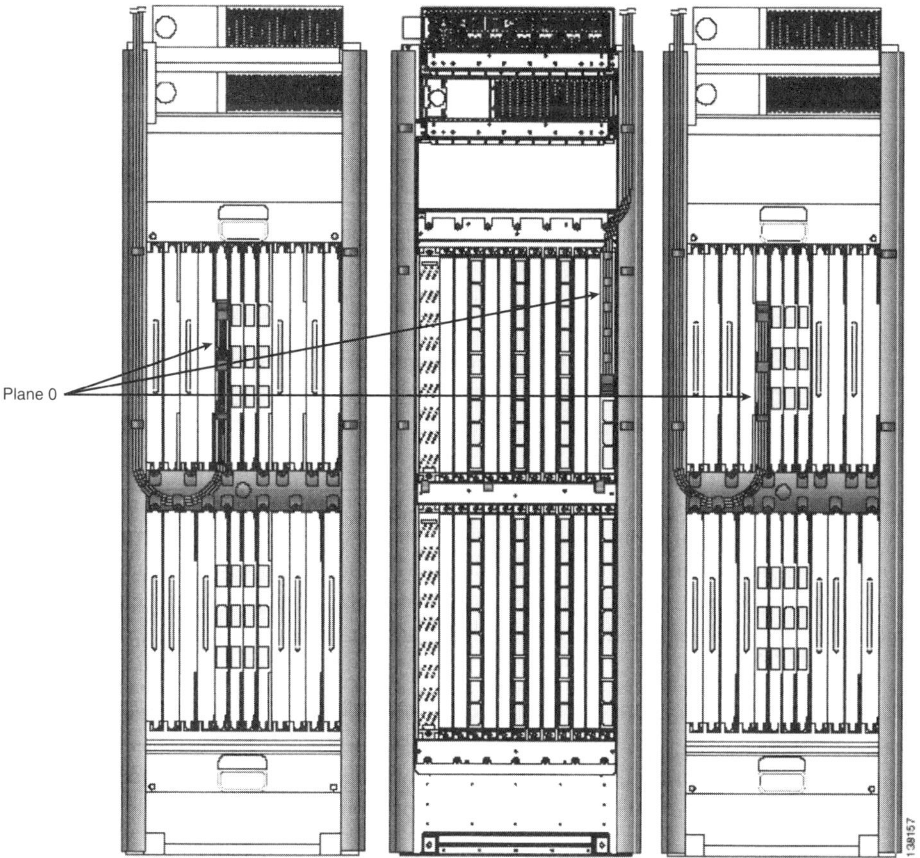

Figure 12-11 *Multishelf 2+1 Connectivity*

The numbering schemes for line card chassis and fabric chassis are important for planning and future growth of the network. The chassis numbering for line card and fabric card chassis follows:

- Line card chassis: 0–239
- Fabric card chassis: 240–248

It is important to capture the serial number of each chassis prior to multishelf configuration. The system cannot be configured properly without the chassis serial number of each LCC and FCC. The serial number will be used in the initial setup on the DSC. You must choose which chassis will initially be the DSC. The DSC will be selected as LCC0 in the setup configurations.

The network administrator has the option to install the optical array cables prior to initial CLI configuration or afterward. The external control Ethernet cabling is required during initial configuration. The external control Ethernet cabling will perform a discovery and download IOS XR to each of the chassis identified in the system.

The serial number is captured in CLI or ROMMON on the CRS-1. Example 12-1 displays capturing the serial number by CLI. Note that all commands to configure the multichassis are admin mode commands.

Example 12-1 *Output of* show diag chassis

```
RP/0/RP0/CPU0:router(admin)#show diag chassis
RACK 0 :
MAIN: board type 0001e0
800-24872
dev 075078
S/N TBA000072774
PCA: 73-7640-05 rev 20
PID: CRS-16-LCC
VID: V01
CLEI: IPM6700DRA
ECI: 445022
```

The output in Example 12-2 displays the serial number in ROMMON. The chassis serial number is displayed in the row 00050.

Example 12-2 *Output of* dumpplaneeeprom *in ROMMON*

```
rommon B3 > dumpplaneeeprom
EEPROM data backplane
000000 ff 00 01 e2 ff ff ff ff ff ff ff ff ff ff ff ff ................
000010 ff ff ff ff ff ff ff ff ff ff ff ff ff ff ff ff ................
000020 ff ff ff ff ff ff ff ff ff ff ff ff ff ff ff ff ................
000030 ff ff ff ff ff ff 08 00 45 3b 61 01 04 00 ff ff ........E;a.....
000040 ff ff ff ff ff ff ff ff ff ff ff ff ff ff ff ff ................
000050 54 42 43 30 36 33 36 36 30 36 39 30 30 30 30 30 TBA0000000072774
000060 ff ff ff ff ff ff ff ff ff ff ff ff ff ff ff ff ................
000070 ff ff ff 00 ff ff ff ff ff ff ff ff ff ff ff ff ................
000080 ff ff ff ff ff ff ff ff ff ff ff ff ff ff ff ff ................
000090 ff ff ff ff ff ff ff ff ff ff ff ff ff ff ff ff ................
0000a0 ff ff ff ff ff ff ff ff ff ff ff ff ff ff ff ff ................
0000b0 ff ff ff ff ff ff ff ff ff ff ff ff ff ff ff ff ................
0000c0 ff ff ff ff ff ff ff ff ff ff ff ff ff ff ff ff ................
0000d0 ff ff ff ff ff ff ff ff ff ff ff ff ff ff ff ff ................
0000e0 ff ff ff ff ff ff ff ff ff ff ff ff ff ff ff ff ................
0000f0 ff ff ff ff ff ff ff ff ff ff ff ff ff ff ff ff ................
```

Viewing the Configuration

After you have captured the serial number for all line card chassis and fabric card chassis, you can begin the next step to configure the system.

Displaying the command output of **show running-config** in Admin EXEC mode displays the serial number configured for each rack number. This command is used to verify that the configuration is correct. The serial numbers displayed are those entered by an operator. If this number is wrong due to an entry error, the number is still displayed but the DSC does not recognize the chassis, and the offended chassis will not be part of the multishelf system.

In Example 12-3, the configuration was created in admin config-exec mode. Serial number TBA000072774 is the serial number of the DSC, which is designated as rack 0. If you do configure your own serial number as rack 0, the router will assume it is the DSC. The FCC configuration for serial number TBA00000003 is numbered 240. This is the first rack numbered for the fabric card chassis. The output display of various commands will use F0 to denote the first fabric card chassis. The two are used interchangeably.

Example 12-3 *Output of* show running-config

```
RP/0/RP0/CPU0:router#admin
RP/0/RP0/CPU0:router(admin)#show running-config
Building configuration...
dsc serial TBA00000003 rack 240
dsc serial TBA000072774 rack 0
dsc serial TBA00000002 rack 1
```

Example 12-4 displays a multishelf configuration. This configuration is listed below the output of Example 12-3 in admin configuration. **controller fabric plane** *n* is created for each plane. The configuration shown represents single-module configuration because the **oim count** is 1. Multimodule configuration is represented with the command **oim count 3**. The third line under each defined plane establishes the plane on the configured slot. For example, F0/SM9/FM dedicates slot 9 as plane 0 on the FCC.

Example 12-4 *Output of Fabric Plane Configuration*

```
(admin-config)#controllers fabric plane 0
(admin-config)#oim count 1
 (admin-config)#oim instance 0 location F0/SM9/FM

(admin-config)#controllers fabric plane 1
(admin-config)#oim count 1
 (admin-config)#oim instance 0 location F0/SM6/FM

(admin-config)#controllers fabric plane 2
(admin-config)#oim count 1
 (admin-config)#oim instance 0 location F0/SM3/FM
```

```
(admin-config)#controllers fabric plane 3
(admin-config)#oim count 1
 (admin-config)#oim instance 0 location F0/SM0/FM

(admin-config)#controllers fabric plane 4
(admin-config)#oim count 1
 (admin-config)#oim instance 0 location F0/SM12/FM

(admin-config)#controllers fabric plane 5
(admin-config)#oim count 1
 (admin-config)#oim instance 0 location F0/SM15/FM

(admin-config)#controllers fabric plane 6
(admin-config)#oim count 1
 (admin-config)#oim instance 0 location F0/SM18/FM

(admin-config)#controllers fabric plane 7
(admin-config)#oim count 1
 (admin-config)#oim instance 0 location F0/SM21/FM

RP/0/RP0/CPU0:router(admin)#show controllers fabric rack all detail
Rack Rack Server
Num Status Status
-- --- ---
0 NORMAL PRESENT
1 NORMAL PRESENT
F0 NORMAL PRESENT
```

Examples 12-5 and 12-6 display all eight planes with operational state and status.

Example 12-5 *Output of* show controllers fabric plane

```
RP/0/RP0/CPU0:router(admin)#show controllers fabric plane all detail
Plane Admin Oper  Down  Total   Down
Id    State State Flags Bundles Bundles
-------------------------------------------
0       UP     UP           0           0
1       UP     UP           0           0
2       UP     UP           0           0
3       UP     UP           0           0
4       UP     UP           0           0
5       UP     UP           0           0
6       UP     UP           0           0
7       UP     UP           0           0
```

For Example 12-6, the expected output should contain a series of 1s for each of the fabric planes active in the system. If a fabric plane is administratively shut down, the output of the command remains the same. If the fabric card is physically removed or powered down, the 1 changes to a dot (.).

Example 12-6 *Output of* show controllers fabric connectivity

```
RP/0/RP0/CPU0:router(admin)#show controllers fabric connectivity all
  Flags: P - plane admin down,       p - plane oper down
         C - card admin down,         c - card  oper down
         L - link port admin down,   l - linkport oper down
         A - asic admin down,         a - asic oper down
         B - bundle port admin Down, b - bundle port oper down
         I - bundle admin down,       i - bundle oper down
         N - node admin down,         n - node down
         o - other end of link down  d - data down
         f - failed component downstream
         m - plane multicast down

 Card        In  Tx Planes  Rx Planes
 R/S/M       Use 01234567   01234567
--------------------
0/0/CPU0     1   11111111   11111111
0/1/CPU0     1   11111111   11111111
0/3/CPU0     1   11111111   11111111
0/9/CPU0     1   11111111   11111111
0/RP0/CPU0   1   11111111   11111111
0/RP1/CPU0   1   11111111   11111111
1/3/CPU0     1   11111111   11111111
1/RP0/CPU0   1   11111111   11111111
1/RP1/CPU0   1   11111111   11111111
```

In Example 12-7, you can verify control Ethernet connectivity. The SCGE-22 gigabit Ethernet cabling connects to each route processor on the line card chassis. Each route processor has two (redundant) connections to the SCGE-22 card. We can then expect that each line card chassis will have four connections to the fabric chassis—two for the active and two for the standby processor.

Example 12-7 *Control Ethernet Connectivity Verification*

```
RP/0/RP0/CPU0:router(admin)#show spantree mst 1 detail location 0/RP0/CPU0
Instance                  1
Vlans mapped:             1

Designated Root          00-15-c7-27-f2-00
Designated Root Priority 1 (0 + 1)
Designated Root Port     GE_Port_0
```

```
Bridge ID MAC ADDR        00-0b-fc-f8-a4-4b
Bridge ID Priority        32769 (32768 + 1)
Bridge Max Age  8 sec     Hello Time  1 sec   Forward Delay  6 sec   Max Hops 4

Switched Interface    State Role    Cost    Prio   Type
------------------    ----------    ------  ----   ----------------
FE_Port_1             FWD desg      200000  128    P2P
GE_Port_0             FWD root      20000   128    P2P
GE_Port_1             BLK altn      20000   128    P2P
```

In Example 12-8, we utilize a very effective command for verification and troubleshooting. The unidirectional link detection (UDLD) feature is enabled by default on all control Ethernet links. We can use this feature to determine our far-end connected port. Determining port connectivity is very useful for physical connectivity and troubleshooting. Notice in Example 12-8, Interface_GE_Port_0 and Interface_GE_Port_1 provide details on local and remote connectivity. Under each interface, the shaded entries are for demonstrative purposes only. Each gigabit port identifies the far end card on the fabric chassis as well as the port number. We can determine with which node gigabit port 0 is connected by referencing the device name. The remote node is fabric chassis 0 or (F0) and shelf controller 0 (SC0). The port ID references the far end port, port #1 on F0, SC0.

Example 12-8 *Control Ethernet UDLD Verification*

```
Production - please preserve shading
RP/0/RP1/CPU0:cwdcrs-mc1(admin)#show controllers switch udld location 0/rp0/CPU0

Interface FE_PORT_1
---
Port enable administrative configuration setting: Enabled
Port enable operational state: Enabled
Current bidirectional state: Bidirectional
Current operational state: Advertisement - Single neighbor detected
Message interval: 7
Time out interval: 5

    Entry 1
    ---
    Expiration time: 17
    Device ID: 1
    Current neighbor state: Bidirectional
    Device name: node0_RP1_CPU0_INT
    Port ID: FE_PORT_0
    Neighbor echo 1 device: node0_RP0_CPU0_INT
    Neighbor echo 1 port: FE_PORT_1
```

```
    Message interval: 7
    Time out interval: 5
    CDP Device name: BCM_SWITCH

Interface GE_Port_0
---
Port enable administrative configuration setting: Enabled
Port enable operational state: Enabled
Current bidirectional state: Bidirectional
Current operational state: Advertisement - Single neighbor detected
Message interval: 7
Time out interval: 5

    Entry 1
    ---
    Expiration time: 14
    Device ID: 1
    Current neighbor state: Bidirectional
    Device name: nodeF0_SC0_CPU0
    Port ID: Gig port# 1
    Neighbor echo 1 device: node0_RP0_CPU0_INT
    Neighbor echo 1 port: GE_Port_0

    Message interval: 7
    Time out interval: 5
    CDP Device name: BCM_SWITCH

Interface GE_Port_1
---
Port enable administrative configuration setting: Enabled
Port enable operational state: Enabled
Current bidirectional state: Bidirectional
Current operational state: Advertisement - Single neighbor detected
Message interval: 7
Time out interval: 5

    Entry 1
    ---
    Expiration time: 15
    Device ID: 1
    Current neighbor state: Bidirectional
    Device name: nodeF0_SC1_CPU0
    Port ID: Gig port# 1
    Neighbor echo 1 device: node0_RP0_CPU0_INT
```

```
    Neighbor echo 1 port: GE_Port_1

    Message interval: 7
    Time out interval: 5
    CDP Device name: BCM_SWITCH
RP/0/RP1/CPU0:cwdcrs-mc1(admin)#
```

Line Card Chassis to Multishelf Preparation

Let's assume your network has a single CRS-1 16-slot chassis installed in the network. You are looking to expand by adding a second LCC to your existing network and have your LCC participate as a multishelf. If you already have multiple existing LCC, you will have to decide which chassis will assume the role of the DSC or rack 0. To do this migration, the minimum required software image is IOS XR 3.4.1 and ROMMON version of 1.45. From hardware point of view, the chassis must have at least RPs, S123 cards, alarm cards, and fan controllers. The PLIMs and MSC can be inserted at any time because they are used to forward traffic and do not manage the system. The following is a checklist of what should be prepared during installation:

- The fabric card chassis is installed, ready, and powered. It should be populated with the SCs, S2 cards, OIMs, and OIM-LED modules and connected to the power feed.
- Keep the array cables ready, not connected yet.
- Unpack and keep S13 cards ready for the LCC (rack 0) to replace its existing S123 cards.
- The S2 cards in FCC are strategically placed to attain power redundancy across various power zones.
- Keep the serial numbers of all chassis handy.

Step 1 and step 9 that follow recommend you enable and disable line card chassis 1 in *install-mode*. This command instructs the chassis to accept fabric connectivity and operations and not forward "production" data traffic to the line card until the command is removed.

The single chassis to multishelf conversion steps (2+1) follow:

1. Configure LCC (rack 0) as DSC using the following commands:
   - **dsc serial** *serialNumber* **rack 0**
   - **dsc serial** *serialNumber* **rack 240**
   - **dsc serial** *serialNumber* **rack 1 d**
   - **controllers** *fabric rack* **1 install-mode**
2. Now boot up the FCC. The FC chassis will boot up partially and wait for the continuity of fabric connectivity (S1-S2-S3) to be established.

Note: If there is more than one FCC, the following steps should be carried out for all the FCC desired to be a part of the system.

3. Execute the following for all S123 cards:
   a. Shut down the plane on an S123 card on LCC (rack 0) using **controllers fabric plane** *planeNumber* **shutdown**
   b. Power down the plane on an S123 card on LCC (rack 0) using **hw-module power disable location** *rack*/SM*slot*/SP
   c. Replace the S123 card with an S13 card and allow it to boot up (**check LED = IOS-XR-RUN**)
   d. Configure the fabric plane mappings:
      ```
      controllers fabric plane planeNumber
      oim count 1
      oim instance 0 location rack/slot/FM
      ```
   e. Power up the plane for that S13 card using the **no** form of the CLI in Step 3.
4. Issue the command **no hw-module power disable location** [*rack*/SM*slot*/SP]

   Wait for the FC to power up and boot. Power up the plane for that S13 card using the **no** form of the CLI in steps 3a and 3b:
   ```
   no controllers fabric plane planeNumber shutdown
   ```
5. Connect the three fiber bundles to S13 connectors on LCC and OIM on FCC. Verify that the fabric plane comes up using the **show controller fabric plane [n]** command on DSC. Additionally verify the LEDs light up for each connection on the OIM LED Panel in FCC.
6. Repeat Step 3 until all planes are upgraded.
7. Now power on the LCC1 and let it synchronize the image through the control Ethernet port, after which it waits for the fabric connectivity. LCC0 will transfer the IOS XR image through the control Ethernet network and reload LCC1. This process will take approximately 45 minutes.
8. Connect the fiber bundles to their S13 connectors and OIM on FCC. Check the LED status to verify the connectivity. Verify the rack, plane, and connectivity status using **show controller fabric.**
9. After successfully cabling both the LCCs to the FCC and verifying the plane status to be UP for rack 0 and rack 1, remove the LCC1 from the install mode using the command **no controllers fabric rack 1 install-mode.**
10. Finally, verify that all fabric planes are functional using the following **show** commands on DSC:
    a. Status of fabric connectivity (no "." state of planes for all rack 0 and 1 PLIMs)
    b. Status of planes (admin and oper status is UP)
    c. Status of the fabric bundles (0 down links)
    d. Status of racks in the system—all racks visible

Troubleshooting Multishelf Fabric Planes

This section describes the commands to execute when troubleshooting various components of the fabric card or fabric connectivity on a multishelf system.

There are a few factors that can cause a fabric card or plane to perform adversely. You should verify the following:

1. Verify all fabric planes are operational with the following command:

   show controllers fabric plane all detail

2. Verify cells are traversing with the plane without significant drops by using the following commands:

   show controllers fabric plane all statistics

   show controllers fabric plane *plane_id* **statistics detail**

3. Verify all links between S1, S2, and S3 are up and identify any down links:

   show control fabric sfe s1 all | include UP.*DOWN

   show control fabric sfe s2 all | include UP.*DOWN

   show control fabric sfe s3 all | include UP.*DOWN

   show control fabric sfe ingress all | include UP.*DOWN (for MSC fabric interface ASICs)

   show control fabric sfe fabricq all | include UP.*DOWN (for MSC fabric interface ASICs)

In Example 12-9 the output displays the verification of the fabric planes. Notice all eight planes are in an UP state. You will notice the column of down bundles has an integer of three downed bundles for each plane. This is expected behavior for a multishelf system 2+1. Refer to Figure 12-7. There are nine OIM bundles on the fabric card chassis. In a multishelf 2+1, LCC 0 and LCC 1 will occupy the first six OIM bundles of the nine bundles occupying S2 fabric card. On each plane, the first three bundles are dedicated for LCC 0 and the second three are dedicated for LCC 1. Therefore, in a multishelf 2+1 system, the last three OIM bundles will remain unused and it is expected behavior to see three down bundles. If a multishelf 3+1 system is implemented, you should expect to see down bundles displayed as zero because LCC 2 will occupy the final set of bundles per plane.

Example 12-9 *Verifying the Fabric Planes*

```
RP/0/RP0/CPU0:router(admin)#show controllers fabric plane all detail
Flags: P - plane admin down,           p - plane oper down
       C - card admin down,            c - card  oper down
       L - link port admin down,       l - linkport oper down
       A - asic admin down,            a - asic oper down
       B - bundle port admin Down,  b - bundle port oper down
       I - bundle admin down,          i - bundle oper down
       N - node admin down,            n - node down
       o - other end of link down   d - data down
       f - failed component downstream
       m - plane multicast down,    s - link port permanently shutdown
       t - no barrier input
```

```
Plane   Admin  Oper    Down   Total     Down
Id      State  State   Flags  Bundles   Bundle
------------------------------------------------
0       UP     UP             9         3
1       UP     UP             9         3
2       UP     UP             9         3
3       UP     UP             9         3
4       UP     UP             9         3
5       UP     UP             9         3
6       UP     UP             9         3
7       UP     UP             9         3
```

In Example 12-10, the fabric plane in plane 1 is operational, but not all destination fabric queue ASICs can be reached through this fabric plane, according to the ingress MSC perspective. Due to the dynamic nature of multicast in the fabric architecture, destinations of multicast traffic cannot be predetermined. The fabric plane is shown as MCAST_DOWN. Multicast traffic use the other fabric planes to deliver data to the appropriate egress MSCs. Unicast traffic will continue to use the affected fabric plane if traffic is destined to a reachable fabric queue ASIC. If traffic is destined for a fabric queue ASIC that is deemed unreachable, the other remaining available fabric planes are used. Notice the "m" displayed under Down Flags, indicating the plane is multicast down. To change the operational state of a fabric plane from MCAST_DOWN to up, check the external fiber cabling connected to the fabric cards on the LCC and the OIM of the FCC. For further assistance, contact Cisco Technical Support if you suspect an issue with hardware.

Example 12-10 *Output of* **show controllers fabric plane all detail**

```
RP/0/RP0/CPU0:router(admin)#show controllers fabric plane all detail
Flags: P - plane admin down,          p - plane oper down
       C - card admin down,           c - card  oper down
       L - link port admin down,      l - linkport oper down
       A - asic admin down,           a - asic oper down
       B - bundle port admin Down,    b - bundle port oper down
       I - bundle admin down,         i - bundle oper down
       N - node admin down,           n - node down
       o - other end of link down     d - data down
       f - failed component downstream
       m - plane multicast down,      s - link port permanently shutdown
       t - no barrier input

Plane   Admin  Oper    Down   Total     Down
Id      State  State   Flags  Bundles   Bundles
------------------------------------------------
0       UP     UP             9         3
1       UP MCAST_DOWN  m      9         6
```

```
3        UP      UP              9       3
4        UP      UP              9       3
5        UP      UP              9       3
6        UP      UP              9       3
7        UP      UP              9       3
```

Example 12-11 displays the output of an administratively shut down fabric. Because the card has power but is administratively down, the down flags will display only a P, indicating the plane is administratively shut down. It is important to note that multicast traffic can identify the plane; however, software will reroute traffic to another plane in operation.

Example 12-11 *Output Displaying Fabric Plane 1 mcast_down*

```
RP/0/RP0/CPU0:router(admin)#show controllers fabric plane all detail
Flags: P - plane admin down,           p - plane oper down
          C - card admin down,          c - card  oper down
          L - link port admin down,     l - linkport oper down
          A - asic admin down,          a - asic oper down
          B - bundle port admin Down, b - bundle port oper down
          I - bundle admin down,        i - bundle oper down
          N - node admin down,          n - node down
          o - other end of link down   d - data down
          f - failed component downstream
          m - plane multicast down,     s - link port permanently shutdown
          t - no barrier input

Plane  Admin    Oper        Down        Total      Down
Id      State    State       Flags       Bundles    Bundles
 ----------------------------------------------------
 0      DOWN     DOWN        P           9          3
 1      UP       UP                      9          3
 2      UP       UP                      9          3
 3      UP       UP                      9          3
 4      UP       UP                      9          3
 5      UP       UP                      9          3
 6      UP       UP                      9          3
 7      UP       UP                      9          3
```

Example 12-12 displays fabric plane 4 as administratively shut down and powered off. The output displays down flags of pPm. The lowercase p represents plane operation down, uppercase P represents plane admin down, and lowercase m represents plane multicast down. When these three flags appear in sequence, it is an indication a user has taken the card out of service.

Example 12-12 *Output of Fabric Displaying Plane 4 Powered Down*

```
RP/0/RP0/CPU0:router(admin)#show controllers fabric plane all detail
Flags: P - plane admin down,          p - plane oper down
         C - card admin down,         c - card  oper down
         L - link port admin down,    l - linkport oper down
         A - asic admin down,         a - asic oper down
         B - bundle port admin Down, b - bundle port oper down
         I - bundle admin down,       i - bundle oper down
         N - node admin down,         n - node down
         o - other end of link down   d - data down
         f - failed component downstream
         m - plane multicast down,    s - link port permanently shutdown
         t - no barrier input

Plane  Admin  Oper     Down     Total    Down
Id     State  State    Flags    Bundles  Bundles
 ----------------------------------------------
 0     UP     UP                9        3
 1     UP     UP                9        3
 2     UP     UP                9        3
 3     UP     UP                9        3
 4     DOWN   DOWN     pPm      9        6
 5     UP     UP                9        3
 6     UP     UP                9        3
 7     UP     UP                9        3
```

Troubleshooting Fabric Links

The commands described in this section can be instrumental when troubleshooting fabric bundle links between stages in the fabric. In a multishelf system, the fiber bundles are external between each ASIC stage within each fabric plane. Using the set of following commands can provide a baseline to troubleshoot fabric bundles and links. As a review, the array cables connect Stage 1 (S1) fabric from the LCC to the Stage 2 (S2) fabric on the FCC, and then to Stage 3 (S3) on the egress LCC.

The output from the **show controllers fabric bundle port all** command shown in Example 12-13 displays the status of the bundle ports from each card on each chassis, including each line card chassis and fabric chassis. The bundle represents the links in the array cables connecting the fabric ASICs.

Example 12-13 *Output of* show controllers fabric bundle port all

```
RP/0/RP0/CPU0:router(admin)#show controllers fabric bundle port all
Flags: P - plane admin down,          p - plane oper down
         C - card admin down,         c - card  oper down
         L - link port admin down,    l - linkport oper down
         A - asic admin down,         a - asic oper down
```

```
        B - bundle port admin Down, b - bundle port oper down
        I - bundle admin down,      i - bundle oper down
        N - node admin down,        n - node down
        o - other end of link down  d - data down
        f - failed component downstream
        m - plane multicast down
Bundle Port Admin Oper
R/S/M/P State State
----------------
0/SM0/SP/0 UP UP
0/SM0/SP/1 UP UP
0/SM0/SP/2 UP UP
0/SM1/SP/0 UP UP
0/SM1/SP/1 UP UP
0/SM1/SP/2 UP UP
0/SM4/SP/0 UP UP
0/SM4/SP/1 UP UP
0/SM4/SP/2 UP UP
0/SM5/SP/0 UP UP
0/SM5/SP/1 UP UP
0/SM5/SP/2 UP UP
1/SM0/SP/0 UP UP
1/SM0/SP/1 UP UP

!Output omitted for brevity
```

When performing verification and troubleshooting commands on the fabric architecture, there are three main categories to verify the normal operation. The fabric architecture is complex, and it is difficult to document every troubleshooting scenario. However, be sure to monitor the following:

- Verify operational fabric planes
- Verify (down) links within a fabric bundle
- Verify any cell loss or corrupted cells (cell errors)

Example 12-14 displays fabric statistics for all fabric planes to view cell status. Verify whether any planes experience a high count of UCE. You typically see a very small increment of CE counters.

Example 12-14 *Output of* **show controllers fabric plane all statistics**

```
RP/0/RP0/CPU0:router(admin)#show controllers fabric plane all statistics
In                          Out          CE            UCE           PE
Plane                        Cells                      Cells        Cells         Cells           Cells
```

```
-----------------------------------------------------------------
 0             15243690             17909592          0          0          0
 1                    0                    0          0          0          0
 2             12020673             14334201          0          0          0
 3             11019177             13276976          0          0          0
 4             10999896             13263122          1          0          0
 5             11035779             13323585          0          0          0
 6             11018346             13308959          1          0          0
 7             10997478             13279968          1          0          0

CE  = Errored cell with a correctable error detected using FEC code
UCE = Errored cell with an uncorrectable error detected using FEC code
PE  = Parity error present within a cell when processed by SFE
```

Check for the individual down links in a fabric bundle. The **show controllers fabric bundle all detail** command will help identify individual links that are not in operation.

When individual links are down in a bundle of an (external) array cable, it is likely the individual links have been contaminated. In this case, the fiber cable might require cleaning with a dedicated fiber cleaning kit. Contact your Cisco representative if you require a fiber cleaning kit. The last three bundles shown in Example 12-15 with a down flag of "bo" represent the fabric card without connectivity from the LCC to the FCC.

Example 12-15 *Output of Link Verification in Fabric Array Cable Bundle*

```
RP/0/RP0/CPU0:DSC-RP0(admin)#show controllers fabric bundle all detail
  Flags: P - plane admin down,       p - plane oper down
         C - card admin down,        c - card  oper down
         L - link port admin down,   l - linkport oper down
         A - asic admin down,        a - asic oper down
         B - bundle port admin Down, b - bundle port oper down
         I - bundle admin down,      i - bundle oper down
         N - node admin down,        n - node down
         o - other end of link down  d - data down
         f - failed component downstream
         m - plane multicast down

 Bundle        Oper      Down     Plane Total Down   Bundle        Bundle
 R/S/M/P       State     Flags    Id    Links Links  Port1         Port2
-------------------------------------------------------------------------
 F0/SM4/FM/0  UP                  1      72    0      F0/SM4/FM/0  0/SM1/SP/0
 F0/SM4/FM/1  UP                  1      72    0      F0/SM4/FM/1  0/SM1/SP/1
 F0/SM4/FM/2  UP                  1      72    1      F0/SM4/FM/2  0/SM1/SP/2
 F0/SM4/FM/3  UP                  1      72    3      F0/SM4/FM/3  1/SM1/SP/0
 F0/SM4/FM/4  UP                  1      72    0      F0/SM4/FM/4  1/SM1/SP/1
 F0/SM4/FM/5  UP                  1      72    0      F0/SM4/FM/5  1/SM1/SP/2
```

```
F0/SM4/FM/6  DOWN      bo   1    72    72     F0/SM4/FM/6  2/SM1/SP/0
F0/SM4/FM/7  DOWN      bo   1    72    72     F0/SM4/FM/7  2/SM1/SP/1
F0/SM4/FM/8  DOWN      bo   1    72    72     F0/SM4/FM/8  2/SM1/SP/2
```

The command **show controllers fabric link port ?** allows you to verify operational or down links at each stage of the fabric architecture. The output displays links with a valid far-end port. You may shut down this switch fabric element (SFE) port as shown in Example 12-16 to place the link out of service.

Example 12-16 *Output of* fabric link ports

```
RP/0/RP0/CPU0:DSC-RP0(admin)#show controllers fabric link port ?
  fabricqrx    Fabricq Rx port
  ingressqtx   Ingressq Tx port
  s1ro          S1 Out-of-Band Rx port
  s1rx          S1 Rx port
  s1tx          S1 Tx port
  s2rx          S2 Rx port
  s2tx          S2 Tx port
  s3rx          S3 Rx port
  s3tx          S3 Tx port

RP/0/RP0/CPU0:DSC-RP0(admin)#show controllers fabric link port s2rx all | include
  UP.*DOWN.*SM
  Flags: P - plane admin down,        p - plane oper down
         C - card admin down,         c - card  oper down
         L - link port admin down,    l - linkport oper down
         A - asic admin down,         a - asic oper down
         B - bundle port admin Down,  b - bundle port oper down
         I - bundle admin down,       i - bundle oper down
         N - node admin down,         n - node down
         o - other end of link down   d - data down
         f - failed component downstream
         m - plane multicast down
Sfe Port          Admin Oper  Down    Other              Near-end    Far-end
R/S/M/A/P         State State Flags   End                Bport       Bport
------------------------------------------------------------------------
F0/SM4/SP/0/0     UP    DOWN  l       N/A                F0/SM4/8    2/SM1/2
F0/SM4/SP/0/1     UP    DOWN  l       N/A                F0/SM4/7    2/SM1/1
F0/SM4/SP/0/2     UP    DOWN  l       N/A                F0/SM4/8    2/SM1/2
F0/SM4/SP/0/3     UP    DOWN  l       N/A                F0/SM4/7    2/SM1/1
F0/SM4/SP/0/5     UP    DOWN  l       1/SM1/SP/1/54      F0/SM4/3    1/SM1/0
F0/SM4/SP/0/9     UP    DOWN  l       N/A                F0/SM4/8    2/SM1/2
F0/SM4/SP/0/11    UP    DOWN  l       N/A                F0/SM4/6    2/SM1/0
F0/SM4/SP/0/18    UP    DOWN  l       N/A                F0/SM4/7    2/SM1/1
F0/SM4/SP/0/19    UP    DOWN  l       N/A                F0/SM4/7    2/SM1/1
```

```
F0/SM4/SP/0/20    UP    DOWN  1      N/A              F0/SM4/6    2/SM1/0
F0/SM4/SP/0/21    UP    DOWN  1      N/A              F0/SM4/6    2/SM1/0
F0/SM4/SP/0/27    UP    DOWN  1      N/A              F0/SM4/8    2/SM1/2
F0/SM4/SP/0/29    UP    DOWN  1      N/A              F0/SM4/6    2/SM1/0
F0/SM4/SP/1/0     UP    DOWN  1      N/A              F0/SM4/8    2/SM1/2
F0/SM4/SP/1/1     UP    DOWN  1      N/A              F0/SM4/7    2/SM1/1
F0/SM4/SP/1/2     UP    DOWN  1      N/A              F0/SM4/8    2/SM1/2
F0/SM4/SP/1/3     UP    DOWN  1      N/A              F0/SM4/7    2/SM1/1
F0/SM4/SP/1/9     UP    DOWN  1      N/A              F0/SM4/8    2/SM1/2
F0/SM4/SP/1/11    UP    DOWN  1      N/A              F0/SM4/6    2/SM1/0
F0/SM4/SP/1/18    UP    DOWN  1      N/A              F0/SM4/7    2/SM1/1
F0/SM4/SP/1/19    UP    DOWN  1      N/A              F0/SM4/7    2/SM1/1
F0/SM4/SP/1/20    UP    DOWN  1      N/A              F0/SM4/6    2/SM1/0
F0/SM4/SP/1/21    UP    DOWN  1      N/A              F0/SM4/6    2/SM1/0
```

The command **show controller fabric link port [s2rx] all statistics** is useful to check whether there are incrementing cell losses due to cell errors. The output in Example 12-17 provides insight as to whether there are (SFE port) corrupted packets on the link or the link status may be set as down.

Example 12-17 *Output of Statistics of Receive Side of S2 Fabric Links*

```
RP/0/RP0/CPU0:DSC-RP0(admin)#show controllers fabric link port s2rx all statistics
Total racks: 3

Rack 0:

     SFE  Port            In                In       CE       UCE       PE
     R/S/M/A/P         Data Cells       Idle Cells   Cells    Cells     Cells
--------------------------------------------------------------------


Rack 1:

     SFE  Port            In                In       CE       UCE       PE
     R/S/M/A/P         Data Cells       Idle Cells   Cells    Cells     Cells
--------------------------------------------------------------------


Rack F0:

     SFE  Port            In                In       CE       UCE       PE
     R/S/M/A/P         Data Cells       Idle Cells   Cells    Cells     Cells
--------------------------------------------------------------------
  F0/SM4/SP/0/0                  0                0        0        0         0
  F0/SM4/SP/0/1                  0                0        0        0         0
  F0/SM4/SP/0/2                  0                0        0        0         0
  F0/SM4/SP/0/3                  0                0        0        0         0
```

```
  F0/SM4/SP/0/4            22201       990874147913       0        0        0
  F0/SM4/SP/0/5                0                  0       0        0        0
  F0/SM4/SP/0/6           456073       990814555174       0        0        0
  F0/SM4/SP/0/7           456074       990816053446       0        0        0
  F0/SM4/SP/0/8         71623829       990743269845       0        0        0
  F0/SM4/SP/0/9                0                  0       0        0        0
 F0/SM4/SP/0/10            22202       990874209532       0        0        0
 F0/SM4/SP/0/11                0                  0       0        0        0
 F0/SM4/SP/0/12           973868       990873231836       0        0        0
 F0/SM4/SP/0/13           973869       990793994623       0        0        0
 F0/SM4/SP/0/14           973869       990873151319       0        0        0
 F0/SM4/SP/0/15         71623829       990743363567       0        0        0
 F0/SM4/SP/0/16         71623829       990744862570       0        0        0
 F0/SM4/SP/0/17           456073       990814414809       0        0        0
 F0/SM4/SP/0/18                0                  0       0        0        0
 F0/SM4/SP/0/19                0                  0       0        0        0
!Output omitted for brevity
```

Summary

The multishelf system supports scalability to meet growth demands needed by service providers. The multishelf system supports the migration from single (LCC) shelf system to multishelf system by leveraging in-service hardware upgrade. Complexity of managing a multishelf system does not increase as the system grows with the network. Multishelf help reduces the complexity of networks by collapsing the core, edge, and peer layers in a unified system. The reduction in systems to manage and monitor reduces network operating expenses. The multishelf system is built by interconnecting multiple line card shelves using one or more fabric shelves. Multishelf systems can grow to as many as 72 line card shelves interconnected using eight fabric shelves. The multishelf system provides bandwidth capabilities and nondisruptive scalability from 1.2 to 92 terabits per second (Tbps).

Reference

- **Cisco.** http://www.cisco.com/en/US/products/ps5763/products_tech_note09186a0080772675.shtml

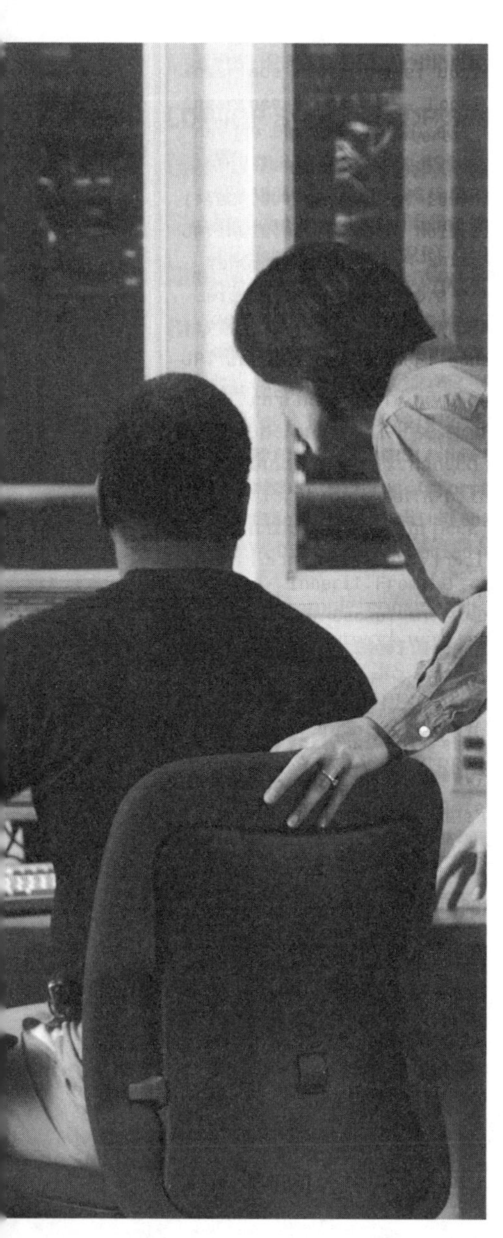

APPENDIX A

ROMMON and Configuration Register Settings

Tables A-1 and A-2 provide a handy reference to some commonly used configuration register settings as well as ROMMON variable settings, respectively. Table A-3 provides a reference to commonly used ROMMON commands.

Table A-1 shows common configuration register settings.

Table A-1 *Configuration Register Settings*

Configuration Register Values	Explanation
0x0	Router boots into ROMMON following a reload. The configuration register setting of 0x0 should be made in admin mode so that it applies to both the active and the standby route processor.
0x102	Normal configuration register setting that boots the system image. It disallows the Break key except during the first few seconds of bootup.
0x42	Password recovery.

Table A-2 shows ROMMON variables.

Table A-2 *ROMMON Variables*

Variable	Example	Notes
BOOTLDR	**BOOTLDR=bootflash:c12kprp-boot-mz.120-31.S0a**	Location of IOS Boot Helper image. This variable is specific to the c12000 platform.
BOOT	**disk0:hfr-os-mbi-3.6.2/mbihfr-rp.vm,1;**	Used when autoboot is set to on.

Variable	Example	Notes
TURBOBOOT	TURBOBOOT=on,disk0 TURBOBOOT=on,compactflash, format TURBOBOOT=on,disk0,clean	Installs Cisco IOS XR onto selected device. The format option removes the install and configuration related files. The admin configuration is not removed. The clean option only removes the installation-related files.
IP_ADDRESS	IP_ADDRESS=172.16.1.1	Sets the IP address of the management port.
IP_SUBNET_MASK	IP_SUBNET_MASK=255.255.255.0	Sets the subnet mask.
TFTP_FILE	TFTP_FILE=comp-hfr-mini.vm	Location of the TFTP_FILE.
DEFAULT_GATEWAY	DEFAULT_GATEWAY=172.16.1.2	Sets the default gateway.

Table A-3 shows the commonly used ROMMON commands.

Table A-3 *ROMMON Commands*

ROMMON-Level Commands	Explanation
set	Typing **set** and then pressing the Enter key displays the current rommon settings.
unset	The **unset** command unsets a rommon variable; for example, **unset TURBOBOOT**.
sync	Saves ROMMON variables into NVRAM.
reset	Resets the route processor or the distributed route processor from ROMMON. It reloads the rommon code and reinitializes the RP or DRP.
confreg	Sets the configuration register from ROMMON; for example, confreg 0x102.
boot	Allows booting of a .vm file; for example, **boot tftp://172.16.1.10/IOX/comp-hfr-mini.vm**

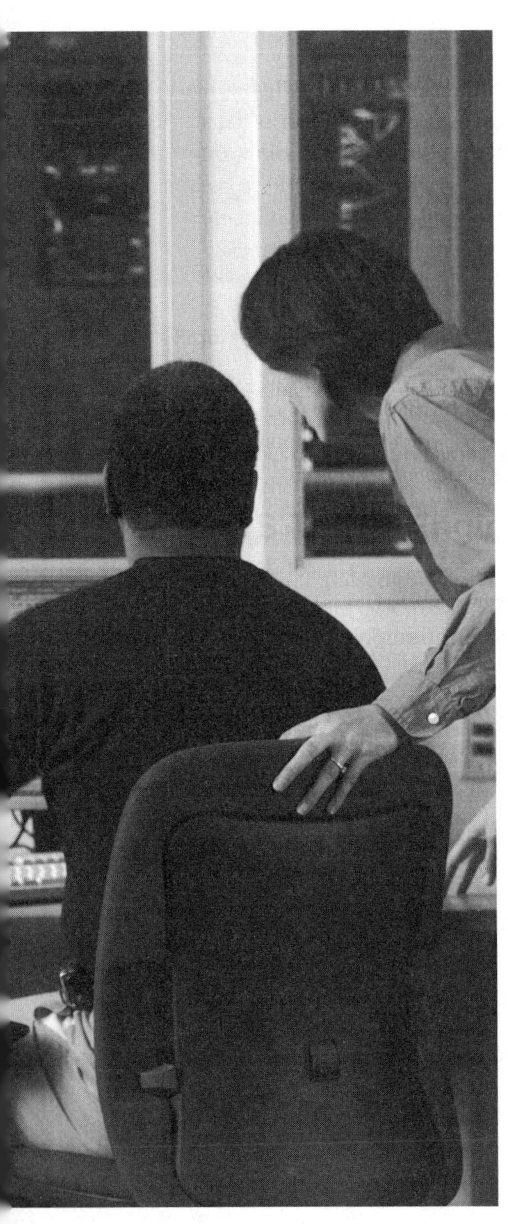

APPENDIX B

Multishelf 2+1 Array Cable Mapping

This appendix provides a cabling map of a multishelf 2+1 system. The table provides Cisco's leading practice of array cable configuration of planes on the fabric card chassis. This configuration takes advantage of the fabric card chassis power zones. The cabling map that follows provides an approach to minimize impact if the chassis loses one or more power zones.

Plane	LCC Rack and Slot	Adapter	FCC Rack and Slot	Adapter
0	Rack 0, SM0	A0	Rack F0, OIM 9	J0
		A1		J1
		A2		J2
	Rack 1, SM0	A0	Rack F0, OIM 9	J3
		A1		J4
		A2		J5
1	Rack 0, SM1	A0	Rack F0, OIM 6	J0
		A1		J1
		A2		J2
	Rack 1, SM1	A0	Rack F0, OIM 6	J3
		A1		J4
		A2		J5
2	Rack 0, SM2	A0	Rack F0, OIM 3	J0
		A1		J1
		A2		J2
	Rack 1, SM2	A0	Rack F0, OIM 3	J3
		A1		J4
		A2		J5

Plane	LCC Rack and Slot	Adapter	FCC Rack and Slot	Adapter
3	Rack 0, SM3	A0	Rack F0, OIM 0	J0
		A1		J1
		A2		J2
	Rack 1, SM3	A0	Rack F0, OIM 0	J3
		A1		J4
		A2		J5
4	Rack 0, SM4	A0	Rack F0, OIM 12	J0
		A1		J1
		A2		J2
	Rack 1, SM4	A0	Rack F0, OIM 12	J3
		A1		J4
		A2		J5
5	Rack 0, SM5	A0	Rack F0, OIM 15	J0
		A1		J1
		A2		J2
	Rack 1, SM5	A0	Rack F0, OIM 15	J3
		A1		J4
		A2		J5
6	Rack 0, SM6	A0	Rack F0, OIM 18	J0
		A1		J1
		A2		J2
	Rack 1, SM6	A0	Rack F0, OIM 18	J3
		A1		J4
		A2		J5

Plane	LCC Rack and Slot	Adapter	FCC Rack and Slot	Adapter
7	Rack 0, SM7	A0	Rack F0, OIM 21	J0
		A1		J1
		A2		J2
	Rack 1, SM7	A0	Rack F0, OIM 21	J3
		A1		J4
		A2		J5

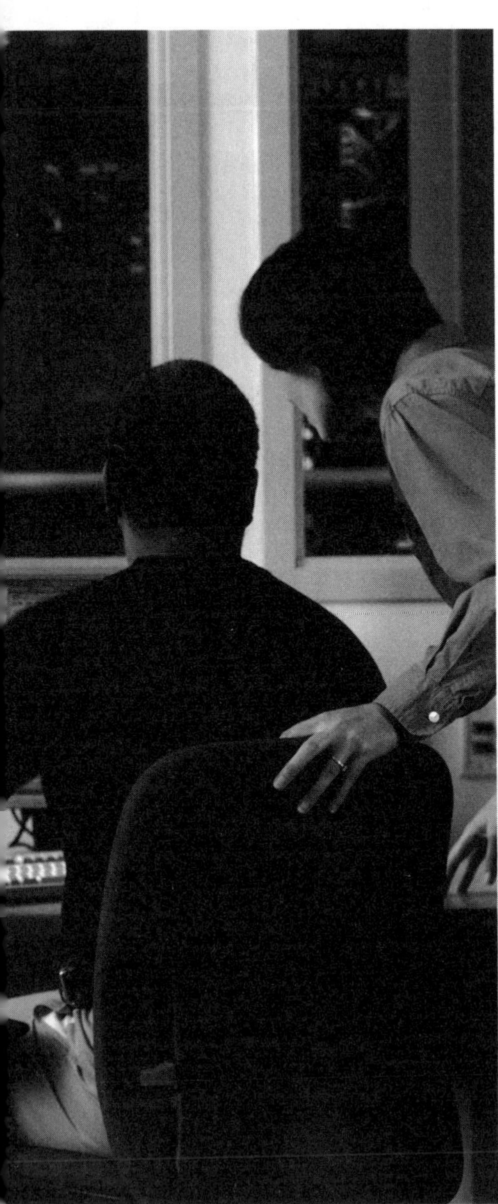

APPENDIX C

Switch Fabric Down Flags

This appendix lists common flags with common commands displaying output of the switch fabric. Note that the flags' characters uppercase and lowercase provide different flag descriptions.

Flag	Flag Meaning	Flag Description
P	plane admin down	Plane has been taken out of service by administrative action.
p	plane oper down	Plane is not able to operate or has been taken out of service by administrative action.
C	card admin down	Card has been taken out of service by administrative action (reserved for future use).
c	card oper down	Flag is set in response to system notification that a card will soon be powered off. This is a transient condition lasting a few seconds before power is withdrawn. Unusual to see this flag in practice.
L	link port admin down	Link has been taken out of service by administrative action.
l	linkport oper down	Flag is set or cleared in response to messages from the ASIC driver code. Flags are enabled when the ASIC is first discovered. Flag is set if the ASIC driver has signaled that an individual link port is not usable for fabric traffic or that the driver has confirmed that the link is ready. Two common reasons for seeing an l flag are Initialization is not complete Sufficient errors have been seen at a receive port so that the ASIC driver shuts the port down
A	asic admin down	ASIC has been taken out of service by administrative action. If the A flag is set, it is seen on all links connected to that ASIC.

Flag	Flag Meaning	Flag Description
a	asic oper down	Flag is set or cleared in response to messages from the ASIC driver code. Flags are enabled when the ASIC is first discovered. Flag is set if the ASIC driver has signaled that a SEA ASIC is not usable for fabric traffic. If the a flag is set, it is seen on all links connected to that ASIC.
B	bundle port admin down	Bundle port has been taken out of service by administrative action. If the B flag is set, it is seen on all links associated to that bundle.

Index

A

B

D

E

F

G - H

I

J - K - L

M

N

O

Q - R

S

T

U

V

W - X - Y - Z